THE ORIENTAL INSTITUTE OF THE UNIVERSITY OF CHICAGO

STUDIES IN ANCIENT ORIENTAL CIVILIZATION NO. 36

THE HILLY FLANKS AND BEYOND

Section 2. "Ubaid Mesopotamia Reconsidered" by Joan Oates

ERRATUM

Please note that the chart on p. 263 was originally
intended to have arrows associated with the question marks
as illustrated on the re-drawn chart below.

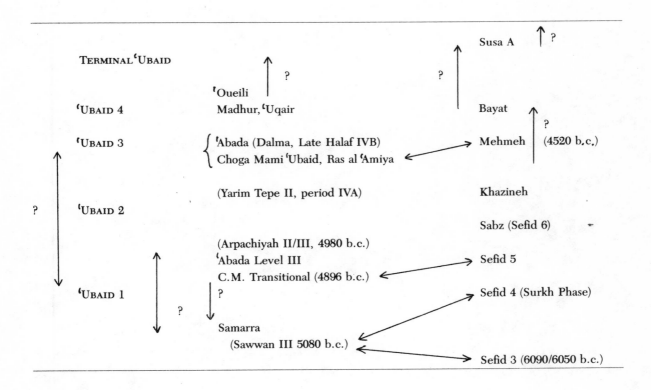

THE HILLY FLANKS AND BEYOND

ESSAYS ON THE PREHISTORY OF SOUTHWESTERN ASIA

PRESENTED TO

ROBERT J. BRAIDWOOD

NOVEMBER 15, 1982

Edited by

T. Cuyler Young, Jr.

Philip E.L. Smith

Peder Mortensen

STUDIES IN ANCIENT ORIENTAL CIVILIZATION NO. 36

THE ORIENTAL INSTITUTE OF THE UNIVERSITY OF CHICAGO

CHICAGO • ILLINOIS

Library of Congress Catalog Card Number: 82−62879

ISBN: 0−918986−37−0
ISSN: 0069−3367

The Oriental Institute, Chicago

CONTRIBUTORS

Robert McC. Adams
Harold H. Swift Distinguished Service Professor
Oriental Institute and Departments of Anthropology and Near Eastern Languages and Civilizations,
   University of Chicago; Director, Oriental Institute

Ofer Bar-Yosef
Professor, Institute of Archaeology
Hebrew University of Jerusalem
Jerusalem, Israel

Jacques Cauvin
Maître de Recherches au Centre National de la Recherche Scientifique
Directeur de l'Unité de recherches archéologiques 17
Centre de recherches d'écologie humaine et préhistoire
07460 St. André de Cruzières
Chargé de cours aux Universités de Paris I—Sorbonne and Lyon II
Maison de l'Orient méditerranéen, 1, rue Raulin, Lyon, France

Marie-Claire Cauvin
Maître de Recherches au Centre National de la Recherche Scientifique
Chargée de cours a l'Université de Paris X—Nanterre
Maison de l'Orient méditerranéen, 1, rue Raulin, Lyon, France

Lorraine Copeland
Institute of Archaeology
University of London
London, England

H. de Contenson
Directeur de Recherches au Centre National de la Recherche Scientifique
Paris, France

Geneviève Dollfus
Centre National de la Recherche Scientifique
Unité de recherches archéologiques 19: Iran-sud
10, rue de Quatrefages
75005 Paris, France

Kent V. Flannery
Curator of Environmental Archaeology
Museum of Anthropology
University of Michigan
Ann Arbor, Michigan

Frank Hole
Department of Anthropology
Yale University
New Haven, Connecticut

Francis Hours sj
Centre National de la Recherche Scientifique
Maison de l'Orient
1, rue Raulin
69007 Lyon, France

Carol Kramer
Associate Professor of Anthropology
Herbert H. Lehman College and The Graduate Center
City University of New York
New York City, New York

Dr. Andrew M.T. Moore
Visiting Associate Professor
Department of Anthropology
University of Arizona
Tucson, Arizona

Peder Mortensen
Director, Forhistorisk Museum, Moesgaard
Hoejbjerg, Aarhus
Denmark

Dr. Hans J. Nissen
Professor of Near Eastern Archaeology
Institute of Archaeology
The Free University of Berlin
Berlin, Federal Republic of Germany

Mrs. Joan Oates, Ph.D.
Fellow of Girton College
University of Cambridge
Cambridge, England

Jean Perrot
Directeur de Recherches au Centre National de la Recherche Scientifique
Centre de recherches français de Jérusalem
BP 547 Jérusalem, Israël

Charles L. Redman
Professor, Department of Anthropology
State University of New York
Binghamton, New York
Staff Associate in Anthropology
National Science Foundation
Washington, D.C.

Ralph S. Solecki
Professor, Department of Anthropology
Columbia University
New York, New York

Rose L. Solecki
Lecturer, Department of Anthropology
Columbia University
New York, New York

Philip E.L. Smith
Professeur, Département d'Anthropologie
Université de Montréal
Montréal, Quebec, Canada

Patty Jo Watson
Professor, Department of Anthropology
Washington University
St. Louis, Missouri

T. Cuyler Young, Jr.
West Asian Department
Royal Ontario Museum
Near Eastern Department
University of Toronto
Toronto, Ontario, Canada

TABLE OF CONTENTS

ix

LIST OF ILLUSTRATIONS

LES RAPPORTS ENTRE L'ANATOLIE ET LA SYRIE DU NORD À L'ÉPOQUE DES PREMIÈRES COMMUNAUTÉS VILLAGEOISES DE BERGERS ET DE PAYSANS

Carte 1. — Des Premiers Paysans aux Premiers Potiers, 7,600–6,000 B.C. 88
Carte 2. — Premiers Entités Culturelles, 6,000–5,000 B.C. 89
Carte 3. — Premiers Contacts entre Civilisations, 5,500–5,000 B.C. 90

THE FIRST FARMERS IN THE LEVANT

Fig. 1. — Approximate Duration of each Stage of the Epipaleolithic and Neolithic 104
Fig. 2. — Temperature Change During the Late Pleistocene and Early Holocene
Related to Stages of the Epipaleolithic and Neolithic 105
Fig. 3. — Distribution of Epipaleolithic 1 Sites 106
Fig. 4. — Distribution of Epipaleolithic 2 Sites 107
Fig. 5. — Distribution of Neolithic 1 Sites 108
Fig. 6. — Distribution of Neolithic 2 Sites 109
Fig. 7. — Distribution of Neolithic 3 Sites 110
Fig. 8. — Distribution of Neolithic 4 Sites in Southern Syria, Lebanon, and Palestine 111

THE FORCE OF NUMBERS: POPULATION PRESSURE IN THE CENTRAL WESTERN ZAGROS, 12,000–4500 B.C.

Fig. 1. — The Study Area 157
Fig. 2. — The Early Neolithic: Sites in the Immediate Neighborhood of Ganj Dareh and Sarab .. 158
Fig. 3. — The Later Neolithic: Sareb Period Sites within the Entire Study Area 159
Fig. 4. — Early Chalcolithic Sites in the Study Area 160
Fig. 5. — Late Chalcolithic–Ubaid Period Sites in the Study Area 161

REGULARITY AND CHANGE IN THE ARCHITECTURE OF AN EARLY VILLAGE

Fig. 1. — Map of Çayönü 197
Fig. 2. — Grill Plan Building EF 2 198
Fig. 3. — Grill Plan Building EF 2 198
Fig. 4. — Grill Plan Building K 5 199
Fig. 5. — Excavated Portion of Grill Plan Building U 22 199
Fig. 6. — Cell Plan Building H 3 200
Fig. 7. — Cell Plan Building U 9 200
Fig. 8. — Close-up of Cells in Building U 9 201
Fig. 9. — Cell Plan Building S 6 201
Fig. 10. — Cache of Limestone Pieces 202
Fig. 11. — Views of Clay Model House found in Cell Plan Building U 9 203
Fig. 12. — Fallen Fragment of Clay Roofing from Cell Plan Building U 9 204
Fig. 13. — Tauf and Stone Foundation of Buildings in Lower Level of Jarmo 204
Fig. 14. — Example of Corridor Building and Adjacent Large Room from Level 2 of Beidha 205
Fig. 15. — Cell-Planlike Mud and Mud-Brick Architecture from Level D
of Ganj Dareh Tepe, Iran 205
Fig. 16. — Plan of Advanced Cell Plan Buildings from Levels 3 and 4 at Umm Dabaghiyah
in Northern Iraq 206

PATTERNS OF INTERACTION BETWEEN SEASONAL SETTLEMENTS AND EARLY VILLAGES IN MESOPOTAMIA

Fig. 1. — Umm Dabaghiyah: Amorphous, Semichipped Flint Nodules 221
Fig. 2. — Umm Dabaghiyah: Small, Irregular Flake Cores; Cylindrical Blade Core;
Conical Blade Cores; Various Core Fragments 222
Fig. 3. — Umm Dabaghiyah: Arrowheads 223
Fig. 4. — Umm Dabaghiyah: Borers; Beaked Blades; Side-Blow Blade-Flake "Cores";
Side-Blow Blade Flakes 224

INTRODUCTION

T HE IDEA for this volume was conceived in the most appropriate of contexts: on a hot and starry night high in the Zagros mountains of western Iran, not forty kilometers from Bob Braidwood's old excavation area in the Kermanshah Plain. Two of us (Mortensen and Smith) were spending the summer of 1977 making a survey of early sites in the adjoining valleys — in the easternmost limits, if you will, of the "Hilly Flanks" of the Fertile Crescent. Young, in Iran on other business, dropped by for a two-day visit. On his first evening the three of us sat up late in the courtyard of the village school, the expedition's headquarters. We sipped our hoarded Scotch and wine, munched pistachios (without reference to possible inclusions; cf. Flannery 1969, n. 71), and talked of many things from high theory to low gossip. The moon rose over the poplar trees and the village slowly went to sleep while we wrestled with the problems of Guran and Ganj Dareh, Asiab and Sarab. Perhaps it was the subliminal influence of these last two sites, dug by Braidwood in 1960, that made us realize how much and yet how little we had learned since then. With such thoughts — could it really have been seventeen years? — came the sudden realization that Bob was about to retire officially at the University of Chicago. Was a festschrift in the works? A second realization: no rumors of such an effort had come along the grapevine. At this point an eavesdropper would have heard various semi-incoherent denunciations of the archeological profession, competing with the howls of the village dogs, before silence at last fell on Kurdistan. Next day, three weary prehistorians went out on survey as planned, and the subject of the night before was not mentioned again.

Then, six months later, Smith found himself sitting at a dinner party with Bob Adams of the Oriental Institute. It was now Montreal, and the night was cold and wintry. Perhaps it was the wine that stirred up recollections of that summer evening in Iran and of the question, Was a publication dedicated to Bob Braidwood being planned? Since it was at once agreed that something should be done, Adams fixed Smith with his customary no-nonsense stare and sprang the trap: If a festschrift volume were to be born, who could be the midwives? The implication of this question was inescapable: the trio of the previous summer was an obvious target. Within weeks Adams had submitted a proposal to the Oriental Institute, which was fully supported by the Institute's administration. Young and Mortensen enthusiastically agreed to be coeditors. By the end of the summer of 1978 the three fledgling editors had a fixed formula, a timetable (we *were* optimistic), and a list of contributors. Every person invited accepted, most manuscripts were in on time, and this book is the end result. Now let us hope that our readers will not come to wish that we had gone to bed early that night in Kurdistan — as, of course, all good archeologists should do when in the field.

One difficulty that had to be faced in organizing a festschrift in honor of Robert J. Braidwood is that a single volume is not nearly enough to reflect properly his multiple interests and contributions. We had to cope with this problem from the start as we thought about possible contributors. Braidwood is an Old World prehistorian. He was the modern pioneer of cooperation between archeologists and natural scientists in investigating the prehistory of the Near East. His contributions to general anthropology are notable. Thus, it would have been perfectly appropriate to ask for articles from a very wide spectrum of scholarly fields: geomorphology, paleobotany, paleozoology, ethnoarcheology, paleolithic archeology, social anthropology — to name but a few. What could we do when faced with such a range of choice?

1

The only way out of the difficulty was to adopt a Draconian policy. We would restrict the topics to be covered to the food-producing time range within Southwestern Asia, and more particularly to the period between roughly 10,000 to 4000 B.C. in the upland zone of the Fertile Crescent from the Mediterranean to western Iran — that is, the period and the regions in which Bob himself has done most of his fieldwork. And we would limit ourselves to contributions by archeologists. We are more than pleased with the results of our policy, and we think that the quality of the articles in this volume justifies our decision in favor of a narrow spectrum of contributors and a more intensive focus than is the rule in most festschriften.

Our editorial thanks are due to several people who helped in the preparation of this book. First, a grateful nod to Robert McC. Adams, who has encouraged the project from the start. J.A. Brinkman, director of the Oriental Institute in 1978, made the whole effort possible by generously giving the idea the backing of the Institute and by arranging for funds needed in the editorial process. Bardy Hart and Carole Richards-Gilbert, of the West Asian Department of the Royal Ontario Museum, did a considerable amount of cheerful retyping of manuscripts and redrawing of illustrations, even though such work was not in their normal line of duty. Jean Luther, managing editor of the Oriental Institute, has coped professionally with manuscripts in two languages, typescripts that sometimes were less than finished products, and drawings and tables in different hands and different formats. Finally, our editorial thanks go also to all contributors. Any delays in the appearance of this volume are our fault, not theirs. In the main, they accepted with good grace our criticisms of and suggestions for their manuscripts. They have been enthusiastic in support of the project. This, then, is their book.

Before the reader turns to these various contributions, however, a brief word about Robert J. Braidwood and his career as a scholar is appropriate.

A full biographical essay, or scholarly appraisal, would be out of place and, in any case, premature. Rather, we would like to muse in a somewhat impressionistic manner (a good Braidwoodian technique) on four specific aspects of Braidwood's contribution thus far: first, his undoubted pioneering efforts to direct archeological attention to the study of the Neolithic (tenacious neogrecism) or Food-producing Revolution in the Near East; second, his contribution to the difficult and often frustrating task of developing multidisciplinary research in prehistoric studies; third, his influence on the discipline of anthropology and, more important, on the public's understanding of that discipline; and fourth, his impact on students of ancient languages and archeology working on the historic ancient Near East.

Braidwood himself has often suggested that what he tried to do can best be understood in terms of the so-called Gap Chart (fig. 1) which graphically outlines what was not known at the end of the Second World War about the shift from hunting and gathering subsistence systems to settled village farming in the Near East. Braidwood compiled the data — or rather details about the lack of data — necessary to draw this chart while he was a student in Henri Frankfort's famous seminar in Chicago in the late thirties and early forties, and he developed the chart for a class in anthropology, which he taught jointly right after the war with Sol Tax and W.M. Krogman. As far as we are aware, the chart itself was first published in 1946 (Braidwood, 1946, p.183).

A brief look at the chart drives home the now astonishing point that in 1945 we had no sites excavated and, effectively, none surveyed that dated after the Zarzian and Natufian and before Hassuna and Garstang's Jericho. In other words, despite V.G. Childe's plea for "Light from the East," made in an effort to complete the picture, as he then saw it, of the diffusion of an agricultural way of life from the Near East into Europe, Near Eastern archeology had simply not addressed the problem in any systematic way. Seton Lloyd and Fuad Safar had published their excavations at Tell Hassuna in 1945, and, as a result, scholars were just beginning to realize that fully developed village farming life was much more ancient in the Tigris and Euphrates valley than once thought. Yet no known site provided a link between that sixth millennium agricultural community and the late hunting and gathering subsistence system that Garrod had documented as the Zarzian of the terminal Pleistocene. In Syro-Palestine the information gap between the last Paleolithic of the region and the earliest known farming villages was, if anything, even wider than in Greater Mesopotamia. Today it is sometimes hard to realize how little we knew such a few years ago.

Braidwood made his most significant contribution to Near Eastern prehistory — if not to prehistoric studies in general — by consciously deciding in 1947 to do something *systematic* to fill this information gap. Looking back today we see that at least two score archeologists eventually joined him in this attack on the big blank in the Gap Chart, with the result, as Nissen observes in this volume, that some 110 aceramic Neolithic sites alone are now known from the Near East. But Braidwood led the way. Remarkably enough, he has been directly involved in the exploration and excavation of over a score of pre-Hassuna and post-Zarzian sites (to say nothing of numerous Paleolithic, Hassuna/Samarra, and post-Hassuna sites). To a considerable extent, inspired by Childe's keen interest in the Near East as a possible hearth of agriculture, it was Braidwood who brought the issues into focus and then led us into the field.

When we look at Braidwood's second major contribution to the discipline, we see that he was once again a genuine pioneer, at least in a Near Eastern context. His drawing of the Gap Chart outlined the problem from a strategic point of view; his field projects were the tactical answer to the strategic problem as he saw it. First, like any good historian or archeologist would have, he developed a testable hypothesis about the Neolithic Revolution. Because it was the upland fringes of the Fertile Crescent that were today the natural habitat of the plants and animals first domesticated in the Near East, Braidwood felt that agriculture probably began in that region, not in the lowlands. Thus was born the hypothesis of the Hilly Flanks. Second, he constructed a field program suitable for the testing of his proposition. Thus was reborn — this time to survive in a Near Eastern context — the idea of a cooperative venture, in the field and laboratory, of natural scientists and archeologists.[1] If, said Braidwood, we archeologists are going to study the processes by which man in the Near East domesticated plants and animals, then we will have to have help from botanists and zoologists at least. But there was more. It was also Braidwood's goal to break out of the old Near Eastern mold of site-oriented fieldwork. Just to dig a site would be an inappropriate field tactic, given his hypothesis and the problem as he understood it. Building on his prewar experiences in the Amuq, he now insisted that we must be interested in a region — in more than one site, in sites in different time ranges, and in the environmental setting of those sites. Hence, at a minimum, his team needed a geologist and, preferably, other natural scientists interested in the past and present landscape rather than in only the artifacts and specimens that the archeologist dug up. And so, the multidisciplinary team came to have dimensions it had never had before. For most prehistorians today this is a commonplace approach. In 1947 in the Near East it was a new idea.[2]

1. Before World War II, such cooperation, usually on a more limited scale than that envisioned by Braidwood, had often been tried on Paleolithic excavations and research projects. Pumpelly had even introduced the idea to Near Eastern archeology back at the turn of the century, when he set out to study the oasis and site of Anau in Russian Turkmenistan, but the concept had died aborning (Pumpelly 1908).

2. As a distinguished contemporary of Braidwood puts it: "The excavations undertaken by the Oriental Institute of Chicago [i.e., Braidwood's excavations after World War II] and those inspired by its initiative, accomplished far more than extending the stratigraphy of a region of key importance to the history of civilisation. As befits fieldwork undertaken to test ideas, the campaign as a whole has helped to alter the whole climate of thought about the true nature of the process of economic transformation at one time

Braidwood's impact on anthropology follows from all we have said thus far about his work. As a pioneer he influenced his discipline by leading the way for others; and together he and others have made the study of the Food-producing Revolution as a vital process in human evolution one of the most popular topics among prehistorians and anthropological archeologists — perhaps, it might now even be said, to the detriment of the study of certain other critical issues in the prehistory of the Holocene Near East.[3] Be that as it may, Braidwood's scholarly contribution to anthropology as a comparative discipline is clear — in his own work and in the work of those who have followed him, both chronologically and intellectually, and, we might add, he has by example been far more influential in demonstrating to colleagues in Europe and other parts of the Old World the advantages of the anthropological approach to prehistory than many who rely on exhortation alone.

What may not be so very well known is what his work, his personality, and his attitudes have done for anthropology and prehistory in a world beyond the limits of the discipline. The theme of the XIth International Congress of Anthropological and Ethnological Sciences, soon to be held in Canada, is "Anthropology and the Public." Braidwood would make a good keynote speaker. His clear and eminently readable elementary textbook, *Prehistoric Men*, is today in its eighth edition and may very well go into still more printings. It is used widely, not only in introductory courses in anthropology but also in many university and some secondary school courses outside anthropology, and it has now influenced more than one generation of beginning students. His little book *The Near East and the Foundations of Civilization* is another classic of its kind that has stimulated many undergraduate students to a vision of the prehistoric and early historic Near East. In yet another effort to reach the wider public, Braidwood put together a small display on the Neolithic Revolution in the Oriental Institute Museum (the first strictly prehistoric display the museum ever mounted). Many saw and enjoyed that exhibit. It also caught the eye of *Time* magazine's science editor. An article with pictures followed, and suddenly the concepts — that people had to domesticate plants and animals before they could stop hunting and gathering and start farming and that agriculture was the necessary foundation for more complex civilizations — were known to much of the general public in North America. Such a chain of events was not surprising, for Braidwood has a style and a presence that appeals to the wider public. In sum, Braidwood's ability to reach beyond the confines of pure scholarship to a larger audience has been good both for his own disciplines — anthropology and Near Eastern prehistory — and for that larger audience itself.

Finally, we come to Bob Braidwood's impact and influence on more traditional Near Eastern studies. We have heard him criticized (with a touch of envy?) for having sometimes published essentially the same paper in many different journals and scholarly publications, both in North America and abroad. Bob himself has mused aloud about the wisdom of that tactic, We would challenge his critics. To diffuse the results of a piece of prehistoric research and thinking across a wide range of scholarly publications is to reach more minds than is possible with a single article in one journal. Therefore, on one level this practice of repeat publications simply stems from Braidwood's dedication to spreading the message as widely as possible. On another level, however, this tactic has brought the excitement of Near Eastern prehistory to the attention of scholars who are not prehistorians — who would never read the standard journals of the field.

---

telescoped in the slogan 'The Neolithic Revolution.' Indeed, the Chicago initiative was one of those most influential in transforming prehistory from a hobby into a disciplined field of scholarship uniquely equipped to test historical hypotheses in terms of extended periods of time" (Clark 1980, p. 9).

3. One senses today something of a renewed interest in the so-called Chalcolithic period and its developments — a consequence, though not a necessary consequence, of the Food-producing Revolution. Articles in this volume by Oates, Watson, Hours-Copeland, Dollfus, Hole, and Nissen are cases in point. Braidwood himself, of course, began his career working on these time ranges and problems in Syria.

How many Near Eastern prehistorians have published as much as Braidwood has in such periodicals as the *Journal of Near Eastern Studies* or the *Journal of World History*?

Of all the scholars who work beyond the confines of anthropology and prehistory those who study the ancient Near East of postprehistoric times have probably been the most influenced by Braidwood's work. This is no doubt due in part to his having had a joint appointment in the Department of Anthropology and the Oriental Institute of the University of Chicago; his office was in the Institute, he taught classes in the building, he shared lab space with other archeologists. Thus he was personally known by many of the philologists and historic archeologists who have been the Institute's strength since it was founded by James Breasted, and they, being distinguished savants of the wider world of ancient Near Eastern studies, helped Braidwood spread the word to many who might not otherwise have had the slightest knowledge of anything that happened at Jericho before Joshua is said to have blown it down. More important, however, are Braidwood's articles and lectures published and given outside the scholarly channels normally used by prehistorians and anthropologists. To a considerable extent, Braidwood is responsible, in North America at least, for the interest that Near Eastern historians have come to evince over the past thirty years in events that happened before 4000 B.C. and for the importance now attached to preliterate periods by those same historians.

More or less at random we plucked two histories of the ancient Near East from a library shelf. A. Leo Oppenheim, in his *Ancient Mesopotamia: Portrait of a Dead Civilization*, has a section, albeit brief, on The Background, in which he mentions botanists and zoologists, "centers of domestication," "lines of diffusion," and the "study of transition" — and then footnotes Braidwood's *Prehistoric Investigations*. W.W. Hallo, the cuneiformist, and W.K. Simpson, the Egyptologist, in their book, *The Ancient Near East, A History* go even further. They entitle a whole chapter "The Near East to the end of the Stone Age," and it begins with a section headed, Introduction: Half of History. Bob Braidwood is well footnoted in this section. We suggest that prehistory probably would have been ignored in these two works (and others like them) had they been written twenty-five years ago. As a case in point, note the following contrast. Whereas Hallo and Simpson are willing to give seven pages to the Paleolithic period alone, Breasted in his *History of Egypt* says, "They [Paleolithic men] cannot be connected in any way with the historic or prehistoric civilization of the Egyptians, and they fall exclusively within the province of the geologist and anthropologist" (Breasted 1950, p.25). Prehistory has become a respectable subject in ancient Near Eastern studies, and Braidwood has been a leader of those responsible for this felicitous development.

Robert J. Braidwood is seventy-five years old in this year of 1982. To a prehistorian's way of thinking, that is not many years — it is really nothing more than a most acceptable standard deviation on a first-class radiocarbon date! Yet it is fair to say that Braidwood's career as a prehistorian did not begin in earnest until after 1945, so he has really been at it for only thirty-five years. In that short time he has pioneered a new kind of factual interest in the Neolithic Revolution of the Near East; he has proved that the interdisciplinary and regional approach to archeology (regardless of the time range) is the only one that makes sense; he has stimulated his anthropological colleagues and a larger public into understanding the importance of the development of food production to wider issues; and he has broken down barriers between the disciplines that study the ancient Near East. He has not been alone in these efforts, but he has often been in front of others. Sometimes, as Bob Braidwood knows, "in front" is a dangerous place; but it is the place where the best of the good scholars will always be.

T. Cuyler Young, Jr.
Philip E. L. Smith
Peder Mortensen

BIBLIOGRAPHY

Braidwood, R.J.
    1946   The biography of a research project. *Chicago Today* 2(3):14—27.

Breasted, J.H.
    1950   *A history of Egypt.* New York: Scribner's.

Clark, G.
    1980   *Mesolithic prelude: the Palaeolithic-Neolithic transition in old world prehistory.* Edinburgh: Edinburgh University Press.

Flannery, K.V.
    1969   Origins and ecological effects of early domestication in Iran and the Near East. In *The domestication and exploitation of plants and animals*, ed. P.J. Ucko and G.W. Dimbleby, pp. 73—100. London: Duckworth.

Pumpelly, R.
    1908   *Explorations in Turkestan: prehistoric civilization of Anua.* Washington, D.C.: Carnegie Institution.

THE EDITORS regret that the economics of present-day publishing have not allowed for cross-checking between specific parts of a contribution, except where the need was obvious.

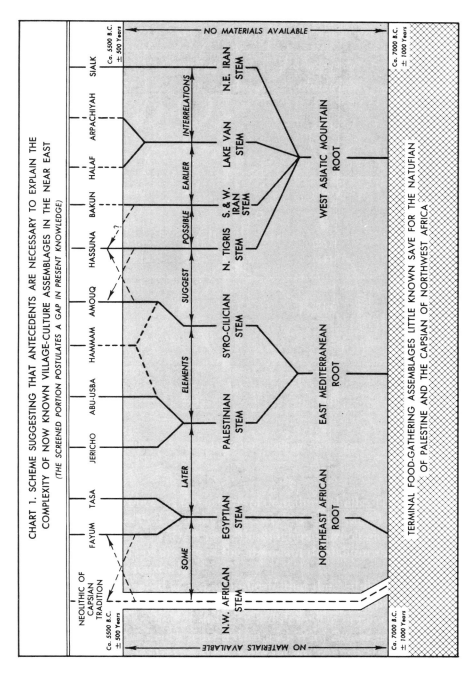

The "gap chart" was first drawn in 1945. The gray portion suggests a period of development completely unknown at that time. The "roots" and "stems" were wholly speculative, and may now be disregarded. The dates were "guess dates," reckoned before the development of radioactive carbon determination. [This is the original caption. — EDS.]

Fig. 1.

SECTION I:
SYRO-PALESTINE

THE NATUFIAN IN THE SOUTHERN LEVANT

Ofer Bar-Yosef

INTRODUCTION

SINCE the first discoveries of D. Garrod and R. Neuville in the caves of Mt. Carmel and the Judean Desert, the Natufian culture has received special attention in the prehistory of the Levant and particularly in relation to the origins of the agricultural revolution (Childe 1952; Braidwood 1952, 1965). A large number of Natufian sites were uncovered by those who were at the same time pioneers of Stone Age research in the Holy Land (Garrod and Bate 1937; Garrod 1932, 1942; Turville-Petre 1932; Neuville 1934, 1951). In an extensive review published almost three decades after the first excavations, Garrod announced the new stage of research initiated with the uncovering of the large open-air sites of Eynan (Ain Mallaha) and Nahal Oren (Wadi Fallah) (Garrod 1957).

Today, almost a generation later, only preliminary reports of these two important sites are available. These, with the earlier publications, despite their lack of crucial details form the main basis for overall summaries of the Natufian (Perrot 1968; Redman 1978; Hassan 1977; Braidwood 1973, 1975).

Therefore there is no need to justify the continued study of Natufian sites, either in the original territory of the Galilee, Mt. Carmel, and Judean Hills or in adjacent regions such as the Beka'a valley in Lebanon or the Negev. Several of the previously investigated sites have been the subjects of renewed excavation. These included the terraces of El-Khiam and Nahal Oren, Eynan, and, lately, the terrace of El-Wad (Echegaray 1964, 1966; Noy et al. 1973; Perrot 1974; Valla 1975–77). New sites were discovered through systematic surveys and have been partially excavated or tested (Henry 1976a, b; Marks and Larson 1977; Bar-Yosef et al. 1974; Valla et al. 1979). The distribution of known Natufian sites in the southern Levant is shown in figure 1.

With the new wave of fieldwork in Natufian sites came efforts to interpret Natufian material culture in different terms. Following critiques of Childe's and Braidwood's models, and with the exposition of new paradigms, more elaborate interpretations of the Natufian were stressed (Binford 1968; Flannery 1969; Wright 1977; Hassan 1977; Redman 1978). The Natufian became an example of the archeological expression of intensive hunting and gathering, along with a number of agricultural preadaptations as reflected in certain utensils and installations. Efforts were even made to differentiate between Natufian sites occupied primarily in vegetal food collection and those occupied primarily in hunting (Hassan 1977). However, many of these interpretive efforts were too often based on very fragmentary evidence and on intelligent guesses rather than on solid facts. It is instructive at this point in our research to present a critical review of the Natufian in the light of the most recent discoveries made in Israel.

Neither the theoretical questions concerning the definition of the Natufian as an archeological entity nor the uncertainties of what constitutes a site will be discussed here. Instead, a brief list of suppositions and pragmatic working hypotheses based on experience gained in fieldwork, laboratory work, recently published data of ethnographical observations from the Near East, and living hunter-gatherer societies from temperate and semiarid zones, is given here.

> 1. All lithic assemblages included within the Natufian entity demonstrate that the same basic technology was always used for flint knapping. Variations of the specific (secon-

dary) technology, such as microburin technique, are used as markers for subentities, either chronological or territorial.

2. Quantitative typological variability between the different flint, bone, and ground stone assemblages is expected. Additional data (faunal remains, microwear analysis, and so forth) could serve to differentiate between chronological and seasonal (functional) changes. Intrasite variability can be expected as a consequence of deflation/erosion during interoccupation periods or as an expression of different activity areas. The latter can be discerned only when well recorded and well sealed loci are excavated carefully.

3. The geographical distribution of the various sites is expected to concur with the territorial behavior of the main species of available game. If wild stands of cereals were exploited, their exact location should be reconstructed on the basis of palynological evidence compared with their recent distribution.

4. Neighboring archeological entities coeval with the Natufian should be reconstructed on the basis of the same pragmatic assumptions (1−3) in order to establish the uniqueness of the latter.

Following the observable differences between the various Natufian sites and in view of the difficulties that stem from the identification with the Natufian of every assemblage containing lunates, a site classification was proposed (Bar-Yosef 1970). Large sites containing structures, burials, numerous heavy ground stone tools, and a rich bone industry were labeled *base camps*. Small sites without structures and graves, but with a rich lithic industry, located within a reasonable radius from the base camps (ca. 30−50 km) were called *seasonal camps*. Neither of these terms was meant to indicate precisely the degree of occupancy, i.e., ephemeral, permanent, and so forth, or the major economic activity carried on at the site. This terminology was aimed primarily at suggesting a site hierarchy in order to permit the definition of various Natufian territories, working on the assumption that under Levantine Mediterranean conditions each such territory would have included one base camp and several seasonal ones (Bar-Yosef 1975).

The Natufian as an archeological entity is therefore defined on the basis of the contents of its base camps. Taking into account both their constituents and their distribution in the southern Levant, the base camps can be divided into two major regions: the Galilee-Judea and the Negev Highlands. This assessment has nothing to do with other possible Natufian territories in Lebanon and Syria. Detailed publications of sites from these adjacent regions will enable us to make a better definition of the Natufian. Meanwhile, this paper will present some basic facts and offer some questionable hypotheses related to the chronological framework of the Natufian in the southern Levant, to reconstructed paleoenvironment, to the structures and graves built by the Natufians, and to their lithic, bone, and ground stone industries, their art objects, and their jewelry. The final parts of the paper will raise some problems concerning the interpretations of site size.

CHRONOLOGICAL FRAMEWORK AND CLIMATIC RECONSTRUCTION

Stratigraphy remains the basic tool for the relative chronological placement of any archeological entity. The Natufian culture, in its restricted definition, has been found in a stratified sequence in only two sites. These are Yabrud Rock-shelter III (Rust 1950), where a small Early Natufian assemblage lies above a Geometric Kebaran A (once called Falitian), and Hayonim Terrace (Henry 1976b), which has a similar sequence. This situation, which exists in spite of the large number of known Natufian sites (fig. 1), demonstrates a shift in the settlement pattern when compared with that of preceding cultural complexes (Bar-Yosef, forthcoming).

More accurate chronological placement of the Natufian is based on the following list of radiocarbon dates (table 1). When these dates are accompanied by the dates of preceding and

Table 1. — Radiocarbon Dates from Natufian Sites

	Material (charcoal, bone)	*B.C.*	*Lab. no.*
Early Natufian			
Hayonim Terrace D	CH	9970±90	SNU-231
El-Wad B₂ (Cave)	B	9970±660	UCLA
El-Wad B₂ (Terrace)	B	9525±600	ULCA
Kebarah B	B	9200±400	UCLA
Jericho	CH	7850±240	GL-72
Jericho	CH	7900±240	GL-69
Jericho	CH	9216±107	P-376
Eynan (Mallaha) IV sol b	CH	9640±540	LY-1660
Eynan III sol	CH	9790±570	LY-1661
Eynan III sol	CH	9360±880	LY-1662
Late Natufian			
Rosh Horesha	CH	11,140±200	I-5496
Rosh Horesha	CH	8540±430	SMU-9
Rosh Horesha	CH	8930±280	SMU-10
Nahal Oren V	B	8096±318	BM-764
El-Wad B₁	B	7845±600	UCLA
Mureybet Phase IA	CH	8400±150	Mc-663
	CH	8220±200	Mc-731
	CH	8280±170	Mc-732
	CH	8150±150	Mc-674
	CH	8080±150	Mc-733
"Epi-Natufian"			
Mureybet Phase IB	CH	8640±140	Lv-607
Harifian			
Abu Salem	CH	8020±150	I-549
	CH	8220±150	I-5499
	CH	8280±150	I-5500

succeeding cultural complexes, one can cautiously estimate the duration of the Natufian as from ca. 10,300 B.C. through 8500 B.C. (fig. 2).

In figure 2 the available data from within the main geographical units of the southern Levant are used to show the distribution of the various archeological entities between ca. 11,000–7500 B.C. An examination of this chronological chart indicates that no Natufian sites are as yet recorded from northern Sinai. Only three small ephemeral sites assigned to the Early Natufian have been located in the western Negev to date, while none have been securely attributed to the Late Natufian, in spite of the continuous surveys still being conducted (A. N. Goring-Morris, pers. comm.).

The chronological placement of the Natufian within a critical climatic period — the transition from the Pleistocene to the Holocene — necessitates a brief discussion of the fragmentary evidence related to this subject. Contrary to the prevailing agreement during the 1950s and even the early 1960s that no major climatic changes occurred in the Levant, a different picture has emerged from the palynological records, alluvial sequences, paleozoological studies, and so forth (Van Zeist and Bottema 1977; Wright 1977; Butzer 1978; Tchernov 1976; Davis 1978). As yet, however, the clearest records are still those of the northern Levant. In that vast region the presence of lakes has permitted the preservation of pollen grains and the possibility of obtaining long detailed cores. Unfortunately, the same is not true for the southern Levant.

The reconstruction of Van Zeist, Bottema, and Wright shows the dominance of cold and dry conditions in the northern Levant from ca. 12,000–9000 B.C. Following the possible division of the Levant into three main climatic transversal zones (Butzer 1978) one may infer for this period a cold and wet climate prevailing in the southern Levant. This tentative conclusion is supported by the fragmentary geomorphological evidence (Butzer 1978; Goldberg 1976) and the dispersion of numerous sites, radiocarbon dated, over the deserts (Bar-Yosef, forthcoming). However, it is as yet unclear exactly when the transition from the Pleistocene to the Holocene climate occurred in the various subzones of the Levant.

Today, it seems that this climatic change in Israel was not less marked than it is in the palynological record of the northern Levant. This is well demonstrated in the marine cores from the Gulf of Eilat (Z. Reiss, pers. comm.), the fragmentary palynological evidence from the Jordan valley (Horowitz 1979), and the sediments of Natufian open-air sites showing an increase in colluvial accumulation (Bar-Yosef et al. 1974). The interpretation of the few examples of pollen spectra from archeological sites is still controversial (A. Leroi-Gourhan, Th. Henry 1976b; Horowitz 1976). Strong arguments suggest that pollen grains from these sites and many others were the result of the infiltration of recent and subrecent pollen grains as well as of selective preservation. It is therefore advocated that paleoclimatic inferences be primarily based on the detailed study of cores from the sea shelf and existing or dried-up lakes.

Until the results of this kind of research are available, the following reconstruction is proposed. From ca. 12,000 B.C. to ca. 9000 B.C., the northern zone, incorporating most of the Galilee, was characterized by cold and dry conditions. Southward, ranging into the Negev and Sinai, a zone of cold and wet climate prevailed. Around 9000 B.C. this zone moved northward, causing the expansion of forests into higher altitudes in the Zagros and the Ghab (Van Zeist and Bottema 1977). Therefore, during the early Holocene, the climate of the southern Levant was Mediterranean to semiarid and the area had better rain distribution than it has today. A moister spell, less marked than the previous one, occurred during the seventh millennium B.C.

STRUCTURES, GRAVES, AND POPULATION

Characteristic features of the Natufian are partially subterranean habitation structures and graves. In spite of the limited evidence, it is nevertheless clear that building activities were rare in some earlier Kebaran and Geometric Kebaran sites but more impressive and common in the Natufian.

Architectural relics are best known from Eynan (Ain Mallaha), where they can be separated into three major layers (Perrot 1966, 1974; Valla 1975, 1981). In the earliest layer three structures were exposed. The largest was a semicircular dwelling about 8–9 m in diameter; seven postholes indicated possible roofing. The second structure was smaller (4 m in diameter), and the third had a benchlike outline made of simple lime plaster. The second layer provided smaller structures (6–3 m in diameter) and installations that were organized in what seemed to be three terraces (a phenomenon known from the later PPNA occupation at Nahal Oren). The uppermost layer contained only a few relics. In every layer a repeated set of rebuildings, modifications, and so forth, was recognized, indicating continued return to the place by people who knew, or even built, the original structures. The redigging and rebuilding created small stratigraphical problems as well as difficulties in isolating discrete lithic assemblages, but the overall picture of the site remained the same.

Hayonim Cave revealed, in its main occupation layer, a series of small, oval structures (2.5–3.5 m in diameter) built of undressed stones brought inside the cave by the Natufians. Each structure was used as a habitation for at least one phase of its history. One of them (locus 4) served later as a kiln for burning limestone. Pounded lime was found on the edges of pestles both at Hayomin Cave and at Eynan, where structure 1 and a few plastered pits indicate that the use of this mixture had already started during Natufian times.

The relics on Hayonim Terrace and El-Wad Terrace were fragmentary, built up in the same manner as at Eynan, forming a terrace wall and not a free-standing wall. Similar walls were uncovered at Nahal Oren but have not been published. In the latter site, postholes, similar to those of Eynan, were uncovered around the large fireplace in the cemetery area (Stekelis and Yizraeli 1963, pl. 3A).

Flimsy, poorly preserved circular structures were exposed in Rosh Zin (Henry 1976); the clearest one has a pavement with a stone pillar at its edge. Rounded structures are also visible on the surface of Rosh Horesha, the southernmost Natufian site in the Negev Highlands (Marks and Larson 1977).

Among the numerous installations within the Natufian sites two types are quite discrete: the hearths and the circular, paved binlike installations. Plastered pits at Eynan increase the variability of this category. No plant remains have yet been found in any of the installations to testify to their possible usage.

Natufian graves were uncovered in all base camps in the Galilee-Judean Hills region. The exact relationship between the dwellings and the graves is as yet unclear. There are indications at Eynan that the graves were dug in deserted habitation structures and under the floors. At Hayonim Cave the graves of the main occupation layer were in the area of the cave, outside the structures. But from the earlier occupation one grave was uncovered from under the floor.

The graves were formed from either shallow or deep pits and were rarely paved with stones. At Hayonim Cave two tombs were constructed of limestone slabs. Similar slabs were used to cover simpler graves at Eynan, Erq el-Ahmar, and also Hayonim. But, in general, ordinary graves were closed with cobbles or simply with earth. Sealed graves were marked at Nahal Oren by the deep "stonepipes" (also considered mortars broached or broken at the bases). Both in Nahal Oren and in Hayonim Cave, small cup marks were made in one of the stones above or beside the graves.

Special installations in cemeteries or burial grounds were scarce. It is claimed that the large fireplace (1.2 m in diameter) surrounded by limestone slabs in Nahal Oren belongs to the ensemble of inhumations around it (Stekelis and Yizraeli 1963).

The burials themselves showed significant variability, both in burial patterns and in grave goods. Almost as a rule, the pattern of the body disposition varied in primary burials from supine to semiflexed to flexed position. The number of inhumations also varied from single to collective. Secondary burials were either isolated or mixed with primary burials, and it is nearly impossible to characterize the typical Natufian burial (Perrot 1966; Valla 1975a, 1975–77; Bar-Yosef and Goren 1973). Scattered human bones occurred also within excavated occupational deposits.

The categorization of single or collective burials according to the chronological order of the Natufian cultural sequence needs quantitative support, but it looks as if the early observations made by Garrod and Neuville were correct and single burials were more numerous during the Late Natufian.

The common grave goods were head decorations, necklaces, bracelets, and belts worn around the thighs. Dentalium shells and bone pendants were frequently the constituents of this jewelry. Necklaces made of partridge tibia and perforated wolf canines were exceptional examples found at Hayonim Cave.

The direct relationship of other grave goods to the burials is rarely clear. At Hayonim Cave a bone dagger 30 cm long was found under the right arm of a woman lying in a supine position. In Nahal Oren the bone figurine of a young gazelle, as well as other art objects, is attributed to a burial (Cauvin 1972). A limestone man's head from El-Wad was located near skeleton H.10. Four gazelle horn cores were found in a grave at Eynan, but more doubtful as grave goods are the horse teeth assigned to the secondary burials in Erq el-Ahmar.

The contents of a special grave at Eynan stand out: a young child and a puppy dog were found buried together (Valla 1975–77; Davis and Valla 1978). Besides being new evidence of domestication of the dog, it provides an insight into man–animal relationship.

The failure of the research to give a better picture of Natufian mortuary practices is also exemplified in the study of the skeletal remains. Of the very large number of burials uncovered since the excavations of Garrod in Shukbah, in 1928, only a small portion has been adequately published. A brief survey shows that the following numbers of inhumations have been mentioned in the literature: Erq el-Ahmar, 7; Shukbah, 45; Kebara, ?; El-Wad, 87; Eynan, ca. 40; Nahal Oren, ca. 45; Hayonim, ca. 35. But of an expected total of 250–300 skeletons (complete and fragmentary) only about 30 or 40 have been published along with metrical data (Arensburg 1973; Arensburg et al. 1975; Ferembach 1977).

There is a consensus that the Natufian population is a Proto-Mediterranean one, i.e., an autochthonic population with some similarities to Mousterian ancestors as well as to the scarce remains from the Upper Paleolithic and earlier Epipaleolithic deposits (Arensburg 1977). The Natufians were "short to medium in stature (males 160–165 cm; females 150–155 cm). Their mean age at death was about 30 years, and maximum life-span may have been around 50 years. Their crania were generally gracile, with a relatively large capacity (1484 cc, males). The males tended to be dolichocranial (mean index, 72.9); females were mesocranial (mean index, 77.8); brachycrany occurred in some 20% of the skulls. The vault was generally high, orthocrane to hypsicrane in relation to length, and acrocrane to metriocrane in relation to breadth. The frontal region was metriometope to eurymetope. The face was broad, euryene and euryprosope in the males (no female faces were available for measurement); the nose was chamaerrhine; and the orbits were chamaechonche. The mandible was brachygnathic, with a relatively wide ramus and medium bigonial-bichondylar proportion." (Arensburg et al. 1975, p. 206.)

Slightly different, but still falling within this population, were those from Eynan who were more robust, perhaps due to greater calcium consumption in their daily diet (Ferembach 1977).

Finally, observed dental pathological variations exhibited a high incidence of caries in the populations at Eynan, El-Wad, and Nahal Oren, slightly less than a high incidence at Hayonim Cave, and a low incidence at Kebara Cave (Smith 1972). The last-named site provided some unique archeological features as well. The preliminary report of the excavator (Turville-Petre 1932) indicates the presence of about 1,000 sickle blades, a figure not reached in any other site. Moreover, the number of pounding stones (kept in the Rockefeller Museum in Jerusalem) is very small. Unfortunately, the Natufian layer was completely removed from the cave and therefore additional digging is not a viable option.

Smith concluded her studies by stating that the Natufians consumed pounded or ground cereals, probably after roasting them; by this activity they differed from their predecessors and were similar to the population of Neolithic Jericho.

A serious effort to ascertain the distribution of age groups of the Natufians has yet to be made. The data are scarce and indicate that only about 30% of the dead were children up to 10 years of age. The frequency of those who reached 30 is about 5% to 10%. There is an urgent need for paleodemographic studies of the Natufian populations, as these may provide insights into the question of possible evidence for demographic pressures.

In short, questions concerning the reconstruction of social hierarchies, kinship among the dead, the relationship of grave goods to the buried people, and so forth, are impossible to answer at this time.

Natufian mortuary practices themselves (including the filling of graves with large stones and consequent skeletal deformation) and geomorphological processes have complicated these studies significantly. More serious, the absence of adequate reporting, including the presentation of maps, photos, and lists of accompanying artifacts, has severely hampered research efforts.

FLINT, STONE, AND BONE INDUSTRIES

The lithic industries, in the framework of a systematic study, are analyzed on three different levels: basic technology (the methods for blank production and their metric results), specific technology (methods of secondary trimming, including microburin technique and resharpening), and morphological typology. Functional typology, based on microwear studies, will not be considered here in spite of its importance for the interpretation of discrete, well-excavated assemblages (Cahen et al. 1979).

The main difficulties in studying the basic technology stem from the lack of agreement on descriptive attributes and methods of measurement. The difficulty in distinguishing between direct and indirect percussion in Epipaleolithic industries and the identification of the striking platforms on cores struck from various directions are examples of these problems. No less problematic are the measurements of length, maximum width, and thickness of blades and bladelets, which cast doubt on the boundary of 12 mm as a boundary between the two categories (Tixier 1963). These questions and others only indicate that the study of what is now commonly called debitage (blanks, cores, and debris) is still in its infancy, and even certain aspects related to the availability and nature of raw material in a given region are as yet not well studied.

A pioneering technological study made a few years ago by D. Henry presented a large body of data from several Natufian sites. Also included were additional assemblages considered as belonging to the same entity, due to the presence of lunates (Henry 1973, 1977). Although Henry's work had shown the uniqueness of the Natufian basic technology, further accumulation of data concerning various other Epipaleolithic industries blurred its distinctiveness. Nevertheless, anyone who has handled Levantine Epipaleolithic assemblages is capable of distinguishing between Natufian products and most of the other ones. This capability reinforces the feeling one gets, from reading the available reports, that every scholar uses his own attributes to describe and classify the debitage types. In comparing Natufian technology to other Epipaleolithic industries it is sufficient to characterize it as a predominantly blade/bladelet industry. The blades and bladelets were generally short and wide and had blunt tips (as opposed to convergent distal ends). Cores were exploited intensively from more than one striking platform and more than one knapping direction, which resulted in the scarcity of flat striking platforms. (Of the blanks, blades/bladelets were regularly used for shaping mainly microlithic tools.)

Specific technological features found in Natufian assemblages include the use of microburin technique and the special shaping method known as Helwan retouch (bifacially oblique retouch). This type of retouch became the "fossile directeur" marking the Early Natufian manifestations and their contemporaries. It also played an important role in the suggested subdivisions of the Natufians as proposed by Garrod and Neuville. Recently, another trial to test this hypothesis was made on the basis of the following criteria: the intensity of use of the microburin technique (excluding the Krukowski burins, which resulted from a different process of retouching), the relative frequency of Helwan retouch on the total population of lunates, and the average length of lunates (see fig. 3 and Bar-Yosef and Valla, 1979). All reliable radiocarbon dates from Natufian sites that are not in contrast with either later or earlier industries were incorporated in the analysis; the results — the distribution of the assemblages according to time and units and technological facies — are presented in table 2.

It is thus clear that Garrod and Neuville's hypothesis must be modified to include two contemporaneous technological facies of the Natufian. More work and radiocarbon dates are obviously required, but the outcome of this analysis has already undergone two field tests. An excavation at Eynan (summer 1979) in the uppermost layer (Ib) revealed the higher frequency of

Table 2. — Suggested Chronological Division of Natufian Sites Following
Technological Criteria and Size Decrease of Lunates

	With Microburin Technology	*Without Microburin Technology*
Late *Natufian*	Taibé	Salibiya I
	Nahal Oren VI−V	Shukbah Cave B
	Fazael IV	Eynan Ib
	Rosh Zin	Eynan Ic
	Rosh Horesha	
	El-Wad B_1	
	Tor Abu Sif	
	P. 508	
	Umm ez-Zuwetina	
Early *Natufian*	Beidha	Eynan IV−III−II
	El-Wad B_2	Hayonim Cave B
	Hayonim Terrace	El-Wad B_2(?)
		Kebara B
		Umm Qalaa
		Erq el-Ahmar

short lunates made by abrupt retouch. Similarly, a small sounding in El-Wad Terrace produced a Late Natufian sample (from Garrod's layer A, which is mixed with Byzantine sherds) with very small, abruptly retouched lunates. Further investigations will, perhaps, lead to an even better spatial and chronological division of the Natufian.

On the third level of technological analysis, most of the blanks chosen by the Natufians were shaped by various specific technologies (burin blow, retouch, microburin technique, and so forth) into those forms that quantitatively characterize the Natufian assemblages. The number of recently studied assemblages using accepted type lists or well defined categories is rather small; therefore, it is better to remain on the level of tool-group descriptions. Table 3 presents the figures from several already published works and gives a general idea about the typological variability among Natufian sites (fig. 4). This compilation requires a few comments and clarifications concerning certain tool types.

While the indices of end scrapers are more or less the same in various sites, those of the burins fluctuate quite considerably. However, the burins on truncations are the most common ones and were generally made with one burin blow. Retouched blades (which are considered a posteriori tools) and backed blades grade into the retouched and backed bladelets, traditionally defined as microliths. The boundary of 9 mm for the retouched bladelets (Tixier 1963), while very useful in earlier industries, is less effective for Natufian assemblages. In spite of the different approaches adopted by various researchers, the general group of microliths and geometrics reaches about 40% or more in every site. The index of the geometrics varies, and it seems that in the Late Natufian it tends to overrun the index of plain microliths. Among the geometrics the lunates generally dominate, but there is an interesting variability in the appearance of other types, such as the trapeze-rectangle, the triangle, and the parallelogram. Some sites, like Hayonim Cave, are devoid of these geometric forms, but in others, like Hayonim Terrace or Salibiya I, they are well represented.

Two special tool types occur consistently for the first time in the Natufian: picks and sickle blades. The first, which might be considered the forerunner of the axe group in the succeeding

Neolithic industries, is an elongated (8–10 cm) bifacially or trifacially flaked chunk (fig. 4, nos. 6–7). These have been recovered from Eynan, Hayonim Cave and Terrace, Nahal Oren, and El-Wad. Microwear studies might enable us to determine whether they were used for shaping ground stone artifacts, such as mortars, or for other tasks.

Sickle blades, showing luster that covers a relatively wide area on both faces of the blade, make their first quantitatively significant appearance in the Natufian and continue to be made through the succeeding seven millennia (through at least the Iron Age). There is little doubt that they were used for cutting grasses, especially the wild and, later, domesticated cereals. One may cautiously conclude that this tool type was more common in the Galilee-Jordan valley area than in the Negev. A similar phenomenon was observed among the Pre-Pottery Neolithic sites.

Ground stone tools occur in large numbers in Eynan, Hayonim, Nahal Oren, El-Wad, and Erq el-Ahmar (fig. 5). Only moderate or small numbers have been found so far at sites in the Lower Jordan valley (such as Fazael IV and Salibiya I), in the Judean Desert (Ain Sakhri, Umm ez-Zuwetina, Tor Abu Sif), and in the Negev. The ground stone tools are mainly pounding tools such as bedrock mortars, mobile mortars, bowls of various types, cup marks, and pestles. Of special interest are those boulder "mortars" pierced in heavy limestone cobbles (up to 100–150 kg) with a hole 70–80 cm deep, also called "stone pipes." As mentioned above, they were found in erected position in graves in Nahal Oren Terrace and around the platform at Jericho (Stekelis and Yizraeli 1963; Kenyon 1960). More were found on Hayonim Terrace and at Hayonim Cave (only as broken pieces). Among the mortars one finds a quasi-goblet shape (fig. 5, nos. 14–15). A meander relief decoration was found at both Eynan (Perrot 1966, fig. 15) and Shukba (unpublished). Some of the mortars and bowls as well as many of the pestles are made of basalt. An archeometric study is necessary in order to locate the actual sources, since in some cases the minimum distance to the closest basalt source is 30–50 km.

Within this group of artifacts two types of grooved stones are also included. The first and the simplest to interpret are the whetstones made of sandstone (the origins of which have also not been located). The second type, sometimes mistakenly included in the former category, is made of basalt (rarely of limestone) and has a parallel-sided groove that sometimes shows dark burning marks. These are probably the "shaft straighteners" known from the ethnographic literature. They attest indirectly to the use of archery in Natufian times. Supportive evidence comes from a recent study of a bone shaft straightener from El-Wad (Campana 1979).

The Natufian bone industry was undoubtedly far richer in quantity and forms than any earlier or later cultural entity. The variety of objects made of bones, teeth, and horn cores of gazelles, wolves, fallow deer, roe deer, and birds is presented in table 4 and figure 6.

The type list of the bone objects in table 4 is organized according to possible function. The first six types are thought to belong to skin-working and sewing activities. Fully shaped points or barbed ones (types 7–9) are considered parts of hunting devices (spears or arrows) and were well distributed over various ecological zones. Gorgets and hooks were possibly used in fishing and were found only in the Natufian sites close to the sea. Sickle hafts are among those objects whose function as a component of a cutting tool is exhibited by the complete specimens (from El-Wad, Umm ez-Zuwetina, and Zawi Chemi Shanidar). For the same reason the function of the various pendants is clear.

Whether the functional interpretation of each category is correct is still unknown, but the uneven geographical distribution is clear and the possibility of delineating cultural territories has already been discussed in the literature (Bar-Yosef and Tchernov 1970; Stordeur 1979; Bar-Yosef, forthcoming). Unfortunately, the lack of counts of bone objects (apart from Hayonim Cave and Terrace) prevents a serious discussion of this point. Relying only on presence and absence of certain types can lead to false conclusions. A few examples follow. At Hayonim Cave, in spite of the large excavated surface and volume there were no pendants made of gazelle phalanges or

Table 3. — Examples of Lithic Assemblages of Natufian Sites

	Eynan IV–III (741)	Eynan Ib (620)	Hayonim Cave Loc. 5 (504)	Hayonim Terrace Lay. C (747)	Salibiya I (423)	Fazael IV (1163)	Rosh Zin (1216)	Rosh Horesha (3173)
Scrapers on flakes/blades	2.7	2.0	5.3	5.6	2.3	1.0	7.2	2.7
Multiple tools	0.5	0.4	1.4	0.3	--	--	0.6	0.5
Burins	14.4	10.9	24.4	3.7	3.8	0.1	10.5	12.3
Retouched and backed blades	7.8	8.5	2.0	15.6	8.7	16.0	3.6	10.1
Truncated pieces	3.1	4.1	1.8	3.6	2.8	4.1	8.0	7.7
Microliths	32.0	27.9	21.6	40.0	36.4	20.8	8.7	9.6
Geometrics	8.0	11.7	15.2	14.6	21.7	25.7	37.6	32.5
Notches and denticulates	10.9	14.3	13.2	14.1	7.0	14.0	15.5	16.3
Perforators	2.7	2.7	0.8	0.8	1.9	1.7	2.0	1.5
Various tools	17.6	16.7	14.0	1.1	15.1	16.4	6.0	6.7
	99.7	99.2	99.7	99.4	99.7	99.8	99.7	99.9

SOURCES: Valla 1975a; Bar-Yosef and Goren 1973; Henry 1976; Marks and Larson 1977.

Table 4. — The Distribution of Various Bone Objects in Natufian Sites

Type	Hayonim Cave	Hayonim Terrace	Eynan	Nahal Oren	El-Wad	Kebara	Shukbah	Erq-el Ahmar	Umm ez-Zuwetina	Umm ez-Zuwetina	Salibiyah I	Jericho	Ain Sakhri	Rosh Horesha
1. Burnisher	x	--	x		x	--	--	--	--	--	--	--	--	--
2. Spatulae	x	--	x		--	x	--	--	--	--	--	--	--	--
3. Awl	x	x	x		x	x	--	x	x	x	x	--	x	x
4. Point with articulation	x	x	x		x	x	x	x	x	x	x	--	x	x(?)
5. Pierced point (needle)	--	--	x		x	x	x	--	--	--	x	--	--	--
6. Elongated point	--	--	x		--	--	--	x	--	--	--	--	--	--
7. Fully shaped point	x	--	x		x	x	x	x	--	--	--	--	--	--
8. Bi-point	--	--	x		--	x	--	x	--	--	--	--	--	--
9. Barbed point	--	x	--	x	x	x	--	x	--	--	--	x	x	--
10. Gorget	x	--	--	x	x	x	--	--	--	--	--	--	--	--
11. Hook	--	--	--	x	--	x	--	--	--	--	--	--	--	--
12. Sickle haft	x	--	x	x	x	x	--	--	x	x	--	--	--	--
13. Pendant, phalange	--	--	x		x	x	--	x	--	--	--	--	--	--
14. Pendant, tooth	x	--	--		x	--	--	--	--	--	--	--	--	--
15. Pendant, shaft	x	x	x		x	x	--	--	--	--	--	--	x	--
16. Pierced bone	--	--	x		x	--	--	--	--	--	--	--	--	--
17. Various bone objects	x	x	x		x	x	x	--	--	--	--	--	--	--

SOURCES: Bar-Yosef and Tchernov 1970; Henry 1976; Noy et al. 1973; Garrod and Bate 1936; Perrot 1966; Valla, pers. comm.; Garrod 1942; Neuville 1951; Kenyon 1960; Marks and Larson 1977.

bone points with the metapodial articulation in place. However, the latter was found in Hayonim Terrace. Perforated elongated bone pieces were found at Eynan and only recently on the surface of El-Wad Terrace. The possible relationship between the Natufian sites within a reconstructed societal framework is still untested, and while the bone industry might help in this matter, it should first be checked against the results obtained from the studies of various other archeological features.

ART OBJECTS AND ORNAMENTS

Natufian art can be divided into two basic categories: naturalistic figurines and decorations and abstract decorations. The naturalistic art objects are made of bone and limestone and are either portable figurines or decorations on utensils in daily use. The inventory includes five sculpted sickle hafts from El-Wad and Kebara and a broken bone figurine from Nahal Oren decorated with young ruminants, possibly gazelles. Two portable objects found in the cemetery area of Nahal Oren show a different feature at either end. One has an awl (?) at one end and a limestone dog's head at the other. The other is a horn core, which has a man's head carved at one end and a bovid's head carved at the other. Additional limestone (or calcitic) figurines represent a human body, a human face, and a schematic face from Eynan, a man's head from El-Wad, a mating couple from Ain Sakhri, a tortoise (?) from Eynan, and the famous kneeling gazelle (?) from Umm ez-Zuwetina (figs. 7–8).

Abstract decorations include the net, chevron (or zigzag), meander patterns, and numerous lines, either straight or curved. Most of these patterns appear as ornaments on tools in daily use, such as spatulas, stone bowls, shaft straighteners, ostrich-egg containers (?), and so forth. Peculiar are the series of regular unfinished drillings on bone tubes (?) found at Hayonim Cave (fig. 6, no. 18). A more thorough study of all of the above-mentioned objects is necessary in order to ascertain whether the various types of decoration of the mobiliary art pieces are representative of specific human groups in the Natufian culture.

It is still quite difficult to characterize Natufian art. It is similar to art from other hunting societies and perhaps shows a special emphasis on the exploitation of young ruminants (Cauvin 1972). This emphasis conforms with the frequency of young gazelles in the bone counts of Natufian sites, which amounts to 33% (Davis 1978). However, the combination of sickles and young gazelles is rather curious, unless the zoological identification is erroneous or the sickles had something to do with cutting grasses for feeding gazelles. One may hypothesize that a unique religious relationship existed between these two elements, which seem to be the two basic subsistence resources of Natufian communities in the Galilee-Judean Hills area (Cauvin 1972).

A large variety of marine molluscs was used by the Natufians for fabricating decorations such as headdresses, necklaces, belts, and so forth. These, in their probable original arrangements, are known from the finds in various graves (El-Wad, Eynan, Hayonim Cave). If these are marine molluscs, consideration of their frequencies in various sites and of their possible use as a primitive medium of exchange has been neglected.

Reports that include quantitative studies with the identification of the possible origins of the various shells are rare (Avnimelech 1937; Tchernov in Bar-Yosef et al. 1974b; Tchernov 1976; Mienis 1977). Table 5 presents the frequencies of species from identified sources. In order to place the Natufian sites within a framework, I have added several Kebaran sites and a few Neolithic ones. The ties between the Natufian and the Mediterranean world are clear, especially when the distribution of species at Rosh Horesha is compared with the distribution at Abu Salem, the Harifian site located only three km away. The Harifian is dominated by Red Sea shells as are the Neolithic sites of southern Sinai. Although Red Sea shells were also imported into Natufian sites, their number decreases with distance, as known from other examples of primitive trade.

Table 5. — Number of Species of Marine Molluscs and Their Origins in Selected Kebaran, Geometric Kebaran, Natufian, and Neolithic Sites

| | Gastropoda | | | Scaphopoda | Polecypoda | | |
	M	RS	Unknown	Dentalium	M	RS	Unknown
Ksar Akil (Phase 1)	1(5)	--	--	(14)	--	--	--
Ein Gev I	2	--	--	--	--	--	--
Ein Gev III	2	--	--	+	--	--	--
Hayonim Cave	9(40)	--	--	(490)	--	--	--
Hayonim Terrace	5	--	--	+	1	--	--
El-Wad	5	1	--	+	9	--	--
Rosh Zin	3(18)	1(1)	--	(281)	1(1)	1(1)	--
Rosh Horesha	6(21)	2(2)	1(5)	(441)	2(9)	--	--
Abu Salem (Harifian)	3	25	1	(318)	--	2	2
Jericho PPNA and PPNB	4	2	1	--	2	--	1
Ujerat el Mehed (S. Sinai, PPNB)	1(5)	13(89)	--	(3)	--	3(24)	--
G. Rubsha (S. Sinai, PPNB)	--	8(43)	--	(6)	--	2(9)	--

M = Mediterranean.
RS = Red Sea.
SOURCES: Mienis 1977; Biggs 1963; Garrod and Bate 1937; Tchernov, in Bar-Yosef et al. 1974a; Inizian and Gaillard 1978.
NOTE: Parentheses indicate actual counts.

One major problem concerns the origins of dentalium shells. These may be obtained from the Mediterranean and the Red Sea shores as well as from raised beaches of Plio-Miocene age (Avnimelech 1937; Mienis 1977). A new, thorough paleozoological study is needed urgently in order to enable the study of the use of the abundant dentalium shells within the framework of a possible Natufian trade network.

Obsidian pieces uncovered at Eynan indicate that the Natufians engaged in the trade of this raw material prior to the Neolithic. Green stones, shaped as beads and pendants and either defined as phosphorite or thought to be of a different mineralogical variety that originated in Transjordan or Syria, have been recovered from El-Wad, Eynan, and Fazael IV. Malachite beads, possibly brought from the Arava valley, were found in Rosh Horesha.

Thus, in spite of the richness of Natufian malacological assemblages and variegated jewelry, there has been no systematic effort to analyze exchange networks or other aspects of Natufian trade. All that can be said at this point is that Natufian culture seems most closely connected to the Eastern Mediterranean.

THE NATUFIAN SUBSISTENCE

Most of the known Natufian sites were excavated before the various techniques for flotation were introduced into archeological research. However, even the trials in recent years at Eynan, Hayonim Cave, Hayonim Terrace, Rosh Zin, Rosh Horesha, and so forth, with various methods failed to retrieve floral evidence. The most systematic effort at Nahal Oren produced 50 carbonized seeds (Noy et al. 1973, p. 92). Of those, 11 were of vetch and one was of vine. At Eynan and Hayonim Cave, scarce carbonized seeds of wild barley and broken pieces of almond crust were found. But none of these finds is conclusive quantitatively significant evidence.

The poor preservation of vegetal remains in Natufian sites can be partially explained by the nature of the deposits. In the Mediterranean zone, where the large sites are located, terra rosa soils predominate and most commonly the sediments in the sites are clays and colluvium. The sediments are soaked each winter and dry up and crack in summer, thus destroying paleobotanical relics. Although the desertic loess in the Negev better preserves charcoal flecks, on the whole the lack of carbonized material is well expressed in the overall scarcity of C^{14} dates from Natufian sites (table 1). In spite of indirect evidence such as the sickle blades and the food-processing utensils (mortars and pestles), the interpretation that wild cereals were probably harvested should await the retrieval of more plant remains.

The faunal evidence seems to be more informative. Recent studies of Epipaleolithic and Neolithic bone assemblages of ungulates present the following picture (fig. 9): in spite of the uneven sample sizes, the data lead to the conclusion that the Natufians constantly practiced the hunting of gazelles along with other types of game, depending on the geographical location of each site. Such is the case at Eynan, in the Upper Jordan valley (the Hula valley), where wild boar was abundant, or Rosh Horesha, in the Negev Highlands, where ibex constituted half of the game.

Suggestions proposing a kind of primitive "domestication" of the gazelle (Legge 1972) are now untenable in the light of published evidence on the gazelle's behavior (Simmons and Ilani 1975–77; Davis 1978), although a higher incidence of young gazelles was noted in Hayonim Terrace and Nahal Oren (Davis 1978; Legge 1972). The Natufians' strategy for hunting game seems to have been based on the exploitation of the available mammals within their immediate territory. Much more can be learned when tables giving the counts by the various parts of the skeletons are published.

Fishing was practiced by the Natufians, as evidenced by the scarce fish vertebrates collected at Hayonim Cave and by the bone gorgets and hooks found at Nahal Oren, El-Wad, and Kebara Cave. The largest quantities of fish remains were collected at Eynan. The extent to which the Natufians exploited fish and fowl as food resources is still unclear. It seems likely, however, that vegetal resources and a small range of ungulates were the main staples of their diet.

INTER- AND INTRASITE VARIABILITY

Modern research in archeology has raised questions concerning site size, the nature of sites as determined from their remains, and the distribution of sites and its possible meaning within a framework of the reconstructed activities of past societies. Without going into the theoretical background, a few of these aspects as related to the Natufian sites will be discussed here.

Natufian sites vary in size from several dozens of square meters to several thousands of square meters. Their size frequencies contrast with earlier Epipaleolithic sites (of the Kebaran, Geometric Kebaran cultural complexes, etc.) and have been used by us and others to determine and demonstrate the cultural change that took place with the establishment of the Natufian society (Bar-Yosef 1970, forthcoming; Braidwood 1975; Hassan 1977).

Natufian sites fall into three size categories: small — 15–100 m² (Hayonim Cave, Sefunim Cave, Usba Cave, Rakefet Cave, Ala Safat Cave, Erq el-Ahmar Rock-shelter, Umm ez-Zuwetina Cave, Ain Sakhri Cave, Umm Qala'a Cave, and Tor Abu Sif); medium — 400–500 m² (Kebara Cave, El-Wad Cave and Terrace, Rosh Zin, Salibiya I, Fazael IV), and large — more than 1,000 m² (Eynan, Hayonim Terrace, Nahal Oren, Nahal Ein Gev II, Rosh Horesha).

It is not surprising that all the small sites are cave sites. It was only there and perhaps in the deserts that small, ephemeral sites could be preserved. It is worth mentioning here that the total collection from Sefunim Cave contains four sickle blades (which might be from one sickle) and a dozen lunates (perhaps from a few arrows). Contrary to this kind of evidence, the site at Hayonim Cave, which seems to be no larger than 150 m², contained, in the excavated 85 m², several structures, evidence for three layers, 16 graves, and so forth. Therefore it is the contents of the site combined with its size and interpreted as part of a network of similar sites that will help in understanding Natufian settlement patterns.

Dealing with the contents of sites, I proposed a decade ago to attempt to differentiate between base camps and seasonal camps. Even with the increasing amount of data, these basic definitions still seem helpful in the study of the Natufian as an archeological entity.

In classifying the relationships between sites the interest was to define intuitively (on the basis of available data) some organized social systems. Base camps were believed to contain structures, graves (which symbolize the personal/group ties to a certain locale), heavy-duty tools, and a rich bone industry. Seasonal camps were those sites that demonstrated the presence of flimsy structures (for short-period dwelling), scarce heavy-duty tools, a few bone tools, and no graves. Under the Mediterranean climatic regime the repeated occupation of such camp sites is expected. This process will result in the accumulation of considerable lithic and bone refuse, but the attributes of a "base camp" will remain relatively rare.

The requirement that every newly discovered site be assigned to the Natufian on the basis of such a classification avoided the identification of lunate-bearing assemblages as necessarily Natufian. Such a cursory identification is exemplified by the unproven claim that the Natufian stretches from the Nile Valley to southern Anatolia. The restricted definition of the Natufian culture to a certain territory also implies that this term cannot be used as an equivalent to a "time entity." Within the area of the southern Levant at least two Natufian territories can be discerned when the contents of the sites are taken into account: the Galilee-Judea zone and the Negev. Northern Sinai was probably occupied contemporaneously with the Early Natufian by certain small groups of hunter-gatherers (called the Negev Kebaran of Helwan Phase) and in Late Natufian times by a still ill-defined entity (see also fig. 2).

The issue of Natufian sedentism was raised by Perrot (1966) when he suggested that Eynan could in actuality be considered a small village. This hypothesis was accepted by Braidwood (1973, 1975) and Cauvin (1978) as well as others. However, the determination of whether a site was a permanent settlement requires assessments based on independent — i.e., nonarchitectural — sources of evidence. Such a source is exemplified in the presence of human commensals. The large collections of microvertebrates from Hayonim Cave, accumulated there through the activities of birds of prey, exhibit high frequencies of house mouse, house rat, and house sparrow (Tchernov, in Bar-Yosef et al. 1974b). These human commensals live only in and around sedentary settlements, indicating, therefore, that Hayonim Terrace (in front of the Cave) was a permanent Natufian settlement.

Accepting the possible sedentism of several Natufian sites requires explanations as to the nature of the repeated occupations observed in the stratigraphic records. The data from Eynan and Hayonim Cave point to the continual return of the same population. If this is correct, then for how long were these sites occupied each year?

The Natufian differed from preceding cultural complexes in the amount of energy spent in digging and building. Therefore, while the processes of accumulation and destruction in a Paleolithic or early Epipaleolithic site in the Levant were basically dominated by natural agencies, the processes in operation in a Natufian site were the result of a combination of both human and natural agencies. Unfortunately, there are as yet no detailed sedimentological studies of Natufian open-air sites and only rare ones of Natufian habitations in caves (Goldberg 1979).

In spite of this deficiency there still exists the possibility that the ratio of tools per cubic meter

Table 6. — Frequencies of Tools per m³ in Various Sites

Site	Nature of Deposit	Tools per m³
Natufian		
El-Wad Cave and Terrace	Silt, clay, building cobbles, some colluvium, etc.	32
Erq el-Ahmar Rock-shelter	Silt	50
Hayonim Cave	Silt and building cobbles	94−167
Salibiya I	Clay and silt	476
Hayonim Terrace	Clay and colluvium	1,067
Rosh Horesha	Silt and colluvium	1,040
Eynan Ib	Clay and colluvium	2,055
Eynan IVa (floor)	Clay, some colluvium	1,342
Fazael IV	Clay and colluvium	2,022
Mushabian		
Mushabi XIV-1	Sand	97
Mushabi V	Sand	165
Geometric Kebaran A		
Mushabi XIV-2	Sand	211
Lagama North VIII	Sand	180
Kebaran		
Fazael III-4	Clay	1,150
Fazael III-6	Clay	427
Fazael VII	Clay and fine gravel	390
Late Upper Paleolithic		
Fazael IX	Clay and colluvium	760
Fazael X	Clay and colluvium	867

SOURCES: Bar-Yosef and Phillips 1977; Marks and Larson 1977; F. Valla, pers. comm.; N. Goring-Morris 1980.

might reflect the intensity of occupation, keeping in mind the possible interference of natural agencies such as sheetwash, leaching, colluviation, and so forth. Table 6 presents figures from Natufian sites along with a few from preceding cultural complexes.

The low figures for El-Wad and Erq el-Ahmar seem to be the results of poor sieving. However, the possibility that cave sites present lower frequencies when compared to open-air sites should be taken into account, as in the case of Hayonim Cave.

The Natufian ratios for open-air sites range between 500−2,000 tools per m³. In spite of similar deposits, these high values were not reached by any known earlier site. If the high figures for Rosh Horesha, Eynan, and Fazael IV were interpreted as being a result of the intensity of occupation (perhaps increased by the natural wash of the sediments of the time), they could give some insight into the Upper and Epipaleolithic sites. Obviously, however, the available numbers are only tentative as are averages for larger excavated surfaces. It will be interesting to see the actual frequencies for discrete layers presented in maps, especially where the actual distribution of tools and artifacts on floors cannot be obtained.

Before discussing the geographical distribution of Natufian sites, a few comments regarding their specific locations are essential, in view of the old paradigm still extant in the literature — that man moved out of caves at the beginning of the Holocene (Noy et al 1973, p. 91; Cauvin 1978, pp. 3, 9; Wright 1977, p. 297). In reality, more open-air sites than caves were used by the hunter-gatherers, whose residues were defined in the Levant as Late Upper Paleolithic, Keberan, Geometric Kebaran A, Mushabian, and so forth (Bar-Yosef, forthcoming; Bar-Yosef and Martin 1981). Caves and rock-shelters in the early part of the Epipaleolithic sequence constitute only 15% of all known sites, and the use of this type of habitation increased in Natufian times to about 40% of the sites. Therefore, it appears that Natufians entered caves rather than abandoned them. One possible explanation for this phenomenon is the temperature increase, which restricted the dripping activity in caves and made them habitable and perhaps even suitable for storage, as noticed by Solecki in Shanidar (Solecki 1963).

The geographical distribution of Natufian sites (fig. 10) shows its ties with the Mediterranean and Irano-Turanian vegetational zones. Even those sites in marginal locations and present-day ecotones were probably in a more favorable environment, if the reconstruction of paleoclimatic conditions is correct. Although small sites exist within the Saharo-Arabian zone and the semiarid region, until now the largest Natufian sites have been found only in environments where sources of subsistence were secure year-round. This observation is supported by the negative evidence collected in surveys in the higher mountains of Lebanon and the deserts of the western and southern Negev as well as of northern Sinai.

In considering the adaptive strategy of the Natufians one may examine a hypothetical reconstruction of a spatial distribution of Natufian base camps and seasonal camps in a known region such as Mt. Carmel. The intensive surveys carried out in this region for many years indicate that we do indeed know the total number of Natufian sites (Ronen and Olami 1978; Olami 1975). A few small sites were undoubtedly erased by development and agricultural activities, but the remainder indicate the presence of two important Early Natufian sites, Kebara and El-Wad, and the two Late Natufian ones, El-Wad and Nahal Oren. Seasonal sites included Rakefet Cave, Abu Usba Cave, Sefunim, and an unknown number of open-air sites. Even the most approximate calculations of population size will show that the Natufians lived, like hunter-gatherers of today, under the carrying capacity of their environment.

Concluding Remarks

While studying cultural processes through the archeological record it is quite common to identify units representing fully developed entities forming clear-cut stages within a sequence. Rarely, we can trace formative phases, ones during which the forthcoming phenomena are in their infancy. These "transitional" phases are generally not very well defined. In the Southern Levant we are quite lucky to have a great deal of data of this sort from the Natufian culture, even if it is not fully studied and as yet not very well reported. This phase spans the transition from one way of life to a new one, from hunter-gatherers to the earliest farmers.

The Natufian culture, as defined on the basis of its stone industry, is still Epipaleolithic. Its character as such is reinforced by a richness in microliths and an intensity of occupation as exhibited by the enormous quantities of tools and debitage relative to the volume of sediments, and so forth. However, site size, dwellings, graves, and so forth, express features that typify the periods that follow it. It is the combination of those traits that makes the task of excavating a Natufian site a complicated and intriguing operation.

The old excavations, and even the more recent ones where better techniques were used, have introduced many new questions. We have only scarce data related to intrasite variability, the number and extent of the occupations and reoccupations of the same sites, the vegetal diet of the Natufians, or the amount of trade goods.

The intensive fieldwork of the last decade has produced an overwhelming body of additional data about the period that immediately preceded the Natufian. At that time, small bands of hunter-gatherers occupied the whole area of the Levant in its various ecozones. With such a background the uniqueness of the Natufian culture with its various territories, base camps, and seasonal/exploitation camps is very evident. The social evolution that occurred in parts of the Proto-Mediterranean population seems to be a autochtonic change, resulting in differentiation between the human occupations of the Mediterranean and the Irano-Turanian zones and those of the higher mountains and the deserts. This differentiation is reinforced in the following millennia and appears to be one of the basic cultural components of the Levant.

The social agglomerations of the Natufian are remarkable when compared to the preceding level of small bands and exhibit as well additional changes in settlement pattern, increase in shell trade, and flourishing of the bone industry. Economically, previous strategies were intensified. Intensification, as possibly testified by the use of sickles (intensive harvesting of wild cereals) and the specialized hunting of antelopes formed the main economic activities until the beginning of the eighth millenium B.C. (based on radiocarbon dates). The appearance of mobiliary art and decoration marked the onset of a local cultural development in the Levant.

For various reasons the Natufian population made much more use of caves and rock-shelters than did preceding and succeeding populations. Therefore, the old European idea that human remains were to be found mainly in caves caused the Natufian to be more intensively studied than earlier or later stages of human development. The open-air sites, still not fully explored by any means, offer a stimulating potential for future research.

BIBLIOGRAPHY

Arensburg, B.
    1973   The people in the land of Israel from the Epi-Palaeolithic to present times: a study based on their skeletal remains. Ph.D. diss., Tel-Aviv University.
    1977   New Upper Palaeolithic remains from Israel. In *Stekelis memorial volume*, ed. B. Arensburg and O. Bar-Yosef, *Eretz-Israel* 13:208–15.

Arensburg, B.; Goldstein N.; and Nathan, N.
    1975   The Epipalaeolithic (Natufian) population in Israel. *Arquivos de Anatomia e Antropologie* 1:205–17.

Avnimelech, M.
    1937   Sur le mollusques trouvés dans les couches préhistoriques et proto-historiques de Palestine. *Journal of the Palestine Oriental Society* 17:81–92.

Bar-Yosef, O.
    1970   The Epi-Palaeolithic cultures of Palestine. Ph.D. diss., Hebrew University, Jerusalem.
    1975   The Epi-Palaeolithic in Palestine and Sinai. In *Problems in prehistory: north Africa and the Levant,* ed. F. Wendorf and A.E. Marks, pp. 363–78. Dallas, Texas: Southern Methodist University.
    forth-   The mediterranean Epi-Palaeolithic as the background to the "Neolithic Revolution." In
    coming   *The origins of agriculture and technology: east or west Asia?* ed. P. Sørensen and P. Mortensen, University of Aarhus.

Bar-Yosef, O.; Arensburg, B.; and Tchernov, E.
    1974   *Hayonim Cave: Natufian cemetery and settlement remains.* Bemaaravo Shel Hagalil, ed. M. Yeda'aya. Regional councils of Sulam Zor and Ga'aton.

Bar-Yosef, O.; Goldberg, P.; and Levenson, T.
    1974   Kebaran and Natufian sites in wadi Fazael, Jordan valley. *Paléorient* 2:415–28.

Bar-Yosef, O., and Goren, N.
    1973   Natufian remains in Hayonim Cave. *Paléorient* 1:49–68.

Bar-Yosef, O., and Martin, G.
    1981   Le problème de la "sortie des grottes" au Natoufien: répartition et localisation des gisements Epipaléolithques du Levant méditerranéen. *Bulletin de la Société Préhistorique Française* 78:187−92.

Bar-Yosef, O., and Phillips, J.L.
    1977   *Prehistoric investigations in Gebel Maghara, Northern Sinai.* "Qedem" 7, Monographs of the Institute of Archaeology, Hebrew University, Jerusalem. 269 pp.

Bar-Yosef, O., and Tchernov, E.
    1970   The Natufian bone industry from Ha-Yonim Cave. *Israel Exploration Journal* 20: 141−50.

Bar-Yosef, O., and Valla, F.
    1979   L'évolution du Natoufien, nouvelles suggestions. *Paléorient* 5:145−52.

Biggs, J.
    1963   On the mollusca collected during the excavations at Jericho 1952−58 and their archaeological significance. *Man* 63:125−28.

Binford, S.R.
    1968   Early Upper Pleistocene adaptations in the Levant. *American Anthropologist* 70(4): 707−17.

Braidwood, R.J.
    1952   *The Near East and the foundations of civilization.* Eugene, Oregon: Oregon State System of Higher Education.
    1960   The agricultural revolution. *Scientific American* 203:130−52.
    1973   The early village in southwestern Asia. *Journal of Near Eastern Studies* 32:34−39.
    1975   *Prehistoric men*, 8th ed. Glenview, Illinois: Scott, Foresman.

Butzer, K.W.
    1978   The late prehistoric environmental history of the Near East. In *The environmental history of the Near and Middle East since the last ice age*, ed. W. Brice, pp. 5−12. London: Academic Press.

Cahen, D.; Keeley, L.H.; and Noten, F.L. van
    1979   Stone tools, toolkits and human behavior in prehistory. *Current Anthropology* 20: 661−83.

Campana, D.V.
    1979   A Natufian shaft straightener from Mugharet el-Wad, Israel: an example of wear pattern analysis. *Journal of Field Archaeology* 6:237−42.

Cauvin, J.
    1972   *Religions néolithiques de Syro-Palestine.* Paris: Librairie d'Amérique et d'Orient.
    1978   *Les premiers villages de Syrie-Palestine du IXème au VIIème millénaire avant J.C.* Collection de la Maison de l'Orient Méditerranéen Ancien, 4. Série Archéologique, 3. Lyon: Maison de l'Orient.

Childe, V.G.
    1952   *New light on the most ancient East.* New York: Praeger.

Clutton-Brock, J.
    1978   Early domestication and the ungulate fauna of the Levant during the pre-pottery Neolithic period. In *The environmental history of the Near and Middle East since the last ice age*, ed. W. Brice, pp. 29−40. London: Academic Press.

Davis, S.
    1974   Animal remains from the Kebaran site of Ein Gev I, Jordan valley, Israel. *Paléorient* 2:453−62.

1978   The large mammals of the Upper Pleistocene-Holocene in Israel. Ph.D. diss., Hebrew University, Jerusalem.

Davis, S., and Valla, F.
1978   Evidence for domestication of the dog 12,000 years ago in the Natufian of Israel. *Nature* 276:608−10.

Echegaray, J.G.
1964   Excavaciones en la terraza de "El Khaim" (Jordania), vol. 1. In *Estudio del Yacimiento y los Niveles Paleoliticos.* Bibliotheca Praehistorica Hispana, vol. 5. Madrid: Artes Gráficas Gonzalo Bedia.
1966   Excavaciones en la terraza de "El Khaim" (Jordania), vol. 2. In *Los niveles Meso-Neoliticos, estudio de la fauna, flora y analisis de las tierras del Yacimiento.* Bibliotheca Praehistorica Hispana, vol. 5. Madrid: Artes Gráficas Gonzalo Bedia.

Ferembach, D.
1977   Les Natoufiens de Palestine. *Eretz-Israel* 13:240−51.

Flannery, K.V.
1969   Origins and ecological effects of early domestication in Iran and the Near East. In *The domestication and exploitation of plants and animals*, ed. P.J. Ucko and G.W. Dimbleby, pp. 73−100. London: Duckworth.

Garrod, D.A.E.
1932   A new Mesolithic industry: the Natufian of Palestine. *Journal Royal Anthropological Institute* 62:257−69.
1942   Excavations at the cave of Shukbah, Palestine 1928. *Proceedings of the Prehistoric Society* 8:1−20.

Garrod, D.A.E., and Bate, D.M.
1937   *The stone age of Mount Carmel.* Oxford: Oxford University Press.

Goldberg, P.
1976   Upper Pleistocene geology of the Avdat/Aqev area. In *Prehistory and paleoenvironments in the central Negev, Israel*, vol. 1: *the Avdat/Aqev area, part 1*, ed. A.E. Marks, pp. 25−55. Dallas, Texas: Southern Methodist University Press.
1979   Micromorphology of sediments from Hayonim Cave, Israel. *Catena* 6:167−81.

Goring-Morris, N.
1980   Upper Palaeolithic sites from Wadi Fazael. *Paléorient* 6:173−92.

Hassan, F.A.
1977   The dynamics of agricultural origins in Palestine: a theoretical model. In *The origins of agriculture*, ed. C.A. Reed, pp. 589−609. The Hague: Mouton.

Henry, D.O.
1973   The Natufian of Palestine: its material culture and ecology. Ph.D. diss., Southern Methodist University, Dallas, Texas.
1976   The excavation of Hayonim Terrace: an interim report. *Journal of Field Archaeology* 3(4):391−406.
1976b   Rosh Zin: a Natufian settlement near Ein Avdat. In *Prehistory and paleoenvironments in the central Negev, Israel*, vol 1: *the Avdat/Aqev area, part 1*, ed. A.E. Marks, pp. 317−48. Dallas, Texas: Southern Methodist University Press.
1977   An examination of the artifactual variability in the Natufian of Palestine. *Eretz-Israel* 13:229−40.

Horowitz, A.
1976   Late Quaternary paleoenvironments of prehistoric settlements. In *Prehistory and paleoenvironments in the central Negev, Israel*, vol 1: *the Avdat/Aqev area, part 1*, ed. A.E. Marks, pp. 57−68. Dallas, Texas: Southern Methodist University Press.

1979   *The quaternary of Israel*, Academic Press, New York.

Inizian, N.L., and Gaillard, J.M.
1978   Coquillages de Ksar-'Aquil: éléments de parure? *Paléorient* 4:295–306.

Kenyon, K.M.
1960   Excavations at Jericho 1957–1958. *Palestine Exploration Quarterly* 22:1–21.

Legge, A.J.
1972   Prehistoric exploitation of the gazelle in Palestine. In *Papers in economic prehistory,* ed. E.S. Higgs, pp. 119–24. Cambridge: University Press.

Marks. A.E., and Larson, P.A. Jr.
1977   Test excavations at the Natufian site of Rosh Horesha. In *Prehistory and paleoenvironments in the central Negev, Israel,* vol 2: *the Avdat/Aqev area, part 2; and the Har Harif,* ed. A.E. Marks, pp. 191–232. Dallas, Texas: Southern Methodist University Press.

Marks. A.E., and Simmons, A.H.
1977   The Negev Kebaran of the Har Harif. In *Prehistory and paleoenvironments in the central Negev, Israel,* vol 2: *the Avdat/Aqev area, part 2; and the Har Harif,* ed. A.E. Marks, pp. 223–69. Dallas, Texas: Southern Methodist University Press.

Mienis, H.K.
1977   Marine molluscs from the Epi-Paleolithic and Harifian of the Har Harif, central Negev (Israel). In *Prehistory and paleoenvironments in the central Negev, Israel,* vol. 2: *the Avdat/Aqev area, part 2; and the Har Harif,* ed. A.E. Marks, pp. 347–53. Dallas, Texas: Southern Methodist University Press.

Neuville, R.
1934   Le préhistorique de Palestine. *Revue Biblique* 43:237–59.
1951   Le Paléolithique et le Mésolithique du desert de Judée. *Archives de l'Institut de Paléontology Humaine,* vol. 24. Paris: Masson.

Noy, T.; Legge, A.J.; and Higgs, E.S.
1973   Recent excavations at Nahal Oren, Israel. *Proceedings of the Prehistoric Society* 39:75–99.

Olami, Y.
1975   Prehistoric sites on Mount Carmel. *Mitekufat Haeven* 13:21–35.

Perrot, J.
1966   Le gisement Natoufien de Mallaha (Eynan), Israël. *L'Anthropologie* 70:437–84.
1974   Mallaha (Eynan), 1975. *Paléorient* 2:485–86.

Redman, C.
1978   *The rise of civilization.* San Francisco: Freeman.

Ronen, A., and Olami, Y.
1978   *'Atlit map.* Archaeological Survey of Israel, Jerusalem.

Saxon, E.
1976   The evolution of domestication: a reappraisal of Near Eastern and North African evidence. In *IX° Congrès de l'Union-Internationale des Sciences Préhistoriques et Protohistoriques* [Nice, 1976], Colloque XX: *Origine de l'élevage et de la domestication,* pp. 180–226. Paris: Editions du Centre National de la Recherche Scientifique.

Schroeder, B.H.
1970   A prehistoric survey in the northern Bekaa valley. *Bulletin Musée de Beyrouth* 23:193–204.

Simmons, A.H., and Ilani, G.
1975–   What mean these bones? Behavioral implications of gazelles' remains from archaeological
77   sites. *Paléorient* 3:269–74.

Smith, P.
1972   Diet and attrition in the Natufians. *American Journal of Physical Anthropology* 37:
            233–38.

Solecki, R.S.
1963   Prehistory in Shanidar valley, northern Iran. *Science* 129:179–93.

Stekelis, R.S., and Yizraeli, T.
1963   Excavations at Nahal Oren: preliminary report. *Israel Exploration Journal* 13:1–12.

Stordeur, D.
1979   Quelques remarques préliminaires sur l'industrie de l'os du Proche Orient du Xème au
            VIème millénaire. In *L'industrie en os et bois de Cervidé durant le Néolithique et l'Age de
            Métaux*, ed. H. Camps-Fabrer, pp. 37–45. Paris: Editions du Centre National de la
            Recherche Scientifique.

Tchernov, E.
1976   Some late Quaternary faunal remains from the Avdat/Aqev area. In *Prehistory and
            paleoenvironments in the central Negev, Israel*, vol 1: *the Avdat/Aqev area, part 1*, ed.
            A.E. Marks, pp. 69–73. Dallas, Texas: Southern Methodist University Press.

Tixier, J.
1963   *Typologie de l'Epipaléolithique du Maghreb*. Mémoires du Centre de Recherches
            Anthropologiques Préhistoriques et Ethnologiques, Alger. Paris: Arts et Métiers
            Graphiques.

Turville-Petre, F.
1932   Excavations in the Mugharet el Kebarah. *Journal Royal Anthropological Institute*
            62:270–76.

Valla, F.R.
1975   *Le Natoufien: une culture préhistorique en Palestine*. Cahiers de la Revue Biblique 15.
            Paris: Gabalda.
1975–   La sépulture H 104 cd Mallaha (Eynan) et le problème de la domestication du chien en
77   Palestine. *Paléorient* 3:287–92.
1981   Les établissements Natoufiens dans le nord d'Israël. In *Préhistoire du Levant: chronol-
            ogie et organisation de l'espace depuis les origines jusqu'au VIe millénaire*, ed. J. Cauvin
            and P. Sanlaville. Actes du Colloque International du Centre National de la Recherche
            Scientifique [Lyon 1980], no. 598. Paris: Editions du Centre National de la Recherche
            Scientifique.

Valla, F.R.; Gilead, I.; and Bar-Yosef, O.
1979   Prospection préhistorique dans le Néguev septentrional. *Paléorient* 5:221–31.

Wright, H.E. Jr.
1977   Environmental change and the origin of agriculture in the Old and New worlds. In *The
            origins of agriculture*, ed. C.A. Reed, pp. 281–318. The Hague: Mouton.

Zeist, W. van, and Bottema, S.
1977   Palynological investigations in western Iran. *Palaeohistoria* 19:19–85.

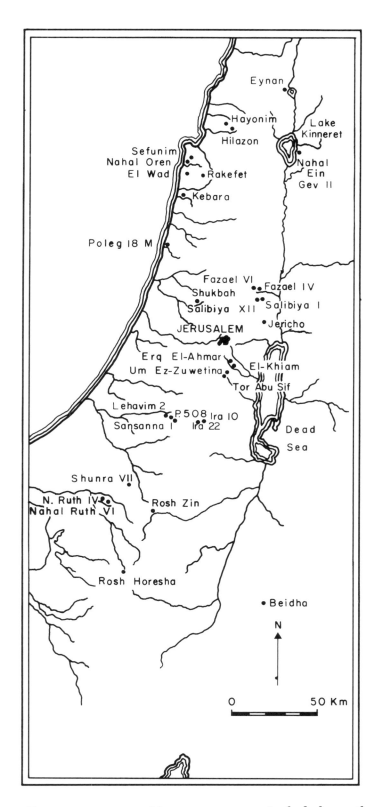

FIG. 1. — DISTRIBUTION OF NATUFIAN SITES. Included are those sites discovered during surveys in 1979−1980, as yet unpublished.

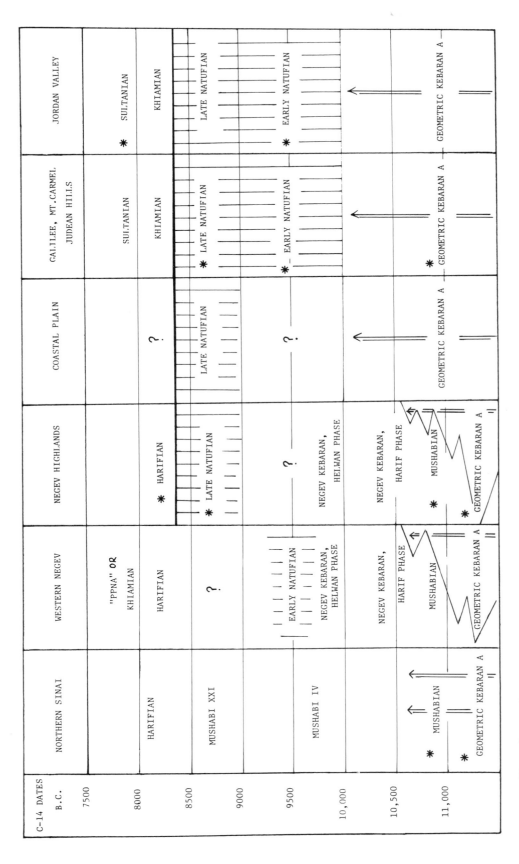

FIG. 2. — CHRONOLOGICAL TABLE SHOWING THE PLACE OF THE NATUFIAN CULTURE AMONG OTHER EPI-PALEOLITHIC ENTITIES. The asterisk marks those units already radiocarbon-dated.

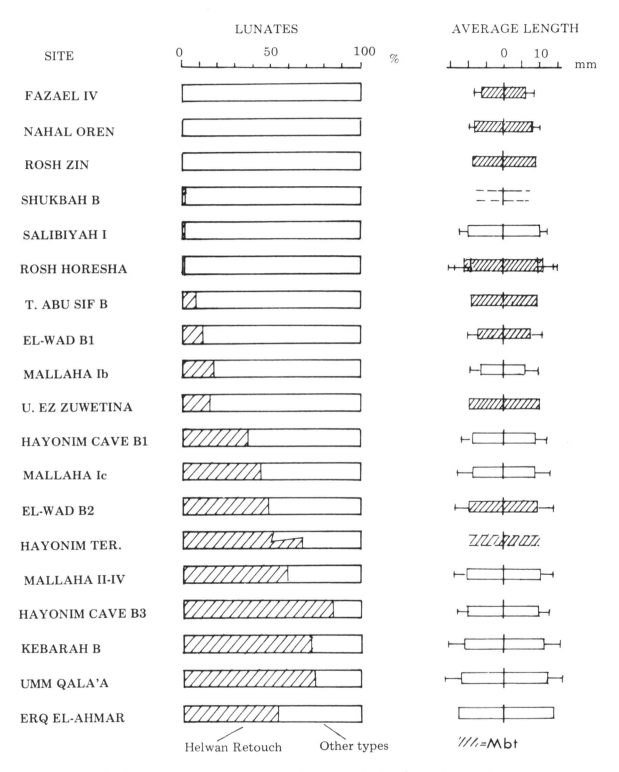

	LUNATES	AVERAGE LENGTH

FIG. 3. — THE RELATIVE FREQUENCIES OF HELWAN (striped areas) AND OTHER LUNATES. Shown are the average length of each, with one standard deviation (after Bar-Yosef and Valla, 1979).

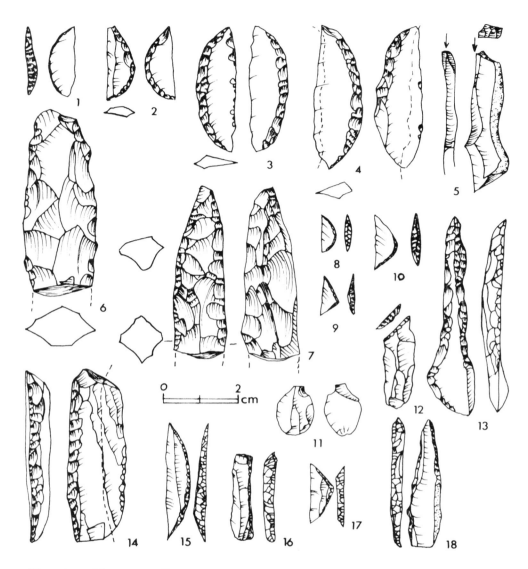

FIG. 4. — NATUFIAN FLINT TOOLS FROM HAYONIM CAVE, FAZAEL IV, ROSH ZIN, AND ROSH HORESHA. (After Bar-Yosef and Goren 1973; Bar-Yosef et al. 1974; Henry 1976; Marks and Larson 1977.)

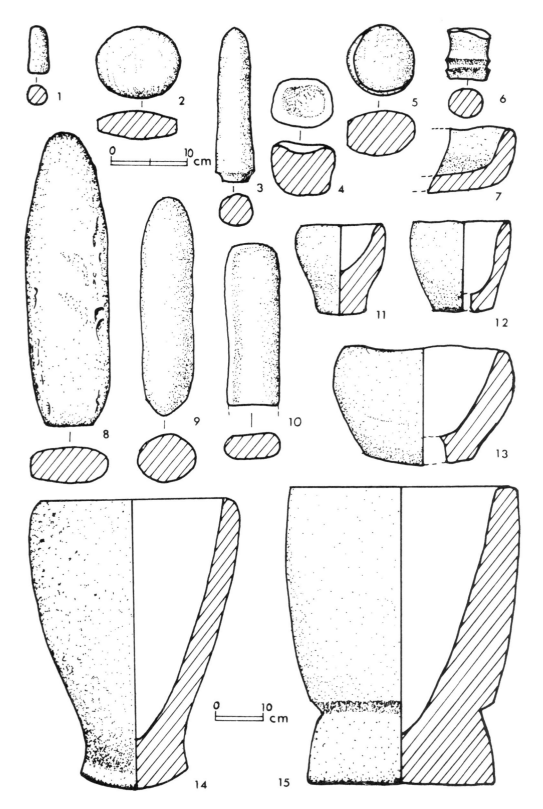

Fig. 5. — Natufian Ground Stone Tools from Eynan and Hayonim Cave. (After Perrot 1966; Bar-Yosef and Goren 1973.)

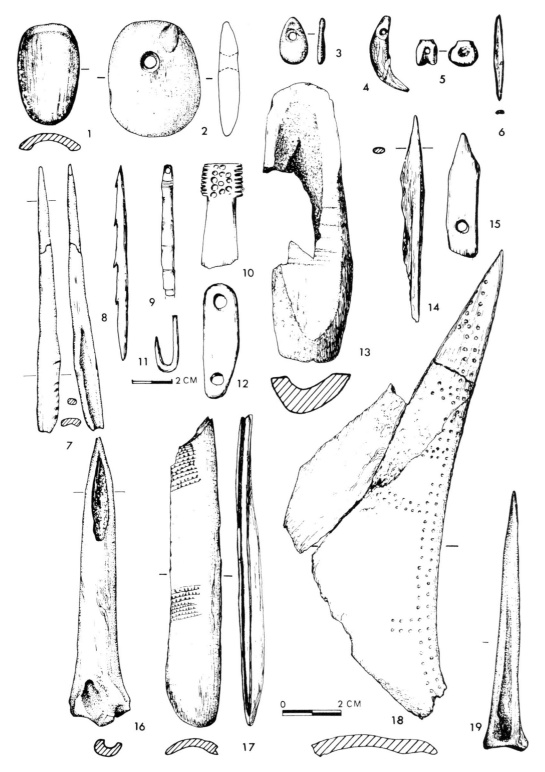

Fig. 6. — Natufian Bone Tools and Pendants from Hayonim Cave, Kebara Cave, and Eynan. (After Bar-Yosef and Tchernov 1970; Turville-Petre 1932; Perrot 1976.)

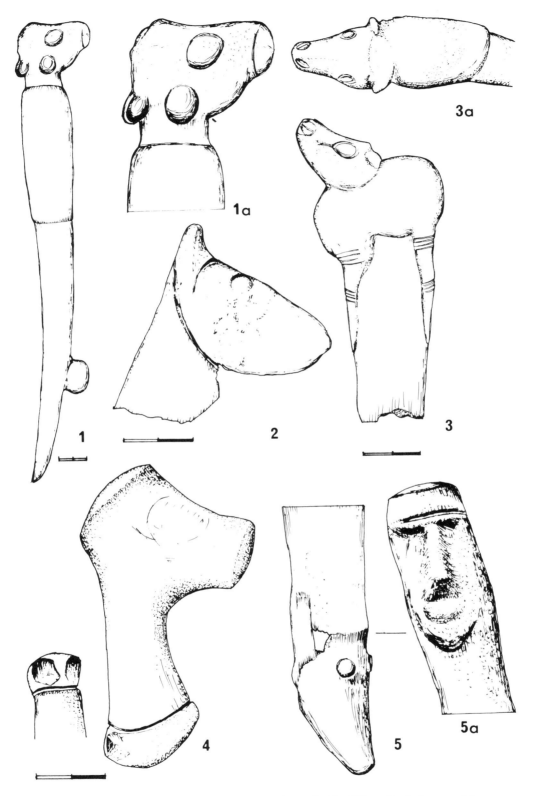

Fig. 7. — Art Objects from Kebara (1, 1a), El-Wad (3, 3a), and Nahal Oren (2, 4). Shown are young gazelles on sickle hafts (1 and 3) and as isolated object (2); double-feature figurines: dog's head and an awl (4); bovid's head and man's head (5). Note the different scales, each of 2 cm.

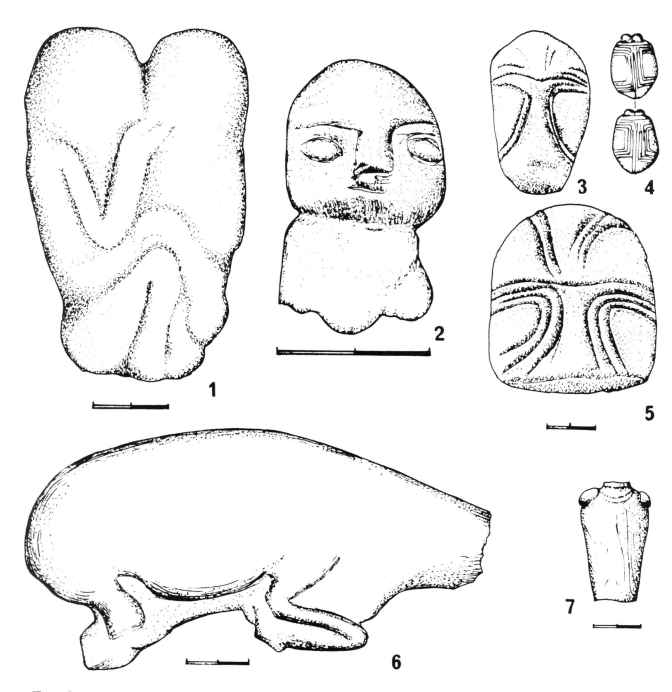

FIG. 8. — ART OBJECTS FROM AIN SAKHRI (1), EL-WAD (2), EYNAN (3, 5, 7), AND UMM-EZ-
ZUWETINA. Erotic figurine (1), man's head (2, 3), man's body (7), schematic representation of a man's
head (5), tortoise (4), and kneeling gazelle (6). Note the different scales, each of 2 cm.

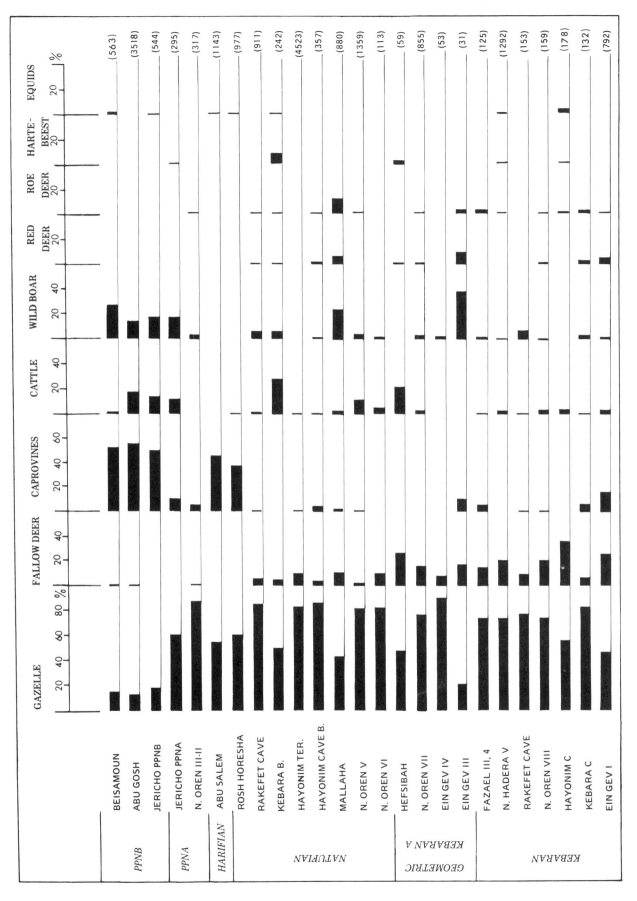

FIG. 9. — FREQUENCY DISTRIBUTION OF UNGULATE REMAINS IN EPI-PALEOLITHIC AND PRE-POTTERY NEOLITHIC SITES. (After Davis 1974, 1978; Ducos 1968; Clutton-Brock 1978; Legge, in Noy et al. 1973; Saxon 1976.)

NATUFIAN ●

NEGEV KEBARAN △
(HELWAN PHASE)

N

0   50 Km

FIG. 10. — A DISTRIBUTION MAP OF NATUFIAN (dots) AND NEGEV KEBARAN HELWAN PHASE SITES (triangles). A hatched line marks the border between the Mediterranean and Irano-Turanian zones and those of the Saharo-Arabian vegetation.

ORIGINES DE L'AGRICULTURE AU LEVANT
FACTEURS BIOLOGIQUES ET SOCIO-CULTURELS

Jacques Cauvin et Marie-Claire Cauvin

L E PASSAGE des économies de chasse — cueillette héritées du Paléolithique aux premières communautés agropastorales constitue bien le problème essentiel auquel se sont voués les préhistoriens travaillant au Proche-Orient depuis la fin de la dernière guerre mondiale. Nous sommes tous redevables à R. J. Braidwood d'avoir véritablement lancé ce type de recherche en traçant d'avance, bien avant la mode actuelle des "modèles", le cadre conceptuel et méthodologique auquel nous devions tous nous référer.

Rappelons les points principaux de cette hypothèse initiale (Braidwood et Braidwood 1953; Braidwood 1962):

1. Les débuts de l'agriculture ne pouvaient s'être effectués que dans la zone semi-aride à céréales sauvages *(nuclear zone)*, où l'environnement présentait une large gamme d'espèces végétales et animales domesticables.

2. L'étude de l'environnement était donc primordiale et l'on sait que Braidwood fut le premier au Proche-Orient à considérer l'archéologie comme une entreprise pluridisciplinaire avec une large participation des naturalistes.

3. Mais cet environnement devait avoir tout au plus un rôle "permissif". Il ne fallait chercher ni dans ses pressions, ni dans ses éventuelles modifications, auxquelles Braidwood au départ croyait peu, une impulsion décisive pour l'invention des nouvelles économies.

4. L'accent était donc porté plutôt sur la maturation sociale et culturelle des petits groupes humains, qui, dans ce milieu favorable mais encore exploité suivant l'ancien système, y auraient élaboré peu à peu les conditions de la "production" à venir: tendances au regroupement et à la sédentarisation, perfectionnement technologique (polissage de la pierre, mobilier lourd, etc.). Si bien que dans cette optique l'"era of incipient domestication" était réellement pressentie comme un "événement culturel" (Braidwood 1962), le milieu favorable restant subordonné à l'initiative socio-technologique susceptible d'en tirer parti.

Il est toujours redoutable pour un "modèle" d'être confronté avec le résultat des recherches vingt ans après. Si nous entreprenons quand même une telle confrontation pour le domaine syro-palestinien, ce n'est pas seulement parce que nous pensons montrer que la plupart de ces idées n'ont guère "vieilli", mais parce que ces hypothèses comme les contre-hypothèses qui leur furent opposées sont au coeur d'un débat fondamental sur la nature même de l'évolution humaine.

D'autres modèles d'explication, en réaction parfois contre celui de Braidwood, ont en effet été récemment proposés. Les archéologues qu'influencent les théories démographiques de Boserup (1965) admettent que l'agriculture (et l'élevage) sont bien nés dans la "zone nucléaire", mais

43

comme la conséquence d'une pression démographique exigeant que fussent artificiellement intensifiées les ressources alimentaires. C'est la même croissance démographique qui justifie dans la "théorie des zones marginales" de Binford non plus une origine de l'agriculture dans la zone nucléaire mais l'éclatement et l'émigration de ses cueilleurs protosédentaires trop nombreux vers la périphérie de la zone, où un environnement moins riche constituerait alors le stimulant indispensable à la naissance de l'agriculture comme économie de remplacement. Dans les deux cas c'est donc un facteur biologique, la croissance de la population, qui est mis en avant, complété chez Binford (et Flannery) par la pression mobilisatrice d'un milieu appauvri. Ces hypothèses qui font de l'agriculture le résultat d'une *nécessité*, nous mènent loin de l'hypothèse braidwoodienne où les facteurs biologiques ne sont en rien déterminants.

L'intensification récente des recherches en Syrie-Palestine a livré nombre de documents sur cette période cruciale. Un bilan est possible où toutes ces diverses "variables" dont l'agencement fait problème (le développement technologique et culturel, l'évolution démographique, celle du milieu et ses manipulations par l'homme) peu à peu se précisent, s'ordonnent dans le temps, passent du domaine de l'hypothèse à celui de la constatation et révèlent peu à peu leurs rôles respectifs.

D'abord le cadre naturel. Tout est loin d'être clair dans les résultats de la paléoclimatologie au Levant. Toutefois, pour la période qui nous occupe, le diagramme pollinique d'Hayonim (Leroi-Gourhan, à paraître) montre que le climat sec et froid du Kébarien devient plus humide et chaud, avec apparition des céréales sur le littoral palestinien, vers 10.000 B.C., soit juste avant le Natoufien. Après une phase plus sèche, correspondant sur ce site à la fin de la séquence natoufienne qui pourrait correspondre à la base de Mureybet vers 8500 (Leroi-Gourhan 1974), une nouvelle fluctuation humide a été reconnue à Mureybet entre 8000 et 7700 B.C. Or ces deux épisodes d'humidification, à conséquences évidentes sur la richesse du milieu naturel en céréales, interviendraient, si leur généralité se confirme, juste à la veille de deux événements fondamentaux pour le développement de la sédentarisation: la première période vers 10.000 va voir en effet la création des premiers villages de Natoufien à chasse-cueillette intensifiée, la seconde est celle où apparaissent à Jéricho et Mureybet les premières traces d'agriculture.

Les modifications du climat ont donc pu jouer un rôle plus important qu'on ne l'a cru, mais non pas, suivant l'ancien modèle hérité de Childe et Toynbee, au moment d'épisodes critiques créant, par leur "défi", la nécessité de ripostes culturelles de compensation (l'agriculture était pour Childe une de ces ripostes), mais au contraire en accentuant, si l'on peut dire, la bienveillance du milieu. Il convient donc de suivre à présent chronologiquement la mise en place des éléments culturels qui, de leur côté, paraissent converger vers l'établissement de la sédentarisation agricole.

LA FIN DU PALÉOLITHIQUE ET LES PREMIÈRES INNOVATIONS TECHNIQUES

On commencera l'étude de l'évolution culturelle à la fin du Paléolithique Supérieur, pendant la période qui va d'environ 13.000 à 10.000 B.C., et qui est aussi la seconde phase des cultures de famille Kébarienne. Elle englobe le "Kébarien classique évolué" (Bar-Yosef 1970) et ces industries palestiniennes assez diversifiées que Bar-Yosef a regroupées sous le terme générique de *Kébarien Géométrique A*, caractérisées par l'abondance des microlithes géométriques tels que trapèzes et rectangles. Il s'y ajoute le "Mushabien" du Sinaï et les gisements apparentés au Kébarien Géométrique A, récemment découverts au Liban (Hours 1976), et en Syrie dans la région de Palmyre (Fujimoto 1979), d'El Kowm (Cauvin, Cauvin, Stordeur 1980) et sur l'Euphrate: Nahr el-Homr (Roodenberg 1977). Cette occupation s'avère très dense en Palestine surtout, où, en plus des grottes déjà connues, les gisements de plein air se comptent à présent par dizaines. L'important est que l'on rencontre déjà sur plusieurs d'entre eux les architectures en fosses aménagées que développeront plus tard les Natoufiens et le mobilier de broyage indispensable à la consommation des céréales. Sur le lac de Tibériade la gisement Kébarien d'Ein Gev I (Bar-Yosef 1970) a ainsi livré une cabane en fosse à paroi retenue par un mur en pierres sèches semi-circulaire. Au Kébarien Géométrique A, Ein Gev III a livré deux habitats analogues à mur de pierres demi-circulaire ainsi qu'une cabane ovale. Il y a aussi des murs à Haon III (Bar-Yosef 1975) et Ein Gev IV (Martin et Bar-Yosef 1975-77). Tous ces sites ont du mobilier lourd en pierre.

Sur le littoral palestinien, le site Kébarien de Hadera V, ceux "Kébarien Géométrique A" de Hadera I et IV (Ronen 1976) et d'Umm Khalid (Bar-Yosef 1970) ont tous du mobilier de broyage (meules, mortiers). Il en est de même pour les gisements "Kébarien Géométrique A" et mushabiens du Sinaï (Mushabi XIV et V, Lagama N. VIII); Lagama N. VIII a livré en outre des structures en fosses dont un foyer cerné de dix trous de poteaux disposés en cercle (Bar-Yosef et Goring Morris 1977), caractère qui semble préfigurer les supports de charpente d'Aïn Mallaha (Perrot 1974).

Nous attirons l'attention sur l'importance pour notre problème de ces découvertes récentes. Avant 10.000, on ne saurait encore parler de "villages", le degré de sédentarité des groupes humains n'est pas encore nettement établi et il n'est même pas sûr que le mobilier de broyage ait été utilisé pour les céréales (celui de Mushabi V présente des traces d'ocre). Il reste que la possibilité même de construire des villages sédentaires est conditionnée par une certaine maîtrise des techniques d'habitat et celle d'utiliser largement les céréales sauvages, puis de les cultiver, par la possibilité de les broyer.

Ce que nous constatons ici, c'est qu'un certain savoir technique qui paraît fondamental pour les économies futures paraît s'être préparé *avant* le Natoufien[1], avant même l'optimum climatique qui, en faisant sortir les céréales de leurs zones-refuges où elles se cantonnaient dans les périodes froides, définira la "zone nucléaire" suivant l'acception de Braidwood.

DE 10.000 À 8300 B.C.: LES PREMIERS VILLAGES NATOUFIENS

La carte des gisements reste toujours très dense au Natoufien. Les limites de la culture semblent les mêmes qu'au Kébarien. L'efficacité des prospections israéliennes a multiplié les découvertes en Palestine, mais du Natoufien ancien, caractérisé par ses segments à retouche Héluan et déjà signalé en Syrie à Yabrud (Rust 1950), a été récemment découvert dans la région d'El Kowm (Cauvin, Cauvin, et Stordeur 1980) et sur l'Euphrate à Nahr el-Homr (Boerma et Roodenberg 1977). C'est au Natoufien récent (IXe millénaire) que sont fondés sur l'Euphrate Abu Hureyra et Mureybet. Les sites natoufiens paraissent plus dispersés en Syrie qu'en Palestine, mais les prospections y ont été moins intenses.

L'un de nous a déjà suggéré (J. Cauvin 1978) que si l'occupation de sites en plein air, au Natoufien, n'est pas nouvelle, c'est toutefois à cette époque que la grotte, espace abrité mais de dimensions réduites, ne paraît plus suffire à l'installation de certains groupes humains devenus plus importants. La plupart des grottes "kébariennes" du Mont Carmel et de Judée voient leur occupation déborder sur leurs terrasses désormais aménagées. Par ailleurs certains gisements de plein air peuvent eux-mêmes atteindre 2.000 m² (Aïn Mallaha), voire 3.000 m² (Rosh Horesha). Surtout les plus importants de ces gisements s'avèrent à la fouille être de véritables villages où se réinvestissent ces inventions kébariennes que sont la maison ronde en fosse aménagée et le mobilier de broyage. Ces villages sont sédentaires et vivent d'une économie de pêche−chasse−cueillette largement diversifiée où la cueillette des céréales sauvages paraît à présent jouer partout un rôle important.

---

1. Il en est de même pour les lames lustrées, naguère considérées comme apparaissant au Natoufien, qui lui préexistent en fait.

La multiplicité même des stations natoufiennes de dimensions très diverses montre qu'une importante mobilité subsiste parmi les groupes humains. Il est encore difficile de déterminer, autrement que sur un plan spéculatif, la part exacte qui revient dans cette diversité à une véritable alternance saisonnière dans l'occupation de certains sites[2] ou aux simples déplacements que requiert dans une économie de chasse—cueillette la dispersion dans l'espace des ressources alimentaires: ces déplacements peuvent alors ne concerner que de très petits groupes fonctionnels gravitant autour de leur habitat permanent.

Donc beaucoup de traits longtemps réputés caractériser le Natoufien (maisons, meules, faucilles, etc.) lui préexistent: il reste pour singulariser cette période, outre son outillage typique à base de segments, un phénomène général d'intensification de la cueillette et surtout l'existence de groupes humains plus importants et la sédentarisation en villages d'une partie d'entre eux. La "sortie des grottes" dont on parle à leur propos n'a aucune signification écologique: ce dont témoigneraient les derniers habitats cavernicoles qui subsistent tout en "débordant", c'est simplement leur manque d'espace à l'échelle des nouvelles communautés.

LA FIN DU IXe MILLÉNAIRE ET SES PROGRÈS TECHNOLOGIQUES

La culture natoufienne paraît prendre fin vers 8300 B.C. La fin du IXe millénaire a révélé son originalité depuis qu'ont été découverts et datés la culture harifienne du Negev et les niveaux IB et II de Mureybet, ce site permettant lui-même de mettre par comparaisons à leur place chronologique exacte les gisements à pointes d'El Khiam (M.-C. Cauvin 1974b) désignés en Palestine par le terme de *Khiamien* (Echegaray 1966).

Cette période forme transition entre le Natoufien et les cultures de type PPNA de Jéricho.

Il convient d'abord de remarquer que la carte de ces installations (fig. 1) recouvre les zones occupées au Natoufien et qu'une continuité sans rupture avec cette culture se manifeste par la persistance des segments dans le Harifien et leur très progressive disparition de Mureybet IB à Mureybet II. En même temps une certaine diversification culturelle ressort de l'analyse des mobiliers.

Le terme de *Harifien* a été proposé par Bar Yosef (1975) pour désigner les gisements du Negev et du Sinaï où l'on observe, avec la persistance des segments, la présence d'un type de flèche particulier, la pointe d'Harif. Les sites du Sinaï (Lagama IV, Mushabi III, XV, et XX: Phillips 1977) peuvent en outre présenter un autre type de pointe, variante de celle d'Harif, la "pointe de Mushabi", attestée à Mushabi XV et XX. Tous ces sites de vallée, petits et nombreux, sont interprétés comme des haltes de chasse sans doute reliées à des établissements permanents d'un plateau du Negev (Djebel Hallal) non encore prospecté.

Au Negev même on connaît les sites de la région d'Harif (Abu Salem, G8, G20, K3: Marks et al. 1972) et ceux de la région d'Halutza (H4, H87, H404, et Lavan 110).

Cependant il existe au Sud du Sinaï un gisement, Abu Madi (Bar Yosef comm. pers.) qui, sans doute contemporain des précédents, appartient à une autre culture: c'est un épinatoufien à pointes d'El Khiam. Il laisse supposer qu'à l'époque envisagée des incursions khiamiennes se sont dévelopées vers l'Ouest:[3] on en trouve d'ailleurs des traces jusqu'au delta du Nil, à Helwan.

Le Khiamien paraît en effet "chez lui" en Palestine orientale et littorale: à Dhra (Raikes 1980), à El Khiam 4 d'Echegaray (base de B1 de Perrot), et à Gilgal (Noy 1976). Sur le littoral on retrouve

---

2. Telle qu'elle a été proposée par exemple pour le Mont Carmel et Hayonim (Vita Finzi et Higgs 1970, 21).

3. On trouve aussi des pointes d'El Khiam en plein coeur de la région "harifienne" d'Halutza, à Lavan 108 (Noy s.d.) et sporadiquement sur les sites harifiens eux-mêmes (par exemple Mushabi XX: Phillips, ibid., fig. 99, no. 22).

avec des segments les pointes d'El Khiam dans les grottes du Mont Carmel à El Wad B1 (Garrod et Bate 1937), à Nahal Oren "early PPNA" (Noy, Legge, et Higgs 1973) et, semble-t-il, à Rakefet. On constate aussi leur présence sur les gisements des dunes littorales: Michmoreth 26 A, Alexander 26, Poleg 18 M (Burian et Friedman 1965), et au Nord jusqu'aux Sables de Beyrouth (Hours 1976).

C'est enfin un faciès du Khiamien chargé de traits culturels propres à l'Euphrate (erminettes de Mureybet, bâtons polis) que l'on retrouve en Syrie à Mureybet IB et II, où il succède comme en Palestine au Natoufien.[4]

Signalons enfin un troisième ensemble culturel encore mal connu et non daté précisément, que la stratigraphie de Jéricho oblige pourtant à situer aussi à la fin du IXe millénaire. C'est celui qui correspond au "Protoneolithic" de K. Kenyon caractérisé par l'abondance de ses tranchets bifaces, la persistance de microlithes mais sans géométriques, et la très grande rareté des flèches à encoches. Cet exemple serait bien isolé si on ne songeait au nombre considérable de stations de surfaces repérées autrefois par Mallon (1925) sur les collines de Judée, caractérisées précisément par l'abondance de leurs tranchets et l'absence de flèches. Il est possible qu'un environnement boisé (oasis, montagnes) ait alors favorisé d'abord dans certains secteurs très limités l'invention d'un outil à bois(?), le tranchet, qui par la suite persistera au PPNA (dans le Sultanien de Crowfoot-Payne 1976).

Il en résulte pour cette fin du IXe millénaire un type d'occupation de l'espace finalement très dispersé en de multiples points, en contraste avec ce qu'on observera à la période suivante, mais bien dans la ligne, en revanche, de l'occupation natoufienne et de signification analogue. Là encore il existe des petites stations à occupation temporaire et de vrais villages sédentaires à maisons rondes ou ovales à présent plus souvent construites en surface que naguère. Le mieux connu est harifien: c'est Abu Salem (Marks et Scott 1976). Le Khiamien a aussi des maisons rondes à Gilgal, à Abu Madi, et à Mureybet IB et II. Enfin ce sont des structures de même type que révèle sans doute la coupe du sondage de K. Kenyon dans le "Protoneolithic" de Jéricho (Kenyon 1957). Il n'apparaît pas que les dimensions des villages eux-mêmes se soient accrues depuis le Natoufien. L'économie telle qu'on la perçoit à Abu Salem ou Mureybet II reste du type à "large spectre", tournée préférentiellement vers la cueillette des céréales, la chasse des petits herbivores, chèvre et gazelle à Abu Salem, gazelle surtout à Mureybet, tandis que la pêche joue à Mureybet un rôle aussi important qu'au Natoufien.

Ce n'est donc pas dans le domaine de l'économie que s'effectuent les changements importants, mais bien et uniquement, dans celui, culturel, des outillages avec l'apparition des flèches et d'outils lourds du genre tranchet. Ce sont ces instruments nouveaux qui sont à la base d'une certaine diversification des cultures dans l'ensemble syro-palestinien.

LA RÉVOLUTION SOCIO-ÉCONOMIQUE DU VIIIe MILLÉNAIRE

C'est la première moitié du huitième millénaire qui est en Syrie-Palestine la période fondamentale pour la naissance de l'agriculture. Si tant d'hypothèses ont pu être avancées pour expliquer celle-ci, c'est que cette phase était aussi jusqu'à tout récemment particulièrement mal connue. Pendant longtemps seul le site de Jéricho représentait, au PPNA, cette période: encore a-t-il fallu attendre un long délai pour que soient connues les bases de son économie.

Ce "silence" de la recherche n'est pas un hasard: il reflète d'abord l'étonnante raréfaction des gisements. Le premier aspect de la révolution dont nous parlons concerne en effet l'occupation

---

4. L'abondance des perçoirs et microperçoirs est un autre trait commun entre Mureybet IB–II et les gisements khiamiens de Palestine (El Wad B1, El Khiam 4, Dhra etc). On sait qu'ils sont très rares dans le Harifien.

de l'espace. La carte des installations paraît se vider; la liste des sites occupés à cette période est, même aujourd'hui, vite faite: c'est en Palestine, Jéricho, Nahal Oren, El Khiam, en Syrie Tell Aswad, Mureybet, et Cheikh Hassan.[5] Il n'y a plus de sites en grottes,[6] ni non plus les petites stations secondaires des périodes précédentes qui multiplient les points sur une carte. Tout au plus peut-on supposer que dans des régions qui n'ont révélé jusqu'à présent aucun site PPNA important, des petits groupes ont pu encore perpétuer l'état culturel du IXᵉ millénaire.[7]

Le second aspect du changement est que les sites connus, plus rares, sont en revanche plus étendus. Un seuil est franchi dans la dimension des villages: à Jéricho, Mureybet, Cheikh Hassan, ils atteignent 2 à 3 hectares. Aussi bien, si la raréfaction des sites va évidemment à l'encontre de l'hypothèse d'un accroissement démographique global, il n'est pas certain qu'elle reflète en sens inverse une forte dépopulation. L'impression est celle d'une concentration démographique en quelques points choisis (où les oasis et bords de fleuves, chers à Gordon Childe, joueraient un rôle important) et surtout la disparition de la plupart de ces lieux d'activité transitoire qu'une mobilité persistante des populations au IXᵉ devait multiplier sur leurs parcours. Le VIIIᵉ millénaire est donc en Syrie-Palestine un progrès décisif de la sédentarisation à laquelle, semble-t-il, presque plus rien n'échappe.

Que sont ces villages? L'impression qui prévaut de sites comme Mureybet ou Nahal Oren est qu'à l'intérieur des limites villageoises l'habitat se resserre, devient plus dense qu'au IXᵉ millénaire à la faveur de contiguïtés entre les maisons rondes rendues possibles par les progrès de la maçonnerie. Surtout la région du Moyen Euphrate, qui est la seule à offrir à moins de 20 km l'un de l'autre deux sites de cette période, découvre la technique des murs rectilignes d'abord comme division interne des habitats circulaires, puis vers 7700 B.C. pour la construction en dehors d'eux de structures rectangulaires en damiers qui paraissent être dans un premier temps des silos, avant de devenir vers 7500, des habitats (J. Cauvin 1978; Aurenche 1979).

Or, c'est dans ce contexte villageois agrandi et architecturalement perfectionné que surgissent les premières expériences agricoles archéologiquement perceptibles. On sait (Leroi-Gourhan 1974) qu'à Mureybet les indices de proto-agriculture qui apparaissent, en III B, vers 7700 B.C. sont palynologiques, les graines d'orge et d'engrain ne témoignant pas encore de modifications morphologiques. Ces modifications sont chose faite à Jéricho (Hopf 1969) bien que les graines trouvées (blé amidonnier, orge à deux rangs) soient peu nombreuses, ce qui était normal avant l'intervention des techniques modernes de flottation. A Tell Aswad (Contenson 1973; M.-C. Cauvin 1974a) près de Damas, c'est au cours de la phase IB, c'est-à-dire vers 7700 B.C. comme à Mureybet, que le diagramme pollinique dénote une brusque montée des céréales "provenant très certainement d'une phase agricole" (Leroi-Gourhan, à paraître).

Pourquoi ce changement? L'un de nous (J. Cauvin 1977) a déjà exposé ce qui rendait le modèle des "zones marginales" de Binford et Flannery irrecevable dans le cas présent. C'est bien dans la "zone nucléaire," qu'ainsi que le pensait Braidwood, l'agriculture est née.

Une fois admise cette localisation centrale des premières expériences, faut-il y voir la conséquence d'un accroissement démographique global rendant les ressources, même spontanément enrichies, encore insuffisantes en regard d'une multiplication des consommateurs? On a vu que cette interprétation conforme au modèle de Boserup peut être exclue par un simple examen de la

5. Hors de Syrie, mais toujours en Haute Mésopotamie, il faudrait sans doute ajouter base de Cayönü (Braidwood et al. 1971).

6. Seule exception la petite grotte de Nacharini (Schroeder 1976) dans les montagnes de l'Anti-Liban.

7. On peut interpréter ainsi la récolte d'une lame-faucille à dos obtenu par retouches obliques bifaces (comme à Jéricho PPNA ou Nahal Oren) sur une station de Judée, Beit Taamir, et une autre sur les dunes de Ramleh (Mallon 1925).

carte des occupations. Il y a bien en revanche une sorte de regroupement démographique dans des villages sédentaires à population localement accrue.

On peut considérer comme une tentative de sauver, en lui faisant changer d'échelle, l'hypothèse démographique avec tout ce qu'elle implique de pression biologique en faveur du changement, l'interprétation que donne Ducos (1978) des mutations économiques de Mureybet au début du VIIIᵉ millénaire. Ducos constate la transformation de la chasse, qui privilégie désormais les grands herbivores (âne, boeuf) alimentairement plus "rentables", et le développement démographique simultané du village. Il considère ce second facteur comme la cause du premier, et aussi comme la cause de l'apparition au même moment de la protoagriculture.

Ces nouvelles stratégies alimentaires mieux organisées répondraient en effet à la nécessité biologique d'accroître l'approvisionnement en fonction d'une population du village plus nombreuse.[8] Autrement dit le modèle de Boserup est ici ramené du niveau macrogéographique où il n'est pas vérifié au niveau microgéographique à l'échelle d'un village particulier et de sa croissance locale.

Nous restons sceptiques sur la possibilité d'expliquer de la sorte les phénomènes constatés. La corrélation entre l'accroissement du groupe humain et l'organisation de ses activités alimentaires n'implique en rien le déterminisme biologique qui est ici proposé. Si la pression démographique était vraiment la variable indépendante du processus, on pourrait s'étonner qu'elle n'ait pas commencé par intensifier l'exploitation de ressources traditionelles, dans un environnement aussi privilégié que les rives du Moyen Euphrate, environnement qui ne dut jamais, à si haute époque, être exploité pleinement. On a noté à l'inverse, à Mureybet III, un quasi abandon de la pêche et de la chasse aux petits ruminants de la steppe, attestant qu'on n'était pas réellement dans une situation de pénurie mais au contraire de libre choix.

Surtout il revient à Flannery, d'avoir montré (Flannery 1972) sur des exemples ethnographiques convaincants que ce "plafond", qui à partir d'un certain seuil interdit à un groupe humain de s'accroître davantage, n'a souvent rien à voir avec un problème alimentaire. Une tendance bien actuelle à considérer les hommes comme des consommateurs peut occulter cette autre donnée d'expérience qu'un système social efficace pour assurer la cohésion d'un groupe d'une dimension donnée peut devenir inopérant si le groupe s'accroit trop. Celui-ci, alors, réduit artificiellement ses naissances, ou bien essaime et va fonder ailleurs d'autres communautés. Seul un changement au niveau des structures de la société peut donc éviter cet éclatement.

La pression démographique est un phénomène certain mais banal, commun à tous les temps, en vertu des lois de multiplication de l'espèce. Elle peut certes engendrer des situations critiques sur le plan biologique par excessive concurrence en face des ressources disponibles, mais cela ne semble pas être encore le cas dans le Levant du VIIIᵉ millénaire ni à l'échelle régionale, ni à celle des sites particuliers. En revanche si les techniques nouvelles d'acquisition, plus collectives, ont effectivement pour résultat de rentabiliser tant la chasse que la collecte des végétaux, il ne faut pas oublier que cette même "organisation" est aussi la *condition* préalable de l'agrandissement des villages parce qu'elle améliore leur capacité culturelle à "vivre ensemble" sans tension préjudiciable à la cohésion du groupe.

C'est dans ce domaine précis qu'il se produit du nouveau au VIIIᵉ millénaire. L'agriculture, la chasse organisée, le protoélevage qui lui succède vers 7500 B.C. à Mureybet nous ont paru être

---

8. "Même dans ces périodes d'équilibre apparent entre les groupes humains et leur environnement, il existe des contraintes tenant à des facteurs biologiques propres aux groupes humains eux-mêmes. Ces contraintes sont assez fortes pour que des processus adaptatifs, progressifs ou mutatifs, jouent, induisant des changements plus ou moins profonds dans l'organisation des groupes et les techniques d'acquisition de la nourriture" (Ducos, ibid., 133).

avant tout des façons de mettre en oeuvre *à travers* les activités alimentaires une nouvelle pratique sociale qui se manifeste aussi dans les constructions "monumentales", donc collectives, de Jéricho PPNA.

C'est pourquoi invoquer comme déterminantes des contraintes biologiques qui n'ont rien de particulier à cette époque risque d'affadir le phénomène sans rendre compte de sa spécificité historique. Nous retrouvons le problème qui a préoccupé Braidwood: pourquoi l'agriculture à ce moment et pas, par exemple, au Natoufien? Les recherches récentes au Levant semblent bien confirmer ses intuitions, qui, sans négliger les variables écologiques et biologiques qui trouvent naturellement leur place dans une approche "multifactorielle" (Redman) de la préhistoire, privilégient cependant nettement l'agent humain et la maturation progressive de son milieu social et culturel.[9]

BIBLIOGRAPHIE

Aurenche, O.
  1979   La maison orientale: l'architecture du Proche Orient des origines au milieu du IVe millénaire. Thèse d'Etat Université de Lyon II.

Bar-Yosef, O.
  1970   The Epi-Paleolithic cultures of Palestine. Ph.D. diss., Hebrew University, Jerusalem.
  1975   The Epi-Paleolithic in Palestine and Sinai. In *Problems in prehistory: North Africa and the Levant*, ed. F. Wendorf and A.E. Marks, pp. 363–78. Dallas, Texas: Southern Methodist University.
  1975   Les gisements "Kébarien Géométrique A" d'Haon, vallée du Jourdain, Israël. *Bulletin de la Société Préhistorique Française (Comptes Rendus Séances Mensuelles)* 72(1):10–14.

Bar-Yosef, O., et Goring Morris, A.N.
  1977   Geometric Kebaran occurrences. In *Prehistoric investigations in Gebel Maghara, northern Sinai*, O. Bar-Yosef and J.L. Phillips, pp. 115–48. Monographs of the Institute of Archaeology, Hebrew University, Qedem 7. Jerusalem: Hebrew University.

Binford, L.R.
  1968   Post-Pleistocene adaptations. In *New perspectives in archaeology*, ed. S.R. Binford and L.R. Binford, pp. 313–41. Chicago: Aldine-Atherton.

Boerma, J.A.K., et Roodenberg, J.J.
  1977   Une deuxième industrie Epipaléolithique sur le Nahr el-Homr. *Palaeohistoria* 19:8–17.

Boserup, E.
  1965   *The conditions of agricultural growth*. Chicago: Aldine.

Braidwood, R.J.
  1962   The earliest village communities of southwestern Asia reconsidered. In *Atti del Sesto Congresso internazionale delle Scienze preistoriche e protoistoriche*, vol.1, pp. 115–26. Florence: Sansoni.
  1967   *Prehistoric men*, 7e ed., Glenview, Illinois: Scott, Foresman.
  1972   Prehistoric investigations in southwestern Asia. *Proceedings of the American Philosophical Society* 116(4):310–20.

9. Article rédigé en Mars 1980.

Braidwood, R.J., et Braidwood, L.S.
    1953   The earliest village communities of southwestern Asia. *Journal of World History* 1(2):278−310.

Braidwood, R.J.; Çambel, H.; Redman, C.L.; et Watson, P.J.
    1971   Beginnings of village-farming communities in southeastern Turkey. *Proceedings of the National Academy of Sciences* 68(6):1236−40.

Braidwood, R.J., et Reed, C.A.
    1957   The achievement and early consequences of food production: a consideration of archeological and natural-historical evidence. In *Population studies: animal ecology and demography*, pp. 19−31. Cold Spring Harbor Symposia on Quantitative Biology, vol. 22. Cold Spring Harbor, Long Island: The Biological Laboratory.

Burian, F., et Friedman, E.
    1965   Ten years of prehistoric survey in the coastal plain from Nahal Hadera to Nahal Lachish. *Mitequfat Haeven* 6/7:1−33.

Cauvin, J.
    1977   Les fouilles de Mureybet (1971−1974) et leur signification pour les origines de la sédentarisation au Proche-Orient. In *Archeological reports from the Tabqa dam project — Euphrates Valley, Syria*, ed. D.N. Freedman, pp. 19−48. Annual of the American Schools of Oriental Research, vol. 44. Cambridge, Mass.: American Schools of Oriental Research.
    1978   *Les premiers villages de Syrie-Palestine du IXe au VIIe millénaire avant J−C*. Collection de la Maison de l'Orient Méditerranéen Ancien 4, Série Archéologique, 3. Lyon: Maison de l'Orient.

Cauvin, M.-C.
    1974a   Outillage lithique et chronologie à Tell Aswad (Damascène, Syrie). *Paléorient* 2(2):429−36.
    1974b   Flèches à encoches de Syrie: essai de classification et d'interprétation culturelle. *Paléorient* 2(2):311−22.

Contenson, H. de
    1973   Chronologie absolue de Tell Aswad (Damascène, Syrie). *Bulletin de la Société Préhistorique Française (Comptes Rendus, Séances Mensuelles)* 70(9):253−56.

Crowfoot-Payne, J.
    1976   The terminology of the aceramic Neolithic period in the Levant. In *IXe Congrès de l'Union−Internationale des Sciences Préhistoriques et Protohistoriques* [Nice, 1976], Colloque III, pp. 131−37. Paris: Editions du Centre National de la Recherche Scientifique.

Ducos, P.
    1978   *Tell Mureybet, étude archéozoologique et problèmes d'écologie humaine*. Paris: Centre National de la Recherche Scientifique.

Echegaray, J.G.
    1966   *Excavaciones en la terraza de "El Khiam" (Jordania)*. Vol 2: *Los niveles Meso-Neoliticos, estudio de la fauna, flora y analisis de las tierras del yacimiento*. Bibliotheca Praehistorica Hispana, vol. 5. Madrid: Artes Gráficas Gonzalo Bedia.

Flannery, K.V.
    1972   The origins of the village as a settlement type in Mesoamerica and the Near East: a comparative study. In *Man, settlement and urbanism*, ed. P.J. Ucko, R. Tringham, and G.W. Dimbleby, pp. 23−53. London: Duckworth.
    1973   The origins of agriculture. *Annual Review of Anthropology* 2:271−310.

Fujimoto, T.
    1979   The problems of the Upper and Epi-Paleolithic assemblages in the Palmyra basin. *University Museum, University of Tokyo* 16:77–130.

Garrod, D.A.E., et Bate, D.M.A.
    1937   *The stone age of Mount Carmel; excavations at the Wady el-Mughara.* Oxford: Clarendon Press.

Hopf, M.
    1969   Plant remains and early farming in Jericho. In *The domestication and exploitation of plants and animals,* ed. P.J. Ucko and G.W. Dimbleby, pp. 355–60. London: Duckworth.

Hours, F.
    1976   L'Epipaléolithique au Liban: résultats acquis en 1975. In *IXᵉ Congrès de l'Union—Internationale des Sciences Préhistoriques et Protohistoriques* [Nice, 1976], Colloque III, pp. 106–130. Paris: Editions du Centre National de la Recherche Scientifique.

Kenyon, K.M.
    1957   *Digging up Jericho.* London: Benn.

Leroi-Gourhan, A.
    1974   Etude palynologique des derniers 11000 ans en Syrie semi-désertique. *Paléorient* 2(2):443–51.
    à   Diagrammes polliniques de sites archéologiques au Moyen-Orient. *Symposium de*
    paraître   *Tübingen Férrier 1978.*

Mallon, A.
    1925   Stations préhistoriques de Palestine. *Mélanges de l'Université Saint-Joseph* 10:188–214.

Marks, A.E.; Crew, H.; Ferring, R.; et Phillips, J.
    1972   Prehistoric sites near Har Harif. *Israel Exploration Journal* 22:73–85.

Marks, A.E., et Scott, T.R.
    1976   Abu Salem: type site of the Harifian industry of the southern Levant. *Journal of Field Archeology* 3:43–60.

Martin, G., et Bar-Yosef, O.
    1975–   Ein Gev III, Israël (1974–1975). *Paléorient* 3:285–86.
    1977

Noy, T.
    1970   Prehistoric sites in the Halutza dunes (survey). *Mitequfat Haeven* 10:1–11.
    1976   Gilgal. *Israel Exploration Journal* 26:48.
    s.d.   *(ed.) In the footsteps of early hunters: arrowheads from the collection of F. Burian and E. Friedman, cat. no. 151.* Jerusalem: The Israel Museum.

Noy, T.; Legge, A.J.; et Higgs, E.S.
    1973   Recent excavations at Nahal Oren, Israel. *Proceedings of the Prehistoric Society* 39:75–99.

Perrot, J.
    1951   La terrasse d'El Khiam. In *Le Paléolithique et le Mésolithique du désert de Judée,* ed. R. Neuville, pp. 134–78. Paris: Masson.
    1968   La préhistoire Palestinienne. *Supplément au dictionnaire de la Bible,* no. 8, cols. 286–446. Paris: Letouzey et Ané.
    1974   Mallaha (Eynan), 1975. *Paléorient* 2(2):485–86.

Phillips, J.L.
    1977   The Harifian. In *Prehistoric investigations in Gebel Maghara, northern Sinai.* O. Bar-Yosef and J.L. Phillips, pp. 199–218. Monographs of the Institute of Archaeology, Hebrew University, Qedem 7. Jerusalem: Hebrew University.

Raikes, T.D.
    1980   Notes on some Neolithic and later sites in Wadi Araba and the Dead Sea valley. *Levant* 12:40–60.

Redman, C.L.
    1978   *The rise of civilization.* San Francisco: Freeman.

Ronen, A., et Kaufman, D.
    1976   Epipaleolithic sites near Nahal Hadera, central coastal plain of Israël. *Tel Aviv* 3:16–29.

Ronen, A.; Kaufman, D.; Gophna, R.; Bakler, N.; Smith, P.; et Amiel, A.
    1975   The Epipaleolithic site of Hefziba, central coastal plain of Israël. *Quartär* 26:53–72.

Roodenberg, J.J.
    1977   An Epipaleolithic industry on the Nahr el Homr. In *Archeological reports from the Tabqa dam project — Euphrates valley, Syria,* ed. D.N. Freedman, pp. 9–17. Annual of the American Schools of Oriental Research, vol. 44. Cambridge, Mass.: American Schools of Oriental Research.

Rust, A.
    1950   *Die Höhlenfunde von Jabrud (Syrien).* Neumünster: K. Wachholtzm.

Schroeder, B.
    1976   The Antilebanon cave of Mughara en-Nacharini: a preliminary report. In *IXe Congrès de l'Union Internationale des Sciences Préhistoriques et Protohistoriques* [Nice, 1976]. Paris: Editions du Centre National de la Recherche Scientifique.

Stekelis, M., et Yisraely, T.
    1963   Excavations at Nahal Oren: preliminary report. *Israel Exploration Journal* 13(1):1–12.

Vita Finzi, C., et Higgs, E.S.
    1970   Prehistoric economy in the Mount Carmel area of Palestine: site catchment analysis. *Proceedings of the Prehistoric Society* 36:1–37.

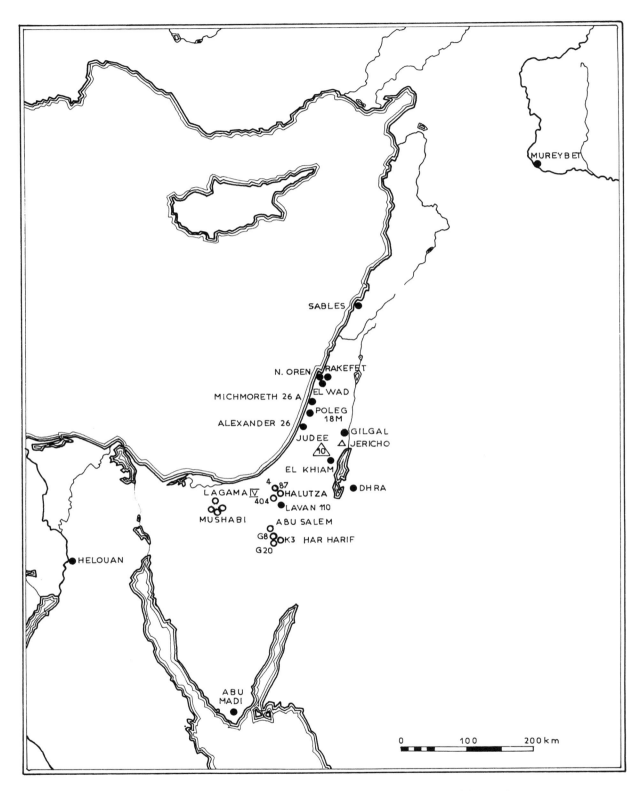

Fig. 1. — Carte des Installations du Levant entre 8300 et 8000 b.c. Points: gisements khiamiens; cercles: gisements harifiens; triangles: gisements de type Jéricho Protonéo (le grand triangle désigne dix gisements de Judée).

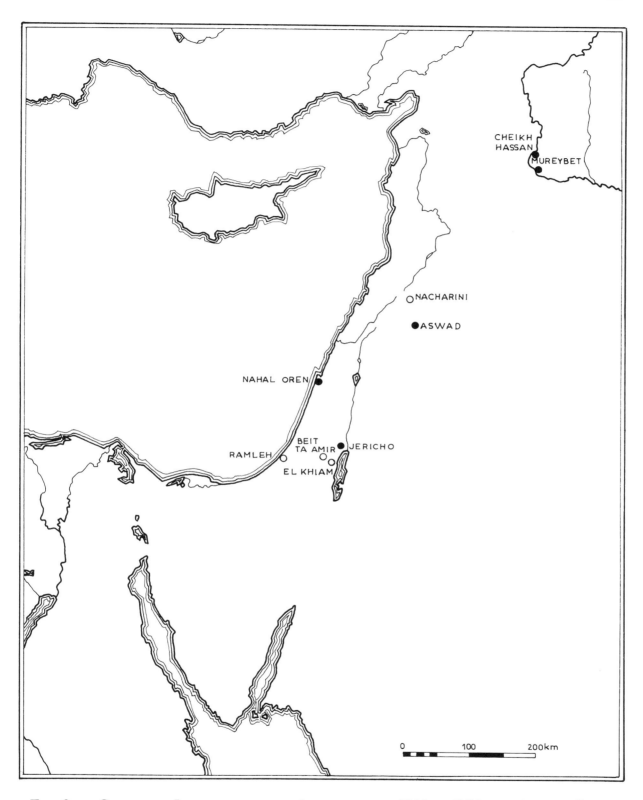

Fig. 2. — Carte des Installations du Levant entre 8000 et 7500 b.c. Points: villages agricoles; cercles: trouvailles d'industrie PPNA.

EARLY AGRICULTURE IN WESTERN ASIA

Henri de Contenson

THE EMPHASIS given to research on early agriculture in Syria by W. van Liere and the writer on behalf of the Syrian General Directorate of Antiquities and Museums began in 1963 in the Damascus area (de Contenson 1971) and the Euphrates (van Liere and de Contenson 1966) and continues today. While outstanding results were achieved in the Euphrates area (Cauvin 1978; Moore 1975) and test excavations were undertaken at Tell Assouad in the Djezira and El Kowm near Palmyra, work was resumed by the writer in the Damascus area in 1974 and continued at coastal Ras Shamra until 1976 (de Contenson 1978a).

Prompted by Robert Braidwood's inspired approach toward the development of food production, environmental studies are in process on all the sites excavated. They include sampling and investigation of paleobotanical remains (W. van Zeist, S. Bottema, and J. Bakker-Heeres, University of Groningen), palynology (Arl. Leroi-Gourhan, Musée de l'Homme), wood identification (M. Dupeyron, University of Paris), archeozoology (P. Ducos, Centre National de la Recherche Scientifique [C.N.R.S.]), fish remains (J. Blot, Muséum National d'Histoire Naturelle), and geomorphology (P. Sanlaville, University of Lyons). The results available up to now point to an early occurrence of cultivation and a relatively late development of herding in western Syria.

This general process of development is reinforced by what has survived of the tool kit: flint artifacts (M.C. Cauvin, C.N.R.S.), bone industry (D. Stordeur, C.N.R.S.), clay tokens (D. Schmandt-Besserat, University of Texas), and ceramics (L. Courtois, C.N.R.S.). Drawing and photography of material remains have been completed by J. Dufour, C.N.R.S. Anthropological remains were examined by D. Ferembach, C.N.R.S.

Neutron-activation analyses for source exploitation of obsidian were conducted at first by J. Cann, University of Cambridge, and C. Renfrew, University of Southhampton, and later by S. Warren, University of Bradley. Radiocarbon dating has been completed by G. Delibrias, C.N.R.S., and W. Mook, University of Groningen. An attempt to date by obsidian hydration was undertaken by J. Michels, University of Pennsylvania, but the results remain rather inconclusive.

TELL ASWAD

Tell Aswad remains the earliest settlement known in western Syria. The site lies on ancient Pleistocene marshes east of the Ghuta, between the two lakes of Hijjane and Ateibe.

The mean annual rainfall is less than 200 mm, and nowadays the area is cultivated by irrigation. Even if climatic conditions were slightly moister at the time of its first occupation it is assumed the area was unsuitable for dry-farming. It appears, however, from ancient records, that Lake Ateibe extended close to the northeastern edge of the settlement. In the last century its size has been drastically reduced, due to the growing use of the waters from Wadi Barada for agriculture in the Ghuta and the urban requirements of Damascus.

Part of the mound is a natural clayey hillock, like those strewn across the surrounding plain. The size of the settlement is approximately 275 m north-south by 250 m east-west and covers about 5 hectares. The maximum depth of archeological deposits is 4.50 m, but the light ashy earth, which is the bulk of the "Black Mound," was no doubt seriously affected by erosion during the centuries of nonoccupation.

Throughout the whole occupation no solid architecture was encountered. Pits are the most common feature at all levels; they are either large (reaching several meters in diameter) and shallow, possibly being pit dwellings, or deep and narrow, resembling rubbish pits. Remains of reed wattle-and-daub structures are presumably from the walls and roofs of the huts, which were probably of the *zarifa* type until recently visible in the marshy areas of the Ghab and coastal districts. Planoconvex mud bricks, when found in situ, seem to have been used only to build platforms in open spaces between the pits; they are similar to contemporaneous Jericho PPNA hog-backed bricks. Also unchanged in all levels are flexed burials in pits, occasionally strewn with red ochre; some are individual tombs, others are collective. No changes were evidenced in either dwellings or burials throughout the sequence.

The artifactual assemblage shows marked differences from the lowest levels to the surface, thus dividing the development of the settlement into two main phases.

Level I, the earliest occupation, was found only in the eastern part of the site. In antiquity it was sheltered by the natural mound from the west winds, which were presumably then already prevailing, and was the level nearest to the shore of the lake. Study of the tool kit gave evidence of two stages.

The lowest, labeled IA (4.50−2.25 m), is dated in the first half of the eighth millennium B.C. by two radiocarbon determinations: GIF-2633: 7790±120 B.C.; GIF-2372: 7690±120 B.C. Characteristic of this stage are long sickle blades (fig. 3), often serrated, and notched arrowheads; flat retouch is used only to thin down the butt of flint tools. The assemblage resembles that of contemporaneous Mureybet III but shows few connections with Jericho PPNA. Although both Syrian and Palestinian industries have a Natufian background they differ markedly.

Stage IB (2.25−1.80 m) follows in the second half of the eighth millenium B.C., according to two radiocarbon dates: GIF-2370: 7390±120 B.C.; GIF-2371: 7320±120 B.C. Arrowheads become more numerous, being mostly of the pressure-flaked, narrow-tanged Byblos type. The tool kit can be compared to that from Mureybet IVA, which is also dated in the same period (M.C. Cauvin 1974c). Obsidian is imported in small quantities, almost entirely from the Ciftlik area in central Anatolia. Clay is used to model animal and conical pawnlike figurines.

From the very beginning of the occupation, agriculture was practiced, emmer wheat (*Triticum dicoccum*) being the main crop. Pulses, such as lentil (*Lens culinaris*) and pea (*Pisum sativum*), were also cultivated. W. van Zeist suggests utilization of surface water for agricultural purposes; planting the crops on the shore of Lake Ateibe would have provided the plants with several weeks of extra moisture at the beginning of the dry season. This assumption is supported by the proportion of marsh-plant seeds and pollens recovered from the Aswad samples (van Zeist and Bottema 1977, p. 82). Barley is also present, but according to W. zan Zeist belongs to the wild variety (*Hordeum spontaneum*), which was the most widespread of Near Eastern cereals and could have been gathered in the vicinity of Tell Aswad. The inhabitants occasionally collected wild fruits: almonds (*Amygdalus*), pistachio (*Pistacia*), and figs (*Ficus*), the occurrence of which was possible in the original natural environment.

Hunting remained apparently more important than farming for the economy of Tell Aswad. Gazelle became extinct in the area only about eighty years ago, and wild boar, still found nowadays in the northeastern mountains, is even today a favorite game for nearby villages. The inhabitants in antiquity also exploited the available resources, such as fowl and fish, from the lake.

The establishment of permanently settled life at Tell Aswad in the eighth millennium B.C. seems to have been made possible because of the proximity of Lake Ateibe, which provided building materials and protein food and allowed a certain amount of farming activity.

With Level II the settlement reaches its greatest extent, which includes the top of the natural mound. From these upper layers five dates are available: GrN-6678: 6935±55 B.C.; GrN-6679: 6915±60 B.C.; GrN-6677: 6825±75 B.C.; GrN-6676: 6700±55 B.C.; GIF-2375: 6610±110 B.C.

Level II can safely be assumed to cover the first half of the seventh millennium B.C. The prosperity of the community appears to be the result of a reduced dependency on the natural environment: cerealia and leguminous plants become an important component of the pollen diagram; the possibility of rotating crops has been suggested by Arl. Leroi-Gourhan. Besides numerous remains of emmer wheat, the seeds of einkorn (*Triticum monococcum*) and free-threshing wheat (*Triticum durum/aestivum*) have been recovered. Barley seems now to be domesticated; it is mostly two-row (*Hordeum distichum*) but is also naked (*Hordeum nudum*). Pulses remain an important diet component. Wild fruits are still collected.

Presumably connected with the increase in agricultural activities and characteristic of Level II are the prominence and variety of flint sickles, which now include not only serrated blades, often truncated and pressure flaked, but also retouched blades and truncated sickle elements with overlaying retouch. Arrowheads are quite diversified; there are Byblos points, Amuq points, oval points, notched points, and rare Jericho barbed points (fig. 4). These implements agree with the evidence, from faunal remains, of the continuation of hunting activities. Among flint tools the burins come next, followed by the scrapers, the borers, and the drills. A few bifacial axes also occur. Level II is especially rich in flint artifacts, which are sometimes struck from bipolar naviform cores; the result is an increase in crested blades. Connections are patent both northward with Mureybet IVB and southward with the PPNB culture.

The use of obsidian increases markedly, originating in approximately equal quantities from central Anatolia (Ciftlik) and eastern Anatolia (Nemrut Dağ and possibly Lake Van). Ground axes, limestone vessels, and basalt querns or rubbers remain conspicuously rare, which is not surprising, considering the scarcity of stones in the vicinity of Tell Aswad. Various attractive stones were neatly ground for manufacturing small objects, such as beads, pendants (fig. 5), tiny cylinders, and balls, some bearing incisions. The raw materials — limestone, alabaster, cornelian, greenstone, soapstone, and obsidian — provide evidence of far-reaching trade relations. Besides their use as adornment, including their possible use as labrets, the function of a number of these tokens is not clear. Bone tools (fig. 6), consisting of awls, spatulas, and helves, are not frequent but are quite elaborate.

Other than flaked flints, however, most of the artifacts in Level II are made of baked clay. Animal figurines and conical figurines are more common. They are associated with a large number of new types. Several varieties are anthropomorphic: upright flat figurines akin to those found by J. Perrot at Munhata (Perrot 1966, pl. VI, 1–6, 9–11) and a remarkable series of seated female figurines, either tall, with hands clasped under their breasts, or squat and triangular shaped (figs. 7, 8, 9). The latter type recalls "mother goddess" figurines from Çayönü and Jarmo (Mellaart 1975, figs. 20 and 35). Among other baked clay objects the most common are balls, discs, and small cups, which are utterly different, on technical grounds, from the ceramics.

Although Aswad II is strongly related to other PPNB sites, such as Mureybet, Saaide, Beisamoun, and Beidha, the evidence from obsidian and clay figurines suggests it is also linked with northern Mesopotamia.

GHORAIFÉ

Ghoraifé, 15 km farther north than Tell Aswad and directly west of Lake Ateibe, was settled during the same kind of environmental conditions as those of Tell Aswad, presumably as its offspring. The site extends over approximately the same amount of area as Tell Aswad, 300 m north-south by 200 m east-west, and exceeds 6 m at its highest point. The first occupation of Ghoraifé seems to be earlier than the time of the desertion of Tell Aswad, but the former outlived the latter.

Lower Level I (6.40 to 3.50 m) yielded three dates, all in the first half of the seventh millennium B.C.: GIF-3376: 6760±190 B.C.; GIF-3375: 6530±190 B.C.; GIF-3374: 6450±190 B.C. As on Tell

Aswad, structures are restricted to pits, remains of reed walling, and planoconvex mud bricks. Flaked-flint industry is characterized by long naviform cores, long serrated sickle blades, tanged arrowheads, burins, and scrapers. Obsidian is imported from the same sources as those of Aswad II. Baked clay is frequent and includes spheres, discs, cylinders, and a few figurines such as animals and seated or conical statuettes. A unique pawnlike figurine, 5.8 cm high, is especially elaborate because of its incised pedestal; it is assumed to represent a male divinity (fig. 10).

Floral and faunal remains give the same picture as Aswad II; according to W. van Zeist, "The inhabitants could likewise have cultivated their cereals and leguminous crop plants on the shore of Lake Ateibe" (Van Zeist and Bottema 1977, p. 83). The close relationships between Aswad II and Ghoraifé I link the latter with the early PPNB culture.

Level II (3.50 m and upward) offers a poorer assemblage, which is based mostly on chipped flint. Besides a few naviform cores, most of its material comes from tabular flint, shaped into small cores. Arrowheads are mainly pressure-flaked Byblos points, associated with a few notched points. Sickle blades are much less numerous; they usually show an abrupt retouch and small denticulation, but some show an overlaying flat retouch. Scrapers are now more common than burins. Obsidian seems more frequent too; possibly there was an increasing reliance on eastern Anatolian sources. If stone artifacts and baked clay are very scarce, the bone industry is particularly rich; it consists mainly of spatulas, made from animal ribs, but includes awls and helves. A complete spatula measures 28 cm long. Most conspicuous in the upper layers at Ghoraifé is the large amount of animal bones, which suggests that this settlement, without giving up its farming activities, was relying more than previously on game resources. This shift from agriculture to the hunting of herbivorous animals could possibly be related to the dryness, assumed by Arl. Leroi-Gourhan on palynological grounds, of the second half of the seventh millennium B.C. (Arl. Leroi-Gourhan 1974), which is precisely the date given by one single determination (GIF-3372: 6200±190 B.C.) for Ghoraifé II. A slight climatic trend toward dessication could also account for the abandonment of the site and the apparent lack of settled communities in the eastern part of the Damascus area during the following millennia.

TELL RAMAD

The close connections of two late PPNB exposures such as Ghoraifé II and Ramad I are strengthened by the dating of the latter to the same period as the former: GrN-4426: 6260±50 B.C.; GrN-4428: 6250±80 B.C.; GrN-4821: 6140±50 B.C. Climatic conditions, however, were notably different, Tell Ramad being at the foot of Mount Hermon in the well-watered area favorable for dry-farming. The settlement was established at the point of contact of two plateaux, one of basalt and the other of limestone. Both plateaux unfailingly provided raw materials.

Such an environment accounts for the appearance at Ramad I of solid architecture, with semisubterranean clay dwellings, plastered hearths, boulder stone platforms, and stone artifacts such as numerous basalt querns and grinders and frequent limestone bowls. Bone and flint implements are similar to those recovered from Ghoraifé II; unique in the bone industry are an arrowhead and a carding comb (fig. 12). Flint axes are more common, as could be expected in a better-wooded environment. Plastered skulls made their first appearance, as far as we know, in the Damascus area, firmly linking Tell Ramad with the PPNB-Natufian culture (Jericho, Beisamoun). Trade relationships were not severed with Anatolia: obsidian still arrived mainly from Çiftlik but also from Nemrut Dağ. Greenstone artifacts and a bead drilled from a nugget of native copper also point to central Anatolia.

The same varieties of crops were grown at Tell Ramad as at Ghoraifé and Aswad: emmer wheat, two-row barley, and lentil remaining predominant. Flax (*Linum usitatissimum*) is now cultivated as an oil plant. Among wild fruits, almond, pistachio, and hawthorn (*Crataegus*) are common, but fig does not occur. Hunted animals are gazelle and equid from the steppe and deer and wild cat from wooded slopes of Mount Hermon.

Without any break in the development of the tool kit, which is, however, now dominated by coarse-denticulated sickle-blade sections, Level II yields rectangular mud-brick houses, with plastered floors and stone foundations, of a typical PPNB style (Abou Gosh, Munhata, Beisamoun). Dwellings line narrow lanes. The village is not half as large as the former ones, its surface being about 2 hectares and extending from 175 m east-west to 150 m north-south. The filling is made up mainly of salty ashes, as expressed in the name of the site, "Hill of Ashes." This development took place during the first half of the sixth millennium B.C. according to radiocarbon dates: GrN-4427: 5970±50 B.C.; GrN-4822: 5950±50 B.C.; GrN-4823: 5930±55 B.C. Characteristic of Ramad II are lime White-ware vessels (fig. 13) and soft ware. Baked clay objects are common but less elaborate: animal figurines, pawnlike figurines, and balls are well represented, while seated figurines are rare (de Contenson 1967, fig. 8; de Contenson 1970, fig. 10).

The last stage at Tell Ramad, Level III, does not show any change in the flint industry but is characterized by a lack of solid architecture and the digging of deep pits, the use of dark-faced burnished ware, and the breeding of definitely domesticated animals (goat, sheep, pig, ox, and dog, according to D. Hooijer). Burnished ceramic heads of figurines (fig. 14) are reminiscent of those found at Byblos *Néolithique ancien* (J. Cauvin 1972, fig. 28, 1) and Hassunan levels at Yarim Tepe (Mellaart 1975, fig. 85). Whether these developments are the effect of some climatic change or of a drastic shift toward pastoralism, or both, is difficult to ascertain.

Finally, settled life seems to come to an abrupt end in the Damascus area toward the end of the sixth millennium B.C. In contrast, there is no evidence of any disturbance in the coastal area, a better-watered Mediterranean environment.

RAS SHAMRA

The Ras Shamra sequence, on the northern coast of Syria, begins in only the mid-seventh millennium B.C. The available radiocarbon dates for basal Level VC (14.80−13.20 m) are as follows: P-460: 6414±100 B.C.; P-459: 6192±100 B.C.; GIF-3960: 5950±140 B.C. The first inhabitants settled on a limestone ridge overgrown with pine trees; very soon, arboreal pollens decreased and cerealia appeared, no doubt as an effect of agricultural activities. As in the Damascus area, the main crop plants were emmer wheat, barley, lentil, pea, and flax; a little einkorn was also cultivated. Besides the wild fruits mentioned for Aswad — pistachio, almonds, and figs — gathering included olives (*Olea*) and cornel berry (*Cornus*). Hunting remained an essential food resource; the game included wild boar, roe deer, fallow deer, goat, and possibly ox. Large sea fish, presumably tunny, were captured.

The culture is aceramic; there are a few limestone and soapstone bowls. Characteristic is the large number of flints; the prominent tool is the scraper, which is followed by tanged arrowheads. The latter are either of the Byblos type or have a broad, notched, bulbous tang, produced by the so-called Ugarit technique. Finely serrated sickle blades are present but are not very common. Obsidian is more frequent than in southern Syria (3% of the chipped stone industry instead of the average 1%) and comes exclusively from central Anatolia (Ciftlik). Bone spatulas are an important component of the assemblage. Soapstone was used to carve two stamp seals and a bull statuette, only one leg of which has survived. Baked clay figurines are very scarce; a triangular incised figurine is related to the seated-female type from the Damascus area (de Contenson 1962, fig. 28).

Rectangular stone houses appear in the upper strata of Level VC (fig. 15). There are many links between the artifacts from this stage and those from contemporaneous sites such as Abu Hureyra in the Later Aceramic Phase and Ramad I. Toward the end of this level pine groves once again spread over the landscape.

With Level VB (13.20−12.20 m), tree pollen declines, while cerealia become superabundant in the pollen spectrum, which indicates a renewal of cultivation. Massive rectilinear stone foundations have been uncovered in this stage (fig. 15), which belongs to the first half of the sixth millennium B.C.: P-458: 5736±112 B.C. There is no evidence of any break in the development of the flaked-flint industry: naviform cores, at first more frequent than in the former stage, fall out of use and are replaced by small cores. Truncated sickle blades of the same type as in Level VC become the most common tool, followed by burins and arrowheads of Byblos, Ugarit, and Amuq types (fig. 18). Obsidian remains well represented (8.5% of the total chipped stone industry). Soft limestone is often carved into figurines or slabs of limestone are incised with checkered patterns (fig. 16). Dark-faced burnished ware and soft ware appear from the beginning of Level VB; they are similar to the ceramics from the Amuq A period. The latter yields, on the whole, the same type of assemblage, including, in addition, butterfly beads (*perles à ailettes*), which are also known in the Later Aceramic Phase at Abu Hureya.

Level VA (12.20–10.20 m) shows a declining cerealia percentage, which is presumably not the result of a decline in agriculture but of a removal of the fields, due to the concentration of the dwellings. Although still isolated, small rectangular stone houses, with plastered floors (fig. 17), seem to have been built closer together. Cultivation was, therefore, now practiced on the outskirts of the settlement. Dark-faced burnished ware and soft ware are now associated with white-coated ware, Hassuna "husking trays," and lime White ware. The flint industry is basically the same as that of Level VB. Obsidian amounts to about 5% of the chipped stone implements, a ratio comparable to that of Abu Hureyra. Double-notched limestone and sandstone pebbles were probably used as net weights for fishing, which was more intensively practiced on large sea fishes, such as tunny and shark. Soft limestone is still used for making figurines (fig. 19). Burnished ware is also shaped into figurines, loom weights, and stamp seals. Carbonized wood from the end of this stage provided a radiocarbon dating: P-457: 5234±84 B.C.; the chronological boundaries should be ca. 5750–5250 B.C., on the same horizon as Amuq B, Sukas Neolithic, Abu Hureyra Ceramic Neolithic, and Byblos *Néolithique ancien*.

Level IV (10.20–6.25 m) follows immediately and shows evidence of Mesopotamian influence. Along with local ware, often pattern burnished, there appears painted pottery of Halafian style. New types of stamp seals are made out of carnelian and soapstone (fig. 20). Obsidian is abundant and used for adornment. Attempts are made to use timber and mud brick for the building of multiroomed houses, which now cluster together in a restricted area. Facilities such as stone-built ovens with plastered sill are quite common. The breeding of small cattle, goat, and sheep, although already known, becomes more important in the economy of the settlement. All of these innovations point to strong links with the Halafian focus. The evidence, however, excludes any significant change in the population; it points instead to acculturation due to exchange with an area that had reached a higher standard of culture. The development of this new stage during the fifth millennium B.C. pushes Ras Shamra toward urban civilization.

Although herding seems to have developed rather late in western Syria, the earliest settled communities cultivated a variety of cereal and leguminous crops from at least the eighth millennium B.C. onward, and in many respects their inhabitants were not very different from the peasants who are tilling the same fertile soil today.

BIBLIOGRAPHY

Braidwood, Robert J.
    1972   Prehistoric investigations in southwestern Asia. *Proceedings of the American Philosophical Society* 116:310–20.
    1973   The early village in southwestern Asia. *Journal of Near Eastern Studies.* 32:34–39.

Braidwood, Robert J., and Braidwood, Linda S.
    1960   *Excavations in the plain of Antioch*, vol. 1: *the earlier assemblages: phases A —J.* Oriental Institute Publications, vol. 61. Chicago: University of Chicago Press.

Cauvin, Jacques
    1972   *Religions néolithiques de Syro-Palestine.* Paris: Maisonneuve.
    1977   Les fouilles de Mureybet (1971—1974) et leur signification pour les origines de la séden-tarisation au Proche-Orient. In *Archeological reports from the Tabqa dam project — Euphrates valley, Syria*, ed. D.N. Freedman, pp. 19—48. Annual of the American Schools of Oriental Research, vol. 44. Cambridge, Mass.: American Schools of Oriental Research.
    1978   *Les premiers villages de Syrie-Palestine du IXème au VIIème millénaire avant J-C.* Collection de la Maison de l'Orient Méditerranéen Ancien 4, Série Archéologique, 3. Lyon: Maison de l'Orient.

Cauvin, Marie-Claire
    1974a   Flèches à encoches de Syrie: essai de classification et d'interprétation culturelle. *Paléo-rient* 2:311—22.
    1974b   Outillage lithique et chronologie à Tell Aswad (Damascène, Syrie). *Paléorient* 2:429—36.
    1974c   Note préliminaire sur l'outillage lithique de la phase IV de Mureybet (Syrie). *Annales Archéologiques Arabes Syriennes* 24:59—63.
    1977   Outillage lithique et chronologie de Tell Ghoraifé C (Damascène, Syrie). *Paléorient* 3:295—304.

Cauvin, Marie-Claire, and Stordeur, Danielle
    1978   *Les outillages lithiques et osseux de Mureybet, Syrie (fouilles van Loon, 1965).* Cahiers de l'Euphrate, vol. 1. Paris: Editions du Centre National de la Recherche Scientifique.

Crowfoot-Payne, Joan
    1976   The terminology of the aceramic Neolithic period in the Levant. In *IX° Congrés de l'Union Internationale des Sciences Préhistoriques et Protohistoriques*, Colloque III, pp. 131—37. Paris: Editions du Centre National de la Recherche Scientifique.

de Contenson, Henri
    1962   Poursuite des recherches dans le sondage à l'Ouest du temple de Baal (1955—1960). In *Ugaritica*, vol. 4, ed. Claude Schaeffer, pp. 477—519. Paris: Geuthner.
    1963   New correlations between Ras Shamra and al-'Amuq. *Bulletin of the American Schools of Oriental Research* 172:35—40.
    1967   Troisième campagne à Tell Ramad, 1966: rapport préliminaire. *Annales Archéologiques Arabes Syriennes* 17:17—24.
    1970   Septième campagne de fouilles à Tell Ramad en 1970: rapport préliminaire. *Annales Archéologiques Arabes Syriennes* 20:77—80.
    1971   Tell Ramad, a village of Syria of the 7th and 6th millennia B.C. *Archaeology* 24:278—83.
    1972   Tell Aswad: fouilles de 1971. *Annales Archéologiques Arabes Syriennes* 22:75—84
    1973a   Chronologie absolue de Tell Aswad (Damascène, Syrie). *Bulletin de la Société Pré-historique Française* 70:253—56.
    1973b   Le niveau halafien de Ras Shamra: rapport préliminaire sur les campagnes 1968—1972 dans le sondage préhistorique. *Syria* 50:13—33.
    1975   Les fouilles à Ghoraifé en 1974. *Annales Archéologiques Arabes Syriennes* 25:17—24.
    1976a   Nouvelles données sur le Néolithique précéramique dans la région de Damas (Syrie) d'après les fouilles de Ghoraifé en 1974. *Bulletin de la Société Préhistorique Française* 73:80—2.
    1976b   Précisions sur la stratigraphie de Tell Aswad (Syrie). *Bulletin de la Société Préhistorique Française* 73:198—99.
    1977   Le Néolithique de Ras Shamra V d'après les campagnes 1972—1976 dans le sondage SH. *Syria* 54:1—23.

1978a   Recherches sur le Néolithique de Syrie (1967–1976). In *Académie des Inscriptions et Belles Lettres, comptes rendus des séances de l'année 1978: 820–25*. Paris: Editions Klincksieck.

1978b   Le niveau V de Ras Shamra: rapport préliminaire des campagnes 1972–1976 dans le sondage SH. *Annales Archéologiques Arabes Syriennes* 17/18:9–28.

1978c   Tell Aswad: fouilles de 1972. *Annales Archéologiques Arabes Syriennes* 17/18:207–15.

de Contenson, Henri, and Liere, Willem J. van

1963   A note on five early Neolithic sites in inland Syria. *Annales Archéologiques de Syrie* 13:179–205.

1966   Premiers sondages à Bouqras en 1965: rapport préliminaire. *Annales Archéologiques Arabes Syriennes* 16(2):181–92.

Ferembach, Denise

1970   Etude anthropologique des ossements humains néolithiques de Tell Ramad, Syrie (campagnes 1963–1966). *L'Anthropologie* 74:247–54.

France-Lanord, Albert, and de Contenson, Henri

1973   Une pendeloque en cuivre natif de Ramad. *Paléorient* 1:107–15.

Hooijer, D.A.

1966   Preliminary notes on the animal remains found at Bouqras and Ramad in 1965. *Annales Archéologiques Arabes Syriennes* 16(2):193–96.

Kirkbride, Diana

1960   A brief report on pre-pottery flint cultures of Jericho. *Palestine Exploration Quarterly* 92:114–19.

1968   Beidha: early Neolithic village life south of the Dead Sea. *Antiquity* 42:263–74

Lechevallier, Monique

1978   *Abou Gosh et Beisamoun: deux gisements du VII° millénaire avant l'ère chrétienne en Israël*. Paris: Association Paléorient.

Leroi-Gourhan, Arlette

1973   Palynologische Befunde aus Quartärablagerungen in Damaskus Becken und seine Rahneberichen. *Zeitschrift für Geomorphologie* N.F. 17:303–18.

1974   Etudes palynologiques des derniers 11.000 ans en Syrie semi-désertique. *Paléorient* 3:443–51.

Liere, Willem J. van, and de Contenson, Henri

1964   Holocene environment and early settlement in the Levant. *Annales Archéologiques de Syrie* 14:125–28.

Mellaart, James

1975   *The Neolithic of the Near East*. London: Thames and Hudson.

Moore, Andrew M.T.

1975   The excavations of Tell Abu Hureyra in Syria: a preliminary report. *Proceedings of the Prehistoric Society* 41:50–77. (With contributions by G.C. Hillman and A.J. Legge.)

Mortensen, Peder

1970   A preliminary study of the chipped stone industry from Beidha. *Acta Archaeologica* 41:1–54.

Perrot, Jean

1966   La troisième campagne de fouilles à Munhata (1964). *Syria* 43:49–63

1968   La préhistoire palestinienne. *Supplément au dictionnaire de la Bible*, vol. 8, cols. 286–446. Paris: Letouzey and Ané.

Redman, Charles L.

1978   *The rise of civilization. From early farmers to urban civilization in the ancient Near East*. San Francisco: Freeman.

Renfrew, Colin; Dixon, John E.; and Cann, John R.
  1966   Obsidian and early cultural contact in the Near East. *Proceedings of the Prehistoric Society* 32:30—72.

Schmandt-Besserat, Denise
  1977   The earliest use of clay in Syria. *Expedition* 19(9):28—42.

Stordeur-Yedid, Danielle
  1976   Les pointes d'os à poulie articulaire: observations techniques d'après quelques exemples syriens. *Bulletin de la Société Préhistorique Française* 73:39—42.

Zeist, Willem van
  1976   On macroscopic traces of food plants in southwestern Asia: with some reference to pollen data. *Philosophical Transactions of the Royal Society of London B (Biological Sciences)* 275: *The early history of agriculture*, pp. 27—41. London: The Royal Society.

Zeist, Willem van, and Bakker-Heeres, J.A.H.
  1975   Evidence for linseed cultivation before 6000 B.C. *Journal of Archaeological Science* 2:215—19.

Zeist, Willem van and Bottema, S.
  1966   Palaeobotanical investigations at Ramad. *Annales Archéologiques Arabes Syriennes* 16(2): 179—80.
  1977   Palynological investigations in western Iran. *Palaeohistorica* 19:19—85.

Chronology of Main Stratified Syro-Palestinian Neolithic Sites.

Date B.C.	Amuq Plain	Ras Shamra	Mureybet	Abu Hureyra	Buqras	El Kowm	Aswad
5000 —	---------	------------					
	C	IVC					
5250 —	---------	------------					
5500 —	B	VA		--------------	------------	--------------	
				Ceramic Neolithic	III	Upper	
5750 —	---------	------------			============	============	
	A	VB			II	Middle	
6000 —	=========	============		============	------------	--------------	
				Late Aceramic Neolithic	I		
6250 —		VC			------------	Lower	
6500 —		------------		--------------		--------------	-----------
6750 —		Slenfe					II
				Early Aceramic Neolithic			
7000 —			--------------				-----------
			IVB				
7250 —			--------------				IB
			IVA				
7500 —			--------------	--------------			-----------
7750 —			III				IA
8000 —			--------------				-----------
			II				
8250 —			--------------				
			I				
8500 —			--------------	--------------			
8750 —				Mesolithic			
9000 —				--------------			

NOTE: Double line shows first occurrence of ceramics.

Ghoraifé	Ramad	Beqa'a	Coastal Lebanon	Northern Palestine	Jericho	Beidha	Date B.C.
		Ard Tlaili Lower	Byblos "Néolithique Ancien"	Munhata 2 B 1			— 5000
				Munhata 2 B 2	PNA		— 5250
	III	Labwe II					— 5500
	II	Labwe I					— 5750
II	I						— 6000
				Munhata 3–6	Late PPNB	II–V	— 6250
I							— 6500
		Saadiyeh	Dik el Mehdi	W. Fallah III	Early PPNB	VI–IX	— 6750
							— 7000
							— 7250
							— 7500
					PPNA		— 7750
							— 8000
				W. Fallah II	"Proto-Neolithic"		— 8250
							— 8500
				W. Fallah I	Natufian	Natufian	— 8750
							— 9000

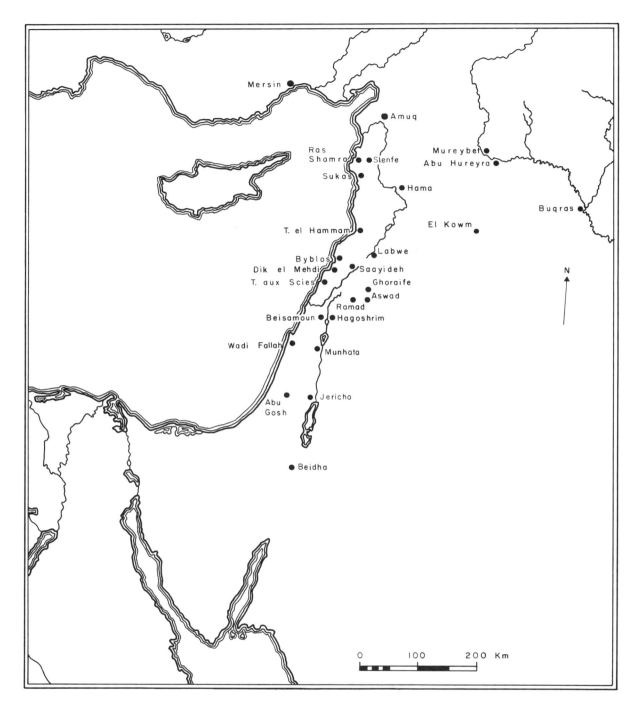

FIG. 1. — MAIN NEOLITHIC SYRO-PALESTINIAN SITES.

FIG. 2. — NEOLITHIC SITES OF THE DAMASCUS AREA. FIG. 3. — ASWAD I: FLINT SICKLE BLADE. Scale, 1:1. FIG. 4. — ASWAD II: FLINT ARROWHEAD OF JERICHO TYPE. Scale, 1:1. FIG. 5. — ASWAD II: STONE PENDANTS. Scale, 1:1. FIG. 6. — ASWAD II: BONE TOOLS. Scale, 3:5.

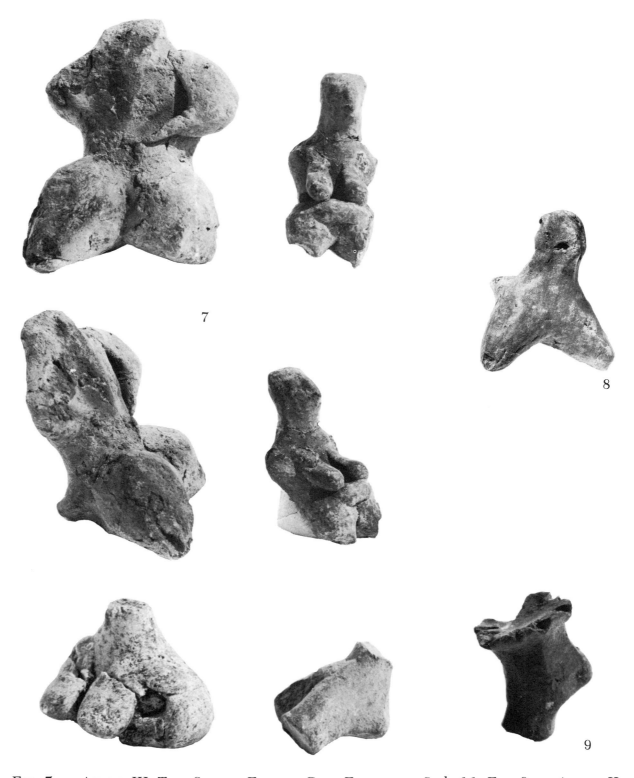

FIG. 7. — ASWAD III: TWO SEATED FEMALE CLAY FIGURINES. Scale 1:1. FIG. 8. — ASWAD II: SEATED CLAY FIGURINE. No Scale. FIG. 9. — ASWAD II: FRAGMENTS OF CLAY FIGURINES. Torso, legs, and head. Scale, 2:1.

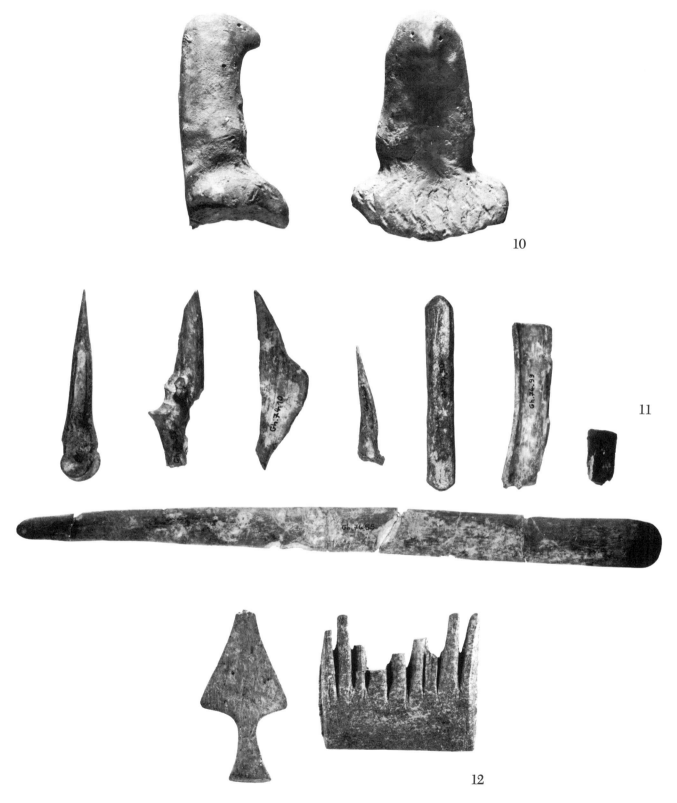

10

11

12

Fig. 10. — Ghoraife I: Pawnlike Clay Figurine. Scale, ca. 1:1. Fig. 11. — Ghoraife II: Bone Tools. Scale, 3:5. Fig. 12. — Ramad I: Bone Implements; Arrowhead and Carding comb. Scale, 1:1.

72

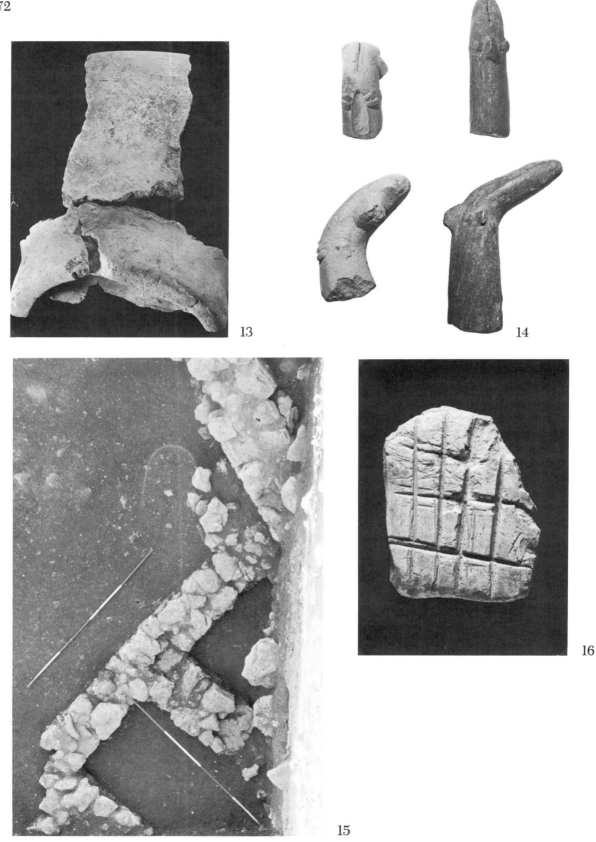

13

14

15

16

Fig. 13. — Ramad II: Fragments of Lime White Ware Bowl. Scale, 1.5:5. Fig. 14. — Ramad III: Burnished Clay Figurine Heads. Scale, 1:1. Fig. 15. — Ras Shamra VC: Stone Architecture. Upper right corner: VB wall. Fig. 16. — Ras Shamra VB: Incised Limestone Slab. Scale, 1:1.

Fig. 17. — Ras Shamra VA. House with stone walls and plastered floor.

18

19

20

FIG. 18. — RAS SHAMRA VA: FLINT ARROWHEADS. Ugarit, Amuq, and Byblos points. Scale, 4:5. FIG. 19. — RAS SHAMRA VA: CARVED LIMESTONE ANIMAL HEAD. Scale, 1:1. FIG. 20. — RAS SHAMRA IV: CARNELIAN AND SOAPSTONE STAMP SEALS. Scale, 1.5:1.

LES RAPPORTS ENTRE L'ANATOLIE ET LA SYRIE DU NORD À L'ÉPOQUE DES PREMIÈRES COMMUNAUTÉS VILLAGEOISES DE BERGERS ET DE PAYSANS 7600−5000 B.C.

Francis Hours and Lorraine Copeland

ENTRE 7600 et 5000 B.C.,[1] le genre de vie établi dans le Levant septentrional se concrétise en petits villages groupant des maisons de plan rectangulaire plus ou moins complexe, habités par des paysans qui ont adopté définitivement la culture du blé et de l'orge, la domestication du mouton et de la chèvre, bien que la chasse occupe encore une place importante, la chasse à l'aurochs en particulier. Cela se traduit dans l'équipement technique par la présence d'un mobilier lourd (meules, mortiers, et pilons destinés au broyage), de faucilles et de pointes de flèches pédonculées, avec ou sans épaulements (pointes de Byblos ou pointes d'Amuq). Avec des variantes, cette civilisation s'étend depuis le sud du plateau anatolien au nord, de la plaine de Konya à la vallée du haut Tigre, jusque dans le Negev au sud, tandis qu'à l'est on la rencontre encore dans le Sinjar. Elle recouvre donc à peu près tout l'espace levantin.

Après 5000 B.C., on trouve répandue sur tout le piedmont sud du Taurus, et jusque dans la Beqaa centrale au Liban, la céramique peinte dont on a fait le critère de la civilisation halafienne. En 2.600 ans, le Levant septentrional est passé d'une organisation de l'espace uniforme et peu structurée à l'hégémonie d'une influence dont on peut suivre le point de départ et les débuts, l'expansion et les limites.

Notre propos est de suivre ce qui s'est passé durant ces 2.600 ans (7600−5000 B.C.) dans le sud de la Turquie et le nord de la Syrie actuelle, au contact de domaines biogéographiques différents: bordure littorale méditerranéenne, montagnes soit occidentales du Liban et des Alaouites, soit plus septentrionales du Taurus, collines et avant-monts, plaines et plateaux steppiques du croissant céréalier, et frange occidentale du désert. Il est présomptueux de vouloir expliquer les changements de civilisation qui se sont opérés dans cette région à cette époque, car les données dont nous disposons sont encore trop maigres, mais on peut décrire et préciser les points qui devront être, un jour, expliqués, lorsque nous en saurons davantage.[2] En nous appuyant sur les dates publiées, nous tâcherons de suivre la succession de ces changements, époque par époque, de façon synchronique à travers toute la région, et non pas de façon diachronique continue dans chaque province prise isolément, comme on le fait d'ordinaire. Chaque étape culturelle fera l'objet d'une carte, ce qui permettra l'ébauche d'une analyse spatiale rudimentaire.[3] Chemin faisant, on signalera les explications qui ont été avancées pour rendre compte des transformations vécues par la région.

1. Le système de référence employé pour toute notre chronologie utilise les dates de 14-C avec 1/2 vie conventionnelle de Libby: 5.568 ± 30 ans, calculées en B.C., sans calibration.

2. La distinction entre explication et description se réfère au vocabulaire de la "Nouvelle Archéologie" (voir Hours 1980, 217−20). Des extrapolations "explicatives" ont été effectuées par certains auteurs, comme on le verra plus loin.

3. Nous utiliserons pour cela l'ensemble des fouilles et des prospections, publiées ou non, dont nous avons pu avoir connaissance, notamment: Archi et al. 1971; Besançon et al. 1980; Bostancı 1971, 1973; Braidwood 1937; Braidwood R. et L. 1960; Buccellati G. et M. 1967; Çambel et Braidwood 1980; Cauvin 1970; Copeland 1979; Davidson et McKerrel 1976; French 1964, 1965a, 1965b, 1970, 1972; Kirkbride 1972; Lloyd 1938; van Loon 1967; Mallowan 1937; Matthers, à paraître; Maxwell-Hyslop et al. 1942; Mellaart 1954, 1961; Merpert et al. 1977; Özdoğan 1977; Seton-Williams 1954; Todd 1965, 1966.

DES PREMIERS AGRICULTEURS AUX PREMIERS POTIERS (7600—6000 B.C.)

Entre 7600 et 6600 B.C., on connaît quatre sites datés:[4] Aşıklı Hüyük, Çayönü, Mureybet (niveau IV) et Abu Hureyra *(Early Aceramic)*. Ils ont en commun, semble-t-il,[5] de connaître l'agriculture et l'élevage, d'ignorer la céramique. On y a utilisé des pointes de flèches à pédoncules, façonnées par des retouches obtenues par pression (sauf à Aşıklı), ce qui n'existe pas avant 7600. A Çayönü (L. Braidwood, c.p.), l'outillage d'obsidienne porte souvent des stries sur la face ventrale des lames et des éclats, et on rencontre des faucilles aux deux bords utilisés, avec une tête élargie, qui se retrouvent dans les environs à Cafer Harabesi (J. Cauvin, c.p.), plus à l'est à Magzaliya (N. Bader 1979), et, plus tard, dans le Zagros à Shimshara (Voigt 1976). A Mureybet et Abu Hureyra, un débitage laminaire particulier s'opère à partir de nucleus à deux plans de frappe opposés, dits "naviformes", dont l'épannelage façonne le dos en forme de coque de navire.

A partir de 6600, des nouveautés apparaissent, comme la hache en pierre dure polie, qui témoigne moins d'une nouvelle technique de fabrication que d'une orientation vers le défrichage ou le travail du bois. Mais surtout, les efforts pour résoudre le problème du récipient commencent à aboutir, avec la "vaisselle blanche" en chaux ou en plâtre (Frierman 1971) et les premiers pots en argile cuite avec dégraissant (J. Cauvin 1974). Cependant, le fond commun de l'outillage lithique reste le même: pointes de flèches du type de l'Amuq ou de Byblos, nucleus naviformes, faucilles. Datés de cette époque, entre 6600 et 6000, on connaît Çatal Hüyük (niveaux XII—IX), Can Hasan III (7—2) (Ergin 1975), Ras Shamra (V c), Abu Hureyra *(Late Aceramic)*, Bouqras (l'ensemble du site) (Akkermans et al., sous presse), tell Assouad/Aswad (Balikh).

Les critères fournis par les sites datés donnent autant de variables permettant de regrouper autour de ces points forts d'autres gisements, dont on connaît le matériel mais non la date exacte. Lorsque les publications sont suffisamment précises et font état d'une typologie un peu détaillée, il est possible de tenir compte de la ligne de démarcation que nous avons tracée aux environs de 6600 B.C. Mais, étant donné que bien des éléments: architecture rectangulaire, pointes de l'Amuq ou de Byblos, nucleus naviformes, se retrouvent tout au long de la période, il est parfois difficile de trancher, et nous devons nous résoudre, pour donner l'image complète de ce que nous connaissons aujourd'hui dans cette région, à traiter comme un tout les 1.600 ans qui aboutissent à l'adoption de la céramique (carte 1).

Sur le plateau d'Anatolie, Aşıklı Hüyük d'abord, puis Çatal Hüyük (XII—IX) et Can Hasan III (7—2), auxquels on peut joindre Reis Tümeği, forment un groupe qui ignore le nucleus naviforme. Çatal Hüyük est à part, en ce que la céramique y est présente, de façon intermittente, sous forme de récipients non peints, mais lustrés. Il est à noter que la céramique intermittente existe plus à l'ouest à la même époque à Suberde. De toute façon, ces trois ou quatre points restent séparés, et ne sauraient former un "ensemble" *(system)* car ils ne sont pas contemporains, Aşıklı étant plus ancien, comme l'indique la forme des pointes de flèches, d'allure plus archaïque que ce que l'on trouve d'ordinaire à cette époque, et qui évoque la phase III de Mureybet (J. Cauvin 1978, 92, n. 4). D'autre part, nous ne connaissons pas les assemblages lithiques des niveaux anciens de Çatal Hüyük, qui n'ont pas été étudiés par Bialor 1962.

Dans les vallées du Taurus, autour de Çayönü, on trouve Boy tepe, et Cafer Harabesi sur l'Euphrate, dont l'architecture rappelle Çayönü (J. Cauvin, c.p.). Les étranges faucilles signalées plus haut forment un lien supplémentaire, et on pourrait peut-être parler ici de sous-ensemble, avec des prolongements vers Magzaliya à l'est, et même les grottes de Sakce Gözü à l'ouest

4. Pour les dates précises, voir les listes de Mellaart 1975, 283—88 et de Henry et Servello 1974. Ces deux listes ne sont pas à jour, ni exemptes d'erreurs, et doivent êtres vérifiées. Elles sont cependant utiles.

5. Aşıklı Hüyük n'a pas été fouillé: Todd 1966 et 1968.

(Waechter et al. 1951). Il faut néanmoins se rappeler que le matériel d'aucun de ces sites n'a été vraiment publié.

Dans le domaine méditerranéen, non loin de Ras Shamra mais sur le prolongement des montagnes alaouites, se trouve Janoudiyeh, site non fouillé et important, dont les pointes de flèches de type Amuq (Contenson 1969) indiquent une occupation à cette époque, entre autres.

Les dernières prospections ont permis de reconnaître, le long du cours moyen de l'Euphrate, les sites de Gritille et Hayaz en Turquie (Özdoğan 1977), Qara Dere et Molla Assad sur le Sajour (Besançon et al. 1980), Dibsi Faraj et Krein II sur l'Euphrate,[6] auxquels on peut joindre Pınar Başı (Bostancı 1971) et Carchemish (Woolley 1934, 1952), en ré-interprétant de vieilles références. Le long du Balikh, outre tell Assouad/Aswad, découvert par Mallowan, fouillé par lui et par Cauvin, diverses prospections, publiées ou non (Mallowan 1946 et Copeland 1979), permettent de signaler, datant de la même époque, tell Breilat, tell Hammam, tell Mafraq Slouq. Il y aurait d'autres sites à placer sur la carte, mais on ne connaît rien des récentes prospections allemandes ou hollandaises le long du Khabour. La seule indication publiée faisant allusion à une occupation remontant peut-être à cette époque dans la région signale des grattoirs-perçoirs, décrits par L. Braidwood (in McEwan et al. 1958), et récupérés dans les briques d'une forteresse assyrienne à Fakhariya, à la frontière syro-turque. On retrouve les mêmes outils à tell Molla Assad sur le Sajour, plus à l'ouest, dans un contexte acéramique, mais avec de la vaisselle blanche.

Au confluent du Khabour et de l'Euphrate, tell es Sin, découvert par les Hollandais, semble contemporain de Bouqras. Plus à l'est, tell Magzaliya, dans le Sinjar (N. Bader 1979), se rattache à la tradition levantine par ses pointes de flèches, tandis que ses faucilles à tête élargie en font un intermédiaire entre le Taurus (Cafer et Çayönü) et le Zagros (Shimshara). Plus au sud, un petit tell près de Umm Dabaghiya, Umm Dabaghiya 4? (Kirkbride 1972), serait à mentionner. Enfin, dans le désert syrien, El Kowm est un relais entre Mureybet, Abu Hureyra, Bouqras et la côte.[7]

Le tableau qui émerge de ce bref inventaire et des critères choisis est forcément très provisoire, car on ignore beaucoup de choses. Un fond commun, défini par les pointes de flèches, dont il faut nuancer la typologie (M.C. Cauvin 1974), et par l'architecture rectiligne, dénote l'unité d'un genre de vie où la chasse garde une certaine importance. D'autre part, l'adoption de cabanes rectangulaires, qu'on peut agglomérer en ensembles complexes, mais qui gardent cependant chacune une identité distincte, signifie peut-être que la famille nucléaire commence à acquérir quelque autonomie (Flannery 1972). L'ensemble correspond, en gros, au p.p.n.b. de Palestine.

Cependant, on peut distinguer quelques nuances. L'Anatolie forme une région à part, avec un centre à Çatal Hüyük, dont la céramique intermittente marque l'avance technique. La typologie des pointes de flèches, l'obsidienne striée, les faucilles à tête élargie (peut-être en relation avec l'utilisation de l'obsidienne, car on n'en connaît pas qui soient fabriquées en silex) marquent une parenté entre les sites de la bordure méridionale du Taurus: grottes de Sakce Gözü, Cafer Harabesi, Çayönü, jusqu'à Magzaliya et le Zagros vers l'est. Un type spécial de débitage du silex, avec les nucleus naviformes, commence à dessiner une province levantine, dont la frontière septentrionale, à partir de Ras Shamra, remonte dans le fossé Amuq-Marash, rejoint l'Euphrate à Hayaz et le descend jusqu'à Bouqras, intégré de ce point de vue au Levant. En revanche, sur le plan de l'architecture, avec les grandes maisons complexes à murs rectilignes, les enduits décorés et les portes en chatières (*port holes*), de Abu Hureyra à Bouqras les parentés semblent aller vers l'est, pour rejoindre plus tard la vallée du Tharthar. La vallée moyenne de l'Euphrate forme donc un sous-ensemble très vivant. Outre le lieu de rencontre entre l'ouest (nucleus naviformes) et

---

6. Prospection non publiée de Moore, cf van Loon 1967.
7. Signalé par Buccellati G. et M. 1967, sondé par Dornemann (1969), fouillé aujourd'hui par J. Cauvin.

l'est (architecture), elle est le théâtre de l'éclosion d'une céramique intermittente (Mureybet, Assouad/Aswad, Bouqras) et de l'utilisation de la vaisselle blanche en plâtre et/ou en chaux (Abu Hureyra, El Kowm, Bouqras).

Sans vouloir trop insister sur le rôle de l'environnement, et avec toute la prudence qu'impose la rareté des documents, on peut toutefois faire remarquer que le plateau anatolien, l'arc sud du Taurus, la steppe syrienne et la vallée de l'Euphrate, toutes régions diverses du point de vue de l'écologie, sont chacune le siège de sous-ensembles archéologiques différents. L'interaction de ces sous-ensembles ne donne pourtant pas l'impression d'un espace vraiment structuré, où l'on pourrait discerner des provinces culturelles bien définies.[8] Il faut cependant retenir le rôle que joue l'Euphrate, à la fois comme frontière, comme point de rencontre d'influences diverses, et comme centre d'inventions.

Premières entités culturelles (6000—5500 b.c.)

A partir de 6000 b.c., voir carte 2,[9] la céramique est partout présente sur les confins syro-anatoliens, ce qui donne des possibilités de critères précis, mais d'un autre côté, par voie de facilité, a conduit bien des auteurs à ne pas mentionner autre chose que des tessons dans les notes brèves qui ont été publiées.

En prenant comme point de repère Çatal Hüyük, niveaux VIII à II (5900—5700 b.c.), on peut définir un sous-ensemble appelé par J. Mellaart: *Early Pottery Neolithic of the Konya Plain*, qui occupe le plateau anatolien depuis le Tuz Gölü (Değirminözü-6) jusqu'à Can Hasan-3 (Can Hasan III, sommet: 5800. Ergin 1975), et de Çatal Hüyük-4 à Kumluk-16. Cette civilisation utilise une céramique non décorée mais lustrée, dont la pâte est plutôt claire, à dégraissant minéral, avec des formes globulaires. Les pointes de flèches sont toujours pédonculées, mais plates et trian-

---

8. Ce n'est pas le cas plus au sud: Syrie centrale et méridionale, Liban, Palestine, où les choses sont plus précises.

9. Les sites sont désormais trop nombreux et trop près les uns des autres pour qu'on puisse inscrire tous leurs noms sur une carte. Nous les avons donc numérotés, en les regroupant par régions. Ce sont ces numéros qui figurent sur les cartes. La liste suivante donne la correspondance entre les noms et les numéros.

Plateau anatolien: 1 Avla Dağ, 2 Can Hasan I, 3 Can Hasan III (niveau I), 4 Çatal Hüyük est, 5 Çatal Hüyük, 6 Değirminözü, 7 Igdeli Çeşme, 8 Ilıcapınar, 9 Kara Hüyük Yarma, 10 Kayardı tepe, 11 Kerhane, 12 Keyren, 13 Koca Hüyük, 14 Köşk Pınar Bor, 15 Küçük Köy, 16 Kumlak, 17 Pınarbaşı, 18 Sapmaz Köy, 19 Tepecik Çiftlik.

Cilicie: 20 Ada tepe II, 21 Boz tepe, 22 Çavuşlu, 23 Çükür Köprü, 24 Domuz, 25 Hacı Bozan, 26 Hacılar (Cilicie), 27 Incirlik, 28 Kabarsa, 29 Mersin, 30 Misis, 31 Pascu, 32 Şamşin, 33 Sultan tepe, 34 Tarmıl, 35 Tarse, 36 Tatarlı, 37 Tılan Hüyük, 38 Tirmil, 39 Velican.

Côte méditerranéenne, Amuq, Rift: 40 Bırtlan, 41 Boz Islahiye, 42 Davut Pasha, 43 Dhahab, 44 Faruq, 45 Gültepe, 46 Hama, 47 Hammam (cave), 48 (wadi) Hammam, 49 Hasanuşaği Üçtepe, 50 Hasanuşaği Yerküyü, 51 Jedaideh, 52 Kanisah, 53 Karataş, 54 Mahmutliye, 55 Qaddahiyat Ali Bey, 56 Qalaat Mudiq (Apamée, niveau V), 57 Qinanah, 58 Ras Shamra, 59 Sakce Gözü, 60 tell Sukas, 61 Tabbat el Hammam, 62 Turundah.

Qoueiq, Jabbul, Euphrate: 63 Abu Hureyra, 64 Abu Zanne, 65 Aïn et Tell, 66 Akhterine, 67 Archaq, 68 Bahouerte, 69 Battal, 70 Bouheira, 71 Carchemish, 72 Chair, 73 Deir Hafir, 74 Fafine, 75 Hmaine, 76 Jededieh Jabbul, 77 Kadrich, 78 Maled, 79 Shaikh Ahmad, 80 Soussiane, 81 Suran, 82 Turlu.

Balikh, Khabour: 83 Agab (Aqab), 84 Ambara, 85 Assouad/Aswad, 86 Chagar Bazar, 87 Chatal Hüyük (wadi Dara), 88 tell Habesh, 89 Hajji Nasser, 90 tell Halaf, 91 Hammam (Balikh), 92 Hasan Rumi, 93 Mounbateh.

Steppe, Tharthar: 94 Bouqras, 95 Ghazala, 96 El Kowm, 97 Kül tepe (Sinjar), 98 Rafia al Janubi, 99 tell Sotto, 100 Thalathat II, 101 Umm Dabaghiya, 102 Yarim tepe I et II, 103 Hawa, 104 Ki Juyuk Kebir, 105 Khunaifes, 106 Umm Dhiyaba.

gulaires, et amincies sur les deux faces par des retouches obtenues par pression. On connaît 13 sites se rattachant à la même civilisation, qui pour Çatal Hüyük est l'époque de la "supernova" (Mellaart 1967).[10] Mais, en dépit d'efforts récents (Bartel 1972), il est très difficile d'apprécier le rôle exact joué par Çatal Hüyük sur le plateau anatolien durant cette première moitié du VIe millénaire, et de caractériser le genre de lien, en dehors des similitudes de la céramique, qui relie entre eux les 13 sites en question.

Plus au sud, en Cilicie, le long des côtes de la Méditerranée, dans le bassin de l'Amuq et la vallée du Qoueiq, un autre ensemble est formé par les sites où l'on a trouvé de la céramique lustrée à pâte sombre, la DFBW décrite par R. Braidwood, une des caractéristiques qui ont permis à ce dernier de définir sa civilisation syro-cilicienne. En l'absence d'indications un peu détaillées, il est aventureux de placer tel ou tel site dans la première phase de cette civilisation: Amuq A, ou la seconde: Amuq B. Néanmoins, à travers les publications concernant l'Amuq, la Cilicie et le Qoueiq, on peut estimer à une vingtaine le nombre des villages relevant de cette civilisation à l'époque de l'Amuq A.[11] Leur distribution, très concentrée dans les fonds alluviaux, indique pour la première fois la recherche systématique de sols aptes à l'agriculture. Tous ces villages sont situés d'autre part à l'intérieur de l'isohyète actuel de 200 mm, qui marque aujourd'hui la limite théorique des possibilités de l'agriculture non irriguée. Il est évident que ce vaste ensemble, qui se prolonge au sud jusqu'à la latitude de Byblos, comprend, en ce qui nous occupe, plusieurs sous-ensembles facilement isolables, dont l'unité interne et les rapports mutuels restent à préciser.

Des points communs existent entre l'Anatolie et la Syro-Cilicie: usage d'une céramique lustrée non peinte, similitude de l'outillage lithique, mais ce sont pourtant des ensembles distincts, car l'architecture et l'utilisation de l'obsidienne diffèrent. De plus, entre le plateau d'Anatolie et le domaine méditerranéen de la Syro-Cilicie, le contraste dans l'environnement est tel que l'adaptation aux conditions naturelles a certainement influé sur le comportement. La partie fouillée de Çatal Hüyük donne en effet l'image d'une agglomération compacte, dont les maisons serrées les unes contre les autres avec un minimum d'ouvertures sur l'extérieur semblent particulièrement adaptées à la rigueur hivernale du plateau anatolien. Ce que l'on connaît de la Cilicie, de l'Amuq, et du Qoueiq (nous ne possédons pas le plan entier d'une seule maison) indique une occupation de l'espace plus lâche, ce qui est assez naturel dans une région où les hivers, pluvieux mais doux, n'exigent pas qu'on s'agglutine pour lutter contre le froid et la neige. Il est de plus à noter que l'arc montagneux du Taurus proprement dit est, autant que nous le sachions, déserté à cette époque. Contrairement à ce qu'on a dit (Mellaart 1975, pp. 124—25), il n'y a donc pas eu beaucoup de relations entre l'Anatolie et la Syro-Cilicie durant la période de l'Amuq A.

Au même moment, dans les hautes vallées du Khabour et de ses affluents, un autre ensemble se dessine, dont la caractéristique est l'emploi d'une céramique à pâte sombre, lustrée, non décorée, qui se distingue de celle de l'Amuq en ce qu'elle est épaisse, plus grossière, et à dégraissant végétal.[12] Notée pour la première fois à tell Halaf et datée de 5600, elle a été retrouvée, précédant la civilisation halafienne, par Mallowan à Chagar Bazar-86 et par Davidson à Habesh-88. Nous sommes, là encore, à l'intérieur de la limite actuelle des cultures sèches.

Ces trois ensembles concernent directement les rapports entre l'Anatolie et la Syrie, mais il faut aussi tenir compte d'un quatrième, situé entre le Tigre et l'Euphrate, le long de la vallée du

10. Il faut noter que les niveaux plus anciens, XIII ou XII à IX, n'ont été atteints que par des sondages très restreints.

11. Deux dates: Ras Shamra V B, 5736; et Mersin 33—28, 6000.

12. Distinction non comprise la plupart du temps. La "Altmonochrom" de von Oppenheim (Oppenheim et Schmidt 1943) n'est pas la même chose que la DFBW de Braidwood.

Tharthar, bien qu'il soit différent, car il appartient plus au Moyen-Orient qu'au Levant. Il s'agit de la civilisation découverte récemment à Sotto-99, Umm Dabaghiya-101 et dans cinq autres villages, avec une date pour Thalathat II-100, niveau 15, de 5570. Ici, la céramique est peinte, l'architecture aligne en longues rangées des enfilades de pièces rectangulaires. Ces traits existaient déjà dans la période précédente à Bouqras, dont le niveau le plus récent est daté de 5900, et ne sont pas sans ressemblance avec ce qu'on trouve à El Kowm.

Pour conclure, entre 6000 et 5500, les confins syro-anatoliens offrent une image extraordinairement différente de celle qu'on pouvait constater auparavant (comparer les cartes 1 et 2). Au nord d'une ligne marquée par le Sinjar, la jabal Abd el Aziz et le Bichri, des populations qui n'ont pas besoin de pratiquer une agriculture irriguée utilisent une céramique lustrée, non peinte. Elles forment trois groupes séparés, non seulement à cause des caractéristiques de la céramique, mais aussi parce qu'elles sont isolées géographiquement dans des domaines bioclimatiques dissemblables. Le "Néolithique céramique ancien de la plaine de Konya", sur les plateaux d'Anatolie, ne franchit pas au sud la chaîne du Taurus. La civilisation syro-cilicienne de l'Amuq A reste cantonnée dans le domaine méditerranéen, et ne dépasse pas à l'est la vallée du Qoueiq. Dans le bassin du haut Khabour, la "Altmonochrom" reste isolée. Au sud de l'alignement des montagnes de la zone steppique, un quatrième groupe d'affinités plus orientales rassemble les villages de la civilisation Sotto-Umm Dabaghiya, dont la céramique est peinte, et qui se trouvent le long de la vallée du Tharthar dans un contexte écologique beaucoup plus aride: il est difficile d'imaginer qu'on puisse subsister là sans quelque pratique d'irrigation.

Bref, le phénomène le plus frappant est le changement dans l'organisation de l'espace qui se produit entre 7000–6000 et 6000–5500 B.C. Au lieu d'une dispersion quasi aléatoire et peu structurée de sites plutôt individualisés comme à la période précédente, nous avons, après 6000, des entités qui groupent plusieurs villages proches les uns des autres, partageant la même civilisation. Autant qu'on puisse le savoir aujourd'hui, les contacts entre ces ensembles culturels sont négligeables. De plus, la vallée moyenne de l'Euphrate semble avoir perdu le rôle civilisateur que nous avons souligné pour la période précédente, et le fleuve apparaît maintenant comme une barrière. Cette organisation de l'espace en entités distinctes soulève un certain nombre de questions, non résolues.[13]

Et d'abord celle de leur apparition. Si le groupe anatolien paraît assez naturellement se développer à partir de ce qui existe lors de la période précédente à Can Hasan et à Çatal Hüyük, où la céramique n'est pas une nouveauté absolue, en revanche, partout ailleurs, l'introduction des récipients en argile cuite et la diversité de leurs types s'expliquent mal. On pourrait penser que le centre d'inventions que constitue l'Euphrate entre 7000 et 6000, avec la céramique monochrome intermittente de Mureybet et la céramique peinte de Bouqras, aurait pu servir de point de départ aux développements de la Syro-Cilicie et du Tharthar. Mais il faudrait alors rendre compte de la désertion de la vallée moyenne de l'Euphrate après 6000 B.C.

De plus, il est assez vraisemblable que la nouvelle organisation de l'espace correspond à une transformation de la structure sociale des populations, tant à l'échelle du village qu'à celle de la région. Il n'est malheureusement guère possible de donner un contenu un peu précis à cet énoncé. En effet, à l'échelle du village, une structure sociale hiérarchisée devrait se traduire par l'existence de bâtiments un peu exceptionnels, témoignant de fonctions particulières, ou du rang supérieur de leur propriétaire. Mais aucun des villages qui ont été fouillés dans cette région ne l'a été dans son intégralité, et nous ne connaissons pas, par conséquent, leur organisation interne.

---

13. Les tentatives d' "explication" proposées ici, et plus loin dans la troisième partie, ont été rajoutées à la demande des organisateurs de ces mélanges.

Au niveau de la région, la plupart des sites ont été signalés par des prospections sommaires, qui ne permettent pas d'apprécier l'importance relative des uns ou des autres, ni même le plus souvent de préciser s'il y avait des rapports effectifs entre les divers points qu'on peut placer sur la carte. Pour résoudre ces problèmes, nous avons besoin d'un certain nombre de renseignements précis, qui ne peuvent être fournis que par des fouilles, et non par des théories, qu'il s'agit précisément de tester.

Premiers contacts entre civilisations (5500—5000 b.c.)

A partir de 5500, l'occupation de l'espace, au contact de la steppe syrienne et du domaine anatolien, donne les premières indications de ce qui sera la règle à partir du Ve millénaire: l'unification culturelle, sinon politique, de la région (carte 3).

En Anatolie, le bassin du Tuz Gölü paraît abandonné. Celui de Konya est d'abord occupé par quelques villages, dont la céramique est qualifiée de *Late Pottery Neolithic of the Konya Plain*: niveaux supérieurs de Çatal Hüyük est-4, Küçük Köy-15, Keyren-12, Koca Hüyük-13 et Can Hasan I, niveaux 7—4. La céramique semble en continuité avec ce qui existait à la période précédente: non peinte, avec des poignées verticales et un dégraissant à base de coquilles, ce qui permet des comparaisons avec l'ouest. Mais plus tard, juste avant 5000, apparaît une nouvelle céramique: peinte, rouge sur fond clair, à Çatal Hüyük ouest-5, Kara Hüyük Yarma-9, et Can Hasan I-2 (niveau 3, b—c. Le niveau 3 a, postérieur, est daté de 4800). Sans qu'on sache bien pourquoi, la nouvelle civilisation est appelée "chalcolithique ancien". Quoi qu'il en soit, l'apparition dans cette région de la céramique peinte, assimilée pour la circonstance à l'usage du cuivre forgé, est une nouveauté.

En Syro-Cilicie, les développements du décor de la céramique de l'Amuq A en Amuq B s'accompagnent d'une occupation de l'espace plus dense, surtout dans le bassin de l'Amuq, la vallée du Qoueiq, le bassin de Jabbul, la vallée de l'Oronte et la côte. On peut dénombrer une quarantaine de villages, dont la date est indiquée par Ras Shamra Va: 5234. C'est durant cette période qu'apparaît en Cilicie une céramique peinte à décor caractéristique: des zig-zags verticaux rouges sur fond blanc (Yıldırım, en turc: éclair), dont on retrouve des traces à Can Hasan en Anatolie. On peut voir l'influence de cette céramique dans certains décors de l'Amuq B: Sakce Gözü-59, ainsi que dans la vallée du Qoueiq et le bassin de Jabbul: tell Maled-78, Ain et Tell-65, Jededieh-76, et Shaikh Ahmed-79. Il semble que les décors de l'Amuq B atteignent la région de l'Euphrate à Carchemish-71 et Turlu-82. Par ailleurs, comme nous l'avons signalé plus haut, des tells en nombre non négligeable (une quinzaine) ont été identifiés dans cette partie du Levant comme relevant de la civilisation de l'Amuq, mais avec trop d'imprécision pour qu'on puisse les placer avant ou après 5500, bien qu'ils aient sûrement été occupés entre 6000 et 5000: ils ne sont marqués sur aucune carte, pour ce présent article.

A la même époque, dans le haut Khabour et le ouadi Dara, apparaît une nouvelle civilisation, avec une céramique aux décors caractéristiques (rosettes, bucranes, etc.) rouges et noirs sur fond clair, comprenant des formes carénées, et avec des bâtiments dont certains sont à plan circulaire. Elle a été identifiée pour la première fois à tell Halaf, sur le Khabour, et datée sur ce site de 5600. T. Davidson (Davidson 1977) a tenté de préciser l'évolution du Halaf, et pense que ses manifestations les plus anciennes, antérieures à 5000, se retrouvent à tell Aqab-83 (Davidson et Watkins 1981), Ambara-84, Chagar Bazar-86, Çatal Hüyük-87, tell Habesh-88, tell Hajji Nasser-89, Hasan Rumi-92, et que Halaf-90 et Mounbateh-93 marquent l'extension vers l'ouest de cette civilisation, dans une première étape, antérieure au début de Arpachiyah, selon ce que l'on connaît pour le moment.

Enfin, sur le territoire occupé auparavant par la civilisation de tell Sotto-Umm Dabaghiya, fleurit le complexe Hassouna-Samarra, sans liens avec l'ouest, sauf des traces fugitives à Chagar

Bazar-86 et Mounbateh-93. Nous indiquons la position de quelques-uns des villages les plus occidentaux de ces civilisations, sans vouloir prendre parti sur les rapports entre Umm Dabaghiya et Hassouna I A, ni entre les civilisations de Hassouna et Samarra: ces problèmes en effet concernent des régions qui se situent en dehors des limites géographiques de cet article. La dizaine de sites (97 à 106) marqués sur la carte 3 ne fait que suggérer ce qui existe plus à l'est.

Entre 5500 et 5000, l'organisation de l'espace, telle qu'on peut la percevoir pour le moment, montre donc des différences assez nettes avec ce qu'on a pu noter auparavant. L'abandon des montagnes se poursuit avec la désertion du Tuz Gölü en Anatolie centrale. L'occupation des terres arables à l'intérieur des limites du territoire propice à l'agriculture non irriguée s'intensifie en Cilicie, dans l'Amuq, le Qoueiq, Jabbul, et le Khabour, et témoigne de la recherche systématique des sols fertiles. A l'est du Sinjar et de l'Euphrate, le Moyen-Orient amorce un nouveau développement (Hassouna-Samarra), qui ne s'étendra pas à l'ouest. L'Euphrate moyen, complètement abandonné, et les montagnes de la zone steppique jouent plus que jamais un rôle de frontière. Mais l'élément nouveau est que, entre l'Anatolie et la Cilicie, l'Amuq et le Qoueiq, le Khabour et le Balikh, on perçoit des contacts. Les entités culturelles entrent en communication les unes avec les autres.

Pour la période qui nous occupe, ces contacts ne sont perceptibles que grâce à quelques tessons de poterie. La céramique peinte passe de l'Anatolie en Cilicie, et le décor dit Yıldırım se retrouve de Can Hasan jusque dans l'Amuq. De même, dans le bassin de Jabbul, à Jededieh et Shaikh Ahmad, on trouve des tessons peints qui rappellent ceux de Cilicie. Tell Mounbateh, sur le Balikh, a livré quelques fragments, décorés de "*dancing ladies*" et de rosettes (Copeland 1979), qui témoignent de rapports avec le Halaf et Samarra.

Que signifient, du point de vue de la civilisation, ces contacts au niveau de la céramique? Il est, là encore, extrêmement difficile de le préciser. S'agit-il de la simple circulation de marchandises utilitaires, et sous quelle forme? S'agit-il de la diffusion d'objets considérés comme véhiculant une valeur de prestige? On concevrait assez bien que la céramique halafienne paraisse d'une qualité telle que la possession d'un vase décoré de bucranes puisse susciter l'envie, et qu'un villageois du bassin de Jabbul désire l'acquérir, sans que cela signifie nécessairement que son village soit passé sous l'influence des territoires où la céramique halafienne est abondante, et sans doute autochtone.

D'autre part, il se pourrait que nous soyons en présence d'une situation analogue à celle invoquée pour expliquer, dans d'autres circonstances, le passage à l'économie de production (L. Binford 1968). Le petit noyau halafien fait figure de centre en expansion, tandis que la région syro-cilicienne, qui paraît avoir épuisé son capital d'inventions, représente une aire réceptrice, accueillant les nouveautés de l'est et de l'ouest. A moins que la présence conjuguée de précipitations relativement abondantes et de sols fertiles n'ait rendu l'ensemble Cilicie-Amuq-Qoueiq attractif au point d'attirer les occupants de provinces voisines moins favorisées, qui seraient arrivés en apportant leurs pots avec eux. On peut encore imaginer que la densité de l'occupation en Syro-Cilicie ait eu pour conséquence une exploitation des ressources produisant des surplus, dont l'exportation vers l'Anatolie ou le Khabour aurait eu pour contrepartie l'importation de quelques vases. Tout cela est, bien entendu, invérifiable.

Les contacts entre entités culturelles, quelle qu'en soit la cause, impliquent-ils au sein de ces dernières une transformation de la structure sociale? A ce genre de question, que certains se posent, les réponses sont nombreuses, et dépendent des options préalables de chacun en matière de sociologie.[14]

---

14. Quel que soit leur contenu, ces réponses ne sont ni vérifiables, ni réfutables. C'est-à-dire (Popper 1978) que, ne pouvant être soumises au critère de la "falsifiabilité" — néologisme dû à Popper — elles ne

Dans des perspectives marxistes, le Levant septentrional, à l'époque qui nous occupe, en est à la phase de "Barbarie", qui succède à la "Sauvagerie", et dans laquelle l'homme a acquis le contrôle de la reproduction du bétail, les techniques d'agriculture, et a appris à accroître par son travail la productivité naturelle (Engels 1884). La sédentarisation, qui est le corollaire de ces activités de production, a pour effet de valoriser le rôle des femmes et, à l'agriculture comme mode de production, correspond le matriarcat comme structure de la société dans les communautés villageoises. Mais il arrive un moment où la concentration des villages suscite une concentration des moyens de production, et une sorte d'unification de la région sous un pouvoir plus ou moins central, afin de résoudre les contradictions qui surgissent au sein de ces sociétés. De là la formation d'entités plus larges, dont on peut percevoir l'extension géographique, et les contacts avec d'autres entités du même genre. Cela correspond à une reprise de l'influence masculine qui amène la fin du matriarcat, et à une structure politico-économico-sociale nouvelle, dont un modèle a été décrit par Marx à partir de l'Inde du XIXe siècle et appelé "mode de production asiatique". Ce dernier mode de production devrait précéder un système de plus grande centralisation: l' "Esclavagisme". Selon ce schéma, très simplifié, les confins syro-anatoliens, entre 5500 et 5000, se trouvent au point de passage entre le système des communautés villageoises autonomes (barbarie) et un début de centralisation (mode de production asiatique), qui prépare l'esclavagisme de Sumer et d'Akkad.

Dans les perspectives anglo-saxonnes de l'empirisme néo-évolutionniste (Sahlins 1968; Service 1962), le schéma est moins théorique, et se veut plus descriptif. La structuration de la société s'opère aussi suivant une concentration progressive, mais commence par de petits groupes: les "bandes." Celles-ci s'organisent ensuit en "tribus." Ces deux formes de société sont égalitaristes et non hiérarchisées, ce qui veut dire que les fonctions sociales ne sont pas héréditaires. Lorsque la succession héréditaire apparaît avec un début de centralisation, on a alors des "chefferies", qui préludent aux "états". On peut interpréter notre carte 3 en pensant que la densité des sites en Syro-Cilicie, la naissance du noyau halafien dans le haut Khabour et ses affluents, ainsi que les timides contacts entre ces entités culturelles amorce la phase des chefferies, dont la complète réalisation serait l'expansion halafienne à l'époque suivante, 5000−4500 B.C. (P.J. Watson, ce volume). Il ne s'agit là pourtant que d'une vision sommaire des choses, car pour Service et Sahlins la phase des chefferies implique des liens entre les systèmes de parenté, la répartition des terres et l'organisation politique, toutes données dont nous ne connaissons absolument rien pour les civilisations qui nous occupent.

Prises à un certain niveau de généralité, les deux théories énoncées ci-dessus ne sont pas sans points communs. Elles aident à mieux voir que, dans le période entre 5500 et 5000, sur les confins entre l'Anatolie, le Levant méditerranéen et la steppe syrienne, se développe une situation dans laquelle les villages autonomes paraissent être intégrés dans des unités plus vastes. Dépouillés de leur appareil théorique, Marxisme ou empirisme néo-évolutionniste ne disent au fond rien de plus. Quant à savoir si cela s'accompagne de la disparition du matriarcat ou de l'avènement des chefferies . . .

Quoi qu'il en soit, ces premiers contacts préparent l'expansion de l'influence halafienne qui, entre 5000 et 4500, atteindra la Méditeranée à l'ouest et l'Iran à l'est.

---

peuvent être considérées comme scientifiques. Le critère de la falsifiabilité s'énonce comme suit: "Les énoncés ou systèmes d'énoncés communiquent une information relative au monde empirique dans la seule mesure où ils sont capables d'entrer en conflit avec l'expérience ou, plus précisément, dans la seule mesure où ils peuvent être *soumis à des tests* systématiques, c'est-à-dire où ils peuvent être soumis (conformément à une "décision méthodologique") à des tests qui pourraient avoir pour résultat leur réfutation" (Popper 1978, 319).

Conclusion

Cette brève revue du Levant septentrional entre 7600 et 5000 b.c. permet donc de distinguer des étapes dans l'organisation de l'espace. Après 1.500 ans d'une occupation aléatoire, individualiste et peu différenciée, durant laquelle, malgré le jeu de certaines influences, il est pour le moment difficile de reconnaître des civilisations différentes (carte 1), des ensembles s'organisent en Anatolie, Syro-Cilicie, sur le haut Khabour et le Tharthar (carte 2). On peut éventuellement regrouper les trois premiers en un super-ensemble, celui des céramiques non peintes lustrées. Puis, tandis que le plateau anatolien se vide à partir de 5500, les fonds de vallées et les bassins de piedmont du Taurus sont occupés de façon dense, et des contacts s'établissent entre les principales régions, contacts repérables surtout dans le transport de quelques types de céramique (carte 3). Dans cette optique, les influences orientales ne paraissent pas dépasser le Sinjar et la dépression du Tharthar.

La localisation des centres levantins de civilisation à l'intérieur de l'isohyète de 200 mm et dans les fonds de bassin montre que l'environnement a certainement joué un rôle dans le peuplement, mais non pas uniquement le climat. Les paysans d'alors ont été attentifs aux précipitations, et aussi à la qualité des sols. Mais cela n'explique pas tout, et les motifs et la signification de certains faits signalés plus haut nous échappent: abandon des montagnes et du plateau anatolien, par exemple, expansion de la civilisation syro-cilicienne, origine du Halaf, limite occidentale de la céramique peinte de Mésopotamie. Nous n'avons même pas idée de ce que signifient, sur le plan de l'organisation sociale et politique des groupes humains, les différences constatées dans la répartition de la céramique ou les formes d'architecture.

En attendant, à défaut d'explications, il est tout de même utile de mieux connaître les modalités de l'occupation de l'espace dans une partie de cette bordure de collines du croissant fertile, *the hilly flanks of the fertile crescent*, où est née notre civilisation.

Bibliographie

Akkermans, P.; Loon, M.N. van; Roodenberg, J.J.; et Waterbolk, H.T.
    sous   The 1976–1977 excavations at Tell Bouqras. *Annales Archéologiques Arabes Syriennes.*
    presse

Archi, A.; Pecorella, P.; et Salvini, M.
    1971   Gaziantepe la sua régione. *Incunabula Graeca.* t. 48. Rome: Edizioni Dell'Atheneo.

Bader, N.O.
    1979   *Tell Magzaliya: an early Neolithic site in the northern Iraq. Sovietskaya Arkheologica* 1979 no. 2:117–33.

Bartel, B.
    1972   The characteristics of the Çatal Hüyük supracommunity. *American Journal of Archaeology* 76:204–5.

Besançon, J.; de Contenson, H.; Copeland, L.; Hours, F.; Muhesen, S.; et Sanlaville, P.
    1980   *Etude géographique et prospection archéologique des plateaux de la région de Menbij (Syrie du nord): rapport préliminaire.* Travaux de la recherche coopérative sur programme 438. Lyon: Maison de l'Orient Méditerranéen.

Bialor, P.
    1962   The chipped stone industry of Çatal Hüyük. *Anatolian Studies* 12:67–110.

Binford, L.
  1968   Post-Pleistocene adaptations. In *New perspectives in archaeology,* ed. S. Binford et L. Binford, pp. 313–41. Chicago: Aldine-Atherton.

Bostancı, E.
  1971   A research on the Solutrean and Adıyaman cultures surrounding Adıyaman. *Antropoloji* 5:45–49.
  1973   A new research on the palaeoanthropological, prehistoric and Quaternary problems of the Adıyaman province in the south east of Anatolia. *Antropoloji* 6:89–114.

Braidwood, R.
  1937   *Mounds on the plain of Antioch: an archeological survey.* Oriental Institute Publications, vol. 48. Chicago: University of Chicago Press.

Braidwood, R., et Braidwood, L.
  1960   *Excavations in the plain of Antioch*, vol. 1: *the earlier assemblages: phases A–J.* Oriental Institute Publications, vol. 61. Chicago: University of Chicago Press.

Braidwood, R.; Çambel, H.; Redman, H.; et Watson, P.J.
  1971   Beginnings of village farming communities in southeastern Turkey. *Proceedings of the National Academy of Sciences* 68(6):1236–40.

Buccellati, G., et Buccellati, M.
  1967   Archaeological survey in the Palmyrene and Jebel Bishri. *Archaeology* 20:305–6.

Çambel, H., et Braidwood, R.J.
  1980   *The joint Istanbul and Chicago Universities prehistoric research project in southeastern Anatolia: I.* Faculty of Letters, University of Istanbul.

Cauvin, J.
  1970   Mission 1969 en Djezireh (Syrie). *Bulletin de la Société Préhistorique Française (Comptes Rendus Séances Mensuelles)* 67:286–89.
  1972   Sondage à Tell Assouad. *Annales Archéologiques Arabes Syriennes* 22:85–96.
  1978   *Les premiers villages de Syrie-Palestine du IXème au VIIème millénaire avant J.C.* Collection de la Maison de l'Orient Méditerranéen Ancien 4. Série Archéologique, 3. Lyon: Maison de l'Orient.

Cauvin, M.C.
  1974   Flèches à encoches de Syrie: essai de classification et d'interprétation culturelle. *Paléorient* 2:311–22.

Contenson, H. de
  1969   Contribution à l'étude du Néolithique de Syrie: description de diverses trouvailles de surface. *Mélanges de l'Université Saint Joseph* 45:61–84.

Copeland, L.
  1979   Observations on the prehistory of the Balikh valley, Syria, during the 7th–4th millennia B.C. *Paléorient* 5:251–275.

Davidson, T.
  1977   Regional variation within the Halaf ceramic tradition. Ph.D. diss., Edinburgh University.

Davidson, T., et McKerrell, H.
  1976   Pottery analysis and Halaf period trade in the Khabur headwaters region. *Iraq* 38:45–46.

Davidson, T., et Watkins, T.
  1981   Two seasons of excavation at Tell Aqab in the Jezirah, N.E. Syria. *Iraq* 43:1–18.

Dornemann, R.H.
  1969   An early village. *Archaeology* 22:65–68.

Engels, F.
  1884   *L'origine de la famille, de la propriété privée et de l'état.* Paris.

Ergin, M.
1975   Türk Kronologisinin tesinde C-14 yöntemyle yapilan çalişmalar. *Türk Belleten Tarih wa Archeologii Kurumu* V (Bilim Kongresi): 143–57.

Flannery, K.V.
1972   The origins of the village as a settlement type in Mesoamerica and the Near East: a comparative study. In *Man, settlement and urbanism*, ed. P.J. Ucko, R. Tringham, and G.W. Dimbleby, pp. 22–53. London: Duckworth.

French, D.
1964   Recent archaeological research in Turkey. *Anatolian Studies* 14:35–36.
1965a   Surface finds from various sites. *Anatolian Studies* 15:38–39.
1965b   Prehistoric sites in the Göksu valley. *Anatolian Studies* 14:177–201.
1970   Notes on site distribution in the Cumra area. *Anatolian Studies* 20:139–48.
1972   Settlement patterns on the Konya plain, south central Turkey. In *Man, settlement and urbanism*, ed. P.J. Ucko, R. Tringham, and G.W. Dimbleby, pp. 231–38. London: Duckworth.

Frierman, J.D.
1971   Lime burning as the precursor of fired ceramics. *Israel Exploration Journal* 21:212–16.

Henry, D., et Servello, F.
1974   Compendium of 14-C determinations from Near Eastern prehistoric sites. *Paléorient* 2:19–44.

Hours, F.
1980   Archéologie théorique et nouvelle archéologie: à propos du livre de J.C. Gardin. *Etudes* 355:215–33.

Kirkbride, D.
1972   Umm Dabaghiya 1971: a first preliminary report. *Iraq* 34:3–15.

Lloyd, S.
1938   Some ancient sites in the Sinjar district. *Iraq* 5:123–42.

Loon, M. van
1967   *The Tabqa reservoir survey, 1964*. Damascus: Direction Générale des Antiquités et des Musées.

McEwan, C.; Braidwood, L.S.; Frankfort, H.; Güterbock, H.G.; Haines, R.C.; Kantor, H.J.; and Kraeling, C.H.
1958   *Soundings at Tell Fakhariyah*. Oriental Institute Publications, vol. 79. Chicago: University of Chicago Press.

Mallowan, M.
1937   The excavations at Tell Chagar Bazar and an archaeological survey of the Habur region: second campaign, 1936. *Iraq* 4:91–177.
1946   Excavations in the Balikh valley (1938). *Iraq* 8:111–39.

Matthers, J.; Kenrick, Philip M.; and Bernus-Taylor, Marthe
1978   Tell Rifa'at 1977: preliminary report of an archaeological survey. *Iraq* 40:119–62.

Matthers, J.
1981   *The Nahr Qoueiq, Northern Syria, and its catchment*. British Archaeological Reports.

Maxwell-Hyslop, R.; Taylor, Du Plat; Seton-Williams, V.; et Waechter, J.
1942   An archaeological survey of the plain of Jabbul, 1939. *Palestine Exploration Quarterly* 74:8–20.

Mellaart, J.
1954   Preliminary survey of pre-classical remains in southern Turkey. *Anatolian Studies* 4:175–89.

1961   Early cultures of the south Anatolian plateau. I: Neolithic cultures of the south Anatolian
            plateau. II: the early chalcolithic of the Konya plain. *Anatolian Studies* 11:159−84.
1967   *Çatal Hüyük: a Neolithic town in Anatolia.* London: Thames and Hudson.
1975   *The Neolithic of the Near East.* London: Thames and Hudson.

Oppenheim, M. von, et Schmidt, H.
1943   *Tell Halaf,* vol. 1: *die prähistorische Funde.* Berlin: Walter de Gruyter.

Özdoğan, M.
1977   *Lower Euphrates basin 1977 survey.* Middle East Technical University Lower Euphrates
            Project Publications, series 1, no. 2. Istanbul: Middle East Technical University Keban
            and Lower Euphrates Projects.

Popper, K.R.
1978   *La logique de la découverte scientifique.* Paris: Payot.

Sahlins, M.D.
1968   *Tribesmen.* Englewood Cliffs, N.J.: Prentice-Hall.

Service, E.R.
1962   *Primitive social organization.* New York: Random House.

Seton-Williams, V.
1954   Cilician survey, 1951. *Anatolian Studies* 4:121−74.

Todd, I.
1965   Surface finds from various sites. *Anatolian Studies* 15:34−36.
1966a   Aşıklı Hüyük: a Protoneolithic site in central Anatolia. *Anatolian Studies* 16:139−63.
1966b   Surface finds from various sites: central Anatolia. *Anatolian Studies* 16:43−48.
1968   The dating of Aşıklı Hüyük in central Anatolia. *American Journal of Archaeology*
            72:157−58.

Voigt, M.
1976   *Hajji Firuz Tepe: an economic reconstruction of a sixth millennium community in western
            Iran,* 2 vols. Ann Arbor, Mich.: University Microfilms International.

Waechter, J.; Göğös, S.; et Seton-Williams, V.
1951   The Sakce Gözü cave site, 1949. *Belleten* 15: 193−201.

Watson, P.J.; LeBlanc, S.A.; et Redman, C.L.
1971   *Explanation in archeology: an explicitly scientific approach.* New York: Columbia Uni-
            versity Press.

Woolley, L.
1934   The prehistoric pottery of Carchemish. *Iraq* 1:146−54.
1952   *Carchemish: report on the excavations at Jerablus on behalf of the British Museum,* part
            III: *the excavations in the inner town and the Hittite inscriptions.* Oxford: British
            Museum Publications. (With a contribution by R.D. Barnett.)

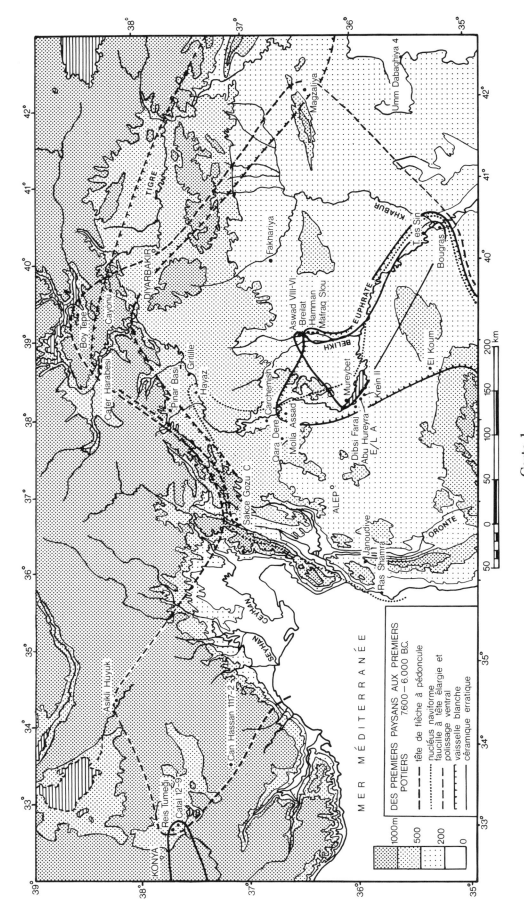

Carte 1

DES PREMIERS PAYSANS AUX PREMIERS POTIERS
7600 — 6.000 B.C.

- - - tête de flèche à pédoncule
.... nucléus naviforme
········ faucille à tête élargie et polissage ventral
---- vaisselle blanche
—— céramique erratique

MER MÉDITERRANÉE

KONYA
Reis Tümeği
Çatal 12-9
Can Hassan 1117-2
Aşıklı Hüyük

SEYHAN
CEYHAN

Çater Harabesi
Çayönü
Boy Tepe
DIYARBAKIR
TIGRE
KHABUR

Pınar Başı
Gritille
Havaz
Sakçe Gözü C
Qara Dere
Carchemish
Molla Assad
Dibsi Faraj
Abu Hureyra
E/L A
Krein II
El Koum

Janoudiye
Ras Shamra
ORONTE
ALEP

Mureybet
BELIKH
Mafraq Slou
Hamman
Breilat
Aswad VIII-VI
Faknariya
Magzaliya
Umm Dabaghiya 4

EUPHRATE
T. es Sin
Bougras

km
200   150   100   50   0   50

1000m
500
200
0

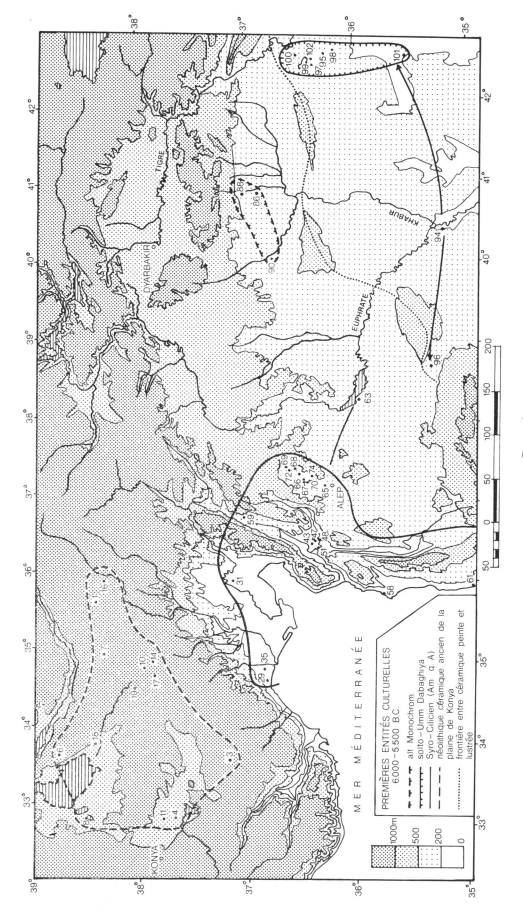

Carte 2

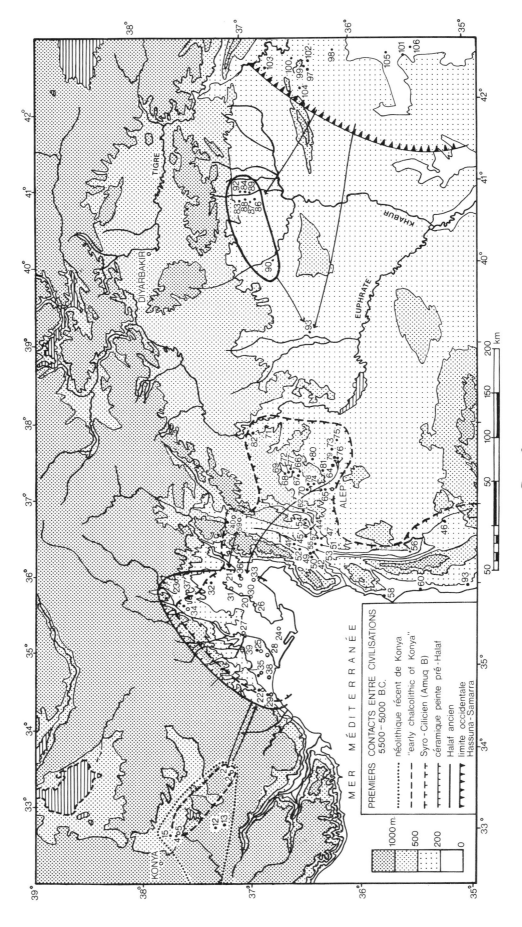

Carte 3

MER MÉDITERRANÉE

PREMIERS CONTACTS ENTRE CIVILISATIONS
5500-5000 B.C.

.... néolithique récent de Konya
– – – – "early chalcolithic of Konya"
ᵀᵀᵀᵀᵀ Syro-Cilicien (Amuq B)
⊥⊥⊥⊥⊥ céramique peinte pré-Halaf
——— Halaf ancien
——— limite occidentale Hassuna-Samarra

1000 m.
500
200
0

KONYA

DIYARBAKIR

TIGRE

KHABUR

EUPHRATE

ALEP

0 50 100 150 200 km

THE FIRST FARMERS IN THE LEVANT

Andrew M.T. Moore

T HE PURPOSE of this essay is to determine the circumstances in which and the reasons why a farming economy and sedentary way of life developed in the Levant. The study of the transition from hunting and gathering to farming in this region is of particular importance for several reasons. Throughout the late Pleistocene and early Holocene, as today, the Levant was a distinct geographical region bounded by natural frontiers: the Taurus mountains to the north, the Syrian desert to the east and southeast, Sinai and the Gulf of Suez to the southwest and the Mediterranean to the west. These geographical boundaries served as cultural frontiers during the Epipaleolithic and Neolithic. Also, the Levant has been more intensively investigated than any other region of western Asia by archeologists interested in Epipaleolithic and Neolithic communities. It is thus possible to examine the origins of the first agricultural societies in greater detail here than elsewhere. Finally, it seems that, on present evidence, agricultural societies crystallized in the Levant earlier than in any other neighboring region.

I suggest that the transition from hunting and gathering to settled farming was conditioned principally by five factors. These were the environment, population, economy, pattern of settlement, and social organization. Changes in these factors and their influence upon each other largely explain why agricultural societies came into existence in the Levant.[1] The development of farming and the formation of permanent villages brought about a permanent alteration in the pattern of existence of the inhabitants of the region; some of the immediate consequences of these developments should be considered.

This essay falls into three parts. The changes in environment that occurred in the late Pleistocene and early Holocene will be discussed first, since I believe that these had an important influence on the development of agriculture. The Epipaleolithic societies that inhabited the Levant between about 18,000 and 8500 bc[2] will be considered in the second part. An agricultural way of life began to crystallize in the region during this period. The Neolithic itself will form the subject of the third part. The Neolithic of the Levant, which lasted from about 8500 to 3750 bc, may be divided into four successive stages, which I have called Neolithic 1 to 4. The development of the new economy will be considered within this framework.

ENVIRONMENTAL CHANGE DURING THE EPIPALEOLITHIC AND NEOLITHIC

We have known for many years that in the Levant the change from mobile hunting and gathering to a sedentary, agricultural way of life happened about the time of the transition from Pleistocene to Holocene. This coincidence suggests that the amelioration of the environment that took place at the close of the Pleistocene created conditions that were favorable for the development of the new economy. Three factors governed this improvement in the environment: temperature, rainfall, and vegetation.

---

1. Many of the arguments presented here were first put forward in a doctoral thesis (Moore 1978). A more detailed consideration of the supporting evidence may be found there.

2. All the dates given in this essay are based on radiocarbon determinations calculated on the Libby half-life without further calibration. I have, accordingly, followed the convention whereby all such dates are expressed in radiocarbon years bc.

Evidence from deep-sea cores taken from the Atlantic, the Caribbean, and the Pacific has shown that during the Pleistocene the surface of the earth was subject to major, regular cycles of climatic change. During the last cold phase (oxygen-isotope stage 2) the temperature fell worldwide. This caused sea levels to be lowered at least 100 m (Shackleton and Opdyke 1973, p. 45). Amounts of precipitation also fluctuated markedly, which led to substantial adjustments of vegetation zones. These changes had a profound effect upon the environment of the Levant.

It has been estimated that the drop in mean annual temperature during isotopic stage 2 lowered the snow line in the mountains of Lebanon and in the Taurus by about 1,000 m (Messerli 1966, p. 61, 1967, p. 139; Kaiser 1961, pp. 142ff, fig. 1). Depression of the snow line by this amount would have required a fall in temperature of about 6° or 7° C (Messerli 1967, p. 207; Farrand 1971, p. 550). This estimated fall in temperature is of the same order of magnitude as that obtained by Thunell in a recent study of cores drilled in the floor of the eastern Mediterranean. He has calculated that the drop in surface water temperature was about 4° to 6° C (Thunell 1979, p. 365). The temperature was at its lowest between 18,000 and 13,000 bc (Shackleton and Opdyke 1976, p. 456). It slowly began to rise before the end of stage 2 and then increased quite rapidly, though with fluctuations, until it reached its postglacial maximum about 3000 bc. Thus, throughout the Epipaleolithic and Neolithic the temperature in the Levant was cooler than it is today (fig. 2).

The fluctuations in precipitation during the late Pleistocene and early Holocene in the Levant were partly independent of the changes in temperature. These fluctuations do not seem to have been very great, but in a semiarid area as sensitive to minor changes in environmental variables as the Levant their effects were considerable upon the water levels of lakes and the extent of vegetation zones, particularly the latter.

When the temperature reached its minimum about 18,000 bc the climate of the Levant became arid. The reduction in precipitation was partly responsible for a fall in the levels of the lake in the Damascus basin, the Lisan lake, and the Jafr lake (Kaiser et al. 1973, pp. 279ff, 348ff; Neev and Emery 1967, p. 26; Huckriede and Wiesemann 1968, pp. 80, 82). It also caused the zone of what is now Mediterranean forest to contract until it was confined to the coastal mountains. Oak forest gave way to maquis near Lake Huleh (Horowitz 1971, p. 267), but Palestine and the areas to the south seem to have enjoyed slightly higher levels of precipitation than north Syria. The Ghab core from the Orontes valley indicates that during the most arid phase (subzone Y5) Jebel Zawiye was steppic, while the only forest to be found was on the seaward side of the Jebel Alawiye (Niklewski and van Zeist 1970, p. 750, fig. 5). Beyond the Levantine coast to the east and south lay a broad zone of steppe.

The environment changed toward the end of the Pleistocene as the temperature rose. The climate became not only warmer but moister as well. This caused the level of the Dead Sea and the lake in the Damascus basin to rise, while mud flats were formed in the Jafr basin. There is a date of 7900±150 bc for this phase from the Dead Sea (Neev and Emery 1967, p. 28).

The increase in precipitation had a marked effect upon the vegetation. The zone of Mediterranean forest expanded considerably until it clothed not only the hills and mountains of the coastal region but also the edge of the plateau to the east (Niklewski and van Zeist 1970, pp. 750ff; Kaiser et al 1973, pp. 307ff; Horowitz 1971, p. 260). There are indications from the pollen cores with the most detailed records that the expansion of forest took place earlier in the southern than in the northern Levant. The process began about 12,000 bc on the evidence of a well-dated core from the Huleh basin (Bottema and Van Zeist 1981, after Tsukada), but not until 10,000 bc along the Orontes (Bottema and Van Zeist 1981). It is also clear from these studies and from Leroi-Gourhan's work in Lebanon and the Damascus basin (1973, p. 46) that the extent and density of the forest zone fluctuated at the end of the Pleistocene and the beginning of the Holocene.

During this phase the vegetation of the Levant reached a particularly rich climax (fig. 4). Then as now there were three principal vegetation zones, the boundaries of which were determined mainly by rainfall (Zohary 1970). The inland edge of the Mediterranean forest lay along the 300 mm isohyet. This forest zone extended farther to the east and south than it does now. It was also composed of a greater variety of species than it is today; among these species were hornbeam and silver lime, which indicates that the climate was cooler and moister.

Between the 300 mm and 150 mm isohyets lay the steppe, which then covered the entire inland plateau and Sinai. It was the most extensive of the vegetation zones, spreading over a much larger area than now. The steppe, like the Mediterranean forest, was richer in species than it is at present. Remains of hackberry, turpentine, and feather grasses were all recovered from the Mesolithic deposits of my excavation at Tell Abu Hureyra, for example, but these species are not found in the surrounding steppe today (Hillman 1975, table 1). Between the forest and the steppe proper lay an intermediate zone of open woodland. This intermediate open woodland and the better-watered steppe were important because they were the most attractive areas in which to found early agricultural settlements. Beyond these zones, in regions that received less than 150 mm of rainfall, lay the desert, which was much less extensive than it is now.

Thus, at the close of the Pleistocene the climate of the Levant was both cooler and more humid than at present. Much of the region consisted of Mediterranean and intermediate open forest with a broad zone of steppe beyond. The climax vegetation in each of these zones was also particularly rich.

These favorable environmental conditions persisted into the early Holocene. Reconstructions of atmospheric circulation patterns by Lamb and others have shown that, as the Holocene advanced, rainfall became more seasonal and gradually diminished (Lamb 1971). The temperature continued to rise, which brought about an increased rate of evaporation. The forest zones shrank, to be replaced by steppe that, in its turn, diminished in area as the desert expanded (fig. 7). These trends were accentuated by man, whose activities had a deleterious effect upon the steppe and forest zones.

The changes in climate began to influence the vegetation in northern Palestine after 8000 bc (van Zeist and Bottema 1980, after Tsukada). The forest cover diminished significantly during the seventh millennium, increased during the late sixth and fifth, and was then reduced still further. The Dead Sea was not affected so swiftly since it remained at a relatively high level until well into the Holocene (Neev and Emery 1967, p. 28). Then, during the fifth millennium, increasing evaporation caused the level of the lake to fall sharply.

Similar trends affected the vegetation in both Lebanon and Syria. Forest cover remained extensive in northwestern Syria until as late as perhaps 6000 bc (Bottema and Van Zeist 1981), but thereafter it was adversely affected by climatic change and man's activities. The evidence of the plant remains from Abu Hureyra would suggest that these influences had already caused some degradation of the steppe by the seventh millennium.

Epipaleolithic

In this section I shall consider the pattern of settlement and economy of the Epipaleolithic inhabitants of the Levant against the background of the environmental changes already outlined. The Epipaleolithic may be divided into two stages for the purposes of this essay (fig. 1), Epipaleolithic 1 and 2, traditionally known in Palestine as the Kebaran and Natufian respectively.

For much of Epipaleolithic 1 the climate of the Levant was cool and dry. Sites of this stage were widespread throughout the region from the coast east and south, extending as far as the interior plateaux (fig. 3). Their inhabitants seem to have avoided the high hills and mountains, which would have been still quite thickly forested. They preferred the open woodland of the foothills and lowlands and the steppe beyond. They did not, however, penetrate very far east into the dry steppe and desert of the plateaux or into southern Sinai, almost certainly because these areas were too arid and excessively cool in winter.

About 90 Epipaleolithic 1 sites have been identified in the Levant (fig. 3), principally on the basis of the typology of their flint assemblages. These sites were all inhabited briefly at some time during this stage, which lasted a maximum of 8,000 years. They were small, few exceeding 300 m², which would indicate that the groups that camped at them consisted of no more than 20 or 30 people. The evidence of plant, animal, and other remains suggests that these groups were mobile hunter-gatherers and that they followed a regular, seasonal pattern of movement. They practiced selective hunting of one principal species, usually gazelle but sometimes fallow deer or goats. They also hunted a wide range of other game, both large and small, and took birds, fish, and shellfish when available. Vegetable foods were certainly eaten and may have formed a major portion of the diet but, for the moment, there is very little evidence of this aspect of the economy.

The improvement in environment toward the close of the Pleistocene began late in Epipaleo-lithic 1. Epipaleolithic 2 thus coincided with a period of relatively cool, moist climate and rich forest and steppe vegetation, conditions that were particularly favorable for human settlement and that had a marked effect upon the way of life of the people of the Levant. A map of the distribution of Epipaleolithic 2 sites (fig. 4) shows that they were spread over the same geograph-ical area as the sites of Epipaleolithic 1, the only significant difference being that they extended farther into the highland zone. On the other hand, the extent of the vegetation zones was now very different. Nearly all Epipaleolithic 2 sites were situated in the Mediterranean and inter-mediate open forest, while only a few, such as Abu Hureyra, were in the better-watered steppe.

About 75 Epipaleolithic 2 sites are known, slightly fewer than for Epipaleolithic 1, but they were occupied during a much shorter period, about 1,500 years. Assuming that the ratio of sites discovered to those that once existed is about the same for both stages, there was a substantial increase in the population of the Levant from Epipaleolithic 1 to Epipaleolithic 2.

The main reason for the growth in population was probably the environmental improvement that began toward the end of Epipaleolithic 1. The rise in temperature and increase in rainfall brought about a luxuriant growth in vegetation and, thus, a great increase in the biomass. Human populations can rise rapidly to a level somewhat below carrying capacity in the absence of other constraints (Birdsell 1968, p. 230). In this instance the carrying capacity itself increased markedly. It thus seems probable that the population of the Levant grew in response to the increase in the quantity of wild plant and animal foods that were available.

Most Epipaleolithic 2 sites were less than 500 m² in area and so were little larger than Epipaleolithic 1 sites. Some, however, were considerably bigger, from 800 to 2,000 m² or more. These settlements usually consisted of a series of circular huts or pit dwellings. They were inhabited by relatively numerous groups of people who had perhaps come together through the coalescing of smaller bands typical of Epipaleolithic 1 society. There is evidence from Abu Hureyra, Hayonim, Ain Mallaha, and elsewhere indicating that these large Epipaleolithic 2 sites and also some of the smaller ones were occupied both longer and more intensively than any in Epipaleolithic 1. Thus in Epipaleolithic 2 there was a trend toward larger group size and a semisedentary way of life based on villages. These trends would have brought about wholly new social configurations. Larger groups living together for much of the year would have required new forms of social organization and would also have enjoyed more intense and sustained social intercourse than their ancestors.

Changes took place in the economy during Epipaleolithic 2 that were quite as important as these modifications in environment, settlement pattern, and social organization. The inhabitants of many sites continued to practice selective hunting of the species most common in the vicinity — gazelle at Nahal Oren and Mugharet el Wad, goats at Beidha, gazelle and onager at Abu Hureyra and Mureybat. This kind of animal exploitation was more intensive at some sites, however, than in Epipaleolithic 1. An indication of such relatively intense culling was the high proportion of immature animals killed at several sites, 55% of the gazelle at Nahal Oren (Noy et al.

1973, table 5) and 75% of the goats from Beidha (Perkins 1966, p. 67), for example. Such evidence implies that man was in close contact with these species and that he was taking care to conserve their herds, for otherwise his principal supply of meat would rapidly have diminished. Nonetheless, the inhabitants of most Epipaleolithic 2 sites continued to take a wide range of other game, birds, fish, and shellfish where they were available.

The best evidence for the changes that were taking place in the exploitation of plants comes from the excavation of Abu Hureyra.[3] The site is a large tell, 11.5 hectares in area, situated on the Syrian Euphrates. It was first settled about 9000 bc during Epipaleolithic 2 and then abandoned during the ninth millennium. It was reoccupied in Neolithic 2 about 7500 bc and reached its greatest extent during the seventh millennium. It was finally abandoned during the sixth millennium, perhaps as late as 5500 bc.[4]

We wanted to reconstruct the economy of the site in as much detail as possible for each phase of occupation and so we used special methods such as flotation to recover large samples of organic remains, in all, more than 1,000 liters of plant remains and 2 metric tons of animal bones. Gordon Hillman of the University of Wales, who is studying the plant remains, has found that cereal grains were particularly abundant in samples from the Epipaleolithic 2 settlement. The most numerous were grains of wild-type einkorn, but wild-type barley and wild rye were also present (Hillman 1975, table 1). This suggests that cereals were an important constituent of the diet. Also present were vetches and wild-type lentils. A wide range of other plants was gathered from the wild for food, including feather grass, capers, hackberry fruits, and turpentine nutlets.

The presence of cereals in such large quantities, and of the pulses, in the Epipaleolithic 2 settlement at Abu Hureyra leads one to ask how the inhabitants obtained them. Were these seeds simply gathered from the wild or were they deliberately planted and harvested? The cereals and pulses recovered were, for the most part, morphologically wild types, yet these species were among the first to be domesticated in the Levant. The earliest domestic mutants have been found in Neolithic 1 settlements at Jericho and Nahal Oren, which were occupied only a few centuries later. Thus, it would be reasonable to suppose that the people of the Levant had already been cultivating these plants for some time before any morphological change became apparent.

The middle Euphrates is too arid today for wild einkorn to grow in the vicinity of Abu Hureyra or at the site of Mureybat nearby, where many einkorn grains have also been found in a ninth millennium settlement (van Zeist and Casparie 1968, p. 45). Since the climate was both cooler and more humid in Epipaleolithic 2, einkorn could have grown there then. It could have been harvested wild, but there are indications that it may have been cultivated. Hillman has carried out experiments on stands of wild einkorn in the Munzur mountains of eastern Turkey. These experiments concerned the application of various methods of harvesting and crop rotation to wild cereals. He concluded that if the most simple methods of harvesting and husbandry were used, then the morphology of wild einkorn would have remained the same over long periods of time. Only if novel harvesting and other cultivation techniques were applied, again over many centuries, would domestic mutants arise. Thus wild einkorn and perhaps other plants could have been deliberately planted and harvested by the inhabitants of Epipaleolithic 2 Abu Hureyra without any change taking place in the morphology of the seeds.

Cultivation of einkorn and possibly of other cereals and pulses would have disturbed the natural vegetation in the vicinity of the site. It is significant, therefore, that seeds of weeds such as *Lithospermum arvense, Alyssum, Atriplex,* and *Polygonum arenastrum* were found in samples

---

3. A summary account of the excavation has been published (Moore 1975).

4. There are radiocarbon dates of 8842±82 bc BM-1121 for the Epipaleolithic 2 (Mesolithic) settlement and 7424±72 bc BM-1122, 6726±72 bc BM-1423, and 6240±77 bc BM-1424 for the Neolithic village that succeeded it.

from the Epipaleolithic 2 levels. They might indicate that the land around the site had been severely trampled by humans and animals but, since they are characteristic of cultivated ground in the area today, their presence does suggest that the inhabitants were practicing simple tillage.

Seeds have not yet been recovered in large quantities from contemporary sites, but there is other evidence to support the view that simple agriculture was beginning to play a part in the Epipaleolithic 2 economy. Several Epipaleolithic 2 sites — Abu Hureyra, Mureybat, and Dibsi Faraj East on the Euphrates and Saaideh, Qornet Rharra, Ain Mallaha, and Jericho farther south — had much potentially cultivable land in their immediate vicinities. This cannot be said of many Epipaleolithic 1 sites. It is also significant that Epipaleolithic 2 settlements have been discovered at the bottom of five tells that were later the sites of flourishing Neolithic villages, namely, Abu Hureyra, Mureybat, El Kum, Jericho, and Beidha. Only at El Kum has an Epipaleolithic 1 site been found in such a location.

The sites at which cereals were likely to have been a staple food are those such as Abu Hureyra that were situated in the better-watered steppe and intermediate forest zone, since it was there that sufficiently open conditions existed for cereals to flourish. It has been suggested, however (Mellaart 1975, p. 30; Henry 1973, p. 188, 1981), that wild cereals would have been abundant in the Mediterranean forest and would have provided a major part of the diet of the inhabitants of sites in this zone. This hypothesis seems improbable to me: the Mediterranean forest would have been relatively dense during this stage, and thus the growth of wild cereals would have been inhibited. On the other hand, it would have been rich in other potential plant foods and there is indirect evidence to suggest that the inhabitants of sites in this zone were exploiting them. Bedrock mortars, pestles, and deep mortars, either intact or, in the case of the so-called stone pipes, with their bases broken, have been found on many sites in this zone, such as Ain Mallaha, Mugharet el Wad, Hayonim, and Saaideh. Such tools are poorly designed for grinding cereals but would have enabled their makers to process acorns efficiently. Acorns were an abundant food resource of the Mediterranean zone that, if collected and stored, would have permitted semi-sedentary settlement. In this connection it should be noted that deep mortars have not been recovered from sites in the steppe zone where ground stone tools of any kind are rare. The main ground stone objects found at Abu Hureyra were saddle querns and rubbers, which would have been suitable, of course, for processing cereals.

These developments may now be summarized. The evidence indicates that the population of the Levant greatly increased in Epipaleolithic 2 in circumstances of environmental affluence. There was much more food available from wild resources, which allowed some of the small groups typical of Epipaleolithic 1 society to coalesce and to establish much larger settlements. They then occupied these new sites on a semisedentary or, perhaps, even sedentary basis. These trends would have had important social consequences. The inhabitants of the large sites would have needed new forms of social organization to regulate subsistence activities and to maintain community harmony over extended periods of time. Life in these settlements would have encouraged regular, sustained social contacts with a substantially greater number of people than had earlier been possible. This development may have created a desire to keep these larger groups together for as much of the year as possible, to become fully sedentary, in fact. Only a more systematic exploitation of plants and animals would have made this possible. The productivity of traditional methods of hunting and gathering was increased, while care was taken to conserve wild food resources. Other methods of obtaining food, in particular the cultivation of cereals, were introduced. The reality was probably exceedingly complex, but the improvement in environment, the growth of population, and the new patterns of social organization do much to explain why these novel adaptations in the economy took place.

Neolithic

The development of the new agricultural economy brought about far-reaching changes in the level of population and in social organization during the Neolithic. This period may conveniently be divided into four stages (fig. 1), each stage being defined principally by a characteristic constellation of material remains. It will be seen that modifications also occurred in the economy, population, and settlement pattern from one stage to the next. Neolithic 1 and 2 had certain general features in common, in particular in aspects of their economies, so that they may be referred to as the Archaic Neolithic. The economies and settlement patterns of Neolithic 3 and 4 were significantly different from those of the Archaic Neolithic, so that these two stages may be usefully called the Developed Neolithic.

There was no abrupt break with the Epipaleolithic in the Archaic Neolithic but, rather, a slow process of adaptation as the new economy, based on a mixture of simple agriculture and continued exploitation of wild resources, took hold. This economy was in time developed as far as prevailing environmental conditions permitted, and the consequences for the level of population and settlement patterns were remarkable.

The distribution of sites in Neolithic 1 was broadly similar in its geographic spread to that of Epipaleolithic 2 (fig. 5). The main difference in location was that most Neolithic 1 sites were situated on lower ground in more open country, reflecting a greater need for arable and pasture as the new economy was adopted. The most striking feature of the settlement pattern is the decrease in the number of sites occupied. About 30 may be attributed to Neolithic 1 whereas the total for Epipaleolithic 2 was 75. Epipaleolithic 2 lasted approximately 1,500 years, while the duration of Neolithic 1 was about 900 years; one might therefore predict a modest decrease in the number of sites occupied. On the other hand, most Neolithic 1 settlements were much larger than those of Epipaleolithic 2. The largest settlement, Jericho, was 4 hectares, while Tell Aswad may have extended over 1 hectare in this stage. These settlements were of a wholly new order of size, being many times bigger than any site previously inhabited in the Levant. Thus, although there were fewer Neolithic 1 than Epipaleolithic 2 sites they were much bigger than any Epipaleolithic ones; this implies that the population was becoming concentrated on fewer, larger sites. One other fact should be noted: people were becoming more sedentary. They were not moving regularly from one site to another during the year as their predecessors had done, so the number of sites occupied by a given population was declining. If these facts are considered together there is no reason to suppose that the population either decreased or increased very much during Neolithic 1, although the pattern of occupation was changing.

The economy of some Neolithic 1 sites was based upon collecting wild plants and herding or hunting. This pattern did not differ much from that of many Epipaleolithic 2 sites. At others, such as Nahal Oren and, in particular, Jericho the inhabitants depended upon the cultivation of cereals, principally emmer and barley, and pulses (Noy et al. 1973, table 6; Hopf 1969, p. 357). Even at these settlements they still collected a wide range of wild plant foods. At Jericho and some other sites the inhabitants selectively hunted or culled gazelle (Clutton-Brock 1971, p. 48) in such a manner that the herds were conserved. In other words, they were practicing a form of animal husbandry. They also continued to hunt a number of other species, as in Epipaleolithic 2. Thus agriculture and herding were conducted more systematically in Neolithic 1 in order to sustain the growing population of the larger sites. On the smaller sites, less intensive practices still served to provide an adequate food supply.

Simple agriculture was adopted throughout the Levant during Neolithic 2. At Abu Hureyra several cereals were cultivated, among them emmer, einkorn, and barley, and also lentils, vetches, chickpeas, and other pulses. As time went on, cereals provided more of the food that was eaten, and a greater variety of pulses was grown. Anthony Legge of the University of London, who is studying the animal bones, has found that early in Neolithic 2 much of the meat came from controlled herds of gazelle. This pattern changed during the Neolithic 2 occupation of the site when gazelle were abruptly displaced by the introduction of sheep and some goats (Legge 1975, p. 76, 1977, pp. 56ff), which were probably domesticated. Cattle, deer, pigs, equid, and hare were regularly hunted, while fish, shellfish, and birds were also eaten. Numerous plants and fruits were collected in season to supplement the diet. Thus, throughout the Neolithic 2 sequence at Abu Hureyra, wild food resources were intensively exploited to supplement agriculture and herding.

The economy of the Pre-Pottery Neolithic B or Neolithic 2 settlement at Jericho was also based on crops and herds and regularly supplemented by hunting and gathering. Emmer, einkorn, and barley as well as lentils, chickpeas, and horse beans were all grown (Hopf 1969, p. 356), as at Abu Hureyra. Herded ovicaprines, principally goat, provided more meat than did gazelle from the beginning of the Pre-Pottery Neolithic B occupation (Clutton-Brock 1971, p. 53). The other species killed were cattle and pigs. Here, as at Abu Hureyra, wild plants and game were also regularly exploited.

The economies of Abu Hureyra and Jericho were typical of Neolithic 2 villages whose inhabitants, one may now assume, were sedentary. Some smaller sites still functioned as hunting stations, but, otherwise, simple agriculture was practiced everywhere.

A map of the distribution of Neolithic 2 sites illustrates two major developments that took place during this stage. Figure 6 shows the location of about 140 sites certainly inhabited in Neolithic 2, that is, over a period of 1,600 years from 7600 to 6000 bc. This is very many more than the 30 sites known to have been occupied during the 900 years of Neolithic 1. Furthermore, in Neolithic 2 there was another general increase in the size of settlements, which were also occupied for a longer period than before. All the evidence points to a substantial growth of the population of the Levant during this stage. This increase in numbers was a result of the widespread adoption of simple agriculture and herding, which permitted support of a much higher population from the available resources.

The growth of the population would have occasioned greater pressure on the usable land. This may account for the second novel aspect of the Neolithic 2 distribution of sites, the major expansion of settlement into the steppe zone. It is probable that the adoption of sheep and goat herding in Neolithic 2 permitted this zone to be successfully exploited for the first time by groups of pastoralists. This was the only stage of the Neolithic during which the steppic interior was regularly inhabited.

The economy of the Archaic Neolithic — simple agriculture and herding combined with intensive hunting and gathering — proved remarkably successful when practiced in the favorable conditions of the prevailing environment. It permitted a huge increase in the population and an attendant rise in the number and size of sites. It also made possible the exploitation of the steppic interior for the only time during the Neolithic. These processes were accompanied by changes in society that were quite as far-reaching in their consequences as the adoption of the new agricultural economy.

Large villages such as Jericho were first established in Neolithic 1, but by Neolithic 2 the pattern was widespread. Sites such as Abu Hureyra, Ras Shamra, Buqras, and Jericho would have housed populations of several thousands during the seventh millennium. Such large, densely crowded settlements were a new phenomenon. Their inhabitants would have required an effective system of community government to regulate not only affairs between families but also to oversee the well-being of the village as a whole, to apportion rights to land around the settlement, and even to arrange simple irrigation works.

The change in economy, the growth in population, and the formation of such large villages brought about a new form of social organization. The typical houses at Abu Hureyra, Buqras, and elsewhere were rectilinear, multiroomed structures separated from each other by narrow lanes and courts. These individual houses were generally similar from one end of a settlement to the other. They were large enough to have been inhabited by a single family. Houses of similar construction, external shape, and dimensions, though with fewer internal divisions, are common in north Syria and some other areas of the Levant today; the families living in them are composed of children, parents and, frequently, other relatives. This analogy would suggest that Neolithic 2 houses were inhabited by nuclear or extended families, as Flannery suggested several years ago (1972, p. 39). Such dwellings were so much alike and so widespread that one may suppose that the families occupying them made up the core of the social system. This pattern first became general with the construction of relatively large subcircular family huts at Jericho and Mureybat (Aurenche 1980, p. 52) in Neolithic 1, but its roots lay in the equally large circular huts built in the early phases of occupation at Ain Mallaha in Epipaleolithic 2 (Valla 1981).

All of the houses at Abu Hureyra had the same variety of contents. This observation was supported by the general similarity of the remains deposited in burials beneath the house floors. Such evidence from this and other sites suggests that there was no significant difference in wealth or status from one family to another in the Archaic Neolithic. Although this society may have been egalitarian, its members would have enjoyed more intense and complex social relationships than ever before, because they were living so closely together in such large settlements the year-round. This richer pattern of social organization would have given the population of the Levant a fresh incentive to maintain the size of their settlements even if economic and environmental circumstances changed.

The early Holocene rise in temperature and decrease in rainfall began to affect the vegetation of the Levant seriously late in the seventh millennium. The forest zones contracted, to be replaced by steppe, while the desert in its turn began to encroach upon the steppe (fig. 7). These trends continued, with only minor respites, throughout the Developed Neolithic of the sixth and fifth millennia.

This deterioration in the environment was partly responsible for the changes in economy and settlement pattern that took place in Neolithic 3. The Archaic Neolithic economy depended upon a delicate balance between agriculture, herding, and wild resources. As conditions in the intermediate open forest and steppe worsened, the supply of wild foods would have diminished. There would have been insufficient grazing for stock and game, while simple farming would have been seriously impaired by drought. In time, this would have necessitated a change of adaptation, but the process was hastened by the actions of man himself. The evidence of the plant remains from Abu Hureyra makes it plain that he was exerting too much pressure on the environment of sites in the more marginal areas by overgrazing the natural vegetation and clearing land for agriculture and fuel (Hillman 1975, p. 70). This pressure was only intensified by the rise in population that took place during Neolithic 2. The adverse effect of man's exploitation of the environment would have made necessary major adjustments in his economy and pattern of settlement even without the onset of warmer, drier conditions.

Man responded by abandoning the intensive pursuit of hunting and collecting of wild foods and concentrating instead on agriculture and herding. Mixed farming based on the cultivation of several cereals and pulses and the herding of domesticated sheep, goats, cattle, and swine became the economic basis of sites throughout the Levant. The new adjustment was so successful that it has remained the basis of the economy of villages in the Levant until modern times.

The mixed-farming economy was most productive when practiced in the Mediterranean forest zone of the coast and northern plains. Accordingly, the inhabitants of sites in the open forest and steppe, that is, along the Euphrates, in central Syria, Transjordan, and Sinai, abandoned their settlements and moved northward and westward (fig. 7). Even Palestine was almost completely deserted for several centuries in the early sixth millennium. The migrants founded new settlements throughout the now reduced Mediterranean forest, particularly along the coast and in the rift valley. Once the new economic adjustment had been fully assimilated, some people returned to Palestine later in the sixth millennium.

A comparison of figures 6 and 7 makes clear just how dramatic was the relocation of settlements during Neolithic 3. The adjustment to the new agricultural and herding economy and the movement of people must have imposed considerable strains on society, yet these changes were evidently accomplished successfully. As a result, the population of the Levant remained about the same during the sixth millennium as it has been in the seventh.

The final stage of the Neolithic of the Levant is Neolithic 4, which lasted from about 5000 bc until the early fourth millennium. Northern and central Syria passed into the Halaf sphere about this time, so the stage may be followed only in southern Syria, Lebanon, and Palestine. Here the economy changed little from the adaptation established in Neolithic 3, but the settlement pattern was modified. The density of settlement in this stage was greater than ever before, while new sites were founded high in the hills and mountains. About 80 village sites of this stage have been found in southern Syria, Lebanon, and Palestine (fig. 8), as compared with 45 for the same area in Neolithic 3. Since both stages lasted about a millennium it appears that there was another substantial increase in population during Neolithic 4.

The new economic adjustment of almost complete dependence on mixed farming seems to have been so productive, even when carried out on a fraction of the land area exploited in Neolithic 2, that this adaptation was able to support a much greater population. Yet settlement remained confined to the Mediterranean forest and its fringes, the area best suited to arable agriculture combined with stockbreeding. There was no spread of settlement into the steppe, which remained almost deserted. The growth in population did lead, however, to increased penetration of the upland zone. Sites like Kleat, Jba'a, and Wadi Salhah are at such high altitudes that they can only have been occupied in the summer months. Their material remains are also so restricted in range that few activities can have been carried out on them. It seems that these sites were transhumant camps exploited on a seasonal basis by pastoralists who wintered in agricultural settlements on lower ground.

I have argued from the evidence reviewed in this essay that the genesis of the agricultural way of life in the Levant occurred in the Epipaleolithic. During the Archaic Neolithic the new way of life spread throughout the region, although in this stage, farming and herding were always balanced by continued exploitation of wild resources. The formation of agricultural villages brought about changes in social and community organization that were quite as far-reaching in their importance as the development of the new economy itself. There was a period of adjustment in Neolithic 1 when agriculture and sedentary life became widely established. These developments made possible the marked increase in population and expansion of settlement far out into the steppe zone in Neolithic 2.

This configuration was substantially modified after 6000 bc in the Developed Neolithic. The growth in population and overintensive exploitation of the fragile vegetation and soil of the steppe obliged man to modify his economy once more to maintain the higher level of population and new pattern of social organization. Climatic changes in the early Holocene intensified these environmental pressures. Agriculture and stock breeding were developed further until they supplied virtually all the food required. This kind of peasant farming was most productive when it was practiced on the moister soils of the Mediterranean forest, which made necessary a major relocation of settlement in Neolithic 3. The developed agricultural economy was capable of supporting a much greater population on a relatively small area of land. A major consequence of this capability was the further growth in population that took place in the final stage of the Neolithic.

Bibliography

Aurenche, Olivier
  1980   Un exemple de l'architecture domestique en Syrie au VIIIe millénaire: la maison XLVII
           de Tell Mureybat. In *Le moyen Euphrate: zone de contacts et d'échanges: Actes du
           colloque de Strasbourg* [Mars 1977], ed. J. Cl. Margueron, pp. 35–53. Université des
           Sciences humaines de Strasbourg, Trauvaux du Centre de Recherche sur le Proche-
           Orient et la Grèce Antiques, 5. Leiden: Brill.

Birdsell, Joseph B.
  1968   Some predictions for the Pleistocene based on equilibrium systems among recent
           hunter-gatherers. In *Man the hunter*, ed. R.B. Lee and I. DeVore, pp. 229–40. Chicago:
           Aldine.

Bottema, S., and Zeist, W. van
  1981   Palynological evidence for the climatic history of the Near East, 50,000–6000 B.P. In
           *Préhistoire du Levant: chronologie et organisation de l'espace depuis les origines jusqu'au
           VIe millénaire*, ed. J. Cauvin and P. Sanlaville, pp. 111–32. Actes du Colloque Interna-
           tional du Centre National de la Recherche Scientifique [Lyon, Maison de l'Orient
           Méditerranéen, 10–14 juin 1980], no. 598. Paris: Editions du Centre National de la
           Recherche Scientifique.

Clutton-Brock, Juliet
  1971   The primary food animals of the Jericho tell from the Proto-Neolithic to the Byzantine
           period. *Levant* 3:41–55.

Farrand, W.R.
  1971   Late Quaternary paleoclimates of the eastern Mediterranean area. In *The late Cenozoic
           glacial ages*, ed. K.T. Turekian, pp. 529-64. New Haven: Yale University Press.

Flannery, Kent V.
  1972   The origins of the village as a settlement type in Mesoamerica and the Near East: a
           comparative study. In *Man, settlement and urbanism*, ed. P.J. Ucko, R. Tringham and
           G.W. Dimbleby, pp. 25–53. London: Duckworth.

Henry, D.O.
  1973   The Natufian of Palestine: its material culture and ecology. Ph.D. diss., Southern
           Methodist University, Dallas, Texas.
  1981   An analysis of settlement patterns and adaptive strategies of the Natufian. In *Préhistoire
           du Levant: chronologie et organisation de l'espace depuis les origines jusqu'au VIe
           millénaire*, ed. J. Cauvin and P. Sanlaville, pp. 421–32. Actes du Colloque International
           du Centre National de la Recherche Scientifique [Lyon, Maison de l'Orient Méditerra-
           néen, 10–14 juin 1980], no. 598. Paris: Editions du Centre National de la Recherche
           Scientifique.

Hillman, Gordon C.
  1975   The plant remains from Tell Abu Hureyra: a preliminary report. In The excavation of
           Tell Abu Hureyra in Syria: a preliminary report, A.M.T. Moore, pp. 70–73. *Proceedings
           of the Prehistoric Society* 41:50–77.

Hopf, M.
  1969   Plant remains and early farming in Jericho. In *The domestication and exploitation of
           plants and animals*, ed. P.J. Ucko and G.W. Dimbleby, pp. 355–59. London: Duck-
           worth.

Horowitz, A.
  1971   Climatic and vegetational developments in northeastern Israel during Upper Pleisto-
           cene-Holocene times. *Pollen et Spores* 13:255–78.

Huckriede, R., and Wiesemann, G.
1968   Der Jungpleistozäne Pluvial-See von El Jafr und weitere Daten zum Quartär Jordaniens. *Geologica et Palaeontologica* 2:73–95.

Kaiser, K.
1961   Die Ausdehnung der Vergletscherungen und "periglazialen" Erscheinungen während der Kaltzeiten des quärtären Eiszeitalters innerhalb der Syrisch-Libanesischen Gebirge und die Lage der klimatischen Schneegrenze zur Würmeiszeit im östlichen Mittelmeergebeit. In *Report of the VI International Congress on the Quaternary* [Warsaw 1961], vol. 3: *geomorphological section*, ed. Jan Dylik, International Association for Quaternary Research, pp. 127–48. Lódź: Pánstwowe Wydawnictwo Naukowe.

Kaiser, K.; Kempf, E.K.; Leroi-Gourhan, A.; and Schütt, H.
1973   Quartärstratigraphische Untersuchungen aus dem Damaskus-Becken und seiner Umgebung. *Zeitschrift für Geomorphologie* 17:263–353.

Lamb, H.H.
1971   Climates and circulation regimes developed over the northern hemisphere during and since the last Ice Age. *Palaeogeography, Palaeoclimatology, Palaeoecology* 10:125–62.

Legge, A.J.
1975   The fauna of Tell Abu Hureyra: preliminary analysis. In The excavation of Tell Abu Hureyra in Syria: a preliminary report, A.M.T. Moore, pp. 74–76. *Proceedings of the Prehistoric Society* 41:50–77.
1977   The origins of agriculture in the Near East. In *Hunters, gatherers and first farmers beyond Europe*, ed. J.V.S. Megaw, pp. 51–67. Leicester: Leicester University Press.

Leroi-Gourhan, A.
1973   Les possibilités de l'analyse pollinique en Syrie et au Liban. *Paléorient* 1:39–47.

Mellaart, J.
1975   *The Neolithic of the Near East*. London: Thames and Hudson.

Messerli, B.
1966   Das Problem der Eiszeitlichen Vergletscherung am Libanon und Hermon. *Zeitschrift für Geomorphologie* 10:37–68.
1967   Die Eiszeitliche und die gegenwärtige Vergletscherung in Mittelmeerraum. *Geographica Helvetica* 22:105–228.

Moore, A.M.T.
1975   The excavation of Tell Abu Hureyra in Syria: a preliminary report. *Proceedings of the Prehistoric Society* 41:50–77. (With contributions by G.C. Hillman and A.J. Legge.)
1978   The Neolithic of the Levant. Ph.D. thesis, University of Oxford. Ann Arbor, Mich.: University Microfilms.

Neev, D., and Emery, K.O.
1967   The Dead Sea. *Bulletin of the Geological Survey of Israel* 41:1–147.

Niklewski, J., and Zeist, W. van
1970   A late Quaternary pollen diagram from northwestern Syria. *Acta Botanica Neerlandica* 19:737–54.

Noy, T.; Legge, A.J.; and Higgs, E.S.
1973   Recent excavations at Nahal Oren, Israel. *Proceedings of the Prehistoric Society* 39:75–99.

Perkins, D., Jr.
1966   The fauna from Madamagh and Beidha: a preliminary report. In Five seasons at the pre-pottery Neolithic village of Beidha in Jordan: a summary, Diana Kirkbride, pp. 66–67. *Palestine Exploration Quarterly* 98:8–72.

Shackleton, N.J., and Opdyke, N.D.

1973   Oxygen isotope and palaeomagnetic stratigraphy of equatorial Pacific core V28-238: oxygen isotope temperatures and ice volumes on a 10^5 and 10^6 year scale. *Journal of Quaternary Research* 3:39–55.

1976   Oxygen-isotope and paleomagnetic stratigraphy of Pacific core V28-239. Late Pliocene to latest Pleistocene. In *Investigations of late Quaternary paleoceanography and paleoclimatology*, ed. R.M. Cline and J.D. Hays, pp. 449–64. Geological Society of America, Memoir No. 145. Washington, D.C.: Geological Society of America.

Thunell, R.C.

1979   Eastern Mediterranean Sea during the last glacial maximum: an 18,000 years B.P. reconstruction. *Quaternary Research: an Interdisciplinary Journal* 11:353–72.

Valla, F.R.

1981   Les établissements natoufiens dans le nord d'Israël. In *Préhistoire du Levant: chronologie et organisation de l'espace depuis les origines jusqu'au VIᵉ millénaire*, ed. J. Cauvin and P. Sanlaville, pp. 409–19. Actes du Colloque International du Centre National de la Recherche Scientifique [Lyon, Maison de l'Orient Méditerranéen, 10–14 juin 1980], no. 598. Paris: Editions du Centre National de la Recherche Scientifique.

Zeist, W. van, and Bottema, S.

1981   Palynological evidence for the climatic history of the Near East, 50,000–6000 B.P. In *Préhistoire du Levant: chronologie et organisation de l'espace depuis les origines jusqu'au VIᵉ millénaire*, ed. J. Cauvin and P. Sanlaville. Actes du Colloque International du Centre National de Recherche Scientifique [Lyon, Maison de l'Orient Méditerranéen, 10–14 juin 1980], no. 598. Paris: Editions du Centre National de la Recherche Scientifique.

Zeist, W. van, and Casparie, W.A.

1968   Wild einkorn wheat and barley from Tell Mureybit in northern Syria. *Acta Botanica Neerlandica* 17:44–53.

Zohary, M.

1970   Vegetation of Israel and the Near East. In *Atlas of Israel*, ed. D.H.K. Amiran, J. Elster, M. Gilead, N. Rosenan, N. Kadmon, and U. Paran, Botany VI/I. Jerusalem: Survey of Israel.

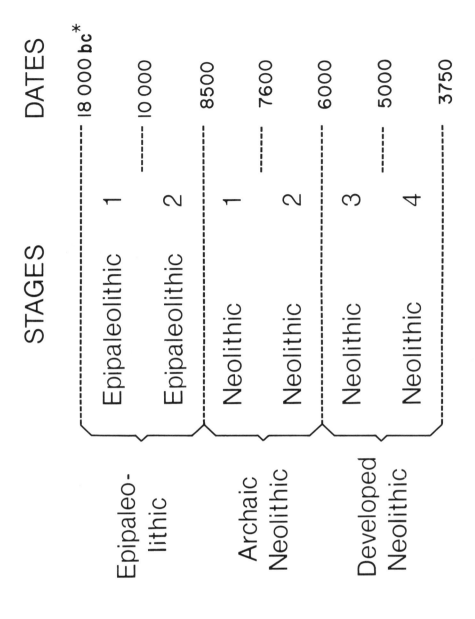

Fig. 1. — Approximate Duration of each Stage of the Epipaleolithic and Neolithic.

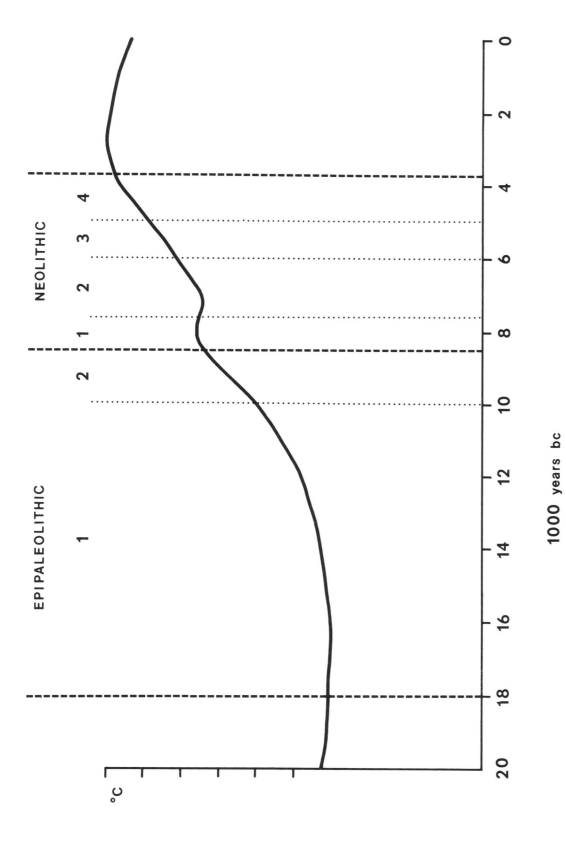

Fig. 2. — Temperature Change During the Late Pleistocene and Early Holocene Related to Stages of the Epipaleolithic and Neolithic. Vertical axis calibrated for a difference of 6 degrees C between late glacial minimum and postglacial maximum. (After Emiliani, Shackleton, Opdyke, and others.)

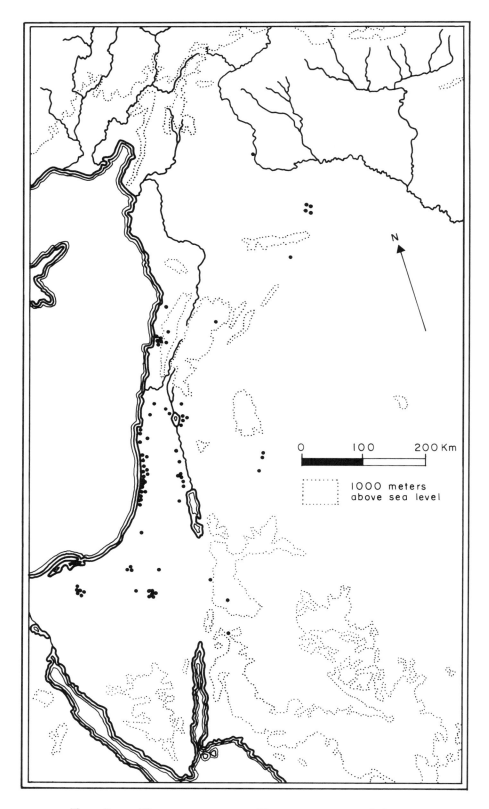

FIG. 3. — DISTRIBUTION OF EPIPALEOLITHIC 1 SITES.

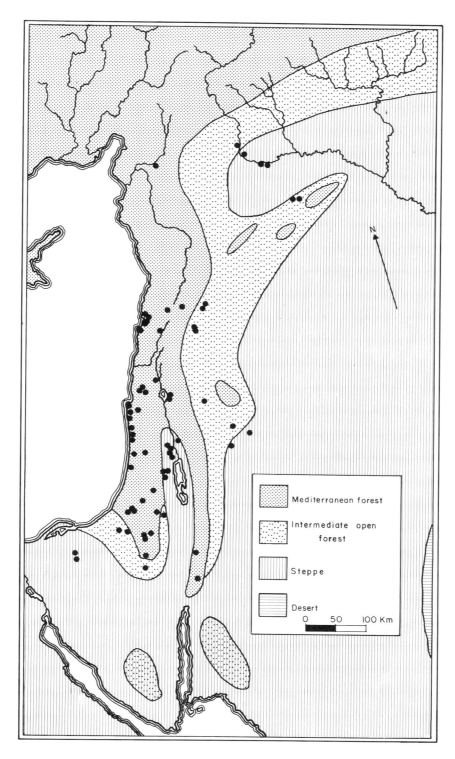

Fig. 4. — Distribution of Epipaleolithic 2 Sites. These are related to probable extent of vegetation zones ca. 9000 B.C.

108

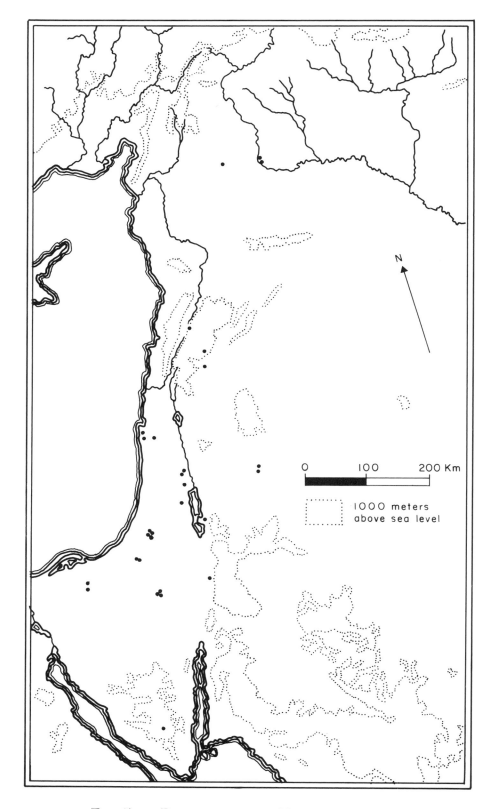

FIG. 5. — DISTRIBUTION OF NEOLITHIC 1 SITES.

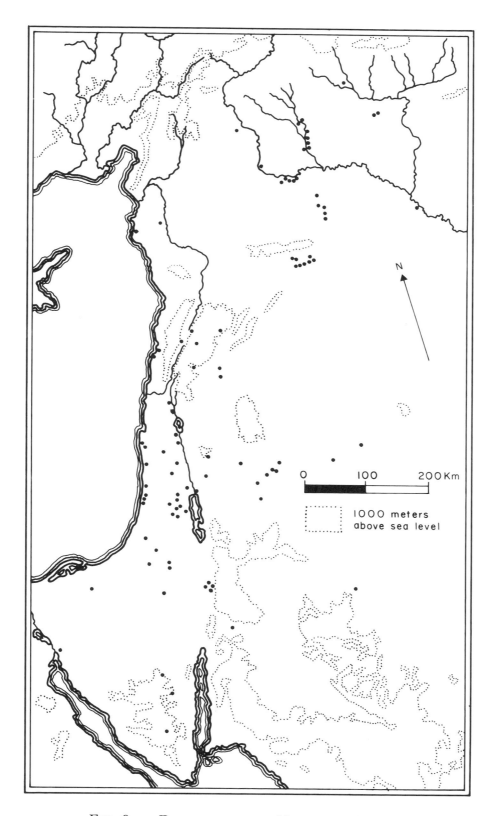

Fig. 6. — Distribution of Neolithic 2 Sites.

110

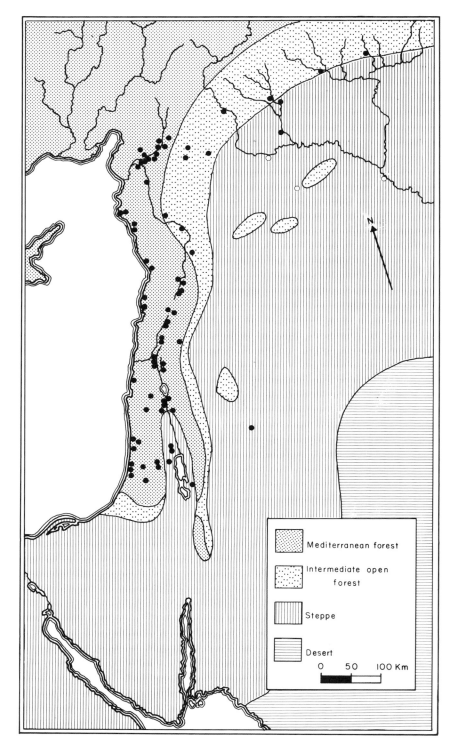

FIG. 7. — DISTRIBUTION OF NEOLITHIC 3 SITES. These are related to probable extent of vegetation zones during the sixth millennium bc. The open circles mark sites abandoned during Neolithic 3.

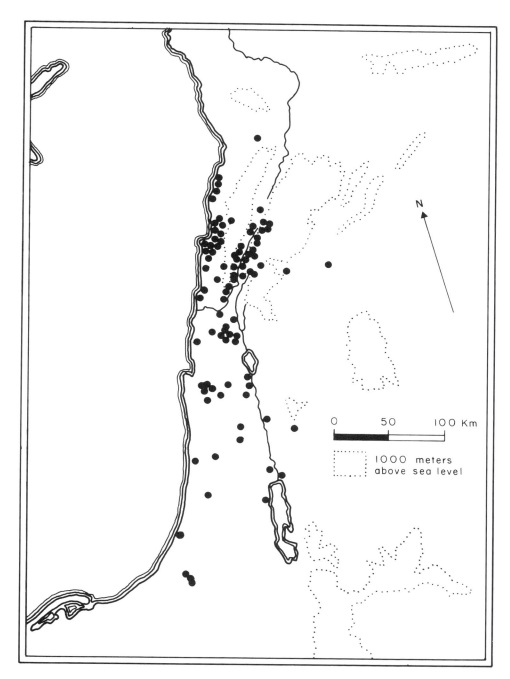

Fig. 8. — Distribution of Neolithic 4 Sites in Southern Syria, Lebanon, and Palestine.

TERMINOLOGIE ET CADRE DE LA PRÉHISTOIRE RÉCENTE DE PALESTINE

Jean Perrot

IL Y A PRÈS d'un demi-siècle, René Neuville, décrivant la préhistoire récente de la Palestine sur la base des découvertes de D. Garrod dans les grottes du Carmel et des siennes propres dans les grottes et abris du désert de Judée, se trouvait dans une position plus aisée que la nôtre aujourd'hui pour proposer une image du Paléolithique supérieur et du Mésolithique palestiniens. Rendons hommage toutefois à son intuition; les progrès de la recherche, l'affinement des techniques de fouille et d'analyse, n'ont pas, pour l'essentiel, infirmé ses conclusions (Neuville 1934).

Les difficultés présentes viennent d'abord de l'abondance des données et, en même temps, de leur insuffisance qualitative. Ces données ont alimenté une prolifération d'hypothèses et de modèles; tout a été dit sur les origines possibles de la culture des céréales et de l'élevage des animaux, sur le mode de vie des anciennes populations du Proche-Orient, sur leur organisation sociale, voire sur leurs plus secrètes pensées. Nous n'en demeurons pas moins, et sur tous ces points, dans le domaine des hypothèses. Nous sommes devant un amas d'incertitudes. Les analyses les plus fines ne rendront pas plus solide la documentation dont nous disposons actuellement. Il faut attendre les résultats de nouvelles fouilles, amples et rigoureuses.

Les données actuelles permettent, sans doute, de dégager quelques traits technologiques, typologiques, et culturels. La plus grande attention portée depuis trente ans à l'environnement et à ses variations, le souci de préciser la distribution géographique des sites, leur importance, la densité de leur population et ses activités, la précision plus grande des mesures radiométriques, autorisent dès aujourd'hui une première esquisse de l'évolution culturelle du Proche-Orient. Mais celle-ci se heurte aussitôt à des difficultés en ce qui concerne le cadre et la terminologie.

La terminologie traditionnelle est usée par les manipulations qu'elle a subies depuis un demi-siècle; tiraillée par les adaptations qu'on en a voulu faire, elle paraît impuissante à rendre compte clairement des divers aspects du développement. La tentation est donc grande de créer des termes nouveaux; avec pour résultat, le plus souvent, d'ajouter à la confusion. Faut-il faire table rase du passé et créer une terminologie nouvelle ou s'efforcer à plus de clarté en serrant le sens des termes en usage?

Sans refaire l'historique de l'emploi des termes les plus couramment utilisés, termes qui sont propres aux domaines de l'environnement, de l'archéologie, de l'économie ou des techniques, on fera quelques remarques sur la terminologie et sur le cadre de la préhistoire récente de la Palestine, région où s'est élaborée la préhistoire du Levant. L'étude comparative directe des gisements et du matériel entre la région palestinienne et la région syro-libanaise n'est pas possible aujourd'hui. Il importe donc de préciser le sens du vocabulaire propre à la préhistoire de la Palestine avant d'étendre celui-ci à la préhistoire de la Syrie et du Liban.

Il y a une quinzaine d'années, j'avais préféré le terme *épipaléolithique* à celui de *mésolithique* pour l'horizon du Natoufien (Perrot 1966). Ceci en raison d'abord de l'évidente filiation de l'outillage en silex de Mallaha avec celui du Paléolithique supérieur. Le Natoufien apparaissait comme représentant au Levant un développement comparable à celui observé sur le pourtour méridional du bassin méditerranéen et décrit comme épipaléolithique. Il paraissait souhaitable aussi d'écarter les risques de confusion qu'il y avait à suivre de trop près en Palestine la terminologie européenne qui avait déjà induit en erreur les premiers préhistoriens de la région.

Par ailleurs, l'âge du Natoufien se trouvait reculé sur l'horizon du Pléistocène. L'économie natoufienne ne se distinguait pas essentiellement de celle du Paléolithique; sur la base de l'analyse de la faune faite par P. Ducos, j'avais montré qu'elle demeurait basée sur la chasse, la pêche et la cueillette. L'idée d'un début de "néolithisation" sur l'horizon du Natoufien était abandonnée.

Le terme *épipaléolithique* fut repris au colloque de Londres sur la terminologie, en 1969, et étendu par H. Hours et L. Copeland (Hours 1974) à l'ensemble des complexes industriels à microlithes postérieurs à l'Aurignacien du Levant, c'est-à-dire plus précisément au Kébarien et au Natoufien. Ce qui est commode en considération des difficultés que soulevaient les classifications de Garrod et de Neuville, mais ce qui ne les résoud pas. Les limites de cet "Epipaléolithique" demeurent mal définies; il existe des industries à microlithes antérieures au Kébarien, et les microlithes, s'ils se raréfient, ne disparaissent pas avec le Natoufien. Il conviendrait donc de s'attacher à préciser les articulations de cet Epipaléolithique du Levant avec ce qui précède et avec ce qui suit. Pour l'instant, c'est un peu l'aile de Pégase dont le peintre masque habilement l'attache par un opportun petit nuage.

A l'Epipaléolithique fait suite encore parfois dans la littérature un "Néolithique", précédant un "Chalcolithique" ou "Enéolithique". Ces termes fatigués ont été abandonnés, et avec raison, il y a trente ans par R. J. Braidwood et l'équipe de Chicago. Leur fortune cependant paraît inépuisable. Tant que l'on reste dans le domaine de l'économie et des techniques, le terme *néolithique* est commode pour désigner l'horizon des premières tentatives de production de la nourriture. Mais ce niveau de développement n'a pas été atteint partout au même moment dans les différentes régions du Proche-Orient; le terme *néolithique* ne peut y avoir de sens chronologique que dans d'étroites limites géographiques; il serait dangereux de l'étendre sans discernement à l'ensemble du Levant qui est loin de constituer une zone biogéographique homogène au développement continu.

A l'intérieur de la périodisation "lithique", qui reste floue, s'inscrit la séquence des grands complexes industriels: Kébarien, Natoufien, etc. Cette séquence s'est enrichie de termes qui cherchent à rendre compte de la variabilité géographique, chronologique, ou stylistique, variabilité d'autant plus grande que devient plus étroite l'adaptation à l'environnement. Aux "Nébékien" et "Falitien" de Jabroud, plus ou moins tombés en désuétude, est venu s'ajouter le "Mushabien" du Sinaï, etc.

Les travaux d'O. Bar-Yosef ont éclairé l'horizon du Kébarien au sens large (Bar-Yosef 1970). L'image d'un Kébarien ancien ou "classique" semble généralement acceptée, précédant un "Kébarien à géométriques" aisément identifiable. A l'intérieur des complexes industriels ainsi désignés, il existe des variantes typologiques ou des nuances de style; mais elles n'apparaissent ni si évidentes ni si assurées qu'elles puissent dès à présent justifier des appellations distinctes. Ainsi, la présence de lamelles à dos arqué, de pointes de la Mouillah ou de la technique du microburin dans les industries du groupe de Mushabi au Sinaï (Phillips et Mintz 1977) ne suffit pas à en faire une industrie essentiellement différente du Kébarien au sens large et ne paraît pas justifier l'introduction d'un "Mushabien". La littérature s'encombre progressivement de termes qui n'ont même pas le mérite de l'euphonie! Pourquoi ne pas parler simplement d'un Kébarien à géométriques du Sinaï, voire de Mushabi, ou de telle couche d'un des gisements de Mushabi. De même pour Jabroud. On conçoit très bien des variantes géographiques ou biogéographiques et il importe de les souligner.

On s'attend à ce qu'un Natoufien du Néguev se distingue d'un Natoufien de Galilée, un Natoufien "méditerranéen" d'un Natoufien de la zone semi-aride, mais dans l'état actuel des connaissances, et tant que ces variantes ne pourront être définies avec toute la précision souhaitable, il suffira de les désigner selon leur province. On saura gré à M.-C. Cauvin de s'en tenir à un Kébarien à géométriques et à un Natoufien de la cuvette d'el Kowm! De même, les variantes chronologiques, lorsqu'elles peuvent être établies, seront exprimées de manière satisfaisante, pour l'instant, par "ancien, moyen et récent". On parlera clairement d'un Natoufien récent du Moyen Euphrate, etc.

La difficulté de la séquence lithique réside surtout dans le fait que ses termes se chargent d'ambiguïté au fur et à mesure que l'on avance dans le temps et que s'étendent les catégories de matériel archéologique. Nous sommes ici au point d'articulation de deux méthodologies, celle de la préhistoire proprement dite et celle de la préhistoire récente et de la protohistoire. La séquence lithique est venue se confondre dans la pratique avec la séquence culturelle. Si le Kébarien "ancien" évoque encore, pour l'essentiel, un outillage en silex, le "Kébarien à géométriques" associe déjà à l'industrie du silex des fonds de cabane, avec un outillage lourd, en pierre, important. Quant au terme *Natoufien* il fait naître aussitôt l'image d'une culture matérielle riche et variée qui ne s'applique évidemment pas à tous les gisements ou niveaux à industrie natoufienne. La confusion s'installe vite entre les deux sens, lithique et culturel, du terme. Il importe donc de préciser dans quel sens on l'emploie.

En ce qui concerne le Natoufien — au sens strict du terme appliqué à l'outillage en silex — ses variantes chronologiques, écologiques, technologiques, typologiques, ou stylistiques ne sont pas encore définies avec précision. La seule subdivision du Natoufien que l'on ait pu introduire jusqu'ici avec un semblant d'assurance repose sur l'évolution techno-typologique des segments de cercle, là où elle a pu être observée sur des bases stratigraphiques, c'est-à-dire à Mallaha et à Hayonim. Les patientes analyses de Bar-Yosef et Valla (1979) ont confirmé l'intuition de Neuville et ont permis à ces auteurs de proposer un *Natoufien ancien* et un *Natoufien récent*, en attendant sans doute la définition d'un Natoufien moyen, qu'ils paraissent pressentir. En dehors de cette distinction, qui semble fondée, il serait préférable de s'en tenir pour les industries à des distinctions d'ordre géographique ou biogéographique, sans faire de chaque autre site un site éponyme.

La fin de la période marquée par le Natoufien voit s'amplifier la variabilité technologique, typologique, et stylistique des outillages; ceux-ci sont généralement caractérisés sur cet horizon par des outils typiques tels que pointe de flèche, tranchet, pic, hache, etc. Les gisements d'el Khiam, d'Oren, et de Jéricho (Tell es Sultan) qui ont livré ce matériel ont donné naissance à un "Khiamien", à un "Sultanien", auxquels est venu s'ajouter plus récemment un "Harifien". Sans doute conviendra-t-il un jour d'introduire de nouvelles appellations pour rendre compte des différents aspects de l'industrie lithique sur cet horizon. Pour l'instant, ces distinctions sont prématurées en raison de l'insuffisance qualitative des données sur lesquelles elles reposent.

Le matériel archéologique d'el Khiam et du N. Oren n'a pas été recueilli dans des conditions stratigaphiques satisfaisantes. Les couches d'el Khiam, sur un talus en forte pente, sont de nature géologique; elles résultent de l'érosion des dépôts formés en avant des abris qui s'ouvrent au pied de la falaise. Les niveaux de la terrasse d'Oren (O. Fallah) (T. Noy et al. 1973) n'ont pu être séparés avec la rigueur nécessaire.

Les niveaux "Proto-neolithic" de Jéricho, qui ont donné un "Proto-sultanien", ont été fouillés sur 5 m². Au-dessus, le matériel archéologique des niveaux p.p.n.a. se distingue surtout par la présence de haches cylindriques en basalte à taillant ogival poli. L'outillage en silex reste dans la tradition du Natoufien. Les niveaux de Jéricho devraient permettre d'introduire des distinctions au cours d'une période qui, à en juger par la puissance des dépôts, a dû être longue; mais les données actuelles sont insuffisantes; il faut attendre la publication et, éventuellement, une reprise de l'exploration.

L'industrie des sites de la montagne de Harif, dans le Néguev, et des hauteurs du Sinaï (Marks 1973; Phillips 1977) présente moins d'affinités avec la tradition natoufienne et devra être distinguée. Sa position cependant demeure incertaine. Du point de vue de l'évolution technologique et typologique, on notera que la "pointe de Harif", petite pièce à dos ou troncature oblique, souvent pédonculée, n'est pas une véritable pointe de flèche comme l'a justement fait remarquer A. Marks (1973) ni un outil spécifique au même titre, par exemple, qu'une hachette. Dans son ensemble, et en considération de son contexte culturel, l'industrie de Harif paraît moins évoluée que celle de Jéricho. Dans ces conditions il est hasardeux de la placer sur l'horizon de celle des niveaux p.p.n.a. sur la base des seules déterminations radiométriques; d'autant plus que la position chronologique des niveaux de Jéricho n'est pas elle-même assurée.

Du point de vue économique, social, et culturel, certaines modifications peuvent être observées sur cet horizon, la plus notable concernant l'importance numérique de la population de Jéricho. Rien n'indique toutefois que le processus de "néolithisation" soit déjà amorcé.

Les niveaux p.p.n.a. de Jéricho n'ont livré aucune trace d'élevage des animaux. La culture des céréales n'y est pas davantage prouvée. La présence de deux grains de blé et de six grains d'orge ne permet pas de conclure à une "mutation des stratégies alimentaires" (Cauvin 1978). Les conclusions de M. Hopf (1969) sont réservées. On ne trouve pas dans les niveaux p.p.n.a. de Jéricho ces "innovations décisives" qui marquent la "phase III" de Mureybet. Le polissage de la pierre n'est pas une nouveauté en Palestine; il était attesté dans le Natoufien ancien, notamment à Mallaha. Le seule nouveauté est la présence d'obsidienne qui pourrait indiquer une influence septentrionale en Palestine. Pour le reste, les niveaux p.p.n.a. de Jéricho se rattachent nettement à ce qui précède et non à ce qui suit.

Pour ces raisons, et dans l'attente d'une information plus complète, l'horizon des niveaux p.p.n.a. de Jéricho, pour individualisé qu'il paraisse, ne doit pas être séparé de l'horizon du Natoufien proprement dit, le terme *Natoufien* étant pris ici dans son sens culturel le plus large. Il serait préférable pour l'instant de rassembler sous l'appellation de *Natoufien final* ou d'Epinatoufien les complexes archéologiques entrevus à el Khiam, au N. Oren, à Jéricho p.p.n.a., etc. Il conviendrait en tout cas d'abandonner le sigle p.p.n.a. qui tend à renforcer l'idée d'une continuité entre cette phase de développement et celle que représentent les niveaux p.p.n.b. de Jéricho. Cette continuité, en effet, n'est pas évidente; le fouilleur la récuse formellement: "there is an absolute break stratigraphically, structurally and in all equipment between A and B" (Kenyon 1959).

Les niveaux p.p.n.b. de Jéricho apportent une première et timide indication d'un proto-élevage et d'une proto-agriculture; peut-être même, avec l'introduction de *T. monococcum*, peut-on parler d'un début de culture des céréales. Ce brusque développement, qu'attestent encore d'autres traits technologiques, typologiques, et culturels, a conduit à conclure à une influence extérieure et à rechercher hors de Palestine et plus précisément dans la province syrienne (Perrot 1968) la phase formative de cette civilisation.

En considération de l'indéniable homogénéité technologique, économique, et culturelle que l'on observe sur cet horizon dans les provinces du Levant, du Taurus au Sinaï, on n'a pas tardé à utiliser hors de Palestine le sigle p.p.n.b. forgé pour les niveaux p.p.n.b. de Jéricho et les niveaux des sites palestiniens contemporains. On peut certes adopter cette appellation pour l'ensemble de la région et parler d'un p.p.n.b. du Levant; il faut préciser cependant que ce terme n'est illustré en Palestine, où il est né, que sous un aspect "moyen"; la phase "ancienne" ou "formative" du p.p.n.b. du Levant n'est pas représentée en Palestine ailleurs, peut-être, qu'à Beidha où les niveaux 5−3 permettent d'assister, en ce qui concerne le plan des habitations, à une évolution comparable à celle enregistrée à Mureybet III−IV. De même la phase finale du p.p.n.b., telle qu'elle est décrite sur les sites septentrionaux avec la généralisation de l'usage de la céramique, n'est pas connue en Palestine tout au moins sur les sites du bassin jordanien; ceux-ci paraissent avoir été abandonnés avant l'introduction de la céramique.

La durée de la phase "ancienne" du p.p.n.b. est difficile à apprécier. En Palestine cette phase correspond, à Jéricho, au hiatus observé par K. Kenyon entre les niveaux p.p.n.a. et p.p.n.b. On prendra en considération les observations stratigraphiques de K. Kenyon: "Jericho of the p.p.n.a. stage comes to an abrupt end. Over the remains of the first phase appears an entirely new type of occupation. A period of erosion intervenes between the two, with buildings on the edge of the mound denuded, and rain water gullies cutting down to a considerable depth in more than one place. It is, however, impossible to estimate whether the erosion was the result of a succession of heavy rains in a single winter or whether it took place over decades" (Kenyon 1967, p. 271). Et ailleurs: "This break corresponds to a layer of soft silt over the tower in squares D1 + F1 and to the silting up against the face of the great wall" (Kenyon 1956, p. 73). On est davantage tenté d'évaluer la durée de cette période en décennies, sinon en siècles, plutôt qu'en jours de pluies d'un mauvais hiver. L'hypothèse d'envahisseurs "B" détruisant les défenses de la ville "A" est peu vraisemblable. On notera à ce propos que la gracilisation du squelette des hommes de Palestine est un phénomène attesté dès le Natoufien ancien (Crognier et Dupouy-Madre 1974) et qu'il ne saurait être mis en relation avec le hiatus p.p.n.a.–p.p.n.b. de Jéricho.

Les niveaux p.p.n.b. de Jéricho ont leur équivalent à Beidha (niveaux supérieurs) et, en Palestine cisjordane, à Munhata (6–3), à Beisamoun et à Abou Gosh. Il n'y a plus aucune raison, à la suite des fouilles conduites de 1968 à 1972 par M. Lechevallier à Beisamoun et à Abou Gosh (Lechevallier 1978), d'abaisser la date de ces gisements, comme j'avais proposé de le faire (Perrot 1968) sur la base d'indices fournis par des ramassages de surface. J'avais cru alors pouvoir conclure à une occupation des sites de la zone méditerranéenne de Palestine prolongée au-delà de l'abandon des villages de la zone semi-aride du bassin jordanien. Cette idée reste correcte, semble-t-il, en ce qui concerne les établissements de la région côtière (Ascalon, Givat ha-Parsa); mais il faut l'écarter en ce qui concerne Abou Gosh, dans la montagne de Jérusalem, et Beisamoun, dans la haute vallée du Jourdain, au bord du lac Houleh. Rien ne permet de penser que ces sites ont été occupés plus longtemps que Munhata, Jéricho, ou Beidha; des modifications climatiques et biogéographiques défavorables ne suffiraient donc pas à expliquer la brusque disparition des villages de la vallée du Jourdain avant la fin du VIIᵉ millénaire.

Sur le plan de l'économie et de l'évolution sociale on s'accorde généralement pour reconnaître que Jéricho (niveaux p.p.n.b.) et, dans leur ensemble, les sites p.p.n.b. du Levant représentent l'horizon des *premiers villages*, notion correspondant au "level of primary village farming communities" de R. J. Braidwood.

Précédemment, sur l'horizon du Natoufien au sens large, la Palestine a connu un niveau de *cueillette intensive à large spectre* avec, là où les ressources naturelles sont suffisantes en toute saison — et la pêche joue alors un rôle plus important peut-être que celui des céréales — l'apparition d'*établissements permanents*. Cette permanence elle-même devient facteur de développement technologique (techniques de construction des habitations, de fabrication et usage de la chaux, techniques relatives à la conservation et à la préparation des aliments, polissage de la pierre, etc.).

Le passage du stade "cueillette intensive à large spectre" avec "village" occasionnel au stade des "premiers villages" se fait en Palestine de manière abrupte, discontinue, cette discontinuité se plaçant sur l'horizon du premier hiatus stratigraphique (p.p.n.a.–p.p.n.b.) de Jéricho. Les données actuelles de l'archéologie ne permettent pas d'étudier ce changement en Palestine ailleurs peut-être qu'à Beidha, dont on attend la publication définitive. Le gisement de Hatula, dans les collines de Judée (Ronen et Lechevallier 1980), paraît correspondre à cet horizon, mais son exploration ne fait que commencer. Dans l'état actuel des recherches, c'est en Syrie seulement, à Mureybet, sur le Moyen Euphrate, à travers les niveaux de la Phase III, que l'on observe les modifications qui interviennent alors et nous font franchir le seuil entre les deux stades de développement. D'où l'intérêt exceptionnel de Mureybet et des sites sur cet horizon.

Une remarque s'impose ici concernant le terme *village*. Le caractère permanent de l'occupation du site de Mallaha a paru suffisamment évident pour que s'impose, faute de mieux, le terme *village* pour désigner une agglomération d'une vingtaine d'habitations, à en juger par ce que l'on sait de l'étendue du gisement et de la densité de l'occupation dans les 300 m² du secteur fouillé (Perrot 1968). Il convient cependant d'écrire "village" entre guillemets. On parle couramment aujourd'hui de village de pêcheurs; et Mallaha pourrait être considéré comme tel, étant donné l'abondance remarquable des restes de poisson. Mais dans le contexte qui est celui du Natoufien, sur un horizon où se pose justement le problème de savoir où se placent les premières tentatives de production des aliments, il n'est pas indifférent d'employer un terme dont le sens accepté est celui "d'agglomération d'habitations construites, occupées de façon permanente par des gens qui produisent leur nourriture".

On préférera en tout cas le terme *village* à l'expression *camp de base* qui implique un système de relations avec un ou plusieurs établissements satellites. Le schème se conçoit dans le Zagros en fonction de la transhumance: à un campement d'été sur le plateau correspond un village ou campement d'hiver dans le piémont. Mais rien d'analogue n'a jamais été observé en Palestine; les relations supposées entre tel ou tel établissement natoufien relèvent de la simple conjecture.

Devant les difficultés que rencontre la construction d'un cadre à partir des données stratigraphiques et des considérations d'ordre archéologique, typologique, économique, ou culturel; devant l'insuffisance actuelle des données; devant aussi l'ambiguïté de la terminologie traditionnelle, il a pu paraître souhaitable de faire table rase et de proposer un cadre indépendant qui s'appuierait sur les déterminations radiométriques, aujourd'hui plus nombreuses.

Certes, les datations par le C^{14} ont donné à la préhistoire récente du Proche-Orient une profondeur naguère insoupçonnée. Neuville et Garrod, il y a cinquante ans, dataient le Natoufien du VIᵉ millénaire avant l'ère chrétienne. On s'accorde aujourd'hui pour le placer entre le XIᵉ et le IXᵉ millénaires avant l'ère chrétienne.

Les déterminations radiométriques offrent un degré satisfaisant de fiabilité lorsqu'elles sont nombreuses et cohérentes; ces conditions, toutefois, ne sont pas souvent réunies. Même alors, les déterminations radiométriques ne sauraient à elles seules autoriser des rapprochements; surtout lorsque ces rapprochements ne sont pas en accord avec les indications de la stratigraphie et de l'archéologie. Un cadre construit sur des données stratigraphiques et archéologiques peut recevoir une dimension chronologique relative des datations C^{14}; mais les datations C^{14} à elles seules ne permettent pas d'établir un tel cadre.

Elles le pourraient qu'on se heurterait à d'autres difficultés. A partir du moment où les corrections par la dendrochronologie ne sont plus, pour l'instant, possibles, c'est-à-dire au-delà du VIᵉ millénaire, le calendrier C^{14} présente des décalages importants avec l'âge réel. L'écart est de 600 ans environ au VIᵉ millénaire; il s'accroît peut-être encore au-delà; à moins qu'il ne se réduise et se manifeste en sens inverse (Evin 1980). Le calendrier C^{14} présente donc par rapport au calendrier en âge réel des écrasements ou des étirements qui sont loin d'être négligeables, et qui faussent l'idée que l'on peut se faire de la vitesse de l'évolution et du dynamisme historique. Que peuvent valoir dans ces conditions des rapprochements serrés de province à province sur la base de synchronismes radiométriques?

Dans l'état actuel de la question il ne paraît d'ailleurs pas nécessaire de s'enfermer dans la fausse précision de tranches de temps dont les indicatifs devront demain être modifiés. Une approximation de l'ordre du demi-millénaire sur l'horizon du Natoufien, par exemple, correspond à la précision, qui est de 5%, et jugée fort satisfaisante, qu'apporte couramment en Palestine, sur l'horizon du premier millénaire avant l'ère chrétienne, le calendrier céramique; la marge d'erreur est de ± 25 ans; la précision est la même, de l'ordre du demi-siècle, pour le IIᵉ millénaire, et de l'ordre du siècle pour le IIIᵉ millénaire, ce qui est suffisant pour les reconstructions que l'on peut espérer faire aujourd'hui. Sur l'horizon de l'Epipaléolithique, une précision de l'ordre du demi-millénaire, calculée sur une moyenne des déterminations C^{14} apparues en longues séries cohérentes, suffit pour déterminer la position chronologique relative des grandes entités archéologiques et culturelles.

En conclusion, tout en reconnaissant la nécessité d'introduire un ordre nouveau, il serait préférable de ne pas bouleverser trop vite le fragile équilibre du cadre et de la terminologie en usage, mais de prendre conscience de ses faiblesses et de rechercher les moyens d'y remédier. Il est certainement peu satisfaisant de recourir au vocabulaire de la séquence lithique, à des termes tels que "Kébarien" et "Natoufien" pour désigner au-delà des complexes industriels les grandes entités archéologiques et culturelles de l'Epipaléolithique. Parler de "Natoufien final" suffit mal à rendre compte de l'évolution buissonnante apparente sur cet horizon. De même, à la période suivante, l'emploi du sigle p.p.n.b. ne soulève guère moins de difficultés que l'emploi du terme *Néolithique*. Il convient cependant de conserver provisoirement ces termes pour une première mise en place générale des faits raisonnablement établis. A l'intérieur des enveloppes larges ainsi délimitées, il existe incontestablement des variantes technologiques, typologiques, stylistiques, écologiques et culturelles; toutefois, ces variantes ne sont pas encore identifiées et leur position relative n'est pas encore déterminée avec une suffisante certitude; les nommer dès à présent autrement que par référence aux sites ou aux régions qui les ont fait connaître ne peut que conduire à obscurcir le tableau en donnant une égale importance aux grandes lignes et aux détails.

Le tableau ci-dessous apparaîtra donc comme en retrait des connaissances actuelles. Il n'a d'autre prétention que de fournir un point de départ, une référence intelligible, soulignant les points d'articulation et les problèmes de la séquence palestinienne.[1]

Millénaires av. J.C.	Stades de développement	Entités archéologiques et culturelles		Sites clés de Palestine
XVIIIe−XVIe	EPIPALEOLITHIQUE — cueillette intensive à large spectre — "villages"	KEBARIEN	"classique"	Kebara
XVIe−XIe		KEBARIEN	à géométriques	Haon III
XIe−IXe		NATOUFIEN	ancien (moyen)	Mallaha 4−2, Hayonim
IXe−VIIIe		("PPNA")	récent final	Mallaha 1b / Jericho p.p.n.a.
			--	hiatus p.p.n.a.−p.p.n.b.
VIIIe−VIIe	premiers villages	"PPNB"	moyen	Beidha 5−3 (?) / Jericho p.p.n.b. / Munhata 6−3
			--	(Grand hiatus palestinien)
				Munhata 2B (Shaar Hagolan)

1. Je tiens à remercier mes collègues O. Bar-Yosef et F. Valla qui ont bien voulu relire un premier état de cette note et me faire part de leurs observations. Achevée après le colloque "Préhistoire du Levant", organisé par le CNRS à Lyon du 10 au 14 juin 1980, cette note n'ignore pas le schéma chronologique présenté à ce colloque par O. Aurenche, J. Cauvin, M.-C. Cauvin, L. Copeland, F. Hours, et P. Sanlaville, "Chronologie et organisation de l'espace dans le Proche Orient de 12.000 à 5.600 av. J.C."; elle tient compte aussi de remarques faites par O. Aurenche et J. Cauvin relatives à la région palestinienne; ces remarques m'ont amené à souligner quelques aspects de la préhistoire palestinienne qui n'avaient peut-être pas été suffisamment mis en évidence jusqu'ici.

Bibliographie

Bar-Yosef, O.
1970   The Epi-Palaeolithic cultures of Palestine. Ph.D. diss., Hebrew University, Jerusalem.

Bar-Yosef, O., et Valla, F.R.
1979   L'évolution du Natoufien: nouvelles suggestions. *Paléorient* 5:145–52.

Cauvin, J.
1978   *Les premiers villages de Syrie-Palestine du IXe au VIIe millénaire avant J-C.* Collection de la Maison de l'Orient Méditerranéen Ancien 4, Série Archéologique, 3. Lyon: Maison de l'Orient.

Crognier, E., et Dupouy-Madre, M.
1974   Les Natoufiens du Nahal Oren, Israël: étude anthropologique. *Paléorient* 2(1):103–201.

Evin, J.
1980   Communication personnelle.

Hopf, M.
1969   Plant remains and early farming in Jericho. In *The domestication and exploitation of plants and animals*, ed.P.J. Ucko and G.W. Dimbleby, pp. 355–60. London: Duckworth.

Hours, F.
1974   Remarques sur l'utilisation de listes types pour l'étude du Paléolithique supérieur et de l'Epipaléolithique du Levant. *Paléorient* 2(1):3–18.

Kenyon, K.
1956   Excavations at Jericho. *Palestine Exploration Quarterly* 88:67–82.
1959   Some observations on the beginnings of settlement in the Near East. *Journal of the Royal Anthropological Institute* 89:34–43.
1967   Jericho. *Archaeology* 20(4):268–75.

Lechevallier, M.
1978   *Abou Gosh et Beisamoun: deux gisements du VIIe millénaire avant l'ère chrétienne en Israël.* Mémoires et Travaux du Centre de Recherches Préhistoriques Français de Jérusalem, vol. 2. Paris: Association Paléorient.

Marks, A.
1973   The Harif point: a new tool type from the terminal Epi-Palaeolithic of the central Negev, Israel. *Paléorient* 1(1):97–99.

Neuville, R.
1934   Le préhistorique de Palestine. *Revue Biblique* 43:237–59.

Noy, T.; Legge, A.J.; and Higgs, E.S.
1973   Recent excavations at Nahal Oren, Israel. *Proceedings of the Prehistoric Society* 39:75–99.

Perrot, J.
1966   Le gisement Natoufien de Mallaha (Eynan), Israël. *L'Anthropologie* 70(5/6):437–83.
1968   La préhistoire palestinienne. In *Supplément au dictionnaire de la Bible*, no. 8, cols. 286–446. Paris: Letouzey et Ané.

Phillips, J.L.
1977   The Harifian. In *Prehistoric investigations in Gebel Mayhara, northern Sinai*, O. Bar-Yosef and J.L. Phillips, pp. 199–218. Monographs of the Institute of Archaeology, Hebrew University, Qedem 7. Jerusalem: Hebrew University.

Phillips, J.L., and Mintz, E.
  1977   The Mushabian. In *Prehistoric investigations in Gebel Mayhara, northern Sinai*, O. Bar-Yosef and J.L. Phillips, pp. 149–63. Monographs of the Institute of Archaeology, Hebrew University, Qedem 7. Jerusalem: Hebrew University.

Ronen, A., et Lechevallier, M.
  1980   *Hatula 1980*. Rapport au Département des Antiquités d'Israël. Unpublished mimeograph.

LATE PLEISTOCENE—EARLY HOLOCENE CULTURAL TRADITIONS IN THE ZAGROS AND THE LEVANT

Rose L. Solecki and Ralph S. Solecki

INTRODUCTION

THIS paper deals with the late Pleistocene and early Holocene cultures of the Near East, specifically those of the Levant and the Zagros region where we have the most relevant archeological information. This period ranges from ca. 15,000 B.C. to 8000 B.C.,[1] and although the cultures in the two regions may be viewed roughly as belonging to the same horizon, differences reflecting local environmental conditions, traditions, and contacts are evident. Of the two regions, the Levant is the much better known, through extensive work in northern and central Palestine, the Negev, the Sinai, and Lebanon.

A word about terminology is needed here, as different designations are used in various parts of the Near East for roughly similar, coeval cultures. In the Levant, the term *Epipaleolithic* is used to include all the microlithic industries that postdate the Levantine Aurignacian C and predate the Pre-Pottery Neolithic (Bar-Yosef 1975, p. 363). Henry and Servello (1974, p. 23) note that the Epipaleolithic may be divided into two phases: an earlier one, characterized by a continuation of the regional Upper Paleolithic lithic tool traditions, with a subsistence base, site size, and settlement patterns little different from the local Upper Paleolithic ones, and a later one (ca. 10,000 B.C. to 8000 B.C.), which witnessed a major shift in the subsistence base from hunting to greater emphasis on plant collecting and even some domestication of animals. For the Zagros region we prefer to separate this time span (from ca. 15,000 B.C. to 8000 B.C.) into two distinct sections and assign one to the very end of the Paleolithic and one to the very beginning of the Neolithic. We propose restricting the term *Epipaleolithic*, at this writing, to the Zarzian culture and use the term *Protoneolithic* (R.L. Solecki 1964; R.S. Solecki 1963) for the Zawi Chemi/Karim Shahir complex. We prefer this system for the Zagros because, on the basis of subsistence, settlement pattern, and technology, the Zarzian seems clearly to represent the very end of the Paleolithic way of life while the Zawi Chemi/Karim Shahir seems to foreshadow the Neolithic. In addition, the Zagros cultures at this time do not seem to have utilized the microlithic technology to as great an extent as those in the Levant, nor is the microburin technique characteristic of any known Zagros lithic industry. Also, microlithic tools continue in use in later Neolithic contexts in the Zagros, e.g., Jarmo (Braidwood and Howe 1960, p. 44), and other sites as well; and in other parts of the world microlithic industries are even found in still later contexts. As a final note, we do not feel that the term *Mesolithic* is appropriate for these early village sites that we would call Protoneolithic.

THE CULTURES

The Epipaleolithic cultural picture of the Levant seems to be extremely complex. Briefly discussed here will be those well-described cultural units that seem relevant to this study. Some of these units belong to widespread industrial phases; others — e.g., the Moshabian, the Negev Kebaran, and the Harifian — appear to be limited to parts of the Negev and the northern Sinai. The Kebaran is the earliest of the Levant Epipaleolithic cultures, with radiocarbon dates

---

1. All the radiocarbon dates in this paper follow Henry and Servello (1974).

ranging from ca. 16,000 B.C. to 12,000 B.C. Bar-Yosef (1975, pp. 364, 368) has suggested a beginning date of from 18,000 B.C. to 15,000 B.C. for the Kebaran and that it lasted 3,000 years. Sites are concentrated near the Mediterranean coast of Palestine, in a number of open sites and some caves.

A summary of the Kebaran follows (ibid., p. 368). Microliths (retouched and backed bladelets) form from 50% to 90% of the total assemblage, and geometric microliths (e.g., trapezes and scalene triangles) occur in many of these assemblages. Other tool groups that are well represented are scrapers, burins, truncated pieces, and notches and denticulates. Also present in several Kebaran sites are rare bone tools (mainly points and burnishers) and grinding and pounding stones. Dentalium shells are already present in small numbers in the Kebaran and the Geometric Kebaran A. At Ein Gev I there seems to be evidence for a hut dug into a sandy hill, outlined by a shallow basin 5 m to 7 m in diameter.

Although the Geometric Kebaran A is not as well known as the Kebaran, its stratigraphic position is recorded from a number of sites, and a date of ca. 12,500 B.C. has been proposed as the beginning date (Marks 1977, p. 11). Bar-Yosef (1975, p. 369) has suggested that at several sites there seems to be a direct typological connection with the earlier Kebaran.

A description of the Geometric Kebaran A industry follows (ibid, p. 369). The trapezes-rectangles (occasionally with a few triangles and lunates) constitute at least half of the microlithic category, and at several sites these tools constitute an absolute majority. They have been added to the classic Kebaran tool inventory. Scrapers made on blades are most numerous. The appearance of the microburin techniques is noted, but they cannot yet be considered a traditional element. Pounding and grinding tools are associated. At the site of Iraq ez-Zigan, Wreschner and Ronen (1975) report rectangular and round stone-walled structures associated with a Geometric Kebaran industry, probably Geometric Kebaran A.

The Geometric Kebaran A is the earliest Epipaleolithic culture in the central Negev (Marks 1977, p. 6) and northern Sinai (Bar-Yosef and Phillips 1977, p. 115), and for the northern Sinai there is the possibility of at least a partial contemporaneity of the Geometric A and the Moshabian (ibid, pp. 142–43).

The Moshabian has been radiocarbon-dated from sites in the central Negev and the northern Sinai to ca. 12,000 B.C. to 11,000 B.C., a span of some 1,000 years (ibid, p. 182). It shares a number of tool types with the Geometric Kebaran A, but unlike the latter it has a well-developed microburin technique and large numbers of arch backed bladelets. Bar-Yosef and Phillips (ibid, p. 183) report that the Moshabian bears a striking resemblance in some features to assemblages found in North Africa and the Nile Valley.

The Negev Kebaran, divided into an early and a late phase, has been identified for the central Negev region as a separate unit within the larger Kebaran complex (Marks and Simmons 1977), although no radiocarbon dates are available. It may possibly derive from the Moshabian, and the early phase (Harif) could be contemporary with the Moshabian (Marks 1977, p. 25). The late phase (Helwan) has a suggested contemporaneity with the Early Natufian, ca. 10,000 B.C. to 9000 B.C. The Negev Kebaran is placed in the Kebaran complex because of the importance of its microlithic industry, with its emphasis on the production of nongeometric microliths (especially backed and truncated bladelets); but the microburin technique is characteristic, and in the late phase, Helwan lunates are added to the inventory.

The term *Geometric Kebaran B* has been used by Bar-Yosef (1970, 1975) to refer to a number of assemblages with typological traits different from, but yet reminiscent of, the Natufian. There appears to be some cultural overlap with materials from the Helwan phase of the Negev Kebaran, and the nature of the relationships between these industries is not altogether clear.

The Natufian, dated at ca. 10,000 B.C. to 8000 B.C., ushers in important cultural changes in the Levant. Sites are much larger, and the villages were possibly settled year-round. Bar-Yosef (1975,

p. 371) reports important differences in intrasite activity at Natufian sites and the earlier Kebaran. At the Natufian sites much energy was devoted to excavation, building, and the making of ground stone tools. Also there are elaborate burials with grave furnishings and art pieces and personal adornments. Although no evidence has been found for the domestication of plants (or animals), the presence of food-processing tools, sickle blades, and possibly storage pits suggests that plant material was being intensively exploited. The flint industry has been summarized by Henry and Servello (1974, p. 24): ". . . high frequencies of geometric microliths (primarily lunates), pieces bearing sheen (sickle blades), and large massive pieces (scrapers, denticulates and notches). In addition to these diagnostic tool types, the microburin technique is associated with the Natufian, particularly from those assemblages of southern Palestine."

Natufian sites have a wide distribution in the Levant. Evidence now seems to indicate that two chronological divisions are present in the Natufian: an earlier phase of more limited distribution within the Mediterranean vegetational zone and a later, more widespread phase of penetration into the Negev and other regions (Bar-Yosef 1975, p. 370). Henry (1974) points out that there is an obvious decrease in the use of the Helwan retouch technique from Early to Late Natufian and an opposite trend in the use of microburin technique during the entire Natufian period. Bar-Yosef (1975, p. 370) suggests the Geometric Kebaran A assemblages of the northern Levant as one possible source for the Natufian.

Long-range contacts within the Levant are evident during the Natufian period. Basalt objects are common in Natufian sites, far from the source of this material in eastern Galilee. Dentalium shells were traded from the Mediterranean Sea inland and from the Red Sea northward.

The Harifian, like the earlier Moshabian and Negev Kebaran, was a local Negev/Sinai development dating after the Late Natufian penetration into the region. The Harifian seems to have been a short-lived culture, flourishing only from ca. 8200 B.C. to 8000 B.C., when increasing dessication forced the abandonment of village life in the area. Although there is a general similarity of the Harifian to the Natufian, Kebaran, and Moshabian, and the aceramic Neolithic, it is felt to be different enough to deserve a separate industry designation (Scott 1977, p. 284). The Harifian industry has been summarized by Marks (1977, p, 25): it was basically a microlithic industry with such characteristic elements as Harif points; extensive use of the microburin technique; backed blades and bladelets; end scrapers, many and well made; strongly truncated pieces; minute lunates and triangles; and few burins. Massive tools were also an important element. Many of these have strong denticulate retouch; others, called choppers, resemble chipped axes, and picks are reported. Harifian ground-stone artifacts are noted for "their many forms, the use of a wide variety of raw materials, and the varying degrees of expertise exhibited in the use of this technological system" (Scott 1977, p. 308). All the grinding stones from the Harifian site of Abu Salem, it should be noted, were stained pink from ochre grinding. Bone tools were rare and were mainly piercing tools. Exotic materials in the form of shells come from both the Mediterranean Sea and the Red Sea; the latter, however, are more common, and there is evidence to suggest that some of the shells may have come from the Indian Ocean. The Harifian was characterized by large villages with circular or oval stone-walled houses. The economy was similar to that of the Natufian.

The Epipaleolithic/Protoneolithic sequence in the Zagros region is not as well known as that of the Levant, due to the limited amount of archeological investigation of sites of that period in the Zagros region. Only two cultures have been outlined in the Zagros during this time period, the Zarzian and the Zawi Chemi/Karim Shahir complex.

The Zarzian was first excavated at the type site, Zarzi, by D. Garrod in 1928 (Garrod 1930) and since then at Shanidar Cave (Solecki 1955, 1963), Palegawra (Braidwood and Howe 1960), Pa Sangar (Hole and Flannery 1967), Warwasi (Braidwood 1960), Ghar-i Khar (Young and Smith 1966), and Mar Ruz, Mar Gurgalan Sarab, and Dar Mar (Mortensen 1974, 1975). Several other occurrences, including a number of open sites, have been suggested as Zarzian (Braidwood and Howe 1960; Hole and Flannery 1967; Mortensen 1974; and Wright and Yaghmā'i n.d.), but certain Zarzian affiliation is not possible, we feel, without fuller cultural samples and/or radiocarbon dates. Hole and Flannery (1967, fig. 2) have suggested a time range of ca. 20,000 B.C. to 10,000 B.C. for the Zarzian, but the radiocarbon dates from Shanidar and Palegawra are limited to the later part of this time range: Shanidar B2 is dated at 10,050±400 B.C., and Palegawra has five dates that range from 12,530±75 B.C. to 11,110±110 B.C. and one possibly contaminated date from 9640±95 B.C. Hole and Flannery (1967, p. 153), on the basis of their work in Luristan, believe that the Zarzian developed directly out of the Baradostian. This is not the situation at Shanidar Cave, where a time gap of ca. 15,000 years and a cultural gap are present between the earlier Baradostian (Upper Paleolithic) and the Zarzian (Epipaleolithic). However, for the upper end of the Zarzian sequence we see possible evidence in Shanidar valley for the direct development of the Zawi Chemi out of the Zarzian. Citing Hole and Flannery, this suggests a local Zagros sequence from the Baradostian to the Zarzian to Zawi Chemi. However, many more data are needed to substantiate this hypothesis and before we can understand the cultural processes that took place here.

The type site at Zarzi was dug by D. Garrod, and the material recovered was described in her report (1930). Recently Bar-Yosef (1970), as part of his study of the Epipaleolithic cultures of the Levant, restudied and reclassified part of the Zarzi material. The general discussion of the Zarzian (from Zarzi) that follows here incorporates both of these studies. It should be noted that Bar-Yosef (1970, p. 187) believes that more than one industry is present in the Zarzi layer.

At the site of Zarzi, according to Garrod (1930, pp. 22–23), somewhat less than 25% of the industry is microlithic; it includes a large number of microscrapers, followed by scalene triangles (some could be called backed blades with retouched or truncated ends), backed bladelets (some of which are almost lunate shaped), and a small number of burins. Garrod (ibid, p. 21) notes that the scalene triangle is the only geometric form found at Zarzi and that it was confined to the upper part of Layer B. She does not illustrate any microburins but does report (ibid.) that "one micro-graver of the Tardenoisian type was found."

According to Garrod (ibid, pp. 22–23), in the full-sized industry notched and denticulated pieces (primarily on blades) are most common, followed in popularity by a variety of scrapers (including such types as discoidal, rostrate, steep, core, and so forth), a rather large group of end scrapers on blades and flakes, also variable in size, backed blades (here are placed specimens Garrod called Gravette points as well as the backed blades), a small number of burins, and other minor types. She lists no borers, but Bar-Yosef (1970, p. 189) reports "there is a borer of the Natufian types and a small awl." Of special note is the presence of two shouldered points. Also of special note are two small fragments of obsidian. One of these has been analyzed for source and has been identified as coming from an Armenian source, Nemrud Dağ (Renfrew, Dixon, and Cann 1966, p. 42).

Also found in Layer B at Zarzi are two fragments of worked bone, one worked to a sharp point and the other shaped to a blunt point, a grooved stone of schist, and a schist pendant. These objects may be attributable to a Protoneolithic occupation at the site.

Shanidar Cave Layer B can be divided into two horizons, a lower one (B2), referable to a Zarzian occupation, and an upper one (B1), referable to the Zawi Chemi. The inhabitants of Shanidar Cave dug pits into the ground during both the Zarzian and the Protoneolithic periods, possibly for food storage.

When the material from Zarzi Layer B is compared to that of Shanidar Layer B it is evident that the two are closely related, although differences are present. Each contains a microlithic industry, which at first glance seems to be more important at Zarzi. However, if one removes the microscrapers from the microlithic category, which is evidently what Bar-Yosef (1970) has already done in his reappraisal, then at each of the two sites the proportion of the microlithic components to the chipped stone industry is quite similar — i.e., ca. 11%. The microlithic component at Shanidar Cave is composed primarily of backed blades, both those that are simple backed (with some tendency to curved or gibbous backs) and the more numerous ones with retouched ends. The latter grade into the scalene triangles, which are a popular geometric form. Other geometrics include lunates and rare isosceles triangles and trapezoids. Again one possible microburin is present.

Notched and denticulated pieces make up the largest category in the regular-sized tools, as at Zarzi. Also common at both sites are end scrapers, but much less frequent at Shanidar Cave are the thick-core scrapers so numerous at Zarzi (this apparent difference is no doubt due to differences in classification). It should be noted that these two groups, notched and denticulated pieces and end scrapers and other scrapers, make up more than 50% of the total chipped-stone industry. Burins are more common at Shanidar Cave (perhaps due to admixture from the Baradostian layer), as are borers. Backed blades occur in almost the same percentage at the two sites, and two shouldered points have also been found at Shanidar Cave. Important differences between the two assemblages are evident in the presence of the following items at Shanidar Cave and their absence at Zarzi: *pièces esquillées*, truncated pieces, truncated backed blades, and lunates. Obsidian also has been found at Shanidar Cave in Layer B; in fact, Layer B has proportionally the largest number of pieces of worked obsidian found in the cave (Solecki 1955, p. 412). None of the pieces from the Zarzian layer have been analyzed for source, but two from the Baradostian layer have (Renfrew, Dixon, and Cann 1966): one of these is from the Nemrud Dağ source in Armenia (as is the specimen from Zarzi); the other, on the basis of analysis, could have come from either a Cappodocian source or the Kars district in Armenia (to the north of Nemrud Dağ). The latter seems the more likely interpretation.

The site of Palegawra (Braidwood and Howe 1960) also contained a Zarzian occupation, also apparently mixed with later Zawi Chemi/Karim Shahir materials. Generally, the industry seems very much like that of Shanidar Cave. Braidwood and Howe (ibid, p. 58) note that it looks like a Late Zarzian phase, strongly marked by geometric microliths (scalene and isosceles triangles, trapezes, and one that looks like a crescent). Also characteristic are large numbers of backed blades and microlithic bladelets; various end, round, and other scrapers, both large and small; smaller, coarse side scrapers; various burins, drills, and fabricators; and a large number of notched and otherwise used flakes and blades. Howe also reports microburins, but no counts are given. Obsidian again is present here, worked into a number of tools. Some items (e.g., ground stone and bone objects) found in the Palegawra deposits must date from the Protoneolithic or even later.

Five cave/shelter sites containing Zarzian occupations have been tested in Iranian Kurdistan-Luristan and briefly described: Pa Sangar (Hole and Flannery 1967), Warwasi (Braidwood 1960), Ghar-i Khar (Young and Smith 1966), and Mar Ruz and Mar Gurgalan Sarab (Mortensen 1975).

The site of Pa Sangar Rock-shelter has both a Baradostian and a Zarzian occupation. Appearing for the first time in the Zarzian at Pa Sangar are notched blades and geometric microliths (including scalene triangles, crescents, and trapezoids); backed microlithic blades replace backed blades. Microburins are reported, but no counts are given. Unique to the Pa Sangar Zarzian were imported seashells used as ornaments; there were two large scallop shells, and scattered through the debris were a number of dentalium shells. Bone tools, especially awls, were fairly common beginning in the Baradostian, and unshaped sandstone abraders, occurring first in the lower Baradostian, were common in the Zarzian layers.

The rock-shelter of Warwasi and the cave of Ghar-i Khar are fairly close to each other, northeast of Kermanshah. Warwasi contains Mousterian, Baradostian, and Zarzian occupations. The Zarzian industry has been described by Braidwood (1960, p. 695): "Has the usual list of end and round scrapers, both normal and microlithic in size, some burins, and various forms of blunted backed microlithic bladelets and scalene triangles. It lacks not only the geometric microlithic lunates, trapezoids, and triangles, but also the larger, handsome backed blades found at some sites in Iraq." No mention is made of the notched and denticulated pieces so characteristic of other Zarzian sites. There is also no report of the microburin technique.

At the site of Ghar-i Khar, Young and Smith (1966) report several occupations from Middle Paleolithic to Upper Paleolithic, one of which has tentative cultural and temporal correlations with some phase of the Zarzian. This industry has tools that represent a continuation of earlier traditions, such as backed bladelets and blades, retouched blades, and certain scraper types. New elements found in this layer are microburins (one only, P.E.L. Smith, pers. comm.), triangles, truncated backed blades, Gravettelike points, and curved backed bladelets. Also present are the following items, which suggest later periods: chipped stone axes (?), grinding stones, and worked bone awls.

Mortensen's (1974, 1975) investigations in the Hulailian valley have turned up a number of cave/shelter, open-air, and single-find sites that are placed in the Upper Paleolithic period. At least three of the cave/shelter sites belong to the Zarzian period. Two of these sites, Mar Gurgalan Sarab and Mar Ruz, have been tested and have revealed a typical Zarzian industry: many small scrapers and notched/denticulated blades, some burins, rare shouldered points, backed blade-lets, and a small number of geometrics (Mortensen 1975).

Open-air Zarzian sites have also been reported from Iraqi Kurdistan, Luristan, and south-western Iran, but, as already discussed, more cultural and chronological information is needed for these locations.

To review, the Zarzian presently is definitely known from a number of cave/shelter sites, representing both base camps and temporary (butchering?) encampments; possible open-air sites have also been located. The known Zarzian cave/shelter sites can vary from quite small shelters to large cave sites such as Shanidar. They are characteristically located in the valleys of the broad Zagros mountain chain, but in a wide altitudinal zone ranging from Shanidar Cave at an elevation of ca. 750 m to Warwasi and Ghar-i Khar at over 1300 m, and in valleys of various sizes. All of the sites seem to have been chosen for their easy access to water, strategic location for long-range siting, and suitability as a domicile. Most, if not all, of them face south/southeast for good light and warmth, especially attractive during cold periods.

The Zarzian people seem to have been primarily hunters; there is no good evidence for the wide-scale use of plant food (e.g., from food processing tools such as querns, mullers, and so forth), although pits, possibly for food storage, have been found at Shanidar Cave. In culture, settlement, and subsistence strategy, the Zarzian, therefore, seems to fit well into an Epipaleo-lithic pattern.

The regular-sized chipped-stone tools (from Zarzi and Shanidar Cave, where counts are available) comprise ca. 75% to 90% of the total chipped-stone industry. This is certainly evidence that the Zarzian was not primarily a microlithic industry. Notched and denticulated pieces and scrapers of various types and sizes (including end, core, discoidal, thumbnail, etc.) are by far the most common tool types in the Zarzian industry. These are probably for the most part skin-working and woodworking tools. Backed blades are still an important element in most Zarzian sites but are lacking at Warwasi (Braidwood 1960, p. 695) and reported to have been replaced by backed bladelets at Pa Sangar (Hole and Flannery 1967, p. 159). Simple burins of various types are found in Zarzi sites in small to moderate numbers, and borers also are present. Rare shouldered points are found at Zarzi, Shanidar, and sites in the Hulailan valley. Shanidar Cave has *pièces esquillées* and crescents, items not yet reported from other Zarzian sites. The Zarzian layers from Zarzi, Shanidar Cave, and Palegawra, the three more westerly sites, all contain some obsidian pieces.

The Zarzian microlithic industry includes backed blades and backed blades with retouched ends ranging into scalene triangles. The scalene triangle is the most characteristic geometric microlithic form and apparently at some sites is the only geometric form. Present at Shanidar Cave, Pa Sangar, and Palegawra are rare lunates and trapezoids, and at Palegawra, even rarer rectangles, perhaps suggesting a somewhat later date for these sites. Only very rare occurrences of microburins have been reported for Zarzian sites, suggesting that this manufacturing technique was not commonly used for the production of geometric microliths or other items. No definite pieces with Helwan retouch are found at any of the Zarzian sites.

It should be pointed out here that Zarzi, Shanidar Cave, Palegawra, Ghar-i Khar, and possibly Pa Sangar contain objects characteristic of the later Protoneolithic period. In some cases these pieces may truly belong to the Zarzian occupation, but when many such tools are present or, as in the case of Shanidar Cave, a Protoneolithic cemetery is present, we feel certain that two separate and distinct occupations are indicated.

The second Zagros culture to be discussed here is best known from Shanidar Cave, Zawi Chemi Shanidar, and Karim Shahir. In this paper, for the sake of simplicity, we shall refer to the culture as Protoneolithic. Two radiocarbon dates have been obtained for it: 8920±300 B.C. from Zawi Chemi Shanidar and 8650±300 B.C. from Layer B1 at Shanidar Cave.

This culture (Braidwood and Howe 1960; R.L. Solecki 1964; and R.L. Solecki, 1981) is known from both cave and open village sites. The same sort of changes in settlement pattern, subsistence strategy, and technology that took place in the Levant in the immediate post-Pleistocene period were also taking place here in the Zagros. The site of Zawi Chemi Shanidar is an open village site with simple, rounded, stone-walled architecture. Plant food of some kind was being processed at the site in sizable amounts, to judge by the abundant milling stones found there, and a study of the animal bones suggests that sheep were being kept by the end of the Zawi Chemi occupation, although hunting was still important (Perkins 1964). There was an abundant pecked- and ground-stone industry, including such common types as mullers; querns; various abraders, pounders, hammerstones, pecking stones, and rubbers; grooved stones; shaped slabs; chipped celts with polished bits; ornamental items such as pendants and beads; and other miscellaneous pieces. There was also an important flaked-stone industry, characterized by choppers, very common spall tools, chisels, flake knives, and so forth. An important worked-bone industry was associated; it included such items as sharp pointed awls, blunt-ended tools, spatulas, handles for microliths and regular-sized blades, beads of various kinds, and so forth. Limited horn, antler, and ivory industries were also present. Some of the bone tools and even some of the stone pieces were decorated with simple designs (Solecki 1980).

A cemetery area and a single isolated burial were associated with the Zawi Chemi occupation of Shanidar Cave. The cemetery area contains 31 individuals in some 26 graves, or burials; including the one isolated burial, there is a total of 32 individuals. The Shanidar Cave burials and the associated grave goods exhibit a number of parallels with Natufian burials, the only comparable sample for this time period in the Near East. Fire was evidently used as a burial ritual in both areas, possibly for a funeral feast or other attribute. The one burial outside the cemetery, that of a "box burial" at Shanidar Cave, was associated with red ochre, which was found in a grinding stone interred with the individual, a woman. The stone pavings at Shanidar Cave were not found over the graves. Individuals were found in flexed burial positions in both areas, although at Shanidar Cave there was a variety of positions. Both the Shanidar Cave and the Natufian people interred their dead with burial goods. However, while the Natufians usually decorated the adults with beads, the Shanidar people placed the beads with children. One child was found with 1,500 beads. Some children were heavily decorated with beads, others hardly or not at all. There was no set compass direction for the burials, and they appear to have been buried in all directions, although more seem to be oriented to the east. Most of the Shanidar Cave burials appear to have been disturbed; only fourteen were found in sufficiently good condition to determine how the bodies had originally lain. Most of the burials had been placed in an area above a bed of charcoal and ashes; presumably these came from the hearths surrounding the cemetery area. The individuals were predominantly subadults.

Denise Fermbach (1970) studied the skeletal remains of eight individuals from Shanidar Cave. She puts them all into the Eurafrican type (Atlanto-Mediterranean) of the Proto-Mediterranean race. They constitute a local variety of a population presenting characteristics more modern than those of the Natufians of Palestine, who lived somewhat earlier and about the same time as the Zawi Chemi people of Shanidar Cave.

A summary of the Zawi Chemi chipped-stone industry follows. Microliths make up about 25% of the total chipped-stone tool count. Backed blades of various kinds are by far the most common microlith, and many of these are blades with retouched ends, which grade into the scalene triangle category. Of the classified geometrics only the lunates are common; triangles and trapezoids are very rare. Characteristic are several types of small-sized borers, denticulated or notched pieces, and truncated pieces.

As in the earlier Zarzian, in the full-sized lithic industry denticulated and notched pieces are most numerous, but here they are followed closely in popularity by a varied class of pieces lumped under the heading of *pièces esquillées*. Side scrapers of several different types — especially, thick ones, often with denticulated edges — and steep scrapers are also characteristic. End scrapers are poor specimens, being mainly crude ones on flakes. Borers are another characteristic type, especially the double-backed variety. Backed blades, truncated pieces, and crude burins occur in modest numbers.

In brief, the chipped stone industry of the Zawi Chemi culture seems to represent the very end of the Upper Paleolithic tradition. However, what characterizes it most are the new technologies and the whole host of new tool groups that foreshadow the Neolithic way of life.

COMPARISONS AND CONCLUSIONS

A preliminary statement on the environmental picture is necessary to set the background for the comparative discussions, even though environmental studies have not yet provided broad schemes for the Late Pleistocene — Early Holocene (ca. 15,000 B.C. to 8000 B.C.) in the Near East. In fact, Butzer (1977, p. 389) notes that "the results now available suggest that climatic changes within the Near East do not necessarily follow the same pattern from region to region; hence, broad interregional correlations are precluded." Discrete local conditions and local environmental changes (e.g., changes in sea levels and local rainfall patterns, tectonic activities, and so forth) make general interpretations difficult.

Horowitz (1977, p. 220) divides the Würm in Israel into three pluvial phases: Early, Middle, and Late. The Late Phase dates from ca. 14,000 B.C. to 9500 B.C., and thus the start of the Holocene is placed at ca. 9500 B.C. General agreement puts the beginning of the Holocene at about this time, and such a date is accepted in this paper. Horowitz (ibid., p. 223) notes that during the Würmian period almost all of Israel was occupied, that the northern and central parts of the country were well populated, and that during the wetter Atlantic period even the southern Negev and parts of Sinai were occupied. Recent studies in the central Negev add to this picture. Marks (1977, p. 5) has pointed out that this region in the very southern end of the Levant underwent climatic oscillations during the Würm, but its position would make these less intense and of shorter duration. By ca. 14,000 B.C. to 13,000 B.C. the central Negev was dry, and there is no evidence for human occupation (the same appears true for the northern Sinai as well). After ca. 12,500 B.C., climatic amelioration set in, and by 10,000 B.C. the climate of the central Negev was again of Mediterranean type. The Late Natufians spread to the area ca. 9000 B.C. as the climatic optimum was reached there. After 8000 B.C., drier conditions set in once again, and village life was abandoned in the region.

For parts of the Levant, at least, and based on a variety of evidence (geomorphic, pollen, flora and fauna, and so forth) Bar-Yosef (1977, p. 365) notes that "a shift from drier to humid and a return to drier conditions can be plotted for the period of 20,000–18,000 B.C. to 8000 B.C."

Pollen evidence from Lake Zeribar and other sites in the Zagros region has provided climatological evidence on the Late Quaternary and Early Holocene period (Van Zeist and Wright 1963; Van Zeist 1967). From ca. 12,000 B.C. onward, the evidence shows that although changes occurred slowly, the annual precipitation as well as the temperature increased, i.e., conditions gradually were becoming warmer and wetter. Mme. Leroi-Gourhan's study of the pollen from Zarzi (1976) indicates that at that time the environment at Zarzi was that of a steppe, very dry and cold, almost without trees. She believes that the pollen indicates the end of the steppe period, ca. 12,000 B.C., already mentioned for the Lake Zeribar area. She noted that cerealia-type pollens were extremely rare.

Of particular interest to the later phase of the time period discussed in this paper is the evidence relative to the development of agriculture. As Butzer (1977, p. 403) points out, there is no evidence to indicate that a post-Pleistocene dessication was related to the development of agriculture. In fact, he points out (ibid.) for the Levant-Zagros region, "Instead, the close of the Pleistocene opened up extensive arable lands and lush pastures in the high country." Pollen studies from Natufian, Harifian, and Zawi Chemi sites provide interesting data relevant to this subject. At both Rosh Horesha (Late Natufian) and Abu Salem (Harifian), sites in the Negev, Horowitz (1977, p. 324) has found evidence of cereal pollen, while none is present in the Recent spectrum. He further notes that the presence of cereal pollens at both sites (although presently it is not possible to determine if they came from wild or domesticated species), associated with plant-processing tools, suggests that cereal grasses were being used. Although these specimens may have come from wild plants collected in the region, the possibility that they were domesticated should not be ruled out. In reference to this, Horowitz (ibid., p. 326) concludes, "The absence of cereal pollen from temporally earlier spectra from the Central Negev (Horowitz 1976), however, supports the position that these cereals were, in fact, cultivated." A similar situation is present at the roughly coeval site of Zawi Chemi Shanidar. Mme. Leroi-Gourhan (in R. L. Solecki 1981), on the basis of her study of the pollen from the site, noted that during the Zawi Chemi occupation there was a definite increase in the gramineae pollen, cerealia type, which she feels could be ascribed to a change in agricultural techniques.

In the Levant, thanks to recent extensive archeological investigations, we have a fairly complete sequence for most of the time period under consideration here. The earliest, the Kebaran, which may be tentatively dated from 16,000/15,000 B.C. to 13,000/12,000 B.C., is followed by the Geometric Kebaran A, for which a beginning date of ca. 12,500 B.C. has been suggested. In the northern and central portion of the area, the Geometric Kebaran A is followed in the sequence by the Natufian (with a time range of ca. 10,000 B.C. to 8000 B.C.), while in the Negev and the northern Sinai a number of local cultures (e.g., Moshabian, Negev Kebaran, and Harifian) as well as a Late Natufian occupation fill in the later portion of the Epipaleolithic sequence. This appears to have been a rather complex period in Levantine prehistory, with numbers of local cultures reflecting local traditions, environmental factors, and perhaps contacts with cultures outside the immediate area.

The Zagros region has unfortunately not had such extensive archeological investigations in sites of this period, and our knowledge accordingly is much more limited. However, we can make some tentative comparisons, even on the basis of our presently limited knowledge. When we look at the radiocarbon dates for the Zarzian we find them all in the range of ca. 12,500 B.C. to 10,050

B.C., i.e., roughly the same date as for the Geometric Kebaran A and other coeval Levant industries. In the Zarzian, as in the Geometric Kebaran A, geometric microliths form an important part of the microlithic assemblage. Perhaps in much of the Zagros region it was too cold and dry for human occupation during the earlier part of the Epipaleolithic (i.e., from ca. 16,000 B.C. to 13,000 B.C.), at the time of the Kebaran in parts of the Levant. As noted above, the pollen sample from the site of Zarzi indicates a very dry and cold steppe environment (Leroi-Gourhan 1976). The radiocarbon dates from Shanidar Cave indicate a gap in the sequence of some 15,000 years, from ca. 25,000 B.C. to 10,050 B.C. It is difficult to see why so inviting a site as Shanidar Cave would have been left unoccupied for such a long time if the climatic/environmental picture was suitable for human activity. From Luristan, Hole and Flannery (1967) report a continuous developmental sequence from the Baradostian to the Zarzian. Perhaps climatic conditions were more favorable there and man was able to live there during the cold/dry period indicated for the Zagros at that time.

The Epipaleolithic cultures of the Levant and the Zagros obviously share many traits, and both may be viewed not only as the final carriers of a long-lived Paleolithic tradition but as cultural innovators as well. In both areas, at ca. 12,500/12,000 B.C., climatic conditions were beginning to ameliorate, and man began to move into new areas as areas became more suitable for human occupation. In the Levant, man was living in both open sites and caves. There is some evidence for the construction of stone-walled shelters at the open sites, and some pounding and grinding tools are associated. These Kebaran-related people were mainly hunters, although probably some plant food was being processed, as evidenced by the milling stones. Dentalium shells have also been reported from Kebaran and Geometric Kebaran sites. The Zarzian is definitely known from cave/shelter sites and possibly from open air sites as well. No architectural remains have been identified with the Zarzian. Zarzian peoples were hunters, and although they must have gathered wild foods as well, there is no good evidence (e.g., grinding stones) for the processing of grains. Perhaps this is a reflection of environmental conditions in the Zagros at that time. Some simple bone tools, primarily piercing tools, seem to be associated, and Hole and Flannery (1967) report that unshaped sandstone abraders are common in the Zarzian layers of Pa Sangar. They also report some dentalium shells, items not found at other Zarzian sites. More complex ground-stone pieces and other objects occur at a number of Zarzian sites, but there are problems of possible admixture with later, Protoneolithic materials.

Although microliths are found in both the Zarzian and the Kebaran/Geometric Kebaran industries it is important to note here that on the basis of the Zarzi and Shanidar Cave collections[2] the Zarzian, unlike the Kebaran, is not primarily a microlithic industry. In fact, only about 25% of the total chipped-stone industry at most could be put in the microlithic category. Notched and denticulated pieces and scrapers of various sizes and shapes make up well over 50% of the total chipped-stone industry. Of special note are the rare shouldered points found at two Zarzian sites, Zarzi and Shanidar Cave, at least. Obsidian occurs in varying amounts in at least three of the known Zarzian sites. Obsidian from two of these sites has been provenienced, and in both cases an Armenian source was indicated,[3] which suggests possible long-term relation between the two areas. Obsidian has not yet been found in any Epipaleolithic site in the Levant.

The microburin technique for the manufacture of geometrics as well as of other pieces was popular in various Levantine Epipaleolithic industries, e.g., the Natufian, the Moshabian, the

2. It should be pointed out that all the earth removed from Shanidar Cave was screened and processed twice.

3. Note should be made that the obsidian from Shanidar Cave that was identified as to source was from the Baradostian layer, not the Zarzian layer.

Negev Kebaran/Geometric Kebaran B, and the Harifian (Henry 1974). There seems to have been a concentration of this technique in the southern Levant, and there is evidence that even in the Natufian the technique decreased in use from south to north and was especially related to the Late Natufian phase. The microburin technique, therefore, was used in the southern Levant from ca. 12,000 B.C. (beginning of the Moshabian) to at least ca. 8000 B.C. (end of the Harifian) and spread northward sometime during the Natufian period. Henry (ibid., p. 395) also suggests that concerning the question of the microburin technique there might have been a "stimulus-diffusion relationship" between the southern Levant and North Africa during the Epipaleolithic; at least there seems to have been a greater potential for this than for it to have been between the southern Levant and the rest of the Middle East. The Zagros data reinforce, at least, the latter part of this proposition. Information on the use of the microburin technique for the Zarzian (and the Protoneolithic as well) is meager indeed, even though geometric microliths are characteristic. A single possible example of microburins has been reported from Zarzi, Shanidar Cave, and Ghar-i Khar; none are mentioned for Warwasi; and their presence is reported for Palegawra and Pa Sangar but no counts are given. This evidence indicates that the microburin technique was, at best, very rare in the Zarzian industry and not regularly used for the manufacture of geometric or other pieces.

In the later part of the Epipaleolithic/Protoneolithic sequence in both the Levant and the Zagros, important changes, as already described, were taking place, changes that anticipated and ushered in the Neolithic economy, technology, and way of life; such things as semipermanent or permanent villages, extensive processing of plant food and possibly some use of domesticated cereals (Horowitz 1977, p. 326, and Leroi-Gourhan 1981), some domesticated animals (Perkins 1964), elaborate burials with grave goods, greatly expanded worked-bone and ground-stone industries, exotic items and adornments. Many of these traits indicate more complex socioeconomic and technological patterns, but others suggest humanistic and aesthetic advances as well. We have already mentioned the Natufian/Zawi Chemi burials and their elaborate grave goods. Special note should also be made of the appearance of decorated portable or mobiliary art in both the Natufian and the Zawi Chemi and of a special study of this art (R.S. Solecki 1980) that has shown that the Natufian and Zawi Chemi share a number of design elements and other features as well. The Zawi Chemi design elements on both stones and bones range from curvilinear or wavy-line decorations to linear parallel-line elements and hachures or chevrons. These design elements are duplicated in the Levant, in a more or less general way. The marks were undoubtedly incised in both areas with the sharp end of a flint or the edge of a flake, or possibly a burin. The geometric design elements such as the plats or hachures can be explained as possibly originating from designs formed in twilled weaving or plaiting. There is evidence for matting or basketry in the Protoneolithic at Shanidar Cave. Other elements cannot find support in this hypothesis. These are the lozenge elements and the banded wavy-line elements. One of the latter forms looks like a snake motif.

Epipaleolithic chipped-stone traditions continue in both areas, and geometric microliths characteristically in the form of lunates are present. The Natufian has been described as following local tradition, i.e., being a predominantly microlithic chipped-stone industry, although larger-sized and even massive tools are associated, while in the Zawi Chemi the microlithic component (here like the Zarzian) represents only about 25% of the total chipped-stone industry. There are no microburins at Zawi Chemi, nor any definite pieces with Helwan or bifacial retouched backing. The Early Natufians, as well as some of the Negev/Sinai Late Epipaleolithic peoples, used this very distinctive backing method. This entire complex of Helwan retouch/microburin technique appears not to have been characteristic of the Zagros region.

Also virtually absent at Zawi Chemi are sickle blades, items characteristic of the Natufian, while such items as the following are very common at Zawi Chemi: notched/denticulated pieces, *pièces esquillées,* and side scrapers of various sizes and types. Other differences between the two chipped stone industries are present, but they both fit into the very end of the Paleolithic tradition.

A comparison of the pecked- and ground-stone and worked-bone industries at the two sites also provides some interesting information. Zawi Chemi has considerably more, and more varied, ground-stone tools, reflecting environmental conditions and cultural needs as well as different traditions or even chronological differences. It is interesting that in a comparative study of Natufian-Zawi Chemi bone tools (Campana 1979) it has been shown that different manufacturing techniques were used in the two areas. Almost all of the Natufian implements were shaved into shape with flint tools with the use of techniques that had probably been applied to the manufacture of wooden tools and objects since very early times and therefore represent a continuation of Upper Paleolithic traditions. The Zawi Chemi bone tools, on the other hand, were manufactured almost entirely by the use of abrasive/grinding techniques, which is another reflection of the importance of this method of tool manufacture in the Zawi Chemi. Also it should be noted that many woodworking tools, such as axes, adzes, gouges, and possibly the denticulated and notched pieces, are characteristic of the Zawi Chemi.

In summary, geographically there are obvious differences between the habitats of the early cultures of the Levant and the Zagros under discussion here; and, understandably, the characteristics of the habitats must have made an impress upon the indigenous populations. For instance, in the Levant the exploitable areas ranged from the maritime border and lowland marsh areas to inland sea- and lakeshores and from seashore to upland and low mountain areas. In the Zagros, on the other hand, we are dealing with a more rugged environment of mountain valleys, high plateaus, and turbulent rivers.

There appears to be substantial agreement among investigators that the Epipaleolithic in both the Levant and the Zagros (i.e., the Kebaran in the former and the Zarzian in the latter) seems to have indigenous roots, although we would like to see more evidence that the Zarzian stems from the Baradostian. More radiocarbon-dated Zarzian sites are badly needed for tracing the Baradostian-Zarzian relationship and especially for understanding the internal cultural developments within the Zarzian itself. The origin of the Natufian is still something of a mystery, and some investigators are unwilling to commit themselves in print. There is even some vacillation in the much-quoted paragraph of Garrod (1957, p. 212), though one scholar, Bar-Yosef (1975, p. 370), stands up to declare himself, albeit rather tentatively. He thinks that the Geometric Kebaran A might be pointed to as a source for the Natufian. In any case, if we examine the C^{14} dates, remembering all of the current problems of dealing with old and new C^{14} dates, qualifications, and so forth, there appears to be a span of ca. four thousand years (ca. 16,000 B.C. to 12,000 B.C.) for the Kebaran in the Levant and a span of two thousand years (12,530 B.C. to 10,050 B.C.) for the Zarzian in the Zagros. Could there be stimulus diffusion for the Epipaleolithic from west to east in southwest Asia? One factor that we must not lose sight of is that it was probably too cold and dry in the high Zagros for human occupation in the millennia just before the appearance of the Zarzian.

Taking a look at the accepted dates for the Natufian time span in the Levant (from 10,000 B.C. to 8000 B.C.), we note that they are not very much different from the C^{14} dates for the Protoneolithic of Shanidar Cave (8650 B.C.) and Zawi Chemi (8920 B.C.). For one thing, these dates show an increase in the tempo of cultural change, and for another, a strong possibility that there was much interchange of ideas, and so forth, between the Levant and the Zagros at this time, given the near contemporaneity of the two cultures.

Impressionally, the Epipaleolithic cultures of the Levant and the Zagros resemble each other. Economically, there appears to be little difference, although we note that grinding stones are present in the Kebaran and absent to date in the Zarzian. (Grinding stones are reported even earlier in northeast Africa, and connections with that continent are hard to dismiss in the light of the mounting evidence.) From a culture that was already predisposed toward experimental food collection and the preparation of such edibles as acorns, nuts, and wild grass seeds, it was a natural step to emphasize vegetal foods (especially the storable varieties) in the Natufian and the Protoneolithic. The bone awls, denticulates, and notched flints were probably used for the manufacture of baskets and fiber bags for the storage of vegetal provender. As we observed above, there appears to have been no knowledge of shaped grinding stones in the Zarzian, or before the Protoneolithic. The hunting techniques do not appear to differ from each other in the two areas of concern, although it is noted that no harpoons or real evidence of fishing have been found in the Zagros cultures. The stone arrowhead was introduced in the Levant toward the end of the Natufian and appears only much later in the ceramic cultures in the Zagros and neighboring areas. Korfmann (1971) debates the point about bows and arrows in the late Natufian and presents a case for that weapon not having been adopted before the Pre-Pottery Neolithic B. However, grooved stone tools with good heat-retention qualities (e.g., chlorite) have been found in the Protoneolithic. We believe that they are cane shaft straighteners and that they suggest an earlier occurrence in the Near East for this weapon (Solecki and Solecki 1970).

Taking Jericho as a prime example, the change to settled village life is manifestly a more dramatic event in the Levant than in the Zagros area. The necessity for a wall around Jericho is indicative of a marked imbalance of wealth and surplus in an early age. Comparing the course of cultural development in the Levant and the Zagros we are impressed by the fact that there are still fairly large gaps in the cultural chronology of the foothills and mountains of the Zagros. Thus, there is a blank of nearly a thousand years between Zawi Chemi/Karim Shahir and Jarmo in Iraqi Kurdistan, filled in Iranian Kurdistan by the sites of Ganj Dareh and Asiab, which form important connecting links between the Protoneolithic and the ceramic cultures of the Zagros.

To summarize, in both the Levant and the Zagros, slowly improving climatic conditions after ca. 12,000 B.C. permitted plants and animals to move out of restricted or refuge areas. Man was thus able to enlarge his geographic range and to develop to adopt new economic strategies, new technologies, and eventually a new way of life.

BIBLIOGRAPHY

Bar-Yosef, O.
> 1970   The Epi-Paleolithic cultures of Palestine. Ph.D. diss., Hebrew University, Jerusalem.
> 1975   The Epi-Paleolithic in Palestine and Sinai. In *Problems in prehistory: North Africa and the Levant*, ed. F. Wendorf and A.E. Marks, pp. 363–78. Dallas, Texas: Southern Methodist University.

Bar-Yosef, O., and Phillips, J.L.
> 1977   *Prehistoric investigations in Gebel Maghara, northern Sinai.* Monographs of the Institute of Archaeology, Hebrew University, Qedem 7. Jerusalem: Hebrew University.

Braidwood, R.J.
> 1960   Seeking the world's first farmers in Persian Kurdistan: a full-scale investigation of prehistoric sites near Kermanshah. *The Illustrated London News*, no. 6325(237):695–97.

Braidwood, R.J., and Howe, B.
> 1960   *Prehistoric investigations in Iraqi Kurdistan.* Studies in Ancient Oriental Civilization, no. 31. Chicago: University of Chicago Press.

Butzer, H.W.
> 1975   Patterns of environmental change in the Near East during late and early Holocene times. In *Problems in prehistory: north Africa and the Levant*, ed. F. Wendorf and A.E. Marks, pp. 389–410. Dallas, Texas: Southern Methodist University Press.

Campana, D.
1979   An analysis of the use-wear patterns on Natufian and Protoneolithic bone implements. Ph.D. diss., Columbia University, New York.

Ferembach, D.
1970   Etude anthropologie des ossements humains proto-néolithiques de Zawi Chemi Shanidar (Iraq). *Sumer* 26(1/2):21−64.

Garrod, D.A.E.
1930   The Palaeolithic of southern Kurdistan: excavations in the caves of Zarzi and Hazar Merd. *Bulletin of the American Schools of Prehistoric Research* 6:8−43.
1957   The Natufian culture: the life and economy of a Mesolithic people in the Near East. *Proceedings of the British Academy* 43:211−27.

Henry, D.
1974   The utilization of the microburin technique in the Levant. *Paléorient* 2(2):389−98.

Henry, D., and Servello, F.
1974   Compendium of C-14 determinations derived from Near Eastern prehistoric sites. *Paléorient* 2(1):19−44.

Hole, F., and Flannery, K.V.
1967   The prehistory of southwestern Iran: a preliminary report. *Proceedings of the Prehistoric Society* 33:147−206.

Horowitz, A.
1977   Pollen spectra from two early Holocene prehistoric sites in the Har Harif (west central Negev). In *Prehistory and paleoenvironments in the central Negev, Israel*, vol. 2: *the Avdat/Aqev area, part 2; and the Har Harif*, ed. A.E. Marks, pp. 323−26. Dallas, Texas: Southern Methodist University Press.

Korfmann, M.
1971   The Natufian, an "indigenous Palestinian culture"?: a consideration of Natufian long-range weapons. *Berytus Archaeological Studies* 20:25−41.

Leroi-Gourhan, A.
1976   Les pollens de Zarzi, dans le Kurdistan Irakien. *Sumer.*

1981   Analyse pollinique de Zawi Chemi. In *An early site at Zawi Chemi Shanidar*, Solecki, R.L. pp. 77−79. Bibliotheca Mesopotamica: Primary Sources and Interpretive Analyses for the Study of Mesopotamian Civilization and its Influence from Late Prehistory to the End of the Cuneiform Tradition, vol. 13, ed. G. Buccellati. Malibu: Undena Publications.

Marks, A.E.
1977   Introduction: a preliminary overview of central Negev prehistory. In *Prehistory and Paleoenvironments in the central Negev, Israel*, vol. 2:*the Avdat/Aqev area, part 2; and the Har Harif*, ed. A.E. Marks, pp. 3−34. Dallas, Texas: Southern Methodist University.

Marks, A.E., and Larson, P.A., Jr.
1977   Test excavations at the Natufian site of Rosh Horesha. In *Prehistory and Paleoenvironments in the central Negev, Israel*, vol. 2: *the Avdat/Aqev area, part 2; and the Har Harif*, ed. A.E. Marks, pp. 191−232. Dallas, Texas: Southern Methodist University.

Marks, A.E., and Simmons, A.H.
1977   The Negev Kebaran of the Har Harif. In *Prehistory and Paleoenvironments in the central Negev, Israel*, vol. 2: *the Avdat/Aqev area, part 2; and the Har Harif*, ed. A.E. Marks, pp. 233−69. Dallas, Texas: Southern Methodist University.

Mortensen, P.
1974   A survey of prehistoric settlements in northern Luristan. *Acta Archaeologica* 45:1−47.
1975   Survey and soundings in the Holailan valley, 1974. In *Proceedings of the IIIrd Annual Symposium on Archaeological Research in Iran* [Tehran, 1974], ed. F. Bagherzadeh, pp. 1−12. Tehran: Iranian Center for Archaeological Research.

Perkins, D.
  1964   Prehistoric fauna from Shanidar, Iraq. *Science* 144:1565–66.

Renfrew, C.; Dixon, J.E.; and Cann, J.R.
  1966   Obsidian and early cultural contact in the Near East. *Proceedings of the Prehistoric Society* 32:30–72.

Scott, T.R.
  1977   The Harifian of the central Negev. In *Prehistory and Paleoenvironments in the central Negev, Israel*, vol. 2: *the Avdat/Aqev area, part 2; and the Har Harif*, ed. A.E. Marks, pp. 271–322. Dallas, Texas: Southern Methodist University.

Simmons, A.H.
  1977   The geometric Kebaran "A" camp site of D101C. In *Prehistory and Paleoenvironments in the central Negev, Israel*, vol. 2: *the Avdat/Aqev area, part 2; and the Har Harif*, ed. A.E. Marks, pp. 119–29. Dallas, Texas: Southern Methodist University.

Solecki, R.L.
  1964   Zawi Chemi Shanidar: a post-Pleistocene village in northern Iraq. In *Report of the VIth International Congress on the Quaternary* [Warsaw, 1961], vol. 4, International Association on Quaternary Research, pp. 402–12. Lódź: Pánstwowe Wydawnictwo Naukowe.
  1981   *An early site at Zawi Chemi Shanidar.* Bibliotheca Mesopotamica: Primary Sources and Interpretive Analyses for the Study of Mesopotamian Civilization and its Influence from Late Prehistory to the End of the Cuneiform Tradition, vol. 13, ed. G. Buccellati. Malibu: Undena Publications.

Solecki, R.L., and Solecki, R.S.
  1970   Grooved stones from Zawi Chemi Shanidar: a Proto-Neolithic site in northern Iraq. *American Anthropologist* 72:831–41.

Solecki, R.S.
  1955   Shanidar cave: a Paleolithic site in northern Iraq. In *Annual Report of the Smithsonian Institution for 1954:* 389–425.
  1963   Prehistory in Shanidar valley, northern Iraq. *Science* 139:179–93.
  1980   Art motifs and prehistory in the Middle East. In *Theory and practice: essays presented to Gene Weltfish*, ed. S. Diamond, pp. 59–77. The Hague: Mouton.

Wreschner, E., and Ronen, A.
  1975   Iraq ez-Zigan, 1975. *Israel Exploration Journal* 25(4):254–55.

Wright, H.T., and Yaghmā'i, T.
  n.d.   Test excavations at Rezā Qoli Abād Sangi: an Epipaleolithic site in southwestern Iran.

Young, T.C., Jr., and Smith, P.E.L.
  1966   Research in the prehistory of central western Iran. *Science* 153:386–91.

Zeist, W. van
  1967   Late Quaternary vegetation history of western Iran. *Review of Paleobotany and Palynology* 2:301–11.

Zeist, W. van, and Wright, H.E., Jr.
  1963   Preliminary pollen studies at lake Zeribar, Zagros mountains, southwestern Iran. *Science* 140:65–67.

SECTION II:
GREATER MESOPOTAMIA

THE FORCE OF NUMBERS: POPULATION PRESSURE IN THE CENTRAL WESTERN ZAGROS 12,000–4500 B.C.

Philip E.L. Smith and T. Cuyler Young, Jr.

> The world is divided and organized according to the force of numbers which gives each living mass its individual significance and fixes its level of culture and efficiency, its biological (and economic) rhythm of growth, and its pathological destiny [Braudel 1974, p. 54].
>
> I have long been of the opinion that demography is much too important to be wasted on demographers [Levy 1974, p. 110].

INTRODUCTION

IN 1970 we proposed an explanation for the rise of agriculture and its early development in Greater Mesopotamia. That model was based on the proposition that human population growth preceded and was a causative factor in the domestication of plants and animals by altering the demographic-economic equilibrium, and that it was subsequent continued population growth and increases in population densities which then permitted and even stimulated the introduction of ever shorter fallow periods in the agricultural cycle. Shorter fallow periods in turn related to certain technological innovations such as the invention of the plough and the development of irrigation techniques (Smith and Young 1972). Painting with a dangerously wide and at times thick-bristled brush, we covered the period from the late Upper Paleolithic to the rise of civilization in Sumer and Elam over a large area of the Near East.

Four major stages in this developmental process were defined. The first, represented in the Zagros mountains by the late Zarzian and probably in the Levant by the Natufian, witnessed the development in small highly favored environments of sedentism based on an intensive exploitation of wild cereal grasses. We argued that population then increased rapidly as one result of sedentism and that

> as population increased *within those environmental limits*, population density increased. As population density increased, the degree of overexploitation of the environment increased. Yet through sedentism man had, in the meantime, developed certain new social and economic patterns that had become cultural norms. We might expect a reluctance to deviate from those norms in some cases at least. Under cumulative pressures resulting from the interaction of his social, economic and environmental circumstances, all influenced by increasing population densities, he gradually began more and more to manipulate the plants and animals with which he was familiar and which were so important to the maintenance of 'normal' patterns of culture [Smith and Young 1972, pp. 33–34].

Thus, we argued, began the food producing or Neolithic revolution in Greater Mesopotamia.

In the second stage of the sequence, the early Neolithic of the Zagros, we saw solid evidence for the first serious efforts at cultivation and animal manipulation in the Near East. This phase is documented at such sites as Karim Shahir, Zawi Chemi, Asiab, Ganj Dareh, and Ali Kosh (Bus Mordeh Phase) as well as others. These are only a handful of sites, but they are found in several different environmental zones within Greater Mesopotamia: the Piedmont, central High Zagros, southern High Zagros, and the border area between the latter region and the lowland alluvium of Khuzistan respectively.

141

In the third stage, the later Neolithic (c. 7000 B.C. to, in places, perhaps as late as 5500 B.C.) there was a considerable increase in the number of sites discovered within the study area, but those sites were found mainly in the same region as were occupations of the previous phase. Only the border fans between the Zagros and the Mesopotamian lowlands, such as those in the area of Mandali and parts of northern Khuzistan, were newly settled. Characteristic sites of the period are Jarmo, Sarab, Guran, and — later — Ali Kosh. Finally, for the fourth stage, the Chalcolithic (in traditional Mesopotamian terminology the Hassuna, Halaf, and Ubaid periods), we noted there was something like an eight-fold increase in the number of known sites and a rapid and complete colonization of the whole of Greater Mesopotamia, including by then the Urmia basin, the central Iranian plateau, and north and south Mesopotamia proper. We observed,

> There is little doubt that much of the population growth of the sixth millennium and the pressure created by that growth was absorbed through colonization and migration. Even so, however, the density of the population must have risen markedly, as the data from Deh Luran and the central western Zagros alone testify, and it is reasonable to assume that, along with colonization, more intensive forms of agricultural exploitation involving still further shortening of the fallow period were a feature of the period [Smith and Young 1972, pp. 42–43].

In brief, thus stood our thoughts when we went to press in 1970.

Since then, over the past decade, the general theme of population pressure as an agency in the evolution of societies has taken some hard knocks. These range from mildly condescending put-downs, in which the word *theory* is preceded by adjectival phrases like "currently fashionable" or "intellectually seductive," to more vigorous attacks, which seek to dismiss the theory as something that explains nothing or even as a dangerous deterministic fallacy (see Young [1977] for an attempt to answer the latter criticism). Of course the hypothesis bore within itself some of the seeds of its own tribulation. It drew partial sustenance from the cultural-materialist school of anthropology just as this approach was being derided as vulgar materialism and — at least in archeology — suffering a decline in popularity. Perhaps it also suffered from seeming to underline certain positive features of population growth and stress and thus went against the grain of the neo-Malthusian doomsday syndrome of recent years. It appeared to be crudely monocausal in a period when multiple causality was becoming the received faith. It was accused by some triumphant critics of being incapable of answering the Big Question, Why do populations grow in the first place? and, therefore, of being theoretically inadequate. It is (not surprisingly) devilishly tricky to answer by archeological means (or even, for that matter, among living populations) the question, At what point in quantitative increases in population do qualitative shifts in technology, in social, economic, and political organization, or in other aspects of cultural life appear? Finally, the hypothesis has perhaps had more to fear from some of its more reductionist friends who have posed oversimplistic applications of the model than from its avowed opponents who chop merrily at its foundations.

Faced with these torments, and bearing the welts inflicted by a phalanx of critics, what should a pair of prehistorians who so blithely, a mere decade ago, launched their own proud little ship on the pond of Near Eastern prehistory now do? Was it all a ghastly error, an illusion of two unsophisticated and linear-minded archeologists who failed to see in time that others were already signing up on more elegant and less vulnerable craft? Our sense of economy rebels. Surely, if the principle of uniformitarianism holds, there was *something* to our hypothesis. So, in an age when salvage and recycling have become near-gospel, we return to our drawing board and try to see, in the light of more experience and of new discoveries, how useful and fruitful the approach still is.

In taking up the issue once again we do not propose to offer a formal or a detailed rebuttal to the criticisms, made by various authors in recent years, of either the concept of population pressure as a factor in cultural evolution, or, more specifically, of the Boserup variant of this concept (Boserup 1965).[1] This would require a considerably longer paper than the editors of this volume will allow. We, and others, have elsewhere made the theoretical arguments for population pressure as a causative agent. Here, rather, we will try to demonstrate that there *is* reasonably good archeological evidence that population was growing immediately before the technological and social changes that are observable archeologically in the central Zagros. While we accept that there will always be differences of opinion on how to interpret this evidence, we insist that the phenomenon itself cannot be dismissed.

Nevertheless, before turning to accentuate the positive we wish to observe in passing that, contrary to what some critics seem to have assumed, we have never argued that the model was a simple one. From this assertion follow other basic points worth stressing once again. (1) We do not see our hypothesis as involving unifactorial or simple linear processes unrelated to many other significant issues,[2] although we continue to believe that in many cases there is a hierarchy of causal variables among which population pressure may be the leading or overriding one — that is, a good old-fashioned prime mover (Smith and Young 1972, pp. 49−57; Smith 1972, pp. 421−22; Young 1972, pp. 837−38. (2) Cowgill (1975) and Hassan (1978) appear to hold that the population-pressure thesis is based on the belief that changes in technology are brought about only when the level of severe food shortage or starvation is reached. They then argue that, since humans do not normally continue to propagate and increase in numbers up to this point, the notion of population pressure is fallacious. In fact, their position is a distortion of the thesis as we see it, and reminds us of the old "nature red in tooth and claw" distortion of the concept of natural selection in biology. We do not propose a dramatic starvation or strictly-from-hunger model. Rather, we maintain that changes can take place in agriculture practices under the pressure of population long before severe food shortages or the threat of starvation develop, as the perception of an unfavorable reward-for-work ratio grows in the minds of the people concerned. (3) We have never argued that it was a universal explanation applicable to all times, places, and situations — a kind of silver bullet — but rather that it is a usually necessary but not necessarily sufficient condition for agricultural and other changes (Smith and Young 1972, pp. 49−57). We shall continue to eschew the true-believer syndrome. (4) We have been at pains to emphasize that the causes for population increases and decreases are both social and biological and to stress the important role of cultural norms in maintaining settled communities through agricultural experimentation (Smith and Young 1972, pp. 32−33). (5) We also continue to believe that on good methodological grounds it is *not* necessary to explain the immediate causes of increasing (or decreasing) population pressure when we are studying its consequences in a given situation, although several critics have appeared to think such a failure to explain causation invalidates the entire hypothesis. A geologist evaluating the consequences of a glacial advance is not

1. We present this contribution in honor of Bob Braidwood in full awareness that he does not really share our belief in the role of population as an explanatory factor in cultural change. Never mind; as a friend and as a friendly critic he has listened to us and encouraged us to explore its possibilities, just as he has cheerfully tolerated among his colleagues a wide range of viewpoints, even those that occasionally pain him on intellectual or esthetic grounds.

2. Much as we admire Redman's excellent and useful summary of the rise of food production and early urbanism in the ancient Near East (Redman 1978), we would take issue with the unilinear interpretation of our thesis that he presents (see esp. fig. 4:4), lacking as it does a single fashionable feedback or backward-pointing arrow.

methodologically obliged to explain just what meteorological or other circumstances caused the advance, however interesting that question might be. Similarly, no one has ever suggested that the changes in climate that came at the end of the Pleistocene and in the early Holocene should not be considered important issues in the study of early agriculture simply because we still lack a satisfactory explanation of what caused those climatic shifts. Rather, we suggest that if population did grow or shrink and affect the ratio of work input to productivity, the result (judging from recent ethnographic and historical examples that, with all due regard for the danger of projecting the present into the past, could be relevant to prehistoric situations) might be along the lines of our hypothesis. That is, while we should, of course, eventually try to understand why population increases and decreases, we should not confuse proximal and distal types of explanation at this level of analysis. (6) Finally, we wish to remark that all of the criticisms of our 1972 paper have to our knowledge been made only on general and theoretical grounds. We know of no serious or detailed attempt to refute the specific we outlined for the archeological data from Greater Mesopotamia, although Wright and Johnson (1975), without specific reference to our article, find it unsatisfactory at a local level in the north Khuzistan plain for explaining the origin of the state.

Setting aside for now these interesting but broader issues and having in mind the theme and purpose of this volume, we propose to return to a few of the basic propositions and specific ideas first outlined in our 1972 argument and to reexamine them on a much more narrow front. That is, in this paper we take a less general approach, putting more emphasis on local details and local processes. There has been a great deal of excavation and survey done in Greater Mesopotamia in the last ten years. We know best the work done in the central western Zagros involving three of the geographic zones discussed in the 1972 article: the Inner Zagros, the central High Zagros, and the southern High Zagros. It is on these regions that we now wish to focus attention; specifically on the Kangavar, Sahneh, Harsin, Kermanshah, Mahi Dasht, and Hulailan valleys (and immediately neighboring valleys where and when data are available), all in western Iran (fig. 1). The time range dealt with is the same as in 1972: the terminal Paleolithic to the end of the Ubaid period.

Naturally, the archeological coverage of these valleys, either by survey or excavation, is somewhat uneven, albeit much progress has been made in data collection over the past decade. Moving roughly east to west, we note that a fairly extensive survey of the Malayer plain is complete but yet to be published in any detail (Howell 1978). The Assadabad, Sahneh, and Nehavand valleys have still been surveyed in only a rather hit-and-miss fashion (Young 1966). The Kanagavar valley, on the other hand, has been intensively surveyed and all sites noticed have been examined (Young 1975), and the local sequence has been well established by excavations at Godin Tepe and Seh Gabi (Young and Levine 1974). In the Harsin region, excavations at Ganj Dareh are now complete (Smith 1976, 1978), and fairly intensive survey has been conducted in the immediate area of this early Neolithic site (Smith and Mortensen 1980). In two field seasons Levine has made much progress with an intensive survey of the Mahi Dasht and other valleys in the Kermanshah region, which provides about a forty-percent coverage of that region (Levine and McDonald 1977); in 1978 he undertook new excavations at Tepe Sarab. This work adds to and complements that done by Braidwood in the same area twenty years ago (Braidwood 1961). The high mountain country of Luristan has been in part surveyed by Goff (1971), and intensive walking surveys have covered a large part of the Hulailan valley, in which the important site of Tepe Guran is located (Mortensen 1974, 1975, 1976). Altogether, since we went to press in 1970 with our 1972 article, upward of 900 new sites of all periods have been located and mapped in the study area, providing a total of something over 1,400 sites. In short, our data base is much improved. So let us see where we now stand.

THE ARGUMENT

THE EPIPALEOLITHIC

The Epipaleolithic of our area — that is, the period of occupation from approximately 12,000 to 10,000/9000 B.C. — is best characterized by the Zarzian, although this may not be the only cultural unit present. (It should also be recalled that not all industries with blades and bladelets need be Zarzian in age or type: some may be vestiges of Zawi Chemi–Karim Shahir occupations, i.e., post-Epipaleolithic in the sense used here. We have kept this possibility in mind when estimating the number of Zarzian sites.) In the main the Zarzian continues the upland-zone adaptation of the preceding Baradostian. Most known sites are at high elevations in the Zagros, and some (perhaps most) represent probably warm-weather occupations. Possible winter sites are not clearly identified in our area, though they may be present at lower altitudes in Khuzistan, Fars, and elsewhere. The sites seem to reflect the exploitation of local resources but — as pointed out by many authors — have some new features, particularly, an emphasis in certain sites (Warwasi, Ghar-i Khar, as well as others outside our area) on the consumption of a land snail, *Helix salmonica*. The postulated shift to a great variety of foods, especially nonungulate food such as wild cereals, molluscs, birds, small game, and fish — the so-called Broad Spectrum Revolution (Flannery 1969) — is an intriguing and even likely possibility but is not yet demonstrated by indisputable archeological evidence.

The climate and environment during Zarzian times remain less well known than one could wish, and our understanding is based too exclusively on the palynological analysis of a few lake and spring cores, particularly from Lake Zeribar in Iran (van Zeist and Bottema 1977) and extrapolations from other areas such as the Persian Gulf and the Levant (McDonald 1979). Apparently, the cool-temperate, dry conditions of Baradostian times were succeeded around 12,000 B.C. by somewhat warmer, moister conditions; increasingly oak-pistachio vegetation replaced the treeless *Artemisia* steppe (although small numbers of trees may have been present even in the Pleniglacial in more sheltered valleys and at lower altitudes). This situation was accentuated after 9000 B.C. with what we may regard as early Holocene conditions. Thus the Zarzian, whatever its time of beginning or its absolute length, did witness toward its close the onset of more favorable conditions for vegetation and quite possibly the spread and proliferation of wild grasses, including cereals. Unfortunately, this reconstruction leaves much room for debate where details and timing of changes are concerned. Thus a broad statement that the final Pleistocene/Zarzian period saw a change from a more to a less severe continental climate is about as far as we need go here.

It would be strange, however, if the environmental shift had no effects on the cultural patterns. It has been suggested already that such effects can be traced in subsistence patterns, which in turn may be reflected in such innovations as grinding stones for food preparation. Perhaps the most striking and significant change is denoted by a sharp rise in the number of sites. For the entire Zagros region of Iran and Iraq we have at least 20 known Zarzian sites; for the Baradostian we have 7. In the area chosen for discussion here there are about 9 known Zarzian sites; there are 2 for the Baradostian. The known Zarzian sites in this region are, it is true, largely concentrated in the Hulailan valley (7), the result of the more intensive survey there by Mortensen (Mortensen 1975, pp. 2–4).[3] And, needless to say, an absolute or relative increase in the number of sites may involve more than one simple explanation. Furthermore, we are aware of the risk of assuming population growth on the basis of a single variable (the number of settlements in a region), but if there are no flagrant discrepancies in site size or in apparent site function the inherent error may

---

3. We thank Peder Mortensen for advice and for information dealing with the Hulailan valley, which we have incorporated into this article.

not be excessive. Nonetheless, even when one has considered the probability that chance of discovery and greater specialization of prehistoric activities may explain some of the Zarzian increase, we are left with the real fact that more spots on the landscape were now being utilized by people than in the preceding (and certainly no briefer) Baradostian period. Although we cannot yet demonstrate the point to our own or our colleagues' complete satisfaction, we believe the most economical explanation of this fact to be that in terminal Zarzian times the population of the Zagros had increased in numbers, in part, at least, as a consequence of the more favorable living conditions then obtaining, especially as plant foods became more abundant. It should of course be pointed out that this may not have been a steady or regular trend even within our area. Thus in the Kermanshah-Bisitun-Harsin sector only two Zarzian sites are known to date, Warwasi and Ghar-i Khar — the same two sites that represent the Baradostian presence. This lack of local site increase is puzzling, we confess, and we do not know whether it is the result of the reconnaissance methods used up to now or of a genuine difference from, say, the Hulailan valley. We suspect that the first possibility is the correct one and that more Zarzian (and Baradostian) sites will be found by more intensive and inclusive surveys in this zone.

How late these Epipaleolithic/Zarzian occupations lasted in our area remains a problem; indeed, none of them can yet be accurately dated and/or correlated with fixed points along the scale of developing environmental changes. The question of the survival of the Zarzian or its derivatives into formally Holocene times is intimately tied up with that of the beginnings of recognizable food production. For the moment we tend to agree with those colleagues who believe that if an "ancestor" must be chosen for the assemblages found in such sites as Zawi Chemi and Karim Shahir, the Zarzian is probably the best candidate.

THE EARLY NEOLITHIC

At the present time it is not clear if we have, in our study area, sites as early as Zawi Chemi and Karim Shahir in Iraq are supposed to be. Basal Ganj Dareh (Level E), though in principle a promising site for this period, has yielded contradictory radiocarbon determinations and must for the time being be placed in abeyance chronologically (although, like nearby Asiab, there are good reasons to believe it is no younger than ca. 7500 B.C.) (Smith 1976, 1978).[4] In any case, Level E has so far yielded no good evidence, direct or indirect, of food producing; Hesse's (1977) analysis of the faunal remains suggests no cultural control was present — a conclusion he reaches for Asiab also, in spite of Bokonyi's (1977) argument for goat domestication at the latter site. At Asiab also there is no evidence for plant *cultivation* so far. Level E at Ganj Dareh, and Asiab, may well be occupations representing hunting and collecting activities. We hesitate in any case to accept that there was a hiatus between the Zarzian and the earliest food-producing sites in this area. Certainly we can think of no unfavorable environmental changes that might have caused hunters and gatherers to abandon entirely an area that had been successfully occupied in Zarzian and earlier times.

For the period down to ca. 7000 B.C. or a few centuries later within our study area we had, until very recently, only two known sites: Asiab in the Kermanshah plain and Ganj Dareh near Harsin. There are no equivalents known in the Hulailan valley before ca. 6500 B.C. (basal Guran), in spite of Mortensen's meticulous searches. Furthermore, no such early agricultural sites are known in other major valleys until even much later, e.g., in the Kangavar valley (see below). At first glance, therefore, our basic hypothesis in this paper — that population had been increasing not only in

---

4. Recently a new suite of charcoal samples has been processed, but it fails to clear up the ambiguity in the determinations, some of which, if taken literally, would make Level E younger than the following levels. An honest struggle with sometimes contradictory radiocarbon dates is of course firmly within the Braidwoodian tradition of scholarship.

the Zagros as a whole but in our study area particularly — would seem to be unfounded or at least unsupported by the archeological evidence. It has seemed puzzling, for example, that only one site (Asiab) has ever been found on the well-examined Kermanshah plain. It is hard to accept that later agricultural practices, or alluviation and erosion, could have destroyed or buried all traces of occupation in this time range in all the large valleys that have been surveyed. But appearances may be deceptive, and a different interpretation is very plausible.

In 1977 one of us, in association with Mortensen, made a reconnaissance in the area near the site of Ganj Dareh (Smith and Mortensen 1980). The area chosen was a rectangle of 25×25 km, in which Ganj Dareh lies in the northeast quadrant. We selected this area of 625 km² as the most practical size for allowing us to sample a number of typical environmental subzones — small valleys, rolling hills, rocky escarpments — in a working season of two months. We make no pretence that it was as thorough a survey as Mortensen carried out over a much longer period at Hulailan or as Levine began on the Kermanshah plain (Levine and McDonald 1977). Nonetheless, much of it was done on foot; each subzone was sampled to some degree; and although we undoubtedly missed much we did locate some 35 prehistoric sites of all periods extending from the earlier Paleolithic to the Iron Age. For our purposes here, however, we need mention only three new sites (Tepe Ghenil, Tepe Qazemi, and Tepe Qala Kamand Bagh), all apparently of the general Asiab–Ganj Dareh type and all (with Ganj Dareh) located within a circle of 7 km radius. Furthermore, although their specific environmental contexts differed somewhat, all four sites are located in small, rather inaccessible side valleys rather than in broad valleys such as the Kermanshah plain or the Hulailan (fig. 2).

The morals or lessons of this example are at least twofold. First, it suggests that more sites of this period than were known up to 1977 probably are present, but the contexts in which to look for them are in the narrow and sometimes high side valleys. Certainly, if we located without much difficulty three new ones in addition to Ganj Dareh in our small rectangle, there seems little reason to doubt that similar sites are to be found throughout the more inaccessible parts of our study area and indeed throughout the Zagros as a whole. Second, there is an interesting possibility that concentrations of such sites are simply not to be expected in the larger, more open valleys, where their rarity or absence has until recently posed a problem. The hypothesis we favor at present is that the early steps toward a formal food production based on plants and animals associated with reasonably sedentary communities (as contrasted with the very likely but amorphous tendencies in the Epipaleolithic to select and even to some extent control certain species) were most suitably and efficiently made in just these small valleys. That is, possibly the initial form of protoagricultural economy was a very special and even unstable type of adaptation, dependent on a certain range of conditions found only in such upland side valleys.

Exactly why this should be the case remains unclear at the moment, and probably much depends on whether we are speaking of ungulate or of cereal utilization. In several parts of the world it has been noted that narrow river valleys permit high stability of residence to hunter-gatherers if a number of ecological zones for food-getting are within easy reach, with the specific resources in specific seasons; see Watanabe (1968) in the case of the Ainu of northern Japan. The proximity of resources such as game, cereals, acorns, and other nuts from several topographical subzones may have been one factor; the easy access to springs, perhaps for simple irrigation of wild plants or the watering of early domesticates, and the existence of a high water table may have been others. Hesse's suggestion (1977) — that a narrow valley, like that at Ganj Dareh, with a number of nearby rocky slopes provides food security for wild goat herds throughout even the most snowy winters (since prevailing wind patterns would ensure that at least one slope and its vegetation would always be clear of deep snow) — offers another explanatory factor. The role of relatively minor climatic and environmental changes in directing and guiding modifications in the human subsistence and settlement patterns has not yet been worked out. The reduction in the number of large mammals such as equids and red deer at the end of the Pleistocene may have been due to milder climatic conditions and the subsequent spread of the oak forest, which reduced the possibilities for migration of herds (Hesse 1977, pp. 327–29). Gazelle also seem to have become rare. One possible consequence of this reduction in the numbers of certain animal species was an increased emphasis on goat and sheep harvesting in the early Holocene, which in turn may have restricted human mobility and hence produced more intense pressure on resources within local zones (see Harris 1977, p. 193) and even a more acute sense of territorial rights. This in turn might have been a favorable context for taking steps ultimately leading to greater control over the wild animals and even the wild cereals. It seems possible that this trend would be more marked in the higher and smaller valleys than in the larger ones, where hunting and gathering may have remained the basic and most sensible means of exploitation until considerably later.

Whatever the true or entire causes, the point we want to make is that present archeological evidence tends to support an argument that the earliest agricultural settlements in the Zagros were not made on the larger valley floors until cultural control of certain species had already advanced to a particular level in the immediate hinterland. At any rate, the evidence from Levels D to A at Ganj Dareh (and possibly from the new sites of the same type nearby, discovered in 1977) argues for the existence in this region before ca. 7000 B.C. of groups living in communities with complex and sophisticated buildings of mud brick; making a simple kind of soft-baked pottery; apparently using rather elaborate lime kilns; controlling to a marked degree the behavior of the local goat herds, although no morphological changes in the skeletons are yet visible; and, judging by the sudden proliferation of grinding and pounding stones, processing some kind of plant food, although the status of the recovered botanical remains is not yet established.[5] Whether these levels reflect year-round occupations or only seasonal residence (the faunal evidence from Ganj Dareh Level D and later suggests they were lived in all seasons of the year), they certainly indicate a more intensive and specialized type of settlement and subsistence economy than obtained in earlier times. They represent, we suggest, a necessary transitional phase in a special zone between the first attempts at cultivation and animal control and the later, more developed phase found at sites like Sarab, Jarmo, and Guran. Whether Tepe Abdul Hosein about 55 km southeast of Ganj Dareh in Luristan is contemporary with the sites mentioned above is not certain, but it seems probable (Pullar 1979). If so, it suggests that formally aceramic groups, with and without brick buildings, may already have been cultivating barley and emmer wheat. A more intensive survey of the area around Abdul Hosein, directed specifically to locating Neolithic occupations, might well recover in similar small upland valley niches further sites analogous to the ones recently found near Ganj Dareh. To test the implications of our hypothesis, similar surveys should be carried out in many other areas as well.

THE LATER NEOLITHIC

It is only in the later Neolithic, perhaps beginning sometime during the seventh millennium B.C., that we find our first evidence for occupations down on *selected* valley floors (fig. 3 — showing a total of some 29 sites for this period in the study area). Sarab and related sites in the Kermanshah and Mahi Dasht valleys and Guran and contemporary sites in the Hulailan are cases in point. Let us focus our attention for now on the Kermanshah region.

A considerable number of Sarab period sites (17) are found in this area, either at the very edges of the relatively recent alluvium that covers the valley bottoms or on the fans beyond the

---

5. The floral materials from Ganj Dareh are now being studied by Professor W. van Zeist of Groningen and, as this article is being completed, some interesting tentative results are emerging.

alluvium.[6] While there can be no doubt that the alluvium covers a good many Neolithic and later sites not large enough to penetrate the overburden, it is also true that no sites contemporary with Ganj Dareh and the early Neolithic are found on the fans surrounding the alluvium (Asiab is a special case to which we shall return). Brooks, Dennell, and Levine (1982) have argued that the late alluvium on the floors of the Kermanshah and Mahi Dasht valleys is so widespread that it completely obscures small early settlement patterns. This is no doubt true for patterns, but we would argue that, since there is an abundance of Sarab-related sites on the nonalluviated fans, there is every reason to expect to find in those same locations sites of the early Neolithic contemporary with Ganj Dareh, were such sites to be found *at all* in the broad, open valleys. Particularly, one would expect such sites in the immediate neighborhood of the several large springs that are characteristic of the Kermanshah region. But no such sites have been found. Given the environmental conditions described above, which seem to be characteristic of the locations where most early Neolithic sites are found — small upland valleys with a wide variety of potential resources near at hand and readily available for exploitation — we here suggest that the broad valleys, fans, or presently alluviated areas, simply were not attractive to the *earliest* manipulators of plants and animals.

The distances involved in a shift from the upland valley niches to the open valley floors and fans are not great, but the environmental variations can be and are considerable. For example, it is probable that wild sheep and goats would have consistently preferred the upland valleys to the valley floors. While the former, as pointed out, provided shelter in winter on certain hill slopes, as well as the security of rocky outcrops to which the animals could retreat quickly in time of danger, the latter provided no such protection either from the elements or from natural and human predators. In much the same way, the upland niches would have been attractive to the wild cereal grasses. Here, in other words, would have been the natural habitat par excellence of the early domesticates: the "Hilly Flanks" of Braidwood's original model in microcosm, if you will.

In other ways as well, the broad open valleys would have presented early farmers with quite different environments from what they were accustomed to in the uplands. Trees would have been rare, for the lower valleys probably would have been covered with fairly thick, rich grasslands. Presumably, heavy turf would thus have been common; perhaps a range of tools quite different from those used for cultivation in the upland valley niches, such as hoes, would have been needed, and, on the Boserup model, shorter fallow periods might have been called for (Smith and Young 1972, pp. 40–41). Springs would have been fewer and farther apart and the digging of wells for drinking water would possibly have been necessary, unless sites were always located near a river (and several are not). In sum, a move down into the broad valleys would demand considerable adaptation to somewhat new environments perhaps at least perceived as being rather inhospitable (except for hunting, fishing, and collecting activities) and very possibly requiring a greater input of labor than had been the case in the upland valleys.

Our hypothesis therefore suggests that two conditions would have to be met before the occupation of the valley floors, witnessed for the first time in the later Neolithic, would be either practicable or desirable. First, a long period of experimentation with the plants and animals native to the upland valley niches would have to occur, in which farmers gradually gained a more certain control over the species being manipulated. A concomitant of such increasing control would be a similar increase in a commitment to a sedentary agricultural way of life. Second, increases in population and population densities would have to have reached a point in the

---

6. Early and late Sarab (late Neolithic) period sites can now be distinguished on the basis of ceramic changes through time at Sarab itself (McDonald 1979) and are differentiated on the map in figure 2, but our discussion considers the period as a unit.

uplands where the move to the rather more challenging and demanding valley floors would be something of a necessity in order to preserve cultural patterns that now included sedentism and primitive agriculture. In other words, why leave a perfectly satisfactory environmental adaptation such as we have postulated for the upland valley niches and move down onto the valley floors unless you must? From whence came the stimulus to undertake the move down onto the open valley floors, where most probably a sedentary agricultural way of life would have required a considerable increase in labor input, except from the pressures of increasing numbers of mouths to feed?

Such a shift of occupation in the later Neolithic did not, of course, mean a complete abandonment of the upland environments — any more than the occupation of the uplands in the early Neolithic had meant the valley floors were ignored. The shift did, however, mean a considerable decline in the number of people occupying the uplands, as witnessed by the lone Sarab-period site found within the area near Harsin surveyed by Mortensen and Smith in 1977 (fig. 2). Perhaps reflecting similar tendencies is the pattern of settlement observed in the Hulailan valley, where no village sites in the Guran time range (later Neolithic) are found off the valley floor (Mortensen 1974). In the earlier period, Asiab, of course, remains the single exception to the general distribution of settlement in the upland valley niches. Given that Hesse (1977) would now argue there is no evidence for goat domestication at Asiab, we would tend to interpret that seemingly anomalous site, particularly in the light of the hypothesis put forward here, as an early Neolithic hunting and clam-collecting station. In other words, we are not suggesting that early Neolithic peoples living in the uplands ignored the valuable resources available on the valley floors but only that they did not farm and thus establish sedentary life patterns in that open environment.

In broad terms, therefore, we would argue that the relatively sudden (only seemingly sudden, given our crude chronological controls) appearance of a fairly extensive Sarab and Sarab-related period occupation on the valley floors in certain parts of central western Iran is evidence of growing population pressures forcing people out of the small and spatially restricted but nevertheless somewhat safer and richer multiple resource uplands into the slightly more challenging environments of the valley floors. Furthermore, it was technological advances such as a greater control of both the plant and animal domesticates — and perhaps the development of hoes that made possible the breaking of heavier sods in the lower valleys — that made this move, this spread into a somewhat new though not foreign environment, possible.

Such population pressures, however, were not so great as to require for their relief any immediate occupation of all the open valleys in the central western Zagros. Fairly intensive survey in the Kangavar valley has yet to reveal there any certain occupation in the later Neolithic period, and more extensive survey in the Assadabad, Nehavand, and Sahneh valleys seems to confirm this picture.[7] McDonald (1979) has argued in considerable detail, and probably as convincingly as the data will allow, that the more eastern valleys of the central western Zagros, such as Kangavar, are and were sufficiently less attractive with respect to climate and soils to have been considered agriculturally marginal by early farmers for some time after more favored areas, such as the Kermanshah and Mahi Dasht valleys, were first occupied. However difficult this proposition is to document for the past, certainly the modern peasant is well aware of the basic facts. Any farmer in Kangavar will tell you that he would prefer to own a comparable amount of

---

7. The appearance of two sherds of late Sarab-period pottery in Mound C at Seh Gabi (McDonald 1979, p.413) is the only evidence from any of the valleys in the higher reaches of the Gamas Ab drainage for an early settlement in this area prior to the foundation of Mound C itself (mid-fifth millennium B.C.). Two sherds do not an occupation make. In other words, no one is suggesting that men of the later Neolithic did not use these valleys in some fashion, but rather we are suggesting that there is not significant agricultural settlement in these areas until much later.

land and water in the Kermanshah region, and when you ask why he replies, "Because the winters are shorter and less cold, the growing season is longer and the soil is better." He knows, in other words, where the good bottomland is. It is with just such reasoning that we should explain why the first move by agricultural and sedentary societies out of the upland valley niches so favored in the early Neolithic, made under the spur of increasing population, seems to have carried them only into selected areas of the open valley system, such as the Mahi Dasht.

THE CHALCOLITHIC

Developments in the time range immediately following the later Neolithic settlement of the valley floors in the central western Zagros suggest a filling in of the landscape. In what can roughly be described as the "J Ware" period in terms of the sequence near Kermanshah (McDonald and Levine 1977), which here includes several other contemporary ceramic cultures as well as that of J Ware, we note that there are considerably more sites in the region (some 120) but that in the main they are still confined to the same valleys occupied in the later Neolithic (Sarab) period (fig. 4).

This pattern reflects a gradual adaptation to the newly occupied environment, a period in which the agricultural implications of the shift of settlement to the wide, open valleys were being worked out and the advantages of the new situation capitalized upon. While the initial move, under pressure, from the upland valley niches may well have been made with some hesitancy, as our model suggests was likely, nevertheless, once the commitment had been made, certain agricultural advantages of the valley floors would have become apparent. Those advantages would have been positively adaptive as men became willing to be farmers and give up the hunting and gathering practices used earlier as insurance to cover periods when, from time to time, early attempts to control sheep, goats, and wild cereals failed. More land ready at hand for cultivation, less erosion because the fields were on more gradual slopes, large stands of wild grasses that provided comparatively abundant grazing for increasing flocks of animals now dependent on and reconciled to human control, and, as simple irrigation came to play a role in overall production, more running water, were all advantages in the new circumstances that, in a fairly short time, could have made the valley floors seem much less challenging and indeed more pleasant and profitable than were the upland valley niches. These broad generalizations are, of course, borne out today in the way in which the present population distributes itself economically, socially, and ethnically across the landscape in this region. The wealthier Kurds, Persians, and Turks farm the valley floors; the poorer Kurds, and the Laki and Lurs, looked down on by all, scratch a living from the upland valley niches. There is, in fact, good evidence to suggest that the upland valleys had a long time ago become so marginal from a fully developed agriculturalist's point of view that they had been abandoned to exploitation almost exclusively by pastoralists and that the present farmers of these regions were forcefully settled on their scruffy plots only in this century. Certainly this is the case with many upland villages, as documented often by simple enquiry. In short, a region that was exploited in Zarzian times by a nonsedentary adaption and that was a paradise for an early Neolithic manipulator of plants and animals who was experimenting with sedentism became in a later period when a complete commitment to agriculture had been made and the larger valley floors were fully settled, marginal from the farmer's point of view and, with the new adaptive strategy of pastoralism, reverted to nonsedentary patterns of settlement — until the locals were told to do otherwise by a strong central government. It is entirely logical in these circumstances to suggest that pastoralism in the Zagros is a development of early Chalcolithic times.

The agricultural advantages of the valley floors in turn would soon have been a considerable spur to population growth. (Critics please note here the ritual introduction of feedback.) All of the factors inherent in fully sedentary conditions that, as we have argued elsewhere, probably resulted in increased population (Smith and Young 1972, pp. 32—33) would have had a similar and perhaps even more pronounced effect among the early agriculturalists in the open valleys around Kermanshah and in the Hulailan. Increased production, given the several advantages of the more open valleys discussed above and given increased labor input, would also have been a positive spur to population growth. And just such growth is, we argue, demonstrable in the considerable increase in the number of sites during the earliest Chalcolithic when occupation was still, in the main, confined to the same limited number of larger valleys that were first occupied in the later Neolithic period.

The longer-term results of that population growth and the pressures it created can be seen in the settlement pattern for the region in the late Chalcolithic or late Ubaid period (fig. 5). First we note an almost 100% increase in the number of sites (ca. 220). Second, and more important, we see that the archeological map of central western Iran has been transformed. Occupation has spread out to include almost all of the larger, open valleys heretofore not settled. By now, population levels and pressure have reached a point where the less agriculturally attractive areas such as the Kangavar valley can not be left unfarmed. Even pockets in the sparse and highly marginal mountain regions of Luristan proper are in part occupied, and for the first time in the sequence one can speak of a more or less continuous spread of settlement over the whole Zagros. Some of this colonization had been postponed for a very long time indeed. Our earliest evidence for any extensive occupation of valleys, such as Kangavar, dates to the period when Dalma pottery was in vogue, the latter half of the fifth millennium B.C. (Young 1975), and any widespread occupation of the Malayer valley had begun still later in the Godin VI time range (Howell 1978).[8]

Conclusions

By the end of the Ubaid, of course, there was hardly any region within Greater Mesopotamia that did not show some human occupation. Thus these patterns of changing settlement, which we have been attempting to trace in microcosm against the background of the more fine-grained environmental variations of the central western Zagros, can also be discussed within the macrocosm of Greater Mesopotamia as a whole. This statement brings us back to our 1972 article, for that is what we tried to do then. Perhaps at that time also we should have begun with the smaller perspective and moved toward the larger, though in 1970 we did not have available the kinds of data we have brought to the argument today. Be that as it may, we find it somewhat encouraging that a second look, with more data, at the original proposition, this time on a much more narrow and restricted front, suggests there is something to the original model after all. And the small-scale approach perhaps reveals certain complexities and pitfalls in the story that the broad-brush technique obscures.

For example, such a finer-grained analysis of the data would have saved us from the mistake of implying, if not actually saying, that the appearance of human occupation in north and south Mesopotamia proper, in the lowlands of the Tigris and Euphrates rivers, came about because the Zagros highlands became filled with people and population pressure forced emigration westward (Smith and Young 1972, pp. 41—42). In fact, of course, population was booming in lowland Khuzistan (Elam); agriculturalists had already made a significant appearance in southern Mesopotamia (Sumer); and settlement was well established on the plains of northern Mesopotamia before people had even bothered to occupy the Kangavar valley (and other less

---

8. Mound C at Seh Gabi (McDonald 1979) almost certainly predates the Dalma (Kangavar valley period X) occupation in the Kangavar valley. Mound C is, however, the only site of its period known in the valley. Thus the Dalma period is the first of which we can speak of a settlement pattern in the region and therefore of anything like a significant occupation of the valley (Young 1975).

favorable highland valleys within the Zagros mountains). Should we be surprised that the course of events turns out to be rather more complex than first thought? Hardly. Yet the broad-canvas approach perhaps drew us into at least sounding simplistic.

Furthermore, more or less as predicted, the new data suggest that the whole course of the prehistory of agriculture in Greater Mesopotamia was one of uneven development. By the time that farmers were ready to cope with the Kangavar valley at a relatively low level of economic and social complexity (both the Dalma and subsequent Seh Gabi period occupations in that region do not suggest anything more than a village agricultural adaptation), others in Greater Mesopotamia were on the threshhold of the Uruk period and a course of change that would fairly quickly lead to the complex civilizations of Sumer and Elam. Simple or complex, however, these changes can in part at least be viewed, either in small or large scale, as responses to population growth and to increases in population densities. Similar variable rates of change and development certainly also characterize the earlier steps in the process as well. All of the people who had become adapted to an early Neolithic subsistence pattern in the multiple-resource upland valley niches of the Zagros, such as the occupants of Ganj Dareh, did not suddenly pack their goatskin bags in the face of congestion and population pressure and move down onto the floor of the Kermanshah and Mahi Dasht valleys. Occupations such as those documented at Tepe Sarab would have been under way while numerous Ganj Darehs were still occupied, just as the Zarzian patterns of hunting and gathering would have continued in certain areas long after sedentism became commonplace at early Neolithic sites. Not all of the Irish left the island or moved to town when the potatoes gave out.

In the long run, however, when any resource becomes scarce as ever greater demands are put on the existing supplies that can be provided at a given level of technology, some people must move out to other regions in search of new supplies and some must adjust their technologies in the face of shortage; even those left behind (either actually or technologically) in the most favored circumstances will eventually be caught up in the new adaptations that have resulted from the stress. Today, as population pressure, measured both in absolute numbers and intensity of demand, puts great strains on existing oil resources, change on several fronts results. On the one hand, new fields that once seemed uneconomical are being developed — e.g., in North Dakota and Montana. Such developments often require people adapted to one kind of environment to move into a new landscape; what self-respecting Texan would, if he had a choice, go north to the oil fields of the Canadian Arctic? On the other hand, new technologies such as the Tar Sands Project in northern Alberta evolve in hopes of solving the supply problem.

Finally, to close on a general point. Robert Braidwood, like Childe and many other great archeologists, shares a basic assumption with Thomas Malthus about agricultural innovations: mankind continually seeks to improve its subsistence and technology as a natural practice or process. Since, in this view, the domestication of plants and animals is a logical improvement over hunting and gathering it will be quickly adopted when the right cultural and technological conditions develop. Population growth would be a normal response to the new and more productive situation. It is unnecessary for us to emphasize here that our perspective is a rather different one, derived as it is from Boserup's thesis that population pressure (a frequent result of population growth) can often be the independent variable that itself brings about changes in agriculture and technology. But although the Boserupian thesis (and our model that is based in large part on it) is sometimes thought of as opposed to Malthusian or "neo-Malthusian" doctrine, we are beginning to realize that this supposition too (like much else that has been said and written about the role of population in cultural change) is a simplification. In reality, as Simon (1977) has pointed out in another context, the traditional Malthusian "invention-pull" hypothesis and the Boserupian "population-push" model are complementary, not opposed. They operate in differ-ent contexts, and both have been important in history. The invention-pull concept accurately describes economic-demographic history in cases where an immediate labor-saving invention appears that produces the same output with less labor compared to the technology currently in use, e.g., a new and profitable plant food; whereas the population-push hypothesis is a looped, or feedback, model that deals with inventions that do not save labor at the time of introduction but can produce higher levels of output albeit with absolutely more labor per person, e.g., full-scale domestication, shorter fallow systems, or more complex methods of irrigation (Simon 1977, pp. 164, 168). We might close, therefore, as we began, with a quotation and by embracing a spiritual comrade heretofore in partial disguise as our supposed opponent, that old scholar Thomas Malthus, who once remarked that if it were not for population increase "I do not see what motive there would be, sufficiently strong, to overcome the acknowledged indolence of man, and make him proceed in the cultivation of the soil" (1803, p. 491). Perhaps after all, the real difference between Malthus and ourselves lies in the fact that the two sides occupy different loci along the sliding scale between pessimism and optimism about the human condition.

BIBLIOGRAPHY

Bökönyi, S.
  1977   *Animal remains from four sites in the Kermanshah valley, Iran: Asiab, Sarab, Dehsavar and Siahbid: the faunal evolution, environmental changes and development of animal husbandry, VIII–III millennia* B.C. British Archaeological Reports, Supplementary Series, vol. 34. Oxford.

Boserup, E.
  1965   *The conditions of agricultural growth.* Chicago: Aldine.

Braidwood, R.J.
  1961   The Iranian prehistoric project, 1959–1960. *Iranica Antiqua* 1:3–7.

Braudel, F.
  1974   *Capitalism and material life 1400–1800.* New York: Harper and Row.

Brooks, I.A.; Dennell, R.W.; and Levine, L.D.
  1982   Alluvial sequence in central west Iran and implications for archaeological survey. *Journal of Field Archaeology* 9(3):285–99.

Cowgill, G.L.
  1975   On causes and consequences of ancient and modern populations changes. *American Anthropologist* 77(3):505–25.

Flannery, K.V.
  1969   Origins and ecological effects of early domestication in Iran and the Near East. In *The domestication and exploitation of plants and animals*, ed. P.J. Ucko and G.W. Dimbleby, pp. 73–100. London: Duckworth.

Goff, C.L.
  1971   Luristan before the Iron Age. *Iran* 9:131–52.

Harris, D.R.
  1977   Settling down: an evolutionary model for the transformation of mobile bands into sedentary communities. In *The evolution of social systems*, ed. J. Friedman and M. Rowlands, pp. 401–7. London: Duckworth.

Hassan, F.
  1978   Demographic archaeology. In *Advances in archaeological method and theory*, vol. 1, ed. M. Schiffer, pp. 49–103. New York: Academic Press.

Hesse, B.
  1977   Evidence for husbandry from the early Neolithic site of Ganj Dareh in western Iran.
                Ph.D. diss., Columbia University, New York.

Howell, R.
  1979   Survey of the Malayer plain. *Iran* 17:156–57.

Levine L.D., and McDonald, M.M.A.
  1977   The Neolithic and Chalcolithic periods in the Mahidasht. *Iran* 15:39–50.

Levy, M.J., Jr.
  1974   New uses of demography. *Comparative Studies in Society and History* 16(1):110–16.

Malthus, T.
  1803   *An essay on the principle of population: or a view of its past and present effects on human
                happiness.* London: J. Johnson.

McDonald, M.M.A.
  1979   An examination of mid-Holocene settlement patterns in the central Zagros region of
                western Iran. Ph.D. diss., University of Toronto.

Mortensen, P.
  1974   A survey of prehistoric settlements in northern Luristan. *Acta Archaeologica* 45:1–47.
  1975   Survey and soundings in the Holailān valley 1974. In *Proceedings of the IIIrd Annual
                Symposium on Archaeological Research in Iran* [Tehran, 1974], ed. F. Bagherzadeh
                pp. 1–12. Tehran: Iranian Center for Archaeological Research.
  1976   Chalcolithic settlements in the Holailān valley. In *Proceedings of the IVth Annual
                Symposium on Archaeological Research in Iran* [Tehran, 1975], ed. F. Bagherzadeh,
                pp. 42–61. Tehran: Iranian Center for Archaeological Research.

Pullar, J.
  1979   Tepe Abdul Hosein. *Iran* 17:153–55.

Redman, C.L.
  1978   *The rise of civilization: from early farmers to urban society in the ancient Near East.* San
                Francisco: Freeman.

Simon, J.L.
  1977   *The economics of population growth.* Princeton: Princeton University Press.

Smith, P.E.L.
  1972   Land-use, settlement patterns and subsistence agriculture: a demographic perspective.
                In *Man, settlement and urbanism*, ed. P.J. Ucko, R. Tringham and G.W. Dimbleby, pp.
                409–25. London: Duckworth.
  1976   Reflections on four seasons of excavation at Tappeh Ganj Dareh. In *Proceedings of the
                IVth Annual Symposium on Archaeological Research in Iran* [Tehran, 1975], ed.
                F. Bagherzadeh, pp. 11–12. Tehran: Iranian Center for Archaeological Research.
  1978   An interim report on Ganj Dareh Tepe, Iran. *American Journal of Archaeology*
                82:538–40.

Smith, P.E.L., and Mortensen, P.
  1980   Three new "early Neolithic" sites in western Iran. *Current Anthropology* 21(4): 511–12.

Smith, P.E.L., and Young, T.C., Jr.
  1972   The evolution of early agriculture and culture in greater Mesopotamia: a trial model. In
                Population growth: anthropological implications, ed. B.J. Spooner, pp. 1–59. Cam-
                bridge, Mass.: Massachusetts Institute of Technology Press.

Watanabe, H.
  1968   Subsistence and ecology of northern food gatherers with special reference to the Ainu. In
                Man the hunter, ed. R.B. Lee and L. DeVore, pp. 69–77. Chicago: Aldine.

Wright, H.T., and Johnson, G.
  1975   Population exchange and early state formation in southwestern Iran. *American Anthropologist* 77(2):267–89.

Young, T.C., Jr.
  1966   Survey in western Iran, 1961. *Journal of Near Eastern Studies* 25(4):228–39.
  1972   Population densities and early Mesopotamian urbanism. In *Man, settlement and urbanism*, ed. P.J. Ucko, R. Tringham and G.W. Dimbleby, pp. 827–42. London: Duckworth.
  1975   An archaeological survey of the Kangavar valley. In *Proceedings of the IIIrd Annual Symposium on Archaeological Research in Iran* [Tehran, 1974], ed. F. Bagherzadeh, pp. 23–40. Tehran: Iranian Center for Archaeological Research.
  1977   Population dynamics and philosophical dichotomies. In *Mountains and Lowlands: essays in the archaeology of Greater Mesopotamia*, ed. L.D. Levine and T.C. Young, Jr., pp. 387–98. Bibliotheca Mesopotamia: Primary Sources and Interpretive Analyses for the Study of Mesopotamian Civilization and its Influence from Late Prehistory to the End of the Cuneiform Tradition, vol. 7. Malibu: Undena Publications.

Young, T.C., Jr., and Levine, L.D.
  1974   *Excavations of the Godin project: second progress report.* Toronto: Royal Ontario Museum.

Zeist, W. van, and Bottema, S.
  1977   Palynological investigation in western Iran. *Palaeohistoria* 19:20–85.

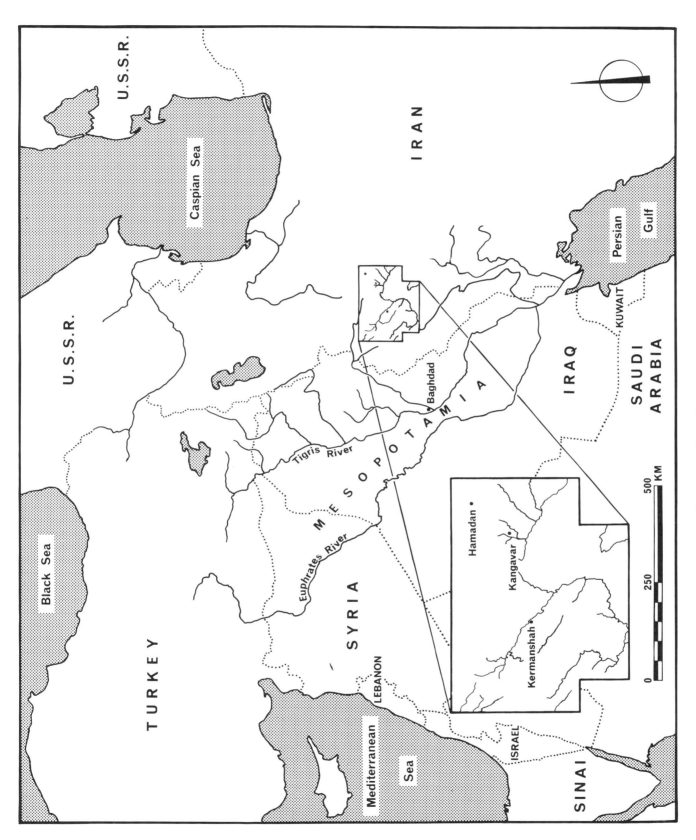

FIG. 1. — THE STUDY AREA.

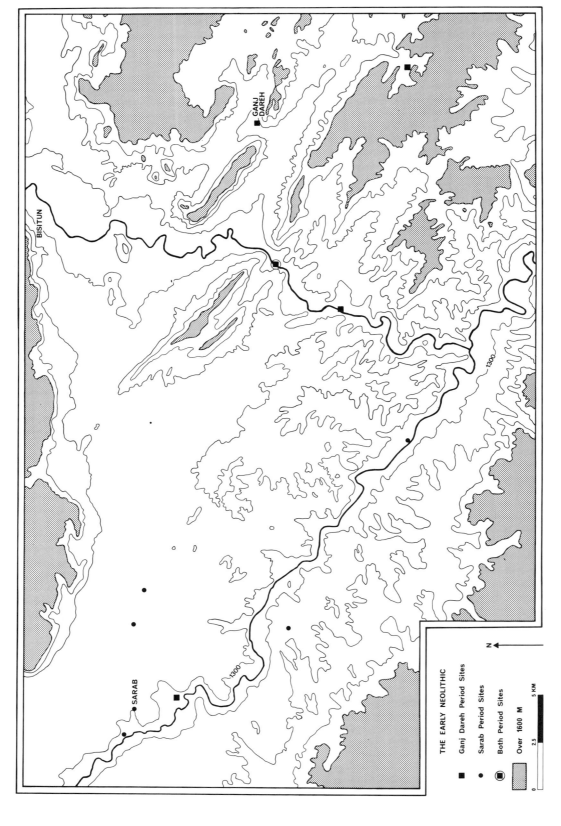

THE EARLY NEOLITHIC

■ Ganj Dareh Period Sites

• Sarab Period Sites

◉ Both Period Sites

▨ Over 1600 M

0   2.5   5 KM

FIG. 2. — THE EARLY NEOLITHIC: SITES IN THE IMMEDIATE NEIGHBORHOOD OF GANJ DAREH AND SARAB.

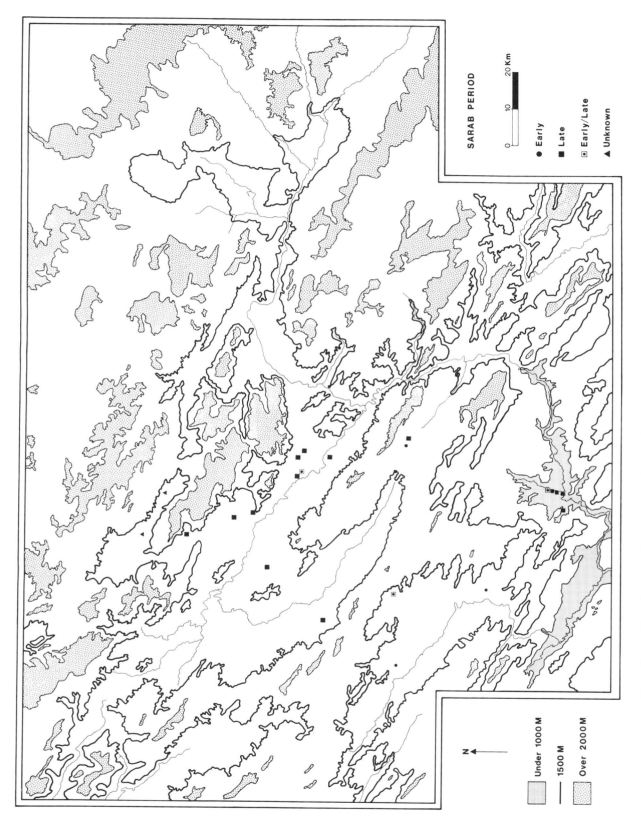

SARAB PERIOD

• Early
■ Late
⊡ Early/Late
▲ Unknown

0 10 20 Km

N

Under 1000 M
1500 M
Over 2000 M

FIG. 3. — THE LATER NEOLITHIC: SARAB PERIOD SITES WITHIN THE ENTIRE STUDY AREA.

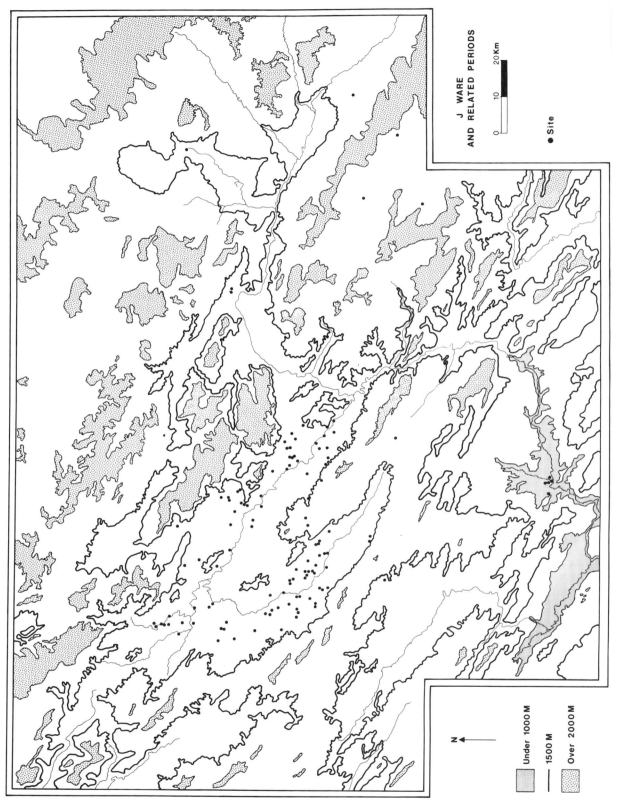

J WARE
AND RELATED PERIODS

0   10   20 Km

● Site

Under 1000 M

1500 M

Over 2000 M

N

FIG. 4. — EARLY CHALCOLITHIC SITES IN THE STUDY AREA.

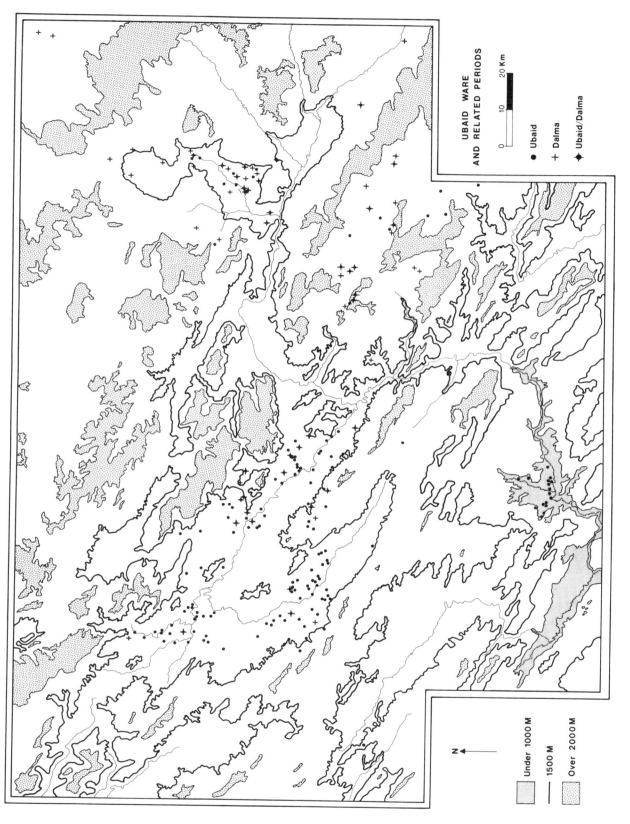

UBAID WARE
AND RELATED PERIODS

0   10   20 Km

● Ubaid
+ Dalma
✦ Ubaid/Dalma

N

Under 1000 M
1500 M
Over 2000 M

Fig. 5. — Late Chalcolithic–Ubaid Period Sites in the Study Area.

EARLY PIG DOMESTICATION IN THE FERTILE CRESCENT
A RETROSPECTIVE LOOK

Kent V. Flannery

INTRODUCTION

IN THE spring of 1959, as I sat taking notes in a World Prehistory course at the University of Chicago, I was startled to hear Dr. Robert Braidwood say, "Would Mr. Flannery please stay after class?" My first reaction was to wonder whether I had flunked the midterm so badly that he was going to advise me to try an alternative career. Instead, luckily for me, I was invited to join the Oriental Institute expedition to Iran. Having heard of my background in the zoology program at Chicago, Braidwood wanted me to serve as a field assistant for Dr. Charles Reed.

Thus began four of the most exciting years of my life, beginning with the excavations at Sarab and Asiab and ending with the excavations at Ali Kosh in 1963. Two of my first assignments from Reed were (1) to review the history of studies on early pig domestication and (2) to devise a method for identifying domestic pigs in Braidwood's archeological material. I began with the osteological collections of Chicago's Field Museum and the faunal remains from Gird Banahilk; I ended up with a series of studies and measurements (Flannery 1961) which have never been fully published.

In the last two decades, new excavations have greatly increased our knowledge of early pig domestication in the Zagros and Taurus Mountains, Khuzistan, northern Mesopotamia, and the Levant. Obviously, in a paper of this length one cannot cover all areas or all new discoveries. Thus I will simply try to review our understanding of early pig domestication in the Fertile Crescent, concentrating mainly on those areas where Bob Braidwood has worked, such as Kurdistan and the Amuq. Unfortunately, such important areas as Anatolia and the Iranian Plateau will have to wait until later.

Because the origins of the following study can be traced to my initial contact with Braidwood, it seems an entirely appropriate offering for a volume honoring his career in archeology. Were it not for him I would never have seen the Near East and possibly never have pursued archeological faunal analysis. Both are experiences I would not trade for anything.

THE PROBLEM

At the time I began my studies with Braidwood, one of the most discouraging problems of Near Eastern prehistory was a perpetuation in the literature of what Reed (1959, p. 1631) had described as "unverified claims" for early animal domestication. The pig, whose wide geographic range and ready exploitation of diverse environments had brought him into contact with prehistoric peoples over most of the world, was a notable example. Near Eastern archeology had only recently emerged from a period when the mere presence of pig remains at a site was taken as proof of domestication, and whole ancient economies were linked to swineherding without the slightest attention to osteological evidence.

Zoologists could hardly claim to have been more objective. One experienced paleontologist (Vaufrey 1951), suggesting the presence of domestic pig at a Natufian site some ten thousand years old, had taken as his evidence a single phalanx, without showing that it differed in any way from the wild phenotype. Seven years later, this same unverified claim was perpetuated in a summary paper by a highly regarded archeologist (Garrod 1958).

163

At that time there were comparatively few reports from the Near East that had utilized available data on how the domestic pig differs structurally from its wild ancestor. Still rarer were studies on how these differences could be wrung from the broken, disarticulated fragments that are usually the only zoological evidence recovered through excavation. The purpose of my original study was to present concrete, metric data on pig remains from several sequences of archeological sites, combining this with radiocarbon dates where possible, and to suggest when and where the domestication of this important food animal took place in the Fertile Crescent in prehistoric times. I quickly discovered that some of Braidwood's sites had samples so large that one could speak of statistical *populations* of pigs with a mean, range, and standard deviation rather than of isolated specimens.

TAXONOMY

It is the opinion of zoologists that all domestic pigs of Europe, Southwest Asia, and northern Africa were derived from *Sus scrofa* Linnaeus; indeed, Ellerman and Morrison-Scott (1951) list no other wild species of pigs for those three regions. Theories that East Asian domesticates were introduced into the area under consideration during prehistoric time, once considered a real possibility, by 1960 seemed improbable in the light of studies by various regional specialists.

Ackerknecht (1950) had found no reason to believe, on the basis of anatomy, that domesticated north and central European pigs were anything but descendants of the local *S. scrofa*. Likewise, Boessneck (1956) had referred pigs of the early Greek Neolithic to this species. Gaillard (1934) had found enough similarity in early Swiss and Egyptian domesticates to refer them to the same subspecies of *S. scrofa*, and Reed (1959) saw a similar origin for prehistoric herd swine in the Near East. The lingering in the literature of older constructs like *Sus palustris* (e.g., in Josien 1956) no longer tended to be taken seriously by other workers. Invalid as a species since 1909, the *palustris* form may nonetheless have been a legitimate prehistoric subspecies of *S. scrofa*, although one might question how appropriate a designation it is for Near Eastern pigs.

In the years since the advent of modern field techniques, skeletal material from prehistoric sites had accumulated rapidly — more rapidly than it could be fully processed by the (then) few available archeologically minded zoologists if it continued to be necessary for each man to work out his own independent skeletal criteria for domestication. In the case of *Sus scrofa* it became evident that there was need of a series of measurements by which wild and domestic pig remains could be quickly distinguished from each other.

To be truly useful for the prehistoric archeologist this set of measurements had to be one that could be applied to small fragments of bone rather than to whole skeletons. Preferably, the part or parts of the body involved should be those most often preserved over long periods of time. Further, to be a reliable tool, the measurements had to be based on as large a statistical sample as possible over as wide a geographic range as seemed relevant to the problem. For stability, the character involved had to be a polygenic one, not highly subject to drift, regional fluctuation, or large sampling error.

An examination of pig remains from a number of the Near Eastern sites already excavated by Braidwood for the Oriental Institute of the University of Chicago revealed that the most frequently preserved skeletal item was dentition — jaws, fragments of jaws, isolated teeth. Molars in particular, because of their size, strength, and hardness of enamel, were preserved in greater quantity than any other part of the body. Distal ends of humeri were only a very distant second; in the case of several sites, molars were the only available evidence of pig. I therefore turned to the literature on the early history of archeological faunal analysis to see what conclusions had been reached by previous investigators regarding differences in the dentition of wild and domestic pigs.

Table 1. — Ranges of Molar and Premolar Length in Three Groups of European Pigs

Race	Length of Tooth or Tooth Row (mm)						Size of sample
	M3 sup.	M1−3 sup.	P1−M3 sup.	M3 inf.	M1−3 inf.	P1−M3 inf.	
Modern wild European Sus scrofa	36−50	77−87	130−141	38−53	76−88	149−154	11
Pigs from "pile-dweller" sites	26−40	58−74	99−120	24−42	57−79	108−136	3?
Modern domestic European pigs	30−32	64−69	100−119	34−43	63−83	117−135	Not given

SOURCE: Figures, taken from Pira (1909), incorporate those of Rütimeyer (1862).

PREVIOUS WORK ON EARLY DOMESTIC PIGS

Switzerland appears to have been one of the first real centers for the study of the prehistoric pig. There the discovery of the fauna from the era of the Swiss "pile dwellings," whose remains were often well preserved in the peat bogs, or *torfmooren*, of the area, led to a series of publications by Ludwig Rütimeyer (e.g., 1860, 1862). Through numerous measurements Rütimeyer established the skeletal phenotype of the modern wild and domestic European *Sus scrofa* and undertook to show that the pig associated with the pile dwellings could not be equated with either of them. The *torfschwein*, as it was nicknamed, received the status of a separate species, which Rütimeyer called *Sus palustris*; later workers (cf. Pira 1909; Gaillard 1934) reduced it to a race, *S. scrofa palustris*.

"The characteristic impression of the *torfschwein*," Rütimeyer wrote in 1862 (p. 45), "lies in its short, low, pointed face . . . ." He eventually concluded that it must be an Asian form or a hybrid Eurasian pig that had "lived wild in the same area of the European wild pig."

This study had the advantage of being based on more complete portions of the skeleton than would likely have been available without the preservation in peat. Many of the statistics are for entire bones and, as such, are of limited use to the Near Eastern prehistorian, who deals in splinters; others, for articular ends alone, are more helpful. The dental measurements given by Rütimeyer in 1862 for wild, domestic, and "pile-dweller" pigs appear to be effective criteria for distinguishing the wild from the domestic phenotype and are repeated in table 1, revised and amplified by the addition of similar figures from Pira (1909).

Rütimeyer's research pointed up the fact that both jaws of the *torfschwein*, as well as those of the European domestic pig, were noticeably shorter than the jaws of wild *Sus scrofa*. Premolars and incisors were drawn closer together, so that the diastema between them was one-third less than that of modern wild forms. Canines were considerably smaller. Premolars were short and the distance between them had lessened, the result being that the total length of the cheek-tooth row was consistently shorter than that of the European wild race. The heel of the third molar was greatly reduced, and the whole molar row, according to Rütimeyer's figures, was significantly shorter in domestic forms. This seemed to accompany an overall shortening of the skull (table 2).

But Rütimeyer, useful as his research may have been, failed to recognize the real historical position of the *torfschwein*. It remained for Adolf Pira of the University of Stockholm to demonstrate that *Sus scrofa palustris* was not an Asian form and not a hybrid, but rather a prehistoric domestic race that developed slowly — through shortening of the snout and the skeletal extremities — from the native wild European pig (Pira 1909, pp. 373−4). With the

Table 2. — Measurements of Length of Skull and Mandible in Three Groups of European Pigs

Race	Basilar Length of Skull (mm)	Length of Lower Jaw at Level of Alveolar Ridge (mm)	Size of sample
Wild *Sus scrofa* from Swedish peat bogs	375–388	316–330	3
Domestic pigs from Middle Ages (Uppsala)	255–261	--	Not given
Modern domestic pigs (Sweden)	310–334	250–306	4

SOURCE: Figures taken from Pira (1909).

discovery of this fact, many of the main trends leading to the domestic phenotype appear in sharper detail; it is also evident that the modern domestic pigs of Europe, having been selectively and efficiently bred for size in the centuries since the Renaissance, are consequently bigger than were the early prehistoric domestic pigs.

Pira was also the first, apparently, to study the long sequence of changes from wild to domestic pig that can be noticed in certain stratified archeological deposits of northern Europe. Working with bones from sites of the Stone, Bronze, and Iron Ages of Sweden he was able to catch the moment at which the domestic phenotype became apparent in Scandinavia (Pira 1909). Pira used two control groups: wild-pig skeletons unearthed in Scandinavian peat bogs and domestic-pig skeletons (dating from the Middle Ages to modern times) in the collections at Uppsala.

Archeological specimens studied by Pira fell into three groups: (1) bones from the "late stone age" sites of Ringsjön and Åloppe; (2) bones from the lowest ("pre-cattle-breeding") levels at the site of Stora Karlsö; and (3) bones from upper ("cattle-breeding") levels at Stora Karlsö and the contemporary Neolithic site of Gullrum. Pigs from Ringsjön and Åloppe were indistinguishable from modern and ancient wild *Sus scrofa*; length of their upper third molars ranged from 40–44 mm. Pigs from the lowest levels at Stora Karlsö, however, had a range of only 36–39 mm for the upper third molar, while those from highest levels at the same site had a range of only 27–32 mm. According to Pira (1909, p. 245), the pigs from Stora Karlsö and Gullrum showed a definite reduction of the snout, including a shortening of both upper and lower jaws; hence they were probably domestic. Pira concluded: "The fact that domestic swine first appear gradually and together with wild pigs, and that at the older sites of the late stone age . . . they are larger than at the later [sites] . . . indicates that our Neolithic swine are not imported, but develop in Sweden as an indigenous race" (ibid, pp. 372–73).

The early studies by Pira and Rütimeyer were pioneering works, which have been followed up by dozens of modern zoologists. It is impossible to summarize here all the studies on European Neolithic faunal remains that are available today, but recent radiocarbon dates suggest that even the North European Neolithic may be pushed back to 4000 B.C., and pig domestication along with it.

POSSIBLE CAUSES OF SNOUT-SHORTENING AFTER DOMESTICATION

The causes of shortening of the snout in early domesticates, of which the shortening of the molar-premolar row is one symptom, have been the subject of much speculation. Some workers have viewed the shortening in terms of reduced selection pressure for the long muzzle associated with the "grubbing and rooting" behavior of the wild pig. Another theory, often advanced by the German school, is that the pig, like some other domestic animals, appears to be merely a pedomorphic race of the wild species. The existence of a process "that in a sense can be called fetalization," by which the short snout of the juvenile developmental stage persists into adulthood, has been claimed by adherents of this theory (e.g., Starck 1954, p. 208).

Not all zoologists agree with this. For example, Kelm, who studied the postembryonic development of the young wild and domestic pig of Europe at various ages, believed that the short snout of the domestic Berkshire hog, at least, was not the result of a persistence of the juvenile stage but of a kind of development completely different from that of the wild pig. "The skull of an eight-day-old Berkshire," he maintained, "clearly differs from the skull of a newborn wild pig. It is in all respects more fully developed. Occipital and bizygomatic width is greater; the first premolar is more fully erupted. In spite of this, the snout region has a shorter and wider form" (1938, p. 520). Kelm's photographs are convincing, but it should be borne in mind that he was examining a large, highly specialized, snub-nosed modern breed of pig, the product of considerable selective breeding, which differs as widely from Rütimeyer's *torfschwein* as it does from the wild *S. scrofa*. The early, primitive domestic pig is perhaps a different problem, and here one of the features that makes the pedomorphic theory attractive is that it does not imply, on the part of prehistoric man, the kind of conscious, scientific breeding that was necessary to produce the Berkshire hog.

Boettger (1958) regards domestic pedomorphism as the result of the domesticate's becoming precociously fertile while still physically immature. This phenomenon in pigs, he feels, "can generally be interpreted as infantilism, for in the young animal the jaw is still short ... the persistence of a juvenile developmental stage in the domestic animal is obviously the consequence of a most premature conclusion of growth ... as a consequence of early sexual maturity, called forth through changed environmental conditions" (Boettger 1958, p. 20). In a footnote on the same page he adds, "The earlier conclusion of growth as a phenomenon of domestication, by reason of which the domestic animals are of lesser size than the wild stock, was generally well established in the early period of animal domestication." Spurway's investigation into the origins of domestication also makes note of a "sexual precocity and increased fecundity, some of which is consequent on lengthening of the reproductive periods and thus due to alterations in hormonal systems" (1955, p. 349).

One striking feature of the domestic phenotype is its impermanence once pigs are released from captivity; the return of the Arkansas "razorback" in the direction of the wild phenotype within a relatively few generations is one of the best-known examples. Whatever the causes of the trend toward short-snouted pedomorphism, it is obviously a readily reversible trend.

EARLY ANALYSES OF NEAR EASTERN PIGS

Perhaps the first serious attempt to apply metric data to the problem of early pig domestication in Western Asia was Duerst's analysis of the faunal remains recovered by Pumpelly (1908) at the oasis of Anau in Turkestan. The Anau excavation has always been a favorite of Bob Braidwood's, and he used to point out to his students that Pumpelly was far ahead of his time in using a team of interdisciplinary specialists to attack the problem of domestication.

The earliest levels of Anau (Period I-A) probably began in the fifth millennium, and Period I-B may have run to roughly 4000 B.C. According to Pumpelly (1908, p. 39), only wild animals were present at first, "out of which were locally domesticated the long-horned ox, the pig and horse, and successively two breeds of sheep." Reed (1960, fig. 7) feels that pigs were "certainly" domestic by the time of Anau II, and the measurements support this; see, for example, the 30-mm-long lower M3 listed by Duerst (1908).

But was Duerst right in feeling that domestic pigs were not present at Anau *before* Period II (perhaps 4000–3000 B.C.)? Considerable light is shed on this question by the discovery that Duerst believed domestic swine to be descendants of the small "*Sus vittatus*" (now reduced to a subspecies of *S. scrofa*). The domesticates themselves he called *Sus palustris*. The skulls of the Anau pigs, he observed, "possess the greatest similarity to the skulls of the *torfschwein*. . . . According to the researches of Rütimeyer, Rollestone, Otto, and others, *Sus palustris* . . . is derived from *Sus vittatus*, which would agree very well with our finding" (Duerst, in Pumpelly 1908, p. 355). One Anau brain case was "decidedly that of a small adult pig, whose front shows a slight convexity, which we usually find in the Indian *Sus cristatus* or *Sus vittatus*" (ibid). Thus it is clear that Duerst would have interpreted any small *Sus* remains from the lowest levels at Anau as being simply the wild form of *Sus vittatus*, since he further concluded that *Sus scrofa* probably reached Anau "only after the south Asiatic wild boar *(Sus vittatus)* had disappeared" (p. 357).

The intellectual atmosphere in 1908 was one that welcomed the concept of migrations out of some "Aryan homeland" into Europe, bearing such creatures as *Sus palustris*. It is far more likely, on the basis of what we now know, that the small pigs in Anau I were locally domesticated *Sus scrofa*.

EARLY PIG DOMESTICATION IN THE FERTILE CRESCENT

When I began to search for pigs in Braidwood's faunal collections we had little more to go on than a handful of studies like Duerst's and a series of European measurements. Before plunging into the archeological material from Southwest Asia it was clearly necessary to establish the dental characteristics of the wild pigs from that area. For use as a control, I measured 21 specimens of wild *Sus scrofa* from Iran, Iraq, Syria, and Israel. From these statistics (table 3) the dentition of *S. scrofa* emerged as being rather uniform over the given range, since there were no size differences between males and females except for the canine[1] and no significant differences between pigs from the lowland marshes, the foothills, and the high mountains.

Only permanent teeth were measured, whether they were from pigs collected in the wild or from those from archeological excavations; all lengths given in this study, unless stated otherwise, are in millimeters. They include: maximal length of each molar, taken along the axis of the tooth row; maximal length of the whole molar row (M1–3); and maximal length of the whole molar-premolar or cheek-tooth row (P1–M3). Since comparisons of wild and domestic pigs indicate that "the shortening of the skull following domestication is also well-established in the length of the molars" (Amschler 1939, p. 75), these measurements are believed to be useful for archeological purposes. Pira's (1909) and Hartmann-Frick's (1960) results tended to support this, and Amschler (1939, p. 68) had called the length of the M3 in particular "a very essential measurement."

Measurements of "zoo specimens" — those born, or raised for much of their lives, in captivity — were not included, in light of the numerous studies on mammals who exhibit pathological skeletal characters as a result of the abnormal life or diet of zoo situations (see, for example, Howell 1925).

The range of measurements shown by my control group fits comfortably with (1) measurements taken by Amon (1938) from 37 specimens of wild pig from the glacial, interglacial, and prehistoric periods of Eurasia; (2) measurements of Algerian, Moroccan, and Egyptian pigs made by Charles Reed; and (3) measurements of more than 40 Israeli wild pigs kindly sent to me by Mr. Gary Nurkin of Tel-Aviv University (personal communication).

---

1. One of the advantages of using dentition is that for many mammals it displays less sexual dimorphism than do the long bones.

Table 3. — Lengths of Cheek Teeth or Cheek Tooth Rows in 21 Specimens of Wild *Sus scrofa* from Southwest Asia.

Provenience	Museum and Number	Length of Tooth or Tooth Row (mm)									
		M3 sup.	M2 sup.	M1 sup.	M1–3 sup.	P1–M3 sup.	M3 inf.	M2 inf.	M1 inf.	M1–3 inf.	P1–M3 inf.
Iran	CAR 502 ♀	36.1	20.7	16.5	73.3	123.6	41.1	23.1	18.0	82.2	143.2
Iran	CAR 543 ♀	33.2	24.1	18.9	76.2	124.6	40.2	23.5	18.8	82.5	148.0
Iran	CAR 551 ♂	41.6	22.6	16.1	80.3	132.7	44.1	24.3	15.7	84.1	148.1
Iran	CAR 552 ♂	36.2	20.4	14.4	71.0	119.0	39.2	21.0	16.6	76.8	147.0
Iran	CAR 555 ♀	36.0	25.2	16.4	77.6	131.9	41.8	26.4	16.1	84.3	147.4
Iran	HBKW; no number; ♂ collected Jan. 1956	37.3	22.4	17.2	69.6	124.9	40.8	23.0	16.3	79.5	142.2
Iraq	CNHM 42439 ♂	38.8	26.3	17.0	81.5	132.4	40.2	24.2	17.4	81.1	141.7
Iraq	CNHM 42440 ♂	37.3	20.8	15.1	73.2	122.0	41.9	21.9	16.0	79.8	139.4
Iraq	CNHM 43325 ♂	35.5	25.0	18.8	79.3	121.3	41.2	24.7	17.1	83.0	147.1
Iraq	CNHM 43327 ♀	42.2	20.7	15.5	78.4	129.8	42.7	21.8	16.0	80.5	145.3
Iraq	CNHM 46077 ♀	42.8	21.5	15.5	79.8	125.2	49.3	22.1	17.2	88.6	146.0
Iraq	CNHM 47417 ♂	37.1	24.2	18.1	79.3	131.2	41.1	24.1	18.5	84.0	151.0
Iraq	CNHM 84476 ♀	35.5	23.1	16.5	74.7	122.4	37.6	22.9	17.0	75.2	- -
Syria	CNHM 44722 ♂	40.2	24.3	19.0	83.5	133.5	38.8	25.2	18.8	82.8	143.8
Israel	HUJ; unlabeled; ♂ shot near L. Huleh	38.1	24.0	18.5	80.6	134.7	38.5	23.6	17.8	79.9	152.3
Israel	BPITA M681 ♂	36.1	24.2	17.9	78.2	130.4	41.2	21.6	15.0	77.8	149.7
Israel	BPITA M683 ♂	36.3	23.6	18.0	77.9	129.2	42.8	23.8	17.9	84.5	152.5
Israel	BPITA M1346 ♂	36.9	24.4	18.6	79.9	130.1	40.1	22.6	17.7	80.4	138.4
Israel	BPITA M1849 ♀	36.0	24.2	17.6	79.5	130.0	41.7	24.1	17.8	83.0	148.3
Israel	BPITA M1928 ♀	37.4	23.5	18.1	79.0	132.7	42.6	23.0	17.7	82.9	156.0
Israel	BPITA MS/45 ♀	34.1	23.9	18.0	75.0	128.0	39.4	23.8	17.9	81.1	152.5
Mean length		37.4	23.3	17.2	77.5	128.1	41.3	23.4	17.2	81.6	147.0
Standard deviation		2.51	1.65	1.36	3.54	4.61	2.43	1.29	1.05	2.96	4.64
Standard error of mean		0.55	0.36	0.30	0.77	1.01	0.53	0.28	0.23	0.65	1.04

On the basis of table 3,[2] the following generalizations about tooth length in wild Near Eastern pigs might be made:

1. The true mean length of the upper third molar in wild Near Eastern *Sus scrofa* is probably between 35.7 and 38.9 mm. Ninety-nine percent (two standard deviations) of all wild pigs should have upper third molars between 30.2 and 44.4 mm in length; the range observed in the control group was 33.2−42.8 mm.

2. The true mean length of the lower third molar is probably between 40.2 and 42.4 mm. Ninety-nine percent of all wild pigs should have lower third molars between 36.3 and 46.3 mm in length; the range observed in the control group was 37.6−49.3 mm.

3. The true mean length of the upper M1−M3 row is probably between 75.4 and 79.6 mm. Ninety-nine percent of all wild pigs should have an upper molar row between 67.8 and 87.3 mm in length; the range observed in the control group was 69.6−83.5 mm.

4. The true mean length of the lower M1−M3 row is probably between 79.7 and 83.5 mm. Ninety-nine percent of all wild pigs should have a lower molar row between 73.1 and 90.2 mm in length; the range observed in the control group was 75.2−88.6 mm.

5. The true mean length of the entire upper cheek tooth row (P1−M3) is probably between 125.1 and 130.9 mm. Ninety-nine percent of all wild pigs should have an upper cheek tooth row between 114.5 and 141.5 mm in length; the range observed in the control group was 119.0−134.7 mm.

6. The true mean length of the entire lower cheek tooth row (P1−M3) is probably between 144.0 and 150.0 mm. Ninety-nine percent of all wild pigs should have a lower cheek tooth row between 133.4 and 160.6 mm in length; the range observed in the control group was 138.4−156.0 mm.

Armed with these figures it is possible now to examine the evidence for early pig domestication in the Near East. I will begin with the Zagros Mountains, where Braidwood first began concentrating his investigations on early food production, and use his faunal collections as my jumping-off place. All measurements, unless stated otherwise, are my own.

THE ZAGROS MOUNTAINS

9000−7000 B.C.

There is no evidence of pig domestication in the Zagros during the period of "incipient cultivation" as defined by Braidwood and Howe (1960). Relevant sites include Karim Shahir (Chemchemal valley, Iraq), Asiab (Kermanshah valley, Iran), Zawi Chemi (Shanidar valley, Iraq), and Ganj Dareh (Gamas Ab valley, Iran).

Karim Shahir was one of the sites included in my original study (Flannery 1961). From the modest sample from Howe's 500 m² excavation (Braidwood and Howe 1960) I was able to cull only one mandible fragment of *Sus scrofa*, although other ungulates are more numerous. The tooth measurements (table 4) fell within the range of wild pigs that I have measured.

The lowest level at Tepe Asiab (Braidwood 1960), some 2.1 m below the surface, yielded the remains of a circular semisubterranean structure 9−10 m in diameter, whose base had been excavated into sterile caliche. This structure contained one of the largest single faunal collections

---

2. Abbreviations for museum collections used in table 3 are as follows:
   BPITA . . . . .Biological-Pedagogical Institute, Tel Aviv
   CAR . . . . .Field number assigned by collector, C.A. Reed,
   in Iran (1960); specimens now in CNHM
   CNHM . . . . .Chicago Natural History Museum (Field Museum)
   HUJ . . . . .Hebrew University, Jerusalem

Table 4. — Lengths of Pig Cheek Teeth or Cheek Tooth Rows in Specimens Dating to the Period 9000–7000 B.C. in the Zagros Mountains

| Archeological Site | Identifying Marks or Period | Length of Tooth or Tooth Row (mm) | | | |
		M3 sup.	M3 inf.	M2 inf.	M1–3 inf.
Karim Shahir (Iraq)	K.I., East Bluff surf. 0–.40	--	39.0	26.3	--
Asiab (Iran)	Km. 27, pig 1	--	40.1	25.9	83.1
Asiab (Iran)	Km. 27, pig 2	--	39.1	--	--
Asiab (Iran)	Km. 27, pig 3	--	42.6	--	--
Asiab (Iran)	Km. 27, pig 4	--	50.1	--	--
Asiab (Iran)	Km. 27, pig 5	41.2	--	--	--
Asiab (Iran)	Km. 27, pig 6	--	41.3	--	--
Asiab (Iran)	Km. 27, pig 7	--	--	24.1	--
Asiab (Iran)	Km. 27, pig 8	--	--	24.9	--
Asiab (Iran)	Km. 27, pig 9	--	--	24.4	--
Asiab (Iran)	Km. 27, pig 10	--	--	23.5	--
Asiab (Iran)	Km. 27, pig 11	--	--	26.1	--
Asiab (Iran)	Km. 27, pig 12	--	--	24.2	--
Asiab pigs {	Mean length	--	42.6	24.7	--
	Standard deviation	--	4.37	0.96	--
	Standard error of mean	--	1.95	0.36	--

NOTE: There is no skeletal evidence of domestication during this period.

of this period; it took Charles Reed and me some three days to excavate the heaped-up animal bones. Best of all, the collection included a sample of pig dentition large enough that one could treat it as a population with a mean and a standard deviation. The molars from Asiab (table 4) should be compared with those of wild Iranian pigs; the impression is that of a homogeneous wild population, which could have come from the thickets along the river below the site. Mean length of the lower M3 of the Asiab pigs is 42.6 mm as compared with 41.3 for the mean of the wild control group.[3] Two more teeth, both second molars, appeared in the upper levels of the site; their lengths match those from the semisubterranean structure. One, from the 1.05/1.20 m level (below datum), measures 25.5 mm. The other, found between the surface and level B, is 23.4 mm long.

Zawi Chemi is another site with some evidence of a circular structure (Rose Solecki 1964). Perkins's (1964) study of the fauna showed no evidence of domestic pig. Similarly, Perkins (personal communication) reports no evidence of pig domestication at Ganj Dareh, a preceramic site with even more impressive architecture and very early evidence of the domestic goat (Smith 1972).

7000–5700 B.C.

According to our present evidence, the domestic pig made its first appearance in the Zagros

---

3. Since my 1961 study, Bökönyi has published the whole Asiab faunal collection. His measurements of the pig teeth (Bökönyi 1977, pp. 75–76) differ insignificantly from mine, the difference being about what one would expect from two persons using two different calipers.

Table 5. — Stratigraphic Occurrence of Pig Dentition at Jarmo

	Operation I				Operation II		
Level	Fragments	Min. indiv.	Potsherds	Level	Fragments	Min. indiv.	Potsherds
				1	76 (D)	15–19	Ca. 5000
	This area mixed with other material; bones not counted.			2	71 (D)	16–20	Ca. 5000
				2⊥	5 (B)	3	Ca. 2000
3, pit 2	5 (D)	3	Ca. 22	3	3 (B)	2	Ca. 100
				4	5	3	68
3	7 (B)	3		5	0	0	65

— POTTERY APPEARS —

4	2	1	None	6	0	0	None
5	8	2	None				
6	3	2	None		Unexcavated		
7⊥	2	1	None				
8	3	1	None				

NOTE: (D): Fragments include clearly domestic pig on basis of length of M3.
    (B): Fragments include pig on borderline between wild and domestic phenotypes on basis of length of M3.

mountains some time between 6500 and 6000 B.C. Because the village of Jarmo (Chemchemal valley, Iraq) provides crucial data for this appearance it will be the site examined in greatest detail. Other relevant sites include Tepe Sarab (Kermanshah valley, Iran) and Tepe Guran (Hulailan valley, Iran).

The seven meters of deposit at Jarmo, first of the early village farming communities excavated in Kurdistan, may represent the debris of some 750 years or more of occupation. Through all strata occur small tauf-walled houses, flint sickle blades, and fragments of grinding stones; the latter were perhaps used in connection with the two strains of wheat and one strain of barley found to be domestic at the site (Helbaek 1960, pp. 102–8). Horn cores of domestic goat indicate the presence of that animal even in lower levels (Reed 1960, p. 131).

There is "an overall consistency of the Jarmo assemblage from bottom to top," according to Braidwood and Howe (1960, p. 49), "with its own implications of inherent cultural continuity." Partway through that continuity, however, a few interesting innovations occurred. Pottery, for example, appeared only after about two-thirds of the occupation had taken place; it was not found more than 2.25 m below the surface. Certain changes in the faunal proportions seem to have accompanied this innovation.

Table 5 shows the stratigraphic occurrence of specimens of pig dentition in the two main operations (I, II) at the site. It will be noted that in all the preceramic levels exposed in I and II, only eighteen fragments were found — the remains, perhaps, of seven individual pigs. Measurements of the dentition from preceramic levels (table 6) show that only the wild phenotype was present and that the wild strain at that time was apparently at least as large as that present at Tepe Asiab. Food production, whether of grain or goats, was not so efficient in these lower levels that hunting could be completely abandoned; accompanying wild pig in preceramic Jarmo were the remains of deer, gazelle, and onager.

Table 6. — Lengths of Pig Cheek Teeth in Specimens from
Prepottery Levels at Jarmo, Iraq (ca. 6750−6000 B.C.)

Identifying Marks	Length of Tooth (mm)				
	M3 sup.	M2 sup.	M1 sup.	M3 inf.	M2 inf.
J−B 0−1	40.5	--	--	44.0	--
J−B 1−2	--	--	--	47.1	--
J−D 0−1	43.2	25.4	--	--	--
J I, 8	--	23.0	--	--	--
J I, 7⊥	--	24.8	--	--	23.2
J I, 6	--	--	--	--	23.0
J I, 5	--	25.0	21.0	38.5	22.2
--	--	--	--	--	21.1

NOTE: There is no skeletal evidence for domestication at this period. (After
Flannery 1961.)

After the appearance of ceramics at about 6000 B.C. there is a rapid increase in numbers of pigs at the site. In all, 172 fragments of jaws and dentition, representing perhaps 40−50 individuals, were found in the pottery-bearing levels shown in table 5. And here in the upper levels of the site — as shown by table 7 — there appear the first domestic specimens seen so far.

Not all the specimens from these upper levels are outside the wild range, but it will be apparent from table 7 that none of the M3's, for example, even approach the mean length of the wild M3. Moreover, the pigs from the pottery-bearing levels form a homogeneous population whose standard deviation from the mean is less than that of the control group.[4] As time progressed, increasing numbers of specimens falling into our "clearly domestic" length range appeared, as did large numbers of juvenile individuals. Of 76 fragments from Level 1 of Operation II about 35 are from immature pigs. And much as at Stora Karlsö Cave (see page 8), "borderline cases" precede the clearly domesticated animals in the stratigraphic sequence (Levels I,3; II,3; II,2). No domestic phenotypes whatsoever are found in the preceramic levels of the site.

The next question is whether *all* the pigs from the pottery-bearing levels at Jarmo were domestic or only those whose dental lengths fall well outside the wild range were. In view of the low standard of deviation it would seem probable that we are dealing with a single closely knit population whose range, in its upper limits, only slightly overlaps the lower limits of the wild, control group. Presumably, therefore, all the pigs from the upper levels were domestic; this conclusion is also reasonable in view of the very limited amount of wild pig hunting reflected in the lower levels.

A possible explanation for the time of arrival of the concept of pig domestication at Jarmo might be sought in an unpublished paper by Adams (1952) on the pottery at the site. Adams states (p. 62):

> The sudden appearance of pottery of a relatively highly developed type at a time corresponding roughly with level 5 in operation II implies that the idea of portable pottery, and probably also its technique of manufacture, was introduced from some outside source at that time . . . . Since sherds from probably no more than 35 vessels are present in the earlier manifestation it is possible that all of the earlier pottery was actually imported.

4. A test for significance of the difference in mean length of the upper M3 between our control group (n = 21) and the pigs from upper Jarmo (n = 11) yields a result of t = 5.07 (significant at greater than the .001 level).

Table 7. — Measurements of Pig Cheek Teeth in Specimens from Upper, Pottery-bearing
Levels at Jarmo (ca. 6000 B.C.)

Identifying Marks	Length of Tooth (mm)						
	M3 sup.	M2 sup.	M1 sup.	M1–3 sup.	M3 inf.	M2 inf.	M1 inf.
J I, 3	33.5	21.3	15.4	70.2	--	--	--
J I, 3	--	--	19.2	--	--	--	--
J I, 3, pit 2	30.9	--	--	--	--	--	--
J I, 3, pit 2	--	--	--	--	--	24.3	18.2
J II, 3	34.5	22.3	--	--	--	--	--
J II, 3	--	--	--	--	36.0	--	--
J II, 2⊥	--	--	--	--	--	23.6	--
J II, 2⊥	--	--	17.9	--	--	--	--
J II, 2	34.1	--	--	--	38.2	--	--
J II, 2	31.8	--	--	--	--	24.3	--
J II, 2	34.4	--	--	--	--	24.4	--
J II, 2	34.3	--	--	--	--	22.3	--
J II, 2	34.0	--	--	--	--	24.2	--
J II, 2	28.5	21.1	--	--	--	--	18.5
J II, 2	--	22.0	--	--	--	--	18.5
J II, 2	--	21.9	--	--	--	--	--
J II, 2	--	23.0	--	--	--	--	--
J II, 2	--	20.7	--	--	--	--	--
J II, 2	--	23.0	--	--	--	--	--
J II, 2	--	20.2	--	--	--	--	--
J II, 2	--	20.6	--	--	--	--	--
J II, 2	--	23.1	17.0	--	--	--	--
J II, 2	--	20.8	17.0	--	--	--	--
J II, 2	--	--	17.2	--	--	--	--
J II, 2	--	--	17.1	--	--	--	--
J II, 2	--	--	18.0	--	--	--	--
J II, 2	--	--	18.6	--	--	--	--
J II, 2	--	--	16.6	--	--	--	--
J II, 2	--	--	17.9	--	--	--	--
J II, 2	--	--	18.5	--	--	--	--
J II, 1	32.9	--	--	--	36.4	--	--
J II, 1	23.8	21.6	16.6	67.2	--	24.0	--
J II, 1	--	24.7	--	--	--	23.6	--
J II, 1	--	17.1	--	--	--	22.8	--
J II, 1	--	19.2	--	--	--	23.5	--
J II, 1	--	24.0	--	--	--	24.0	--
J II, 1	--	22.1	--	--	--	22.7	18.0
J II, 1	--	23.0	--	--	--	--	18.5
J II, 1	--	26.5	--	--	--	--	18.2
J II, 1	21.0	--	--	--	--	--	--

Table 7. — *continued*

Identifying Marks	Length of Tooth (mm)						
	M3 sup.	M2 sup.	M1 sup.	M1−3 sup.	M3 inf.	M2 inf.	M1 inf.
J II, 1	21.1	--	--	--	--	--	--
J II, 1	22.8	18.7	--	--	--	--	--
J II, 1	20.6	17.0	--	--	--	--	--
J II, 1	22.8	18.1	--	--	--	--	--
J II, 1	--	19.1	--	--	--	--	--
J II, 1	--	19.0	--	--	--	--	--
J II, 1	--	17.5	--	--	--	--	--
J II, 1	--	18.4	--	--	--	--	--
J II, 1	--	18.4	--	--	--	--	--
Mean length	32.9	21.9	17.8	68.7	36.9	23.6	18.3
Standard deviation	1.85	1.85	0.98	--	1.17	0.70	0.21
Standard error of mean	0.56	0.37	0.21	--	0.68	0.20	0.09

NOTE: Pigs appear to have been domestic during this period. (After Flannery 1961.)

The "early manifestation" of domestic pig at Jarmo probably involves no more than six to ten individual animals (in the area excavated), which suggests that much the same could be said of the pigs as of the pottery. This leaves us with several unanswered questions. Were the early "borderline" domestic pigs at Jarmo brought in from another site where swineherding had only just begun? If so, were they introduced along with pottery? Or was it merely the knowledge of pottery and swineherding that reached Jarmo, rather than the actual vessels and animals? Alternatively, did pig domestication begin at Jarmo independently of developments elsewhere? So far, no site in the Zagros has produced earlier evidence for swineherding, and most cases are later.

In summary, let us assign a tentative date of ca. 6000 B.C. for pig domestication in Kurdistan, and let us say that it began in the Zagros (1) later than the domestication of sheep and goat but (2) before the local domestication of cattle, which Reed feels were "undoubtedly wild" and fairly rare at Jarmo (Reed 1960, p. 143). We shall see that succeeding pig populations, establishing more firmly the size range of the domestic phenotype, bear out this conclusion.

The site of Tepe Guran in the Hulailan valley of Iran (Mortensen 1964) provides us with another great sequence of village farming levels reminiscent of Jarmo. Here also the lower levels were preceramic, but the upper levels yielded an even longer and more detailed look at the evolution of early pottery in the Zagros than did Jarmo. Of a sample of more than 3,000 identifiable bones, however, only 17 fragments of wild *Sus scrofa* were scattered through all levels (Flannery n.d.). One maxilla fragment from the Operation I trench (at a depth corresponding roughly to Levels O, P, or Q of the main square excavation) had an upper M3 measuring 36.5 mm and an M1−3 row of 71.2 mm. Thus there is no evidence for pig domestication at Guran, even in those levels with painted pottery of the Jarmo style.

Tepe Sarab in the Kermanshah valley of Iran (Braidwood 1960) is a tiny, two-period site (McDonald 1979) contemporary with the upper levels at Jarmo and Guran and radiocarbon-dated to 6000−5700 B.C. It produced more than 8,000 identifiable bones but literally nothing in the way of architecture, and I have never been convinced that Sarab should be considered a village occupied year-round.

Sarab also presents us with one of those little mysteries that sometimes take place between the excavation of a Near Eastern site and the analysis of its materials in another part of the world. In 1960 I participated in the excavations at Sarab and was assigned by Reed the task of separating out all the identifiable bones for packing and shipment. Since I was then engaged in measuring pig dentition I carefully searched all the "unmixed" deposits at Sarab, those in which it was thought there was no possibility of intrusive later material. My notes record "a lone second molar socket, part of a fragment of pig maxilla from Sarab" that measured 22.6 mm; the crown of the tooth would have been longer than that, perhaps 23.0–23.5 mm (Flannery 1961). The collection from Sarab was later studied in detail by Bökönyi (1977), who does not mention the maxilla I measured but reports a lower M3 measuring 38.0 mm of which I have no record and which I evidently never saw. I would very much like to know the exact provenience of this third molar, to see whether it came from one of the superficial levels or borrow pits that I rejected as possibly mixed.

Bökönyi correctly notes that such a molar is in the size range of the domestic phenotype and lists it along with "two unmeasurable extremity bones" as the only concrete evidence for pig domestication at Sarab, adding "there is no trace of local domestication" out of the wild Zagros pig (Bökönyi 1977, p. 30). Perhaps I am being unduly conservative, but I regard three such fragments (from a sample of 8,382 identifiable bones) as inconclusive evidence, especially without knowing the exact findspot of the M3. The situation is analogous to that of the single domestic pig mandible in Bayat phase levels at Tepe Sabz (see below): at best, one could say that pig domestication was being practiced somewhere in the general area, but it would be hard to convince me it was a significant activity either at Sarab or Tepe Sabz. In this case I would prefer to see Bökönyi take the eminently reasonable position he took about the infrequent twisted goat-horn cores at Asiab when he commented that such animals were such an "insignificant minority" that one "cannot speak of real animal husbandry at the site" (Bökönyi 1977, p. 9).

5700–3500 B.C.

In December of 1954, Patty Jo Watson excavated the Halafian site of Gird Banahilk in the mountains of Iraqi Kurdistan (Braidwood and Howe 1960, pp. 33–35). Fifteen measurable specimens of pig dentition were recovered, making Banahilk another site that has provided us with a small population whose mean and standard deviation can be calculated (Flannery 1961). The Banahilk pigs are not only domestic but they are also a uniformly shorter-snouted group than the Jarmo domestic pigs, indicative of a continuing trend in the reduction of tooth length during the sixth millennium. A probable date for Banahilk would lie in the neighborhood of 5000 B.C.

Dimensions of the Banahilk specimens are given in table 8. The lower third molars have a mean length of only 31.7 mm (nearly three standard deviations below the mean of the wild control group); the single upper third molar recovered was 27.6 mm in length (more than four standard deviations below the mean of the wild control group).

Tepe Siahbid in the Kermanshah valley of Iran, excavated by Frederick Matson (Braidwood and Howe 1962), is a small village in the 5000–4000 B.C. time range. Measurements taken by the writer in 1960 (table 9) indicated the presence of a small race of domestic pig, being raised in larger numbers than at any previous period in the Kermanshah plain. Bökönyi (1977, p. 30) also comments on the small size of the pigs at Siahbid, as well as those from the "Uruk" site of Dehsavar, not far away. By the time of Dehsavar (ca. 3500 B.C.), pig domestication may have been widespread in the Zagros.

THE STEPPELAND BELOW THE ZAGROS

The Deh Luran plain lies on the rolling steppe at the base of the Zagros Mountains in north Khuzistan (Hole, Flannery, and Neely 1969). At Tepe Ali Kosh (7000–5800 B.C.) no evidence for pig domestication was found, even in levels contemporary with Jarmo, Guran, and Sarab. At nearby Tepe Sabz (5400–4000 B.C.) the evidence was also scanty. A single left mandible fragment

Table 8. — Measurements of Pig Cheek Teeth in Specimens from the Site of Gird Banahilk, Iraq (ca. 5000 b.c.)

Identifying Marks	Length of Tooth (mm)					
	M3 sup.	M2 sup.	M1 sup.	M3 inf.	M2 inf.	M1 inf.
No. 508	--	--	--	28.6	19.0	15.4
No. 509	--	18.5	15.6	--	--	--
No. 510	--	20.6	15.7	--	--	--
No. 512	27.6	--	--	--	--	--
No. 541	--	23.3	19.8	--	--	--
No. 542	--	--	--	31.2	17.5	13.8
No. 557	--	19.6	16.4	--	--	--
No. 558-A	--	--	--	--	--	16.1
No. 558-B	--	20.0	--	--	--	--
No. 558-C	--	--	--	--	19.5	--
No. 559-A	--	--	15.7	--	--	--
No. 559-B	--	--	--	31.9	--	--
No. 561	--	--	--	32.9	--	--
No. 562	--	18.6	15.4	--	--	--
No. 563	--	--	--	34.0	--	--
Mean length, all specimens	--	20.1	16.4	31.7	18.7	15.1
Standard deviation	--	1.76	1.68	2.04	1.04	1.18
Standard error of mean	--	0.72	0.69	0.91	0.60	0.68

NOTE: All specimens are probably domestic. (After Flannery 1961.)

Table 9. — Measurements of Pig Cheek Teeth from Tepe Siahbid, Kermanshah, Iran

Identifying Marks	Length of Tooth (mm)					
	M3 sup.	M2 sup.	M1 sup.	M3 inf.	M2 inf.	M1 inf.
--	25.5	15.1	13.2	--	--	--
--	--	16.0	13.3	--	--	--
--	--	--	--	--	--	17.0

from what may have been a domestic pig appeared in Level A1 at Tepe Sabz. It was assigned to the Bayat Phase (cf. Susiana d) and radiocarbon-dated to approximately 4100−3800 b.c. This mandible fragment has an M1−M3 length of 66.3 mm, an M2 length of 19.2 mm, and an M3 length of 34.0 mm.[5]

As we suggested in the original Deh Luran report, this isolated mandible can hardly be seen as overwhelming evidence for local swineherding at Tepe Sabz. Since we know that late prehistoric villages in the Zagros (such as Siahbid and Dehsavar) were raising pigs at this time, it may simply be that villages like Tepe Sabz occasionally received domestic pigs from neighboring regions.

5. This length of 34.0 mm for the lower M3 is accurate and corrects a typographical error in Hole, Flannery, and Neely (1969, p. 311), where the measurement is erroneously printed as 45.0 mm.

Another site on the steppeland at the base of the Zagros is Choga Mami near Mandali, Iraq, a 3.5-hectare village of the Samarran period (Oates 1969). Faunal analyses by Bökönyi suggest that domestic pigs were present, representing just under 8 percent of the fauna (Bökönyi 1978, table 1). Since this collection probably dates somewhere between 5500 and 5300 B.C. it provides an interesting contrast with the (broadly contemporaneous) Sabz phase levels at Tepe Sabz, where no evidence of pig domestication was recovered.

Tell Matarrah, on the piedmont steppe of Iraq not far from Kirkuk, is another Hassunan-Samarran village relevant to our discussion of this zone (Braidwood et al. 1952). Unfortunately, the collection of fauna is small, and although pig remains represent 25 percent of the sample (Reed 1969, p. 371), the evidence consists mainly of postcranial bones; no measurable teeth were included in the collection of bones from Matarrah that I studied in 1961. However, the percentage of juvenile pigs was suspiciously high and coupled with the high frequency of pigs makes the presence of the domestic form likely.

THE AL-JAZIRA AND THE MIDDLE TIGRIS

6000–5000 B.C.

The early villages of this region include Tell Hassuna and Umm Dabaghiyah in the al-Jazira west of the Tigris and Tell es-Sawwan on the east bluff overlooking the Tigris near Samarra. Apparently, Hassuna produced a good sample of animal bone; unfortunately, it was never examined by a zoologist, being turned over instead to a staff member of the Royal Iraqi Hospital at Baghdad (Lloyd and Safar 1945, p. 284). "Wild pig" is described as represented by "several good fragments of skulls with teeth" (ibid.), but since no measurements are given we cannot really assess the wild or domestic status of these remains.

For Umm Dabaghiyah (Kirkbride 1972), a site with radiocarbon dates ranging between 5800 and 5300 B.C., Bökönyi (1978) reports "an extremely rich animal bone assemblage" of some 19,000 identifiable specimens. Domestic pig is said to be present but represents only one percent of the fauna. Frankly, given the relatively inhospitable location of the site, I am surprised to learn that domestic pigs were present at all.

The Hassunan-Samarran site of Tell es-Sawwan serves as an example of how important it is to collect large samples of animal bones. A considerable number of excavators (El-Wailly and Abu al-Soof 1965; al-Adami 1968; Wahida 1967) worked at the site in the 1960s, yet recovered only a few hundred animal bones. The collection from Level III that Jane Wheeler and I studied (Flannery and Wheeler 1967) was so small that, although a few pig remains were present, it could not really be determined with certainty whether the domestic phenotype was present. In the words of Bökönyi (1978, pp. 57–58), "Excavations had been going on for several seasons when, in 1972, the energetic young Iraqi archaeologist, Walid Yasin al-Tikruti, took over direction and started to collect carefully the animal remains, recovering as many as 3,073 identifiable specimens in a single season." This much larger sample revealed domestic pigs at es-Sawwan but confirmed their rarity: they constituted less than one tenth of one percent of the fauna (Bökönyi 1978, table 1). As in the case of the rare pig remains from Tepe Sabz and Tepe Sarab, already mentioned above, I consider such a percentage to mean that swineherding was not an important part of the subsistence pattern at Tell es-Sawwan. Since we know that contemporary Samarran sites (such as Choga Mami) were raising pigs, it may be that es-Sawwan occasionally obtained domestic pigs from its neighbors.

THE SYRIAN STEPPE AND THE SOUTHERN TAURUS

9000–6000 B.C.

I will comment only briefly on this huge region because it is one from which our data on early pig domestication are still fragmentary. Several of the best-known sites in the area have produced large faunal samples that apparently contain no domestic pigs. The first of these sites is Tell Mureybit, Syria (van Loon 1968); preliminary faunal analysis was done by Dexter Perkins, Jr. The second is the nearby site of Tell Abu Hureyra (Moore 1975); preliminary faunal analysis was done by A.J. Legge. Perkins reported no domestic animals at all from early Mureybit, and pig remains were apparently rare at Tell Abu Hureyra, even in those levels where domestic sheep and goats occurred (Legge 1975). Even in the Pottery Neolithic levels that Moore aligns with Phase A of the Amuq there is apparently no evidence for domestic pig. This is a significant fact, in light of our evidence for domestic pigs from Tell Judaideh (see below), but certainly not unexpected, given the greatly different environment of Abu Hureyra.

The evidence from the southern Taurus is exciting but apparently still not fully conclusive. Here the crucial collection is from Çayönü in southern Turkey, another site discovered and excavated by Robert Braidwood (Braidwood et al. 1971, 1974); preliminary faunal analysis was done by Barbara Lawrence.

Apparently there is some evidence of domestic pig at Çayönü, but there are disagreements in the literature as to exactly how early it is. There seem to be at least five architectural stages present at the site, originally referred to as I-V (Braidwood et al. 1971) but more recently given verbal designations such as "Cell Plan levels" and "Large Room Plan levels" (Redman 1978). Since the site spans the period from 7300 to 6500 B.C. it could potentially have the oldest domestic pigs in Southwest Asia, and Reed (1977, p. 564) has in fact dated the earliest pigs there at 8800 B.P. (ca. 6800 B.C.). However, the earliest levels (old Phases I and II) have "predominantly (if not completely) wild" fauna (Braidwood et al. 1971, p. 1239), so it is really only the later levels at Çayönü that are relevant here.

According to one member of the excavation team, "Pigs were abundant in all subphases and there is some evidence, although not conclusive, that they had been domesticated by the last subphase" — that is, old Phase V, now called the "Large Room Plan levels" (Redman 1978, p. 163). Redman's figure 5:9 (1978) shows domestic pigs present only from the Phase IV−V transition onward, ca. 6500 B.C., making their appearance only slightly earlier there than at Jarmo. Thus, while the evidence is still "not conclusive," it would appear that, at Çayönü, Braidwood may for the second time have discovered a site with the oldest evidence for pig domestication in its general region.

THE LEVANT

6000−3000 B.C.

The Levant is an area with a mosaic of different habitats, and, as might be expected, the moment of appearance of the domestic pig varies greatly from one locality to another.

Let us begin in the north with Phase A of the Amuq sequence from the Plain of Antioch (Braidwood and Braidwood 1960). An upper third molar of *Sus scrofa* from one of the deepest levels at Tell Judaideh suggests that pig domestication was under way by shortly after 6000 B.C. This upper M3 measures 31.3 mm in length, nearly three standard deviations below the mean of our wild control group.

Pig remains are relatively abundant in the later phases of the Amuq, the domestic phenotype predominating. Table 10 lists the measurements for Phases B, C, and D (ca. 5000−4000 B.C.), a large sample from Phase E (roughly equivalent in time to the later Ubaid), and Phases G and I (the latter carrying us into the time range of the Early Dynastic period).

Occasional large molars crop up in the pig remains from this long sequence (e.g., the 39.5 mm lower M3 shown for Phase E), but this is not surprising. The Amuq is a low intermontane plain, ringed by hills that would have had pine cover and abundant game; wild pigs would have been present in the thickets along the marshes on the valley floor. Considerable hunting went on during these phases, as indicated by the remains of both deer and gazelle. Amschler's unpub-

Table 10. — Measurements of Pig Cheek Teeth from Various Phases of the Amuq Sequence, Antioch

Archeological Period	Identifying Marks	Length of Tooth (mm)			
		M3 sup.	M2 sup.	M1 sup.	M3 inf.
Amuq, Phase A	JK 3, 21⊥	31.3	--	--	--
Amuq, Phase B	JK 3, 19⊥	--	21.5	17.5	--
Amuq, Phase B	None	--	--	18.1	--
Amuq, Phase C	K I 105−110	--	21.8	17.3	--
Amuq, Phase D	K I 65−70	--	20.5	18.0	--
Amuq, Phase D	K I 60	31.4?	--	--	--
Amuq, Phase E	K I 0−150	--	20.0	--	--
Amuq, Phase E	K I 15−20	--	--	--	39.5
Amuq, Phase E	K I 20−25	--	--	17.6	--
Amuq, Phase E	K I 30−35	--	21.9	17.8	--
Amuq, Phase E	K I 50−100	--	23.6	--	--
Amuq, Phase E	K I 50−100	--	--	18.0	--
Amuq, Phase E	K I 50−100	--	--	17.8	--
Amuq, Phase E	K I 50−100	31.4	--	--	--
Amuq, Phase E	K III 1−15	--	--	17.2	--
Amuq, Phase E	None	--	--	17.2	--
Amuq, Phase G	JK 3, 11	--	25.4	--	--
Amuq, Phase I	W 16 ˆ 3	30.5	--	--	--

NOTE: After Flannery 1961.

lished notes (on file in the Oriental Institute) suggest that 27 percent of the Amuq E-I bone fragments were from wild animals.

Moving south to Lebanon we encounter the site of Labweh in the Beka'a valley. Excavated by Diana Kirkbride, the site has been radiocarbon-dated to 6000−5750 B.C. Bökönyi's analysis of more than 1,000 bones showed that domestic pig was present, representing just under 7 percent of the fauna (Bökönyi 1978; table 1).

Farther to the south we encounter the long and complex sequence in Palestine (Israel and Jordan). Here the most extensive work on early domestication has been done by Pierre Ducos (1968, 1978), who reports that "before the Pottery Neolithic period in Palestine and Syria, there was domestication only of *Ovis* and *Capra*" (Ducos 1978, p. 55). To be more specific, domestic pigs were absent in the samples Ducos (1968) studied from the Natufian site of Ain Mallaha, the Pre-Pottery Neolithic levels of Wadi Fallah (= Nahal Oren), El Khiam, and Munhatta 3−6, and possibly even the later site of Hagoshrim (ca. 5000 B.C.). Similarly, no remains of domestic pig were reported from Beidha by Perkins (1966) or from Pre-Pottery Jericho by Clutton-Brock (1971).

Ducos places the beginnings of pig domestication in Israel some time during the Pottery Neolithic period, between 5000 and 4000 B.C. Domestic pigs may have been present as early as Munhatta 2 and were definitely present at Tell Turmus, whose pigs Ducos (1968, p. 91) compares with the race *Sus scrofa palustris*, of which we spoke in an earlier section of this paper. A particularly large sample of domestic pigs came from the Ghassulian site of Metzer, occupied shortly before 3000 B.C. (Ducos 1968, table IV, pp. 157–58).

Ducos makes the significant point that pig domestication was more important in the Mediterranean zone of Palestine than in the arid and semiarid zones. In fact, the relatively late appearance of the domestic pig even in this Mediterranean zone raises the possibility that swineherding in Palestine owes something to the influence of earlier centers of pig domestication in the Beka'a and the Amuq.

The Nile Valley

4000–3000 B.C.

It was not my intention to stray beyond the confines of the Fertile Crescent in this paper, but I feel that brief mention of the Nile Valley is appropriate for two reasons. First, the Nile Delta sites of Ma'adi and Merimde were reported by their excavators to have been major centers of early pig breeding (Menghin 1934, and in Junker 1933), but no actual measurements of the numerous pig remains were published. Second, I have some previously unpublished Predynastic measurements that are relevant to this subject.

The Predynastic village of North Spur Hemamieh was excavated by Gertrude Caton-Thompson in 1924 (Brunton and Caton-Thompson 1928). Hemamieh lies midway between Badari and Qau-el-Kebir in Upper Egypt and revealed both Badarian and Amratian (= Naqada I) levels. In the Amratian levels (ca. 4000–3500 B.C.), Caton-Thompson investigated nine "hut circles" constructed of wattle-and-daub, matting, and thatch. The Hemamieh report makes two specific references to pig remains, as follows:

1. A mandibular ramus resting on the floor of Hut 248, area F–G, in the same locality as a hearth with emmer wheat (Brunton and Caton-Thompson 1928, pp. 84–85)
2. Two unrelated pig mandibles resting on the floor of Hut 252, area E–F (ibid., pp. 85–86)

No faunal report as such was published, but in January 1960 Charles Reed and I were shown a box of faunal material deposited in the British Museum of Natural History by Caton-Thompson. Obviously domestic pig remains include a mandible marked "Hemamieh, N. Spur." Lengths of two complete lower third molars are only 30.2 and 28.5 mm, in the domestic size range (table 11).

These (presumably) Amratian pigs can be compared with four specimens of pig jaws and dentition, illustrated by Gaillard (1934), from the Gerzean (= Naqada II) site of Toukh, 30 km north of Luxor in Upper Egypt. Fortunately, these specimens are illustrated at natural size (Gaillard 1934, pl. VIII, nos. 5–8) so that rough measurements can be taken from the plates. All are of domestic size (table 11) and date to ca. 3500–3000 B.C.

These remains strengthen the credibility of Menghin's claims for early pig domestication in the Nile Delta but do not obviate the necessity of obtaining measurements for comparable specimens from Lower Egypt. How much earlier the domestic pig may have been in Egypt is uncertain, due to lack of data. It is presumed that the domestic race was derived from local wild pig populations which abound in the Nile marshes; Reed (1960, p. 139) mentions the improbability that pigs could have been herded across the Sinai Desert from the Levant.

Where Were Pigs Originally Domesticated?

When I began my study in 1960, near Eastern archeologists appeared confident that all the major domesticates (wheat, barley, sheep, goats, cattle, and pigs) would ultimately prove to have been first domesticated in Southwest Asia. After all, the "hilly flanks" of the Fertile Crescent had the greatest zone of overlap of the natural ranges of the wild ancestors of those major domesti-

Table 11. — Measurements of Pig Cheek Teeth from Predynastic Sites in Upper Egypt

Archeological Site	Identifying Marks	Length of Tooth or Tooth Row (mm)								
		M3 sup.	M2 sup.	M1 sup.	M1–3 sup.	M3 inf.	M2 inf.	M1 inf.	M1–3 inf.	P1–M3 inf.
Hemamieh	None	--	--	--	--	28.5	--	--	62.2	108.4
Hemamieh	"Hemamieh N. Spur"	--	--	--	--	30.2	--	--	--	--
Toukh	5	--	--	--	--	--	--	15.6	--	--
Toukh	6	--	--	--	--	31.1	--	--	--	--
Touhk	7	26.6	20.3	16.7	62.0	--	--	--	--	--
Toukh	8	--	21.4	16.8	--	--	--	--	--	--

NOTE: After Flannery 1961.

cates. And for many of those cultivars the Near East still looks like a good bet. The radiocarbon dates of 14,300−13,800 B.C. for carbonized grains of emmer wheat from a Kebaran level, excavated by Cambridge University at Nahal Oren in Israel, are still our oldest record of that cereal, according to Ofer Bar-Yosef (personal communication). The "insignificant minority" of very early domestic goats proposed for the eighth millennium B.C. site of Asiab by Bökönyi (1977), coupled with the evidence from Ganj Dareh and basal Ali Kosh, suggests the Zagros as one of the oldest areas of domestication for that animal.

For some of the other domesticates, however, the confidence of the Near Eastern archeologists in earlier animal domestication in their area has been steadily eroding for years. Radiocarbon dates in the neighborhood of 16,000−15,000 B.C. for carbonized barley grains in Egypt's Nile Valley (Wendorf et al. 1979) will certainly give Near Eastern archeologists something to think about. And now Bökönyi (1978, p. 59) reports that in a work currently in press he will show that all five of the earliest domestic animals (sheep, goat, cattle, pig, and dog) occurred together as a complex "in the south of the Balkan Peninsula some five hundred years earlier than in the Middle East."

It has been apparent for some time that cattle and pigs were domesticated in southeastern Europe as early as, if not earlier than, they were in the Fertile Crescent.[6] Both are present in Greece between 6500 and 6000 B.C. For example, the Neolithic site of Nea Nikomedeia in Macedonia (Rodden 1962) produced a sample of 65 pig specimens dating to 6220 B.C. There, more than 90 percent of the pigs were juveniles (suggestive evidence for domestication), and measurements of the upper M3's of the adults varied in length from 32 to 34 mm, falling within the range of the domestic pigs from upper Jarmo as well as remaining fully below the mean of the wild pig sample given in table 3 (Higgs 1962, p. 273).

At the present state of our knowledge it would be a mistake to see the origins of pig domestication as a single event occurring in one part of the world and spreading from there to other regions. Rather, there appear to have been several areas in which there was early pig domestication, separated by areas in which there was none. Southeast Europe, the Zagros

6. Bökönyi (1977, p. 59) acknowledges this statement for cattle; his reluctance to do so for the pig is based on a misunderstanding. Citing my study of the domestic pigs at Jarmo he uses a date of "ca. 6500 B.C." for the site (Bökönyi 1977, p. 61). Such a date, however, applies only to the prepottery levels at Jarmo, which lacked domestic pigs. The pottery-bearing levels with domestic pigs, to judge by the dates from Sarab and Guran, must fall closer to 6000 B.C.

Mountains, and (apparently) the southern Taurus seem to have been in the vanguard of pig domestication between 6500 and 6000 B.C., while such areas as the Deh Luran steppe and the middle stretch of the Tigris show negligible swineherding even at 5000 B.C.

As Bökönyi (1977) has suggested, pigs like moist habitats, and it is not surprising that they were important on the swampy plains of Macedonia and Thessaly or the Amuq. This is not the whole explanation for their distribution, however, for the once-swampy Deh Luran plain had no domestic pigs while several of the drier areas of the Zagros and the al-Jazireh did. I remain convinced that one factor influencing whether or not villages took up swineherding was sheep and goat transhumance. As Krader (1955) has pointed out, pigs are incompatible with a nomadic or transhumant way of life, because they do not take kindly to being driven from one elevation to another. Thus it is unlikely that we will find swineherding associated with early Near Eastern societies for which transhumance is important, and this will be an especially crucial consideration in the Zagros.

This issue of transhumance raises a further problem with which future faunal analysts must deal. We know that today in the Near East there are plains and valleys where transhumant herders and fully sedentary agriculturalists live virtually side by side. Some villagers never move, while their neighbors take their sheep and goats to a higher elevation in the summer. What this means is that in some areas of the Fertile Crescent, villages that kept domestic pigs may have been situated almost side by side with villages that did not. Because of such a situation it would be impossible for an archeologist to use only one site to characterize a whole area.

Just because Sarab (for all practical purposes) lacked domestic pigs does not mean that some coeval site in the Kermanshah plain might not have raised many of them. Just because Banahilk had numerous pigs does not mean that every Halaf site in northeast Iraq had them. In the case of pigs — precisely because of the factor of local transhumance — several villages in an area must be excavated and the evidence weighed site by site before we can generalize. This has rarely been done anywhere in the Near East. If only certain villages raised pigs, occasionally providing them for neighboring villages with a different economic focus, it would help to explain why there are so many sites (e.g., Tepe Sabz, Sarab, and Tell es-Sawwan) with only one or two fragments of domestic pig out of thousands of animal bones.

I would also like to urge Near Eastern faunal analysts to try harder to treat early domesticates as populations whose parameters can be statistically described rather than as isolated specimens or tables of measurements. The samples from Tepe Asiab, Jarmo, and Banahilk are important precisely because we can give their mean, range, and standard deviation and can demonstrate at a statistically definable level of confidence that some differ from a sample of wild pigs. It is ironic that even European faunal analysts, who so frequently (and justifiably) criticize their American counterparts for presenting no measurements at all, have only sporadically taken the additional step of treating their samples as populations.

Finally, it seems fitting to close with a reminder that the evidence from two of Bob Braidwood's sites — Jarmo and Çayönü — still gives us our most tantalizing look at the *origins* of pig domestication in the Fertile Crescent. First excavated in 1948, Jarmo focused the world's attention on the food-producing revolution in Southwest Asia. Thirty years later, despite countless subsequent excavations, Jarmo continues to provide us with some of our best data on one of the world's earliest domestic animals.

BIBLIOGRAPHY

Ackerknecht, E.
1950   Anatomische Unterschiede zwischen Wildschwein und Hausschwein. *Zeitschrift für Tierzüchtung und Züchtungsbiologie* 58:465–72.

Adams, Robert McC.
1952   The Jarmo pottery and stone vessel industries. Master's thesis, University of Chicago.

Al-Adami, K.H.
1968   Excavations at Tell es-Sawwan (second season). *Sumer* 24:57–98.

Amon, R.
1938   Abstammung, Arten und Rassen der Wildschweine Eurasiens. *Zeitschrift für Tierzüchtung und Züchtungsbiologie* 40:49–88.

Amschler, J.W.
1939   Tierreste der Ausgrabungen von dem "Grossen Königshügel" Shah Tepé, in Nord-Iran. In *Reports from the Scientific Expedition to the North-Western Provinces of China under the Leadership of Dr. Sven Hedin, the Sino-Swedish Expedition*, publ. 9, vol. 7 (Archaeology), no. 4:35–129. Stockholm: Bokförlags aktiebolaget Thule.
n.d.   *An analysis of faunal remains from early sites on the plain of Antioch.* Files, Oriental Institute of the University of Chicago.

Boessneck, Joachim
1956   Zu den Tierknochen aus neolithischen Siedlungen Thessaliens. *Bericht der Römish-Germanischen Kommission, 1955*, no. 36:1–51.

Boettger, Caesar
1958   Die Haustiere Afrikas. Jena: G. Fischer.

Bökönyi, Sándor
1977   *The animal remains from four sites in the Kermanshah valley, Iran: Asiab, Sarab, Dehsavar and Siahbid: the faunal evolution, environmental changes and development of animal husbandry, VIII–III millennia B.C.* British Archaeological Reports, Supplementary Series, vol. 34. Oxford.
1978   Environmental and cultural differences as reflected in the animal bone samples from five early Neolithic sites in southwest Asia. In *Approaches to faunal analysis in the Middle East*, ed. Richard H. Meadow and Melinda A. Zeder, pp. 57–62. Peabody Museum of Archaeology and Ethnology, Harvard University, Bulletin 2. Cambridge, Mass.

Braidwood, Robert J.
1960   Seeking the world's first farmers in Persian Kurdistan: a full-scale investigation of prehistoric sites near Kermanshah. *Illustrated London News* 237:695–97.

Braidwood, Robert J., and Braidwood, Linda S.
1960   *Excavations in the plain of Antioch*, vol. 1: *the earlier assemblages: phases A–J*. Oriental Institute Publications, vol. 61. Chicago: University of Chicago Press.

Braidwood, Robert J.; Braidwood, Linda S.; Smith, James G.; and Leslie, Charles
1952   Matarrah: a southern variant of the Hassunan assemblage, excavated in 1948. *Journal of Near Eastern Studies* 11:1–75.

Braidwood, Robert J.; Çambel, Halet; Lawrence, Barbara; Redman, Charles L.; and Steward, Robert
1974   Beginnings of village-farming communities in southeastern Turkey: 1972. *Proceedings of the National Academy of Sciences* 71(2):568–72.

Braidwood, Robert J.; Çambel, Halet; Redman, Charles L.; and Watson, Patty Jo
1971   Beginnings of village-farming communities in southeastern Turkey. *Proceedings of the National Academy of Sciences* 68(6):1236–40.

Braidwood, Robert J., and Howe, Bruce
1960   *Prehistoric investigations in Iraqi Kurdistan.* Studies in Ancient Oriental Civilization, no. 31. Chicago: University of Chicago Press.
1962   Southwestern Asia beyond the lands of the Mediterranean littoral. In *Courses toward urban life,* ed. Robert J. Braidwood and Gordon R. Willey, pp. 132–46. Chicago: Aldine Press.

Brunton, Guy, and Caton-Thompson, Gertrude
1928   *The Badarian civilization and Predynastic remains near Badari.* British School of Archaeology in Egypt Publication no. 46. London: Quaritch.

Clutton-Brock, Juliet
1971   The primary food animals of Jericho Tell from the Proto-neolithic to the Byzantine period. *Levant* 3:41–55.

Ducos, Pierre
1968   *L'Origine des animaux domestiques en Palestine.* Institut de Préhistoire de l'Université de Bordeaux Mémoire 6. Bordeaux: Imprimeries Delmas.
1978   "Domestication" defined and methodological approaches to its recognition in faunal assemblages. In *Approaches to faunal analysis in the Middle East,* ed. Richard H. Meadow and Melinda A. Zeder, pp. 53–56. Peabody Museum of Archaeology and Ethnology, Harvard University, Bulletin 2. Cambridge, Mass.

Duerst, J. Ulrich
1908   Animal remains from the excavations at Anau, and the horse of Anau in its relation to the races of domestic horses. In *Explorations in Turkestan: expedition of 1904, prehistoric civilizations of Anau,* vol. 2, ed. Raphael Pumpelly, pp. 339–442. Publications of the Carnegie Institution of Washington, no. 73. Washington, D.C.

Ellerman, J.R., and Morrison-Scott, T.C.S.
1951   *Checklist of Palaearctic and Indian mammals, 1758–1946.* London: Trustees of the British Museum.

Flannery, Kent V.
1961   Skeletal and radiocarbon evidence of the origins of pig domestication. Master's thesis, University of Chicago.
forth-   Hunting and early animal domestication at Tepe Guran. In *Final report on the excava-*
coming   *tions at Tepe Guran,* ed. Peder Mortensen.

Flannery, Kent V., and Wheeler, Jane C.
1967   Animal remains from Tell es-Sawwan, level III (Samarran period). *Sumer* 23:179–82.

Gaillard, C.
1934   Contribution a l'étude de la faune préhistorique de l'Egypte. *Archives du Muséum d'histoire naturelle de Lyon,* 14(3):1–125.

Garrod, Dorothy A.E.
1958   The Natufian culture: the life and economy of a Mesolithic people in the Near East. *Proceedings of the British Academy* 43:211–27.

Hartmann-Frick, H.
1960   Die Tierwelt des prähistorischen Siedlungsplatzes auf dem Eschner Lutzengüetle, Fürstentum Liechtenstein. *Jahrbuch des Historischen Vereins für das Fürstentum Liechtenstein* 59:5–223.

Helbaek, Hans
1960   The paleoethnobotany of the Near East and Europe. In *Prehistoric investigations in Iraqi Kurdistan,* Robert J. Braidwood and Bruce Howe, pp. 99–118. Studies in Ancient Oriental Civilization, no. 31. Chicago: University of Chicago Press.

Higgs, Eric S.
    1962   The biological data: fauna. In Excavations at the early Neolithic site at Nea Nikomedeia,
                Greek Macedonia (1961 season), Robert J. Rodden, pp. 271–74. *Proceedings of the
                Prehistoric Society* 28:267–88.

Hole, Frank; Flannery, Kent V.; and Neely, James A.
    1969   *(eds.) Prehistory and human ecology of the Deh Luran plain.* Memoirs of the Museum of
                Anthropology, University of Michigan, no. 1. Ann Arbor: University of Michigan Press.

Howell, A.B.
    1925   Pathological skulls of captive lions. *Journal of Mammalogy* 6:163–68.

Josien, T.
    1956   Etude de la faune de gisements Néolithiques (niveau de Cortaillod) du Canton de Berne
                (Suisse). In *Archives Suisses d'Anthropologie Général* 21, no. 1, pp. 28–62. Genève:
                Imprimerie Albert Kundig.

Junker, H.
    1933   Vorläufiger Bericht über die Grabung der Akademie auf der neolithischen Siedlung von
                Merimde-Benisalame (Westdelta). *Anzeiger* 1933. Vienna: Kaiserliche Akademie der
                Wissenschaften, Philosophische–Historische Klasse.

Kelm, Hans
    1938   Die postembryonale Schädelentwicklung des Wild- und Berkshireschweines. *Zeitschrift
                für Anatomie und Entwicklungsgeschichte* 108:499–559.

Kirkbride, Diana
    1966   Five seasons at the pre-pottery Neolithic village of Beidha in Jordan. *Palestine Explora-
                tion Quarterly* 98(1):8–72.
    1972   Umm Dabaghiyah 1971: a preliminary report. *Iraq* 34:3–15.

Krader, Lawrence
    1955   Ecology of central Asian pastoralism. *Southwestern Journal of Anthropology* 11:301–26.

Legge, Anthony J.
    1975   The fauna of Tell Abu Hureyra: preliminary analysis. In The Excavation of Tell Abu
                Hureyra in Syria: a preliminary report, A.M.T. Moore, pp. 74–76. *Proceedings of the
                Prehistoric Society* 41:50–77.

Lloyd, Seton, and Safar, Fuad
    1945   Tell Hassuna. *Journal of Near Eastern Studies* 4:255–89.

Loon, Maurits van
    1968   The Oriental Institute excavations at Mureybit, Syria: preliminary report on the 1965
                campaign. *Journal of Near Eastern Studies* 27(4):265–90.

McDonald, M.M.A.
    1979   An examination of mid-Holocene settlement patterns in the central Zagros region of
                western Iran. Ph.D. diss., University of Toronto.

Menghin, Oswald
    1934   Die Grabung der Universität Kairo bei Maadi: drittes Grabungsjahr. *Mitteilungen des
                Deutschen Instituts für Ägyptische Altertumskunde in Kairo* 5:111–18.

Moore, A.M.T.
    1975   The excavation at Tell Abu Hureyra in Syria: a preliminary report. *Proceedings of the
                Prehistoric Society* 41:50–77. (With contributions by G.C. Hillman and A.J. Legge.)

Mortensen, Peder
    1964   Early village-farming occupation. In Excavations at Tepe Guran, Luristan; Jørgen Meld-
                gaard, Peder Mortensen, and Henrik Thrane, pp. 110–21. *Acta Archaeologica* 34:7–133.

Oates, Joan
  1969   Choga Mami 1967−68: a preliminary report. *Iraq* 31(2):115−52.

Perkins, Dexter, Jr.
  1964   Prehistoric fauna from Shanidar Cave, Iraq. *Science* 144:1565−66.
  1966   The fauna from Madamagh and Beidha: a preliminary report. In Five seasons at the
                pre-pottery Neolithic village of Beidha in Jordan, Diana Kirkbride, pp. 66−67. *Palestine
                Exploration Quarterly* 98(1):8−72.

Pira, Adolph
  1909   Studien zur Geschichte der Schweinrassen, insbesondere derjenigen Schwedens.
                Zoologische Jahrbücher, supplement 10:233−426.

Pumpelly, Raphael
  1908   *(ed.) Explorations in Turkestan: expedition of 1904, prehistoric civilizations of Anau*, vol.
                2. Publications of the Carnegie Institution of Washington, no. 73. Washington, D.C.

Redman, Charles L.
  1978   *The rise of civilization: from early farmers to urban society in the ancient Near East.* San
                Francisco: W.H. Freeman and Co.

Reed, Charles A.
  1959   Animal domestication in the prehistoric Near East. *Science* 130:1629−39.
  1960   A review of the archeological evidence on animal domestication in the prehistoric Near
                East. In *Prehistoric investigations in Iraqi Kurdistan*, Robert J. Braidwood and Bruce
                Howe, pp. 119−45. Studies in Ancient Oriental Civilization, no. 31. Chicago: University
                of Chicago Press.
  1969   The pattern of animal domestication in the prehistoric Near East. In *The domestication
                and exploitation of plants and animals*, ed. Peter J. Ucko and G.W. Dimbleby, pp.
                361−80. London: Duckworth.
  1977   A model for the origin of agriculture in the Near East. In *Origins of Agriculture*, ed.
                Charles A. Reed, pp. 543−67. The Hague: Mouton.

Rodden, Robert
  1962   Excavations at the early Neolithic site at Nea Nikomedeia, Greek Macedonia (1961
                season). *Proceedings of the Prehistoric Society* 28:271−74.

Rütimeyer, Ludwig
  1860   Untersuchungen der Tierreste aus den Pfahlbauten der Schweiz. Mitteilungen der
                Antiquarischen Gesellschaft von Zürich, vol. 13(2), no. 2.
  1862   Die Fauna der Pfahlbauten der Schweiz. Allgemeine Schweizerische Gesellschaft der
                Gesamten Naturwissenschaften, Neue Denkschrift, vol. 19.

Smith, Philip E.L.
  1972   Ganj Dareh Tepe. *Iran* 10:165−78.

Solecki, Rose L.
  1964   Zawi Chemi Shanidar, a post-Pleistocene village site in northern Iraq. In *Report of the
                Sixth International Congress on Quaternary* [Warsaw 1961], vol. 4, International Asso-
                ciation on Quaternary Research, pp. 405−12. Łódź: Pánstwowe Wydawnictwo Naukowe.

Spurway, H.
  1955   Causes of domestication. *Journal of Genetics* 53:325−62.

Starck, D.
  1954   Morphologische Untersuchungen am Kopf der Säugetiere. *Zeitschrift für Wissenschaft-
                liche Zoologie* 157:169−219.

Vaufrey, R.
  1951   Mammifères. In *Le Paléolithique et le Mésolithique du désert de Judée*, René Neuville,

pp. 198–233. Archives de l'Institut de Paléontologie Humaine Mémoire 24. Paris: Masson and Co.

Wahida, Ghanim
   1967   The excavations of the third season at Tell es-Sawwan, 1966. *Sumer* 23:167–78.

El-Wailley, Faisal, and Abu al-Soof, Behnam
   1965   The excavations at Tell es-Sawwan: first preliminary report (1964). *Sumer* 21:17–32.

Wendorf, Fred; Schild, Romuald; El Hadidi, Nabil; Close, Angela E.; Kobusiewicz, Michael; Wieckowska, Hanna; Issawi, Bahay, and Haas, Herbert.
   1979   Use of barley in the Egyptian late Paleolithic. *Science* 205:1341–47.

REGULARITY AND CHANGE
IN THE ARCHITECTURE OF AN EARLY VILLAGE

Charles L. Redman

PURSUING a better understanding of the origin of agriculture in the Near East has been a focus of much of Robert J. Braidwood's long and productive career. As a result of his efforts, and the efforts of others, there are now a variety of theories that attempt to explain this most important of transformations in the human existence. The bases of these theories range from an emphasis on the location of natural habitat zones (or their margins) to paleoclimatic change (or the lack of it) and, more recently, to the relation between population growth and productive strategies. Although these approaches include stimulating and plausible explanations for the introduction of agriculture, none seem to completely satisfy the scholarly world. During the past thirty years, since Braidwood's pioneering research at Jarmo, an increasing amount of archeological information has been collected on this problem, but with each new discovery the empirical situation seems to become more complex, rather than clearer. Compounding this situation are the ultimate difficulties archeologists have in dating sites precisely, estimating site and regional populations, and being certain of the limits of the natural habitats for plants and animals or even of whether the discovered examples are truly domesticated. My proposed solution to this apparent conundrum is to proceed in two directions, first to improve our ability to measure the above phenomena accurately, and, second, to change our explanatory focus from the environmental and demographic context of the introduction of agriculture and settled village life to discernment of the crucial elements of the transformation in the nature of the communities themselves.

Fortunately for the latter approach, Braidwood and others, while bringing natural scientists on their expeditions to investigate environment and subsistence resources, have also devoted considerable energy to recording the patterning of additional categories of evidence. Among these categories, architecture has always been a special concern for Braidwood. This concern has involved using architecture in excavation as a context within which to record artifacts and identify stratigraphy and considering architecture as an artifact in itself, to be understood and interpreted in behavioral terms. Given that the beginnings of permanent villages roughly coincide with the introduction of agriculture, issues of architectural patterning may be at the center of the overall transformation. The architecture being built by these people should reflect the increasing use of storage facilities, as well as the restructuring of the entire range of daily activities.

Some progress in examining the changes in architectural forms that accompanied the introduction of agriculture has already been made. Among these changes is the shift from circular to rectilinear buildings manifest in the early villages of the Near East and Mexico, which is described in a stimulating article by Kent V. Flannery (1972). In its simplest form, Flannery's position is that circular dwellings tend to correlate with nomadic or seminomadic societies and rectangular dwellings tend to correlate with fully sedentary, often agricultural societies. My own approach in this chapter is not to pursue his particular line of reasoning but to examine a subset of his second building type, rectilinear village buildings, and to discuss certain variations within it and their possible relationship to specialization of activities within early farming villages.

On the basis of a detailed investigation of the regularities in design of buildings discovered at a single Near Eastern site, I have identified two potentially important building "types" that I suggest have significance for understanding early village life and perhaps the introduction of agriculture as well. In this chapter I will discuss their characteristics and the variability within them and then briefly cite examples of comparable material from contemporary sites in the Near East. Although the published architectural evidence from early village sites remains insufficient for drawing detailed conclusions, this trial formulation is meant to highlight the data I am acquainted with and perhaps to draw out responses that will put it into a broader perspective.

As with so many articles on developments in the early village time range, I rely on evidence from Robert J. Braidwood's excavations. The two building types discussed here are best known to me from the excavations at Çayönü Tepesi, Turkey, that were directed by Braidwood and Halet Çambel of Istanbul University (Braidwood et al. 1969; Braidwood et al. 1971; Braidwood et al. 1974). Other buildings have been discovered at Çayönü in different stratigraphic levels, but I have not attempted to integrate them with this study (in the terminology used in Braidwood et al. 1974, the first set of buildings occurs in subphase G.P. and the second set in subphase C.P.). In addition, Braidwood and Çambel are continuing their excavations at Çayönü, undoubtedly discovering new information relevant to the propositions put forth here, but its use will have to await subsequent studies.

The stratigraphically earlier of Çayönü's two building types was the *grill plan foundation* building, probably dating to about 7300–7000 B.C. (C[14] half-life, 5,570 years, uncorrected). During the 1964 to 1972 seasons of excavations, remains of five separate buildings were uncovered, each with at least one superimposed rebuilding (fig. 1). All five of these buildings occurred in relatively the same stratigraphic position within the sequence of the site, at least tentatively implying that they were the dominant, if not sole, building form for a phase of the site's occupation, and did not continue in use throughout the site's history.

Although the arrangement of foundation walls that characterize this building type is complex in plan, the five structures at Çayönü are consistent in design, size, and orientation to the cardinal directions. This consistency is what leads me to refer to a building "type" that at least for the early villages of Çayönü probably had a particular adaptive significance. The best preserved of the five grill plan foundation buildings (EF 2) is about 5 by 12 m in area and retains much of the plasterlike floor that covers its foundation (fig. 2). The parallel foundation walls are made of stones laid in several rough courses about 45 cm wide. These foundation walls probably supported wood beams on which the plaster floor was laid; because of this, the floor of the building would have been elevated 30 to 40 cm above the ground and would have remained dry throughout the damp winter months (fig. 3). The spaces between the foundation walls of the best-preserved example are about 35 to 40 cm wide, permitting subfloor air circulation that kept the building dry. A row of larger stones was found placed along each of the two longer sides of the K 5 foundation, about 35 cm from them (fig. 4). It is hypothesized that these stones held back the edge of a trench along each side of the building, which allowed air to enter the subfloor spaces between the foundation walls even though they were below the level of the surrounding ground. In cases where preservation permitted identification, it was observed that the spaces between the foundation walls were open to the exterior on one end via a break through or tunnel under the outside wall. These openings occurred on alternate, but not opposite, sides of the building, providing a snakelike passageway for air circulation.

Only in the one well-preserved grill plan building was the flooring above the foundations preserved (fig. 2). Set into this plaster flooring, but above the foundation walls, were bases of interior partitions a single stone wide, which outlined the chambers above the grill walls. There were two long, narrow chambers and three small rectangular cubicles situated down the middle of the building. The three small cubicles, each little more than 1 m², may have been storage bins rather than rooms. A large rectangular area on the southern end of the building was also enclosed by walls but was without the characteristic parallel foundations or the preserved flooring. The remains of a circular bin were found in one corner, and the skeleton of an adult female was found below the level of the ancient surface. As with all of the other grill plan buildings no substantial deposits were associated with this building, so that there was little artifactual or ecofactual material to aid in the identification of areas within the building or of the use of the building itself. Outside the buildings were dense deposits of flint artifacts, animal bones, and carbonized seeds, indicating, among other things, the refuse of a broad range of domestic activities in the immediate vicinity.

Two of the five grill plan buildings have somewhat different characteristics that might justify thinking of them as a separate type or subtype of building. The grill foundation walls are wider, being 50 to 55 cm wide, and the spaces between the foundation walls are narrower, being only 20 cm wide (fig. 5). The second distinguishing characteristic of these two buildings is the area adjacent to the grill-wall portion of the building that is floored with a tightly packed pebble pavement. These are well-rounded stones, probably derived from the river and distinct from the more angular stones used in the wall foundations. In one of these examples, several broad, flat stones were found in place, spanning the space between the grill walls and implying that a portion, or all, of that building's flooring was of stone and not of wood and plaster (fig. 5). In fact, the lack of any traces of preserved plaster flooring in any but the best-preserved example could be taken as evidence that the primary flooring was a perishable material such as matting and/or wood.

Because there are a number of grill plan buildings in the same stratigraphic level and no other substantial architectural constructions in that level, it is reasonable to assume that these are the basic domestic units of the community. Because of the specialized and complex construction technique that seems to be related to keeping the building dry, I suggest that a substantial portion of the space above the grill foundations was devoted to storing grain and other material that might suffer from dampness. This period of Çayönü's occupation was one in which the basic faunal resources utilized were still wild, but a portion of the plant material consumed was already domesticated. These people would have been involved in what Braidwood has referred to as experimentation; I see these rather magnificent buildings as an experiment in designing housing to facilitate the storage and processing of their newly acquired domestic plant foods. Excavation and controlled surface collection has also indicated that during this phase of occupation, Çayönü reached its greatest areal extent, about two hectares. If the pattern of grill plan buildings continues in the unexcavated portion of the site, then the community at the time consisted of at least twenty and perhaps as many as forty of these large buildings, which indicates a substantial population.

The placement of these buildings is also worthy of mention. Each of the five examples seems to have about the same orientation, about 20° west of north; the open, sometimes paved, area is to the south. Although definitive statements about the spacing of buildings are difficult to make with limited horizontal exposures, in at least one case there are two grill plan buildings about 4 m apart on what could have been opposite sides of a pathway (fig. 2). Also, new grill plan buildings frequently are built directly on top of old ones, which implies the importance of their positioning within the village layout. The overall impression provided by the excavated portion of this community of grill plan buildings is that of numerous well-built structures serving as the foci of domestic activities taking place in the spaces between buildings as well as in the open room at the south end of each building. The buildings themselves may have been the location of only a portion of the daily activities that went on within the village. Hence, although the grill plan is certainly a specialized building form, current evidence is that at Çayönü there was little or no specialization of buildings and that probably each building served as the focus of the entire range of activities conducted in locations (e.g., in the open end, to the west, etc.) that were specialized with respect to the building. In terms of the nature of specialization within a village, this architectural phenomenon seems to be a continuation from the preagricultural hut villages described by Flannery (1972) and others.

The stratigraphically later building type discovered at Çayönü is defined by its *cell plan foundation* and probably dates to about 7000 or 6700 B.C. (fig. 1). These structures are referred to as cell plans because their stone foundations form six, eight, or nine small cell-like units. The cells vary in size and number, being in two rows of three, two rows of four, or three rows of three. The foundation walls have been preserved to varying heights, ranging from a single stone high to as many as ten stones high (more than 70 cm). It is not certain whether all seven examples of cell plan buildings discovered at Çayönü functioned in a similar manner. The basic uncertainty is whether the cells were the primary rooms of the building, were less-used subfloor chambers, or were subfloor airspaces analogous to those in the grill plan buildings. The available evidence does not provide a single answer but many, and leads to the conclusion that some of the cells, at least, were used in one or another of the ways I have mentioned.

The spaces between the foundation walls of the one eight-cell building and the two nine-cell buildings are very narrow, leaving almost no question that they were subfloor air spaces to elevate the floor, as in the grill plan buildings (fig. 6). In none of these buildings (nor in the other cell plan buildings) are the floors above the foundation walls preserved, so a discussion of the arrangement of space within the building is not possible. The artifactual contents of these buildings, which have smaller cells, were not distinctive, with the exception of what must have been the purposeful interment, in the southeastern cell of the eight-cell building, of four lower jaws from large wild pigs. All three of these smaller-cell buildings were uncovered in one area on the western part of the site. They appeared to be arranged around a rectangular open space that may have served as a communal courtyard.

Fortunately for us as archeologists, three of the four six-cell buildings seem to have been destroyed in a catastrophic fire that preserved clay features and artifactual contents (fig. 7). The cells in these buildings are the size of a small room 1.0 to 1.5 m wide and 2.5 and 3.5 m long; some stone walls are preserved a half meter or more in height. Because of the burning, mud bricks are preserved in place on top of some of the stone walls and indicate a combination of stone and mud-brick construction. Openings in these well-preserved walls could have functioned as passageways, lending weight to the argument that these cells functioned as rooms while leaving open the possibility that a single more spacious room formed a second story above the cell walls. Each of the three burned six-cell buildings also has a partially enclosed area adjacent to its north end. In one case this area contained a hearth, a handstone, and a quern, the only examples of this sort of artifact to be found in association with any of the cell plan buildings. The implication is that certain domestic cooking and food-preparation activities took place in this more open area, the cells being reserved for other activities.

On the basis of the recovered artifacts, if in fact they do reflect the activities in the cells themselves, it seems clear that at least a portion of the cells were used for manufacturing activities. In two of the buildings with room-sized cells, large quantities of ground stone and antler tools have been preserved. Sickle hafts, adzes, chisels, and pestles are in the inventory. In each of these buildings, certain cells contained certain sets of artifacts, implying that specific parts of a building were used for specific tasks.

A description of some of the objects found in one of the well-preserved cell plan buildings indicates not only the diversity of the implements used in a single building but also the specificity of the use of each cell (fig. 7). The cell in the southeast corner of this building contained the greatest abundance and variety of artifacts, the most numerous of which were small limestone spheres, which may have been used as sling stones (fig. 8). Adzes, two palettes, and a perforated doughnut-shaped object were made of polished stone. Several long flint and obsidian blades were found in the same cell, as were numerous bone objects, an antler-blade haft, and a cylindrical haft of antler. Also found in this cell was a shallow sun-dried clay bowl, which had been modeled in the bottom of a coiled basket — an example of the use of clay for vessels before the introduction of fired pottery. The middle cell on the south was distinctive because of the remains of two small clay model houses (figs. 8 and 11). In addition to several limestone spheres there was a scatter of large chunks of obsidian, which had not yet been worked into tools but seemed to have been smashed from one or more large cores. The southwest cell was characterized by a large number of small highly polished stone adzes and chisels. Several architectural elements of the building, such as roof fragments with beam impressions and a door jamb, had been preserved by a fire in the room. The northwest chamber contained more than twenty marine shells, neatly piled next to a complete antler-blade haft. The most unusual object in the middle room on the north side was a complete scapula of a large *Bos primigenius*, which may have served as an anvil for manufacturing activities. The northeast chamber was almost devoid of artifacts, perhaps being used for sleeping or for a ladder to the upper story or roof.

In each of the two other buildings with room-sized cells, three human skeletons were found in the northwest cell (fig. 9). On one of these skeletons was a long strand of small multicolored stone and shell beads. In the deposit above the other burial group were found a cache of unusually large obsidian implements, including blades, points, and specialized tools that measured as much as 25 cm in length, and a single obsidian flake weighing more than 400 grams, In a nearby, perhaps associated, deposit was a cache of 24 polished limestone objects that resemble chess pawns (fig. 10). All of this material indicates the possibility of elaborate burial practices and subfloor interment.[1]

The clay model houses at Çayönü and the preserved clay architectural remnants in the buildings themselves provide some unusual insights into the building techniques utilized at Çayönü. The hand-modeled clay architectural elements on the models indicate possible functions for similar full-sized elements found in the building in which the model houses were found (fig. 11). The construction technique used in the model houses also seems parallel to the real-life methods. The model's roof was made of clay pressed onto twigs spanning the model's room, and fallen roof fragments of the actual building seem to suggest that a similar method of construction was used (fig. 12). Another feature of the model house, the parapet running around the roof, which has several openings for drainage, was a possible feature of Çayönü's real-life houses, although no such evidence has yet been excavated.

By the time Çayönü was characterized by cell plan buildings its economy had been altered from that of the earlier grill plan building phases. Domestic plants, especially grains, played a more important role in subsistence. Although wild animals continued to be hunted, the major meat source had become domesticated sheep and goats. Technology had changed as well, with the more frequent use of antler hafts for both blades and cylindrical tools, such as scrapers and adzes. Handstones and querns increased in frequency, perhaps as a result of the growing use of grain. Overall, the preliminary interpretation of the community is one in which reliance on domesticated plants and animals has grown, and food-processing and manufacturing activities involving stone, bone, antler, shell, and even clay are substantial. During the cell plan phase there do appear to be variations in the construction and use of the buildings, although all seven excavated buildings are rectangular, free-standing, and about the same size (30 to 40 m²), and they all utilize multiple stone foundations. One difference between the buildings is that the three with room-sized cells appear to have at least a portion of their floor space devoted to specialized manufacturing activities while the others may or may not. The specialization of productive and processing activities within the cell plan buildings and the probable differences between the buildings indicate that the overall organization of activities at Çayönü had probably changed from the earlier grill plan phase. Individual buildings were probably still the basic community unit, but

1. See Schmandt-Besserat 1979 for an interesting perspective on similar pawnlike objects.

more activities went on within the buildings and there might have been some specialization and subsequent exchange of goods between inhabitants of the buildings. In the two areas of the site where more than one cell building has been excavated they seem to have been arranged around large rectangular open spaces. This leaves open the possibility that there may have been an intermediate level of community organization based on groups of cooperating households situated around a large open courtyard. The community at Çayönü during the cell plan phase was smaller than that of the grill plan phase, covering only about 1.5 hectares and comprising twenty to thirty houses. However, this phase was also the period when the greatest quantity of obsidian was being brought to the site and the diversity of the tool industry was the greatest (Redman 1973). My own interpretation of cell plan Çayönü is that it was a very successful community where early experimentation with food production had given way to a major dependence on it and the consequent reorganization and specialization to meet the needs of an agricultural way of life.

The grill plan and cell plan buildings have been described here as they occurred at Çayönü, but I believe that similar buildings have been uncovered at other early village sites, which indicates a broader significance for these types. I will briefly mention published parallels in an effort to demonstrate that whatever is responsible for their construction at Çayönü may be shared by others in the Near East. However, it should be noted that my mention of these other structures is taken very much out of the context of their respective communities and more reliable comparisons could be made only by the excavators of these sites.

I know of two examples of what appear to be remains of grill plan foundation buildings at other early villages in the Near East. I supect that other examples may have been discovered, but due to the small size of excavation units it would be easy for sets of parallel rows of stones to go unreported or at least to not be interpreted as a distinct form. One of these examples, of roughly the same period as Çayönü, was uncovered by Braidwood in Jarmo, in the Zagros mountain foothills of northeast Iraq (Braidwood and Howe 1960). It is a combination of stone and tauf (pressed mud) foundation walls that appear to have been part of a building with both grill and open foundations (Operation II, Level 5; fig. 13). A second example comes from the ceramic neolithic levels of Munhata (Level 2A), a site in the Jordan River valley of Israel. A building with a rectangular-outline foundation and several cross foundation walls that probably supported a raised floor is reported along with what is interpreted as a semicircular hearth adjacent to it (Perrot 1968, p. 416). This building, also like the ones at Çayönü, has one section with grill foundations and one section with an open foundation. In both the Jarmo and Munhata situations the community is composed primarily of rectangular buildings.

Examples of what may be broadly conceived of as cell plan buildings have been reported at four other early villages in the Near East. The best known examples are the "corridor buildings" of Levels II and III at Beidha, in southern Jordan (Kirkbride 1966). Each unit consisted of a narrow central corridor that opened into six small rooms, three on each side of the corridor (fig. 14). Each room was approximately 1.5 m by 1.0 m and was separated from adjacent rooms by wide baulks, which implies that the rooms supported a lightly built upper story. The excavator, Diana Kirkbride, hypothesizes that the corridor rooms were workshops for the manufacture of bone tools, beads, and horn objects and that the second story was the living quarters. Several examples of corridor buildings were uncovered at Beidha, sometimes in association with larger rooms in the same complex. There is evidence of other cell-like buildings, from the excavation of Mureybit in the upper Euphrates River valley of Syria (van Loon, Skinner, and van Zeist 1968). The nature of the architecture at that site is diverse, but among the remains in the upper levels there is a building with small, almost square chambers. The third example of cell plan buildings comes from Ganj Dareh in the Zagros mountains of western Iran (Smith 1972, p. 166). In Level D, where the architecture is well preserved, there are structures composed of small chambers or cubicles constructed of mud bricks and pressed mud (fig. 15). The excavator, Philip Smith, suggests that in some cases a second-story living surface supported by wooden beams covered the cubicles. The function of the cubicles may not have been uniform, but at least some of them may have been used for storage purposes, as implied by the presence of small and large clay pots. A fourth example of cell-like buildings is from Umm Dabaghiyah, a sixth-millennium site in the Jezireh of northern Iraq (Kirkbride 1975). This example is from somewhat later than the other cell buildings and from a community that is quite distinct from others I have mentioned, but the example is particularly informative in terms of what early village cell buildings might develop into with further specialization. In Levels 3 and 4 of Umm Dabaghiyah there are at least two large buildings comprised of dozens of small cubicles (1.5 by 1.7 m) arranged in two or three rows (fig. 16). There are few doorways between these cells, and they are thought by the excavator to have been storerooms for the most part. One chamber, apparently an arsenal used for hunting the onagers that dominate the site's faunal assemblage, contained 2,400 baked-clay sling missiles and about 100 large baked-clay balls.

Two levels of significance can be attributed to the existence of the building types described here, first, the significance related to building technology and, second, the significance of the implications of the building types for the nature of the community. As examples of some of the earliest substantial buildings from some of the earliest villages yet known, both the grill plan buildings and the cell plan buildings are astonishingly complex structures for their time. Although their size, 25 to 50 m² of enclosed area, is not unusually large, the design of their foundations seems more sophisticated than one would expect as the solution to housing formulated by people who had just recently started to live in villages. However, the more we learn of this time range the more industrious and inventive the people seem to have been. Modes of existence were changing radically with the beginnings of agriculture and permanent settlements. Housing design must have been an integral part of their overall adaptation to their new activities. Interestingly, this adaptation took relatively specialized forms that did not appear to last long periods of time; that is, for a period of time the people of Çayönü found it worthwhile to build all of their buildings with relatively complex grill plan foundations and to rebuild them repeatedly on the same location and in roughly the same plan. However, grill plan foundations were not adopted at many other sites nor did they even continue in use at Çayönü throughout its occupation. Nevertheless, Çayönü in its time was an extremely successful community, and the grill plan does seem to have been used in other, albeit isolated, instances. This indicates to me that the grill plan building type was not so much a "traditional" idea carried out by one group of people as it was an architectural solution to a particular set of problems of adaptation that might be known and tried by numerous groups, a solution that only some of them would find worthwhile. It is difficult to be certain of exactly how the grill plan buildings were used or what adaptive problems they solved, but evidence points to their being related to storage of food and probably at a single-family level of organization. The cell plan buildings, on the other hand, seem to be related to manufacturing as well as to storage activities. These activities seem to be associated with individual buildings (except at Umm Dabaghiyah) and hence were carried out at an individual-household level, but there is some reason to believe that groups of these households cooperated. The very nature of the cell plans indicates a certain degree of specialization or at least spatial differentiation of activities within the productive unit, and their spatial arrangement at Çayönü is suggestive of higher-level organization of activities as well.

With the advent of agriculture and settled village life there is a growing use of permanent facilities to enhance production. The grill and cell plan houses can be viewed as examples of this developmental process. At the same time these buildings were in use we see evidence of an increasing range of manufacturing and processing activities being carried out in the community, much of it to facilitate food production. To the people of the cell plan buildings of Çayönü, farming was rapidly becoming an accepted fact of life, and increasing proportions of their energy were being devoted to the production of tools and containers, from a wide variety of raw materials, to aid in their subsistence pursuits. The architectural compartmentalization of manufacturing activities does seem to be an idea that emerged in the early villages of the Near East and evolved to become one of the basic patterns within subsequent architectural history. Given this simplified perspective on these very complex archeological remains it is possible to cite them as evidence for two evolutionary trends occurring within the span of a single village site. One trend is from a primary concern with subsistence and storage to a more balanced concern for the production of tools, facilities, and cultural goods as well as for the immediate needs of subsistence and storage. The other trend is toward the increasing use of architecture to facilitate productive specialization. The grill plan and cell plan buildings of Çayönü are small stages in those long-term trends.

BIBLIOGRAPHY

Braidwood, R.J.; Çambel, H.; Lawrence, B.; Redman, C.L.; and Stewart, R.
  1974   Beginnings of village-farming communities in southeastern Turkey: 1972. *Proceedings of the National Academy of Sciences* 71(2):568−72.

Braidwood, R.J.; Çambel, H.; Redman, C.L.; and Watson, P.J.
  1971   Beginnings of village-farming communities in southeastern Turkey: 1972. *Proceedings of the National Academy of Sciences* 68(6):1236−40.

Braidwood, R.J.; Çambel, H.; and Watson, P.J.
  1969   Prehistoric investigations in southeastern Turkey. *Science* 164:1275−76.

Braidwood, R.J., and Howe, B.
  1960   *Prehistoric investigations in Iraqi Kurdistan.* Studies in Ancient Oriental Civilizations, no. 31. Chicago: University of Chicago Press.

Flannery, K.V.
  1972   The origins of the village as a settlement type in Mesoamerica and the Near East: a comparative study. In *Man, settlement, and urbanism,* ed. P.J. Ucko, R. Tringham and G.W. Dimbleby, pp. 23−53. London: Duckworth.

Kirkbride, D.
  1966   Five seasons at the pre-pottery Neolithic village of Beidha in Jordan. *Palestine Exploration Quarterly* 98(1):8−72.
  1975   Umm Dabaghiyah 1974: a fourth preliminary report. *Iraq* 37:3−10.

Loon, M. van; Skinner, J.H.; and Zeist, W. van
  1968   The Oriental Institute excavations at Mureybit, Syria: preliminary report on the 1965 campaign. Part 1: architecture and general finds. *Journal of Near Eastern Studies* 27(4):265−90.

Perrot, J.
  1968   La préhistoire Palestinienne. In *Supplément au dictionnaire de la Bible,* no. 8, cols. 286−446. Paris: Letouzey and Ané.

Redman, C.L.
  1973   Early village technology: a view through the microscope. *Paléorient* 1(2):249−61.

Schmandt-Besserat, D.
  1979   An archaic recording system in the Uruk-Jemdet Nasr period. *American Journal of Archaeology* 83(1):19−48.

Smith, P.E.L.
  1972   Survey of excavations in Iran during 1970−1971. *Iran* 10:165−68.

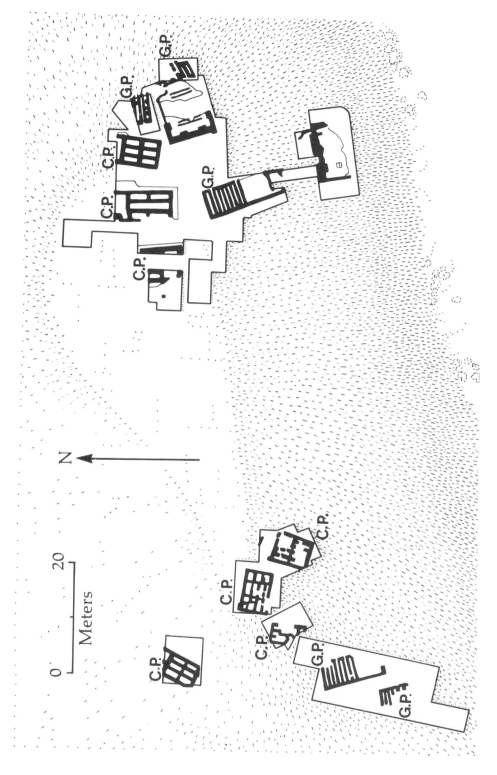

Fig. 1. — Map of Çayönü. The map indicates the location of grill plan (G. P.) and cell plan (C. P.) buildings. (Recorded by T. Rhode, the Joint Prehistoric Project of the Universities of Istanbul and Chicago; reproduced by courtesy of W. H. Freeman and Co.)

2

3

FIG. 2. — GRILL PLAN BUILDING (EF 2). The plasterlike floor is preserved. In the upper left-hand corner of the photograph is a second grill plan building (photographs in figures 2 through 12 are courtesy of the Joint Prehistoric Project of the Universities of Istanbul and Chicago). FIG. 3. — GRILL PLAN BUILDING EF 2. One half of its plasterlike floor has been removed to show its rippled contours and the supporting grill foundations.

5

4

FIG. 4. — GRILL PLAN BUILDING K 5 showing rows of stones along its outside walls and cobbled area at south end of the building. FIG. 5. — EXCAVATED PORTION OF GRILL PLAN BUILDING U 22. This figure shows wider grills, paved area, and a few flat stones spanning grill spaces; an example of the second type of grill plan building.

6

7

FIG. 6. — CELL PLAN BUILDING H 3. This building has small airspace cells and pig-jaw burial in southeast cell. Note adjacent cell building to the left. FIG. 7. — CELL PLAN BUILDING U 9. U 9, with room-sized cells, is well preserved due to fire. Arrows indicate the probable location of doorways.

FIG. 8. — CLOSE-UP OF CELLS IN BUILDING U 9. A cluster of tools in the foreground and a model house and obsidian chunks are indicated by arrows. FIG. 9. — CELL PLAN BUILDING S 6. Skeletons of three individuals are in the northwest corner cell. Note foundations of earlier cell plan exposed below S 6.

Fig. 10. — Cache of Limestone Pieces. The pieces, which resemble chess pawns, are shown in situ in cell plan building S 6.

Fig. 11. — Views of Clay Model House found in Cell Plan Building U 9. Front, top, and underside of roof fragment are shown.

12

13

Fig. 12. — Fallen Fragment of Clay Roofing from Cell Plan Building U 9. Impressions of beams of various sizes that supported the roof are visible. Fig. 13. — Tauf and Stone Foundation of Buildings in Lower Level of Jarmo. Proposed grill plan building is in upper right-hand corner. (Photo courtesy of the Prehistoric Project, The Oriental Institute, The University of Chicago.)

FIG. 14. — EXAMPLE OF CORRIDOR BUILDING AND ADJACENT LARGE ROOM FROM LEVEL 2 OF BEIDHA. (After Kirkbride 1966, reproduced by courtesy of W.H. Freeman and Co.) FIG. 15. — CELL-PLANLIKE MUD AND MUD-BRICK ARCHITECTURE FROM LEVEL D OF GANJ DAREH TEPE, IRAN. (Courtesy of P.E.L. Smith.)

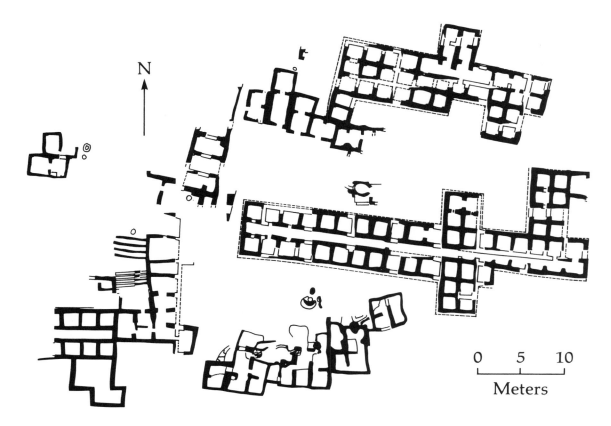

Fig. 16. — Plan of Advanced Cell Plan Buildings from Levels 3 and 4 at Umm Dabaghiyah in Northern Iraq. (After Kirkbride 1975, reproduced by courtesy of W.H. Freeman and Co.)

PATTERNS OF INTERACTION BETWEEN SEASONAL SETTLEMENTS AND EARLY VILLAGES IN MESOPOTAMIA

Peder Mortensen

INTRODUCTION

MORE THAN twenty years ago, when Robert J. Braidwood published the first accounts of his prehistoric investigations in Persian Kurdistan, he suggested that Tepe Sarab, not giving the impression of permanency, might have been occupied during only a portion of the year (Braidwood 1960, p. 695, and Braidwood, Howe, and Reed 1961, p. 2009). Although later analyses of the animal bones from Tepe Sarab have indicated that the site was inhabited year-round (Bökönyi 1977, p. 37; McDonald 1978), I think that Braidwood by this suggestion for the first time stimulated an interest in the relationship between early villages and the seasonal sites contemporary with them.

A number of such nonpermanent sites have since been located in the Zagros area and in Khuzistan (e.g., Hole and Flannery 1967; Hole 1968, 1974; Mortensen 1972, 1979; Smith and Mortensen 1980). The best known and most extensively excavated site of this type, however, is probably Umm Dabaghiyah on the North Mesopotamian plain (Kirkbride 1972, 1973a, b, 1974, 1975, forthcoming).

The present article — in honor of Robert J. Braidwood — is an attempt to consider the function of Umm Dabaghiyah through an analysis of its chipped stone industry and an examination of the patterns of interaction between the earliest nonpermanent sites on the plain and the early permanent villages in the surrounding foothills and intermontane valleys of Northern Mesopotamia.

THE CHIPPED STONE INDUSTRY OF UMM DABAGHIYAH[1]

THE EXCAVATIONS

Umm Dabaghiyah was found and almost completely excavated by Diana Kirkbride during four seasons from 1971 to 1974 (Kirkbride 1972, 1973a–b, 1974, 1975). The mound covers a little less than a hectare and is almost 4 m high. The earliest occupation (Level V) was founded on a thin layer of reddish virgin soil, lying immediately on top of the natural gypsum. It was followed by a number of building phases that can be divided into four main occupations with substantial mud-walled architecture (Levels IV–I). The site seems to span a relatively short period, perhaps three or four centuries, around 6000 B.C.

RAW MATERIALS AND DEBITAGE

Considering that Umm Dabaghiyah is situated in the Jazira, in the middle of a waste and stoneless steppe, it is perhaps surprising that the excavation yielded 13,779 pieces of stratified

1. I am very grateful to Diana Kirkbride for having offered me the chipped stone material from Umm Dabaghiyah for publication. I also wish to express my thanks to the officials of the Iraqi State Organization for Antiquities and Heritage in Baghdad for their cooperation and for the opportunity of having some of the chipped stone materials on loan in Aarhus. Finally, I wish to thank my wife, Inge Demant Mortensen, for her encouragement and help during my preparation of the manuscript and to acknowledge my gratitude to Diana Kirkbride, P.E.L. Smith, T. Cuyler Young, Henry T. Wright, and Helle Juel Jensen for stimulating suggestions and criticism that were of great value.

chipped stone. As noted by Peter Dorrell (1972, p. 69) the saline surface of the steppe consists of redeposited silts and clays more or less cemented by gypsum. But there is no stone easily available on the surface. The raw materials, or the finished tools, had to be brought in from distant sources.

A major part of the materials consisted of flint and chert (93%), a minor part, of obsidian (6.3%), and less than one percent of various other materials, such as white or pink quartz, alabaster, greenstone, and basalt. Compared with flint, the relative amount of obsidian decreases markedly in time from Level IV (22.1%) to Level I (5.5%).[2]

The flint can be separated into two distinct groups, apparently deriving from at least two different sources:

Group 1, including 97.3% of the materials, comprises flint or chert of a bad quality, rather coarse grained and in many cases full of flaws. The color ranges from very light grey (66%) through various shades of darker grey (31.4%) to greyish green (2.6%). Most of the materials belonging to this group can be clearly classified as nodular flint. The pieces are of a moderate size (fig. 1), and they had to be brought in, probably from a deposit of extremely bad flint located by Peter Dorrell about 12 km from Umm Dabaghiyah or from the Wadi Tharthar, which flows north to south some 36 km east of the site. As noted by the excavator, this material was so poor that many chunks had been discarded after one or two blows (Kirkbride, forthcoming).

Group 2 comprises only 2.7% of the flint. The material is very fine grained, the cortex is rarely preserved, and the flint is characterized by a color scheme different from that of group 1, ranging from white (4.2%) through many shades of brown (93.5%) to dark chocolate brown with green veins (2.3%). The latter is common in the mountains of northern Iraq (e.g., Mortensen 1970a, p. 27). It seems most likely, therefore, that this group of flint is derived from a mountainous source of tabular flint, possibly at the Jebel Sinjar, the blue silhouette of which is sometimes faintly visible from the site a little more than 70 km toward the northwest.

Trace element analyses of the obsidian have not yet been carried out, but in transmitted light 43.1% of the 868 pieces of obsidian showed a clear or smoky greyish color, which indicates that the raw material might have come from the Çiftlik area, 800 km toward the northwest on the Anatolian plateau. Of the obsidian, 56.9% had a brownish or greenish tinge, which suggests an origin at one of the two sources of peralkaline obsidian: the volcanic crater of Nemrut Dağ or Bingöl near Lake Van, 450 km north of Umm Dabaghiyah.

The small amounts of quartz, alabaster, greenstone, and basalt used in the lithic industry had to be collected from one of the larger wadis or brought in from the mountains to the north together with the flint and obsidian.

Of the total collection of chipped stone from Umm Dabaghiyah, 92.6% (= 12,770 pieces) is raw materials and debitage, i.e., flint nodules, cores, flakes, blades, and chips without deliberate retouch. This group of materials can be classified roughly as follows:

    a. *Amorphous, semichipped flint nodules* (fig. 1). Irregularly shaped nodules with scars from flaking, often in several directions. In most cases the cortex is left on a substantial part of the surface. Many nodules of this type seem to represent the first stage in the preparation of a flake- or blade core. Others are simply nodules that were discarded after having been tested by one or two blows. Largest diameter: 2.3–10.6 cm, with an average between 3.5–4.0 cm. Total: 1,698 (flint).

    b. *Small, irregular flake cores* (fig. 2a–d). Roughly chipped flake cores, often spherical, with two or three striking platforms. The cortex is sometimes partly preserved, and

2. That obsidian became less important as a trading object in Mesopotamia during the sixth and early fifth millennia B.C. is also exemplified at Choga Mami, where the amount of obsidian compared with flint decreases from 5.7% in the earliest Samarran level (III/Phase 4) to 0.9% at the Ubaid Well (Mortensen 1973, pp. 38–39).

Table 1. — Distribution of Raw Materials and Debitage (Types a—j) at Umm Dabaghiyah

				Levels					
Type	I	I/ II	II	II/ III	III	III/ IV	IV	V	Total Number
a. Amorphous, semichipped flint nodules	323	69	760	171	262	65	47	1	1,698
b. Small, irregular flake cores	23	3	72	38	25	14	9	--	184
c. Cylindrical blade cores	2	--	--	--	--	--	--	--	2
d. Conical blade cores	3	--	8	3	3	1	1	--	19
e. Various core fragments	18	2	27	6	8	2	5	--	68
f. Side-blow blade-flake "cores"	7	1	23	6	10	1	5	--	53
g. Flakes	1,143	85	3,374	810	1,147	243	217	--	7,019
h. Blades	92	16	163	103	118	39	29	1	561
j. Chips	394	52	1,561	526	342	139	150	2	3,166
Total number	2,005	228	5,988	1,663	1,915	504	463	4	12,770

many of the cores show clear battering marks along the edges. Largest diameter: 1.4—4.2 cm. Total: 184 (flint).

c. *Cylindrical blade cores* (fig. 2e). Small cylindrical cores with two opposed striking platforms and with scars from blades having been struck around the entire perimeter. Largest diameter: 2.6—2.8 cm. Total: 2 (flint).

d. *Conical blade cores* (fig. 2f—h). Blade cores with an oval or almost circular striking platform at one end. The cores are widest at the platform and narrow toward a pointed or chisel-shaped lower end. Blades were usually struck around the entire perimeter, but in some cases part of the surface is only roughly prepared by flaking or it shows the cortex from the original surface of the nodule. A few microblade cores are bullet shaped. Height: 1.7—5.1 cm. Total: 19 (flint 18/obsidian 1).

e. *Various core fragments* (fig. 2i—p). Miscellaneous flakes and blades related to the trimming process of cores and the production of blades (cf. Hole, Flannery, and Neely 1969, pp. 100—2; Mortensen 1973, pp. 39—41). The group includes primary and secondary core tablets (fig. 2i—j), edges of striking platforms (fig. 2l—n), and rectangular blade-core flakes (fig. 2o). Total: 68 (flint 67/obsidian 1).

f. *Side-blow blade-flake "cores"* (fig. 4m—n). Trapezoidal blade segments, truncated at one or both ends by the production of side-blow blade flakes (type K, below. Cf. Fukai and Matsutani 1977, p. 55, fig. 3). Length: 0.5—2.4 cm. Total: 53 (obsidian).

g. *Flakes*. Length: 1.2—10.1 cm. Total: 7,019 (flint 6,957/obsidian 62).

h. *Blades*. Length: 1.3—14.1 cm. Total: 561 (flint 373/obsidian 188).

j. *Chips*. Thin flakes, the length of which is less than 1 cm. Most chips are probably debitage from the production of flakes and blades or from the surface trimming of larger tools. Total: 3,166 (flint 2,909/obsidian 257).

The distribution by levels of the various types of raw materials and debitage is indicated in table 1. It shows a rather stable development throughout the sequence with a predominance of unretouched flakes (54.9%), chips (27.7%), and amorphous, semichipped flint nodules (13.2%). Unretouched blades represent only 4.3% of the debitage, which suggests a fairly high exploitation of blades compared to flakes. Within the retouched materials this is confirmed by the fact that 54.5% of the tools are based on blades.

Leaving out of account one fragment of a small conical obsidian blade core there is no evidence of obsidian blades having been produced locally. It seems that the production of obsidian blades took place somewhere else, although further modification of the blades by chipping or retouch was sometimes performed at the site. The presence of a great number of side-blow blade-flakes (fig. 4o−q) and the "cores" from which they were struck (fig. 4m−n) is clear evidence of such activity.

Furthermore, it is important to note that 99.4% of the nodules, cores, core fragments, and debitage of flint can be classified as belonging to group 1. Just seven conical blade cores and a handful of unretouched blades were made of fine-grained tabular flint (group 2), the implication being that the only raw materials that were actually brought to the site for chipping were coarse flint nodules. As we shall see below, these were used for certain categories of tools, produced locally, whereas obsidian blades and implements made of tabular flint from more distant sources were possibly made at another site and carried to Umm Dabaghiyah by the settlers.

IMPLEMENTS

Arrowheads. The arrowheads from Umm Dabaghiyah have been divided into five types:

Type A1 (fig. 3a−d). Small triangular points based on thin flakes or blades with converging edges, occasionally modified by retouch. The tang is short and irregularly formed by ventral chipping, or by edge retouch, along the dorsal and the ventral faces. Length: 2.3−4.2 cm. Total: 13 (flint).

Type A2 (fig. 3e−f). Points based on blades that are sometimes slightly chipped along the edges. The tang has been produced by a semisteep unifacial or bifacial retouch. It is truncated at the base, where the bulb of percussion has been broken off. Length: 2.9−6.2 cm. Total: 8 (flint).

Type A3 (fig. 3g−i). Points based on blades the shape of which is modified by extensive squamous retouch at the ventral face. The tang has been produced by steep ventral retouch. Length: 4.3−5.8 cm. Total: 9 (flint).

Type A4 (fig. 3j−k). Leaf-shaped points with an extensive bifacial retouch. The tang has been produced by a steep ventral retouch. A single fragmentary point, illustrated in figure 3j, is possibly a slender variant of this type. Length: 4.2−5.6 cm. Total: 9 (flint).

Type A5 (fig. 3l−m). Leaf-shaped points, extensively covered on both faces with squamous retouch. The tangs are carefully shaped by bifacial chipping, and the shoulders are clearly indicated. Length: 4.5−5.8 cm. Total: 2 (flint).

Borers

Type B1 (fig. 4a−b). Borers made on flakes, slightly modified by chipping along two converging edges toward the point. Length: 3.3−6.3 cm. Total: 15 (flint).

Type B2 (fig. 4c−e). Borers made on blades. The points are formed at the distal ends by a semisteep dorsal or alternating retouch along the converging edges. Length: 2.6−8.2 cm. Total: 24 (flint 21/obsidian 3).

Type B3 (fig. 4f−g). Like B2 but with a slightly curved point. The proximal ends are modified by retouch so that they form a second point or a kind of tang. Length: 3.5−7.3 cm. Total: 8 (flint).

Type B4 (fig. 4h−i). Lancet-shaped, tanged points bifacially retouched, especially at the distal end. The type is faintly similar to the leaf-shaped arrowheads, but the points of the borers are thicker and slightly worn. Length: 4.2−5.2 cm. Total: 2 (flint).

Type B5 (fig. 4j). Borers made on microblades. The points form half or more than half of the length of the tools. They are narrow and steeply retouched along both edges. Length: 2.1−3.2 cm. Total: 5 (flint 4/obsidian 1).

Beaked blades

Type C (fig. 4k−l). Implements made from thick blades with a steep, lamellar retouch at the ventral face along both edges. A short beak with a strong, burinlike cutting edge has been produced at the distal end by the intersection of the broken end of the blade and the outcurving edge retouch. The proximal end of the blades is usually snapped off. Length: 2.2−5.5 cm. Total: 7 (flint 2/obsidian 5).

Scrapers

Type D 1 (fig. 5a—b). Scrapers made on very small flake cores by steep, secondary retouch along a segment of the largest striking platform. Width: 1.2—3.7 cm. Total: 34 (flint 33/obsidian 1).

Type D 2 (fig. 5c—f). End scrapers made on thick ovoid or subrectangular flakes with a steeply retouched convex edge. The sides and the base are usually formed by retouch on the dorsal side. Length: 1.7—5.5 cm. Total: 49 (flint 46/obsidian 3).

Type D 3 (fig. 5g). End scrapers made on thick rectangular or subrectangular flakes with a steeply retouched oblique edge. Length: 3.7—5.8 cm. Total: 12 (flint).

Type D 4 (fig. 5h). Side scrapers made on thick flakes with a steep convex edge. Length: 3.8—9.5 cm. Total: 7 (flint).

Type D 5 (fig. 5i—j). Scrapers made on thick flakes with an irregular concavo-convex edge. Length: 2.1—6.5 cm. Total: 14 (flint).

Type D 6 (fig. 5k—l). End-of-blade scrapers with a convex edge, produced by a steep or semisteep retouch, sometimes continuing along one or both sides. Length: 2.1—6.5 cm. Total: 16 (flint 11/obsidian 5).

Burins

Type E 1 (fig. 5m). Burins made on flakes. The edge is formed by the intersection at one end of two or more planes produced by burin blows. Length: 2.5—5.6 cm. Total: 14 (flint).

Type E 2 (fig. 5n—o). Burins made on flakes or thick blades. The edge is produced by one or several burin blows struck from a broken or natural transverse truncation. Length: 2.7—10.0 cm. Total: 12 (flint).

Notched flakes or blades

Type F 1 (fig. 5p). Flakes with one or several steeply retouched notches along the edges. Length: 2.3—5.5 cm. Total: 20 (flint 18/obsidian 2).

Type F 2 (fig. 5q—r). Blades with one or several steeply retouched notches along the edges. Length: 2.1—6.9 cm. Total: 30 (flint 22/obsidian 8).

Sickle blades

Type G. Only two pieces of flint had slightly glossy traces of wear along one of the edges: one piece was a flake retouched along the curved back; another piece (fig. 6a) had its cortex preserved along the back. Length: 4.9—6.3 cm. Total: 2 (flint).

Knives

Type H 1 (fig. 6b—c). Flakes with one or two curved, often converging edges. One or both edges are sharpened by a flat retouch along the dorsal or ventral faces, and the edges are in some cases heavily worn. Length: 3.6—11.4 cm. Total: 45 (flint).

Type H 2 (fig. 6d—f). Blades or blade segments with a continuous alternating retouch along both edges. The ventral retouch is often very steep, as if to produce a blunt back. The opposite edge is usually worn from use. Length: 2.8—8.8 cm. Total: 55 (flint 48/obsidian 7).

Type H 3 (fig. 6g—h). Like H 2, but with ventral retouch, and often with heavy traces of wear along both edges. Length: 2.6—10.6 cm. Total: 58 (flint 52/obsidian 6).

Geometrics

A few geometrics were found at Umm Dabaghiyah, but like microliths from most other village sites they constitute a very heterogeneous group in regard to size as well as to morphology. They can roughly be divided into:

Trapezes: type J 1 (fig. 6i—j). Trapeze-shaped blade segments with an oblique truncation at each end. Length: 0.8—3.3 cm. Total: 3 (obsidian).

Crescents: type J 2 (fig. 6k—l). Blade segments, backed by a half-circular retouch. Length: 1.2—2.8 cm. Total: 2 (obsidian).

Side-blow blade flakes

Type K (fig. 4o−q). Small, transverse blade segments, produced by a blow at the central ridge of the dorsal face of a blade (cf. L. Braidwood 1961, pp. 146−47 and Mortensen 1973, p. 46, n. 23). Width: 0.6−2.7 cm. Total: 120 (obsidian).

Firestones

Type L (fig. 7a−b). Very thick flakes with a coarse, steep retouch along the edges. The ventral face is often trimmed by a surface-covering, squamous retouch. One or two restricted areas along the edges are covered with battering marks. Flints with this particular type of wear have been interpreted as firestones (strike-a-lights). They were first identified with some of the rich burials at Çatal Hüyük and at Beidha and have been described in detail elsewhere (Mortensen 1970b, pp. 38−41. Length: 2.8−6.6 cm. Total: 29 (flint).

Picks

Type M (fig. 7c). Heavy core tools, pointed at one end, and irregularly flaked at the surface. The points have a square or a triangular section, and the opposite end is narrowed as if it might have been hafted. Length: 11.5−12.4 cm. Total: 2 (flint).

Choppers

Type N (fig. 7d−f). Large oval or trapezoid pebbles, slightly polished and with a sharp convex edge produced by irregular bifacial flaking. Width: 4.2−9.8 cm. Total: 21 (flint).

Flakes with partial retouch along the edges

Type O. Length: 1.0−5.4 cm. Total: 197 (flint 168/obsidian 29).

Blades with partial retouch along the edges

Type P. Length: 2.2−6.9 cm. Total: 165 (flint 84/obsidian 81).

The temporal distribution by layers of the implements described above is shown in table 2. Just like the raw materials and debitage, the tool groups and types are regularly distributed; there are only minor changes within the sequence. No tools appeared in Level V, however. Three types were not found in the lowest layers (A4−5 and B1); a few other types were absent in Level I (B2, C, D4, E1, and J); and picks (type M) occurred only in Level II. These fluctuations, however, may well be incidental. They do not alter our general impression of a high degree of type stability and of very little innovation during the period of time in which the site was in use.

Consequently, we must conclude that the chipped stone industry of Umm Dabaghiyah seems to represent a relatively short sequence and that there is no evidence of new population elements or of major functional changes at the site. Together with knives (15.8%), scrapers (13.2%), and side-blow blade flakes (12.0%) the material is dominated by a large but heterogeneous group of flakes and blades with irregular retouch along the edges (36.2%). Less predominant are borers (5.4%), notched flakes and blades (4.4%), arrowheads (4%), firestones (2.9%), burins (2.6%), picks and choppers (2.3%), beaked blades (0.7%), geometric microliths (0.3%), and sickle blades (0.2%).

DIANA KIRKBRIDE'S INTERPRETATION OF UMM DABAGHIYAH

We shall proceed with an analysis of the functional and stylistic implications offered by the lithic material. First, however, it is relevant to summarize Diana Kirkbride's current interpretation of the site, which is based primarily on observations derived from the environmental setting of Umm Dabaghiyah, combined with floral, faunal, and architectural evidence (Kirkbride 1974, and forthcoming).

The settlement lies about 200 m above sea level and is surrounded by a hot and arid steppe that is easily transformed into a desert by a slight decrease of the annual rainfall. The precipitation

Table 2. — Distribution of Tools and Implements (Types A–P) at Umm Dabaghiyah

Type	Levels								Total Number
	I	I/II	II	II/III	III	III/IV	IV	V	
Arrowheads: type A1	1	--	3	2	3	3	1	--	13
A2	5	--	2	--	1	--	--	--	8
A3	2	--	3	1	--	3	--	--	9
A4	3	--	1	--	5	--	--	--	9
A5	2	--	--	--	--	--	--	--	2
Borers: type B1	5	4	3	2	1	--	--	--	15
B2	--	--	9	3	2	9	1	--	24
B3	2	--	2	--	2	1	1	--	8
B4	1	--	--	1	--	--	--	--	2
B5	1	--	--	--	2	2	--	--	5
Beaked blades: type C	--	--	4	1	--	2	--	--	7
Scrapers: type D1	6	1	10	2	5	6	4	--	34
D2	11	3	22	6	4	2	1	--	49
D3	5	--	3	3	--	1	--	--	12
D4	--	--	5	--	1	1	--	--	7
D5	2	--	7	1	3	1	--	--	14
D6	2	5	3	5	1	--	--	--	16
Burins: type E1	--	--	6	4	2	2	--	--	14
E2	1	--	6	--	4	--	1	--	12
Notched flakes: type F1	3	--	8	2	2	3	2	--	20
F2	3	--	15	5	4	2	1	--	30
Sickle blades: type G	1	--	--	1	--	--	--	--	2
Knives: type H1	8	--	23	4	3	5	2	--	45
H2	8	1	22	8	4	12	--	--	55
H3	8	1	20	7	6	12	4	--	58
Trapezes: type J1	--	--	--	--	1	1	1	--	3
Crescents: type J2	--	--	2	--	--	--	--	--	2
Side-blow blade-flakes: type K	27	1	59	8	17	1	7	--	120
Firestones: type L	6	--	9	6	2	6	--	--	29
Picks: type M	--	--	2	--	--	--	--	--	2
Choppers: type N	7	--	5	3	1	3	2	--	21
Flakes with retouch: type O	54	--	80	29	20	4	10	--	197
Blades with retouch: type P	36	2	60	24	27	13	3	--	165
Total Number	210	18	394	128	123	95	41	--	1,009

averages between 200 and 250 mm, but the rain often falls heavily, usually concentrated in turbulent thunderstorms. On such occasions a large depression near the site is turned into a lake of salty or brackish water. The floral and faunal remains found at the site seem to reflect that the situation was similar 8,000 years ago.

A preliminary report on the plant remains has been published by Hans Helbæk (1972). In general, the plant list does not seem to differ very much from the species that are found in the area today. A few grains of naked and hulled barley, einkorn, and emmer wheat were found. They may not be of local origin, but as noted by Helbæk their presence could suggest at the most the cultivation of a few small plots. In contrast to this, however, the presence of some fragments of pea and lentil and a single grain of hexaploid wheat seem to indicate that a number of food plants were brought to the site from a more humid and favorable environment.

This was also the case with some of the animal food, remains of which were found during the excavations. As mentioned by Sándor Bökönyi (1973, 1978), aurochs, boar, and badger were probably hunted in the foothills of Jebel Sinjar, about three days walk from Umm Dabaghiyah, whereas small foxes, hares, desert rats, and various birds could be found in the immediate neighborhood of the site, together with wild swine that might occasionally have lived in the bush near the salty depressions. Although bones of five domesticates were found they seem to have played an unimportant role in the daily life. Bones of sheep and goat constitute about 9% of the faunal remains; cattle, pig, and dog less than 2%. The two dominant animals hunted in the vicinity of Umm Dabaghiyah were gazelle (16%) and onager (66−70%).

The central architectural feature of the site, repeated through Levels IV−I, is a courtyard confined along two or three sides by buildings containing more than a hundred small rooms or cells, most of which are without external or internal doors. Nodules of red ochre and thousands of clay sling pellets were found in some of the rooms, but most of the rooms were empty. These central buildings have been interpreted as storage rooms, used by a small group of people living in five or six mud-walled houses on the periphery of the settlement. The doors of some of these houses were blocked, as if they had been left temporarily by the inhabitants.

Diana Kirkbride reaches the conclusion that Umm Dabaghiyah must have been a specialized settlement, occasionally inhabited by a small group of people probably sent out from a more "nuclear society" in order to provide this society with various animal products such as onager hides, sinews, and perhaps even tail hairs. Her hypothesis is based on the exceptionally high frequency of onager bones and on the occurrence of a wall painting showing what has been interpreted as an onager hunt in which a net was used.

FUNCTIONAL AND STYLISTIC IMPLICATIONS

A functional study of the chipped stone industry immediately reveals that there is little or no reflection of agricultural activities within the range of flint tools from Umm Dabaghiyah. At contemporary villages in the Zagros and in Khuzistan the percentage of sickle blades compared to total flint tools varies from ca. 10% to 16.8%. But at Umm Dabaghiyah the two flint blades with faint traces of gloss along the edges might well have been used, for example, for cutting grass or reeds growing by the salty swamps.

Hunting is testified to by various types of arrowheads. Their scarcity may be explained by the fact that there is very little evidence of the use of stone-tipped arrows in Mesopotamia and the Zagros during the seventh and sixth millennia. The few pieces known — from Yarim Tepe II, Telul eth-Thalathat, and Tell Hassuna — are all closely similar to points from northern Syria and are probably imported from that area (cf. Merpert, Munchaev, and Badar 1977, pl. IX, 5−8; Fukai and Matsutani 1977, p. 55. fig. 3:7−8; and Lloyd and Safar 1945, fig. 22:9−10). Bow and arrow and sling pellets of clay could have been used at Umm Dabaghiyah for killing hyenas, wolves, and wild swine in the swamps and small game such as foxes, hares, hedgehogs, and birds. But since the faunal remains point toward hunting gazelle and onager as the main activity, these were possibly hunted by net, as suggested by Diana Kirkbride.

It is remarkable that in comparison with other sites from the late seventh and early sixth millennium (fig. 7) more than 80% of the chipped stone tools from Umm Dabaghiyah are related to scraping and cutting activities. Although many of these tools may have been used for the collecting of plants and roots, the percentage of scraping and cutting tools is high enough that it seems to call for special consideration. If the site — as supposed by the excavator — was based on hunting and the preparation of gazelle and onager hides, a series of specialized cutting and scraping tools, like burins, notched and retouched flakes and blades, knives, and a variety of scrapers would have been required. However, only future analyses of the characteristic traces of wear may reveal the specialized function of some of the more distinct tool types, such as the heavily worn knives of types H2−3, which are numerous at Umm Dabaghiyah but extremely rare at other contemporary sites.

As a basis for our understanding of the special character and function of the site it is important to remember that we can distinguish between a larger group of tools, locally produced of greyish flint or chert of a bad quality (Group 1), and a minor group of tools and implements made of a very fine-grained type of brownish tabular flint (Group 2).

The distribution of flint nodules, cores, core fragments, and debitage at Umm Dabaghiyah shows that the production of tools in Group 1 flint was an open-air task. It was performed primarily in the northern part of the central courtyard between the storage rooms, and in the later periods also in the open area northwest of the storage blocks (Levels I−II). It is notable that this local production included most of the tools roughly shaped of cores and flakes, for example, scrapers of types D1−5, borers of type B1, and the small triangular arrowheads of type A1. Some of the small obsidian implements may also have been produced at Umm Dabaghiyah. Geometric microliths (J1−2) could have been made locally on imported blades, and the presence of obsidian "cores" (f) for side-blow blade-flakes (K) shows with certainty that these were struck at the site.

Although many of the locally produced tools seem to be expressive of the special function of the site they are not stylistically very characteristic. A more distinctive style is reflected by some of the obsidian implements and by most of the tools and implements made of the tabular flint of Group 2. As mentioned above, this kind of flint is found in the mountains toward the northwest, and there is no evidence that it was worked locally at Umm Dabaghiyah.

Almost all of the implements made of this type of flint are blade tools, primarily arrowheads (A2−5), borers made on blades (B3−4), microborers (B5), beaked blades (C), end-of-blade scrapers (D6), and blade knives (H2−3). Stylistically, most of them are closely similar to types found in North Mesopotamia, Syria, and East Anatolia. Thus, arrowheads of types A2−3 are common at seventh millennium sites in northern Syria, e.g., at Tell Ramad II (Contenson and Liere 1964, pl. IIA: 2−3), Bouqras (Akkermans et al., in press, fig. 8:5), Mureybet IV B (Cauvin 1977, p. 39, fig. 20:1), and late Tell Abu Hureyra (Moore 1975, p. 59, fig. 5:5−8). The long fragment of an arrowhead shown in figure 3j is similar to "Amuq points" like those found, for example, at Tell Aswad II (Cauvin 1974, p. 434, fig. 3:7), and arrowheads of type A5 are identical to "Byblos points" found at a number of Syrian sites (cf. Cauvin 1968, p. 56). Beaked blades are known from Çayönü (Braidwood, pers. comm.) and Tell Shimshara (Mortensen 1970a, pp. 33 and 37, fig. 29a−f), and the characteristic blade knives of types H2−3 are paralleled at Yarim Tepe I (Merpert, Munchaev, and Bader 1977, pl. IX: 2−4).

On a more general level the western and northwestern affinities of the people at Umm Dabaghiyah are confirmed by the use of arrowheads and firestones, two cultural elements with a distinct western distribution. Stone-tipped arrows were common in Palestine, Syria, and Anatolia from earliest Neolithic, whereas there is almost no material evidence of the bow and arrow in Eastern Mesopotamia and the Zagros. Possibly this reflects a tradition of using some other type of arrow tip. The use and distribution of firestones are less well studied, but these tools seem to be confined to sites in the Balkans, Anatolia, and the Mediterranean countries, and, so far, all search for firestones in Neolithic materials from other Mesopotamian sites and the Zagros has proved negative (Todd 1966, p. 155; Mortensen n.d., 1970b, pp. 38−40).

To conclude, our preliminary study of the chipped stone industry seems to support Diana Kirkbride's interpretation of Umm Dabaghiyah as a specialized site, seasonally occupied by a small group of people who occasionally spent some time in the Jazira hunting gazelle and onager. They produced many of their stone tools locally, but a number of obsidian and flint implements were imported to the site. Like the fine marble and alabaster bowls and the small basalt axes, usually found in the butchering yards, they were probably brought along by the hunters as personal equipment from their home village, which must have been located somewhere in the foothills or the mountains to the north or northwest.

PATTERNS OF INTERACTION BETWEEN UMM DABAGHIYAH AND OTHER CONTEMPORARY SETTLEMENTS IN NORTH MESOPOTAMIA

In 1978 Charles L. Redman commented on Diana Kirkbride's preliminary formulation of her hypothesis. He wrote: "If this community was a permanent trading outpost organized for the benefit of a powerful central community, then the current concepts of the self-sufficiency and interaction of communities in this period must be reevaluated" (Redman 1978, p. 193). There is a tinge of doubt in this statement, possibly caused by the difficulty of combining or mixing generally accepted concepts of simple organizational bonds between early villages with ideas of a much more complex external structure characteristic of early urban communities. Redman's reservation at this point is well justified if we were to perceive Umm Dabaghiyah as a permanent trading outpost for some large center or town. If that were the case it might be claimed that it is a very early representation of a much later organizational system. On the contrary, however, I tentatively suggest that Umm Dabaghiyah is a late exponent of a much earlier structural system, which I shall briefly attempt to characterize below.

Elsewhere I have described how the settlement patterns in the Zagros theoretically might have developed through three stages from the Late Pleistocene period to ca. 5500 B.C. (Mortensen 1972, pp. 294–95). In the first stage (fig. 8), highly specialized Zarzian hunter-gatherers moved within a certain area from one seasonal base camp to another, thus making a circulating annual movement. In the second stage (the ninth to eight millennium B.C.) the annual movement was still circular, but within a confined system one or two base camps developed into semipermanent settlements that were occupied during longer periods of time. Sites situated in favorable environments where the economy could be supplemented by herding or farming were chosen for this purpose. Karim Shahir, Zawi Chemi Shanidar, and Asiab perhaps represent this transitional stage, which is clearly overlapping with the next phase.

In the third stage the number of semipermanent settlements decreased (the eighth to the early sixth millennium B.C.). Instead, small permanent villages appeared. The circular annual movement was replaced by a radiating pattern in which the permanent village was the center of a settlement system. At this stage a number of small sites were associated with the villages: sites temporarily occupied by small groups of people from the village, moving out to the sites for specific purposes. Characteristic examples of these sites would be hunting stations in the plains, along the rivers, or in caves and shelters, butchering stations, and pastoral camps for herdsmen sent out in the spring with flocks of goat and sheep to pastures in the higher valleys — or in the wintertime, perhaps, to the lower plains (cf. Hole 1968, 1974; Mortensen 1972, 1979).

Although originally developed as a hypothetical illustration of the developments in the Zagros, I think that the third stage of this model can also be applied as a description of the interaction of the earliest settlements in North Mesopotamia. Here the emphasis rests upon the relationship between the nonpermanent settlement in the Jazira and the Assyrian steppe on the one hand and the villages in the foothills and the intermontane valleys on the other.

At the present time we know of a number of villages that existed in the late seventh and early sixth millennia in the valleys and foothills facing North Mesopotamia. Jarmo in the Chamchemal plain, Tell Shimshara in the Dokan valley, and Tell Magzalia, Kully Tepe, Tell Sotto, and Yarim Tepe I in the Sinjar valley are good examples of such villages (Braidwood and Howe 1960;

Mortensen 1970a; Merpert and Munchaev, forthcoming.) At the same time substantial sites such as Bouqras and Tell Abu Hureyra existed along the Euphrates (Akkermans et al., in press; Moore 1975). They were probably specialized settlements, based primarily on stock breeding and hunting.

It is remarkable that the earliest evidence of human occupation on the North Mesopotamian plain belongs to this rather late phase in the development of food production. From the centuries around 6000 B.C. — and preceding the spread of classical Hassunan villages and agriculture over the plain — we have knowledge of only a few settlements, all of a nonpermanent character. This group of sites includes Umm Dabaghiyah in the Jazira and the earliest habitation at four sites situated in the rolling landscape leveling off toward the Assyrian steppe: Telul eth-Thalathat and Tell Hassuna, both not far west of the Tigris valley, Matarrah on a small natural hill southwest of a now normally dry wadi, and Gird Ali Agha on the first major terrace of the left bank of the Greater Zab.

In contrast to what we know of Umm Dabaghiyah, our knowledge of the contemporary layers XV−XVI at Telul eth-Thalathat is very limited. Remains of a mud-walled house and a great number of pits and fire places were excavated. The pottery and the chipped stone industry are similar to those found at Umm Dabaghiyah, but the material is too sparse for a functional analysis. Hunting is indicated by the presence of arrowheads and sling pellets of clay, but only two sickle blades were found (Fukai, Horiuchi, and Matsutani 1970, pp. 14ff.; Fukai and Matsutani 1977, pp. 49ff.).

Hassuna Ia comprises about 1 m of debris, including three "living floors" with pottery, implements, and animal bones centered on hearths, some of which were slightly sunken and paved with pebbles. There were no traces of permanent architecture; not even postholes, which would suggest the presence of huts, were found. On this evidence the three occupations have been explained as campsites for people living in tents or sheltered by weather screens, an interpretation supported by impressions of woven reed matting found in several places (Lloyd and Safar 1945, p. 271). A similar explanation probably applies to the early habitations at Matarrah and Gird Ali Agha. Operation VI:5 at Matarrah revealed a fire place and a number of drains and pits dug into virgin soil, some of them with fire-hardened walls (Braidwood et al. 1952, pp. 7−8). At Gird Ali Agha, three floors of compacted earth layers with irregular pits, flecks of charcoal, and a hearth outlined by small, flat river boulders were found (Braidwood and Howe 1960, pp. 37−38).

The excavators of Tell Hassuna have suggested that the first settlers of the wadi bank were primarily groups of herdsmen and hunters. Two arrowheads of obsidian and a number of sling pellets of clay indicate hunting activities, and a great number of animal bones were recovered; unfortunately, no analysis of this material has been published. Although it is likely that seasonal planting and harvesting took place, the sickle blades from Telul eth-Thalathat, the boulder mortars and pestles found at Hassuna and Gird Ali Agha, and the large stone hoes from Hassuna cannot be interpreted as conclusive evidence of agriculture. It is notable, however, that the four settlements are located in an area watered by 250 to 350 mm of winter rain, creating a natural winter grassland favorable for dry-farming.

The nonpermanent character of the three early occupations of Hassuna, Matarrah, and Gird Ali Agha suggests that they were campsites, seasonally occupied by small groups of villagers from settlements in the mountains who were attracted by the Assyrian steppe because of its great potential as hunting and winter-grazing land.

Unfortunately, a precise location of the villages from which these people might have come is not possible. Although Umm Dabaghiyah and Telul eth-Thalathat XV−XVI may be slightly earlier than Hassuna Ia, Gird Ali Agha, and the earliest occupation at Matarrah, the coarse chaff-tempered pottery found at Umm Dabaghiyah and Telul eth-Thalathat is closely similar to that found at the three other sites. Looking farther afield, there is very little similarity to the ceramics characteristic of the Zagros group (Jarmo, Sarab, Guran, and so forth; cf. Mortensen 1970a, p. 132), but the pottery and a number of elements in the chipped stone industry point toward the north and the northwest as the most likely areas of origin.

In conclusion, then, it is suggested that the North Mesopotamian plain — in the centuries around 6000 B.C., when it was first occupied — was a marginal area within what has tentatively been called a radiating cultural system. The core of this particular system was probably a number of villages situated like Tell Magzalia, Tell Sotto, and Kully Tepe in the intermontane valleys and the foothills north of the plain. The subsistence of these villages would have depended upon hunting, fishing, gathering, herding, and farming. Most of these activities probably took place in the immediate vicinity of the villages or within a radius of a few kilometers from the permanent settlements. Other activities would have been carried out from nonpermanent campsites in marginal areas, at a distance of several days walk from the home village.

The radiating system as represented here can be regarded as the last offshoot of a long series of paleolithic hunting/gathering subsistence systems in which mobility, originally reflected by open, circulating systems, was reduced to that of more closed, radiating systems. At the same time, this stage was also a prelude to an era in which agriculture spread across North Mesopotamia. This happened rapidly, and by the middle of the sixth millennium B.C. the Jazira and the Assyrian steppe was densely populated by farmers and herders living in hundreds of fairly large permanent villages with Hassuna/Samarra pottery (cf., e.g., Oates 1973, pp. 161ff.).

The preceding millennium with its radiating subsistence systems contained the germs of most of the phenomena on which established village agriculture was based. It was a richly differentiated phase, characterized by stylistic and functional variability, by experimentation and expansion, by incipient trade, and by specialization on several levels leading up to new organizational structures. These structures possibly included the first archaic stages of social differentiation in Mesopotamia.

BIBLIOGRAPHY

Akkermans, P.A.; Loon, M.N. van; Roodenberg, J.J.; and Waterbolk, H.T.
    in   The 1976–1979 excavations at Tell Bouqras. *Annales Archéologiques Arabes Syriennes.*
  press

Bökönyi, Sándor
    1973   The fauna of Umm Dabaghiyah: a preliminary report. *Iraq* 35:9–11.
    1977   *The animal remains from four sites in the Kermanshah valley, Iran: Asiab, Sarab, Dehsavar and Siahbid: the faunal evolution, environmental changes and development of animal husbandry, VIII–III millennia B.C.* British Archaeological Reports, Supplementary Series, vol. 34. Oxford.
    1978   Environmental and cultural differences as reflected in the animal bone samples from five early Neolithic sites in southwest Asia. In *Approaches to faunal analysis in the Middle East,* ed. Richard H. Meadow and Melinda A. Zeder, pp. 57–62. Peabody Museum of Archaeology and Ethnology, Harvard University, Bulletin 2, Cambridge, Mass.

Braidwood, Linda
    1961   The general appearance of obsidian in southwestern Asia and the microlithic side-blow blade-flake in obsidian. *Bericht über den V internationalen Kongress für Vor- und*

Frühgeschichte [Hamburg 1958], ed. Gerhard Berser and Wolfgang Dehn, pp. 142–47. Berlin: Mann.

Braidwood, Robert J.
1960   Seeking the world's first farmers in Persian Kurdistan: a full-scale investigation of pre-historic sites near Kermanshah. *The Illustrated London News* 237:695–97.

Braidwood, Robert J.; Braidwood, Linda; Smith, James G.; and Leslie, Charles
1952   Matarrah: a southern variant of the Hassunan assemblage. *Journal of Near Eastern Studies* 11:1–75.

Braidwood, Robert J., and Howe, Bruce
1960   *Prehistoric investigations in Iraqi Kurdistan.* Studies in Ancient Oriental Civilization, no. 31. Chicago: University of Chicago Press.

Braidwood, Robert J.; Howe, Bruce; and Reed, Charles A.
1961   The Iranian prehistoric project. *Science* 133:2008–10.

Cauvin, J.
1968   *Les outillages Néolithiques de Byblos et du littoral libanais.* Fouilles de Byblos, vol. 4, ed. Maurice Dunand. Paris: Librairie d'Amérique et d'Orient, Adrien Maisonneuve.
1977   Les fouilles de Mureybet (1971–1974) et leur signification pour les origines de la sedentarisation au Proche-Orient. *Annual of the American School of Oriental Research* 44:19–48.

Cauvin, M.-C.
1974   Outillage lithique et chronologie à Tell Aswad. *Paléorient* 2:429–36.

de Contenson, Henri, and Liere, W.S. van
1964   Sondages à Tell Ramad en 1963. *Annales Archéologiques de Syrie* 14:109–24.

Dorrell, Peter
1972   A note on the geomorphology of the country near Umm Dabaghiyah. *Iraq* 34:69–72.

Fukai, S.; Horiuchi, K.; and Matsutani, T.
1970   *Telul eth-Thalathat: the excavation of Tell II.* Iraq-Iran Archaeological Expedition, Tokyo University, report no. 2. Tokyo: Yamakawa Publishing.

Fukai, S., and Matsutani, T.
1977   Excavations at Telul eth-Thalathat 1976. *Sumer* 33:49–64.

Helbaek, Hans
1972   Traces of plants in the early ceramic site of Umm Dabaghiyah. *Iraq* 34:17–19.

Hole, Frank
1968   Evidence of social organization from western Iran: 8000–4000 B.C. In *New perspectives in archaeology,* ed. S.R. Binford and L.R. Binford, pp. 245–65. Chicago: Aldine.
1974   Tepe Tūlā'ī: an early campsite in Khuzistan, Iran. *Paléorient* 2:219–42.

Hole, Frank, and Flannery, Kent V.
1967   The prehistory of western Iran: a preliminary report. *Proceedings of the Prehistoric Society* 33:147–206.

Kirkbride, Diana
1972   Umm Dabaghiyah 1971: a preliminary report. *Iraq* 34:3–15.
1973a   Umm Dabaghiyah 1972: a second preliminary report. *Iraq* 35:1–7.
1973b   Umm Dabaghiyah 1973: a third preliminary report. *Iraq* 35:205–09.
1974   Umm Dabaghiyah: a trading outpost? *Iraq* 36: 85–92.
1975   Umm Dabaghiyah 1974: a fourth preliminary report. *Iraq* 37:3–10.
forth-   Aspects of the Dabaghiyah culture. In *Early agriculture and metallurgy: contributions to*
coming   *a symposium on origins in east and west Asia,* ed. Peder Mortensen and Per Sørensen. Studies on Asian Topics, no. 5. Copenhagen: The Scandinavian Institute of Asian Studies.

Lloyd, Seton, and Safar, Fuad
    1945   Tell Hassuna. *Journal of Near Eastern Studies* 4:255–89.

McDonald, Mary M.A.
    1979   An examination of mid-Holocene settlement patterns in the central Zagros region of western Iran. Ph.D. diss., University of Toronto.

Merpert, N., and Munchaev, R.
    forth-   About the sequence of the earliest farming cultures in the Sinjar valley, northern Iraq. In
    coming   *Early agriculture and metallurgy: contributions to a symposium on origins in east and west Asia,* ed. Peder Mortensen and Per Sørensen. Studies on Asian Topics, no. 5. Copenhagen: The Scandinavian Institute of Asian Studies.

Merpert, N.I.; Munchaev, R.M.; and Bader, N.O.
    1977   The investigations of Soviet expedition in Iraq 1974. *Sumer* 33:65–104.

Moore, A.M.T.
    1975   The excavation of Tell Abu Hureyra in Syria: a preliminary report. *Proceedings of the Prehistoric Society* 41:50–77. (With contributions by G.C. Hillman and A.J. Legge.)

Mortensen, Peder
    1970a   Tell Shimshara: the Hassuna period. *Det Kongelige Danske Videnskabernes Selskab Historisk – Filosofiske Skrifter* 5, 2. Copenhagen: Munksgaard.
    1970b   A preliminary study of the chipped stone industry from Beidha. *Acta Archaeologica* 41:1–54.
    1972   Seasonal camps and early villages. In *Man, settlement and urbanism,* ed. P.J. Ucko, R. Tringham and G.W. Dimbleby, pp. 293–97. London: Duckworth.
    1973   A sequence of Samarran flint and obsidian tools from Choga Mami. *Iraq* 35:37–55.
    1979   The Hulailan survey: a note on the relationship between aims and method. *Acten des VII Internationalen Kongresses für Iranische Kunst und Archäologie* [München 1976], pp. 3–8. Berlin: Dietrich Reimer.
    n.d.   The chipped stone industries of Labweh and Ard Tlaili. Unpublished manuscript.

Oates, Joan
    1973   The background and development of early farming communities in Mesopotamia and the Zagros. *Proceedings of the Prehistoric Society* 39:147–79.

Redman, Charles L.
    1978   *The rise of civilization.* San Francisco: W.H. Freeman.

Smith, Philip E.L., and Mortensen, Peder
    1980   Three new "early Neolithic" sites in western Iran. *Current Anthropology* 21(4):511–12.

Todd, Ian A.
    1966   Aşikli Hüyük: a Protoneolithic site in central Anatolia. *Anatolian Studies* 16:139–63.

Fig. 1. Umm Dabaghiyah: Amorphous, Semichipped Flint Nodules (type a). All found in Level II.

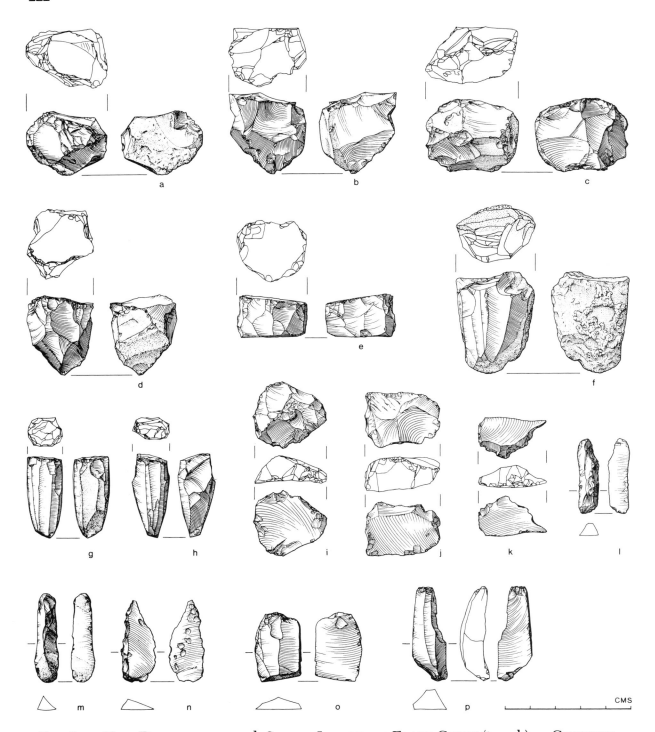

FIG. 2. — UMM DABAGHIYAH: a–d, SMALL, IRREGULAR FLAKE CORES (type b); e, CYLINDRI-
CAL BLADE CORE (type c); f–h, CONICAL BLADE CORES (type d); AND i–p, VARIOUS CORE
FRAGMENTS (type e). All made of flint and found in Levels I (e, i, k, and p), II (a–d, f, h, j, and
l–o), and II (g).

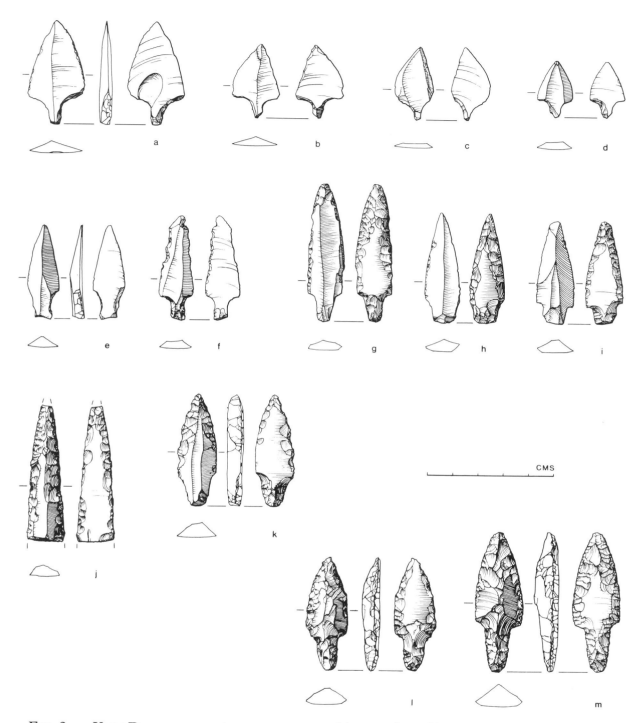

FIG. 3. — UMM DABAGHIYAH: ARROWHEADS; a—d (type A1); e—f (type A2); g—i (type A3); j—k (type A4); and l—m (type A5). All made of flint and found in Levels I (e and k—m), II (f—h), II/III (a), III (b—c and j), III/IV (j), and IV (d).

224

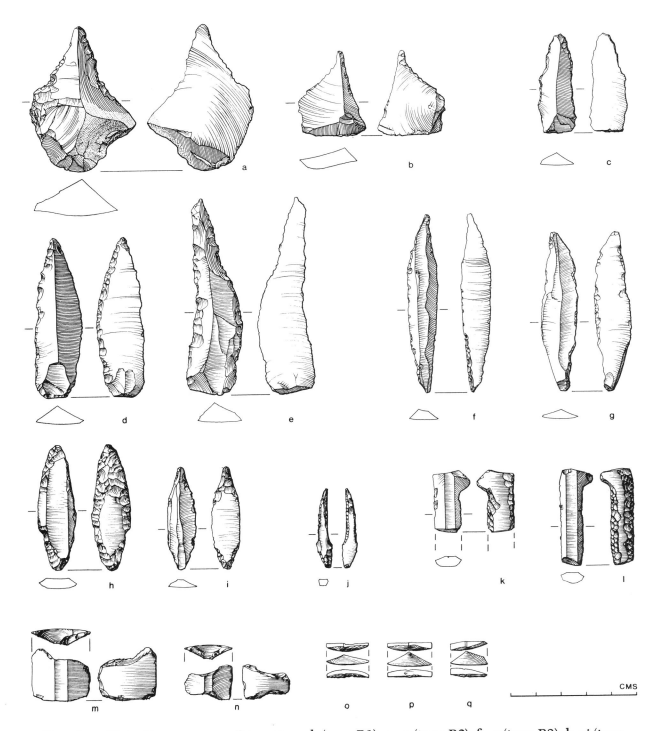

Fig. 4. — Umm Dabaghiyah: Borers; a–b (type B1); c–e (type B2); f–g (type B3); h–i (type B4); and j (type B5). Beaked Blades; k–l (type C). Side-Blow Blade-Flake "Cores"; m–n (type F). Side-Blow Blade Flakes; o–q (type K). a–j are made of flint, k–q of obsidian. Found in Levels I (a, h, and n), II (c, g, k, m, and o–q), and II/III (d and i), III (b, f, and j), and III/IV (e and l).

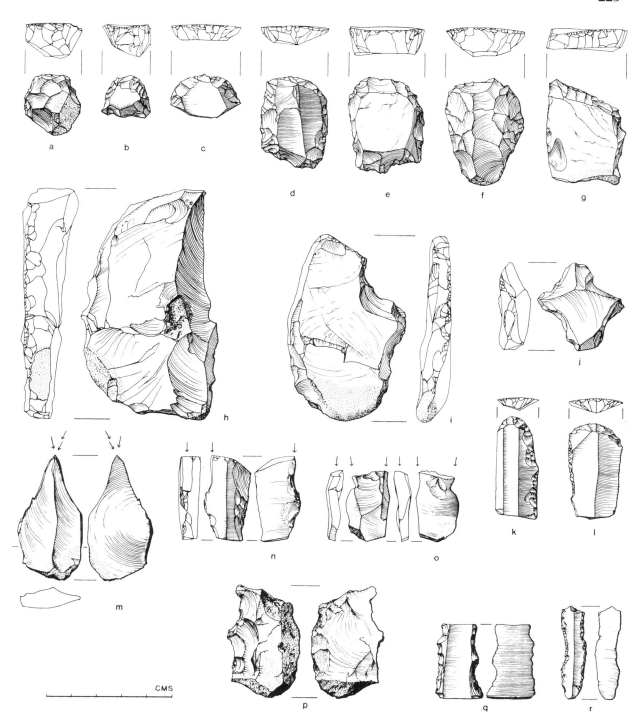

FIG. 5. — UMM DABAGHIYAH: SCRAPERS; a—b (type D1); c—f (type D2); g (type D3); h (type D4); i—j (type D5); and k—l (D6). BURINS; m (type E1) and n—o (type E2). NOTCHED FLAKES AND BLADES; p (type F1) and q—r (type F2). All made of flint and found in Levels I (c), I/II (f and k), II (a—b, d—e, g—h, j, m—n, and p—q), II/III (r), III (i and l), and IV (o).

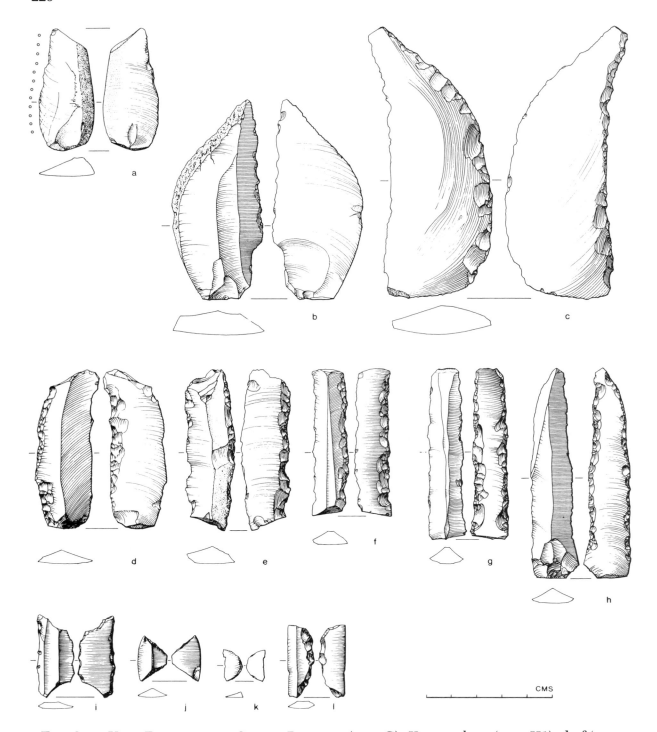

FIG. 6. — UMM DABAGHIYAH: SICKLE BLADE; a (type G). KNIVES; b–c (type H1); d–f (type H2); and g–h (type H3). TRAPEZES; i–j (type J1). CRESCENTS; k–l (type J2). a–h are made of flint, i–l of obsidian. Found in Levels II (b–c, e–g, and k–l), II/III (a and h), III (i), III/IV (j), and IV (d).

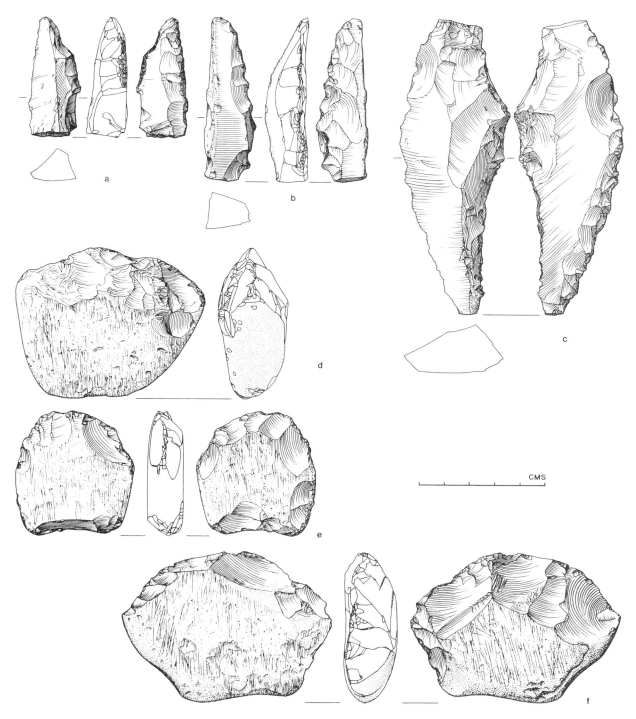

CMS

FIG. 7. — UMM DABAGHIYAH: FIRESTONES; a–b (type L). PICK; c (type M). CHOPPERS; d–f (type N). All made of flint and found in Levels I (d and f), II (b–c and e), and II/III (a).

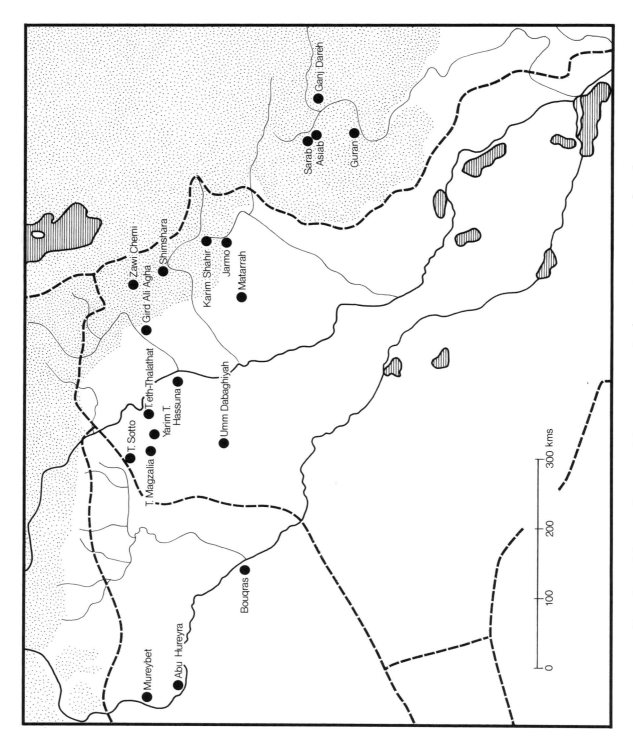

Fig. 8. — Map of Greater Mesopotamia. It shows sites mentioned in the text.

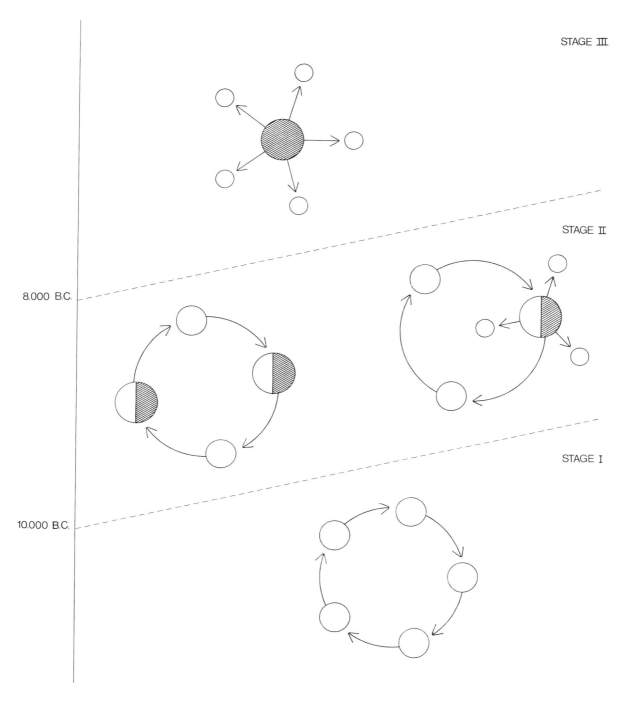

STAGE III

STAGE II

STAGE I

8.000 B.C.

10.000 B.C.

Fig. 9. — Diagram Illustrating how the Settlement Patterns in the Zagros Area may have Developed from the Late Pleistocene Period to ca. 5000 b.c.

THE HALAFIAN CULTURE: A REVIEW AND SYNTHESIS

Patty Jo Watson

INTRODUCTION

ROBERT J. BRAIDWOOD is best known for his contributions to the interdisciplinary study of the food-producing revolution in southwestern Asia. However, he also carried out definitive studies of later time periods in Near Eastern prehistory. In particular, his analyses of the basal Amuq materials (Braidwood 1943; Braidwood and Braidwood 1960) and his various publications on the data pertaining to established and developed village-farming communities (1952, 1958, 1972; with L. Braidwood 1953; and B. Howe 1965) are crucial syntheses.

In this paper, I focus on one of the later cultural horizons to which Braidwood drew attention: the Halafian. In his dissertation he introduced a standardized format for describing not only the shapes and surfaces of vessels in the various Amuq ceramic industries but also their fabrics. Within this ceramological framework he discussed the impact of the Halafian pottery style on the local ceramic sequence. In a later paper he and Linda Braidwood assessed the cultural content of the archeological stages then being used to encompass the prehistory of greater Mesopotamia. They found that the available evidence was insufficient to enable them to define a specific Halafian assemblage in spite of the fact that the distinctive pottery style had been known for several decades (Braidwood and Braidwood 1953, pp. 305–7, especially footnote 59).

When, in 1954, I joined the Iraq-Jarmo Project as archeological assistant (and as a University of Chicago graduate student in search of an M.A. project), it was Braidwood's concern to seek clearer definition of the Halafian assemblage in Iraq that resulted in my supervising a 10-day sondage at the site of Banahilk (Watson 1956 and forthcoming; Braidwood and Howe et al. 1960, pp. 33–35). Some years later we pursued the same topic in southeastern Turkey at a site called Girikihaciyan (Braidwood, Çambel, and Watson 1969; Braidwood, Çambel, Redman, and Watson 1971; Redman and Watson 1970; LeBlanc 1971; LeBlanc and Watson 1973; Watson and LeBlanc ms.). During that time and since, many other archeologists have produced a variety of important data bearing on this prehistoric culture. It has attracted considerable attention not only because of interest in the material itself (especially the pottery) but also because of the critical stage it represents in Mesopotamian culture history.

It is my purpose here to summarize the current state of archeological knowledge and anthropologically based speculation about the Halafian.

A BRIEF HISTORY OF HALAFIAN RESEARCH

John Garstang first referred to Halafian pottery in print (Frankel 1979, p. 2; Garstang 1908), but — until quite recently — knowledge of the style derived primarily from the work of three other archeologists: Max von Oppenheim, Leonard Woolley, and Max Mallowan.

Between 1911 and 1929, from the type site of Tell Halaf, von Oppenheim recovered an abundant and varied sample of the characteristic painted ware, which was described by Hubert Schmidt in a large, well-illustrated report (von Oppenheim 1943). In 1913 Woolley excavated another sample of Halafian pottery from a site near Carchemish (Woolley 1934; Dirvana 1944), but the most significant Halafian excavations until very recently were those of Max Mallowan in the 1930s (Mallowan 1933, 1936; Mallowan and Rose 1935). Mallowan's deep trench at Nineveh defined the stratigraphic position of Halafian wares in northern Iraq, and his Arpachiyah trenches, as well as the Chagar Bazar material, provided data for preliminary ordering of ceramic developments during the Halaf period. Sherds from Tilkitepe near Lake Van indicated a northern limit for the geographic distribution of Halafian pottery (Reilly 1940; LeBlanc and Watson 1973).

In 1945 Lloyd and Safar published stratigraphic information for the Halafian occupation at Hassuna, and a few years after that Ann Perkins synthesized all available Halafian data (Perkins 1949).

The Iraq-Jarmo Project sounding at Banahilk in 1954 was the next Halafian excavation to be carried out, after which there was a hiatus until the work at Turlu in 1963 (Mellink 1964), Girikihaciyan in 1968 and 1970, Yarim Tepe II beginning in 1969 (Merpert and Munchaev 1973; Postgate 1976), Shams ed-Din in 1974 (Radi and Seeden 1974; Azouri et al. 1982), Tell Aqab in 1975 and 1976 (Davidson 1977; Davidson and Watkins, 1981), and Arpachiyah in 1976 (Hijara 1978, 1980; Hijara et al. 1980; Postgate 1977). Halafian pottery has also been reported from Transcaucasia (Merpert and Munchaev 1973, p. 108), from the Elazi ̆g area of Turkey (Davidson 1977, pp. 240–41), from western Iran (Levine and McDonald 1977), from eastern Iraq (Oates 1969, 1972; Postgate and Watson 1979), and from a series of new sites within the previously documented Halafian heartland of northern Iraq and northern Syria (Hijara 1980; Matthers et al. 1978; Copeland 1979; Davidson 1977, 1981; Davidson and Watkins 1981). In the early 1970s, Walter Noll, with several collaborators, began detailed technical studies of early Mesopotamian ceramics, including the Halafian (e.g., Noll 1976, 1977a, 1977b).

SUMMARY AND SYNTHESIS OF HALAFIAN SITE DISTRIBUTION

In the following discussion I use Davidson's (1977) geographic ordering for Halafian sites: Mosul region, Sinjar region, Khabur headwaters, Balikh valley, and Euphrates valley, to which I add the Halafian periphery for material from areas north, south, east, and west of the heartland defined by the regions listed above (see map). Hijara (1980, pp. 232–44) provides a detailed breakdown into six Halafian regions within Iraq. He notes that recent surveys and collation of results from older surveys have yielded a total of just over 200 Iraqi Halafian sites (each of which he briefly describes; Hijara 1980, pp. 292–326), but he suspects the real total is closer to 300. Density of the known sites averages about 1 every 15 or 16 km².

MOSUL REGION

The most important Halafian event here in recent times is the renewal of excavations at Arpachiyah by Ismail Hijara (1980; Hijara et al. 1980; Postgate 1977). This was done during eight weeks in the fall of 1976 when three trenches were cut into the mound summit. The remains in these trenches were dug in 42 layers, which Hijara grouped into 11 stratigraphic levels and four architectural phases, the deposit so investigated being 7.5 m thick. The two earliest phases of the four defined by Hijara predate Mallowan's sequence. These architectural phases are as follows:

1. Village debris associated with rectangular mud-walled rooms (stratigraphic levels XI–IX).

2. Transition to circular architecture, although rectangular structures were also used (Levels VIII–VI). First appearances of mud-walled and plaster-floored tholoi, apparently within a special enclosure. During this phase, two burials (one at each level) were made outside the tholoi walls, one (G2) consisted of four skulls, each was placed within a pottery vessel (Hijira 1978; Hijara 1980, p. 215). A third burial — also a skull within a pot — was found 75 cm west of the tholos in Level VI.

3. The equivalent of Mallowan's TT 10–7 (Levels V–II). Hijara subdivides this phase into two subphases, 3a and 3b. In 3a (Levels IV and V, which are equivalent to

Mallowan's TT 8 and 9) stone foundations appear for the first time, although the tholoi are still simply round in plan. In subphase 3b (Levels III and II, which are equivalent to Mallowan's TT 7 and 8), the tholoi are built with rectangular antechambers.

4. Level I (equivalent to TT 6). The architecture is rectangular again (including, presumably, the famous burned building excavated by Mallowan in TT 6).

A radiocarbon determination on charcoal from a provenience corresponding to the end of Phase 2 and the beginning of Phase 3 yielded a date of 4980 B.C. (Hijara et al. 1980, p. 144; BM 1531, 6930±60 B.P.).

During the 1976 excavations 30 whole vessels and more than 4,400 sherds of Halafian pottery were recovered. Hijara assembles the pottery into four phases:

Arpachiyah Pottery Phase One — layers 42 and 34 (equivalent to part of stratigraphic level XI), with pottery forms 1 through 7 making their first appearance.

Arpachiyah Pottery Phase Two — layers 33 to 24 (stratigraphic levels XI−VIII), with pottery forms 8 to 13 and 22 making their first appearance.

Arpachiyah Pottery Phase Three — layers 23 to 16 (approximately equivalent to stratigraphic level VII), with pottery forms 14 to 21 and 48 making their first appearance.

Arpachiyah Pottery Phase Four — layers 15 to 1 (approximately equivalent to stratigraphic levels VI−I), with pottery forms 23 to 47 making their first appearance.

Davidson's Phases (1977) — Early, Middle, and Late — are all included in Hijara's Arpachiyah Pottery Phase 4. With respect to architectural stratigraphy, Davidson's Early Phase is pre-TT 10 in the Mallowan sequence; Davidson's Middle Phase = Mallowan's TT 10−8; and Davidson's Late Phase = Mallowan's TT 7−6.

The commonest vessel form found by Hijara is the straight- or flare-sided bowl (his F-1 category); sherds of the most popular jar form (F-3) are not nearly so abundant.

Besides the Halafian painted ware, Hijara found 382 sherds of gray burnished plainware throughout the 42 excavated layers. Descriptions of the other artifactual remains are not yet available.

Hijara believes that during the latter part of the occupation period (architectural phases 2, 3, and possibly 4) the community of Arpachiyah took on a special function and significance as a ritual center. During phase 2 the tholos area was walled and ordinary settlement debris is no longer found inside the enclosure, although a number of burials *are* found either inside the tholos area or outside but directly adjacent to it (Hijara 1978). This situation continued through phase 3. In phase 4, site function seems to have altered once more to that of a more or less ordinary village, one that may have been a pottery-producing center (Postgate 1977, p. 304).

The ceramic materials from Hijara's earlier architectural phases (1 and 2) — both of which predate Mallowan's TT 10−6 sequence — should contribute significantly to the definition of a firm chronological seriation for Halafian pottery forms and designs; Davidson (1977) had previously made an initial attempt at such a seriation. His own data from Tell Aqab (see below), added to those from the newly reported strata at Arpachiyah, should go far toward refining Halafian pottery chronology across the north Syrian and north Mesopotamian heartland.

Although there are many Mosul region sites with Halafian occupations besides Arpachiyah, those documented in the archeological literature are Tepe Gawra (Tobler 1950), Hassuna (Lloyd and Safar 1945), and Nineveh (Mallowan 1933), with Banahilk (Watson 1956 and forthcoming; Braidwood and Howe et al. 1960, pp. 33−35) 110 km to the northeast beyond the Rowanduz Gorge. Only for Banahilk, the smallest of these and a Late Phase site in Davidson's terminology (but Pottery Phase 1−2 to 4 of Hijara), is there much information on nonceramic remains.

TEPE GAWRA

Other than Arpachiyah, the most important Halafian site presently known in the Mosul area is Tepe Gawra (Tobler 1950; Perkins 1949, ch. II). No further work has taken place at Tepe Gawra since the University of Pennsylvania excavations. Davidson's recent study of the Halafian pottery from this site (Davidson 1977, pp. 72–83) indicates to him that the present sample belongs to his Late (comparable to TT 6 at Arpachiyah) and Transitional (to Ubaid) Phases (and see the discussion of Halafian trade below), but Hijara finds pottery at Gawra that fits his Phases One and Two (pre-TT 10; Hijara 1980, p. 240).

SINJAR REGION

Major, long-term excavations at a cluster of mounds known collectively as Yarim Tepe have been carried out by a Russian expedition beginning in 1969 (Merpert and Munchaev 1973). Yarim Tepe I is preponderantly Hassunan, while Yarim Tepe II and III were occupied during the Halafian period. So far there are only preliminary reports published in journal and book form, but a wealth of interesting data is indicated that considerably expands our understanding of Halafian communities.

The Yarim Tepe II village covers an area of 150 m in diameter at the maximum, with the deposit between 8 and 9 m in thickness (Merpert and Munchaev 1973, p. 108), and was thus probably comparable in size to Arpachiyah, which is about 150 m in diameter and 8 m thick. The architectural remains indicate a village made up of both round and rectangular mud-brick dwellings, with occasional round rooms having rectangular antechambers like the Arpachiyah TT 7 and 8 tholoi. The largest round houses are between 6 and 6.4 m in diameter (Munchajev and Merpert 1973, p. 10).

Other architectural remains include several kilns and ovens and one or two structures that might have been public buildings of some sort (Merpert and Munchaev 1971, p. 20; 1973, p. 111; Munchajev and Merpert 1973, p. 12; Postgate 1972, p. 150). Many of the burials found so far at Yarim Tepe II are those of children (Merpert and Munchaev 1971, p. 31; Munchajev and Merpert 1973, p. 14), but there are Halafian graves — presumably dug by the Yarim Tepe II people — in the nearby Hassunan mound of Yarim Tepe I (1973, p. 108), at least some of which are a shaft-and-chamber type, and there are several cremations as well as two burials of isolated skulls (Merpert, Munchaev, and Bader 1977, 1978).

Apparently, the large quantity of Halafian pottery recovered from Yarim Tepe II is now in Moscow (Hijara 1980). Hijara's examination of it indicates to him that the bottom levels of Yarim Tepe II belong to the Early Halaf period (Arpachiyah Pottery Phase One). Yarim Tepe III (Postgate and Watson 1979, pp. 157–58) contains Late Halafian and Ubaidian materials; hence the two sites of Yarim Tepe II and III contain an entire stratigraphic sequence for the local Halafian development.

KHABUR HEADWATERS

This region played a very important role in the history of Halafian studies because it was here at Tell Halaf that the diagnostic painted pottery was first recovered in quantity (von Oppenheim 1943), and of course it was from this site that the name for the period characterized by this pottery type was derived. Mallowan's surveys and excavations of the 1930s demonstrated the presence of Halafian wares in the Khabur region to the east of Tell Halaf and provided some important stratigraphic information from the sites of Chagar Bazar and Brak (Mallowan 1936, 1937, 1947; Perkins 1949, ch. II; Davidson 1977, ch. 3). Most recently, a survey team from the University of Edinburgh examined sites along the Wadis Dara and Jaghjagh (Davidson 1977, pp. 86–89) and refined our understanding of Halafian site distribution there. Halafian sites are much more common along the northern branches of the Dara and Jaghjagh than to the south — "Halaf settlement seems to concentrate in an east-west running band through the northern half of the Habur headwaters region" (Davidson 1977, p. 87) — with the northern limit probably being the Jebal Tur.

Davidson defines a developmental sequence for the Halafian pottery of the Khabur area, based on the Chagar Bazar material. He agrees with Mallowan that Halafian pottery from Chagar Bazar Levels 13–15 is closely paralleled by that from pre-TT 10 Arpachiyah. Chagar Bazar Level 12 pottery compares best with the later part of the Middle Phase at Arpachiyah (Middle Phase = TT 10–8), whereas Levels 11–6 equate with Arpachiyah Late Phase (TT 7–6). (It should be remembered that definition of these Halafian phases at Arpachiyah is being modified by Hijara's analyses of his newly excavated material).

On the basis of the Chagar Bazar sequence, Davidson assigns Mallowan's Halafian pottery from Tell Brak to his late Middle to Transitional Phases and that from the type site itself — Tell Halaf — to all four of his phases (Early, Middle, Late, and Transitional), although it is unclear whether the Tell Halaf sequence is a continuous one.

There is also some new information available for the Khabur region from a site 20 km north of Chagar Bazar: Tell Aqab (Davidson 1977, pp. 105–7, 1980; Davidson and Watkins, 1981). Four trenches were dug into this mound by a University of Edinburgh expedition during two field seasons (1975 and 1976). The site is a roughly oval mound rising 9.5 m above the plain and measuring about 225 m by 175 m. The deposits begin with Early Phase (i.e., comparable to the pre-TT 10 materials from Arpachiyah) Halafian strata and continue through Middle, Late, and Transitional phases to Ubaid. The total depth of archeological materials is nearly 12 m. Although the exposures were small, one complete Halafian house was uncovered: a pisé tholos 5 m in diameter.

As to artifacts, the Halafian pottery was accompanied by straw-tempered burnished plainware reminiscent of the *altmonochrom* from Tell Halaf. Also present (in the Late to Transitional Halafian levels) were several female figurines and some stone bowls, beads, and incised pendants, as well as a chipped-stone blade industry that is 80% obsidian.

Davidson and Watkins note that the Aqab pottery is quite similar to that from Arpachiyah and provides no evidence for a major difference between the Mosul and Khabur Halafian traditions. Rather, the Aqab evidence indicates a long developmental sequence in the Khabur area, paralleling that at Arpachiyah and Tepe Gawra. Publication of the Aqab data and the new excavations at Brak by the University of London Institute of Archaeology should very soon refine and modify our knowledge of the Khabur Halafian developments.

BALIKH

As is the case for the Khabur headwaters area, the Balikh drainage was first investigated for archeological sites by Mallowan's 1930s surveys (Mallowan 1946). He discovered two sites with indications of Halafian occupation: Tell Aswad and Tell Mefesh. Recent excavations at Aswad (Cauvin and Cauvin 1972) have not revealed further evidence of Halafian materials, and, in fact, the site seems to have been occupied and then abandoned by bearers of a culture allied to the PPNB of Palestine at a time preceding the Halaf period (see also, Mallowan 1977, p. 151).

Tell Mefesh was tested in a 5-day sondage by Mallowan, who assigned the architectural and artifactual remains to the Ubaid period, but recent reassessment (Copeland 1979, p. 270) indicates a Transitional Halaf/Ubaid placement as more accurate.

A new survey of the lower Balikh was undertaken in 1978 by a CNRS team (Copeland 1979). Their primary objective was to study the Quaternary river terraces near the Balikh's confluence with the Euphrates, but they also compiled information on several mounds, of which at least four (Tell Mounbatah, Tell Zaidan, Chahine, and Subhi Abiad) have Halafian occupations. Zaidan was reported long ago by Albright (1926) and was visited again in 1969 by Cauvin (1970). The Halafian sherds so far available from this site and from Chahine and Subhi Abiad indicate the presence of a Halaf Transitional Phase. Tell Mounbateh was occupied by Halafians possibly by Early Halaf and definitely by Middle Halaf times (Copeland 1979, p. 270); Mounbateh also yielded Late Halaf sherds.

Although it may simply be an error of sampling, on the present evidence there is a gap in the occupational sequence in the Balikh from the PPNB-like horizon represented at such sites as Abu Hureyra, Aswad, and Bouqras to the Middle Halaf Phase exemplified at Mounbateh; and a similar gap apparently exists in the Euphrates valley (Copeland 1979, pp. 268—69).

MIDDLE EUPHRATES VALLEY

Davidson (1977, p. 200) believes the Halafian pottery from sites on the middle Euphrates to form a regional variant, as does the pottery from sites in the Mosul, Sinjar, Khabur, and Balikh regions, respectively. Although a number of middle Euphrates Halaf sites have been reported on the basis of sherds located during surface surveys, only five have been excavated: Carchemish, or Yunus (Woolley 1934), Til Barsib (Thureau-Dangin and Dunand 1936), Tell Turlu (Mellink 1964), Shams-ed-Din (Radi and Seeden 1974; Azoury et al. 1982), and Arslan Tepe near Malatya (the presence of true Halafian pottery here is attested in a personal communication to Davidson from Hauptman; Davidson 1977, p. 225).

The Yunus Halafian pottery is Middle to Late Phase in Davidson's classification (1977, p. 215), whereas that from Turlu is Late or Transitional (Davidson 1977, p. 204), as is also that from Til Barsib (Davidson 1977, p. 225). Shams-ed-Din is one of four Halaf sites discovered by archeological surveys in the Tabqa Dam reservoir. The other three — known only from surface collections — are Tell Mureybit II, Kreyn, and a site near Mumbaqa (no name given; Davidson 1977, pp. 223—24), and all four so far seem to represent Late Phase Halafian occupations.

Davidson's examination of the Halafian pottery from these sites indicated to him that the ceramic tradition in question was late (Middle Phase at best) into the middle Euphrates and — on the present evidence — was not long lived there (Davidson 1977, pp. 225—28). Davidson finds the dividing line between true Halafian sites in the general middle Euphrates area and the Halaf-influenced sites that characterize Syro-Cilicia to lie along the Kurt Dagh (Davidson 1977, p. 257). Tell Turlu and Tell Rifa'at (north of Aleppo) would then represent the most westerly known, excavated, true Halaf sites (see discussion below under Halafian Periphery: West).

HALAFIAN PERIPHERY: NORTH

In the 1930s, excavation by Riley and by Kirsop and Silva Lake at the Urartian mound of Tilkitepe on the shore of Lake Van in eastern Turkey revealed Halafian pottery in the basal levels (Reilly 1940; Davidson 1977, pp. 231—33; Watson 1982). Sir Leonard Woolley (1934) reported Halafian sherds from two mound sites near Urfa, and several other Halafian sites have been found by surveys in southeastern Turkey since that time. In addition, a few other Halafian sites are present in the Elazığ-Keban area (Davidson 1977, pp. 240—41).

The only excavated northern Halafian sites outside the Keban are Tilkitepe and Girikihaciyan, neither being fully published. Davidson's assessment of the available data on the pottery from these two sites indicated to him that Tilkitepe has Middle to Late Phase pottery whereas Girikihaciyan seems to be Late Phase. My own detailed comparison of the Girikihaciyan Halafian ware with Davidson's and Hijara's data (Watson and LeBlanc ms.) bears out a Late Phase (Davidson's terminology) or terminal Pottery Phase 3 to Phase 4 (Hijara's terminology) placement for Girikihaciyan.

In the Keban area, Davidson notes five Halafian sites (Tepecik, Tulintepe, Kortepe,

Korucutepe, and Norşuntepe) and concludes that — on the present evidence — all these sites represent communities producing local versions of Halafian pottery but that they were not true Halafian settlements.

HALAFIAN PERIPHERY: WEST

Halafian occupations are present at Tell Rifa'at near Aleppo and at several sites in the surrounding region (Matthers et al. 1978; Seton Williams 1961; Thomas and Mellaart n.d.) for a total of 22. Twenty-one of these are north of Aleppo, one is southeast, and all are apparently fairly large mounds with two or more periods of occupation. In addition, Lorraine Copeland (personal communication) reports a newly discovered Halafian site — Tell Arab Azzé — on the Sejour (a right-bank tributary of the upper Euphrates) near the Syro-Turkish border northeast of Aleppo. As Mellaart notes, it appears that North Syria was probably within the Halafian sphere.

West of the Aleppo area, however, presently known traces of Halafian wares represent imported or locally produced imitations rather than the products of indigenous Halafian potters (Davidson 1977, pp. 256–59). Most of these Halaf-influenced ceramic industries have been known for a long time (Watson 1965, pp. 69–71) and include Levels II and III at Sakje Güzü (Garstang et al. 1937; Taylor et al. 1950; Davidson 1977, pp. 260–64), Mersin XIX–XVII (Garstang 1953; Mellaart 1975, p. 126; Davidson 1977, pp. 287–91), Amuq C and D (Braidwood and Braidwood 1960; Davidson 1977, pp. 265–72), Ras Shamra IV (de Contenson 1973; Davidson 1977, p. 273–79), and possibly Hama L (Ingholt 1940). Ard Tlaili in the Beqaa in eastern Lebanon seems to represent the most southerly known Halaf-influenced site (Kirkbride 1969; Davidson 1977, pp. 282–84).

On the basis of his recent examination of Halafian pottery from the above sites, Davidson concludes that Halafian influence reaches this Syro-Cilician area near the close of his Middle Phase (Davidson 1977, p. 292) and that the mechanism of spread was trade (see below).

HALAFIAN PERIPHERY: EAST

Hamrin. Salvage work in the Jebel Hamrin area began in 1977 and so far has resulted in the reporting of three sites that contain Halafian occupations (Postgate and Watson 1979, p. 141, 159–80). These three are Tell ar-Rubeidheh, Tell Hasan, and Tell Sungur B. Tell ar-Rubeidheh consists of three small mounds dating to the Uruk, Ubaid, and Halaf periods, respectively. The Halafian mound is said to be badly eroded and was not excavated. Tell Hasan, however, was partially excavated by an Italian expedition in 1978 and 1979. Both Ubaid and Halaf pottery are found in the upper levels; there was a Halafian occupation underneath. All these strata were disturbed by animal burrowing and by early historic period graves, but the Halafian settlement is represented by a small tholos as well as by rectangular houses, all in *tauf*. The Halafian pottery is said to be late in type and includes polychrome decoration (Postgate and Watson 1979, pp. 173–74).

Tell Sungur is actually a set of three mounds — A, B, and C — which are being excavated by a Japanese archeological expedition. Levels III and IV at Sungur B are reported as Late Halafian (the overlying levels, I and II, are Ubaidian and possibly Transitional Halafian-Ubaidian, respectively). No architectural remains had been found as of the initial summary account (Postgate and Watson 1979, p. 179).

Hijara notes several other Halafian sites in the region between the Jebel Hamrin and the Iranian border. Most of these are known only from surface collections, but he believes the partially excavated site of Tell Bagum near the Darbendi Khan Reservoir to be the most important of them (Hijara 1980, pp. 248–49).

Mandali. Although the work of Joan Oates in the area around Mandali (Oates 1968, 1969) revealed the presence of Halafian pottery, she believes the region to have been peripheral: "The rare occurrence of Halaf pottery in the Mandali area strongly suggests that it was never at home there" (Oates 1969, p. 142).

Western Iran and Transcaucasia. Halafian-influenced pottery is present in the Mahidasht area of western Iran within a 50 km radius north, east, and west of Kermanshah (Levine and McDonald 1977; Henrickson 1980). A total of 61 sites examined in 1975 yielded sherds of a local variety of Halafian pottery dubbed "J ware." Shapes are not well known (all this material comes from surface surveys only): "... at least part of this ware bears affinities to the Halaf wares of northern Mesopotamia in both design and method of manufacture, albeit in a rather remote sense for the most part. The ware is perhaps best characterized as a local central Zagros variant of the Halaf" (Levine and McDonald 1977, p. 44).

Together with Halafian-style painted pottery was a red- and/or black-slipped ware, which sounds reminiscent of a few sherds found at Banahilk, where some of the small straight-sided or flare-sided bowls were red- or black-slipped (Watson forthcoming). Further work by the Mahidasht Project in 1978 included sondages at five mounds, one of which — Chogha Maran — yielded J ware sherds in levels dated ca. 4900−4200 B.C. (Henrickson 1980). The ware is characterized as similar to that of Late Halaf in northern lowland Mesopotamia but simpler in decorative style.

Merpert and Munchaev also refer to Halafian pottery in Transcaucasia (Merpert and Munchaev 1973, p. 108).

HALAFIAN SUBSISTENCE AND SETTLEMENT AND THE HALAFIAN ASSEMBLAGE

Available radiocarbon dates indicate a span of approximately 5300 to 4500 B.C. (Libby half-life, uncalibrated) for the Halafian culture (Davidson 1977, pp. 337−39; Hijara 1980, pp. 279−84; Watson, forthcoming).

Although there is remarkably little detailed information available, we can be certain that the Halafians were farmers and pastoralists. Plant remains — emmer wheat and barley — were first recovered in an Halafian context by Mallowan at Arpachiyah (Mallowan and Rose 1935, p. 15). Hijara's recent work at Arpachiyah produced remains of emmer, einkorn, hexaploid wheat, hulled and naked 6-row barley, hulled 2-row barley, and lentils (Hijara et al. 1980, p. 154). Helbaek (1959) reported flax-seed imprints at Brak and Arpachiyah, Davidson refers to emmer wheat at Tell Aqab (Davidson 1977, p. 14), and van Zeist (1980−1981) has identified a variety of cereals and legumes from Girikihaciyan. The Girikihaciyan remains include emmer and einkorn wheat, hulled barley, lentils, bitter vetch, and chickpeas. Flax seeds are also present as are fragments of a few nut and fruit species (pistachio, hawthorn, and almond) and seeds of weedy plants (goat's-face grass, ryegrass, *Lithospermum* sp., and *Anchusa* sp.).

The cultivated plants were probably all dry-farmed. At any rate, Halafian site distribution as now known is confined to areas where crops can be raised without irrigation (Hijara 1980, pp. 250−51). Davidson (1977, pp. 12−13) has observed further that Halafian sites occur primarily on soils of the Brown Mediterranean type, which are particularly suitable for continuous cereal cultivation. Gordon Hillman adds that the use of draft animals for pulling plows would have been highly advantageous in working such soils (personal communication cited in Davidson 1977, p. 15).

The faunal picture is known fairly well for Banahilk and Girikihaciyan (Laffer 1973 and forthcoming; Flannery 1961; McArdle 1973 and ms). At both sites there are domestic sheep, goats, pigs, and cattle. At Banahilk there are also bones of wild sheep, goat, red deer, roe deer, red fox, bear, leopard, birds, and fish as well as many shells of a large land gastropod (*Helix salomonica*). At Girikihaciyan there was domestic dog plus fox, red deer, equid (probably onager), hare, tortoise, bird (possibly partridge), fish, and about 100 fragments of freshwater mussels.

Domestic cattle, sheep, goat, and pig are among the Yarim Tepe II faunal remains (Merpert and Munchaev 1973, p. 112). Bone recovered during the 1976 excavations at Arpachiyah included remains of domestic cattle, pig, goat, sheep, and dog (Hijara et al. 1980, p. 153). Thus, the Halafians had a variety of domestic food animals and at least one possible draft animal (cattle).

Davidson (1977, pp. 17–19) has summarized the available data on Halafian settlement size and concludes that most of the known sites for which sizes can be obtained (Arpachiyah, Gawra, Hassuna, Chagar Bazar, Aqab, Brak, Tell Halaf, Yarim Tepe II, Turlu, Yunus, Shams-ed-Din, Girikihaciyan, and Banahilk) are all relatively small, ranging from under 1 hectare to 8 hectares in area. Davidson adds that this generalization holds true for the Halaf sites located by the University of Edinburgh survey of the Khabur headwaters.

While it is true that 8 hectares is less than the size of the largest known prehistoric site in the Near East (Chatal Hüyük, which covers about 13 hectares), an 8-hectare site is still a substantial community, and an 8-fold difference in sizes among known sites is a significant amount of variation.

Hijara adds that the Iraqi Halafian sites are all 1 to 2 hectares in size but that in the Halafian nuclear zone (between Jebal Sinjar and the area just east of Mosul) there is a recurring pattern of large sites, each surrounded by several small sites (Hijara 1980, pp. 272, 252).

Apart from the well-known painted pottery, which is extremely homogeneous stylistically across the expanse of Halafian territory in northern Iraq and Syria, there is a certain broad similarity from site to site in a few other categories of Halafian materials. The most obvious nonceramic Halafian hallmark is the "tholos" type of building first reported by Mallowan from Arpachiyah and later found at Tepe Gawra, Yarim Tepe II, Yunus, Tell Aqab, Shams-ed-Din, Turlu, Girikihaciyan, and probably Chagar Bazar.

As to artifacts, incised pendants and female figurines are diagnostic, as are well-made stone bowls and large, flat beads of ground obsidian. Davidson (1977, p. 20) suggests that Halafian chipped stone industries are blade based, but this is not true of the chert tools at either Banahilk or Girikihaciyan (although it is of the obsidian). Biconical clay sling missiles are present at several Halafian sites, whereas clearly recognizable stone projectile points are absent.

At a more detailed level of comparison than that just outlined there are significant differences between Halafian sites. For example, although most Halafian sites have tholoi, with and without rectangular antechambers, the later tholoi at Arpachiyah (TT 7 and 8) have walls two to three times as thick as those of any other reported examples (1.65 to 2.0 m vs. .40 to .50 m at other sites). The materials of construction also vary: at Arpachiyah the foundations just referred to are of rock fragments packed together, whereas at Girikihaciyan limestone boulders were used. The Arpachiyah and Girikihaciyan tholoi were apparently *tauf*-walled structures, whereas the one at Tepe Gawra is mud brick.

There is probably a good deal of difference in the forms of painted pottery vessels at the various sites. At any rate, for Girikihaciyan and Banahilk — where sherd counts were made — some striking contrasts are apparent. Less than 3% of the approximately 850 bowl sherds at Girikihaciyan are round-sided bowls, whereas 71% of the approximately 740 bowl sherds at Banahilk are round-sided bowls. Flare-rimmed bowls make up 19% of the bowl sherds at Girikihaciyan but less than 4% at Banahilk. Hole-mouthed bowls comprise 19% of the Banahilk bowl sherd total but less than 2% at Girikihaciyan. Bowl/jar ratios at the two sites also differ somewhat (52.5:47.5 at Girikihaciyan vs. 44.9:55.1 at Banahilk). A further interesting comparison here is from Tell Aqab, where jars make up only 7% to 12% of all Halafian vessels from any level (Davidson 1981, p. 75). Painted ware to plainware ratios also differ markedly (15:85 at Girikihaciyan, 65:35 at Banahilk, and 66:34 at Arpachiyah, 1976 (Hijara 1980, p. 187). With respect to chipped stone, obsidian makes up 30% (by count) of the total fragments of chipped stone recovered from the 1970 excavations at Girikihaciyan; and at Banahilk the obsidian/chert ratio is nearly the same (29% obsidian, 61% chert). However, at Tell Aqab (Davidson 1977, p. 332), obsidian made up 80% to 85% of the chipped stone industry, while at Shams-ed-Din, obsidian is much less common than flint or chert, the proportions being approximately 89% chert to 11% obsidian (Azoury et al. 1982). Hence, there is marked fluctuation simply in gross quantities of obsidian present at different Halafian sites, and when detailed analysis of the chipped stone industries at the new sites (including the newly excavated portions of Arpachiyah) are available there will probably be even greater demonstrable variation. One major difference is already apparent: Davidson (1977, p. 20) notes that the Halafian chipped stone industries are blade based, but this is definitely not true for the chert industry at either Girikihaciyan or Banahilk. Obsidian at both sites does tend to be present as blades (58% at Girikihaciyan, 39% at Banahilk), but the percentage of chert blades is only 7% at Girikihaciyan and 2% at Banahilk.

Enough has been said to demonstrate the heterogeneity in artifactual and architectural categories of Halafian sites. There is also some evidence of variation in functions of Halafian sites. Childe (1952, p. 112) once suggested that Tilkitepe might have been an Halafian outpost established to obtain and export obsidian from Nemrut Dagh on Lake Van. (This interpretation is perhaps somewhat dubious, however. In the first place, Tilkitepe is on the opposite side of the lake from the obsidian source, not a very efficient arrangement for a mining and exporting settlement. In the second place, there are now known to be a number of other Halafian sites distributed at least as far north as Tilkitepe.)

Andrew Moore (personal communication) reports noting an Halafian site, Qadahiye, in northern Syria, located on the right bank of the Euphrates below Jerablus, at a crossing place that the community's inhabitants might have monitored during the time of occupation. Oates (1972, pp. 299–300) also speaks of "bridgehead sites" on the Tigris and Euphrates that were probably occupied from early village times on, and — as Redman notes (1978, p. 210) — Arpachiyah and Nineveh are examples of such sites on the Tigris.

The "burnt house" at Arpachiyah (Mallowan and Rose 1933, pp. 16ff. and 105ff.) has long been recognized as a special establishment of some kind (Mallowan suggests a craftsman's shop), and results of Hijara's recent work in that part of the site confirm the specialized nature of this area. No similar phenomenon has as yet been described for any other Halafian site, but Davidson's investigation of trace-element patterning in Halafian pottery indicates the presence of centers that dominated the pottery trade in particular places (Davidson 1977, pp. 297–336; 1981; Davidson and McKerrell 1976).

Arpachiyah was apparently a major pottery-exporting center within the Mosul region, as were Brak, Chagar Bazar, and Tell Halaf for portions of the Khabur region. Davidson and McKerrell carried out elemental analyses on pottery from Chagar Bazar and five smaller sites above it on the Wadi Dara (the stream bed beside which Chagar Bazar is located), as well as from one site (Ambara) on the Wadi Jaghjagh some 17 miles northeast of Chagar Bazar. Chagar Bazar seems to have been exporting pottery to at least five of the six outlying sites (including Ambara), and Davidson suspects that some of the outlying sites were heavily dependent on Chagar Bazar for various special types of vessels (Davidson and McKerrell 1976; Davidson 1981).

Similarly, a great deal of the Halafian pottery at Tepe Gawra was apparently imported from Arpachiyah, including at least a few entire vessel categories. Davidson further emphasizes Mallowan's suggestion that the Arpachiyah TT 6 community was producing and trading, or at least redistributing, a number of craft products.

In both the Chagar Bazar and Arpachiyah cases the pottery trade was nonreciprocal, i.e., Chagar Bazar and Arpachiyah exported fairly large amounts of ceramics but did not import wares in exchange from those sites. Thus, local trade in Halafian pottery was apparently dominated by specific production centers, such as Chagar Bazar in the Wadi Dara portion of the Khabur region and Arpachiyah in the Mosul region. Furthermore, by Middle and Late Halafian times (in Davidson's terms) at least some of these centers were trading with other sites and with each other in wider intraregional and interregional patterns (Davidson 1977, pp. 312–26). There is pottery at Chagar Bazar that seems to have been made in the lower Wadi Jaghjagh (the Tell Brak area) and at Tell Halaf in the Khabur valley. On the other hand, some of the Halafian sherds from Tell Brak have compositional patterns matching samples from the Wadi Dara, where Chagar Bazar is located. Finally, the composition of some sherds from Tell Halaf is reported to resemble that of Wadi Dara area clays.

At the interregional level, pottery from Tell Arpachiyah (Mosul region) was apparently exported to Tell Brak and Tell Halaf in the Khabur reigon, while Tell Halaf was exporting pottery to Mureybit (and probably also to Shams-ed-Din) in the Euphrates valley. The quantities involved were much smaller than those being exchanged in local or even regional trade, but interregional trade took place not only between production centers (Arpachiyah, Halaf, Brak) but also from such centers (Tell Halaf) to noncenters (Mureybit and Shams-ed-Din).

The communication patterns beginning to emerge from these analyses are compatible with a suggestion that those Halafian sites dominant in the pottery trade were chiefly centers, i.e., places of residence of local strongmen or chiefs, functioning within a ranked society (LeBlanc and Watson 1973; Service 1962). The settlement pattern noted by Hijara as being common in the Sinjar-Mosul region — a big site surrounded by several small sites (Hijara 1980, p. 252) — might also be expressive of a center-hinterland or center-periphery settlement hierarchy.

Alternative explanations for the distribution and homogeneity of Halafian pottery might include settlers migrating from one Halafian community to another or itinerant or localized groups of pottery specialists functioning more or less autonomously and distributing their products from one community to another (Watson 1973).

In discussing the organization of Halafian society, Hijara refers to Rowton's detailed studies of tribal society in early historic Mesopotamia (Rowton 1973, 1974). He does so because be believes Halafian society to have been tribally organized and because he believes ethnographic or ethnohistoric information from the geographic area in question (Mesopotamia) to be more valid than information from distant geographic areas (Hijara 1980, pp. 278–79). I do not agree with this latter point (i.e., that a direct historical approach is categorically better than a general comparative approach), but Rowton does provide some very interesting data on interrelationships between nomadic and sedentary groups in greater Mesopotamia during the third and second millennia B.C. that are relevant to the origins of full-scale nomadic pastoralism there (see Hole 1978, pp. 135–39). However, the tribal organization that concerns Rowton must have been significantly different from that present in Mesopotamia 2,000 years prior to the appearance of city-states. Similarly, ethnographic information on contemporary so-called tribal or tribally-organized nomadic pastoralists indicates how closely tied they are politically and economically to the larger, state-based society that encloses them (Barth 1961; Beck 1980, 1981). It is not clear from Hijara's brief discussion just what he means by "tribe," but if he is thinking of such groups as the Qashqa'i, the Shammar, or the Anezeh (Beck, forthcoming; Dickson 1949, p. 111), then one should note that — although they are usually called tribes — these are ranked societies with hereditary aristocracies, hence chiefdoms in Service's original terminology (Service 1962; it is in the context of Service's 1962 formulation that Hijara's discussion takes place).

At any rate, directionally controlled, nonreciprocal, extensive, and intensive trade in pottery definitely occurred during the Halafian period. From what is known ethnographically about trade in nonurbanized, nonindustrialized societies, such a situation is much more likely in a ranked society than in a nonranked one (recent discussions of trade by anthropologists and archeologists include Adams 1974, 1975; Earle and Erickson eds. 1977; Goad 1978; Sabloff and Lamberg-Karlovsky eds. 1975).

Halafian trading networks must have functioned to transport a variety of information and many materials (minimally: obsidian, marine shells, and gem stones) besides pottery. The majority of the interregional communication would be expected to occur largely between centers, but at least one small Euphrates site that does not seem to have been a center (Tell Mureybit), and perhaps another nearby small site (Shams-ed-Din), received pottery imported from the major Khabur site of Tell Halaf (Davidson 1977, pp. 323–25). However, the Tell Halaf pottery might have gone to a Euphrates area center before being entered into localized trade and transshiped to smaller places like Mureybit and Shams-ed-Din.

The quantities of pottery (and perhaps obsidian, also) that were traded and the great distances over which they were moved might indicate the use of draft animals, a suggestion made by Renfrew et al. (1966). Cattle, at least, were available by the 6th millennium to serve in this capacity.

SUMMARY AND CONCLUSIONS

In conclusion I should like to turn to the question of the divergence between northern and southern Mesopotamia traditions, which first becomes apparent during the Halafian time range, by referring to a recent formulation of Sanders and Webster (1978). These authors discuss the evolution of ranked versus stratified societies, basing their argument on a distinction originally made by Fried (1960, 1967). In stratified societies, differential status (presence of economic classes) results from unequal access to vital subsistence resources, a situation not true of ranked (chiefdom) societies where differential status (presence of social classes) is apparently based primarily on real or fictive lines of kinship and descent (i.e., some clans and lineages are believed to be inherently better than others) and is upheld by more or less elaborate sumptuary rules. Social and economic classes overlap even in nonindustrialized societies, and there is certainly a continuum of tribal-level egalitarian societies to "Big Men" societies/low-level chiefdoms/developed chiefdoms (with paramount chiefs and lesser chiefs)/stratified societies (in Fried's sense), and complexly hierarchical state-based societies. Nevertheless, distinctions among these variants, made for analytical purposes, can be justified.

For example, Sanders and Webster (1978, pp. 281–301) describe a series of alternative cultural-evolutionary sequences beginning with egalitarian societies and culminating in chiefdoms or states. They believe most chiefdoms to be hierarchical organizations alternative to state-based society. That is, they think the usual pristine sequence to state-based society goes from egalitarian to stratified society, and then to the state. Chiefdoms develop instead of stratified societies and states in environmental and ecological situations that are relatively less constrained or circumscribed than those giving rise to states. (This conclusion is similar to one reached earlier by Malcolm Webb [1975].)

Although the data are far from conclusive, it may be useful to consider the Mesopotamian case as an illustration of the processes Sanders and Webster discuss. The Halafian heartland would seem to fit their description of a low risk/low diversity environment (Sanders and Webster 1978, pp. 252–67; and see Hijara 1980, p. 288). Human societies inhabiting it would be expected to develop more slowly than those in high risk and/or high diversity environments and would also be expected to evolve into chiefdoms rather than states. In southern Mesopotamia, however, a different sequence would be expected because of the key role necessarily played by irrigation and the shortage of arable, irrigable land. For a society applying appropriate irrigation techniques (which the Samarrans apparently were doing [Oates 1972, 1978, pp. 468, 470]), vital resources were limited in a way they were not in northern Mesopotamia. For such a society (the Samarran) in such an environment (southern Mesopotamia), there would also be a premium on sociopolitical organization of a kind not necessary in northern Mesopotamia, where rainfall agriculture is productive and there is plenty of good grazing land.

Although he does not think the Halafians were living in chiefdoms, Hijara does believe elements of chiefdom organization were present not only in the Halafian but also in the Samarran (Hijara 1980, pp. 268–75). Samarran pottery is widespread in northern Mesopotamia; at the Samarran site of Tell es-Sawwan there are numerous infant burials in association with large buildings and containing elaborate grave goods. At least the beginnings of craft specialization are indicated by a sophisticated ground stone industry and possibly by the appearance of copper at Tell es-Sawwan (copper is also reported from the Hassunan site of Yarim Tepe I). In reference to the Tell es-Sawwan infant burials, Flannery some time ago (1972) mentioned the possibility of Samarran chiefdoms. Perhaps our own earlier suggestion (LeBlanc and Watson 1973) of the Halafian as a low-level chiefdom was too modest, and one should now consider whether the Samarran might not have been organized as a set of low-level chiefdoms, with the Halafian comprising more developed chiefdoms.

In any case, the factors and processes Sanders and Webster describe might help explain the striking differences between what happened in northern Mesopotamia on the one hand and southern Mesopotamia on the other in the crucial period between 5500 and 3000 B.C., which culminated in civilized city-states in the south, a societal form absent in the north until much later.

ACKNOWLEDGMENTS

The data coverage in this paper has benefited immeasurably from the generosity of several scholars and archeologists currently engaged in Halafian and Halafian-related research.

Lois Beck, Lorraine Copeland, Thomas Davidson, Ismail Hijara, and Andrew Moore kindly read and commented upon a preliminary draft of the manuscript. Several talks with Lois Beck about tribes, chiefdoms, and states and about contemporary pastoral nomadism in the Near East were exceedingly helpful. Helga Seeden generously made available to me the proofs of the detailed report on Shams-ed-Din (Azoury et al.) that appeared in the spring 1982 issue of *Berytus* and also called to my attention a series of articles by Walter Noll and others on the technical details of Halafian, Samarran, and Ubaidian pottery (Noll 1976, 1977a, 1977b). Elizabeth Henrickson and Mary McDonald discussed J ware with me and sent me relevant reprints and papers. Thomas Davidson and Ismail Hijara supplied copies of their dissertations, which were invaluable sources in preparing this review paper. In addition, they have each discussed various aspects of Halafian matters with me on several occasions and have provided several offprints and manuscripts resulting from their own research. Although they — and the others named above — are in no way responsible for the uses to which I have put this information, I know the paper is much better because of their generous assistance.

BIBLIOGRAPHY

Adams, Robert McC.
1974   Anthropological perspectives on ancient trade. *Current Anthropology* 15:239–49.
1975   The emerging place of trade in civilizational studies. J. Sabloff and K. Lamberg-Karlovsky, eds. *Ancient civilization and trade*. Albuquerque: University of New Mexico Press, pp. 451–56.

Albright, William
    1926   Proto-Mesopotamian painted ware from the Balikh valley. *Man* 25:41–42.

Azoury, I.; Bergmann, C.; Gustavson-Graube, C.E.; al-Radi, S.; Seeden, H.; and Uerpmann, H.P.
    1980   A stone-age village on the Euphrates, I–V; report from the Halafian settlement at Shams
                ed-Din Tannira: American University of Beirut rescue excavations 1974. *Berytus Ar-
                chaeological Studies* 28:87–143.

Barth, Fredrik
    1961   *Nomads of south Persia.* London: George Allen and Unwin.

Beck, Lois
    1980   Herd owners and hired shepherds: the Qashqa'i of Iran. *Ethnology.* 19:327–51.
    1981   Economic transformations among Qashqa'i nomads, 1962–1978. In *Modern Iran: dialec-
                tics of continuity and change*, ed. M. Bonine and N. Keddie, pp. 99–122, 404–7. Albany:
                State University of New York Press.
    in   Iran and the Qashqa'i tribal confederacy. In *Tribe and state in Afghanistan and Iran from
    press   1800 to 1980*, ed. R. Tapper. London: Croom and Helm.

Braidwood, Robert J.
    1943   The comparative archaeology of early Syria: from the time of the earliest known village
                cultures through the Akkadian period. Ph.D. diss., University of Chicago.
    1952   *The Near East and the foundations for civilization.* Eugene, Oregon: University of
                Oregon Press.
    1958   Near Eastern prehistory. *Science* 127:1419–30.
    1972   Prehistoric investigations in southwestern Asia. *Proceedings of the American Philo-
                sophical Society* 116:310–20.
    1975   *Prehistoric men.* Glenview, Illinois: Scott, Foresman.

Braidwood, Robert J., and Braidwood, Linda
    1953   The earliest village communities of southwestern Asia. *Journal of World History*
                1:278–310.
    1960   *Excavations in the plain of Antioch*, vol. 1: *the earlier assemblages: phases A–J.* Oriental
                Institute Publications, vol. 61. Chicago: University of Chicago Press.

Braidwood, Robert J.; Çambel, Halet; Redman, Charles; and Watson, Patty Jo
    1971   Beginnings of village-farming communities in southeastern Turkey. *Proceedings of the
                National Academy of Sciences* 68:1236–40.

Braidwood, Robert J.; Çambel, Halet; and Watson, Patty Jo
    1969   Prehistoric investigations in southeastern Turkey. *Science* 164:1275–76.

Braidwood, Robert J., and Howe, Bruce
    1960   *Prehistoric investigations in Iraqi Kurdistan.* Studies in Ancient Oriental Civilizations,
                no. 31. Chicago: University of Chicago Press.
    1965   Southwestern Asia beyond the lands of the Mediterranean littoral. In *Viking fund
                publications in Anthropology*, vol. 32, ed. R. Braidwood and G. Willey, pp. 132–46. New
                York: Wenner-Gren Foundation for Anthropological Research.

Cauvin, Jacques
    1970   Mission 1969 en Djazireh (Syrie). *Bulletin de la Société Préhistorique Française*
                67(9):286–87.

Cauvin, Jacques, and Cauvin, M.-C.
    1972   Sondage à Tell Assoud (Djezireh, Syrie). *Annales Archéologiques Arabes Syriennes*
                22:85–89; 98–101.

Childe, V. Gordon
    1952   *New light on the most ancient East.* New York: Praeger.

Copeland, Lorraine
1979   Observations on the prehistory of the Balikh valley, Syria during the 7th to 4th millennia
        B.C. *Paléorient* 5:251–75.

Davidson, Thomas E.
1977   Regional variation within the Halaf ceramic tradition. Ph.D. diss., University of Edin-
        burgh.
1981   Pottery manufacture and trade at the prehistoric site of Tell Aqab. *Journal of Field
        Archaeology* 8:65–77.

Davidson, Thomas E., and McKerrell, Hugh
1976   Pottery analysis and Halaf period trade in the Khabur headwaters region. *Iraq* 38:45–56.

Davidson, Thomas E., and Watkins, Trevor
1981   Two seasons of excavation at Tell Aqab in the Jezirah, N.E. Syria. *Iraq* 43:1–18. (With a
        contribution by E.J. Peltenburg.)

de Contenson, Henri
1973   Le niveau Halafien de Ras Shamra. *Syria* 50:13–33.

Dickson, H.R.P.
1949   *The Arab of the desert.* London: George Allan and Unwin.

Dirvana, S.
1944   Cerablus Cıvarında Yuns'ta Bulunan Tel Halef Keramikleri. *Türk Tarıh Kurumu Belleten*
        8:403–20.

Earle, Timothy, and Erickson, John
1977   *(eds.) Exchange systems in prehistory.* New York: Academic Press.

Flannery, Kent V.
1961   Skeletal and radiocarbon evidence for the origins of pig domestication. Master's thesis,
        University of Chicago.
1972   The cultural evolution of civilizations. *Annual Review of Ecology and Systematics*
        3:399–426.

Frankel, David
1979   *Archaeologists at work: studies on Halaf pottery.* London: British Museum Publications.

Fried, Morton H.
1960   On the evolution of social stratification and the state. In *Culture and history,* ed. S.
        Diamond, pp. 713–31. New York: Columbia University Press.
1967   *The evolution of political society.* New York: Random House.

Garstang, John
1908   Excavations at Sakje-Geuzi in north Syria: preliminary report for 1908. *Annals of Ar-
        chaeology and Anthropology* 1:97–117.
1953   *Prehistoric Mersin.* Oxford: Clarendon Press.

Garstang, John; Adams, W. Pythian; and Seton-Williams, V.
1937   Third report on the excavations at Sakje-Geuzi: 1908–1911. *Annals of Archaeology and
        Anthropology* 24:119–36.

Goad, Sharon I.
1978   Exchange networks in the prehistoric southeastern United States. Ph.D. diss., Univer-
        sity of Georgia.

Helbaek, Hans
1959   Notes on the evolution of *linum. Kuml* 1959:103–29.

Henrickson, Elizabeth F.
1980   Chogha Maran and the Zagros Chalcolithic: Paper presented at the 79th Annual Meeting
        of the American Anthropological Association, Washington D.C., December, 1980.

Hijara, Ismail
  1978   Three new graves at Arpachiyah. *World Archaeology* 10:125–28.
  1980   The Halaf period in northern Mesopotamia. Ph.D. diss., Institute of Archaeology, University of London.

Hijara, Ismail; Watson, J.P.N.; Hubbard, R.N.L.B.; and Davies, C.
  1980   Arpachiyah 1976. *Iraq* 42:131–54.

Hole, Frank
  1978   Pastoral nomadism in Western Iran. In R. Gould, ed. *Explorations in Ethnoarchaeology.* Albuquerque: University of New Mexico Press, pp. 127–67.

Ingholt, Harald
  1940   *Rapport préliminaire sur sept campagnes de fouilles à Hama en Syrie (1932–1938).* Det Kongelige danske videnskabernes selskab, archaeologist-kunsthistoriske meddelelser, vol. 3, no. 1. Copenhagen: Levin and Munksgaard.

Kirkbride, Diana
  1969   Early Byblos and the Beqa'a. *Mélanges de l'Université Saint-Joseph* 45:45–59.

Laffer, Joanne
  1973   An analysis of the faunal remains of Banahilk, an Halafian site in northern Iraq: with an emphasis on the domestication of cattle. Master's thesis, University of Illinois at Chicago Circle.
  forth-   The Banahilk mammalia. In *Prehistoric archeology along the Zagros flanks,* ed. L.
  coming   Braidwood, R. Braidwood, B. Howe, C. Reed, and P. Watson, chap. 19. Oriental Institute Publications, vol. 105. Chicago: Oriental Institute.

LeBlanc, Steven A.
  1971   Computerized, conjunctive archeology and the Near Eastern Halaf. Ph.D. diss., Washington University, St. Louis.

LeBlanc, Steven A., and Watson, Patty Jo
  1973   A comparative statistical analysis of painted pottery from seven Halafian sites. *Paléorient* 1:117–33.

Levine, Louis D., and McDonald, Mary M.A.
  1977   The Neolithic and Chalcolithic periods in the Mahidasht. *Iran* 15:39–50.

Lloyd, Seton, and Safar, Fuad
  1945   Tell Hassuna. *Journal of Near Eastern Studies* 4:255–89.

Mallowan, M.E.L.
  1933   The prehistoric sondage of Nineveh, 1931–32. *Annals of Archaeology and Anthropology* 20:127–86.
  1936   The excavations of Tall Chagar Bazar and an archaeological survey of the Habur region, 1934–35. *Iraq* 3:1–59.
  1937   The excavations at Tall Chagar Bazar, and an archaeological survey of the Habur region: second campaign, 1936. *Iraq* 4:91–177.
  1946   Excavations in the Balikh valley, 1938. *Iraq* 8:111–62.
  1947   Excavations at Brak and Chagar Bazar. *Iraq* 9:1–266.
  1977   *Mallowan's memoirs: the autobiography of Max Mallowan.* London: William Collins Sons.

Mallowan, M.E.L., and Rose, J.C.
  1935   Excavations at Tell Arpachiyah, 1933. *Iraq* 2:1–178.

Matthers, John; Kenrick, Philip M.; and Taylor, Marthe Bernus
  1978   Tell Rifa'at 1977: preliminary report of an archaeological survey. *Iraq* 40:119–62.

McArdle, John E.
1973 A numerical (computerized) method for quantifying zooarcheological comparisons. Master's thesis, University of Illinois at Chicago Circle.
n.d. Halafian fauna of Girikihaciyan. In *Girikihaciyan: a Halafian site in southeastern Turkey*, P. Watson, and S. LeBlanc.

Mellaart, James
1975 *The Neolithic of the Near East.* London: Thames and Hudson.

Mellink, Machteld J.
1964 Archaeology of Asia Minor: Turlu near Gaziantep. *American Journal of Archaeology* 68:156.

Merpert, N.Y., and Munchaev, R.M.
1971 Excavations at Yarim Tepe 1970: second preliminary report. *Sumer* 27:9−22.
1973 Early agricultural settlements in the Sinjar plain, northern Iraq. *Iraq* 35:93−113.

Merpert, N.Y., Munchaev, R., and Bader, N.
1977 Investigations of the Soviet expedition in Iraq. *Sumer* 33.
1978 Soviet investigations in the Sinjar Plain. *Sumer* 34.

Munchaev, R.M., and Merpert, N.J.
1981 *Earliest agricultural settlements of Northern Mesopotamia; investigations of the Soviet expeditions in Iraq.* Moscow: Publishing house Nauka.

Munchajev, R.M., and Merpert, N. Ia.
1973 Excavations at Yarim Tepe 1972: fourth preliminary report. *Sumer* 29:3−16.

Noll, Walter
1976 Mineralogie und Technik der frühen Keramiken Grossmesopotamiens. *Neues Jahrbuck für Mineralogie* 127(3):261−88.
1977a Techniken antiker Töpfer und Vasenmaler. *Antike Welt* 8:21−36.
1977b Keramik in Vorgeschichte und Antike. *Keramik Zeitung* 29:283−88.

Oates, Joan
1968 Prehistoric investigations near Mandali, Iraq. *Iraq* 30:1−20.
1969 Choga Mami, 1967−68: a preliminary report. *Iraq* 31:115−52.
1972 Prehistoric settlement patterns in Mesopotamia. In *Man, settlement and urbanism*, ed. P.J. Ucko, R. Tringham, and G.W. Dimbleby, pp. 299−310. London: Duckworth.

Perkins, Ann
1949 *The comparative archeology of early Mesopotamia.* Studies in Ancient Oriental Civilizations, no. 25. Chicago: University of Chicago Press.

Postgate, J.N.
1972 Excavations in Iraq, 1971−72. *Iraq* 34:138−50.
1975 Excavations in Iraq, 1973−74. *Iraq* 37:57−67.
1976 Excavations in Iraq, 1975. *Iraq* 38:65−79.
1977 Excavations in Iraq, 1976. *Iraq* 39:301−20.

Postgate, J.N., and Watson, P.J.
1979 Excavations in Iraq, 1977−78. *Iraq* 41:141−81.

Radi, S., and Seeden, H.
1974 Shams-ed-Din. In *Antiquities de l'Euphrate*, p. 59. Aleppo: Musée National d'Alep.

Redman, Charles L.
1978 *The rise of civilization: from early farmers to urban society in the ancient Near East.* San Francisco: Freeman.

Redman, Charles L., and Watson, Patty Jo
1970 Systematic, intensive surface collection. *American Antiquity* 35:279−91.

Reilly, E.B.
    1940   Test excavations at Tilkitepe (1937). *Türk Tarih Arkeologya ve Etnografya Dergisi*
                    4:145—65.

Renfrew, Colin
    1973a   *The emergence of civilization: the Cyclades and the Aegean in the third millennium* B.C.
                    London: Methuen.
    1973b   *Before civilization: the radiocarbon revolution and prehistoric Europe.* London: Jon-
                    athan Cape.

Renfrew, Colin; Dixon, J.E.; and Cann, J.R.
    1966   Obsidian and early cultural contact in the Near East. *Proceedings of the Prehistoric
                    Society* 32:30—72.

Rowton, M.B.
    1973a   Urban autonomy in a nomadic environment. *Journal of Near Eastern Studies* 32:201—15.
    1973b   Autonomy and nomadism in western Asia. *Orientalia* n.s. 42:247—58.
    1974   Enclosed nomadism. *Journal of the Economic and Social History of the Orient* 17:1—30.

Sabloff, Jeremy A., and Lamberg-Karlovsky, Carl C.
    1975   (eds.) *Ancient civilization and trade.* Albuquerque: University of New Mexico Press.

Sanders, William, and Price, Barbara
    1968   *Mesoamerica: the evolution of a civilization.* New York: Random House.

Sanders, William, and Webster, David
    1978   Unilinealism, multilipealism, and the evolution of complex societies. In *Social archeol-
                    ogy: beyond subsistence and dating,* ed. C. Redman, M. Berman, E. Curtin, W. Lang-
                    horne, N. Versaggi, and J. Wanser, pp. 249—302. New York: Academic Press.

Service, Elman
    1962   *Primitive social organization.* New York: Random House.

Seton-Williams, M.V.
    1961   Preliminary report on the excavations at Tell Rifa'at. *Iraq* 27:68—87.

Thomas, Helen, and Mellaart, James
    n.d.   Tell Rifa'at 1978: report of the survey by an expedition from London University. Univer-
                    sity of London: Institute of Archaeology. Unpublished.

Thureau-Dangin, F., and Dunand, M.
    1936   *Til-Barsib.* Paris: Geuthner.

Tobler, A.J.
    1950   *Excavations at Tepe Gawra,* vol. 2. Philadelphia: University of Pennsylvania Press.

von Oppenheim, Max F.
    1943   *Tell Halaf,* vol. 1: *die prähistorische Funde: bearbeitet von Hubert Schmidt.* Berlin:
                    Walter de Gruyter.

Watson, Patty Jo
    1956   New Halafian material from northern Iraq: the Halaf "period" reconsidered. Master's
                    thesis, University of Chicago.
    1965   The chronology of north Syria and north Mesopotamia from 10,000 to 2000 B.C. In
                    Chronologies in old world archaeology, ed. R. Ehrich, pp. 61—100. Chicago: University
                    of Chicago Press.
    1973   Explanations and models: the prehistorian as philosopher of science and the prehistorian
                    as excavator of the past. In *The explanation of culture change,* ed. C. Renfrew, pp. 47—52.
                    London: Duckworth.
    1982   The Halafian pottery of Tilkitepe, seen in the Hittite Museum, Ankara (Citadel), 1955. In
                    Tilkitepe. Die ersten Ansätze prähistorischer Forschung in der östlichen Turkei, by M.
                    Korfman, Anhang II, pp. 203—12. Tubingen: Verlag Ernst Wasmuth.

forth- The soundings at Banahilk. In *Prehistoric archeology along the Zagros flanks*, ed. L.
coming Braidwood, R. Braidwood, B. Howe, C. Reed, and P. Watson, chap. 17. Oriental
        Institute Publications, vol. 105. Chicago: Oriental Institute.

Watson, Patty Jo, and LeBlanc, Steven A.
    1973   Excavation and analysis of Halafian materials from southeastern Turkey: the Halafian
            period reexamined. Paper presented at the 72nd Annual Meeting of the American
            Anthropological Association [New Orleans, November 28–December 2, 1973].
manu-
script   Girikihaciyan: a Halafian site in southeastern Turkey.

Webb, Malcolm
    1975   The flag follows trade: an essay on the necessary interaction of military and commercial
            factors in state formation. In *Ancient civilization and trade*, ed. J. Sabloff and C.
            Lamberg-Karlovsky, pp. 155–209. Albuquerque: University of New Mexico Press.

Woolley, C. Leonard
    1934   The prehistoric pottery of Carchemish. *Iraq*: 1:146–62.

Zeist, Willem van
    1980-81 Plant remains from Girikihaciyan, Turkey. *Anatolica* 7:75–89.

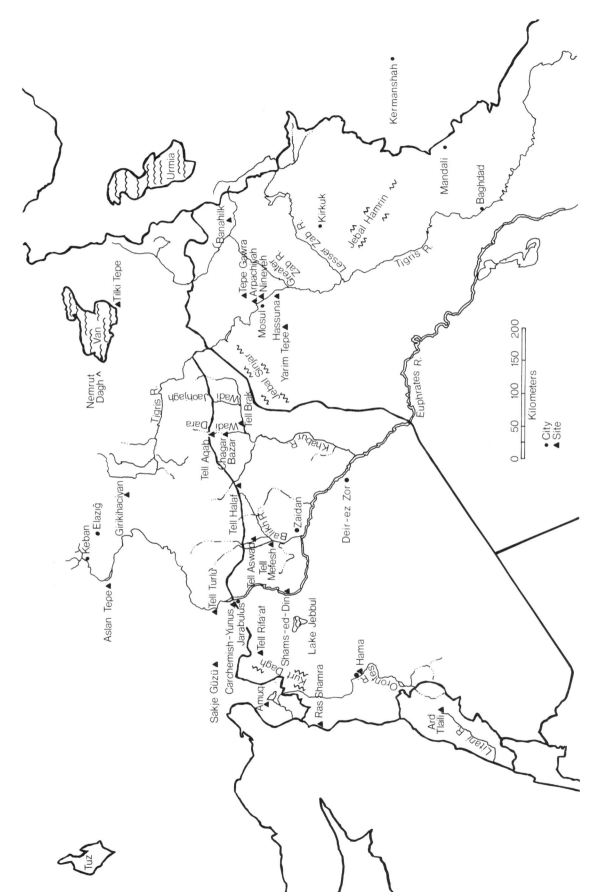

LOCATION OF HALAFIAN SITES REFERRED TO IN THE TEXT.

UBAID MESOPOTAMIA RECONSIDERED

Joan Oates

I T IS with great pleasure that I dedicate this festschrift article to Bob Braidwood, a friend and colleague for many years. Bob's early influence led me both to Near Eastern archeology and to the University of Cambridge; thus it seems appropriate, in this article in his honor, to return to the subject of my first research. In the many years since I first worked in Iraq, the early prehistory of the Near East has altered beyond recognition. At the same time, the later prehistoric periods, Ubaid and Uruk, have attracted relatively little interest, at least in terms of excavation, despite an increasing focus on the theoretical aspects of the rise of urbanism and the state, for the study of which, in Sumer, both periods are of major importance. Perhaps surprisingly, the only discoveries in recent years that have significantly increased our understanding of these prehistoric cultures have lain outside Mesopotamia — the identification of Ubaid sites along the Arabian Gulf and the excavation of substantial Late Uruk "colonies" on the Euphrates in northern Syria. Survey data have expanded our knowledge in certain limited regions, but as a broad generalization it remains true that during the past thirty years the later prehistory of Mesopotamia has not been a major focus of archeological research and that Eridu, dug just after the last war and still unpublished, and Tepe Gawra, excavated some fifty years ago, still provide the basis for any assessment of Ubaid materials.

There have, however, been advances in knowledge. The limited but very rewarding excavation at Ras al Amiya (Stronach 1962) provided confirmation of the essential unity of the long sequence already established at Eridu, while more recent work in Khuzistan, especially in the region of Deh Luran (Hole, Flannery, and Neely 1969; Hole 1977), has strengthened the argument for an indigenous development of Ubaid in southern Mesopotamia. The excavation of Choga Mami provided new evidence for the relationship between Samarra and Eridu and very considerably extended the known geographical range of Ubaid 1- and Hajji Muhammad-related materials (Oates 1969). The work at Choga Mami also provided until now unique evidence for the achievements of Mesopotamian irrigation technology in the sixth millennium bc (Oates and Oates 1976b).

At Warka (Kullaba), various soundings have penetrated Late Ubaid levels in the area of the Steingebäude (Schmidt 1972; Boehmer 1972). Although these have done little to expand our knowledge of the Ubaid ceramic sequence at this site — indeed, they have produced much the same admixture of Ubaid and Uruk types as did the 1931–32 Eanna precinct sounding — they have revealed two very interesting Ubaid shrines (Schmidt 1974), closely reminiscent in plan of the later Uruk temples on the nearby Anu terrace. The facades are elaborately recessed and carefully plastered, and both temples stand on a mud-brick platform of uncertain dimensions. Like the White Temple, one had been carefully whitewashed. Unfortunately, the foundations of the Steingebäude had been dug into the Ubaid mound, thus breaking the stratigraphic connection between these shrines and the high terrace sequence. The newly discovered shrines appear, however, to postdate its foundation (Schmidt 1974, p. 182, 1971, pl. 64). We remain ignorant of the Ubaid high terrace temple plan, but the adjacent "low" shrines are tripartite structures reminiscent not only of Warka Temples D/E (Anu) and the White Temple but also of Temples

251

VIII/VII at Eridu, suggesting little differentiation of temple plan at this period. At Warka, as at Eridu, the virtual identity of the Ubaid shrines and their fitments with those of the Anu Terrace temples provides unequivocal evidence for continuity of religious tradition from Ubaid to Sumerian times.

A brief investigation by German archeologists of a small site near Warka, designated Tell Mismar because of its numerous clay cones, revealed an extraordinary building with rooms of very large dimensions and some cone mosaic ornament still in situ (Schmidt 1978). The exact date of the building is uncertain, but it is possibly to be attributed to a very late or Terminal Ubaid horizon. The earliest sherds recovered from the surface of the site are in the Hajji Muhammad tradition (Schmidt 1978, pl. 1). At Tell el Oueili near Larsa (Warka survey 460, Adams and Nissen 1972) a French expedition under the direction of M. J.-L. Huot has been excavating levels belonging to a late phase of Ubaid occupation. A number of pottery kilns and what appear to have been special storage areas have been found (Huot 1978, pls. 10, 12).

Ubaid materials have been excavated at Yarim Tepe III by the Soviet Archaeological Mission under the direction of Dr. Rauf Munchaev. The tell resembles Arpachiyah in that a small Ubaid site is situated on a larger Halaf mound; Gawra XVIII−XVI provides the closest ceramic parallel. Several large house units and a number of kilns have been found, and there appear to have been many rooms for storage and other special purposes. Of particular interest is a collection of several hundred "grinders in volcanic stone," possibly coming from nearby Kaukab, southwest of Tell Brak in northeastern Syria. Ubaid materials have also been excavated at Qalinj Agha near Erbil (Hijara 1973) and at various sites in the Rania plain (Abu al-Soof 1970), but these remain largely unreported. Ubaid and Ubaid-related materials have also been found on various surveys in western Iran and eastern Syria (inter alia, Levine and McDonald 1977; Goff 1971; Meijer 1978/79), while in 1978 at Tell Brak, Late Ubaid levels were reached some 4.0 m below those containing Late Uruk pottery and a single numerical tablet. Such discoveries, however, have done little more than reinforce existing evidence for the widespread influence of Ubaid Mesopotamia by the late fifth millennium.

HAMRIN BASIN EXCAVATIONS

Undoubtedly, the greatest quantitative addition to the documentation of Ubaid Mesopotamia has resulted from an intensive rescue operation in the Hamrin Basin of the Diyala River, northeast of Baghdad, recently undertaken by the State Organization of Antiquities and Heritage with the cooperation of a number of foreign expeditions. Here, in an area of under 400 sq km, some 10 Ubaid sites have already been investigated. Most are less than a hectare in area, though Tell Abu Husaini, excavated by an Iraqi-Italian expedition under the direction of Dr. A. Invernizzi, has a sherd scatter covering some 6 hectares, and Tell Abada, excavated by Sayyid Sabah Abboud of the State Antiquities Organization, is a low mound of ca 3 hectares. The occupation of most of the sites was of short duration, which has led to some difficulty in relating the various Ubaid occupations chronologically but has also made possible extensive lateral excavation, thereby adding enormously to our hitherto very limited knowledge of village life in this period. Indeed, the fact that so many sites have been investigated in such a small geographical area has provided data of rare quantitative and comparative value.

The most interesting and informative of these new sites is Abada (Hamrin site 7).[1] Oval in shape, some 190 × 150 m in area, and 3.50 m high, it consists of three main levels of Ubaid occupation. The earliest level (III) was excavated over about half of the site. Here the discovery of

---

1. I am very much indebted to Sayyid Sabah Abboud both for information about Tell Abada and for permission to publish plans from his excavations (figs. 1, 2).

a large oven, quantities of red ochre, and grinding stones on which the ochre had been prepared suggests the presence of a pottery workshop. Two rectangular courtyard houses with 12–14 rooms each were also excavated. Many infant urn burials were found in this level.

Level II was the best preserved (fig. 1). Eleven multiroomed building units, separated by streets and narrow lanes, were excavated. The buildings were tripartite and had T-shaped courtyards, clear precursors of the much later cruciform plan well known in the Eanna precinct at Warka. The largest house (fig. 2) had three tripartite units and a buttressed exterior wall. (The cross-wall in the central chamber was a later addition.) To the northeast was an enclosure wall. Since there appeared to be no access to this external "courtyard," it may represent some form of terracing at the rear of the house on the edge of the tell. (Extensive platforms, or terracing, have been discovered at Tell Abu Husaini, site 35.) To the southeast of the main house was an area of circular domed kilns similar to those known at an earlier period at Yarim Tepe I (Oates and Oates 1976a, p. 42). Only the foundations of Level I survived; the house plans closely followed those of Level III.

The painted pottery from Levels I and II at Tell Abada is richly decorated and resembles Ubaid 2/3 materials from Ras al Amiya and Choga Mami (below). A new feature in the Hamrin, however, was the presence of large quantities of incised pottery (fig. 5:14–16), in sherd form often superficially indistinguishable from Hassuna/Samarra. At Abada, incised and painted wares predominated over undecorated and occurred in roughly equal quantity. The Hamrin incised Ubaid is identical with that excavated long ago at Kudish Saghir and Nuzi, some 130 km to the northwest (Starr 1937, pls. 44–46). Similar pottery was also recovered in small quantity at Tepe Gawra (Level XIII) (Tobler 1950, p. 141). Another distinctive feature at Abada (and also at Tell Madhur, see below) was the presence of double-mouthed jars of a type known previously in Late Ubaid and Uruk contexts, for example, at Tepe Gawra (Level XIII). Tortoise vases were found at Abada and resembled those from Ras al Amiya. Also present were large numbers of Dalma impressed or "surfaced-manipulated" sherds (e.g., Hamlin 1975, pls. Ic, II), while Dalma painted ware occurred in Level II. Among the small finds were a number of bent-nail mullers; some were painted, and some had animal protomes.

Some 70 cm of sterile fill separate the earliest level at Abada (Level III) from Levels I and II, and its material culture is distinctively different. Among the pottery are both painted and incised types identical with the Choga Mami "Transitional," together with bowls indistinguishable from Ubaid 1 examples from Eridu, in particular from Levels XVI–XV. A number of vessels in the Hajji Muhammad style and a few Samarran-like sherds were also said to occur. This well-stratified association of Ubaid 1/2 with the so-called Transitional ceramic is of the very greatest importance and confirms the contemporaneity of the latter with early Ubaid, a chronological association tentatively proposed some years ago on the basis of the less unequivocal evidence from nearby Choga Mami (Oates 1969).

Also of chronological significance is the discovery of Late Halaf sherds among the Level II/I deposits, the largest quantity occurring in Level II. There is no Halaf occupation at Abada, nor was any Halaf material recovered from Level I, which is said to have been founded on virgin soil. Nor are there any Halaf sites in the eastern Hamrin, where Abada is situated (S.A. Jasim, pers. comm.). Thus the Level II/I Halaf sherds cannot have been accidentally brought onto the site in mud bricks or plaster made from earlier Halaf debris, either at Abada or at sites nearby. A similar association of Late Halaf and Ubaid 3 materials occurs at a number of Hamrin sites to the west of Abada, for example, at Kheit Qasim 3 (site 65), Tell Hasan (67), and Songor B (42). In this western area, however, marginally earlier Late Halaf levels are also found in which the Ubaid ceramic appears to be absent (e.g., Songor B, T. Hasan). The Hamrin Late Halaf, and indeed that at Choga Mami just to the south, includes large quantities of very fine polychrome vessels, i.e., we are not speaking of a ceramic type comparable to that discovered at Tepe Gawra XIX−XVII, which displays simply a mixture of Ubaid and Halaf features. It is quite clear that in the Hamrin at this time there were potters working in both the Halaf and Ubaid traditions, perhaps even side by side in the same villages. Certainly, the contemporaneity of these two very distinctive ceramic styles cannot be in doubt. Such contemporaneity has always seemed a possible explanation of certain chronological anomalies (Oates 1968, p. 13, 1973, p. 176) and is indeed the only explanation that makes sense of the Late Halaf "intrusion" at Choga Mami, where the Samarran and early Ubaid materials are very closely related. The modern situation may perhaps provide a relevant parallel, in that villages of Arabs, Kurds, Lurs, and Turcomans exist side by side, their inhabitants often distinguishable by their dress and other cultural appurtenances. In the Hamrin we have the first unequivocal evidence of such a situation in Near Eastern prehistory, where previously we had assumed a "chest-of-drawers" sequence of cultures.

Among the other Ubaid sites excavated in the Hamrin Basin is Tell Rashid (site 3), some 12 km south of Abada, also excavated by Sayyid Sabah Abboud. Four levels of Ubaid occupation were identified; pottery and house plans resemble those of Abada. A number of Late Halaf sherds were recovered from the uppermost level. At Kheit Qasim 3 there has been excavated an Ubaid house of unusually regular tripartite plan, with a cruciform central hall and side chambers very like those of the structure to the southeast of the largest Abada house (figs. 1 and 2). Here also the pottery generally resembles that from Abada and includes a number not only of Late Halaf but also of Dalma sherds.[2]

Tell Madhur (site 64) has been excavated by the British Archaeological Expedition in collaboration with the Royal Ontario Museum.[3] It is a low mound less than 100 m in diameter and 2.50 m in height and has two main periods of occupation, Late Ubaid and Early Dynastic I. Virgin soil was reached about 4 m below modern plain level; immediately above this is occupation of the Late Ubaid period (ca. Ubaid 4). One house is particularly well preserved (Level II) and its plan (fig. 3) is of interest. Like those at Abada and Kheit Qasim it is tripartite and has a cruciform central chamber, which at least at Madhur appears originally to have been roofed. The walls remain high enough to preserve external windows in several rooms; rooms 4/5 appear to have been a staircase, although no evidence for either an earthen ramp or fixings for stairs was observed (Roaf n.d.). Room 11 contained a large pot of carbonized grain, which has yielded a radiocarbon determination of 5570 ± 55 b.p. (BM−1458), calibrated after Clark (1975) to 4470 ± 80 B.C. (Killick and Roaf 1979, p. 542).

Large quantities of both incised and painted Ubaid pottery have been recovered from Madhur. The closest parallels of the painted ware lie with Tell Uqair (Lloyd and Safar 1943); flint-scraped bowls also occur at both sites. The incised ware, apparently absent at Uqair, resembles that from Abada. At Madhur, incised decoration occurs mainly on jars (fig. 5:14−16). The most common patterns are incised or gouged herringbone, or combed horizontal and wavy lines or dots; in general, these types closely parallel those illustrated from Kudish Saghir and Nuzi (Starr 1937, pls, 41:R, 44, 46). Cross-hatching is also found, as well as very occasional ribbed examples similar to Gawra nos. 218 and 220 (Tobler 1950).[4] No Halaf pottery was recovered. Although similar incised wares occur at Abada and Madhur, it is clear that Abada is much the earlier settlement.

A number of other sites in the Hamrin have yielded Ubaid pottery (cf. *Sumer* 35, 1979). Among these are Tell Abu Qasim just to the west of Kheit Qasim 3; Tell Rubeidha (site 69), on the west

---

2. I am very grateful to Jean-Daniel Forest for information about Kheit Qasim 3.

3. The excavations at Madhur were directed by Professor T. C. Young, Jr. and J.N. Postgate, with R.G. Killick and M.D. Roaf as field directors. I am indebted to them for permission to publish material from the site, and to Miss Jane Moon for information about the pottery.

4. Cf. also Tobler 1950, pl. LXXVIII:c; Oates 1968, pl. XL:17.

side of the Narin Chai, a tributary of the Diyala that flows along the eastern side of the Jebel; Tulul al Khubari (site 15); and Tell Ayyash (site 17), at which four major Ubaid building levels have so far been identified. At Tell Songor (site 42), near the remarkable site of Tell Gubba with its mazelike Early Dynastic I circular building, Japanese excavators have recovered Ubaid materials from three small mounds, designated A, B, and C (Matsumoto 1979). At Songor B, Late Halaf and early Ubaid 3 materials occur contemporaneously in Level 2, while Levels 3 and 4 have yielded Late Halaf only. In the uppermost level and at Songor C there is pottery reminiscent of Ras al Amiya, while Songor A is of interest because the earliest pottery closely resembles that from Transitional levels at Choga Mami (see below). Here, as at Tell Rihan (Gibson 1979), the closest parallels lie with the very end of the Samarran/beginning of the Transitional occupation at Choga Mami (Oates 1969, p. 121).[5] At Songor A, the house plans of this earliest phase (Matsumoto 1979, fig. 2), which lack the central T-shaped hall characteristic of the Hamrin Ubaid, also closely parallel Choga Mami (Oates 1969, pl. XXIV).

ARABIAN GULF UBAID

Among the most unexpected prehistoric discoveries of the last ten years was the identification of Ubaid 3/4 pottery in the Eastern Province of Saudi Arabia and subsequently in Bahrain and Qatar (Masry 1974; Burkholder and Golding 1970; Roaf 1974; de Cardi 1978; Oates 1976). Some 45 sites have now been found, most of them small, often with only a scatter of surface sherds and flints. Large numbers of aceramic sites with extensive lithic materials have also been identified, and it would appear that the Ubaid ceramic is intrusive, while the stone tools represent indigenous semi-nomadic hunter-collectors. The majority of the Ubaid sherds, painted and plain, tested by neutron activation analysis and by thin section, appear to derive from Sumer, while a contemporary coarse ware (Burkholder 1972, p. 268) differs significantly in both mineralogy and material treatment and is assumed to have been locally manufactured (Oates et al. 1977). Of the Ubaid sherds tested, over 50% can be shown to have come from Ur, Eridu, and Tell al Ubaid (Oates et al., figs. 3, 4).

In Saudi Arabia, soundings have been carried out by Dr. A. Masry (1974) at three of the four large mound sites. Settlement appears to have been both intermittent and impermanent. Nowhere is there evidence of occupation following the Ubaid phase, with the single exception of Al Markh (Bahrain). There, careful excavation has delineated a later phase, characterized by a shift to an aceramic fishing and herding (goats) economy; large numbers of stone tools were associated with the later occupation (Roaf 1974). An important implication of the Al Markh sequence is that not all of the Arabian aceramic flint sites are necessarily *pre*-Ubaid.

The earliest Ubaid sherds so far recovered from the western reaches of the Gulf are Hajji Muhammad in style but are diagnostically not necessarily earlier than Ras al Amiya (early Ubaid 3) (Masry 1974, figs. 18, 39:2; Oates 1976). Most of the Arabian Ubaid is late in style (Ubaid 3/4), while some, in particular that from Ras Abaruk (Qatar) and Al Markh, is possibly to be attributed to an as yet ill-defined "Terminal Ubaid" phase (below, p. 260; de Cardi 1978). On the Iranian side of the Gulf, however, Halilih, an Ubaid site on the Bushehr peninsula, has produced pottery of unequivocal Ubaid 2 attribution.[6] The surface pottery includes a variety of types identical with those from the type site and Eridu XIV–XII. Petrographic and thin-section analysis of sherds from the site, carried out by Dr. D. Kamilli, has revealed that some are possible imports while others show a local or non-Mesopotamian character (M. Prickett, pers. comm.). This is in sharp

5. I am very much indebted to Professor H. Fujii and other members of the Japanese Archaeological Expedition in Iraq for information about the Songor sites.

6. I must thank Miss Martha Prickett for unpublished information about the very interesting site of Halilih.

contrast to the evidence from the western shores of the Gulf, but unfortunately we know nothing of the nature of the Bushehr settlement. It should be noted in this context, however, that in the sixth millennium the sea level in the Gulf may have been significantly below its present level (Nützel 1978). As late as ca. 4900 bc the sea level was possibly still some 4 m below the modern shoreline, a situation that may have permitted a more southerly distribution of early Ubaid settlements than archeologists have so far been able to identify.

Choga Mami

The Mandali survey and subsequent season of excavation at Choga Mami (Oates 1966, 1968, 1969) extended the known range of Hajji Muhammad pottery some 150 km to the northeast of Ras al Amiya and provided the first evidence, albeit still ambiguous, of the relationship between Samarra and early Ubaid. A large number of Ubaid sherds were recovered from the surface of the mound of Choga Mami, together with a type later identified as "transitional," so designated because it displayed many characteristics in common both with the classical Samarran pottery that preceded it at the site and with the early Ubaid ceramic of the south (Oates 1969, 136–38). The Ubaid sherds included a number in the Ubaid 1 and Hajji Muhammad styles (fig. 6:5–13; see also Oates 1968, pl. IX, 1969, pl. XXXII:13, 14, 18) and many that could be attributed to Ubaid 3. Excavation of the site unfortunately revealed that the Ubaid levels had been heavily eroded, but one complete bowl and a single sherd of Ubaid 1 style were found in a Samarran context (Oates 1969, p. 138, pl. XXXII:1, 9); neutron activation and thin-section analysis showed the sherd to have been locally made (H. McKerrell, D. Kamilli, pers. comm.).

The latest levels found at the site were preserved in square J6, owing to the presence nearby of a substantial "guard tower" (illustrated in Mellink and Filip, pls. 77, 78a). Here, five sherds of the most characteristic Hajji Muhammad bowl type (fig. 6:11, 12) were recovered from the uppermost, unsealed deposits of Level 10 (Oates 1969, p. 127, pl. XXIII). In J6, also, was found a well from which a large quantity of Late Halaf pottery was recovered; the well had been dug from a level now lost, suggesting at least the possibility that this Late Halaf material postdated Hajji Muhammad, an observation now confirmed by recent work in the Hamrin. Levels 8 and 9 in squares J6 and J5 yielded pottery of the Transitional type. At the time of the latest level (10), the buildings associated with Levels 8 and 9 had collapsed or been demolished and the area in which they had stood had become an open space with a succession of trodden surfaces. Pottery from this deposit represented the latest stratified Transitional material and afforded the closest parallels with early Ubaid designs, in particular with Eridu levels XVIII–XVI. Similar pottery has been found in Khuzistan at Chagha Sefid (Level 5) and Chogha Mish ("archaic 3") — indeed, many sherds from these sites are indistinguishable — *preceding* deposits of the Sabz Phase (= Sefid 6), which is often equated with Ubaid 1 in Sumer (Hole 1977). As we have already noted, however, the new evidence from Abada confirms our earlier impression from Choga Mami that Ubaid 1 must be at least partially contemporary with the Transitional Phase (= Sefid 5) and must, therefore, predate Sabz (see also Oates 1960, p. 43).

Although the Choga Mami Transitional provides an absolute chronological link between prehistoric Mesopotamia and Khuzistan, we remain uncertain about the true nature of this apparent "transition" from Samarra to Ubaid. It is possible that this material characterizes a purely regional development, representing no more than some degree of contact between potters of Sumer and of central Mesopotamia at this time. Indeed one of the most interesting features of the Choga Mami painted wares is the internal consistency of the potting tradition throughout the Samarran and Ubaid occupation of the site. Some 70 sherds have been analyzed by petrographic thin section by Dr. Diana Kamilli; she reports that although very different kinds of mineral assemblages and technologies were being used at the site simultaneously for different ware types, the same technological tradition was maintained with respect to both material and treatment for the Samarran, Transitional, and Ubaid *painted* wares. This implies a continuity of ceramic tradition at the site that is attested also by stylistic features. The Halaf technology, on the other hand, differs from all the rest.

Generalizations on Choga Mami Ware Types

Mineral Assemblages	*Ware Types*	
Black on buff painted		
Na feldspar	Ubaid 2/3	
Quartz and chert	Transitional	Painted
Simple Fe paint	Samarran	
Rare calcite		
Less than 5% sherd temper		
No chaff, sherd temper		
Halaf painted		
Halaf painted + calcite	Halaf	
5% temper		
No chaff		
Unpainted ware		
Na plagioclase	Unpainted Samarran	
Calcite, quartz, chert	Unpainted Transitional	
Variable % temper	Incised Samarran	
No chaff		
Unpainted ware		
Trace plagioclase, quartz, chert	Coarse Samarran	
Much calcite	Coarse Transitional	
Chaff		

SOURCE: Data from D. Kamilli.

In this context the presence of some Transitional-like material in Sumer should be noted, in particular at Warka survey site 298 where it was found together with some very characteristic Ubaid 1 types, with which it is presumably contemporary (Adams and Nissen 1972). Another small site near Warka (Adams 1975) yielded a group of surface sherds having a surprisingly limited repertoire which seems in general to correspond to the simplest varieties of the Transitional ceramic.[7] A single Transitional sherd has been published along with other surface materials from Tell Oueili (Huot 1971, fig. 2:2), while the small site of Qirawi near Badra has also produced surface sherds of this central Mesopotamian style (Hrouda 1973, fig. 2).

In square 015 at Choga Mami a second well was excavated. This proved to contain Ubaid pottery remarkably like that from Ras al Amiya. Several Transitional sherds were also found, but in general the pottery appears to constitute an essentially homogeneous collection. Figures 4, 5, and 7 illustrate the full range of pottery recovered from this deposit, with the exception of three Hajji Muhammad bowls published in the preliminary report (Oates 1969, pl. XXXII:15–17). As at Ras al Amiya, some of the pottery resembles types found at the site of Hajji Muhammad, but

7. Adams and Nissen 1972, fig. 66:5, and Adams 1975, fig 1:i, are typically Ubaid 1; nos. 8 and 11 (1972) resemble Transitional types. Very general parallels for the remainder of the pottery illustrated in Adams 1975, fig. 1, can be found at both Choga Mami and Eridu.

there is an admixture of what appear stylistically to be later Ubaid types. However, the contemporaneity of these superficially diverse styles is well established at Ras al Amiya.

Among the most distinctive Choga Mami types are fine, carinated bowls of a variety known in Ubaid 2 levels at Eridu, where they constitute the most common single type in Levels XII—X (fig. 4:1—5, 7, fig. 7:1; Lloyd and Safar 1948, type 20; Ras al Amiya type 11). The decoration on the Choga Mami bowls resembles that found on bell-shaped examples from Arpachiyah (Mallowan and Rose 1935, fig. 29) and Gawra XIX—XVII, but the carinated type of Ras al Amiya and Choga Mami would appear, on the basis of the sequence at Eridu, to be the earlier. The latter are also generally finer in quality. Similar sherds have been found at Songor and at Abada, though no complete examples have been recovered from the latter site. Lugged jars are also common on the Mandali and Hamrin sites; they are not recorded at Hajji Muhammad and only one example is reported from the Ubaid 2 levels at Eridu. Ledge-rim jars are found at Eridu (infrequently, but throughout the Ubaid sequence, Lloyd and Safar 1948, p. 124), Ras al Amiya, and Hajji Muhammad; this type is not represented in the relatively small quantity of pottery recovered from the Choga Mami well, but it does occur among surface materials at the site, often decorated with Hajji Muhammad designs (fig. 6:5). Among the most distinctive decorative patterns found on the Choga Mami well pottery is the pendant loop ornament seen on figure 5:12 and figure 7:9. Identical examples as well as variations of this pattern occur at Hajji Muhammad, Ras al Amiya (type 15), and Eridu, Levels XIII—XI. A denticulated pattern of small triangles along the top of the rim (fig. 5:6—9) is also found in Levels XIII—XI at Eridu and at Hajji Muhammad (Ziegler 1953, pl. 12). At Choga Mami such ornament is often found on deep oval dishes that have incised patterns in the base (fig. 5:6; fig. 8). Another very distinctive Hajji Muhammad bowl type (Ziegler 1953, pls. 34:k, 28:d) is found both at Choga Mami (fig. 7:8) and Ras al Amiya (Stronach 1961, pl. XLIV:5). Petrographic thin-section analysis indicates that these strikingly identical bowls were locally made at both Ras al Amiya and Choga Mami. Several sherds of "tortoise vases" were recovered from the Choga Mami well; these, too, were local products. Such vessels occur also in the Hamrin, e.g., in the graves at Songor A and at Kheit Qasim and Tell Ayyash. At both Choga Mami and Ras al Amiya some of the finest pottery (e.g., the bowls of figs. 4 and 7:8, 9) was undoubtedly thrown on some type of potter's wheel.

A new feature of Ubaid decorative technique found at Choga Mami was the use of incised ornament, referred to above, in the base of deep, often oval, bowls (fig. 5:6; fig. 8). A few examples are said to have been found at Abada, and one is illustrated from Kudish Saghir near Nuzi (Starr 1937, pl. 45:B). Similar incised bases occur among the Ubaid materials from Songor (Matsumoto, pers. comm.), and the type is known also at Kheit Qasim 3 (J.-D. Forest, pers. comm.). No identifiable sherds of the more Samarran-like, Ubaid-incised pottery identified at Madhur, Abada, and Nuzi have been found so far at Choga Mami or, indeed, at Songor. A few specimens, however, have been recovered from the surface at Serik, a small site near Choga Mami, where the Ubaid materials generally display many parallels with Abada (fig. 7:11; also Oates 1968, pls. V, XI).[8] Several examples of Dalma impressed ware have also been found at Serik (Oates 1968, pl. V:4); such pottery is so far unknown at Choga Mami.

At both Choga Mami and Ras al Amiya, identical sherds of a handmade straw-tempered ware have been found (Stronach 1961, pp. 121—2; Oates 1969, p. 139). Most of these sherds have been treated with a red slip on both exterior and interior surfaces; many of them are burnished. The

---

8. It should be noted that a sherd from Serik, mistakenly identified as Hassuna (Oates 1968, pl. V:7), should now probably be attributed to the Ubaid incised tradition; ceramic analysis shows it to have been locally made. The discovery of Ubaid incised pottery in the Hamrin also suggests that the earlier identification of the site of Imnethir, north of Mandali, as Hassuna (Oates 1968, 1, n.2) must now be considered doubtful.

surfaces often appear pitted, owing to the burning out of chaff (fig. 7, lower right); the cores sometimes remain unoxidized; and firing clouds occur on the undecorated fragments. The interior surfaces of the larger, undecorated vessels are often rough and gritty. Several examples at both sites bear almost identical vertical patterns of zigzag lines (fig. 6:2–4, fig. 7: lower right); on some examples the edges of the pattern have blurred when fired. Identical sherds were found at Songor C, Level 1, and Songor B, Level 2 (Matsumoto, pers. comm.).

Dr. Diana Kamilli has examined the sherd mineralogy of eight examples of this ware from Choga Mami and four from Ras al Amiya. The results "show a remarkable uniformity of mineralogy, paste texture and paint treatment. The sherd and chaff content (temper) and the tendency to burnish the surface paint and slip mark these sherds as alien to both sites." Clearly, these are imported sherds and their source must be Iran, but I have been unable to find an exact parallel for the very distinctive ornament. The decorated examples of this type from Choga Mami come from the Ubaid well and from unsealed deposits in square H7. Plain red-ware sherds were also discovered in the Halaf well, and a single fragment was found in Level 6 of the water-channel section (Oates 1969, p. 127). One surface example comes from a carinated bowl of a shape characteristic of Tepe Guran (Mortensen 1964, fig. 16:h).

Another discovery from the Ubaid well at Choga Mami is of considerable chronological significance. Three rim sherds, including the complete spout, of a hole-mouth, trough-spouted vessel of a type known from the Mehmeh Phase at Tepe Sabz were found (Mehmeh red-on-red ware, Hole, Flannery, and Neely 1969, fig. 66:a). At Tepe Sabz, three spouted examples are reported in early Mehmeh levels (ibid., p. 165), and the type generally is confined to the Mehmeh Phase, thus providing a very specific synchronism with Ubaid Mesopotamia. Also from the Ubaid well is a lugged vessel (fig. 6:1), handmade in an orange-buff fabric with an orange-red slip, a ware otherwise unknown at Mandali and presumably another Iranian import.

Among the small finds from the Ubaid well are pierced pottery discs and mullers showing definite signs of wear on the rubbing surface as did comparable specimens from Ras al Amiya (Stronach 1961, p. 107). Such objects first appear in Eridu XII. Some chipped stone material was also recovered; this has been published by Peder Mortensen (1973).

OTHER MANDALI SITES AND LOCAL CHRONOLOGY

Of some 20 sites surveyed north of Mandali, seven, including Choga Mami and Serik, have yielded Ubaid surface materials (Oates 1966; Oates and Oates 1976b, fig. 4). One of the most interesting small sites (6a), situated between Serik and Tamerkhan, produced pottery predominantly in the Hajji Muhammad style (Oates 1968, p. 10, pl. IX:23–27). At Koma Sang, to the east of Choga Mami, Iranian black-on-red ware sherds, comparable to those from Ras al Amiya, Songor, and Choga Mami, were also found.

At Choga Mami it is unfortunate that erosion of the site has destroyed all evidence of the stratigraphic relationships between the Halaf well material, the Hajji Muhammad pottery found both on the surface and in unsealed deposits, and the Ubaid well material, which is clearly contemporary with Ras al Amiya and very approximately with Eridu XII/XI. No Hajji Muhammad sherds have occurred within the earlier transitional levels excavated so far, and no Transitional sherds have been found so far at the small Hajji Muhammad site (Mandali survey 6a), situated less than 2 km from Choga Mami. But it remains uncertain whether any of the Hajji Muhammad pottery discovered in Mandali, or indeed the Hamrin, is earlier than the end of Ubaid 2 or even the beginning of Ubaid 3, as defined at Eridu, by which time this style appears to have been common in central Mesopotamia. However, the presence of some sherds of Ubaid 1 type at Choga Mami (e.g. fig. 6:7–9), together with the stylistic similarities between the Choga Mami Transitional and Eridu XVIII–XVI and the presence at Abada III of bowls very like examples from Eridu XVI–XV, does suggest an earlier connection with the south.

The contemporaneity of early Ubaid 3, as identified at Ras al Amiya and Choga Mami, and the early Mehmeh phase in Khuzistan seems reasonably established. The relationship between Choga Mami and Abada is less certain; the presence there of incised sherds of a type so far unknown at Choga Mami or at Songor but present at the later sites of Serik and Madhur would suggest that Choga Mami is the earlier of the two. Nonetheless, there remain many similarities among the painted wares of Ras al Amiya, Abada, Songor, and Choga Mami, and the Ubaid occupation of all four cannot have been far apart in time. The partial contemporaneity of the late phase of Halaf found in the Hamrin and early Ubaid 3 seems also beyond question. It is conceivable, therefore, that the Halaf well pottery at Choga Mami may even postdate the Ubaid materials from the second well (pace Oates 1972, p. 50).

UBAID CHRONOLOGY

Unfortunately, no site among those excavated in the past thirty years has provided a lengthy prehistoric sequence. Eridu and Tepe Gawra remain the only effective points of reference for fifth millennium Mesopotamia, and Eridu remains unpublished. Although Ubaid 1 and 2 appear reasonably well delineated at Eridu, and the transition to Ubaid 3 is fairly clear at Ras al Amiya and Choga Mami, chronological differentiation between later Ubaid materials remains virtually unestablished. To some extent this is a factor of the regional variation noted, for example, in the Hamrin and at Tell Uqair, but the apparent absence at Eridu of any Terminal Ubaid assemblage (Woolley's Ur-Ubaid III; cf. Oates 1960, pp. 41–42, 1976, p. 28) and the lack of significant stratification among the Late Ubaid materials recovered from the various soundings at Warka leave much uncertainty about the attribution of even the most distinctive Late Ubaid types. Among these are the type fossils used to distinguish Ubaid 4 in the Warka survey (Adams and Nissen 1972, p. 99),[9] a simply decorated dish with flattened inverted rim, and open bowls with incised "combing" in the base (e.g., Woolley 1956, pl. 17). Such types are common in both the Eanna and Anu precinct soundings at Warka, along with a distinctive low-necked jar decorated with simple horizonal bands of paint (Boehmer 1972, pl. 57, top). Such types occur also at Oueili[10] but are so far unknown in the Hamrin. Neither this particular jar type nor the comb-incised bowls appear to be represented at Eridu, where by far the most common Ubaid 4 bowl type is the "soup plate" known also at Ur (aU.4; Eridu type 5, Lloyd and Safar 1948). At Warka the Ubaid ceramic is found in association with some apparently Uruk types, e.g., occasional red or grey sherds and Uruk-like spouts (*UVB* IV, p. 37; Boehmer 1972); painted sherds are in a minority: Whether the Warka Ubaid represents a regional variation within Ubaid 4 or a post-Eridu Terminal Ubaid remains to be determined, but the fact that these Warka types are characteristic of the two latest Ubaid sites in the Gulf (Ras Abaruk and Al Markh)[11] suggests at least the possibility of chronological rather than regional differentiation. Excavation at Oueili may eventually answer this question. Radiocarbon determinations, regrettably, tell us little, although the new results from Oueili correlate well with the single sample from Warka. A close examination of figure 9, however, reveals that, in general, recently run samples, such as those from Madhur and Arpachiyah (BM-1531), yield relatively later determinations than, for example, those from Uqair, Gawra, and Arpachiyah, tested many years ago. Indeed, the two groups of dates fail to provide any reliable basis for comparison.

9. It should be noted also that both double rims and the sunburst pattern continue well into Ubaid 3 (pace Adams and Nissen 1972, p. 98).

10. I should like to thank Jean-Louis Huot for information about the second season at Tell el Oueili and for permission to publish the radiocarbon determinations from the site (to be published in *Syria* 1981).

11. A black-painted rim sherd from Al Markh, similar to the Warka type and discovered in the first season, comes from a shallow bowl that was certainly made on a fast wheel.

The relationship between the Mesopotamian Ubaid and various assemblages in Iran remains far from clear; the radiocarbon determinations are equally uninformative. The archeological data from Choga Mami provide two unequivocal synchronisms with the Deh Luran sequence, while the presence of Dalma "surface-manipulated" pottery at Abada, Kheit Qasim, and Serik confirms an Ubaid 3 attribution for at least some of this material. It should be emphasized that Abada II/I was not a settlement of long duration, and that here the association of Ubaid 3, Late Halaf, and Dalma pottery is beyond question. The association of Ubaid and Dalma impressed wares has also been noted in the Mahidasht plain, Iran (Levine and McDonald 1977, p. 43). The two Dalma-period radiocarbon determinations (fig. 9), both falling just before 4000 bc seem late, especially if the association of Dalma with Ubaid in Mesopotamia is "confined to the end of the 5th millennium," as would appear to have been the case in the Kangavar valley (Levine and McDonald 1977, p. 45). Moreover, a date of ca. 4000 bc for the association of Dalma with Late Halaf and Ubaid 3 in the Hamrin, though reasonable in relation to the Madhur date, cannot be reconciled with the more numerous samples from Oueili, which must derive at the earliest from the end of Ubaid 4. Such a date would also leave a gap of a thousand years between Late Halaf and the recent determination from Arpachiyah, which comes from a level some 2.5 m below TT 10 but still 2 m above virgin soil[12] (4980 ± 60 bc, end of Period 2, beginning of Period 3; ca. Level IX, Hijara 1978, p. 127); the latter date, however, accords well with Choga Mami and recent dates from Sawwan.

The most important synchronism between Choga Mami and Khuzistan involves the contemporaneity of the post-Samarran Transitional levels at the former site with Chagha Sefid Phase 5. This places the Choga Mami Transitional and by implication Ubaid 1, if not also early Ubaid 2, *before* the Sabz Phase (Chagha Sefid Phase 6, Susiana a) (see above). A reasonable assumption is that Samarran material in Mesopotamia should therefore be contemporary with Chagha Sefid 4 (Surkh Phase) (Hole 1977, p. 27). However, Samarran levels would also appear to be at least partially contemporary with the earlier Phase 3; at least the painted and incised vessel attributed to this phase at Chagha Sefid is unquestionably Samarran, not Hassunan (Hole 1977, fig. 51:d, g). Unfortunately, many of the most characteristically Mesopotamian sherds from Chagha Sefid are catalogued as "out of context," and one is therefore unable to examine what may be their real stratigraphic distribution. A single example of red-on-cream ware (Sefid Phase 3) found near Choga Mami confirms the connection between Mandali and Deh Luran already at this time.[13]

An examination of the radiocarbon determinations from the two areas, in the context of these relationships, reveals serious discrepancies. The most recent Samarran determinations from Mesopotamia (Sawwan, Level III) cluster very convincingly around 5000 bc (R. Burleigh, pers. comm.).[14] The *latest* Sefid-Phase determinations from C. Sefid and the single Surkh-Phase sample yield dates of ca. 6000 bc (Hole 1977, p. 25). This is in line with the seemingly dubious Samarran dates from highland Shemshara (Oates 1972, n. 8) but is far too early by comparison with determinations from lowland Mesopotamian sites such as Tell es-Sawwan and Choga Mami. Unfortunately, there are no Iranian dates for C. Sefid Phase 5 (C. Mami Transitional), but all three Khazineh-Phase determinations from Tepe Sabz, which are stratigraphically later than Sefid 5, in fact lie roughly contemporary with or chronologically earlier than the Choga Mami Transitional and Samarran dates from Mesopotamia, clearly an impossibility.

The contemporaneity of Mehmeh and Ubaid 3 is certainly established, and the Mehmeh C[14] determination of 4520 ± 20 bc seems reasonable both in relation to the cluster of Bayat dates and

12. I am grateful to Sayyid Ismail Hijara for information about his recent excavations at Arpachiyah and for permission to publish the new radiocarbon determination from the site.

13. I am indebted to Professor Frank Hole for the identification of this sherd.

14. I would like to thank Sayyid Walid Yasin al-Tikriti for permission to publish these radiocarbon determinations of samples excavated by him at Tell es-Sawwan.

to recent determinations from Oueili that cannot be earlier than Ubaid 4. Yet on the basis of Mesopotamian dates this correlation leaves little room for Ubaid 2 unless the latter is at least partially contemporary with the Choga Mami Transitional (which on the evidence from the latter site is certainly possible), or for the Sabz and Khazineh Phases in Khuzistan, which precede the Mehmeh Phase yet must be later than the Choga Mami Transitional (Sefid 5). At the other end of the scale, a Bayat—Ubaid 4 correlation seems not unreasonable; indeed, as figure 9 shows clearly, the recent Oueili determinations are closely comparable to those of Bayat attribution from Tepe Sabz. Current correlations of Ubaid 4 in Mesopotamia with Susa A in Khuzistan (Dyson 1965, pp. 222—23; Wright et al. 1975; Weiss 1977, p. 351) are lacking in conviction, while in Khuzistan itself there is little real evidence for the relationship between Susiana d (?Bayat) and Susa A. In this context it is particularly unfortunate that no Susiana materials have been found at Susa and that the later Susiana phases are absent at Jaffarabad, where Susa A is well represented (Dollfus 1971, 1975, 1978). Certainly there is no convincing argument for equating Susa A with Ubaid 4, and the Susa A radiocarbon determinations from Jaffarabad cluster convincingly around 3200 bc, which is significantly later than any Ubaid date from Mesopotamia. It is true that Susa A displays many parallels with Gawra XII (Le Breton 1957, pp. 91—94; Dyson 1965, pp. 222—23), but the precise attribution of Gawra XII within the Mesopotamian sequence is a matter for debate. Here many non-Ubaid traits appear, and there is a "notable increase in undecorated pottery" (Tobler 1950, p. 147). A new type of pottery appears, "sprig ware," which occurs on some sites to the west, apparently without associated Ubaid wares (e.g., Sinjar site YK 131, where a number of Uruk sherds were also found among the surface materials). Both Tell-i-Ghazir and Susa reveal the presence of a transitional stage between Susa A and Early Uruk as defined by the very inadequate material recovered from Eanna Levels XIII—XII (Dyson 1965, p. 223; Weiss 1977), but we have already seen that the precise attribution of the earlier levels in Eanna is far from certain. At the same time, the early Uruk content of the Deh Luran Terminal Ubaid can clearly be seen in the seal from Sargarab (Wright et al. 1975, p. 137); indeed, the beaded-rim bowls and cable ornament associated with this phase in Khuzistan are characteristic of Uruk levels in Mesopotamia (e.g., Hijara 1972, pl. 14). Basic to these problems is the fact that the *early* Uruk sequence in Mesopotamia remains undefined, while no radiocarbon determinations are available to establish the relative time spans of pre-Uruk IV materials in either Mesopotamia or Khuzistan. Terminal Ubaid and Early Uruk require better definition before these difficulties can be resolved.

Clearly, there is no reason to suppose that ceramically defined archeological periods are likely to be of equivalent length either in the same or separate regions, and the recent evidence from the Hamrin confirms the view that phase by phase "chest-of-drawers" chronologies can no longer be sustained. Nonetheless, there remains little doubt that there are very basic discrepancies between the prehistoric Iranian and the Mesopotamian radiocarbon determinations and that in general the Khuzistan dates lie consistently earlier than those from Mesopotamia, at least in the sixth millennium bc. At the same time, however, recently determined Mesopotamian dates remain reasonably consistent within themselves.

CONCLUSIONS

Recent fieldwork has demonstrated clear regional variation among the pottery styles of Ubaid Mesopotamia and has provided useful chronological data. It has also reinforced the impression of cultural unity throughout the country at this time. The Hamrin excavations have added enormously to our knowledge of village life of the period. Yet chronology continues to present apparently insuperable problems, and, even more important, we remain largely ignorant of the real level of fifth millennium social and economic development. One of the most striking features of Ubaid Mesopotamia is the sheer extent of its influence, yet we remain uncertain what this

				Susa A	?
	TERMINAL UBAID				
		?	?		
		Oueili			
	UBAID 4	Madhur, Uqair		Bayat	
					?
	UBAID 3	Abada (Dalma, Late Halaf IVB)		Mehmeh	(4520 b.c.)
		Choga Mami Ubaid, Ras al Amiya			
		(Yarim Tepe II, period IVA)		Khazineh	
?	UBAID 2				
				Sabz (Sefid 6)	
		(Arpachiyah II/III, 4980 b.c.)			
		Abada Level III		Sefid 5	
		C.M. Transitional (4896 b.c.)			
	UBAID 1	?		Sefid 4 (Surkh Phase)	
		?			
		Samarra			
		(Sawwan III 5080 b.c.)			
				Sefid 3 (6090/6050 b.c.)	

"expansion" means in human terms. Indeed, we cannot even explain the widespread occurrence of identical yet locally manufactured pottery. Who set the fashion? Were there itinerant potters? The evidence at Choga Mami would suggest that there were not. Was there, then, an ancient equivalent of the Sears Roebuck catalogue?

There are hints in the archeological data of growing economic — possibly even "political" — authority, for example, in the association of seal impressions with a Gawra XIII temple, perhaps already suggesting the economic functions of such "religious" institutions; in the increasing size of settlement, implying a need for more formal "political" controls; and in the continuing contact, apparently by sea, with distant parts of the Gulf. Indeed, the evidence indirectly implies an advancement of society that is otherwise ill documented. Until a major Ubaid site is extensively excavated, however, we shall remain in ignorance of such more developed facets of Ubaid life.

Some of our ignorance reflects no more than lack of excavation. For example, little metal has been recovered from Ubaid sites, yet we know that smelting technology was known at the time of Çatal Hüyük and Yarim Tepe I, while the model shaft hole axes of Ubaid Uqair (Lloyd and Safar 1943, pl. XVIII: 2, 5, 7) confirm the presence of cast prototypes by this time. Some metal objects have been found at Abada, and tests now being carried out will certainly add to our knowledge of Ubaid technology. But most of our ignorance unfortunately stems from a basic fact of life in Mesopotamian archeology — that major prehistoric sites tend to be situated in well-endowed or strategic locations where, for these reasons, settlement often persisted for millennia. The overburden of later material at such sites makes lateral excavation of their early levels both a physical and a financial impossibility. Until the day when such a site is extensively excavated we shall undoubtedly continue to underestimate the achievements of the people whose activities almost certainly provided the initial stimulus to the growth of Sumerian society.

BIBLIOGRAPHY

Abboud, Sabah
    1979   Tell 'Abada. *Sumer* 35:525—29.
Abu al-Soof, B.
    1970   Mounds in the Rania plain and excavations at Tell Basmusian (1956). *Sumer* 26:65—104.
Adams, R. McC.
    1975   An early prehistoric site in the Warka region. *Sumer* 31:11—15.
Adams, R. McC., and Nissen, H.J.
    1972   *The Uruk countryside.* Chicago: University of Chicago Press.
Boehmer, R.
    1972   Die Keramikfunde im Bereich des Steingebäudes. In *Vorläufige Bericht über die von
                dem Deutschen Archäologischen Institut und der Deutschen Orient—Gesellschaft aus
                mitteln der Deutschen Forschungsgemeinschaft unternommenen Ausgrabungen in
                Uruk-Warka 1968 und 1969,* vol. 26/27, pp. 31—42. Berlin: Mann.
Burkholder, G.
    1972   Ubaid sites and pottery in Saudi Arabia. *Archaeology* 25:264—69.
Burkholder, G., and Golding, M.
    1970   A surface survey of Al-'Ubaid sites in the eastern province of Saudi Arabia. Third
                International Conference on Asian Archaeology [Bahrain, 1970].
Canal, D.
    1978   La haute terrasse de l'acropole de Suse. *Paléorient* 4:169—76.
Clark, R.M.
    1975   A calibration curve for radiocarbon dates. *Antiquity* 49:251—66.
de Cardi, B.
    1978   *Qatar archaeological report.* Oxford: Oxford University Press.
Dollfus, G.
    1971   Les fouilles à Djaffarabad de 1969 à 1971. *Cahiers de la Délégation Archéologique
                Française en Iran* 1:17—162.
    1975   Les fouilles à Djaffarabad de 1972 à 1974. *Cahiers de la Délégation Archéologique
                Française en Iran* 5:11—222.
    1978   Djaffarabad, Djowi, Bendebal: contribution à l'étude de la Susiane au Ve millénaire et au
                debut du IVe millénaire. *Paléorient* 4:141—67.
Dyson, R.H. Jr.
    1965   Problems in the relative chronology of Iran 6000—2000 B.C. In *Chronologies in old world
                archaeology,* ed. R. W. Ehrich, pp. 215—56. Chicago: University of Chicago Press.
Gibson, McG.
    1979   Chicago-Copenhagen excavations at Uch Tepe, Hamrin. *Sumer* 35:459—67.
Goff, C.L.
    1971   Luristan before the Iron Age. *Iran* 9:131—51.
Hamlin, C.
    1975   Dalma Tepe. *Iran* 13:111—27.
Hijara, I.
    1972   Excavations at Tell Qalinj Agha (Erbil): fourth season 1970. *Sumer* 29:13—34. (Arabic
                section.)

1978   Three new graves at Arpachiyah. *World Archaeology* 10:125−28.

n.d.   *The Halaf Period in Northern Mesopotamia.* Ph.D. dissertation, Institute of Archaeology, University of London.

Hole, F.
1977   *Studies in the archaeological history of the Deh Luran plain: the excavation of Choga Sefid.* Memoirs of the Museum of Anthropology, University of Michigan, no. 9. Ann Arbor: University of Michigan.

1978   The comparative stratigraphy of the early prehistoric periods in Khuzistan. *Paléorient* 4:229−32.

Hole, F.; Flannery, K.V.; and Neely, J.A.
1969   *Prehistory and human ecology of the Deh Luran plain.* Memoirs of the Museum of Anthropology, University of Michigan, no. 9. Ann Arbor: University of Michigan Press.

Hrouda, B.
1973   Ruinbesichtigung im Südostlichen Iraq. *Baghdader Mitteilungen* 6:7−18.

Huot, J.-L.
1971   Tell El Oueili. *Sumer* 27:45−58.

Huot, J.-L.; Bachelot, L.; Braun, J.P.; Calvet, Y.; Cleuzion, S.; Forest, J.D.; Seigne, J.
1978   Larsa: rapport préliminaire VIIe campagne et la première campagne à Tell el 'Oueili (1976). *Syria* 55:183−223.

Killick, R., and Roaf, M.
1979   Excavations at Tell Madhur. *Sumer* 35:530−42.

Le Breton, L.
1957   The early periods at Susa: Mesopotamian relations. *Iraq* 12:79−124.

Levine, L.D., and McDonald, M.M.A.
1977   The Neolithic and Chalcolithic periods in the Mahidasht. *Iran* 15:39−50.

Lloyd, S., and Safar, F.
1943   Tell Uqair. *Journal of Near Eastern Studies* 2:131−58.
1948   Eridu. *Sumer* 4:115−27.

Mallowan, M.E.L., and Rose, J.C.
1935   Prehistoric Assyria: the excavations at Tall Arpachiyah. *Iraq* 2(1):1−178.

Matsumoto, K.
1979   Tell Songor A, B, and C. *Sumer* 35:521−24.

Mellink, M.J., and Filip, J.
1974   (eds.) *Frühe Stufen der Kunst.* Propyläen Kunstgeschichte, vol. 13. Berlin: Propyläen.

Mortensen, P.
1964   Early village-farming occupation: excavations at Tepe Guran, Luristan. *Acta Archaeologica* 34:110−21.

1973   A sequence of Samarran flint and obsidian tools from Choga Mami. *Iraq* 35:37−55.

Nützel, W.
1978   To which depths are "prehistorical civilizations" to be found beneath the present alluvial plains of Mesopotamia? *Sumer* 34:17−26.

Oates, D., and Oates, J.
1976a   *The rise of civilization.* Oxford: Elsevier-Phaidon.
1976b   Early irrigation agriculture in Mesopotamia. In *Problems in economic and social archaeology,* ed. G. de G. Sieveking, I.H. Longworth, and K.E. Wilson, pp. 109−35. London: Duckworth.

Oates, J.
    1960   Ur and Eridu: the prehistory, *Iraq* 22:32−50.
    1966   Survey in the region of Mandali and Badra. *Sumer* 22:51−60.
    1968   Prehistoric investigations near Mandali, Iraq. *Iraq* 30:1−20.
    1969   Choga Mami 1967−68: a preliminary report. *Iraq* 31:115−52.
    1972   A radiocarbon date from Choga Mami. *Iraq* 34:49−53.
    1973   The background and development of early farming communities in Mesopotamia and the Zagros. *Proceedings of the Prehistoric Society* 39:147−81.
    1976   Prehistory in northeastern Arabia. *Antiquity* 50:20−31.

Oates, J.; Davidson, T.E.; Kamilli, D.; and McKerrell, H.
    1977   Seafaring merchants of Ur? *Antiquity* 51:221−34.

Pézard, M.
    1914   *Mission à Bender-Bouchir.* Mémoires de la Délégation en Perse, vol. 15. Paris: Leroux.

Roaf, M.
    1974   Excavations at Al Markh, Bahrain. *Paléorient* 2:499−501.
    n.d.   Excavations at Tell Madhur: the results of the third season.

Schmidt, J.
    1972   Steingebäude. In *Vorläufige Bericht über die von dem Deutschen Archäologischen Institut und der Deutschen Orient-Gesellschaft aus mitteln der Deutschen Forschungsgemeinschaft unternommenen Ausgrabungen in Uruk-Warka 1968−1969,* vol. 26/27, pp. 18−29. Berlin: Gebr. Mann.
    1974   Zwei Tempel der Obēd−Zeit in Uruk. *Baghdader Mitteilungen* 7:173−87.
    1978   Tell Mismar: ein prähistorischer Fundort im Südiraq. *Baghdader Mitteilungen* 9:10−17.

Starr, R.F.S.
    1937,   *Nuzi: report on the excavations at Yorgan Tepa near Kirkuk, Iraq, 1927−1931.* Cambridge, Mass.: Harvard University Press.
    1939

Stronach, D.
    1961   The excavations at Ras al' Amiya. *Iraq* 23:95−137.

Weiss, H.
    1977   Periodization, population and early state formation in Khuzistan. In *Mountains and lowlands: essays in the archaeology of greater Mesopotamia,* ed. L.D. Levine and T.C. Young, Jr., pp. 347−69. Bibliotheca Mesopotamica: Primary Sources and Interpretive Analyses for the Study of Mesopotamian Civilization and its Influence from Late Prehistory to the End of the Cuneiform Tradition, vol. 7. Malibu: Undena Publications.

Woolley, Sir Leonard
    1956   *The early periods: a report on the sites and objects prior in date to the Third Dynasty of Ur discovered in the course of excavations.* Ur Excavations, vol. 4. Philadelphia: American Philosophical Society.

Wright, H.
    1969   Tepe Farukhabad. *Iran* 7:172−73.

Wright, H.T.; Neely, J.A.; Johnson, G.A.; and Speth, J.
    1975   Early fourth millennium developments in southwestern Iran. *Iran* 13:129−48.

Ziegler, C.
    1953   *Die Keramik von der Qal'a des Ḫaǧǧi Mohammad.* Ausgrabungen der Deutschen Forschungsgemeinschaft in Uruk-Warka, vol. 5. Berlin: Gebr. Mann.

CATALOGUE OF FIGURES

FIGURE 4. POTTERY FROM THE UBAID WELL, CHOGA MAMI

1. Open bowl, incomplete. Ht. 5.7 cm, rim dia. ca. 13 cm (possibly oval). Fine, hard, grey-green paste and wash, fine grit temper, surface pared. Shape common in Ubaid 2/early 3. Batch 256, uppermost well deposit.

2. Open bowl, incomplete. Ht. 6.3 cm, rim dia. 17.2 cm. Light grey paste and wash, fine grit temper, surface pared. C.M. 319, Ashmolean Museum, Oxford.

3. Deep bowl, incomplete. Ht. 10.2 cm, rim dia. 20.2 cm. Very fine light grey paste, grit temper, brown paint. Nos. 3–5 and 7 resemble in shape Ras al Amiya type 11 but are decorated in a style known from Arpachiyah, Gawra XVII, Abada, and Eridu XIV–IX (especially Levels XII–X). An identical example is known as early as Eridu XIII. The type is not illustrated from Hajji Muhammad. C.M. 340. Iraq Museum, Baghdad.

4. Deep bowl, incomplete. Ht. 10.6 cm, rim dia. 19.6 cm. Ware identical to no. 3, apparently made on some type of wheel. There were also a number of examples with smaller triangles at the rim, cf. e.g., fig. 7:1. C.M. 339. Columbia University, New York.

5. Open bowl, incomplete. Ht. 11.8 cm, rim dia. 21.6 cm. Buff paste, grey surface, green-black paint, fine ware but slightly coarser than nos. 3,4,7. The bowl was mended in antiquity; there are three pairs of drilled mend holes, two near the rim at opposite sides and one pair near the base. C.M. 348. Cambridge.

6. Open bowl, fragment only. Extant ht. 5.4 cm, rim dia. ca. 10 cm. Buff paste, fine grit temper, green-black paint, blistered where thickly applied; surface of sherds very waterworn. Only certain example of round-based type common at Tepe Gawra and Arpachiyah. Batch 261. Cambridge.

7. Small bowl, incomplete. Ht. 6.3 cm, rim dia. ca. 11 cm. Ware identical to no. 3, black paint, probably pared in the green-hard state. C.M. 325. Ashmolean Museum, Oxford.

Nos. 8–10 and 12–15 are all fragmentary bowls generally similar to nos. 1–7. All are waterworn, and most show signs of having been pared in the green-hard state; this was the most common type recovered from the Ubaid well.

8. Rim dia. ca. 13 cm. Light grey paste, black-green paint.

9. Rim dia. ca. 16 cm. Orange-buff paste, orange-brown paint.

10. Rim dia ca. 15 cm. Orange-buff paste, purple-brown paint; fabric similar to no. 9 but paint better preserved.

11. Open bowl, incomplete. Ht. 8.6 cm, rim dia. 13.2–14.7 cm (deliberately oval?). Gritty buff paste, light wash, dark red paint, faded to orange over most of bowl. The pattern is unique, but it is not clear what is portrayed. C.M. 320. Iraq Museum, Baghdad.

12. Rim dia. perhaps 18 cm. Pale grey paste, black-green paint, paring marks very clear on bowl exterior. Unique pattern.

13. Rim dia. perhaps 10 cm (several sherds of this bowl recovered, but they do not join). Fabric as no. 10.

14. Rim dia. uncertain. Fabric as no. 6.

15. Rim dia. ca. 14 cm. Orange-buff paste, dark red to brown paint, pale orange where worn and thin.

16. Small bowl, incomplete. Extant ht. 7.9 cm, rim dia. 10.2 cm. Grey-green paste, large white grits, black paint, overfired and warped. C.M. 393. Cambridge.

17. Fragment of deep bowl. Rim dia. ca. 14 cm. Buff paste, pale wash, grit temper, brown paint.

18. Large open bowl fragment, probably oval. Extant ht. 7.1 cm, rim dia. ?? 44 cm. Salmon colored paste, orange-buff surface, medium coarse grit temper, purple-brown paint.

19. Fragment of open bowl, deeper than no. 18, also possibly oval. Extant ht. 7.5 cm, rim dia. ?? 36 cm. Buff paste, fine grit temper, dark purple-brown paint. Mended in antiquity. Cf. also *Iraq* 31, pl. XXXII:15, 16.

20. Deep open bowl of which a large number of fragments were recovered. Extant ht. 8.1 cm, rim dia. ca.

24 cm (oval?). Surface very waterworn. Pale buff clay, grit temper, faded orange-brown paint, probably originally a reddish-purple similar to nos. 9 and 19. Cf. Arpachiyah, fig. 26:4.

21. Fragment of large undecorated "casserole," with ledge lugs for lifting. Extant ht. 11.8 cm, rim dia. ca. 25 cm (possibly oval). Yellow-buff paste, grit temper, some chaff, smoothed and scraped surface, waterworn.

FIGURE 5. POTTERY FROM THE UBAID WELL, CHOGA MAMI (1–13); INCISED JARS FROM TELL MADHUR (COURTESY M. ROAF).

1. Lugged jar, incomplete. Rim dia. 7.6 cm, extant ht. 7.0 cm. Buff paste, grit temper, cream wash, warm brown paint. There are four decorated panels between the four lugs, a third, unillustrated, repeating the right-hand illustrated pattern and a fourth consisting of four bands of alternating diagonals, producing a zigzag pattern. Lugged jars of this general type are found at Tepe Gawra (Levels XX–XVII), Arpachiyah, Abada, and Ras al Amiya; they are not reported from Hajji Muhammad and are uncommon at Eridu, though a few examples are known from Level 13 to Level 8 and in the cemetery. C.M. 345. Columbia University, New York.

2. Fragment of lugged jar. Rim dia. 8.0 cm, extant ht. 5.1 cm. Surface very waterworn. Light orange-buff paste, pale surface, grit temper, pale orange-brown paint (originally dark reddish-purple). Three panels of painted ornament preserved as illustrated, fourth missing.

3. Lugged jar, incomplete. Rim dia. 9.6 cm, extant ht. 13 cm. Green-buff paste, grit temper, black paint. The second two panels of ornament repeat those illustrated. See general discussion above, no. 1. C.M. 378. Iraq Museum, Baghdad.

4. Fragment of lugged jar. 10.8 × 7.5 cm. Very friable grey-green paste, green paint; heavily salted and water-soaked, green deposit on surface. Original paint color red-purple (?). Very similar lugged jar in Eridu Level VIII. Batch 261, lower well deposit.

5. Jar fragment. 9.1 × 8.6 cm. Waterworn, buff paste, grit temper, dark brown to purple paint.

6. Fragment of large oval dish. Extant ht. 16.4 cm. Green paste, heavily water-soaked, grit temper including some coarse white grits, green-black paint. Incised pattern in base (cf. figure 8).

Nos. 6 and 7 and possibly also nos. 8 and 9 represent a very distinctive Choga Mami type, so far unrepresented elsewhere although the characteristic incised bases are known also from Kheit Qasim III and Kudish Saghir; a single example has also been found at Tell Brak (1980 season). No pottery of this type has been recovered from Tell Madhur, and it is clear that this particular type of painted and incised Ubaid ware predates the herringbone incised examples known from Madhur, Nuzi, Tell Abu Husaini, Abada, and so forth. Comparable incised bases are found on Late Halaf painted pottery from Baqum north of Halabja (Hijara n.d.).

The painted triangles on the upper rim surface are also a common feature at Choga Mami. Such rim ornament is found as early as Level 16 at Eridu, and very similar examples are known from Levels 13–10 and at Hajji Muhammad. None is illustrated from Ras al Amiya, nor does the type appear to be known at Gawra. Cf. also *Iraq* 31, pl. XXXII:17.

7. Fragment of deep oval dish similar to no. 6. Extant ht. 11 cm. Ware similar to no. 6. It should be noted that nos. 6–9 all have single narrow bands of painted ornament on the exterior surface at the rim (not illustrated).

8. Fragment of open bowl. Ware similar to no. 6, purple-brown paint, exterior surface heavily salt encrusted.

9. Fragment of deep open dish similar to no. 6. Heavily waterworn, paint faded to green. Exterior band of painted ornament ca. 12 mm in width.

10. Globular jar, incomplete. Ht. 17.0 cm, rim dia. 11.5 cm. Gritty cream-colored clay, surface badly water-soaked and decayed; only faint traces of design survive, painted in red. C.M. 352. Iraq Museum, Baghdad.

11. Fragment of large oval dish. Extant ht. 4.2 cm. Very well-levigated cream-colored paste, fine grit temper, pale wash, brown-purple paint; well finished. An identical sherd was found at Eridu, Level 11; a similar type is known at Hajji Muhammad (Ziegler 1953, *taf.* 24:f).

12. Deep oval bowl, incomplete. Ht. 16.0 cm, rim dia. 43.0 × 29.2 cm. Reddish clay, grit temper, pale wash, red paint. No trace of exterior ornament. A very distinctive type, of which a number of examples are known from Choga Mami and Ras al Amiya. Closely comparable examples were found at Eridu, Level 13; see also Ziegler 1953, *taf.* 37c:82 and Oates 1976, p. 26 and fig. 2. C.M. 391. Iraq Museum, Baghdad.

13. Undecorated urn, almost complete. Ht. 21 cm, rim dia. 29.3 cm. Coarse chaff-tempered paste, smoothed cream surface. C.M. 350. Cambridge.

14. Large globular jar. Ht. 48.3 cm, rim dia. 24.5 cm. Chaff-tempered, greenish-buff ware; incised ornament "gives impression of having been scraped as if by the ragged end of a split piece of reed/cane." Cf. Nuzi, R.F.S. Starr 1937, pl. 44. Tell Madhur. 6F:169. Level II house, room 6.

15. Incised jar, incomplete. Extant ht. 17 cm. Greenish-buff paste and surface, straw tempered, handmade but neck wheel-finished; incised diagonal hatching. Fire-blackened. Tell Madhur. 5F:384/TM 306. Level II house, room 3.

16. Incised jar. Ht. 23.2 cm, rim dia. 12.6 cm. Medium-fine buff ware, pale surface, chaff tempered; decorated with diagonal slashes. Tell Madhur. 5F:487/TM 314. Level II house, room 7.

FIGURE 6. IRANIAN BLACK-ON-RED WARE FROM CHOGA MAMI (2–4) AND SURFACE SHERDS OF ERIDU AND HAJJI MUHAMMAD TYPES (5–13).

1. Lugged jar, incomplete. Extant ht. 8.7 cm, rim dia. 8.1 cm. Light orange-buff paste, orange-red slip, surface possibly lightly burnished but too worn for certain identification, heavy chaff temper. No evidence for number of lugs. A unique specimen from Choga Mami and presumably an Iranian import. Batch 261. Ubaid well.

Nos. 2–4 are rim sherds of Iranian black-on-red ware bowls; for description of ware, see p. 277. Several small fragments were found in the Ubaid well.

2. Well-burnished red slip on interior: edges of pattern blurred. Batch 253, upper fill, north slope of "canal X," Oates and Oates 1976a, fig. 5 (square 017).

3. Lightly burnished interior and exterior; this is the same sherd as the one illustrated on figure 7, lower right (lower right-hand corner removed in sampling for neutron activation analysis and thin sectioning). Orientation of sherd uncertain. Surface find, Choga Mami.

4. See above. Possibly lightly burnished, but little trace preserved. Same sherd as fig. 7:10; right-hand side removed for analytical studies. Batch 160. Topsoil, square H7.

5. Sherd of ledge-rim jar. Inner dia. ca. 17 cm, outer dia. ca. 21 cm. Cream-colored paste, grit temper, brown paint. For discussion of type, see p. 277. The unusual orientation can be paralleled at Ras al Amiya (Stronach 1961, pl. LIV). Surface find, Choga Mami.

6. Sherd from bowl or beaker. Extant ht. 6.0 cm. Buff paste, grit temper, dark purple paint. Two examples known from Choga Mami; the pattern occurs at Eridu (Level 14) and Hajji Muhammad, but generally in the base of a bowl (e.g., Ziegler 1953, *taf.* 17).

7. Rim sherd of thin-walled bowl or beaker. Extant ht. 2.7 cm. Very hard, overfired grey core, cream surface, very thick dark purple (blistered) paint. Similar rims are found in Ubaid 1 levels at Eridu; the overall decoration is also reminiscent of Ubaid 1. Surface find, Choga Mami.

8. Body sherd of open bowl. 4.7 × 3.5 cm. Dark buff, "sandy" paste, surface heavily weathered, black-green paint. Design reminiscent of Ubaid 1, especially the fine diagonals on the exterior. Surface find, Choga Mami.

9. Rim sherd of open bowl. 3.0 × 2.6 cm. Cream paste, grey core, cream slip, dark purple paint. Design reminiscent of Ubaid 1. Surface find, Choga Mami.

10. Body sherd of open bowl. 2.8 × 3.4 cm. Buff paste, pale surface, grit temper, paint faded to green on interior, reddish purple on exterior. Transitional or early Ubaid? Batch 190. Square J6, Level 10 (Transitional); upper level in area disturbed by modern graves.

Nos. 11 and 12 are two examples of one of the most distinctive Hajji Muhammad types, which has an Ubaid 2/early Ubaid 3 distribution. Five sherds from vessels of this type were recovered from the latest (unsealed) Transitional level at Choga Mami.

11. Rim sherd of open bowl. Extant ht. 4.0 cm. Buff clay, fine grit temper; interior paint purple faded to green-brown where thin; the exterior of the sherd is completely covered in a purple-green paint. Surface find, Choga Mami.

12. Body sherd from bowl of same type as no. 11. 5.6 × 3.0 cm. Buff paste, fine grit temper, pale slip or wash on interior surface, dark purple paint. Batch 172. Square J6, Level 10 (Transitional).

13. Fragment of deep bowl. Extant ht. 10.2 cm, sherd too warped to enable determination of rim diameter. Overfired green paste, grit temper including large white grits, green-black paint. Ubaid 2/early 3 shape and ornament; cf. Stronach 1961, type 14. Surface find, Choga Mami.

FIGURE 7. PAINTED POTTERY FROM CHOGA MAMI; INCISED UBAID SHERD FROM SERIK.

1. Rim sherd of thin-walled open bowl identical with figure 4:7. Extant ht. 5.6 cm. A number of sherds of this type were recovered from the Ubaid well.

2. Sherd from open bowl identical with an example from Ras al Amiya (Stronach 1961, pl. XLIV:10). Gritty buff paste, pale surface, brown paint. Ubaid well.

3. Lugged jar sherd, similar to figure 5:2; gritty off-white paste, brown paint fading to green. Ubaid well.

4. Shoulder sherd from thick-walled jar. Gritty buff clay, cream surface, brown paint. Ubaid well.

5. Painted sherd, probably from jar shoulder. Buff paste, fine grit temper, cream surface, warm brown paint. Ubaid well.

6. Painted sherd, open bowl probably similar to Ras al Amiya type 2, thin walled. Cream paste and wash, warm brown to purple paint. Ubaid well.

7. (Small triangular fragment beneath nos. 5 and 6.) Painted sherd, jar shoulder. Well-levigated green-buff paste, fine grit temper, brown to purple paint. Ubaid well.

8. Rim sherd of open bowl identical with Hajji Muhammad *taf.* 34:k and Ras al Amiya pl. XLIV:5. Extant ht. 8.2 cm. Warm buff paste, fine grit temper, cream wash, brown to purple-black paint. Thin-section examination shows both the Ras al Amiya and Choga Mami examples to have been locally manufactured. Ubaid well.

9. Rim sherd of open bowl. Extant ht. 5.1 cm. Green-buff paste, fine grit temper, very dark purple (black) paint. Cf. discussion of figure 5:12. Sherd no. 9 is illustrated in Oates 1976, fig. 2:8 (thin section now removed from upper left corner). Batch 264. Square H25, below red clay level in "canal Y," Oates and Oates 1976a, fig. 5.

10. Cf. figure 6:4.

11. Rim sherd from incised Ubaid jar/bowl from Serik (Oates 1968, p. 5). Extant ht. 3.5 cm. Buff paste, grit and chaff temper, traces of pink wash along rim?. Similar incised ornament inside and out. Comparable incised pottery has been found at Hamrin sites such as Madhur and Tell Abu Husaini; cf. also Tepe Gawra Level XIII (Tobler 217) and R.F.S. Starr 1937, pl. 46.

12. Cf. figure 6:3.

FIGURE 8. Incised oval bowl bases from the Ubaid well, Choga Mami. All are either of salmon or buff-colored paste, grit tempered. Cf. figure 5:6,7; also R.F.S. Starr 1937, pl. 45:B. A few similar sherds are known from Kheit Qasim III in the Hamrin and are reported also from Abada; none has been found at Tell Madhur.

FIGURE 9. Ubaid and other relevant radiocarbon determinations.

Dates are quoted in standard form: years before 1950, 5568 half-life; calibration after Clark 1975. R. = Radiocarbon reference.

Tell es-Sawwan Level III	BM-1434	7069 ± 66 bp (5119 b.c.)	W. Yasin, R. Burleigh
	BM-1435	7015 ± 66 bp (5065 b.c.)	W. Yasin, R. Burleigh
	BM-1436	7052 ± 57 bp (5102 b.c.)	W. Yasin, R. Burleigh
	BM-1437	7037 ± 69 bp (5087 b.c.)	W. Yasin, R. Burleigh
	BM-1438	6980 ± 59 bp (5030 b.c.)	W. Yasin, R. Burleigh
mean date		7030 ± 28 bp (5080 b.c.)	Burleigh
Choga Mami Transitional	BM-483	6846 ± 182 bp (4896 b.c.)	R.xix 151
Arpachiyah layer 25 (Hijara period 2/3)	BM-1531	6930 ± 60 bp (4980 b.c.)	I. Hijara
TT 8 (Hijara period 4B)	P-584	7027 ± 83 bp (5077 b.c.)	R.vii 188
Chagar Bazar 11–12 (Hijara period 4B)	P-1487	6665 ± 77 bp (4715 b.c.)	R.xv 373
Yarim Tepe II, Level VI	LE-	6500 ± 100 bp (4550 b.c.)	Hijara
Yarim Tepe II, Level VI (Hijara period 4A)	LE-	6400 ± 120 bp (4450 b.c.)	Hijara
Banahilk "Middle Halaf"	P-1504	6854 ± 72 bp (4904 b.c.)	R.xv 373
Banahilk "Middle Halaf" (Hijara 4A/4B)	P-1502	6752 ± 85 bp (4802 b.c.)	R.xv 373
Banahilk "Late Halaf" (Hijara 4B)	P-1501	6309 ± 78 bp (4359 b.c.)	R.xv 373
Gerikihaciyan "Late Halaf"	GrN-	6465 ± 100 bp (4515 b.c.)	
Siyahbid ("Dalma")	P-442	5815 ± 83 bp (3865 b.c.)	R.v 91
Dalma Tepe	P-503	5986 ± 87 bp (4035 b.c.)	R.v 90
Tepe Gawra XIX	P-1494	7002 ± 82 bp (5052 b.c.)	R.xv 371
Tepe Gawra XVIII	P-1495	6420 ± 61 bp (4470 b.c.)	R.xv 371
Tepe Gawra XVII	P-1496	5991 ± 72 bp (4041 b.c.)	R.xv 371
Tepe Gawra XII	P-1497	5787 ± 72 bp (3837 b.c.)	R.xv 371
Tell Uqair "Late Ubaid"	P-1498	6599 ± 107 bp (4649 b.c.)	R.xv 372
Warka "Late Ubaid"	H138/123	6070 ± 160 bp (4120 b.c.)	
Madhur "Late Ubaid"	BM-1458	5570 ± 55 bp (3620 b.c.)	N. Postgate
Tell el Oueili Level 1 (Late Ubaid)	MC-2382	5980 ± 100 bp (4030 b.c.)	J-L. Huot
below Level 2	MC-2383	6190 ± 90 bp (4240 b.c.)	J-L. Huot
below Level 2	MC-2384	5650 ± 90 bp (3700 b.c.)	J-L. Huot
below Level 2	MC-2385	6170 ± 90 bp (4220 b.c.)	J-L. Huot
below Level 2	MC-2386	5800 ± 100 bp (3850 b.c.)	J-L. Huot
Tepe Sabz			
Khazineh Phase	I-1501	7460 ± 160 bp (5510 b.c.)	R.x 290
Khazineh Phase	UCLA-750B	6925 ± 200 bp (4975 b.c.)	R.vii 355
Mehmeh Phase	I-1493	6470 ± 160 bp (4520 b.c.)	R.x 290
Mehmeh Phase	I-1500	5410 ± 160 bp (3460 b.c.)	R.x 290
Bayat Phase, A3	UCLA-750A	6070 ± 100 bp (4120 b.c.)	R.vii 355
Bayat Phase, A3	I-1502	6060 ± 140 bp (4110 b.c.)	R.x 290
Bayat Phase, A3	SI-156	5770 ± 120 bp (3820 b.c.)	R.viii 419
Bayat Phase, A2	SI-204	6060 ± 200 bp (4110 b.c.)	R.ix 379

Bayat Phase, A2	I-1503	5860 ± 230 bp (3910 b.c.)	R.ix 379
Bayat Phase, A2	SI-205	5700 ± 250 bp (3750 b.c.)	R.ix 379
Bayat Phase, A1	SI-203	6170 ± 200 bp (4220 b.c.)	R.ix 379
Bayat Phase, A1	I-1499	6050 ± 140 bp (4100 b.c.)	R.ix 379
Susa (Susa A)	TUNC-58	5665 ± 121 bp (3715 b.c.)	R.xv 596
Susa (Susa A)	P-912	5418 ± 70 bp (3468 b.c.)	R.viii 352
Susa (Susa A)	GrN-6052	5370 ± 40 bp (3420 b.c.)	Stève and Gasche, MDAI 46, n. 38
Susa (Susa A)	GrN-6054	5275 ± 75 bp (3325 b.c.)	Stève and Gasche, MDAI 46, n. 38
Susa (Susa A)	SPr-1	5093 ± 105 bp (3143 b.c.)	Stève and Gasche, MDAI 46, n. 38
Jaffarabad III (Susa A)	TUNC-46	5141 ± 122 bp (3191 b.c.)	R.xv 596
Jaffarabad III (Susa A)	TUNC-48	5133 ± 94 bp (3183 b.c.)	R.xv 596
Jaffarabad III (Susa A)	TUNC-44	5096 ± 121 bp (3145 b.c.)	R.xv 596
Jaffarabad III (Susa A)	TUNC-43	4966 ± 84 bp (3016 b.c.)	R.xv 596
Jaffarabad II (Susa A)	TUNC-6	5250 ± 75 bp (3300 b.c.)	R.xiv 457
Jaffarabad II (Susa A)	TUNC-5	5243 ± 75 bp (3293 b.c.)	R.xiv 457
Jaffarabad II (Susa A)	TUNC-4	5170 ± 75 bp (3220 b.c.)	R.xiv 457
Jaffarabad I (Susa A)	TUNC-3	5066 ± 70 bp (3116 b.c.)	R.xiv 457

Late Uruk/Jamdat Nasr dates

Nippur Inanna XVII (Warka VI/V)	P-530	4672 ± 74 bp (2722 b.c.)	R.v 85
Warka IVa		4765 ± 85 bp (2815 b.c.)	UVB 21, 1965, 20
Susa 17/16	TUNC-59	4646 ± 93 bp (2696 b.c.)	R.xv 596
Habuba Kabira South	GrN-	5085 ± 65 bp (3135 b.c.)	*AfO* 24, 170
Jebel Aruda	GrN-7989	4495 ± 35 bp (2545 b.c.)	G. van Driel
Jebel Aruda	GrN-8463	4490 ± 45 bp (2540 b.c.)	G. van Driel
Jebel Aruda	GrN-8464	4410 ± 80 bp (2460 b.c.)	G. van Driel
Godin V	Gak-1072	4474 ± 103 bp (2524 b.c.)	Young 1969
Tal-i-Malyan (Banesh Phase)	TUNC-31	4671 ± 88 bp (2721 b.c.)	R.xv 594
Sharafabad	TUNC-32	4382 ± 55 bp (2432 b.c.)	R.xv 594
Sharafabad	TUNC-33	4331 ± 50 bp (2381 b.c.)	R.xv 594
Susa "Jamdat Nasr"	GrN-6051	5035 ± 40 bp (3085 b.c.)	Stève and Gasche
Susa "Jamdat Nasr"	GrN-6053	5015 ± 90 bp (3065 b.c.)	Stève and Gasche
Susa "Jamdat Nasr"	SPr-43	4770 ± 218 bp (2820 b.c.)	Stève and Gasche

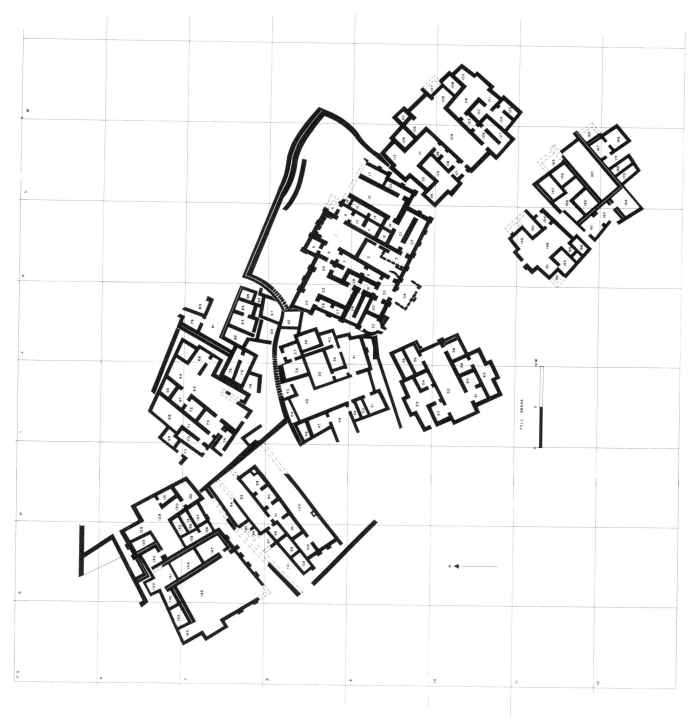

Fig. 1. — Level II Plan. Tell Abada. (Courtesy of S.A. Jasim.)

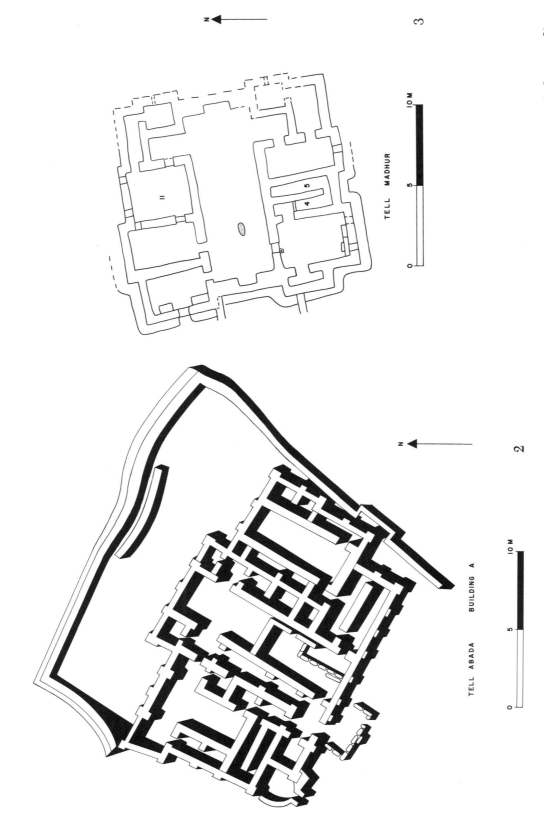

TELL MADHUR

TELL ABADA   BUILDING A

Fig. 2. — Tell Abada, Level II House. (Courtesy of S. A. Jasim.) Fig. 3. — Tell Madhur, Level II House. (After Roaf.)

FIG. 4. — POTTERY FROM THE UBAID WELL, CHOGA MAMI.

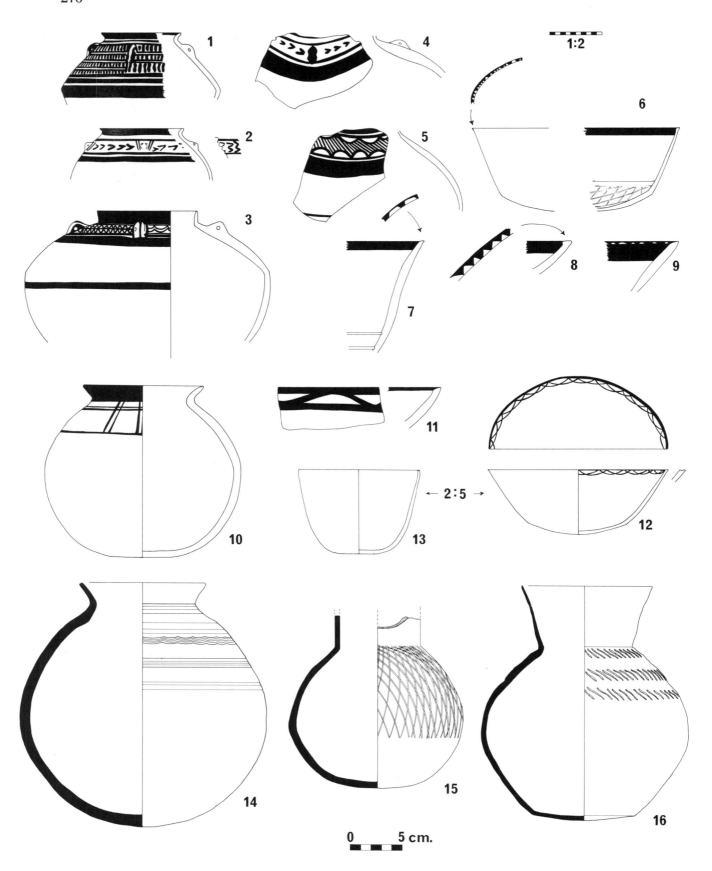

FIG. 5. — POTTERY FROM THE UBAID WELL, CHOGA MAMI (1–13); INCISED JARS FROM TELL MADHUR.
(Courtesy M. Roaf.)

FIG. 6. — IRANIAN BLACK-ON-RED WARE FROM CHOGA MAMI (2—4) AND SURFACE SHERDS OF ERIDU AND HAJJI MUHAMMAD TYPES (5--13).

FIG. 7. — PAINTED POTTERY FROM CHOGA MAMI; INCISED UBAID SHERD FROM SERIK.

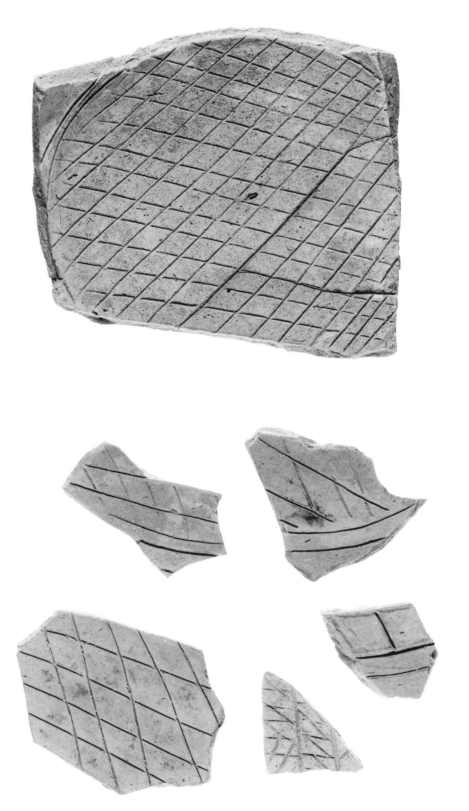

Fig. 8. — Incised Oval Bowl Bases from the Ubaid Well, Choga Mami.

280

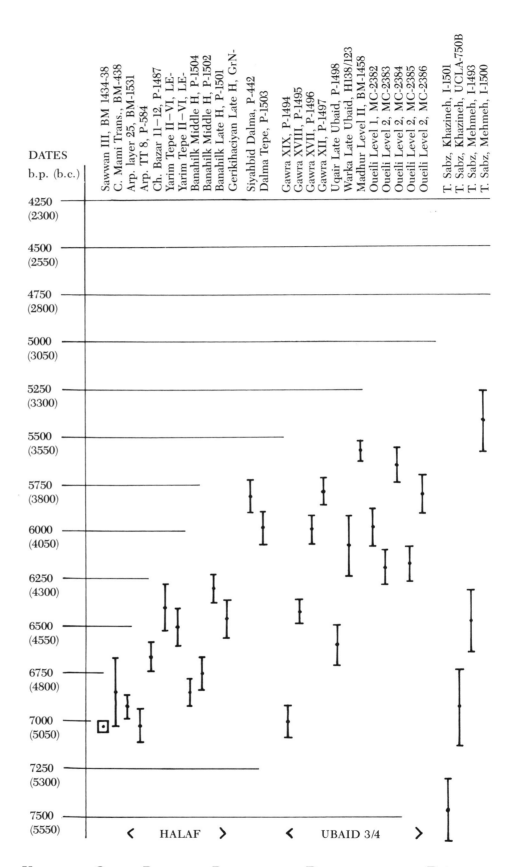

FIG. 9. — UBAID AND OTHER RELEVANT RADIOCARBON DETERMINATIONS. Dates are

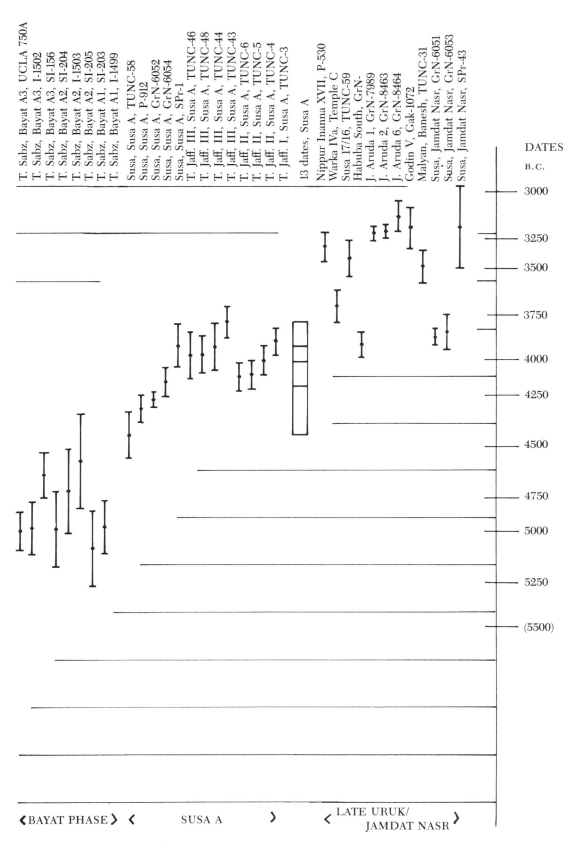

DATES
B.C.

— 3000

— 3250

— 3500

— 3750

— 4000

— 4250

— 4500

— 4750

— 5000

— 5250

— (5500)

❬BAYAT PHASE❭ ❬   SUSA A   ❭ ❬ LATE URUK/
JAMDAT NASR ❭

quoted in standard form: years before 1950, 5568 half-life; calibration after Clark 1975.

REMARQUES SUR L'ORGANISATION DE L'ESPACE DANS QUELQUES AGGLOMÉRATIONS DE LA SUSIANE DU Ve MILLÉNAIRE

Geneviève Dollfus

DEUX DATES — 1957 et 1962 — devaient marquer de leur sceau jusqu'à une époque récente les recherches effectuées dans l'actuelle province du Khuzistan, au sud-ouest de l'Iran.

1957, L. Le Breton propose une tentative de périodisation pour la Susiane pré- et protohistorique;[1] 1962, R. McAdams rend compte de la première prospection systématique effectuée dans la région.[2]

Périodisation et prospection, ces deux volets du diptyque une fois ouverts furent le point de départ de travaux complémentaires. Leurs objectifs étaient, lorsque la séquence serait bien établie, de montrer les diverses sortes d'établissements, leur répartition et, au delà, les types de sociétés; d'examiner aussi les variétés de population au cours des différentes périodes dans les plaines du sud-ouest de l'Iran et de tenter d'en expliquer les causes. Limité jusqu'alors essentiellement à la plaine centrale du Khuzistan, le cadre géographique se trouva bientôt élargi au nord-ouest de la province grâce aux travaux effectués dans la plaine de Deh Luran (Hole et al. 1969; Hole 1977; Wright 1980) et vers le nord-est par les recherches dans les vallées de Dasht-e-Gol et d'Izeh (Wright, ed. 1979).

Ainsi, au cours des deux dernières décades, les connaissances concernant la protohistoire de cette région se sont trouvées très renouvelées. Ce renouveau est dû, non seulement au nombre plus élevé de chantiers ouverts ou de zones prospectées mais également aux orientations diverses qui ont été données aux recherches. Une collaboration amicale entre chercheurs de formation différente a permis aux uns — rompus de par leur formation d'anthropologues aux méthodes modernes des sciences sociales — d'insuffler des idées nouvelles aux autres qui préféraient dans un premier temps de leur recherche ne s'appuyer que sur l'observation directe afin d'édifier sur des bases aussi fermes que possible la séquence archéologique.

Pour la plaine centrale, plus communément désignée sous le terme *Susiane*, et pour celle de Deh Luran, au nord-ouest de la province, des séquences fondées sur des bases stratigraphiques solides ont été établies (tableau 1). Elles ont été exposées lors d'une conférence qui a réuni tous les chercheurs travaillant dans la région sur ces mêmes problèmes puis publiées sous forme de tableaux exposant la périodisation propre à chaque site et les corrélations existant de gisement à gisement (Dollfus 1978; Hole 1978). Cependant, jusqu'à présent aucun consensus sur la terminologie à adopter pour la périodisation générale de la région n'a été obtenu.[3]

---

1. Antérieurement à la synthèse de Le Breton, mentionnons celles de McCown, 1942, et de Vanden Berghe, 1952. Le travail de Le Breton se distingue de celles-ci en ce que l'auteur a pu s'appuyer pour son étude sur des rapports et lettres inédits de Mecquenem ainsi que sur l'étude directe du matériel archéologique.

2. Avant lui, reconnaissance de Gautier et Lampre dans la plaine de Deh Luran (1905) et travaux de Mecquenem et de ses collaborateurs en Susiane (Mecquenem 1934, 1943; Le Breton 1947).

3. A Oxford, en 1972, à Münich en 1976 lors des VIe et VIIe congrès internationaux d'art et d'archéologie de l'Iran, j'ai proposé pour la Susiane une tentative de périodisation mais celle-ci rencontra auprès de P. Delougaz et H. Kantor une vive opposition.

Tableau 1.

	Plaine Centrale					
	Sites					
Choga Bonut	Tépe Tula'i	Boneh Fazili	Choga Mish	Djf.	Djowi	Bend.
			Late Susiana	1 2 III 3		III
						11
					5	
Middle Susiana 3		Middle Susiana 3	Middle Susiana 3	GAP	8 II 10	18 19
				3 mn II	11 12 13 I	22 II
		2	2			
		1	1	GAP	17	27
		Early Susiana Archaic	Early Susiana Archaic	4 5 I 6		28 I
						?
		3	3			
GAP		2	2			
I	Sefid	1	1			
Formative						
Aceramic						

Les tentatives de reconstitution de l'environnement ancien devaient aller de pair avec les travaux des archéologues. Jusqu'aux années 60, les plaines du Khuzistan n'avaient été l'objet d'aucune étude spécifique. On se référait pour leur formation aux études générales concernant la plaine mésopotamienne de Morgan (1900) et Lees et Falcon (1952).[4] Les années 60 marquèrent

4. Voir récemment, outre les contributions de Nützel (1975, 1978) celle de Larsen (1975) qui remet en cause la théorie de Lees et Falcon.

Deh Luran

| Qabr Sheyk. | Suse | Phases | | Sites | | | |
		Région Deh Luran	Ali Kosh	Choga Sefid	Tépé Sabz	Farukhabad
	22					
	23					
	24					
	25 I					
	27					
		Farukh				A23−31
1						
5						
?		Bayat			x	A33−36
		Mehmeh			x	
		Khazineh			x	
		Sabz		x	x	
		Ch. Mami Transit.		x		
		Surkh		x		
		Sefid		x		
		Moh. Jaffar	x	x		
		Ali Kosh	x	x		
		Bus Mordeh	x			

également un tournant: les recherches récentes menées d'une part par les experts de la F.A.O. et du Khuzistan Water and Power Authority, d'autre part par M. Kirkby (1977) apportèrent des renseignements sur les périodes d'active sédimentation, la localisation et la nature des dépôts alluviaux, la formation des terrasses fluviatiles et l'incision des rivières, les changements de cours de celles-ci, toutes observations indispensables pour l'interprétation des données recueillies lors de prospections (Kirkby et Kirkby 1976); elles aidèrent aussi à définir la qualité et la nature des sols, leur drainage, leur degré de salinité, phénomènes importants lors de l'établissement des villages et, donc pour la compréhension du choix de leur emplacement.

Les études palynologiques (Hole et Woosley 1978), celle des macrorestes végétaux (Helbaek 1969; Miller 1977, 1980), des vestiges animaux recueillis (Flannery 1969; Redding 1980) devaient donner un aperçu de la couverture végétale, du climat proche de l'actuel et de ses variations réduites, semble-t-il, à de faibles oscillations, enfin des différents éco-systèmes.

Toutes ces études ont contribué à replacer les établissements mis au jour aussi bien dans leur cadre chronologique que dans leur paléo-environnement.

Aussi, alors que les recherches sur le terrain dans cette région subissent un arrêt momentané, il a paru utile d'examiner dans quelle mesure aujourd'hui les connaissances acquises permettent de concevoir l'organisation de l'espace à l'intérieur des communautés de la Susiane au Ve millénaire et s'il est possible d'aborder des problèmes de démographie.

Le découpage chronologique retenu, fin VIe au début du IVe millénaire, correspond à celui qui voit l'avènement de villages bien développés à économie mixte, élevage et agriculture: élevage de chèvres et de moutons — ces derniers semblant prédominer tout du moins dans le Deh Luran à la fin de la période (Helbaek 1969; Redding 1980)[5] — et dans une faible proportion de bovidés; agriculture dépendant au nord de la plaine des cultures sèches mais plus au sud de l'irrigation des champs.[6] L'orge, le blé, les lentilles, et les vesces paraissent avoir été les principales cultures. Alors que la chasse semble n'avoir joué qu'un faible rôle, les ressources des rivières à proximité desquelles sont souvent situées les agglomérations sont abondamment exploitées: gibier d'eau, poissons, crabes, tortues . . .

Il semble que vers le milieu du Ve millénaire certains centres commencent à se distinguer par leur importance. Tel paraît être le cas de Choga Mish. Si cela devait se vérifier par ailleurs dans la région, on assisterait alors à un début de hiérarchisation des établissements qui irait de pair avec la spécialisation de certains d'entre eux (Dollfus 1974).

Les sites retenus dans cet essai comme représentatifs sont au nombre de cinq: Djaffarabad et Bendebal à l'ouest de la Dez, Choga Mish, Choga Bonut, Qabr Sheykheyn à l'est. Le critère ayant présidé à leur choix est celui de la surface exposée. Une aire de 300 m² d'un seul tenant nous a semblé un minimum pour obtenir une vision de l'organisation interne d'une habitation mais aussi pour apprécier l'agencement des unités entre elles.[7] Il est dommage que pour Qabr Sheykheyn, site où la fouille a porté pour certains niveaux sur 500 m², aucun plan n'ait été publié et qu'il faille en être réduit pour l'étude de l'architecture à la brève note parue dans *Iran* (Weiss 1972). Les autres sites des Ve et début du IVe millénaires fouillés dans la région l'ont été sur une surface trop réduite pour que les restes mis au jour puissent être signifiants par eux-mêmes; c'est le cas de

5. La faune des sites de Susiane (Choga Mish, Djaffarabad, Suse) a été confiée à J. Wheeler. A ce jour aucun rapport n'a encore été communiqué.

6. Jusqu'à présent aucune trace de canal n'a été retrouvée pour cette époque au Khuzistan (cf. en Mésopotamie, Choga Mami) (Oates, 1973) mais la distribution des établissements, en particulier le changement observé par Hole (1977b) entre celle de la période *Archaic* 3 et celle de la "phase Djaffarabad" ne peut s'expliquer que par la possibilité grâce à l'irrigation d'exploiter des terres nouvelles. Les cultures irriguées sont confirmées par l'analyse des débris végétaux.

7. Le critère de 300 m² a été retenu pour la raison suivante. Les maisons en Mésopotamie légèrement antérieures ou contemporaines couvrent pour Sawwan, niv. III une surface approchée de 70 m² (maisons en T) et sont séparées l'une de l'autre par un espace découvert qui dépasse rarement 100 à 150 m², à Choga Mami elles ont entre 38 et 70 m². Pour plus de données cf. Watson 1978. Dans le Fars, à Tall i Bakun A, au niveau 3, la plus grande unité d'habitation ferait un peu plus de 80 m² alors que la maison XII n'en aurait que la moitié. Ces exemples, ainsi que d'autres de maisons actuelles, montrent qu'en dégageant une surface de 300 m², on doit pouvoir se faire une idée du plan d'une habitation et même de l'agencement des maisons entre elles.

Djowi (Dollfus 1976) en Susiane, de Choga Sefid (Hole 1977), de Sabz (Hole et al. 1969), de Farukhabad (Wright 1980) dans le Deh Luran. A Suse, le problème est autre: les fouilles anciennes d'une part (Morgan 1900; Mecquenem 1943), récentes de l'autre (Stève et Gasche 1971; Perrot et Canal, cf. Canal 1978), ont porté sur la nécropole et la haute terrasse. Le Brun (1971) a mis en évidence quelques vestiges d'habitations mais trop fragmentaires pour qu'ils puissent être d'une quelconque aide pour cette étude. Rien n'est connu de l'agglomération de Suse au début du IVe millénaire (fig. 11b.)

Les données recueillies sur l'habitat seront examinées à la lueur d'études récentes concernant les villages actuels de l'ouest et du sud-ouest de l'Iran (Jacobs 1979; Kramer 1979; Sumner 1979; Watson 1978−1979) et plus particulièrement à la lumière d'études régionales (Gremliza 1962; Rouho Lamini 1973) et d'observations personnelles.

Nous considérerons d'abord les *données contemporaines*.

La zone couverte par le rapport de Gremliza forme un rectangle d'environ 25 km nord-sud, 10 km est-ouest dont l'intérêt principal pour nous réside en sa situation: proximité immédiate des sites de Djaffarabad, Djowi, Bendebal, et faible distance (une trentaine de km seulement) de Choga Mish (fig. 1b). Le village de Raddadeh dont les habitations (fig. 2) ont été décrites par Rouho Lamini se situe juste en dehors de la bordure ouest de l'aire étudiée par Gremliza.

Sur les 223 km² parcourus en 1960−1961 par Gremliza, 55 villages ont été recensés représentant une population de 11.855 habitants, soit une densité régionale de 52 km² (tableau 2). La moyenne de la population par village est évaluée à 203 âmes, la plus petite agglomération n'en comptant que 33, la plus importante 690. Les habitations de Raddadeh décrites par Rouho Lamini font donc partie d'un des grands villages de la région, sa population se situant en 1971 aux environs de 450 personnes.

La superficie des villages[8] varie selon le schéma suivant:

Moins de 0, 3 hectare	2
Entre 0, 3 et 0, 5 hectare	10
Entre 0, 5 et 1 hectare	20
Entre 1 et 2 hectares	12
Plus de 2 hectares	10

La structure des agglomérations est peu diversifiée. Le "ghaleh" village enclos par un mur est le type le plus fréquent. Le "ghaleh" appartient à un propriétaire qui possède le village et les terres sur lesquelles travaillent les paysans. La plupart des villages remontent au XIXe siècle. Le propriétaire du village dessinait l'emplacement de celui-ci, le ceinturait d'un mur et encourageait les paysans à construire leur maison à l'intérieur de celui-ci. Il est intéressant de noter que ces villages, bien que proches les uns des autres, 2 à 3 km en moyenne, parfois moins, n'ont que très peu de liens entre eux. Aussi indique Gremliza, ces villages constituent-ils réellement des "unit rather than a communit(y)".

A côté des agglomérations dénombrées, apparaissent quelques petits hameaux. Ils restent l'exception et ont alors des liens de parenté avec un village proche.

A. Le "Ghaleh", village enclos: 42 villages de 17 à 98 maisons.

B. Le "village éclaté". Ce n'est en fait qu'un "ghaleh" avec une extension hors des murs. Raddadeh, comme Tell-i-Nun dans le Fars (Jacobs 1979) entrent dans cette catégorie: 3 villages de 124 à 139 maisons.

8. Celle-ci a été établie après que nous ayions mesuré, sur les plans des villages dessinés à l'échelle 1/2500 par Gremliza, les zones bâties de chaque établissement.

Tableau 2. — Densité de Population

Territoire des villages		Agglomération	
Hab./hect.	Pop./km²	Hectares	Densité/hectare
--	46	--	--
288	20	0,4225	142
90	70	0,2500	252
115	78	0,1600	145
111	97	0,3750	108
140	80	0,3000	373,3
94	75	0,6225	168
148	77	0,3906	291
208	53	1,2562	87
193	54	0,3750	277,3
274	33	0,6875	133,8
215	51	0,6187	179,4
249	49	0,7218	170,4
131	63	0,4687	177
334	40	0,9737	137,6
303	39	0,6562	179,8
335	42	0,7000	202,8
342	39	0,5625	241,7
284	50	1,6875	241,3
216	53	0,3906	294,4
445	34	0,8906	137,1
156	78	0,6300	312,3
197	69	0,3300	412,1
296	50	1,0312	143,5
166	75	0,5362	198,4
312	40	1,0000	126
461	38	1,2093	211,6
420	36	1,4500	106,2
181	69	0,5543	69,8
275	60	0,7981	206,7
371	53	0,4556	430
470	46	2,5111	73,2
257	75	0,8200	235,2
436	58	0,8691	219,8
340	56	1,0941	191
258	66	0,6475	264
371	50	0,7312	254,3
636	36	1,0000	221
760	26	0,8593	240
62	310	0,5062	395,1
480	54	2,3400	110,6
371	65	0,8750	277
1,459	20	1,0175	295

Tableau 2. — *continued*

Territoire des villages		Agglomération	
Hab./hect.	*Pop./km²*	*Hectares*	*Densité/hectare*
771	33	1,1250	257
429	61	0,7155	368,9
471	68	1,8500	174,5
633	60	3,1875	119,5
864	40	2,0812	168,6
704	55	2,5000	154,8
682	63	1,8500	174,5
1,000	46	1,8281	255,4
787	58	2,3437	197,1
806	73	4,3300	137,4
1,124	61	3,0937	223
820	84	2,4000	288,7
11,855	52	58,814	208,2

C. Le village "ouvert", le plus souvent peuplé d'arabophones ou présentant une population mixte: 10 villages de 7 à 66 maisons.

Le village de type A ne varie guère d'un établissement à l'autre: d'une part le "jardin" planté d'arbres fruitiers; d'autre part les quartiers d'habitation où se trouvent mêlés intimement humains et animaux. La demeure du propriétaire du village, lorsqu'il en existe une, se situe en général entre jardin et agglomération.

Le village de type C est beaucoup plus diversifié. Il ne semble pas répondre à un plan particulier et les maisons sont disposées à l'encan. En règle générale, les villages de ce type ne possèdent pas de "jardins" mais les espaces ouverts, les ruelles sont plus larges que dans le type A. Les complexes ne se touchent généralement pas.[9]

Hors les murs pour le type A, à l'extérieur de l'agglomération pour le type C se trouvent l'aire de battage, les zones d'extraction de la terre pour la fabrication des briques crues et celui où les femmes confectionnent les "pains" de combustible.

Pour les trois types de villages, le cimetière se trouve toujours à une certaine distance des villages. Celle-ci peut varier entre 0,300 et 2 km.[10]

Dans l'espace étudié par Gremliza, 2274 complexes d'habitation ont été dénombrés qui comprennent au total 6965 pièces couvertes. Leur répartition est la suivante:

Habitations proprement dites	2975	49,8%
Cuisines	261	4,4%
Etables/bergeries/réserves	1435	24,0%
Réserves	1275	21,5%

9. Comme me l'a aimablement fait remarquer H. T. Wright, les villages de type C sont tous situés dans la partie sud de la zone prospectée par Gremliza. Ils sont peuplés d'arabophones et répondent à un plan d'organisation tribale. La plupart d'entre eux sont de fondation récente et sont donc postérieurs à l'époque où le banditisme étant de règle, il fallait pouvoir se protéger contre celui-ci, d'où la nécessité du mur.

10. Observation personnelle.

Ces maisons sont habitées par 2289 ménages ("nuclear families") qui comptent en moyenne 5,06 individus. Ceux-ci vivent en général dans une seule pièce, plus rarement en occupent plusieurs. La relation maison/pièces d'habitation peut être évaluée à 1,32%, le nombre de pièces ne dépassant que peu celui des maisons (tableau 3).

Ces données acquises, revenons à *l'aube du V*ᵉ *millénaire*.

CHOGA MISH, ARCHAIC 3 À MIDDLE SUSIANA 1
DJAFFARABAD, PÉRIODE I (NIVEAUX 6−4)[11]

CHOGA MISH

À la fin du VIᵉ millénaire, ce n'est pas une implantation nouvelle. Le site est déjà habité comme l'ont été ou continuent de l'être deux autres villages voisins, Choga Bonut et Boneh Fazili. Mais des premières installations de Choga Mish, il semble qu'à ce jour aucun vestige n'ait pu être dégagé (Kantor 1977).[12]

En revanche à partir de la période définie par les fouilleurs comme archaic 3, des restes de maisons sont attestés dans la partie sud-est du site. L'agglomération couvre un minimum de 0,5 hectare (murs présents dans les tranchées XXV, XII, XXI, XXXII, gully cut) (fig. 3). L'épaisseur des dépôts susjacents n'a permis de dégager que quelques structures d'habitat. L'ensemble le mieux conservé est constitué de trois unités distinctes, non accolées. L'une d'entre elles formait à l'origine une pièce de 45 m² (15 × 3). Plus tard, à la fin de la période *Archaic* ou au début de l'*Early Susiana* (?), cette grande salle aurait été subdivisée ou reconstruite sur un autre plan: la maison se transforme d'une pièce unique en trois de plus petites dimensions, 9 m², 5, 75 m², 6, 50 m². Des deux autres unités, une seule pièce de 8,75 m² a été dégagée (fig. 4a).

Tous les espaces décrits semblent avoir été couverts et représenteraient des pièces d'habitation; la plus petite qui comporte une cloison est peut-être une réserve. Toutefois, dans un autre secteur de l'établissement sont signalées à proximité des maisons, des aires découvertes pavées par endroits de galets (Kantor 1975).

En l'absence de toute structure domestique (des foyers, des fours ont-ils été dégagés?), il n'est pas possible d'évaluer si on est en présence d'un seul complexe d'habitation pouvant appartenir à une famille au sens large ou si les trois unités sont distinctes réellement les unes des autres.

La lecture des rapports de fouille met en relief le fait qu'il n'y a pas la moindre discontinuité de l'occupation dans tout ce secteur. Les vestiges *Archaic* 3 sont le plus souvent en contact et souvent imbriqués dans ceux considérés comme *Early Susiana*.

A la période *Early Susiana*, l'agglomération s'est-elle agrandie, seulement déplacée laissant alors quelques maisons de l'époque précédente abandonnées?

Des dépôts *Early Susiana* sont en effet signalés au centre de la terrasse et sur le flanc méridional de celle-ci (Kantor, communication personnelle). Ces derniers sont-ils l'indice d'une extension réelle de l'établissement qui couvrirait près de 4 hectares; plus simplement ne s'agirait-il pas d'une maison rapidement laissée à l'abandon? Ne peut-on pas aussi envisager l'hypothèse au cas où aucune autre structure n'aurait été relevée que, vu leur faible épaisseur (Kantor 1972) et leur situation par rapport à l'ensemble du site, ces dépôts ne soient dûs à

---

11. Nous avons expliqué ailleurs (Dollfus 1978) les raisons qui nous poussent à regrouper Choga Mish, archaïc 3 à *Middle Susiana* 1, Djaffarabad 6−4, Bendebal 28, Djowi 17−13 en une même phase culturelle.

12. "The absence of any architectural remains for the first two of the Archaic Susiana phases had remained a major gap in our knowledge, even raising the question whether substantial buildings existed at that time" (Kantor 1977). A Choga Bonut, *Archaic* 1, on relève quelques fragments de murs (Kantor 1978−1979). A l'ouest de la Dez, à tépé Tula'i, F. Hole pense avoir retrouvé les traces d'un campement de pasteurs (Hole 1974).

l'érosion du tépé primitif en cours de formation (Kirkby et Kirkby 1976)? Si cette suggestion devait être retenue, l'établissement couvrirait environ 1.500 hectares. En tout état de cause, en l'absence d'un plan de la totalité des vestiges mis au jour qui permettrait d'examiner la relation des différents complexes d'habitations entre eux et l'existence éventuelle de bâtiments à caractère public,[13] il nous paraît difficile d'accepter le statut de ville (Kantor 1974a) pour Choga Mish à l'époque *Early Susiana*.

La tranchée XXI permet de se faire une idée du plan et de l'agencement de quelques habitations (fig. 4b). Dans ce secteur, il semble que sur une surface de 700 m², un minimum de quatre complexes aient été mis au jour. L'examen du plan nous a conduit à en proposer l'interprétation suivante: le complexe 1 comporterait une aire découverte d'au moins 28 m² (secteur dégagé), deux pièces d'habitation, l'une de 9 m², l'autre de 6 m² et une zone de réserves de 7,20 m² formée de quatre réduits d'l, 80 m² chacun, soit au total une surface couverte de 22, 20 m².

Au sud, cette maison serait bordée par un corridor qui la séparerait d'un autre complexe.

Les habitations 2 et 3 sont difficiles à dissocier l'une de l'autre. Peut-être n'est ce qu'une seule demeure que nous avons tort de démembrer.

Le complexe 2 paraît formé de deux pièces d'habitation. La plus spacieuse, 12 m², comporte un muret transversal de partition, et une zone de foyers construits; la plus petite n'a que 6 m². Encastrée entre ces deux pièces se situe probablement une réserve de 4 m². Adossées au mur de la grande salle et de la réserve, deux longues pièces (6 × 0, 90 m), présentant toutes deux une petite cloison, pourraient avoir servi à entasser du combustible (cf. Gawra XV−XVI, Tobler 1950 ou l'occupation contemporaine de Raddadeh, fig. 2b). Quant à la pièce oblongue trapézoïdale située sur le côté oriental de la cour, on la verrait bien utilisée comme abri pour les animaux.

Les complexes 2 et 3 partageraient la même cour. La maison 3 possèderait quatre salles d'habitation (9 m², 8 m², 7,5 m², 5 m²) dont l'une au moins est pourvue d'un foyer. Des réduits peuvent être considérés comme des magasins (2,25 m² et 1 m²). Peut-être trouve-t-on au nord un abri pour les animaux et le long de la cour la réserve à combustible. La disposition serait alors assez voisine pour les deux maisons.

	Complexe 1	*Complexe 2*	*Complexe 3*
Cour	28 m²	------------ 15 m² + -----------	
Surface couverte	24,20 m²	37,80 m²	36,15 m²
Habitation	17 m²	18 m²	29,50 m²
Réserves	7,20 m²	13,80 m²	4,85 m²
Abri/anim.	--	6m²+	1,80 m²?

Les vestiges de construction paraissant denses dans les tranchées où ils ont été mis au jour, il serait intéressant de savoir si, au centre de la terrasse (sondage F ou tranchée XI par exemple), on rencontre également des restes d'habitation ou si certains secteurs étaient maintenus en aires découvertes. On pourrait alors apprécier le plan de l'ensemble de l'agglomération qui paraît déjà être celle d'un gros village.

Lors de la période *Middle Susiana* 1, l'agglomération semble conserver les mêmes dimensions

---

13. Deux structures pourraient ne pas être considérées comme, ou en relation avec des unités d'habitation. Il s'agit d'un bâtiment à saillants dégagé dans la tranchée "gully cut" pour lequel le fouilleur suggère qu'il pourrait s'agir d'un sanctuaire (Kantor 1976) et d'une plate-forme de 8 × 6 m à laquelle aucune structure n'est associée (Kantor 1974a).

Tableau 3.*

			Nombre de personnes/pièce																		
			1	*2*	*3*	*4*	*5*	*6*	*7*	*8*	*9*	*10*	*11*	*12*	*13*	*14*	*16*	*20*			
7	8	4.1	--	--	1	2	3	1	--	--	--	--	--	--	--	--	--	--	1	33	C
12	17	3.5	1	1	2	4	1	1	2	--	--	--	--	--	--	--	--	--	1	60	C
13	15	4.2	2	2	1	2	1	1	3	1	--	--	--	--	--	--	--	--	1	63	A
16	21	4.3	--	2	4	1	3	4	2	--	--	--	--	--	--	--	--	--	2	91	A
	20	5.4	1	1	2	2	2	3	--	3	2	--	--	1	--	--	--	--		108	A
17	23	4.8	--	2	4	2	5	1	1	--	--	--	--	--	--	--	--	--	1	112	A
18	22	3.2	2	5	4	1	5	--	--	1	--	--	--	--	--	--	--	--	2	71	A
	20	5.7	--	1	1	4	4	4	1	3	--	--	--	--	--	--	--	--		114	A
19	21	5.2	1	1	2	4	3	2	2	2	1	--	--	--	1	--	--	--	1	110	A
20	21	5.0	1	1	2	3	5	3	4	--	--	--	--	--	--	--	--	--	1	104	A
21	27	3.4	3	2	5	5	3	1	1	1	--	--	--	--	--	--	--	--	3	92	A
	30	3.7	3	4	1	4	3	--	--	1	1	--	--	--	--	--	--	--		111	A/C
	28	4.4	--	4	3	2	1	3	5	3	--	--	--	--	--	--	--	--		123	A
22	24	13.4	3	4	1	8	3	2	1	--	--	--	--	--	--	--	--	--	2	83	A
	37	3.5	1	5	5	1	3	3	3	3	1	--	--	--	--	--	--	--		134	A
24	49	2.4	3	7	8	3	2	1	--	--	--	--	--	--	--	--	--	--	2	118	A
	48	3.0	2	6	6	6	1	1	1	--	1	--	--	--	--	--	--	--		142	A
25	33	4.1	2	4	6	4	4	2	1	1	--	--	1	--	--	--	--	--	2	136	A
	32	4.5	2	3	1	7	6	1	1	2	1	--	1	--	--	--	--	--		143	A
27	36	3.2	2	5	6	8	4	2	--	--	--	--	1	--	--	--	--	--	3	115	A
	40	3.8	2	4	4	3	5	5	1	2	1	--	--	--	--	--	--	--		154	A
	24	5.0	2	3	7	8	6	1	--	--	--	--	--	--	--	--	--	--		122	A
29	31	4.4	2	6	3	1	5	8	1	11	1	1	1	--	--	--	--	--	3	136	A
	33	4.5	1	4	5	5	1	5	6	1	--	--	1	--	--	--	--	--		148	A
30	32	3.9	3	4	5	8	4	2	2	1	1	--	--	--	--	--	--	--	3	126	A
	52	3.3	3	6	4	7	5	2	2	1	--	--	--	--	--	--	--	--		175	A

	n	x̄																			N	
31	60	2.5	5	10	9	4	–	1	–	1	–	–	–	–	–	–	–	–	154	A
32	44	2.8	3	8	9	5	5	1	–	–	–	–	–	–	–	–	–	1	126	A
33	40	4.1	2	3	7	7	6	3	2	1	1	–	–	1	–	–	–	1	165	A
34	43	4.6	1	5	5	5	6	5	–	–	–	–	–	–	1	–	–	1	196	A
35	47	3.9	2	4	8	6	5	3	4	–	–	–	–	–	–	–	–	1	184	C
	39	4.9	2	2	3	10	4	6	4	2	–	–	–	–	–	–	–	2	193	A
	58	4.3	2	4	8	4	8	3	3	–	3	–	–	–	–	–	–	–	253	A
37	45	4.2	1	5	7	8	8	4	4	–	–	–	–	–	–	–	–	1	191	A
38	41	4.1	3	5	7	8	5	5	1	–	–	2	2	–	–	–	–	2	171	A
	49	3.4	2	6	11	6	3	5	–	–	1	2	2	–	–	–	–	–	186	A
39	50	4.4	3	8	8	1	8	4	4	1	1	1	1	–	–	–	–	–	221	A
	62	3.2	1	10	12	7	2	2	2	–	1	–	–	–	–	–	–	–	201	A
43	56	3.5	2	6	12	8	–	4	4	–	–	–	1	–	–	–	–	1	200	A
49	62	4.1	–	6	8	18	6	4	4	2	3	2	–	–	–	–	–	1	259	C
52	64	3.8	2	11	13	8	5	5	5	4	–	–	1	–	1	–	–	1	243	A
54	73	4.0	4	8	11	11	9	4	4	2	1	1	–	1	–	–	–	2	290	A
	65	4.0	5	9	10	6	12	7	2	2	–	–	1	–	–	–	–	–	259	A
55	75	3.5	4	8	10	7	10	6	3	2	–	–	–	–	–	–	–	1	264	A
66	81	4.0	4	11	18	12	4	7	5	2	3	3	–	–	–	–	–	1	323	C
72	100	3.8	4	6	20	15	15	15	7	2	2	2	1	–	–	–	–	1	381	A
73	91	3.8	6	20	11	12	8	10	3	1	1	–	–	–	–	–	–	1	351	A
79	89	4.3	2	6	16	19	14	10	6	3	3	1	1	1	–	–	–	1	387	C
84	115	3.7	7	13	17	12	14	16	2	6	1	1	1	–	1	–	–	1	431	C
96	116	4.0	4	13	21	19	11	15	6	2	1	1	1	1	–	–	–	1	467	C
98	114	4.0	4	14	21	17	18	10	7	3	3	1	1	1	–	–	–	1	462	A
124	165	3.5	10	20	33	12	16	2	4	4	–	3	–	–	–	–	–	1	595	B
126	163	4.2	7	15	23	12	5	7	6	1	–	–	–	–	–	–	–	1	690	B
139	181	3.8	12	18	31	27	20	15	11	2	2	1	2	–	–	–	2	1	693	B

*Tout les chiffres sont extraits de Gremliza tables 13, 15, 20.

que précédemment. Nous ne poursuivrons pas l'analyse détaillée des vestiges mis au jour. Une remarque s'impose. Le plan des maisons *Early Susiana* (fig. 4b) et *Middle Susiana* 1 est très semblable (fig. 5a−b). Le complexe le mieux préservé est formé de trois pièces dont deux, au moins, ont pu servir de chambres (12,50 m², 6,50m², 4,40m²), des réduits de stockage, une pièce trapézoïdale de 3,40m² ayant servi soit pour les bêtes, soit de réserves.

Cour	13 m²
Surface couverte	31,65 m²
Habitation	23,40 m²
Réserves	3,40 m²

DJAFFARABAD

A l'inverse de Choga Mish, Djaffarabad naît à la fin du VIe ou au début du Ve millénaire. Les limites de l'agglomération sont connues (Dollfus 1975) et la superficie est évaluée à environ 0,2 hectare. Le tiers en a été dégagé (fig. 6). Dès le début de l'occupation, l'établissement paraît couvrir cette surface. A la fin de la période, en revanche, une seule maison semble encore habitée.

Niveau 6. Dès l'origine, les maisons paraissent avoir été pluricellulaires (fig. 7a 1−2), mais aucune n'a été dégagée dans sa totalité. Les deux pièces d'habitation respectivement 16,5 m² et 12,8 m² mises au jour à l'ouest et à l'est de l'établissement présentent des caractères identiques: forme rectangulaire ou très légèrement trapézoïdale, sols réenduits à plusieurs reprises, couverture reposant sur des poteaux de bois dont les trous ou les calages ont été retrouvés et plate-forme dans la partie sud de la chambre. Aucune des deux ne présente de trace de foyer; la cuisine se faisait au moins partiellement ou à certaines périodes de l'année dehors, un tannur (four domestique) ayant été mis au jour à l'extérieur contre le mur d'une des pièces. La surface de 3,15 m² de la deuxième chambre dégagée dans l'habitation occidentale ne permet pas de conclure à une réserve ou à un espace d'habitation. Le sol en était bien enduit mais Kramer (1979) a montré qu'il en était de même pour les réserves dans le village qu'elle a étudié.

Niveau 5 (fig. 6). Les constructions recouvrent immédiatement celles du niveau 6. Nous ne reviendrons pas ici sur la description détaillée des niveaux 5b et a (Dollfus 1975). Nous avons à plusieurs reprises attiré l'attention sur la difficulté qu'il y a à les interpréter. Ainsi, pourrait-on être tenté de rapprocher tout le secteur nord-ouest (complexe III) de l'habitation la plus ancienne de Gawra (Gawra XIX, Tobler 1950), mais la présence de sols de torchis soigneusement enduits et souvent refaits dans l'espace 1039 conduit à conclure à une pièce couverte plutôt qu'à une cour.

L'examen des sols, celui du chaînage des murs nous a amené à discerner dans le secteur fouillé trois principaux complexes (fig. 7b, c, d).

Deux d'entre eux présentent des similitudes de plan: pièces d'habitation disposées en L flanquées de salles plus petites (réserves), mais leurs dimensions varient du simple au double. Le troisième complexe, avec son alignement de chambres dont l'une contient un foyer est très différent et s'apparenterait plutôt à l'unité de Choga Mish, *Archaic* 3, après sa réfection.

A Djaffarabad, il ne semble pas que, comme à Choga Mish, on puisse discerner de pièces trop étroites pour que des humains y vivent et qui pourraient être considérées comme des abris pour le bétail. Eventuellement celui-ci ou seulement les jeunes animaux pourraient avoir été parqués le soir dans de petites pièces (14,4 m²) (complexe IV), construites à l'intérieur de l'établissement dans une zone non couverte. Le sol de ces pièces n'est pas enduit mais est de terre battue; aucun indice de toiture n'a été mis en évidence et la couverture paraît avoir été en branchages.

Sur les 600 m² fouillés à Djaffarabad pour le niveau 5b, 182,75 m² sont certainement couverts. Au nord de l'établissement, se trouve une grande aire découverte, riche en traces de décomposition de matières organiques, creusée par endroits de vastes fosses, qui paraît correspondre aux aires d'activités que l'on a notées hors de l'agglomération dans les villages actuels. Au sud du complexe 3, une autre zone découverte[14] est bordée au sud par une ruelle.

	Complexe 1	Complexe 2	Complexe 3	Complexe 4
Surface couverte	73,4 m²	30,5 m²	64,95 m²	14,5 m²
Habitation	67,6 m²	25,5 m²	46,50 m²	--
Réserves	15,8 m²	5,0 m²	18,45 m²	?
Abris/anim.	--	--	--	14,5m²

CHOGA MISH—*MIDDLE SUSIANA* 3; CHOGA BONUT

Vers le milieu de V^e millénaire, quand toute la plaine se couvre d'un nombre beaucoup plus élevé de villages (de 34 à la période précédente à plus de 100; Adams 1962), phénomène qui peut correspondre à une meilleure maîtrise des techniques d'irrigation et à un développement plus grand des zones de cultures irriguées, Choga Mish paraît prendre l'allure d'un centre.

Celui-ci couvre-t-il, comme l'ont suggéré les fouilleurs, la totalité du gisement soit environ 18 hectares (Kantor 1979)? Il paraît difficile de l'affirmer. La poterie que l'on trouve sur la totalité du site pourrait provenir d'un vaste remaniement de terres lors d'occupations plus tardives.[15] Sur la terrasse qui jusque là avait été la zone de prédilection, il semble que l'on n'ait trouvé à ce jour que les traces d'un bâtiment (*burnt building*), différent par son mode de construction des autres maisons et peut-être celles d'un massif de pisé qui aurait servi de fortification (Kantor 1972). La disparition de toute habitation est attribuée à l'érosion et aux occupants du site un millénaire plus tard. N'y a-t-il pas plutôt eu un déplacement du secteur habité vers le nord? Dans la partie septentrionale du site, des couches en place sont signalées sous les dépôts *Late Susiana*.

Admettons cependant la thèse maximaliste, une question alors se pose: A quel type d'habitat sommes-nous confrontés? Il est difficile de penser que l'intégralité du site ait été bâtie; s'agit-il de plusieurs zones d'habitat à réseau serré, ou d'un habitat lâche qui n'entraînerait pas automatiquement une forte augmentation de la population? Grâce au nombre de tranchées et de sondages ouverts, par l'examen des couches possédant du matériel de cette période, une réponse devrait pouvoir être apportée sans difficulté à cette question.

Dans la partie orientale du site, seule à avoir révélé des vestiges d'architecture, on est en présence d'un bâtiment à saillants bien conservé dont la fonction serait administrative ou religieuse (Kantor 1975).[16] Cet édifice n'a pu être fouillé dans son entier. La surface actuellement exposée représente du fait de l'importance des murs, un espace couvert réduit d'environ 35 m², mais il est vraisemblable que ce bâtiment considéré comme monumental avait un plan symétrique (Kantor 1979) et qu'il se poursuivait vers le nord et vers l'ouest.[17]

Ce monument, différent de par sa construction des maisons ordinaires (cf. infra, Choga Bonut) et le mur épais de sept mètres (Kantor 1975) qui le flanque à l'est donnent un caractère tout à fait nouveau à l'établissement. Ce mur entoure-t-il toute l'agglomération? Vise-t-il à ne protéger

14. Ces espaces découverts sont très différents l'un de l'autre. Dans le second, situé entre les maisons, on ne trouve aucune trace de décomposition de matériaux organiques.

15. Choga Mish a été occupé pendant le IVe millénaire, à l'époque élamite, et, d'une façon plus réduite et par intermittence jusqu'à l'époque parthe.

16. Ayant retrouvé en abondance des produits de débitage du silex, H. Kantor pense que dans ce bâtiment aurait existé un véritable "centre industriel" du silex (Kantor 1975).

17. L'épaisseur des murs pourrait aussi faire penser à une maison à deux étages. H. T. Wright me signale que le matériel retrouvé sur les sols ne se distinguait en aucune manière de ceux que l'on trouve dans les maisons ordinaires. L'épaisseur des murs pourrait ainsi trouver une explication.

qu'un quartier et dans cet espace enclos n'y aurait-il que des édifices publics (administratifs ou religieux)? Autant de questions capitales qui restent posées.

Si de Choga Mish, on n'a jusqu'ici pour cette période connaissance d'aucune maison privée, le gisement voisin de Choga Bonut permet d'apprécier le plan d'une habitation. Selon H. Kantor, la disposition de celle-ci serait, sur une échelle beaucoup plus petite, la même que celle de la partie orientale du bâtiment brûlé. On y trouve une pièce en L de 11,50 m² flanquant une chambre rectangulaire de 4 m². Au sud de celles-ci, une pièce oblongue séparée en deux par une cloison pourrait avoir servi de réserve. Au sud, il y aurait une cour où l'on faisait, semble-t-il, la cuisine.[18]

Cour	12	m²
Surface couverte	20,25	m²
Habitation	15,50	m²
Réserve	5,75	m²

La maison de Choga Bonut est la seule connue à ce jour sur cet horizon. Djowi et Bendebal, d'après l'examen des sections, présentent des niveaux d'occupation denses mais les vestiges sont trop fragmentaires pour pouvoir prêter à analyse. Djaffarabad n'est pas habité, seul un atelier de potier y est attesté.

CHOGA MISH, *LATE SUSIANA*

BENDEBAL 16—11; QABR SHEYKHEYN IV—II

DJAFFARABAD, PÉRIODE III (NIVEAUX 3-1)

CHOGA MISH

Au tournant des Ve—IVe millénaire (période *Late Susiana*), les habitants de Choga Mish semblent avoir tout à fait abandonné la partie méridionale du site et s'être fixés seulement dans la zone nord. De leurs maisons, nulle trace n'a jusqu'alors été retrouvée. Seul est signalé ce qui pourrait être un mur de retenue des terres (Kantor 1976).

Bendebal (période III, niveaux 16—11), à l'ouest de Choga Mish, Qabr Sheykheyn (IV—II) au sud-est sont deux établissements tout à fait contemporains qui ont livré des données intéressantes.

BENDEBAL

A Bendebal, du fait de l'érosion, on ne peut apprécier l'étendue de l'établissement. Au niveau 16 fouillé sur 400 m², cinq unités d'habitation au moins ont été dégagées (Dollfus 1977, 1978, et *Cahiers de la Délégation Archéologique Française en Iran* 13, à paraître en 1983). Nous avons figuré ici (fig. 8) le plan des deux unités les mieux conservées. Ces maisons pluricellulaires (?) sont partiellement accolées l'une à l'autre; chacune était longée par une ruelle, l'une sur son flanc ouest, l'autre à l'est. Chaque maison forme un quadrilatère ceint par un mur. L'une comprend une pièce en L d'environ 22 m², une autre carrée de 4 m² et une réserve de 2,40 m². La deuxième, moins bien préservée, était formée soit d'une pièce en L de 19,50 m² et d'une chambre trapézoïdale de 5,70 m²; soit plus probablement d'une pièce rectangulaire de 18 m² et de deux autres de petites dimensions. Dans l'ensemble, les maisons ne paraissent pas avoir été serrées les unes aux autres. Des ruelles, des espaces non bâtis étaient préservés et les maisons s'étageaient

---

18. Deux fours domestiques ont été mis au jour dans cet espace, mais ils sont notés comme d'un autre niveau. Vu leur emplacement par rapport aux murs, Kantor pense qu'ils devaient préexister au moment de l'occupation de la maison (Kantor 1978).

sur le tépé en formation. Sur les 400 m² dégagés au niveau 16, de l'examen des sols et de certains dépôts de matériel, on peut conclure que seuls 150 à 180 m² étaient couverts. Nous n'avons pu déceler si certains complexes comportaient ou non une cour. Les deux unités décrites n'en avaient pas. Aucun foyer n'a été mis au jour, mais les traces de feu sont abondantes dans les zones non bâties.

	Habitation 1	*Habitation 2*
Cour	--	--
Zone couverte	28,50 m²	26 m²
Habitation	26,00 m²	?
Réserve	2,50 m²	?

QABR SHEYKHEYN

A Qabr Sheykheyn, quatre périodes d'occupation du site qui paraissent s'être succédées dans un bref laps de temps, ont été distinguées (Weiss 1972).

Lors des périodes IV et III, les maisons à l'exception d'une seule formée par une pièce rectangulaire de 15,75 m² et décrite comme ne jouxtant aucune autre, comportent chacune entre trois et quatre pièces de petites dimensions. Des structures d'emmagasinement, des foyers domestiques sont signalés.

Ces maisons ne semblent pas avoir été mitoyennes; entre elles apparaissent des plate-formes de 20 à 25 m² chacune et des espaces découverts jonchés de débris sont également signalés.

A la période II, H. Weiss pense que le caractère de l'établissement change. Une seule habitation plus sophistiquée que celle des périodes précédentes aurait été construite sur une plate-forme. Elle serait formée de deux pièces dont la principale aurait 13,44 m² et d'une cour. Doit-on, comme le pense le fouilleur, réduire l'établissement à cette unique maison (Weiss 1972) qui, suivant l'hypothèse de Hole en 1969, émise à la suite de ses prospections, pourrait représenter la maison d'un "khan"? Ne peut-on envisager que l'érosion ait entraîné la disparition d'autres habitations? La plate-forme,[19] la largeur des murs sont-ils des indices suffisants pour donner une importance telle à une habitation qui, par ailleurs, ne paraît ni particulièrement grande, ni particulièrement complexe?

DJAFFARABAD

Au début du IVᵉ millénaire, l'aspect du village de Djaffarabad (fig. 9) est tout à fait différent de celui que présentait l'établissement un millénaire plus tôt. Il est cependant impossible, compte tenu de l'érosion et de la tranchée de Mecquenem d'en évaluer la superficie.

Les structures sont désormais distribuées tout autour d'une aire découverte (au moins 120 m²) qui occupe, semble-t-il, le centre de l'agglomération. Dans cette zone, au début de la période avait été creusé un puits (diam. 3 m)[20] qui, à la fin de la période, n'était plus en usage mais servait de dépotoir.

19. A Djowi, nous avons noté à plusieurs niveaux (couche 12 et couche 14) des "plates-formes" parfois épaisses de l, 20 m. Il nous a paru clair, lors du démontage de celles-ci qu'il ne s'agissait pas réellement de structures mais bien du nivellement d'habitations antérieures. A Bendebal, en un point de la fouille, nous avons fait la même expérience. Ces exemples corroborent la première partie de l'opinion de Weiss. Ils montrent aussi que ces "plate-formes" ne servaient pas obligatoirement à asseoir des maisons particulièrement importantes . . . tout du moins à Djowi et à Bendebal.

20. A Choga Bonut, Kantor signale également un puits de grand diamètre (2,30 m) creusé à partir de niveaux *Late Susiana* enlevés par le bull-dozer (1978).

Les pièces ne sont pas grandes. Aucune, au niveau 3, ne dépasse 6,50 m²; au niveau 2, 8,65 m² (fig. 11a). Les maisons ne sont pas liées les unes aux autres; elles ne comportent qu'une pièce — au sol bien enduit et parfois recouvert de nattes tressées — à laquelle peuvent s'ajouter un ou deux réduits de réserve. A chaque unité est associé un foyer ou un four domestique, parfois les deux. Ceux-ci se situent habituellement ou à l'extérieur des habitations accolés ou à proximité d'un mur, ou, mais le cas est plus rare, dans un "réduit cuisine" (fig. 11a). Aucun signe d'activité culinaire n'a été mis en évidence à l'intérieur des pièces d'habitation. A l'une des chambres (4 m²) se trouve associée une aire (13,70 m²) de briques soigneusement disposées, une réserve qui contenait encore des graines (3 m²) et un réduit (0,65 m²) où on a recueilli en abondance des produits de débitage du silex (fig. 10b).

Tous ces vestiges d'habitation, intéressants par leur disposition, sont cependant trop fragmentaires pour qu'il soit raisonnable de calculer pour les niveaux supérieurs de Djaffarabad, la proportion d'espaces découverts ou couverts tant pour l'ensemble de l'établissement que pour une seule unité d'habitation.

De l'exposé des données recueillies, il ressort que l'information concernant les agglomérations de la Susiane au Vᵉ millénaire est encore ténue.

Les dépôts alluviaux, les phénomènes d'érosion, les remaniements de terre rendent la superficie des établissements difficile à évaluer. Les mêmes causes alliées à la faible surface d'exposition rendent ardue la compréhension de la disposition des villages et souvent celle des maisons elles-mêmes. Formons le voeu qu'à l'avenir des complexes soient dégagés dans leur totalité.

Pour une période donnée, de site à site, ou même à l'intérieur d'une même agglomération, on ne rencontre guère d'homogénéité. Les plans des maisons sont divers, leurs dimensions varient. Il semble cependant qu'au début du Vᵉ millénaire, les complexes d'habitation aient été plus importants qu'à la fin ou au début du IVᵉ millénaire.

		Cour	Zone couverte			
			Habitations	Réserves	Abri/ animaux	Total
Choga Mish						
Early Susiana 1 Cx 1		28	17	7,2	--	24,2
	2	15	18	13,8	6+	37,8
	3		29,5	4,8	1,8	36,1
Middle Susiana 1 Cx 1		13	23,4	3,4	--	31,6
Djaffarabad I	Cx 1	--	67,6	15,8		73,4
	2	--	25,5	5,0		30,5
	3	--	46,5	18,4		64,9
	4	--	--	--	14?	?
Bonut						
Middle Susiana 3		12	15,5	5,7	--	20,2
Bendebal 16	Cx 1	--	26,5	2,5	--	28,5
	Cx 2	--	?	?	--	26,0

Les maisons au début du Vᵉ millénaire devaient abriter des familles au sens large (*extended families*); celles-ci vivaient soit dans des pièces de très grandes dimensions soit dans des chambres plus petites, chaque ménage (*nuclear family*) avec ou sans enfants possédant la sienne, mais les activités culinaires se faisant en commun. C'est encore le cas dans le village du Zagros étudié par Kramer (1979b): "There is a stated and apparent preference for both virilocal residence and extended families; each nuclear family sleeps in a separate room, around either a hearth or an oven, but coresiding nuclear families jointly participate in food preparation and consumption." Ainsi pourraient s'expliquer les différences constatées à Djaffarabad entre les deux types de maisons.

En revanche, à partir des derniers siècles du Ve millénaire et au début du IVe, il semble que la taille des habitations diminue et que chaque maison soit habitée seulement par un ménage (*nuclear family*). Les maisons à Choga Bonut, Bendebal, Qabr Sheykheyn II, ne comptent guère plus d'une ou deux chambres d'habitation, se rapprochant ainsi de ce que l'on observe dans la région à l'heure actuelle (cf. supra et pour plus de détails, Gremliza 1962).

A Djaffarabad, période III, des structures de combustion (four domestique) sont associées à chaque pièce d'habitation, indiquant ainsi l'indépendance vraisemblable de chaque famille. Qu'on soit en face d'un petit village de 5 à 6 maisons représentant le même nombre de ménages, soit en tout 25 à 30 individus et non en présence d'une ferme abritant une seule famille (*extended family*) comme je l'avais pensé (Dollfus 1971) est vraisemblable. Le puits de grand diamètre mis au jour paraît avoir été d'utilisation communale et apporterait la confirmation que l'aire centrale n'est pas la simple cour d'une maison.

Ces considérations n'excluent pas que, dans le futur, des habitations réellement pluricellulaires soient découvertes. Cela pourrait déjà être le cas à Qabr Sheykheyn, période IV (Weiss 1972).

Les prospections menées ces derniers temps par un très grand nombre de chercheurs, jointes à une meilleure compréhension de la stratigraphie permettent maintenant d'établir avec précision pour chaque période, la distribution des agglomérations dans les plaines du Khuzistan. De nouvelles prospections — beaucoup de sites ayant disparu sous les coups des bull-dozers — n'apporteront que peu de connaissances nouvelles. Seul peut-être l'examen attentif des parois des canaux récemment creusés pourrait faire apparaître des sites jusqu'ici ignorés.

En revanche il est souhaitable, sinon indispensable, que dès la reprise des activités dans la région, les archéologues se concertent et envisagent de faire porter leur effort sur un ou deux sites de chaque période afin de procéder à des dégagements aussi extensifs que possible.[21] Si chacun d'entre nous gardait alors constamment à l'esprit les critères qui permettent de discerner les pièces d'habitation, les zones de réserves, éventuellement les abris pour les animaux ou les aires non couvertes (Kramer 1979), alors, mais alors seulement, un grand pas serait franchi et il deviendrait possible de mieux comprendre l'organisation de l'espace dans les villages. Les conditions climatiques n'ont guère changé, les matériaux de construction sont restés les mêmes qu'au Ve millénaire, on peut donc supposer que, même avec une modification des structures socio-économiques, les populations pratiquaient de façon similaire les activités domestiques tant à l'intérieur qu'à l'extérieur des maisons. Ainsi, à l'aide d'études semblables à celles de Watson, Kramer, Jacobs, avec l'appui du travail de Gremliza si riche en données démographiques, il deviendrait possible de dresser un tableau des agglomérations de la Susiane au Ve millénaire.

---

21. De tels dégagements ont été effectués pour les VIe millénaire dans des sites du Zagros (Hajji Firuz, cf. Voigt 1976) ou du plateau (Zagheh, cf. Malek Shahmirzadi 1977). Il est vraisemblable aussi que les fouilles de sauvetage qui viennent d'avoir lieu dans le Hamrin apporteront pour le Ve et le début du IVe millénaire des éléments nouveaux. Cependant tous ces sites ne sont pas localisés dans les plaines mésopotamiennes ou celles du Khuzistan.

REMERCIEMENTS

Ce travail a été accompli dans le cadre des activités de l'URA 19 du Centre National de la Recherche Scientifique, France. Il a été achevé grâce à une bourse d'échange entre le CNRS et la NSF (exchange grant G. 05 0252) en décembre 1980 à Ann Arbor, Mi., où j'ai été accueillie au Museum of Anthropology, Univ. of Michigan, par son directeur, Richard Ford. Il a bénéficié des conversations que j'ai pu avoir avec H. T. Wright et L. Jacobs. Pour sa réalisation matérielle, J. Alden et F. Hiebert m'ont aidée. Que tous ici trouvent l'expression de mes remerciements. Il va de soi que les idées exprimées n'engagent que moi-même. Lors de la publication de ce travail, différents rapports de fouille seront vraisemblablement parus qui remettront, sans nul doute, les idées avancées en question.

BIBLIOGRAPHIE

Adams, R. McC.
  1962   Agriculture and urban life in early southwestern Iran. *Science* 136:109–22.

Canal, D.
  1978   La terrasse de l'acropole de Suse. *Cahiers de la Délégation Archéologique Française en Iran* 9:11–56. Paris: Association Paléorient.

Delougaz, P.P.
  1966   Excavations at Chogha Mish in Iran. *The Oriental Institute report for 1965–1966*:29–38.
  1976   The prehistoric architecture at Chogha Mish. In *The memorial volume of the VI International Congress of Iranian Art and Archaeology*, pp. 31–48. Tehran: Iranian Center for Archaeological Research.

Delougaz, P.P., et Kantor, H.
  1972   New evidence for the prehistoric and Protoliterate culture development. In *The memorial volume of the Vth International Congress of Iranian Art and Archaeology*, vol. 1, pp. 14–33. Tehran: Iranian Center for Archaeological Research.
  1975   The 1973–1974 excavations at Coǧā Miš. In *Proceedings of the IIIrd Annual Symposium on Archaeological Research in Iran* [Tehran, 1974], ed. F. Bagherzadeh, pp. 93–102. Tehran: Iranian Center for Archaeological Research.

Dollfus, G.
  1971   Les fouilles de Djaffarabad de 1969 à 1971. *Cahiers de la Délégation Archéologique Française en Iran* 1:17–161. Paris: Association Paléorient.
  1974   Djaffarabad et la Susiane au Ve et au début du IVe millénaire. In *Proceedings of the IInd Annual Symposium on Archaeological Research in Iran* [Tehran, 1973], pp. 1–14. Tehran: Iranian Center for Archaeological Research.
  1976   Contrôle stratigraphique sur le tépé Djowi. Paper presented at the Vth Annual Symposium on Archaeological Research in Iran [Tehran, 1976].
  1977a   Djaffarabad 1972–1974: périodes I et II. *Cahiers de la Délégation Archéologique Française en Iran* 5:11–220. Paris: Association Paléorient.
  1977b   Travaux récents sur le tépé Bendebal. Paper presented at the VIth Annual Symposium on Archaeological Research in Iran [Tehran, 1977].
  1978   Djaffarabad, Djowi, Bendebal: contribution à l'étude de la Susiane au Ve et au début du IVe millénaire. *Paléorient* 4:141–67.

Flannery, K.
  1969   The animal bones. In *Prehistoric and human ecology of the Deh Luran Plain*, ed. F. Hole,

K. Flannery, and J.A. Neely, pp. 262–330. Memoirs of the Museum of Anthropology, University of Michigan, no. 1. Ann Arbor: University of Michigan Press.

Gautier, J.E., et Lampre, G.
1905   Fouilles de Moussian. In *Mémoires de la Mission Archéologique en Perse,* vol. 8, pp. 59–148. Paris: Leroux.

Gremliza, F.G.L.
1962   *Ecology of endemic diseases in the Dez irrigation pilot area.* Report to Khuzestan Power Authority and Plan Organization of Iran. New York: Development and Resources Corp.

Hole, F.
1977   *Studies in the archaeological history of the Deh Luran plain: the excavations at Choga Sefid.* Memoirs of the Museum of Anthropology, University of Michigan, no. 9. Ann Arbor: University of Michigan Press.
1977b   Social implications of the prehistoric ceramics of Xuzestan. Paper presented at the VIth Annual Symposium on Archaeological Research in Iran [Tehran, 1977].
1978   The comparative stratigraphy of the early periods in Khuzistan. *Paléorient* 4:229–32.

Hole, F., et Woosley, A.
1978   Pollen evidence of subsistence and environment in ancient Iran. *Paléorient* 4:59–70.

Jacobs, L.
1979   Tell-i-Nun: archaeological implications of a village in transition. In *Ethnoarchaeology: Implications of ethnography for archaeology,* ed. C. Kramer, pp. 175–91. New York: Columbia University Press.

Kantor, H.J.
1972   Excavations at Chogha Mish. *The Oriental Institute of the University of Chicago Report for 1971–1972*:12–18.
1974a   Excavations at Chogha Mish. *The Oriental Institute of the University of Chicago Report for 1973–1974*:20–28.
1974b   The Čogā Miš Excavations 1972–1973. In *Proceedings of the IInd Annual Symposium on Archaeological Research in Iran* [Tehran, 1973], pp. 15–22. Tehran: Iranian Center for Archaeological Research.
1975   Excavations at Chogha Mish. *The Oriental Institute of the University of Chicago Report for 1974–1975*:17–26.
1976a   The excavations at Čogā Miš 1974–1975. In *Proceedings of the IVth Annual Symposium on Archaeological Research in Iran* [Tehran, 1975], ed. F. Bagherzadeh, pp. 23–41. Tehran: Iranian Center for Archaeological Research.
1976b   Excavations at Chogha Mish. *The Oriental Institute of the University of Chicago Report for 1975–1976*:12–21.
1977   Excavations at Chogha Mish and Chogha Bonut. *The Oriental Institute Annual Report 1976–1977*:15–23.
1978   Chogha Mish and Chogha Bonut. *The Oriental Institute Annual Report 1977–1978*: 11–19.
1979   Chogha Mish and Chogha Bonut. *The Oriental Institute Annual Report 1978–1979*: 33–39.

Kirkby, A., et Kirkby, M.J.
1976   Geomorphic processes and the surface survey of archaeological sites in semi-arid areas. In *Geoarcheology, earth sciences and the past,* ed. D.A. Davidson and M.L. Schackey, pp. 230–53. London: Duckworth.

Kirkby, M.J.
1977   Land and water resources of the Deh Luran and Khuzistan plains. In *Studies in the archaeological history of the Deh Luran Plain: the excavations at Choga Sefid,* ed. F. Hole, pp. 251–88. Memoirs of the Museum of Anthropology, University of Michigan, no. 9. Ann Arbor: University of Michigan Press.

Kramer, C.
  1979a   (ed.) Ethnoarchaeology: implications of ethnography for archaeology. New York: Columbia University Press.
  1979b   An archaeological view of a contemporary Kurdish village: domestic household, size and wealth. In Ethnoarchaeology: implications of ethnography for archaeology, ed. C. Kramer, pp. 139–63. New York: Columbia University Press.

Larsen, C.E.
  1975   The Mesopotamian delta region: a reconsideration of Lees and Falcon. Journal of the American Oriental Society 95: 43–57.

LeBlanc, S.
  1971   An addition to Naroll's suggested floor area and settlement population relationship. American Antiquity 36:210–12.

Le Breton, L.
  1947   Note sur la céramique peinte aux environs de Suse et à Suse. In Mémoires de la Délégation Archéologique de Perse, vol. 30, pp. 124–46. Paris: Presses Universitaires de France.
  1957   The early periods at Susa: Mesopotamian relations. Iraq 29:79–124.

Le Brun, A.
  1971   Recherches stratigraphiques à l'acropole de Suse (1969–1971). Cahiers de la Délégation Archéologique Française en Iran 1:163–214. Paris: Association Paléorient.

Lees, G.M., et Falcon, N.L.
  1952   The geographical history of the Mesopotamian plains. Geographical Journal 118:24–39.

McCown, D.E.
  1942   The comparative stratigraphy of early Iran. Studies in Ancient Oriental Civilization, no. 23. Chicago: University of Chicago Press.

Malek Shahmirzadi, S.
  1977   Tepe Zagheh: a sixth millennium B.C. village in the Qazvin plain of the central Iranian plateau. Ph.D. diss., University of Pennsylvania.

Mecquenem, R. de
  1934   Fouilles de Suse, 1929–1933. In Mémoires de la Mission Archéologique en Perse, vol. 25, pp. 177–237. Paris: Leroux.
  1943   Fouilles de Suse 1943–1949. In Mémoires de la Mission Archéologique en Iran, vol. 29, pp. 139–57. Paris: Presses Universitaires de France.

Miller, N.
  1977   Preliminary report on the botanical remains from Tepe Djaffarabad 1969–1974 campaigns. Cahiers de la Délégation Archéologique Française en Iran 7:49–53. Paris: Association Paléorient.
  1980   The plant remains. In An early town on the Deh Luran Plain: excavations at Tepe Farukhabad, ed. H.T. Wright, pp. 227–30. Memoirs of the Museum of Anthropology, University of Michigan, no. 14. Ann Arbor: University of Michigan Press.

Morgan, J. de
  1900a   Etude géographique sur la Susiane. In Mémoires de la Délégation en Perse, vol. 2, pp. 1–32. Paris: Leroux.
  1900b   Travaux au tell de la citadelle. In Mémoires de la Délégation en Perse, vol. 2, pp. 88–137. Paris: Leroux.

Nützel, W.
  1975   The formation of the Arabian Gulf from 14,000 B.C. Sumer 31:101–10.
  1978   To which depths are "prehistorical civilizations" to be found beneath the present alluvial plains of Mesopotamia? Sumer 34:17–26.

Oates, J.
    1973   The background and development of early farming communities in Mesopotamia and the Zagros. *Proceedings of the Prehistoric Society* 39:147—81.

Redding, R.
    1980   The faunal remains. In *An early town on the Deh Luran Plain: excavations at Tepe Farukhabad*, ed. H.T. Wright, pp. 233—79. Memoirs of the Museum of Anthropology, University of Michigan, no. 14. Ann Arbor: University of Michigan Press.

Stève, M.J., et Gasche, H.
    1971   *L'Acropole de Suse: nouvelles fouilles.* Mémoires de la Délégation Archéologique en Iran, vol. 46, Mission de Susiane. Paris: Geuthner.

Sumner, W.M.
    1979   Estimating population by analogy. In *Enthnoarchaeology: implications of ethnography for archaeology*, ed. C. Kramer, pp. 164—74. New York: Columbia University Press.

Tobler, A.J.
    1950   *Excavations at Tepe Gawra*, vol. 1. Philadelphia: University of Pennsylvania Press.

Vanden Berghe, L.
    1952   Les ateliers de la céramique peinte chalcolithique en Iran de sud-ouest. *Revue Archéologique* 29:1—21.

Voigt, M.M.
    1976   The economy of a sixth millennium farming community in western Iran: Hajji Firuz Tepe. Ph.D. diss., University of Pennsylvania.

Watson, P.J.
    1978   Architectural differentiation in some Near Eastern communities: prehistoric and contemporary. In *Social archaeology: beyond subsistence and dating*, ed. C. Redman, E. Curtin, N. Versaggi, and J. Wanser, pp. 131—57. New York: Academic Press.
    1979   *Archaeological ethnography in western Iran.* Viking Fund Publications in Anthropology 57. Tucson: University of Arizona Press.

Weiss, H.
    1972   Qabr Sheykheyn. *Iran* 10:172—73.

Wright, H.T.
    1979   *(ed.) Archaeological investigations in northeastern Xuzestan.* Technical Reports of the Museum of Anthropology, University of Michigan, no. 10. Ann Arbor: University of Michigan Press.
    1980   *(ed.) An early town on the Deh Luran Plain: excavations at Tepe Faruhkabad.* Memoirs of the Museum of Anthropology, University of Michigan, no. 14. Ann Arbor: University of Michigan Press.

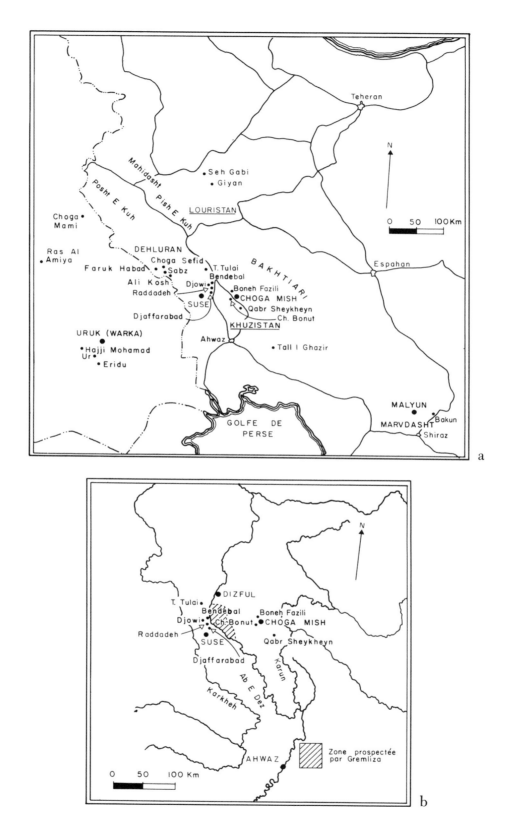

FIG. 1. — (a) CARTE DE SITUATION. (b) CARTE DE DÉTAIL DE LA PLAINE CENTRALE
MONTRANT LES SITES ARCHÉOLOGIQUES ET LA ZONE PROSPECTÉE PAR GREMLIZA.

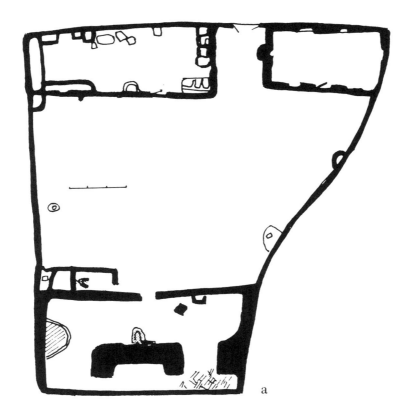

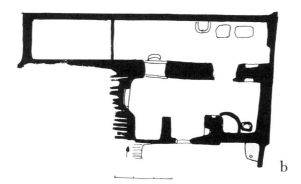

FIG. 2. — (a) UNITÉ D'HABITATION DE RADDADEH. Pièce d'habitation: 18 m²; réserve: 28 m²; ancienne pièce d'habitation transformée en réserve essentiellement de combustible: 43 m²; cuisine: 1,80 m². (b) UNITÉ D'HABITATION DE RADDADEH. Pièce d'habitation: 17,36 m²; réserve: 24 m².

306

FIG. 3. — PLAN TOPOGRAPHIQUE DU SITE DE CHOGA MISH. Dessiné à partir de Kantor et Delougaz 1972 et Delougaz 1976, montrant l'emplacement des sondages et des tranchées ainsi que le lieu de distribution des vestiges de différentes époques: etabli d'après les différents rapports de fouille publiés. a: archaïc; e.s.: early susiana; m.s.: middle susiana; l.s.: late susiana.

Fig. 4. — (a) Choga Mish, Tr. XXV, Archaïc 3. Plan d'unités d'habitation d'après Delougaz 1976. (b) Choga Mish, Tr. XXI, Early Susiana. Plan de 4 unités d'habitation d'après Delougaz 1976.

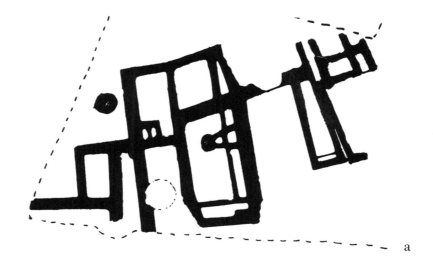

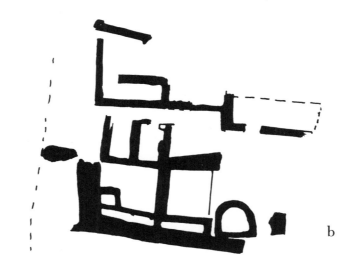

FIG. 5. — (a) CHOGA MISH, TR. XIII, EARLY SUSIANA. Plan
d'une unité d'habitation d'après Delougaz 1976. (b) CHOGA
MISH, TR. XXI, MIDDLE SUSIANA(1?). Plan d'une unité
d'habitation d'après Delougaz 1976.

FIG. 6. — DJAFFARABAD, NIVEAUX 6 ET 5. Plan de l'établissement.

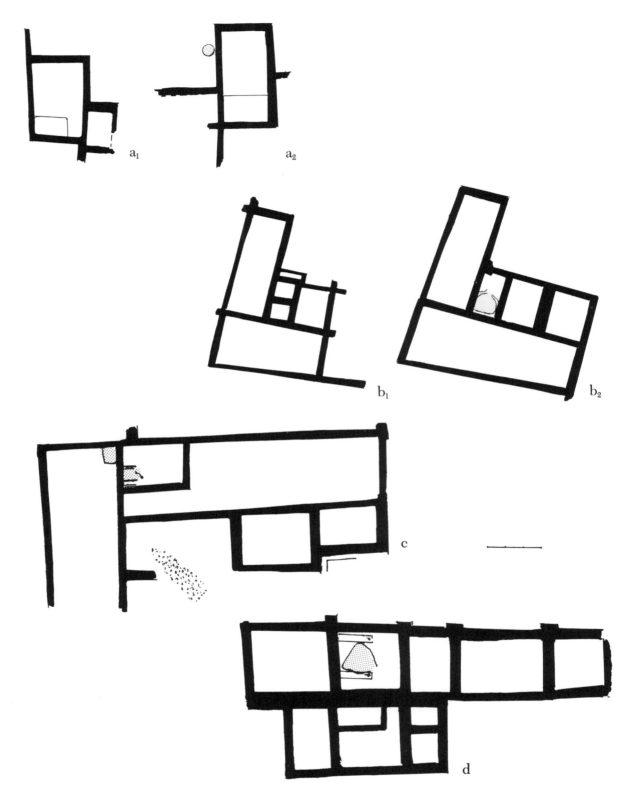

FIG. 7. — (a1−2) DJAFFARABAD, NIVEAU 6. Pièces d'habitation. (b1) DJAFFARABAD, NIVEAU 5b. Unité d'habitation. Cx II. (b2) DJAFFARABAD, NIVEAU 5a. Unité d'habitation remodelée. (c) DJAFFARABAD, NIVEAU 5b. Unité d'habitation. Cx I. (d) DJAFFARABAD, NIVEAU 5b. Unités d'habitation. Cx III.

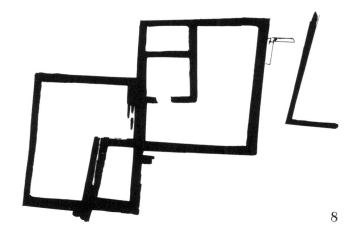

8

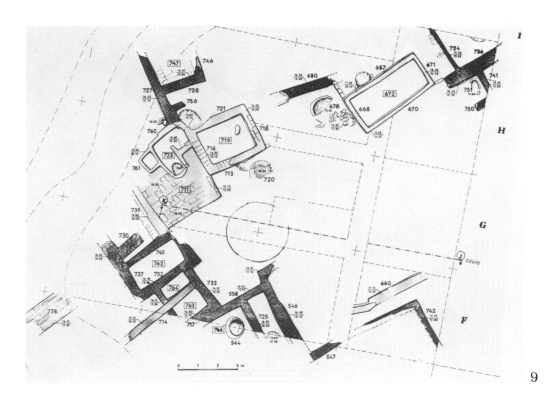

9

Fig. 8. — Bendebal, Niveau 16. Plan de deux unités d'habitation. Fig. 9. — Djaffarabad, Niveau 3. Plan d'ensemble.

312

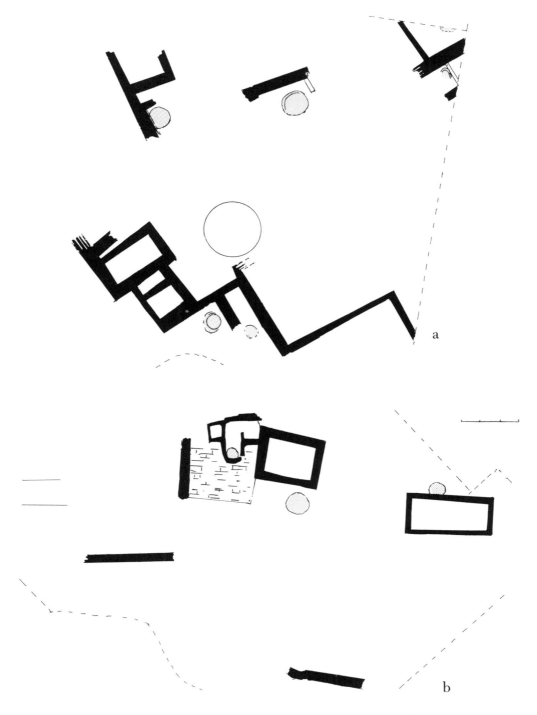

Fig. 10. — (a) Djaffarabad, niveau 3b. Plan des vestiges d'habitat. (b) Djaffarabad, niveau 3a. Plan des vestiges d'habitat.

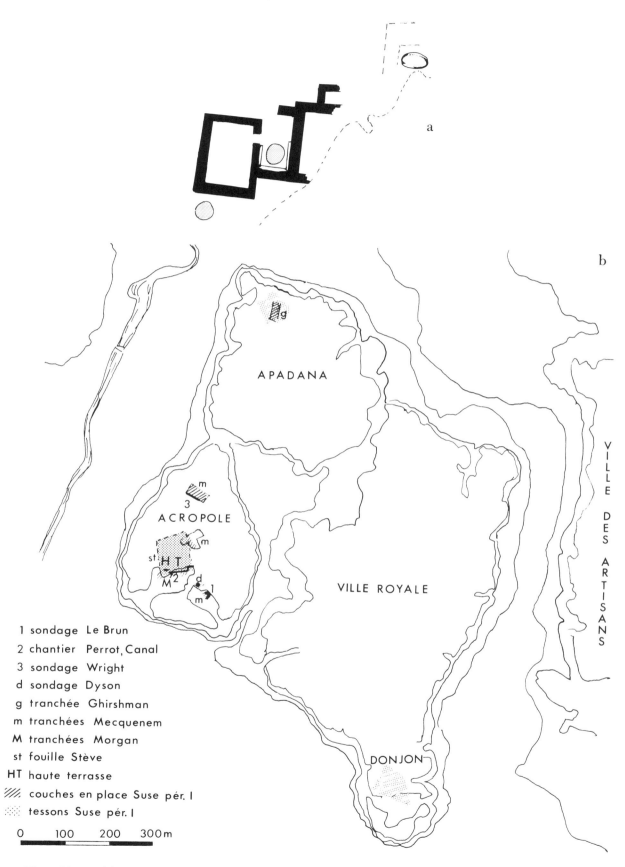

1 sondage Le Brun
2 chantier Perrot, Canal
3 sondage Wright
d sondage Dyson
g tranchée Ghirshman
m tranchées Mecquenem
M tranchées Morgan
st fouille Stève
HT haute terrasse
couches en place Suse pér. I
tessons Suse pér. I

0   100   200   300m

FIG. 11. — (a) DJAFFARABAD, NIVEAU 2. Vestiges d'une maison. (b) SUSE, PLAN TOPO-
GRAPHIQUE DE SUSE (avec l'emplacements des vestiges de la pèriode I).

SYMBOLS OF RELIGION AND SOCIAL ORGANIZATION AT SUSA

Frank Hole

INTRODUCTION

MY INTENT here is to examine "one of the thorniest problems in cultural evolution . . ., the origins of hereditary inequality — the leap to a stage where lineages are 'ranked' with regard to each other, and men from birth are of 'chiefly' or 'commoner' descent, regardless of their individual capabilities" (Flannery 1972, p. 403). I do this by examining Susa, the preeminent site of Khuzistan at the end of the fifth and the beginning of the fourth millennium B.C. Evidence from the cemetery there, excavated three quarters of a century ago, material from the latest stratigraphic excavations, data derived from survey of sites in Khuzistan, and certain textual evidence contribute toward a picture of the organization of society at Susa.

Following a review of the archeological evidence, which has not been presented in this form before, I shall examine various models of social organization. In evolutionist terms Susa is a chiefdom, but this designation obscures the rich variety of potential organizations of advanced agriculturalists. Moreover, Susa was occupied during a period of change, so that flexible rather than static aspects of its organization are appropriately made the center of inquiry. Evidence of a religious focus and of trends that signal increasing institutionalization of religion emerges clearly from the data. The evidence fails to confirm a paramount chief, however, and implies an organization that might best be called an aggregate society.

ARCHEOLOGICAL CONTENT

SUSA

Susa is one of the largest prehistoric sites in Iran, a site that in the late fifth millennium contained a monumental step platform (Canal 1978) and a large cemetery surrounded by a domestic settlement, perhaps as large as 15 hectares. The platform, a massive construction of unbaked clay bricks, is clear indication of a public work carried out under the supervision of a cadre of distinctive personnel whose symbols of status may be seen in the extraordinary crafts found with some of the burials. It would seem unnecessary to defend the proposition that the step platform at Susa is anything other than the foundation of a temple, although we have no direct evidence that it served this purpose. There is, however, a plaque from the Susa period on which is carved the facade of a temple (Stève and Gasche 1971, pl. 39:27), a motif that is often seen on later Uruk seals (Stève and Gasche 1971, p. 184). Moreover, a seal that may also show a temple, as well as a vessel with a temple in carved relief, were both found in levels contemporary with Susa at Jaffarabad (Dollfus 1971, fig. 23:2, pers. comm.). This evidence, if not entirely satisfying, is supported by the finding of actual temples at contemporary sites in southern and northern Mesopotamia.

Susa lies on the western edge of the low Khuzistan plain in southwestern Iran, a region geographically similar to southern Mesopotamia, with which it shared many cultural similarities during the Ubaid, a period that long has attracted attention because of the wide spread (from Syria to Iran) of similarly painted ceramics. We now know that some of the apparent similarity resulted from technical changes in the manufacture of pottery. Nonetheless, the time during which the distinctive pottery was produced saw a great increase in the number of settlements and

315

their spread into previously unsettled regions. In some of these regions, irrigation agriculture provided the means for this expansion.

The Ubaid, referred to in Khuzistan as the Susa I period, was indisputably dynamic. Populations grew. New regions were colonized. New conceptions of the place of man in the universe were portrayed in tangible symbols. New forms of societal organization emerged to meet changing needs and opportunities. The agricultural technology and the crafts to support this dynamism existed already in various parts of southwest Asia, so that the people of the fifth millennium might best be characterized as opportunistic rather than as unusually innovative. They expanded and consolidated their gains while they tinkered with the social frameworks that kept their systems alive in unpredictable and potentially hostile environments. The evidence of their ultimate successes in these human ventures is still ambiguous, at least in Iran, where a decided decline in the number of settlements began to occur before our archeological period — defined on the basis of pottery — ends (various viewpoints on the demographic changes occur in Adams 1962; Hole 1977; Weiss 1977; Wright et al. 1975).

THE CEMETERY

The cemetery is a well-defined locus of artifacts and a context of distinct social significance. Although the cemetery, excavated in 1906 to 1908, contained an estimated 2,000 burials accompanied by pottery, copper and other artifacts, it has attracted attention chiefly for the artistic qualities of the finest ceramic vessels (Morgan 1912; Mecquenem 1943, pp. 1–12; Pottier 1912). The question of the role this cemetery played, in either the site itself or in the region, has been addressed only recently (Dyson 1966, pp. 341–49; Hole 1977). Indeed, there has never been a thorough inventory of the artifacts from the cemetery, let alone a detailed analysis of the material.

We will never know the archeological context of the cemetery precisely, although Perrot and Canal have discovered two more burials recently (Canal 1978a, pp. 33–34; 1978b). As a result of this work the stratigraphic position of the cemetery within the site of Susa is better known but, because Morgan's report is vague, it is impossible to determine it with certainty. Morgan encountered burials during the trenching of the acropolis, an operation that he had carried out in excavation levels five meters thick. At the base of the site, on sterile soil in Level V, Morgan reported finding a cemetery containing approximately 2,000 graves (Morgan 1912, p. 7). He estimated that the cemetery was about 3 m in depth and about 30 m wide (Morgan 1912, p. 2). Mecquenem, who participated in the excavation, later wrote that the cemetery was 3 to 4 m in depth and 12 m in diameter (Mecquenem 1943, p. 6). Morgan reported that the bodies were usually extended but sometimes flexed and were accompanied by ceramic vessels; tombs also contained copper objects and other material. Mecquenem disputed the state of the burials, saying that they were secondary; often, the long bones had been placed in tall beakers and the skulls in open bowls. Canal supports this idea, because the 1972 excavations revealed two secondary burials cut into the side of the "massif funéraire."

The question of whether the burials were primary or secondary is not important here because we are more concerned with the material placed in the graves than with the bones themselves. Unfortunately, there is no information on individual grave lots or on the skeletons. The excavators said that the cemetery contained adults, but the reported lack of any bones in some graves implies burials of infants, cenotaphs for adults interred elsewhere, or ceremonial deposits of ritual goods. Without additional information one cannot distinguish among these possibilities. In Sondage I, north of the cemetery on the opposite side of the step platform, Mecquenem found two burials of children, accompanied by painted vessels (1930, p. 225; 1943, p. 230). No other burials have been found in the extensive Susa period deposits.

Both Morgan and Mecquenem believed the cemetery to be in association with a massive brick wall. The bricks are now known to be part of the low platform (*massif funéraire*) and step platform (*haute terrasse*) (Canal 1978a,b).

The age of the step platform was first recognized by Dyson (1966, p. 344) and then confirmed by Stève (Stève and Gasche 1971, p. 118). The small initial platform that antedated the step platform was identified and exposed by Canal (1978a,b). Canal's work revealed that the first settlers of the Susa acropolis built a low mud-brick platform near their domestic settlement. After some 50–100 cm of debris had accumulated, the step platform, measuring at least 80 m along its southeast face, with a first step 2 m high and a second step 8 m high, was built. The initial low platform continued to be exposed above the surface of the ground until a series of misfortunes struck. The first of these, in Canal's Level 9, was apparently a massive conflagration that resulted in the collapse of the platform's facade. The debris from this collapse contained bricks, "clous" (large, pierced, hollow ceramic cones), burned material, including pieces of wooden beams, and masses of bones (Canal 1978b).

Canal (1978a, p. 38) infers that a charnel house atop the step platform burned, causing bones of decomposing bodies, bricks from the walls, and pieces of the facade of the platform to tumble to the base. This was followed by water erosion of the unstable skin of the platform, resulting in a second, more massive collapse that engulfed the low platform. Under material of the first collapse, at the base of the step platform, lay the skeleton of an adult male.

The initial low platform had been surrounded by no more than 1 m of fill prior to the collapses, and structures with brick walls had been installed between the low platform and the step platform. We can surmise, therefore, that the area around the low platform was not used for burials until material from the collapses had provided sufficient fill into which the bodies could be placed.

In an attempt to reconcile the conflicting accounts of the stratigraphic position of the cemetery, Dyson reviewed the elevations of sterile soil and the depths of Susa I deposits. He concluded that the cemetery may have been on the edge of a natural slope where the burials were cut into accumulated debris. If this were the case, the cemetery dates not to the Susa town whose debris surrounds the low platform but to the age of the step platform. Thus Dyson inferred that the cemetery was late in the history of the Susa-period occupation rather than early. At the time the step platform was built "it was surrounded to the north and south by silos, work areas, and potters' kilns, all of which could, of course, have been connected with a temple economy" (Dyson 1966, p. 369). As for the remainder of the site, he said, "The Susa A occupation extended primarily to the central portion of the Apadana mound and southward across the river through the area of the Acropolis mound" (Dyson 1966, p. 370). Nevertheless, the actual extent of the Susa A occupation remains uncertain (G. Dollfus, pers. comm.). The "river," the cut between the Acropolis and Apadana, may have been either an old course of the Shaur or a canal. It has not been tested archeologically.

It is evident from this discussion that there is still a question about the precise chronology of the cemetery within the Susa settlement. That it is of the Susa perod is not in question: it corresponds with Levels 27–23 of the Acropole sounding (Le Brun 1971) and with Jaffarabad 1–3 (Dollfus 1971). Neither the platform nor the cemetery extends through the final portion of the Susa period, a finding confirmed by Stève's work on top of the platform (Stève and Gasche 1971). In radio-carbon years (corrected) the entire Susa period is between 4200 and 3800 B.C. (see Weiss 1977 for tables of dates and corrections).

CONTENTS OF THE TOMBS

The pottery from the tombs is remarkably varied, a fact whose interpretation is complicated by the absence of information on individual grave lots. The excavators reported that each tomb contained a beaker, one or more open bowls, and a small jar. Also from the burials were numerous copper axes, eleven copper disks, and a copper needle, burin, and chisel; eleven clay or stone cosmetic pots; a few beads; a stamp seal; five fragments of maces; a stone hoe and a microcelt (Morgan 1912, pp. 9–13). In view of the quality of most of the goods it is doubtful that the mace fragments were intentionally placed in the tombs.

Fifty-five copper axes were found, some of which are so large as to represent significant hordes of native copper. Because native copper is relatively soft these objects must be symbolic rather than utilitarian. The absence of copper axes from domestic contexts at Susa and other sites underlines the exceptional nature of these finds and suggests their close identification with individuals. Polished stone axes or celts of the same form are found in domestic contexts (Dollfus 1971, p. 64). Of the eleven copper disks four have holes, possibly for suspension. Although these disks are usually called mirrors their use is problematic. Corrosion has long since obliterated any traces of polish. Both the axes and disks preserve traces of fabric in which they may have been wrapped.

The style and execution of some of the ceramics make these pieces noteworthy in the history of art. Neither they nor the metal are strictly utilitarian. Both suggest the importance of display to certain people of status and of the ability of these people to acquire the finest objects of their time. Although the display centered on individuals, the context in which it was carried out was ceremonial, as I shall discuss below.

SYMBOLISM

MOTIF AND MEANING

Graphics, whether they are designs on pottery or on other media, must result from a combination of conception, skill, style, and nature of the medium involved. A pot results from a combination of the qualities of the clay and the potter's skill and attention to detail, and reflects contemporary values in the painted designs. We generally accept that by the time people were capable of rendering natural and geometric forms of great beauty on curved surfaces they were equally capable of recognizing in these forms ideas that underlay their conception of the world. Thus we look for evidence of symbolism in compositions that go beyond mere stereotyped decoration.

Because production of painted pottery ceased temporarily with the Susa period, one turns to seals and seal impressions for evidence of continuity of symbolism and specific iconography that may be tied to historical sources or that may extend the range of compositional context. To shift from the medium of pottery to that of engraved seals provides continuity but it raises the question whether the two classes of objects functioned in the same ideological domain.

In recognition of the many pitfalls along such a route of investigation, Goff listed five principles that seem "essential for a study of the significance of any symbol in any period. One must:

1. determine the dominant forms as against the relatively incidental;
2. investigate the interrelationships of these forms;
3. emphasize those forms which became a popular style;
4. examine especially the ways in which reality is distorted when a design is representational;
5. utilize the greatest circumspection in drawing inferences about early periods from knowledge about later periods" (Goff 1963, p. xxxiii).

The procedures Goff suggests cannot be carried out generally, because most collections of material are too small, of uncertain provenience, or of different ages. An exception is the Susa cemetery vessels that come from a single context and are numerous enough to be handled quantitatively as well as qualitatively. The problems raised by Goff are more relevant to the use of seal impressions as an aid in recognizing symbolism in the ceramics and in ascribing meaning to the symbols. In the pages that follow I shall keep Goff's injunctions in mind as I deal with one limited set of symbols.

From the time the Susa cemetery was excavated there has been speculation about the meaning of the motifs on the pots. Morgan (1912), like most subsequent writers, believed that one could relate the motifs to Mesopotamian mythology. But it was Pottier, in his detailed description of a selected series of the cemetery vessels, who pointed to the similarities between designs on pottery and seals and to certain cuneiform signs (Pottier 1912, pp. 50ff.). He cautiously refrained from ascribing the underlying meaning to any particular sign: "marque de possession personnelle? marque de tribu? signe religieux?" (Pottier 1912, p. 57). One should not, he said (1912, p. 57), try to *read* designs, as one would read a text. He was particularly critical of Pézard's efforts to attribute meaning to signs, and in a statement to which we should all pay heed he said, "C'est le cas de proclamer le 'droit à l'ignorance' dont les archéologues n'usent peut-être pas suffisamment" (1912, p. 59). In spite of such injunctions many writers have attempted to interpret particular signs.

Morgan (1912, p. 6) related the "arrow" motif to the god Marduk, an attribution that continues to be echoed (Contenau 1927, p. 288; Amiet 1966, p. 43). Pottier himself dealt with this along with the "quiver" motif. "Le carquois de flèches, qui représente son chef ou son dieu posant l'arme de guerre sur un autel. . . . Non seulement il a déja constitué le culte de l'arme de guerre plantée sur un autel, tel qu'on le voit beaucoup plus tard sur les monuments babyloniens, mais il use aussi de symboles pour nous plus mystérieux" (Pottier 1912, p. 38).

Amiet (1966, p. 31) points out that although we can identify some of the subjects, such as birds, goats, or people, we should not assume that we can understand the underlying meaning. Nevertheless, he recognizes the "master of the animals" on both seals and pots. "Le 'Maitre des animaux' est la plus ancienne figure mythologique du répertoire oriental, ancêtre à la fois des héros légendaires et des dieux anthropomorphes" (Amiet 1966, pp. 32, 49).

It is relevant here to refer to the nature of religious conception among early Near Eastern peoples. Jacobsen (1976, p. 3) sees religion as a response to the experience of powers that are not of this world. Further, as such powers are otherworldly they cannot be described directly; thus they are treated metaphorically. Religious metaphors "form a bridge between direct and mediate experience, between the religious founders and leaders and their followers; and they furnish a common bond of understanding between worshippers, and are the means by which religious content and forms are handed down from one generation to the next."

The "master of the animals" that Amiet refers to is such a metaphor, but whether or not we can identify any particular metaphor by name we should be able to recognize its existence by its context and continuity. The master of animals makes a good point of departure. In the next section of this paper we shall deal with graphic expressions whose meanings may well reside partly in religious metaphors.

SIGNIFICANCE OF THE ANTHROPOMORPHIC FIGURES

The vessels from the cemetery, as well as seals from Susa and other sites, exhibit a large corpus of motifs and combinations of design elements that provide rich possibilities for the study of personal emblems, specific iconographic motifs, associations of motifs with one another, stylistic differences and changes, and comparisons outside Susiana. As an analysis of even the cemetery data alone will require monographic treatment, here I shall deal solely with the few cemetery vessels on which there are anthropomorphic figures or signs that are probably emblematic of the offices of these personages, and the seals that bear the same or related motifs.

From the cemetery there are only four vessels that have anthropomorphic figures: one bowl has four figures, each with a "ring" headdress (fig. 1:f,g); one bowl has two figures carrying bows in some sort of hunting scene; and two bowls have figures grasping spades or pointed staffs (fig. 1:a,b).

These bowls have been illustrated repeatedly, with the exception of the one with the ring-headed figures, whose paint is poorly preserved. I shall not discuss the hunters further in the present context.

The conventional interpretation is that the figures grasping spades represent Marduk or his son Nabu, gods associated with agriculture and fertility. By extension, the spades when represented without the figures symbolize agricultural activity. A number of beakers, jars, and bowls from the cemetery have only the spade motif standing in isolation (fig. 1:e); they are sometimes in pairs (fig. 1:c,d) and sometimes singly on or in a base. Only on the open bowls does this motif occur in precisely the same style as it does on the two bowls with the figures, i.e., in a design niche.

If we accept that the spade may stand for the person/shaman/god depicted when the figures are present, then other motifs that occupy the same position on open bowls may have similar significance. For example, also on open bowls are a small series of ring motifs that stand in positions identical to those of the spade motifs — even being set into bases (fig. 1:h,i,j). That these motifs symbolize figures is probable because of the bowl on which four persons with ring-style headdresses appear (fig. 1:f,g); each of these figures stands in a design niche, touching its edges with outstretched arms, in poses like those of the figures with spades. We now see that the free-standing ring motif represents the headdress of a figure, which is absent, and thus the figure itself.

For further insight into these motifs we turn to seals. Le Brun (1971, fig. 35:2) illustrates a seal impression from Level 25 of the Acropole sounding (Susa period) in which the figure wears a "goat-horn" headdress (for a discussion of the "goat-god," see Barnett 1966) and holds a snake in each outstretched hand (fig. 2:a). The posture of the figure holding the snakes is very similar to that of the figures on the pottery. We should note too that the snakes in this seal (and on pottery from the cemetery) have pointed, spadelike heads. None of the snakes appears to emanate from a base as do the spades, however, and none occurs in a design niche of a bowl. The parallels between the seal and the pottery are evident but by no means identical.

The most informative series of seals and sealings come from contexts at Susa that are usually attributed to the Uruk period (Amiet 1972, pp. 219–31). Number 220 (fig. 2:b) depicts an anthropomorphic animal-headed figure wearing a goat-horn headdress, holding two snakes and standing between two objects that may be spades. To suggest reality in what could otherwise be a purely mythological representation, the figure (see also number 219 [fig. 2:c]) is wearing around its neck a disk hung from cords. This detail, perhaps more than anything, suggests that a human is depicted carrying out a ceremony in sacerdotal garb that includes a medallion hung over the chest. The implication is strengthened by the finding in the cemetery of copper disks; that these disks were worn as medallions during religious ceremonies is a more convincing interpretation of their role than any suggestion that they may have been used as mirrors. If this interpretation is correct, we may take one more inferential step and regard the copper axes found in the cemetery as ceremonial versions of agricultural hoes, hence, symbols of agricultural activity, the "spades of Marduk."

We may extend these interpretations by looking at seals 229, 230, and 231 (fig. 2:d,e,f). Each seal depicts several figures dressed in ceremonial clothing. In each there is a figure with a ring-style headdress, a style that was probably misinterpreted as "bulbous" by Amiet, who did not have available as a model the bowl from the cemetery.

We notice that the iconographic contexts of these seals are quite different from those of numbers 219 and 220. The scenes are of libations or offerings, ceremonies in which differently garbed figures are performing separate acts. The spaces are filled with isolated motifs. In view of the fantastic heads and dress it is likely that the seals depict religious mythology. Again there are interesting implications for material found in the cemetery. First, the figures are raising both beakers and bowls. The beaker in 231, with its suggestion of a design, raises the possibility that the seals may actually depict a ceremony of the Susa period, when such beakers were in use. Secondly, the figures (also those in 219) have skirts decorated with bold linear or geometric patterns. The patterns are reminiscent of the large "seals" found in Susa-period context (but not in the cemetery) that have been identified as possible pattern blocks for the imprinting of clothing (Dollfus 1973; Mecquenem 1943, fig. 3:4).

One may legitimately object that I have constructed a picture out of material that is not contemporary. Although there has been some question of the age, Mecquenem (1938, pp. 65–66) clearly states that in the upper part of the Susa I levels, "disséminées sur une surface de 4 mètres carrés, ont été recueillies une dizaine d'empreintes de cachet-boutons sur terre crue; elles montrent des personnages vêtus de robes, coiffés de hautes tiares." These seals, along with others (Amiet 1972), are usually attributed as a single group to the Uruk, although Amiet (1971, p. 219) expressed doubt about this after similar seals were found in unequivocal Susa I context in the Acropole sounding (Le Brun 1971). Also to the point is that none of the seals discussed above is in the style of those excavated under controlled conditions in Uruk Levels 18–17 of the Acropole sounding, where there is the first convincing evidence of writing (Le Brun 1971; Vallat 1978). Although this sounding went down into Susa-period deposits in Levels 27–23, only the sealings and temple model previously mentioned were found. None of this is conclusive evidence that the seals discussed above date from the Susa period, but it is an indication of iconographic continuity.

If this is the case, the seals depict ceremonies like those carried out during the Susa period, if not precisely those of the period. Unfortunately, we have virtually no evidence from secure early Uruk contexts to inform us about ceremonialism.

The lack of seals with the burials, which otherwise contained fine artifacts and evident symbols of office, is curious unless seals were not associated with individuals, that is, unless they symbolized or depicted rites and institutions rather than the persons who participated in them. If this was the case they may have served to mark goods that were brought to the temple for use in the rites depicted or for the shrines of particular deities.

The fact that the earliest depictions are of persons bearing or wearing symbols of office whereas the later seals depict scenes of ceremonies implies a development toward more formal institutionalization of the religion, a trend that might be expected but for which we otherwise have no direct evidence. This implication conforms also to the more personal aspects of religious status as reflected in the burial goods of the Susa period. With increasing institutionalization one would expect "wealth" to take more institutional forms and not to be deposited with the dead.

It is useful now to look back at the wider context of Susa. During the Susa period, Susa, alone among the sites of Khuzistan, contained a large step platform that served as the foundation of a temple at which various rites, probably concerning fertility, were carried out. Surprisingly, the site was founded on the western edge of the plain where there had not previously been a site (Hole 1977). It appeared at about the same time as the demise of the previous center, Chogha Mish. During the Susa period there was a decline in the number of settlements, and most of those remaining or newly founded lasted for relatively short times. The founding of Susa occurred, then, against a background of demographic instability in part certainly occasioned by normal vicissitudes whose causes might lie equally in natural and in social events. Of far more apparent consequence was the abandonment of Chogha Mish and the general decline in population. These events bespeak more fundamental and perhaps shattering experiences.

It may be too strong to suggest that this was a point at which we can see an idea enter history (Redfield 1953, p. 78), but the founding of a ceremonial center on virgin land, far from the sight and influence of Chogha Mish, speaks of the kind of purification that attends rededication to fundamental values and beliefs. We know uncomfortably little about Chogha Mish, except that it contained an architectural complex probably unprecedented in Khuzistan; but whether it was duplicated at Susa remains in doubt. We are even in doubt about whether the complex served sacred or secular purposes. But there is not the slightest doubt that it was burned, which preserved many ceramic vessels whose distributions and types should help us interpret the uses to which the building was put (Kantor 1976).

The settlers of Susa first built a small platform, perhaps to serve chiefly local interests, and then followed by raising the step platform that proclaimed the preeminence of the site in Khuzistan. Whether this massive brick edifice was raised in one frenzy of construction or, like so many other temples, built successively larger in stages should be tested archeologically.

Whatever the precise circumstances, Susa prospered as a center of the craft production epitomized in the elaborately painted vessels found in the tombs. That Susa was the center of this production is likely, inasmuch as vessels identical to those in the cemetery occur at sites throughout Khuzistan. This wide distribution suggests that the fine vessels were used in domestic contexts by persons whose status required them to entertain guests. These same vessels were used also in ceremonies, during propitiation of the deities that, like terrestrial visitors, were offered food and drink.

At Susa itself the priests carried out the ceremonies, garbed in attire and emblems that symbolized the office and the nature of the ceremonies. At death the celebrants took with them into their tombs the signs of their transitory, sacerdotal offices. As Flannery noted, the burial of official symbols with the deceased is one sign that the positions had not yet become hereditary.

We may guess that the minimum number of priests buried at Susa is 55 if each had a single copper axe, or half that number if each had two. The relative scarcity of copper disks implies that they had symbolic referents different from those of the axes. If we assume that there may have been as many as 50 religious functionaries and we take the figure (possibly greatly exaggerated, Dyson 1966, p. 198) of 2,000 tombs as accurate, priests constituted less than 3% of the population. If fine vessels are further indication of status we might enlarge on this figure, but without actual grave lots to examine we would gain little from this exercise. What is evident is that symbols of status, including copper and ceramics, are abundant enough to suggest that there were many persons of high status at any one time at Susa, even allowing 200 years for the use of the cemetery. This impression is reinforced by the lack of specific evidence for exceptional wealth on the part of any individual and by the evident differences in the quality of goods within the total cemetery. Clearly, not all those who were interred enjoyed finely made distinctive display vessels.

The evidence does not point to any particular form of organization at Susa. Clearly, the threshhold of inequality had been passed, presumably some centuries earlier. However, there is no evidence that the shift to hereditary status had yet been made, a point with which I shall deal in greater detail below.

THE SOCIAL FRAMEWORK

CHIEFDOMS

Although the evidence points to the position of Susa as a center for religious ceremonies, it does not inevitably illuminate the internal social organization of the site. There are two matters of concern: the nature of Susa as an organized settlement and the place of Susa along the band-to-state evolutionary continuum. Although the former holds our immediate attention, the latter is the point of departure for most theorists.

The evolutionist approach, delineated by Service (1962), froze social organization into a series of types of increasing complexity. This stimulating delineation reduced a bewildering variability of organizations to a few sharply drawn caricatures and, through its focus on control of production, gave archeologists specific material to look for. Service himself (1971) eventually abandoned his typology, leaving archeologists to labor with the problem. The problem is that if we look at societies instead of society we find a great range of variation even among organizations that might be lumped, let us say, as a tribe or a chiefdom. Moreover, organizations are seldom static and by definition are not so during times of "transition" or "emergence." Service's typology provided a few stills from a long motion picture that illustrated evolution from one stage to the next by emphasizing the control functions of the organization.

In Service's scheme Susa is a chiefdom. No archeologist has given more thoughtful attention to chiefdoms and archeological examples of the form than Colin Renfrew. He (1974, p. 73) lists twenty features of chiefdoms that might be found archeologically. Among these are "the redistribution of produce organized by the chief"; "centers which coordinate social and religious as well as economic activity"; "frequent ceremonies and rituals serving wide social purposes"; "organization and deployment of public labor, sometimes for agricultural work (e.g., irrigation) and/or building temples, temple mounds, or pyramids"; "pervasive inequality of persons or groups in the society associated with permanent leadership"; and "distinctive dress or ornament for those of high status."

Renfrew went on to characterize two types of chiefdoms, the "group-oriented" and the "individualizing." The former have a low level of technology without full-time craft specialization, and there is periodic redistribution by the chief at fixed intervals. In these chiefdoms, where personal wealth is weakly developed, "solidarity of the group [is] expressed most effectively in communal or group activities" (Renfrew 1974, p. 74). The individualizing chiefdoms verge on being kingdoms and are not relevant to the present discussion.

In a later article Renfrew related spatial arrangements to the form of society. He (1978, p. 100) maintained that the most distinctive feature of chiefdoms "in the archaeological record is the presence of central places. For the central person who is the permanent chief is generally situated at a central place, even if this may be a periodic one . . . . The central place was usually dignified by special buildings pertaining to the chief and sometimes by monumental ones relating to ceremonies of life or death." He asks (1978, p. 101), "Is not the most important feature of a chiefdom the existence of a central person, resident at a central place, whether this be periodic or permanent?"

Renfrew's articles concisely and deftly expose the essence of the theoretical problems of dealing with social organization archeologically, and they suggest some means by which we may test for chiefdoms.

Undoubtedly, Susa constitutes what Renfrew would call a center, and since there are no other contemporary centers in Khuzistan, the debate, if any, must focus on the nature of a center. As outlined by Renfrew, centers are invariably occupied by chiefs whose specific functions and authority are related to technological, economic, religious, and other factors. As I have already indicated, we can rule out that Susa's chiefs were individualizing, on the grounds that we have no concentration of wealth. If we follow Renfrew's rubric we are left with the alternative that Susa was a group-oriented chiefdom, under the authority of a central person. It is worth considering chieftainship in greater detail.

CHIEFS

Harris (1977, p. 104) sketches a picture of "big men." "In their purest, most egalitarian phase, best known from studies of numerous groups in Melanesia and New Guinea, 'big men' play the role of hard-working, ambitious, public-spirited individuals who inveigle their relatives and neighbors to work for them by promising to hold a huge feast with the extra food they produce." In this manner, Harris characterized the leaders who first sensed the possibilities of agricultural intensification. These big men attracted a great deal of attention during feasts, but their prestige was fleeting unless they continued to provide on a grand scale.

Harris notes that the big man has only limited authority, a point he emphasizes in a discussion of Indians of the American Southeast. Harris focuses on redistribution, which "undoubtedly provides the key to the understanding of numerous ancient monuments and structures" (Harris 1977, pp. 111–12). Renfrew had already pointed out (1973) the structural similarity between Cherokee council houses and Neolithic henge monuments, but he did not closely examine the organization of the Cherokee society. The Cherokee, and for that matter the Creek, are instructive because they are an alternative to the big man model.

Each of these American Indian societies was organized into semiautonomous conical clans whose heads met in councils (Gearing 1958, p. 1158; Swanton 1928, pp. 277–80). According to Gearing, "The social structure of a human community is not a single set of roles and organized groups, but is rather a series of several sets of roles and groups which appear and disappear according to the tasks at hand" (Gearing 1958, p. 1158). Thus the chief (a clan head selected by other clan heads) acts as "chief" only in certain limited and well-defined situations, accounting for the fact that a Cherokee chief "associates with the people as a common man, converses with them, and they with him in perfect ease and familiarity" (Harris 1977, p. 111, quoting Bartram). Gearing emphasizes that leadership is based on age and experience; its authority is essentially moral (Redfield 1953). What we see in the American Southeast is less a picture of boisterous big men than of old men intent on achieving consensus and preserving tradition through peaceful attention to ceremony and tradition.

In Gearing's study, people shifted routinely from one role to another as daily circumstances changed (Gearing 1958, pp. 1148, 1962). These shifts were in response to human problems: "What is consistent are the social problems. What is recurrent from society to society is solutions to those problems" (Service 1975, p. 9). In any society, large or small, there are persons to tend to these problems. But the possible point that the number of these persons may be large has attracted little discussion. Evolutionists have tended to focus more on one big man than they have on the aggregative nature of the upper strata of many societies that might be called chiefdoms. The accounts of early European settlers in America who tried unsuccessfully to find "chiefs" who had authority over members of their tribes, with whom they could deal, do not correspond with the notion of a big man, let alone an authoritarian leader. The Indians were not without "chiefs," but the chiefly stratum was occupied by many persons. This structure is similar to the "primitive democracy" Jacobsen (1943) described many years ago for Mesopotamia (cf. Oates 1978, pp. 474–75). This organization depends ultimately on a base of essentially interchangeable modules such as corporate clans or lineages, whose members could adopt any of a number of distinct roles according to circumstances and as their progressions through the life cycle permitted.

Although chiefdom has been a seminal concept, particularly in evolutionist studies, it focuses too sharply on centrality rather than on the organizational milieu. Accordingly, we should examine organization in the broad sense rather than continue to emphasize leadership that devolves only from control or regulation. Such an approach would not detract from evolutionist studies, yet it would enable us to deal more explicitly with a greater range of archeological examples, many of which may not be tending directly toward the higher levels of integration specified by evolutionists.

As this point has become clear in the consideration of Susa it is profitable to seek an alternative designation for the group-oriented chiefdom. A convenient model exists in the American Southeast tribes. For our purposes the most striking feature of the Cherokee or Creek organizations is that they aggregate clans. Social anthropologists and ethnographers have felt no need to discuss this structure in terms of chiefdoms, not because chiefly positions did not exist but because they did not see chieftainship in terms of an evolutionary stage of development or even of central social importance. Instead, they were interested in the workings of the society: how warfare, adjudication of disputes, regulation of marriage, or ceremonies were organized. What they found was a society of semiautonomous modules, whose members were graded by age, that could aggregate at times of mutual interest and dissolve at other times. The assumption of any particular role and status was situational (cf. "structural pose," Gearing 1962). That a similar organization could implement complicated affairs without becoming excessively centered on any individual is a message that comes across repeatedly in the Mesopotamian literary tradition (Oppenheim 1967, pp. 6–7) even two thousand years later than Susa.

In terms of Flannery's thorny problem, however, the question at Susa is whether there is social stratification, "institutionalized differentiations of access to positions of differing advantage, rather than in the mere fact of social differentiation" (Smith 1965, p. 160). The question, according to Smith, is whether the highest positions and advantages are open to all. He points out that in many lineage societies, access to positions occurs with age so that in time there is equal access in principle. Such a society is unstratified. According to Smith (1965, p. 149), stratification occurs only when there are means to regulate and thereby strictly limit access to the highest positions. According to this definition of both the nature and the process of stratification, there is no compelling evidence that Susa's society was other than unstratified and acephalous.

We might leave the characterization at this point except that we have still not settled whether Susa can shed any light on the problem of how, in Khuzistan in particular, stratification eventually came about. To do this we shall consider the wider role that Susa, as a center, may have played.

LEADERSHIP AND AUTHORITY

For most, the term *center* implies a person or administrative function that integrates activities over a region wider than that of the center itself. The center takes in and gives out, a process that has profoundly influenced both the center and its hinterland. This is true no matter what the primary function of the center — religious, marketing, or political. The nature of the reciprocal relationships may, however, differ greatly, depending on what kind of center the center is. For example, a market may draw products and customers from a wide region without exercising direct effort to secure either the goods or the customers. Similarly, a religious shrine may be avidly supported by believers and widely ignored by the unfaithful or unpracticing unless there is a resident clergy to enforce matters of belief and participation. The implications of a governmental, or political, center are quite different inasmuch as the business of government is, literally, to govern or regulate the lives of a populace. Here, participation cannot be strictly voluntary. What is required for government, in this sense, is authority.

Can we identify sources of authority at Susa? Authority that would deny access to advantaged positions to all those who were not included by virtue of birth or other principle? We know that persons wearing special garb participated in ceremonies. At least these persons, along with their paraphernalia, were interred at the base of the temple platform. It is unmistakable that these persons held high status during religious ceremonies, but the evidence for stratification on religious grounds is lacking.

Many writers stress the essentially religious nature of the early civilizations. Adams (1966, p. 123) points to "a pervasive and protean preoccupation with fertility." Wheatley (1971, p. 302) stresses that "religion provided the primary focus for social life in the immediately pre-urban period." Jacobsen (1976) devotes a chapter of *The Treasures of Darkness* to the fourth millennium "Gods as Providers," the necessity for which is implied in Adams and Nissen (1972, pp. 85–87); Adams (1974, pp. 4–7), Oates and Oates (1976), and Geertz (1965). Speaking in a more general sense, Service says that chiefdoms "seem universally to be theocratic, and the form of submission to authority [is] that of a religious congregation to a priest-chief." He goes on to say that "ancestor worship is the typical form of the priestly cult" (Service 1975, p. 78).

The close link between religion and status in situations of relatively low social complexity is recognized by all writers (e.g., Norbeck 1961, p. 101). This fact reinforces our impression that

Susa's depicted leaders were sacred rather than secular, but it gives no clues as to the secular side of the coin. It is in no way contradictory that the priests may have been "normal" people in other contexts, as were the Cherokee chiefs.

As I noted earlier, religious status does not automatically confer authority on the holder. The question of whether it does hinges largely on the way priests capitalize on people's beliefs. At this point we have no reason to doubt the faith of the Susians, but equally we have no ready means by which to translate even fervent unquestioning support into political currency that may be used to support a priest's secular goals. It is partly for this reason that writers stress the seductive appeal of feasting, rather than control of minds and hearts, for providing the kick that elevates an egalitarian society to one that is stratified. It is a question of patronage over patriotism. When orchestrated by a big man, a feast cycle can become the center of discussion and activity for the better part of a year and provide opportunities along the way for personal social and economic manipulation. In short, a feast becomes the arena in which many of the daily activities of the group take shape and meaning.

There has never been any question that one can command labor in return for a party. If Stonehenge is not convincing, barn raisings and hayings in our less remote tradition must be. The latter are instructive in that they were carried out in a round robin of mutual aid in which the community prospered through the prosperity of its individual members. The spirit of these gatherings is quite different from the spirit of the big man giveaway, which sought individual elevation at the expense of rivals. The former spirit opened the West. The latter operated within tightly circumscribed and crowded ecosystems.

Giving has come to be seen as essential to a chief who wishes to retain authority. Since feasts are irregular events, the more general form of giving, redistribution, is usually stressed, particularly in societies of emerging stratification (Harris 1977, p. 104). This peculiarly economic view of the origins of hereditary stratification is now so widespread that some authors ignore religion as a "regulatory mechanism" when villages have changed to urban society (Redman 1978).

Redistribution, so often emphasized as a factor underlying the emergence of complex societies, might be taken for granted in Mesopotamia in view of the abundant textual evidence of ration systems in later times (e.g., Gelb 1965). Archeologists have also considered the possibilities of rations during the Uruk period (Johnson 1973, pp. 129ff; Nissen 1970, p. 137). We should recognize, however, that although rations are a form of redistribution, they are distinctly different from what is implied in the big man giveaway feast. They are a formalization of a system that is essentially economic in nature rather than social and symbolic. The Mesopotamian counterpart of a big man feast was associated with certain religious festivals, where distributions of extraordinary, not subsistence, products were made when the goods were available. The underlying, recurring fact in Mesopotamia is the uncertainty of production, a situation diametrically opposed to that of the Pacific chiefdoms. In Mesopotamia, preservation of faith and fertility through ceremonial offerings, rather than ostentatious squandering of readily gained perishable goods, was the norm. At its base, rationing was a matter of economic necessity rather than of social manipulation.

Adams (1966, pp. 48–51) makes a case that there was much room in Mesopotamia for economic diversification, which, if implemented, would have required coordination of production and distribution. Had such a system obtained in Khuzistan during the Susa period, a central organizing function would have been needed, but there is no evidence that production had yet diversified there. In any event, the impetus for any diversification must have come from the organizers rather than the producers, since it was the latter who stood to lose if the system failed. Apart from this, however, each of the Susa-period communities was relatively small, separated, and, to all appearances, much like any other. The most economical explanation of this observation is that they were essentially interchangeable units of production, self-sufficient in many respects.

That there was distribution of goods throughout Khuzistan is not doubted. We have only to examine the ceramics to verify that there was a limited number of production sites, a situation that probably goes back to the early periods of settlement on the plain. What we do not have and clearly need is accurate information on the wares that were being made at Susa. Were these, for example, the fine burial and display wares? If so, what motives underlay their distribution? Patronage, reciprocity, entrepreneurial production? Or what currency purchased them? Labor, grain, other goods, status?

One can run through a list of other endeavors that require leadership and from which authority might be derived: irrigation agriculture, trade, warfare, and so on. The exercise becomes sterile when it becomes apparent that the case you make depends largely on the premise you wish to pursue. The sensible conclusion is that there were human problems in Khuzistan that required human solutions. Susa was situated in a region of relatively low-density settlement, more than a day's walk from the next similar region with a center. In its relative isolation it must have been free from many of the pressures that lead to more complex organizations. It was also in a region of some climatic unpredictability in which both farming and herding were practiced. Essential flexibility through dispersed and small-scale settlements had proven adaptive over the previous two thousand years. What was new was the center. What I have attempted to show is that the nature of centrality at Susa is not well understood. As a center it seems to have served group functions for an area apparently as wide as Susiana itself. Whether there was also a "central person" is problematic. It is more reasonable to assume that Susiana society was headed by clan or lineage leaders, some of whom occupied positions of religious leadership during periodic festivals. Although we can see from the cemetery that the society is distinctly not "egalitarian," we are unable to perceive that it is distinctly "headed." During the Susa period I see not a big man cajoling his relatives and proclaiming his successes but persons with heavy responsibilities for interpreting and attempting to mitigate the awesome forces of nature. It was out of this spirit that the platform of Susa was raised at a sacred spot on the agricultural plain.

CONCLUSIONS

It is difficult to assign Susa a precise segment in an evolutionary trajectory although it is conventional to assume that it represents transitional steps from an egalitarian to a stratified type of society. If we go beyond mere assertion and examine the premises that must underlie such a judgment, we find evidence of a society whose ranking members performed intermittently at religious ceremonies. We are not able, given only a snapshot for a picture, to see whether the society of Susa was trending toward greater stratification, hovering near an equilibrium, or declining. Although we tend, in evolutionist terms, to think that each experiment in social organization was "leading" toward a positive, if incremental, contribution to the reservoir of human experience, many such episodes must have died ingloriously and without issue. Although I am able to suggest iconographic continuities in Susiana, the archeological record also suggests a major cultural/social disjunction at the end of the Susa period. The verdict on Susa's place in human history remains in doubt.

In short, we have not solved that "thorniest of problems" but have moved closer to an understanding of the structure of Susa society, partly through studying its slowly changing religious symbolism and partly through considering alternate forms of organization in light of local factors .

The evidence best conforms with a model of an aggregate society composed of numerous small semiautonomous units (an acephalous, unstratified society, in Smith's terms) that for the most part are demographically coincident with the multiplicity of villages. Both fusion and fission occur along the lines of these kin-based modules, allowing for rapid assembly and disassembly as conditions warrant. This kind of organization was based on clans or estates whose underlying logic was the cooperative work unit essential for carrying out the agricultural tasks specific to this region. A coalescence of such groups into larger aggregates would have been limited more by locally available arable land than by social constraints. The binding force in aggregation would have been identification with the place. Such a community would have been inherently unstable, because particular modular units might have come and gone as situations warranted, precisely as has been described at length by Adams (1974) for early Mesopotamian cities. There is no evident reason why equally easy aggregation and dissolution could not have occurred during the Susa period.

According to this scenario, Susa became a center by design. It was deliberately founded, probably as a sacred site for a temple. In its early history it may have been only a seasonal, intermittently used center whose potential pivotal role in social and economic matters would soon have become apparent. Once its role as a center was appreciated, the infrastructure for developing and supporting new avenues of centrality can hardly have failed to materialize. But rather than creating new forms of society to serve new needs, the citizens of Susa perpetuated and only enlarged the form they already knew: the village or tribal council, probably incorporating pastoral as well as settled elements based on kinship. Kin-based councils, crosscutting lineages when necessary, deriving their authority from tradition and the wisdom of the aged, sought democratic consensus.

This picture of Susian society looks more like the classic Southeast temple mound, flat and broad across the top, than like the classic Egyptian pyramid, for we have seen that the social form of Susa, with its many chiefs or heads, is broad at the top rather than culminating in a pinnacle. The step platform at Susa, therefore, may be the physical metaphor of Susian society, even as the cellular and modular construction of North European Neolithic tombs may recapitulate the society of those times (Renfrew 1978, p. 104, referring to Flemming 1972). At Susa, commoner and priest alike, one in the eyes of their gods, toiled together in life and lay side by side at the base of the platform in death.

ACKNOWLEDGMENTS

Field research relating to this project was supported by National Science Foundation grants to Rice University. A grant-in-aid to support study in European museums of vessels from the Susa cemetery was provided by the American Council of Learned Societies as was a travel grant to attend the Rencontre Internationale de Suse in Iran and the VIth Annual Symposium on Archaeological Research in Iran, 1977. These sources of support are gratefully acknowledged.

BIBLIOGRAPHY

Adams, R. McC.
  1962 Agriculture and urban life in early southwestern Iran. *Science* 136:109–22.
  1966 *The evolution of urban society: early Mesopotamia and prehispanic Mexico.* Chicago: Aldine.
  1974 The Mesopotamian social landscape: a view from the frontier. In *Reconstructing complex societies*, ed. C.B. Moore, pp. 1–20. Bulletin of the American Schools of Oriental Research, Supplement 20. Cambridge, Mass.: American Schools of Oriental Research.

Adams, R. McC., and Nissen, H.J.
  1972 *The Uruk countryside.* Chicago: University of Chicago Press.

Amiet, Pierre
  1966   *Elam.* Paris: Centre National de la Recherche Scientifique.
  1971   La glyptique de l'acropole (1969–1971): tablettes lenticulaires de Suse. *Cahiers de la Délégation Archéologique Française en Iran* 1:217–33.
  1972   *Glyptique Susienne des origines à l'époque des Perses Achéménides: cachets, sceau-cylindres et empreints antiques découverts à Suse de 1913 à 1967.* Mémoires de la Délégation Archéologique en Iran, no. 43. Paris: Geuthner.

Barnett, R.D.
  1966   Homme masqué ou dieu-ibex? *Syria* 43:259–76.

Canal, Denis
  1978a   La terrasse de l'acropole de Suse. *Cahiers de la Délégation Archéologique Française en Iran* 9:11–55.
  1978b   La haute terrasse de l'acropole de Suse. *Paléorient* 4:169–76.

Contenau, G.
  1927   *Manuel d'archéologie orientale.* Paris: Auguste Picard.

de Mecquenem, R.
  1930   Outillage préhistorique d'un nouveau sondage profond dans l'acropole de Suse. *l'Anthropologie* 40:225–32.
  1938   Suse. *l'Anthropologie* 48:65–70.
  1943   Fouilles de Suse, 1933–1939. In *Archéologie Susienne*, R. de Mecquenem, G. Contenau, R. Ffister, and N. Belaiew, pp. 3–161. Mémoires de la Mission Archéologique en Iran, vol. 29. Paris: Leroux.

de Morgan, Jacques
  1912   Observations sur les couches profondes de l'acropole à Suse. In *Mémoires de la Délégation en Perse*, vol. 13, pp. 1–25. Paris: Leroux.

Dollfus, Geneviève
  1971   Les fouilles de Djaffarabad de 1969 à 1971. *Cahiers de la Délégation Archéologique Française en Iran* 1:17–161.
  1973   "Cachets" en terre cuite de Djaffarabad et "cachets" apparentés. *Revue d'Assyriologie* 67:1–19.

Dyson, Robert H., Jr.
  1966   Excavations on the acropolis at Susa and problems of Susa A, B, and C. Ph.D. diss., Harvard University.

Flannery, Kent V.
  1972   The cultural evolution of civilizations. *Annual Review of Ecology and Systematics* 3:399–426.

Fleming, Andrew
  1972   Vision and design: approaches to ceremonial monument typology. *Man* 7(1):57–73.

Gearing, Frederick O.
  1958   The structural poses of 18th century Cherokee villages. *American Anthropologist* 60:1148–57.
  1962   *Priests and warriors: social structures for Cherokee politics in the eighteenth century.* American Anthropological Association Memoir, no. 93. Menasha, Wis.: American Anthropological Association.

Geertz, Clifford
  1965   Religion as a cultural system. In *Anthropological approaches to the study of religion*, ed. Michael Blanton. Association of the Society of Anthropologists Monograph, no. 3. London: Tavistock Publications.

Gelb, Ignace
 1965   The ancient Mesopotamian ration system. *Journal of Near Eastern Studies* 24:230–43.
Goff, B.L.
 1963   *Symbols of prehistoric Mesopotamia.* New Haven: Yale University Press.
Harris, Marvin
 1977   *Cannibals and kings: the origins of cultures.* New York: Random House.
Hole, Frank
 1977   Social implications of the prehistoric ceramics of Xuzestan. Paper presented at the VIth Annual Symposium on Archaeological Research in Iran [Tehran, 1977].
Jacobsen, Thorkild
 1943   Primitive democracy in ancient Mesopotamia. *Journal of Near Eastern Studies* 23:159–72.
 1976   *The treasures of darkness.* New Haven: Yale University Press.
Johnson, Gregory A.
 1973   *Local exchange and early state development in south-western Iran.* Anthropological Papers of the Museum of Anthropology, University of Michigan, no. 51. Ann Arbor: Museum of Anthropology.
Kantor, H.J.
 1976   The excavations at Coǧā Mīs, 1974–1975. In *Proceedings of the IVth Annual Symposium on Archaeological Research in Iran* [Tehran, 1975]. Tehran: Iranian Center for Archaeological Research.
Le Brun, Alain
 1971   Recherches stratigraphiques à l'acropole de Suse (1969–1971). *Cahiers de la Délégation Archéologique Française en Iran* 1:163–216.
Nissen, H.J.
 1970   Grabung in den Planquadraten L/XII in Uruk-Warka. *Baghdader Mitteilungen* 5:101–91.
Norbeck, Edward
 1961   *Religion in primitive society.* New York: Harper and Row.
Oates, Joan
 1978   Mesopotamian social organization. In *The evolution of social systems*, ed. J. Friedman and M.J. Rowlands, pp. 457–85. Pittsburgh: University of Pittsburgh Press.
Oates, David, and Oates, Joan
 1976   Early irrigation agriculture in Mesopotamia. In *Problems in economic and social archaeology*, ed. G. de G. Sieveking, I.H. Longworth and K.E. Wilson, pp. 109–35. London: Duckworth.
Oppenheim, A.L.
 1967   A new look at the structure of Mesopotamian society. *Journal of the Economic and Social History of the Orient* 10:1–16.
Pottier, Edward
 1912   Etude historique et chronologie sur les vases peints de l'acropole de Suse. In *Mémoires de la Délégation en Perse* vol. 13, pp. 27–103. Paris: Leroux.
Redfield, Robert
 1953   *The primitive world and its transformations.* Ithaca: Cornell University Press.
Renfrew, Colin
 1973   *Before civilization.* London: Jonathan Cape. New York: Alfred A. Knopf.
 1974   Beyond a subsistence economy: the evolution of social organization in prehistoric Europe. In *Reconstructing complex societies*, ed. C.B. Moore, pp. 69–88. Bulletin of the

American Schools of Oriental Research Supplement, no. 20. Cambridge, Mass.: American Schools of Oriental Research.

1978　　　Space, time and polity. In *The evolution of social systems*, ed. J. Friedman and M.J. Rowlands, pp. 89–112. Pittsburgh: University of Pittsburgh Press.

Service, Elman R.
1962　　　*Primitive social organization*. New York: Random House.
1971　　　Cultural evolutionism: theory in practice. New York: Holt, Rinehart and Winston.
1975　　　Origins of the state and civilization. New York: W.W. Norton.

Smith, Michael G.
1965　　　Preindustrial stratification systems. In *Social structure and mobility in economic development*, ed. Neil J. Smelser and Seymour M. Lipset, pp. 141–76. London: Routledge.

Stève, M.-J., and Gasche, H.
1971　　　L'Acropole de Suse. *Mémoires de la Délégation Archéologique en Iran*, vol. 46. Paris: Geuthner.

Swanton, J.R.
1928　　　Aboriginal culture of the southeast. *Bureau of American Ethnology, Annual Report*, vol. 42, pp. 673–726. Washington, D.C.: United States Bureau of American Ethnology.

Vallat, François
1978　　　Le matériel épigraphique des couches 18 à 14 de l'acropole. *Paléorient* 4:193–96.

Weiss, Harvey
1977　　　Periodization, population and early state formation in Khuzistan. *Bibliotheca Mesopotamica* 7:347–69.

Wheatley, Paul
1977　　　*The pivot of the four quarters*. Edinburgh: Edinburgh University Press.

Wright, H.T., Jr.; Neely, J.A.; Johnson, G.A.; and Speth, J.
1975　　　Early fourth millennium developments in southwestern Iran. *Iran* 13:129–48.

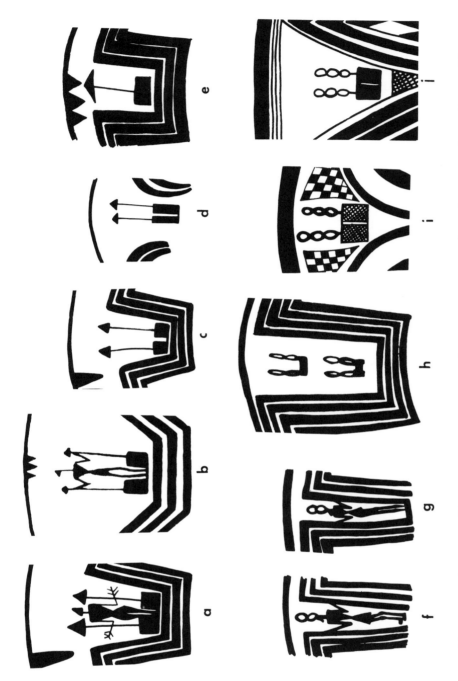

FIG. 1. — MOTIFS ON VESSELS FROM THE SUSA CEMETERY. Drawn from the originals. Scale variable.

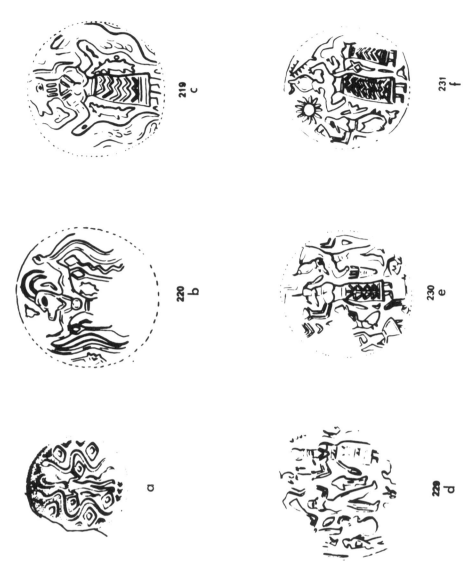

FIG. 2. — SEAL IMPRESSIONS FROM SUSA. a from Le Brun 1971 and b–f from Amiet 1972.

POLITICAL ORGANIZATION AND SETTLED ZONE
A CASE STUDY FROM THE ANCIENT NEAR EAST

Hans J. Nissen

SCHOLARS concerned with the emergence of early civilization in the Near East have always been puzzled by the phenomenon in which wide areas of the Near East, particularly those parts of the "Fertile Crescent" (Breasted 1916) that Braidwood called "The Hilly Flanks of the Near East" (Braidwood 1952), saw the emergence of various kinds of food production and of settled life but remained on a relatively low level of widely dispersed settlements for almost 3,000 years. The development of higher forms of organization, a major leap forward, was centered not in these areas settled earlier but in the large floodplains of Babylonia and Susiana, which in the Neolithic had been marginal areas for human life. Explanations of the latter phenomenon range from blunt attribution of responsibility to the arrival of new, allegedly highly civilized groups; to theories of more favorable ecological conditions; to theories of a constant need to develop better forms of organization in order to cope with the problems of large-scale irrigation.

In view of the results of recent scientific investigations none of these explanations can be proven totally wrong, yet none presents a full answer. Another attempt at understanding will be made here, based on the hypothesis of an interdependence between the level of political organization and the size of the homogeneous and contiguously settled area: the larger that area, potentially the more differentiated the form of political organization. The basic data in support of such a general statement will be taken from developments in the southern part of Mesopotamia and adjoining areas.

We will start by outlining some basic concepts. By definition, central places[1] are places that contain functions of importance not only for themselves but also for a varying array of neighboring settlements. Settlements that, through central places, are tied together by shared interests and thus have closer relations with each other than with other settlements, constitute, by definition, a "settlement system." Again by definition, the simple settlement system, or two-level settlement system, is a system in which the differences in organization between the central place and the minor places of the system are the fewest possible.

The optimal area of a simple settlement system is defined by the needs of the various central functions. The classical central functions, like marketing or central administration, all have as an integral element the inherent possibility of daily movement between the central place and the dependent settlement. Thus, half the daily distance to be covered by the normal means of transport prescribes the maximal radius of such a simple settlement system. We know of other central functions, however, like craft specialization, which are not tied to distance. Their parameter is the minimal number of customers that are needed for the specialization to survive. The more specialized they are, the fewer customers they can find in a given population; or, the more specialized they are, the larger the total population has to be in order to provide enough customers.

This truth has two consequences. On the one hand, the extension of a simple settlement system has a minimal limit that derives from the minimal customer potential of each of the special institutions. As long as this minimal limit lies within the maximal traffic limit mentioned above,

---

1. The principles of the geographers' Central Place Theory have become an integral part of any discussion of archeological theories. For a recent summary, V. Johnson 1977.

the result will be a stable settlement system, the optimal extension of which will normally range around the maximal limit of transport. But we have another consequence as well. While in most cases the maximal limit of transport will be larger than the minimal limit set by the specialized institutions (or will be roughly the same), it is conceivable that some highly specialized institutions could need a larger number of customers than provided by the maximal area allowed by the transport facilities. However, since an enlargement of the potential for customers is not possible because of transportation limit, within simple settlement systems the formation of such highly specialized institutions will not be possible. In other words, the level of specialization within simple settlement systems is tied to the spatial extension of that system, as defined by the capacity of the transport facilities. This restriction would not show up, however, if next to the one simple settlement system there were another, or others, that could partially provide additional customer potential. Such a case would require the existence of a homogeneous geographic area large enough to contain two or more simple settlement systems. Conversely, an area only large enough for one simple settlement system would not lend itself to the formation of such highly specialized institutions.

The existence of a maximal size for simple settlement systems has an additional consequence. Even if the total inhabitable area is larger than the maximal area of a simple settlement system, that system will not be able to enlarge, despite the spatial possibilities. Instead, the area outside the one simple settlement system will be the geographic setting for the formation of another such system. Indeed, this will be the case whenever a relatively large area is settled. Furthermore, this is exactly the situation mentioned above, where specialized institutions of a higher level have the opportunity to develop because they can now draw on a much larger potential of customers. Their development, in turn, is only one aspect of a much more encompassing procedure: the formation of central functions and, consequently, of central places on a higher level than any existing previously. Because in most cases existing central functions also will attain a higher level — for instance, by constructing more elaborate ranking networks for personnel, or more sophisticated internal structures — markedly higher forms of organization will result: central places that must be considered the highest level of a three-level pyramid. At such a point we can speak of three-level settlement systems.

The model outlined so far is a static one; to introduce a historical dimension we have to add a further basic assumption. We may conceive of the early cultural development of man as a slow progress from a total dependence on nonhuman parameters to far-reaching subjection of the nonhuman world to man's needs. From the course of history we can see that a sizeable part of this process consisted of cooperative efforts by men to cope with the problems inflicted by the outside world. These cooperative efforts in themselves brought forth a constant increase in the organization of other such efforts, e.g., the development of such principles as division of labor and craft specialization. Therefore we are entitled to introduce the further basic assumption that the development of division of labor and of craft specialization is closely related to a movement toward an increasing control of nature.

A historical dimension may also be introduced to the discussion by another line of argument, deriving from another general observation. This observation holds that the early stages in the economic development of man should be described in terms of food gathering (hunting, fishing, collecting) and food production, the latter undoubtedly being the historically later stage. Recent research is finding more and more evidence that there was a very long period of time during which both modes of securing subsistence existed side by side. This is easy to accept, since it is obvious that securing subsistence by food production alone presupposes full control of the technologies of agriculture on a level high enough to essentially exclude any occurrence of disasters, such as crop failure or animal plague. It is also obvious that such a level was not attained within a short period, particularly as the improving of subsistence technology is to a large extent an unconscious process. Thus, we have to assume that as food production developed, a changing proportion of food still had to be secured by gathering. This combination of producing and gathering had advantages, since because of it the range of available foods could remain broad and the rather limited variety of food produced by primitive agriculture could be enriched by game and fruits. Further, for a long time this mixed economy was a sheer necessity, as it allowed easy compensation for the failures normal to the early stages of food production.

Clearly, this observation must be an integral part of an answer to the question of where the earliest permanent settlements, which appear roughly at the same time as incipient food production, were able to develop. The hinterland needed by such a settlement could not have been restricted to the narrow limits sufficient for a settlement based on the agricultural production of food alone or even to the much larger area needed for animal breeding. The hinterland of a settlement at the level of a mixed economy would have to have contained areas that were large enough to allow the exploited natural resources to regenerate within a reasonable time. Furthermore, it would have been advantageous for such settlements to lie in areas geographically differentiated to a high degree, since in such areas numerous different ecotopes with different possibilities of exploitation exist in close proximity. Given the necessity for this rather large hinterland, it becomes clear that the distance between settlements would have prohibited the development of close relations of the kind defined as necessary for settlement systems; hence, there would have been a long period in the first few millennia of settled life during which communities would have been isolated.

Underlying subsequent developments was a constant trend toward basing an ever increasing proportion of the total subsistence on food production. This trend in itself even became a stimulus for further development. Thus, efforts to improve the technology of food production, so as to curb the possibility of failure, led to two major results. First, greater technological control of agriculture and consequent lower frequency of failure enabled settlements to become more and more durable and lose their need for a differentiated hinterland. As a result, larger ecotopes, less suited to intensive food gathering, gradually became more interesting for settlers, primarily because such areas offered larger and richer possibilities for farming and herding. Second, an increasing control of food-production technology enabled man to settle in areas that were large enough to support more than one settlement within the same ecotope or, in other words, that were suitable for the formation of settlement systems.

The trends toward food production, however, set off another development, because as food gathering became optional, the hinterland around each settlement could decrease in size. Consequently, the distance between settlements could diminish. Thus, not only were large areas occupied by more than one settlement but also the actual proximity of settlements opened the way for the emergence of more formalized relations between human groups. As mentioned earlier, from then on an increase in local population, and the resultant increase in customer potential, made possible the achievement of new levels of specialization, particularly the formation of central functions and of central places.

After this discussion I believe it redundant to follow up in detail the development of two-level into three-level settlement systems, as that development has similar roots and follows a similar procedure.

If we now ask ourselves what we should look for in order to verify our hypothesis of an interdependence between the level of political organization and the size of the homogeneous and contiguously settled area, we may formulate four theses:

(1) The geographical area of our focus should be the home of wild forms of plants and animals, which easily lend themselves to domestication or at least do not react unfavorably to such attempts.

(2) This geographical area should contain ecological units of various sizes, even the smallest of which should be surrounded by a richly differentiated landscape.

(3) It should be possible to show from our archeological record that those units were settled one after the other, according to increasing size.

(4) The archeological record should show that patterns of organization achieved in the large areas cannot be found in the smaller units.

As stated above, I contend that these conditions can be found in the region north of the Persian Gulf, particularly in the area between the Saudi Arabian desert and the deserts of central Iran. The argument may be summarized as follows:

(1) It is common knowledge today that the ancestors of most species of cereals and of sheep and goat had their natural home in the Hilly Flanks of the Near East, i.e., all those species that later formed the nuclei of food production (Ucko and Dimbleby 1969).

(2) We find here the ideal ecological conditions required of our area, as outlined above. Almost nowhere else are there such contrasts within such small distances: from plains at sea level to mountain ridges of 5,000 meters, from areas almost without rain to areas with a high rate of precipitation, from the large floodplain of Babylonia to the narrow mountain valleys of the Zagros.

(3) Prepottery settlements are located in the small-scale, highly differentiated areas of the Zagros, whereas the large, open plain of Babylonia became settled on a sizeable scale only several thousand years later.

(4) Whereas in the narrow upland valleys we find only isolated settlements, simple settlement systems seem to have developed only in the larger, but still small, intra-montane plains. Multilevel systems (three or more levels) finally emerged only in the large floodplains and cannot be found in the smaller geographical units.

Thus, the area outlined above seems fit for our study. As points one and two are already well documented in literature (and see Smith and Young, this volume), we will focus our attention on points three and four.

Two preliminary remarks are warranted. First, though the several areas discussed do not fall neatly into categories by size, we have to create groups by size for the sake of clarity in our argument. In fact, four such categories can be defined. The smallest encompasses the narrow mountain valleys, some of which include wider pockets of arable land. In some cases landslides closed off such valleys, resulting in the formation of small plains, our second category. These small plains increase in number toward the margins of the Zagros, sometimes opening into the adjoining larger plains. As our third category we note the large floodplain of Susiana, immediately west of the Zagros, formed by the rivers Karkheh and Karun. Greater in size than anything found elsewhere in the Near East is the Babylonian plain, our fourth category, formed by the rivers Tigris and Euphrates.

The second remark concerns the role of artificial irrigation. Undoubtedly, artificial irrigation had a major impact on the development of the Near Eastern culture; there have always existed areas in the Near East where, because of the lack of sufficient rain, agriculture and thus permanent existence were possible only by means of some kind of artificial irrigation. Rightfully, therefore, artificial irrigation has always been credited with having a large influence on events, and much attention has been given to the question of its appearance. Indeed, it has even been assigned an instrumental role in the emergence of early civilization (Wittfogel 1957). On this question, however, I would rather be cautious, for at no point in our discussion do we need to introduce artificial irrigation as an agent in this emergence. Nevertheless, it must play an indispensible part in our considerations for the rather trivial reason that were it not for irrigation we could not talk about Babylonia at all; without artificial irrigation Babylonia would have been a totally barren country for long periods of its history. More important, irrigation intervened at a crucial point in history with critical effect: by accelerating the development of Near Eastern settlement it influenced that development significantly. Taking for granted that irrigated land produces higher yields, let us return to one of our earlier arguments. Since with artificial irrigation the acreage feeding a given number of people can be smaller than with rainfall agriculture, the hinterland necessary for the subsistence of a settlement practicing irrigation agriculture can also be smaller. We noted above that the shift from a mixed economy of agriculture and collecting to one of purely food production permitted a settlement to survive with a smaller hinterland. How much more true this would be with the introduction of irrigation agriculture. Even with small hinterlands for each settlement, more settlements could exploit the same region, and the opportunities for one settlement to impinge or encroach on another would increase, thus accelerating the development of settlement systems. Finally it should be noted that, beyond a certain limit, living too closely together tends to create social problems and conflicts. Thus, at least from the stage of settlement systems onward, the formulation of rules becomes inevitable, as well as the development of institutional measures for punishing any violations. At this stage we obviously encounter those changes we think of as central to any process of urbanization.

Concluding these preliminary remarks, I again stress that the entire development could have taken the same general shape and direction without the introduction of artificial irrigation, but it probably would have taken a much longer time. In looking for the reasons for the development of early civilization we should not include irrigation as a cause, but it merits considerable attention as a reason for the early and rapid development of urbanization in Mesopotamia and adjoining areas.

Turning now to the archeological material from the Near East, we have to be aware that we still do not have enough data to provide a statistically relevant sample and that our material is by no means representative of the whole of the temporal and spatial extent of the process considered here. The reasons for this are that still too little attention has been given to the earliest periods and that the available evidence came to hand too accidentally. Although attempts have been made to acquire a controlled coverage of the entire area, most data remain flawed because the materials were either found by chance or were more readily available. As a result we are still faced with quite a number of gaps, both temporal and spatial, in our data base (Mellaart 1975).

As of now we know of ca. 110 prepottery sites throughout the Near East, an overwhelming number of which are located in highly differentiated mountainous areas like the Taurus or the Zagros ranges. Only very rarely do we find such settlements in areas that come under the heading of larger plains.[2] Among these we might name Ali Kosh in the Deh Luran plain in Khuzestan or Mureybet, Bougras, or Abu Hureira in Syria. A closer look, however, reveals that in these instances, also, the hinterland is rather differentiated, as is the case in Syria because of the ridges following the Euphrates and in Iran because of the proximity of the surrounding outermost chains of the Zagros. In fact, the overall picture looks so uniform that the only known instance of a prepottery site within the Susiana plain seems to stand out as an exception — if it really was a permanent settlement, which remains to be proven.[3]

So far, our findings conform with our proposition except for one point: we have not been able to differentiate in our material between the categories of the narrow mountain valleys and the small

2. I am much indebted to a doctoral candidate of mine, H.G. Gebel, for his permission to use his exhaustive catalogue of aceramic sites in the Near East; cf. Gebel 1980.

3. I thank Professor Helene Kantor, Chicago, for allowing me to use information from an informal report.

intramontane floodplains. Although it may appear that our categories are too rigid, I would rather see in the insufficient evidence the reason for this failure. It is true, however, that we find such prepottery sites associated both with narrow valleys (Jarmo) and with small intramontane plains (Ganj Dareh, Guran). For the time being, our size differentiation does not hold. However, we could formulate our results differently and say that the presence or absence of a differentiated hinterland seems to be the overriding precondition for the location of prepottery sites. Thus, rather than demonstrating a relationship between the earliest settlements and even the smallest geographical category, we end up with a firm statement about a close relationship between these earliest sites and a differentiated landscape.

In part, however, our third point has been proven correct, i.e., that the earliest settlements originated in the smaller geographical units. A look at further developments, with the aim of showing the gradual occupation of larger ecotopes, turns out, on the other hand, to be prohibited by the nature of our material, for in no case can we bridge the large temporal gaps in the data base. For instance, we do not have sufficient material, if any, from the time span connected with the appearance of pottery. Thus, much of our third point can be neither proven nor disproven, and a discussion of isolated cases for which data are available would not get us any further; support for the argument can come only from a continuous chain of information.

In addressing point four we face some of the same difficulties, because again we do not have very much evidence. And there is still another problem, because here we require a different quality of information in order to know whether we are dealing with permanent or nonpermanent settlements or with different levels of highly organized settlements. Apart from the fact that to this very day we do not know what exactly constitutes a central place archeologically, we have too few adequately excavated places at our disposal. If, on the other hand, we simply say that a valley or a small plain just could not support large centers and that thus we should not expect examples of higher forms of organization there, we would be stating a commonplace that would be nothing more than a restatement in the absence of evidence of the original hypothesis. Fortunately, we have better material for the converse, which demonstrates that attempts to transplant a higher form of organization from a large area to a smaller one failed. Indeed, we possess good evidence in Babylonia and Susiana for such a failure, dating to the slightly later Protohistoric periods.

Let us begin with the observation that within a rather short period, the so-called Late Uruk, the archeological inventories of Babylonia and Susiana were essentially the same, so much so, in fact, that we have to conclude a total cultural unity between those two adjacent areas. This is all the more astonishing because we find no such cultural congruence either before or after this brief period. We will discuss this observation in detail before reopening the main argument.

In Babylonia, where we subdivide the Uruk into an early and a late phase, this period was preceded by the Ubaid period. Although, as already reported, Babylonia was not occupied on a large scale before the Late Uruk period, we have enough material to be able to draw a picture of a coherent development in Babylonia, at least based on the most frequent kind of find, pottery (Adams and Nissen 1972; Adams 1981). The pottery of the Ubaid period, by its shapes and decoration, is a subgroup of the last phase of a painted-pottery horizon that, by ca. 4000 B.C., covered much of the Near East. On a light to buff ground we find abstract or geometric patterns painted in a monochrome dark color. Toward the end of that phase two trends become recognizable: first, a steady reduction of the number of patterns of painted pottery until, in the end, they consist almost entirely of simple horizontal bands or wavy lines and, second, a steady increase in unpainted pottery, the surface of which is sometimes treated with a slip of very fine clay. At the same time, two new wares make their first appearance; these are distinguished respectively by a red or a grey coating of the entire surface. Finally, a technical innovation, the potter's wheel, first appears. Thus, at the end of the Ubaid period, in spite of the "poverty" of the painted decoration we are faced with a rather diversified range of pottery.

The pottery of the following early Uruk period continued these trends, with one rather abrupt change: the amount of painted pottery decreased nearly to zero. Shapes became diversified, with a trend from all-purpose shapes to shapes for specific uses. At the same time most of the normal pottery, i.e., not the large vessels, was manufactured on the wheel. A short intervening phase saw a brief renewal of painted pottery, with bold but static designs that nevertheless drew their general character from the Ubaid style of painting. This short revival, however, had already ended before the end of the Early Uruk period (von Haller 1932; Adams and Nissen 1972, pp. 100−101).

The next stage, the Late Uruk period, saw a continuation of the pottery of the previous phase, with a strong emphasis on the diversification of shapes on the one hand and an enormous increase of the total output of pottery on the other. The latter development related directly to the great growth of population in Bablylonia.

The transition from the Late Uruk to the Jemdet Nasr period saw another innovation in pottery making: the technique of throwing from the hump, whereby vessels were turned out from only the uppermost part of a cone of clay shaped on the wheel. This new technique made possible for the first time the manufacture of mass-consumption vessel types on the wheel. It also required a different, more elastic consistency of clay; the resulting different outer appearance of most pottery vessels of the Late Uruk period was merely a consequence of this new technique (Nissen 1970, pp. 139−40). Otherwise, all previous trends continued, though the uniformity in shapes brought forth by mass production stimulated another development, the increase of individualizing accessories like tabs, ridges, cutout decoration, and so forth. The appearance of a polychrome style of painting on a very small number of vessels (luxury ware) probably is also a response to the same stimulus. It has to be stressed, however, that in spite of a different general look, the pottery of the Jemdet Nasr period is part of an uninterrupted line of development from the Ubaid period on. This tradition by no means ends with the Jemdet Nasr period, because the pottery of the subsequent Early Dynastic I period continues these same developments, simply enforcing some of the trends recognizable earlier on. In sum, we should stress the total continuity in the development of early pottery in Babylonia in combination with a forceful drive for internal changes.

If we now turn to the same time range in Susiana, we find first a pottery comparable to the Ubaid pottery from Babylonia. Yet, although the general characteristics are the same, the repertoire of shapes and painted patterns is so markedly different that we may say that this pottery belongs to a different subgroup of the last phase of the larger painted-pottery horizon. This pottery represents a developmental stage within an old tradition, which can easily be shown to follow a long uninterrupted sequence from the Neolithic period on (Hole, Flannery, and Neely 1969). There is no doubt that the phase called Late Susiana, or Susa A, or Susa I (Le Brun 1971) is at least partly contemporary with Ubaid pottery. At the same time we recognize some structural differences. One change we observed in Babylonia finds its counterpart here, the increase of red-slipped ware. At the same time, however, we miss the most intriguing aspect of the later development of Babylonian Ubaid pottery: the dynamic process associated with the reduction of the number of painted patterns. Also, in contrast with Babylonia, we encounter in Susiana no gradual increase in the undecorated pottery. Furthermore, neither the characteristic shapes of the Babylonian Early Uruk nor the sharp fluctuation in the proportion of painted pottery can be observed in Susiana. Rather, the still-flourishing pottery style with vigorous painted designs is quite suddenly replaced by the ceramic group that we know from Babylonia as genuine Lake Uruk pottery. This means that the late phase of Susa A is contemporary with the Early Uruk phase in Babylonia. Except for some grey- and red-slipped vessels the pottery is exclusively unpainted and, as in Babylonia, mostly wheel made. Here is a real "break" in a pottery tradition.

The pottery of the next phase, contemporary with the Babylonian Jemdet Nasr period, remains in the tradition of the Late Uruk pottery. Nevertheless, we do not find here, as in Babylonia, the highly significant replacement of the "bevelled-rim bowls" (BRB) by the so-called conical cups

(Nissen 1970, p. 142). This needs some explanation. BRBs are open cups with a standard capacity, and they occurred by the millions during the Late Uruk period. This first mass-produced pottery was not manufactured on the wheel but cast from molds. Presumably the BRBs served as ration bowls, i.e., containers for the daily barley ration of the employees of the large estates. Given that function they can be taken as diagnostic of a rather complex economic structure in the Late Uruk period. As mentioned above, the introduction in the Jemdet Nasr period of the new technique of throwing from the hump made it possible to use the wheel for mass production, and this way of manufacturing large quantities of vessels apparently proved to be superior to the former use of molds. Although most probably serving the same purpose as the BRBs, the new kind of open bowls, the conical cups, which first appear at the beginning of the Jemdet Nasr period, look quite different and are easily recognizable. Like the BRBs, they can be taken as diagnostic of complex economic organizations.

Applying the same methods of interpretation to the situation in Susiana, we discover that the level of economic organization during the Late Uruk period was the same there as in Babylonia but became different by the Jemdet Nasr period. This proposition is supported by the observation that other pottery shapes found in Susa show that the new technique of throwing from the hump was known and used. Furthermore, not only did the Susa potters not use the shape of the conical cup but they also did not continue the manufacture of mass-produced pottery at all.[4]

If the interpretation of the open bowls as ration bowls and therefore as indicative of a specific, rather highly developed form of economic organization is correct, we find that again in Babylonia there is a continuous development; in Susiana, a discontinuity. Finally, the difference in development in the two regions becomes fully apparent when we note that the pottery of the following phase in Susiana, contemporary with the Early Dynastic I period in Babylonia, is totally unlike the local pottery of the preceding period and, with a predilection for all-purpose shapes and, slightly later, painted decoration, again takes up the tradition of pre-Uruk times (Le Breton 1957, pp. 113–16).

To summarize, what we call the Late Uruk culture in Babylonia continuously grew out of an older local tradition, whereas in Susiana this culture was brought from outside, most probably from Babylonia. If we now note the fact that the Babylonian plain is much larger than the Susiana plain, it becomes obvious that the first part of our proposition — the contention that a higher form of organization was transplanted from a large area into a smaller one — is borne out by the facts.

More difficult to prove is the other part of the proposition, the contention that this transplantation failed. To be sure, we touched upon some of the argument when we talked about the uneven development in Babylonia and Susiana as seen from the pottery: in Babylonia, a constant progress, in Susiana, stagnation and even relapse. Still we have to concede that, so far, our arguments have been based on the evidence from pottery alone, which, for our concerns, is not recognized as the most powerful testimony. We are fortunate, however, to be able to draw on other data as well.

Writing first developed in Mesopotamia in the Late Uruk period. Here again it can be shown that the direction of influence was indeed from Babylonia to Susiana, since in Uruk the first traces of writing were found in the so-called Archaic building level IVa, the very last subphase of the Late Uruk period.[5] In Susa, on the other hand, the earliest traces of the same basic techniques

4. Although shapes 1-4 on fig. 60 of Le Brun 1971 are reported as frequent, the number of such vessels is in no way comparable to the number of BRBs or of "conical cups" in Babylonia; cf. Nissen 1970.

5. The following discussion is based on the findings of A. Falkenstein 1936 and on the preliminary results of work on a comprehensive study of the Archaic texts from Uruk, directed by the writer, supported by a grant of the Deutsche Forschungsgemeinschaft.

and elements used in Babylonia did not appear before Level 16 of the new Acropole sounding, which corresponds to Archaic building level III in Uruk. This time lag is also clear from internal evidence. The signs of the earliest tablets in Uruk were incised with a pointed stylus. Only slightly later, in the next writing stage (IIIc) do we find signs being formed by a combination of varying numbers of straight, impressed wedges, a technique resulting from the use of a triangularly shaped stylus. Proto-elamite writing at Susa is done with such a stylus from the beginning.

The main argument, however, concerns the further history of writing. In Babylonia we find a continuous development, the underlying trend of which was the transformation of the early, clumsy writing system into an easily and universally applicable tool. For instance, one line of development consisted of a simplification of the signs and of the writing technique; another, using the fact that the Sumerian language possesses a large number of homophones, attempted to increase the number of syllabic values of some signs in order to relinquish other, rarely used, signs, i.e., to decrease the number of signs. Ultimately, the system was given such flexibility as to be capable of rendering complex contents, or even other languages, in correct grammar. All this was achieved within a relatively short time span; indeed, the speed of the development was quite remarkable at all stages, including the earliest phase. After the first stage, in which signs were incised, we can differentiate three stages within the Jemdet Nasr period (which was the time of the Archaic building level III in Uruk), each representing a significant improvement of the system.

The situation in Susiana was markedly different. The use of writing ends with Level 14A, or the end of the Jemdet Nasr period. Not until several hundred years later was cuneiform writing imported in its now fully developed form, again from Babylonia.[6] On the whole, Proto-elamite writing gives the impression of being static. Apart from the fact that the Susa scribes had already started the imprinting of signs, during the entire time of its existence, writing in Susiana did not show any changes or improvements comparable to the three developmental stages in Babylonia.

Thus, from a study of early writing, as well as of pottery, it becomes clear that a whole set of cultural phenomena was taken over from Babylonia by Susiana but did not develop there any further. After a short while even these new achievements — at least those we have evidence for — were abandoned altogether.

Although we have been able to gather a considerable amount of evidence for our proposition, we have not yet found an explanation for the facts. Still, from all that has been said, the following sketch may be the most plausible that we can draw.

The sudden opening of the wide Babylonian plain to occupation was based not only on the organizational achievements reached after long developmental processes in other areas like Susiana but also on new requirements and new possibilities. The resulting structures attained new, higher qualities — which we group under the name "Uruk culture" (Nissen 1974). These higher achievements could readily be — and sometimes were — adopted by an area where structures had remained at a previous level. For a while these new structures seemed to suit the needs of that area. However, the long prior tradition there *and the relative small size of the area* prevented the kinds of dynamic ongoing developments we observe throughout early Babylonian history. We should not be surprised by the ultimate breakdown of the system in Susiana, as this development followed a well-known pattern. The adoption of the complex Uruk culture came

---

6. The notion of an inner development of the Proto-elamite writing is hardly touched on by Le Brun and Vallat 1978. The same observation applies to the treatment of the problem of the large temporal gap between the Proto-elamite writing and the introduction of the developed cuneiform system: "Cependant, ce système proto-élamite n'aura qu'une existence éphémère puisque vers le milieu du IIIe mill., il sera abandonné au profit de l'écriture cuneiforme des voisins mésopotamiens." Le Brun and Vallat 1978, p. 40, seem not even to recognize that problem.

close to "living beyond one's means or needs"; participation in the development of newer and still more intricate structures was certainly out of the question. The close relations between these two areas, which was briefly in the late Uruk period a relationship of partners on equal terms, came to an end. Autonomous ongoing development in both regions simply had to conform to the local geographic conditions.

To end this sketch I would like to stress that all the seemingly sudden "cultural breaks," looked at closely, actually meet requirements of our hypothesis. Just as we no longer have to look elsewhere for those superhuman Sumerians who brought the big achievements of mankind along with them to southern Mesopotamia, or for any other deus ex machina for the development of early civilization, so the "breaks" in the Susa sequence before the Late Uruk and after the Jemdet Nasr period do not mark large-scale turmoil in Susiana, or a change in population. They merely represent significant changes in those high-level organizational structures that left the most conspicuous traces in our archeological record.

To return to the main argument, I think I can condense the last part of the discussion into the simple statement that it was the relative smallness of the Susiana plain that led to the final abandonment of the imported structures. To say so means that the second part of my proposition has been proven correct also. Although I have not been able to elaborate on my points three and four in every detail, I trust that the combination of a positive answer to the questions of where and why early permanent settlements were formed and the fairly clear evidence of the impossibility of transplanting complex structures from a larger into a smaller area has made my general hypothesis at least plausible, and perhaps probable.

A word of caution is necessary at the end. Though this study has quite often used rather general terms, it cannot claim any abstract validity beyond an explanation of the case studied. There is a narrow path between the Scylla of mere presentation of facts and the Charybdis of mere abstractions. This is the path that archeology has to tread, as we have been so competently taught by our teacher and friend, Robert J. Braidwood.

BIBLIOGRAPHY

Adams, Robert McC., and Nissen, Hans J.
 1972   *The Uruk countryside*. Chicago: University of Chicago Press.

Braidwood, Robert J.
 1952   The Near East and the foundations for civilization. In *Condon lectures*. Eugene, Oregon: Oregon State System of Higher Education.

Breasted, James H.
 1916   *Ancient times: a history of the early world*. Boston: Ginn.

Falkenstein, Adam
 1936   *Die archaischen Texte von Uruk*. Leipzig: Harrassowitz.

Gebel, Hans Georg
 1980   Frühneolithische Wirtschaftsformen in Vorderasien. Master's thesis, The Free University of Berlin.

Haller, Arndt V.
 1932   Die Keramik der archaischen Schichten von Uruk. In *Vorläufiger Bericht über die von der Notgemeinschaft der Deutschen Wissenschaft in Uruk unternommenen Ausgrabungen*. IV, A. Nöldeke, pp. 31–47. Berlin: Akademie den Wissenschaften.

Johnson, Gregory A.
    1977   Aspects of regional analysis in archaeology. *Annual Review of Anthropology.* 6:479–508.

Le Breton, Louis
    1957   The early periods at Susa, Mesopotamian relations. *Iraq* 19:79–124.

Le Brun, Alain
    1971   Recherches stratigraphiques à l'acropole de Suse (1969–71). *Cahiers de la Délégation Archéologique Française en Iran* 1:163–216.

Le Brun, Alain, and Vallat, François
    1978   L'origine de l'écriture à Suse. *Cahiers de la Délégation Archéologique Française en Iran* 8:11–60.

Mellaart, James
    1975   *The Neolithic of the Near East.* London: Thames and Hudson.

Nissen, Hans J.
    1970   Grabung in den Quadraten K/L XII in Uruk-Warka. *Baghdader Mitteilungen* 5:101–19.
    1974   Zur Frage der Arbeitsorganisation in Babylonien während der Späturuk-Zeit. *Acta Antiqua Hungarica* 22:5–14.

Ucko, Peter J., and Dimbleby, G.W.
    1969   *(eds.) The domestication and exploitation of plants and animals.* London: Duckworth.

Wittfogel, Karl A.
    1957   *Oriental despotism: a comparative study of total power.* New Haven: Yale University Press.

SPATIAL ORGANIZATION IN CONTEMPORARY SOUTHWEST ASIAN VILLAGES AND ARCHEOLOGICAL SAMPLING

Carol Kramer

INTRODUCTION

ROBERT J. BRAIDWOOD's archeological work in the Zagros and Taurus mountains of Southwest Asia has been pioneering both in its use of archeological sampling and in its call for increased attention to details of contemporary village life (Braidwood and Reed 1957, pp. 25ff.; Braidwood and Howe 1960, pp. 38ff.). In the years following Braidwood's work in Iraqi and Iranian Kurdistan, some of his students have gone on to study details of contemporary life in the Zagros (Hole 1978, 1979; Kramer 1979, 1980, 1982; Watson 1966, 1978, 1979). In combination with the other literature on settlements in this area, such ethnoarcheological work may be used to make some preliminary observations on the nature of spatial organization of villages in the Zagros-Taurus mountain arc today.

Largely as a result of the archeological work of Braidwood and his colleagues and students, exposures at a number of prehistoric villages in these "hilly flanks" of Breasted's Fertile Crescent have yielded a wealth of information on their content and organization. Recent reviews by F. Hole (forthcoming), Oates (1973, 1977), and Watson (1978, 1979) clearly show that in many respects early villages are comparable to their modern counterparts. The existence of formal similarities between modern and prehistoric villages in the same area suggests that it is reasonable to use observations of patterning apparent in modern villages in the formulation of archeological sampling designs. The following pages focus on the organization of the individual settlement, from the perspective of the excavator, rather than on the spatial patterning of settlements on a regional scale or the implications that such patterning might have for archeological surface survey. Following a brief review of some salient features of Southwest Asian villages, some of the sampling problems presented by such settlements are considered.[1]

CONTEMPORARY VILLAGES

Systematic investigation of the use of space and building materials in contemporary settlements promises to force archeologists to refine further their approaches to prehistoric settlements. At the very least, such work has already demonstrated that there *is* a range of variation in even the least complex societies (e.g., Yellen 1977) and that because such variability is not exclusively attributable to chronological difference, greater efforts must be made to describe it and specify its causes when it is discerned in archeological contexts. If archeologists can demonstrate that activities within contemporaneous domiciles were essentially the same, for example, then architectural variability from one residence to another cannot be attributed exclusively to "functional variability" related to households' participation in differing activities. It might instead reflect variation in households' economic statuses and/or composition (Kramer 1979). At the same time that they will clarify sources of variability, archeologically oriented investigations of still-functioning societies should go far to pinpoint patterning and repetition that exist along with the diversity and that may reflect comparable human responses to comparable problems or con-

1. I acknowledge with thanks the critical comments made on an earlier draft by Gregory A. Johnson and Lee Horne and regret that I could not incorporate all of their suggestions here.

straints. The material correlates of such behavioral redundancies will, in many cases, be identifiable as archeological residues.

For archeologists working in Southwest Asia it might be useful to attempt to identify redundancies in vernacular architecture (defined here as lacking in standardization and not built by
professional specialists), particularly that of warm, arid habitats. McIntosh (1974, 1976) has
discussed the characteristics of decay of mud structures in West Africa, elucidating one aspect of
the formation of archeological residues there and elsewhere, including much of Southwest Asia.
Vernacular architecture in such habitats displays patterns found not only in Southwest Asia but
also in large portions of South Asia, much of Africa, the circum-Mediterranean, and the American
Southwest (Denyer 1978; Doumanis and Oliver 1974; Oliver 1971; Prussin 1969). Such apparent
redundancies in construction reflect common responses to a limited range of building materials
and to other environmental constraints. They affect house plans, village layouts, and the formation of archeological residues. House plans and village layout seen today appear to have considerable time depth, and in Southwest Asia, patterns of building and of abandonment are clearly
related to the formation of mounds, surely the most prominent type of archeological site.[2]

At least in Southwest Asia, spatial organization within settlements is not wholly unrelated to
spatial relations among settlements. The locations, spatial relations, and density of structures in
villages are not like those in cities. In addition, settlements' areas today are variable, and it
appears that settlements' areas are at least partly related to their relationships with one another
within a larger regional framework.[3] Recent research based on literature for the contemporary
Zagros and adjoining areas shows that some settlements are quite small (i.e., less than one
hectare) whereas others, usually termed *towns, cities*, or *centers*, are substantially larger — in
area and/or in population (Kramer 1980). Within single regions, larger centers appear generally
to be those having more numerous and diversified economic and political functions, and they
generally serve as foci for the collection and redistribution of goods, services, and information
(Costello 1977; Lapidus 1969; Kramer 1982). A wide range of publications for many geographic

2. For example, chaff-tempered mud plaster may retard wall deterioration and is often applied on a
regular basis, particularly to external walling. There is some evidence to suggest that frequency of
application varies with economic rank. Mud absorbs daytime heat slowly and radiates it during cooler
nights; thick house walls delay heat penetration into rooms, as do small windows. Internal courtyards
remain cool for much of the day, partly because they are shaded by building walls except at noon. The
interior courtyard provides both a sleeping area and a summer cooking area, which helps to minimize the
concentration of indoor heat. Nucleation or clustering of houses in blocks minimizes the surface area
exposed to solar radiation and serves to shadow the narrow, winding alleys separating blocks. Pale exterior
surfaces reflect heat, and small windows, which usually open onto a house's courtyard rather than the
adjacent alleys, minimize the amount of direct sunlight entering rooms (al-Azzawi 1969; Cockburn 1969;
Kramer 1982; Rapoport 1969). While the causes of settlement nucleation are not the subject of this paper, it
should be noted that settlements may assume a nucleated form not only because of some of the factors
mentioned above but also because it can be an efficient use of land, and it may reflect a defensive posture
with respect to predators. In any case, such nucleated settlements of mud tend — all other factors being
equal — to form mounds. In contrast to his "n-transforms," Schiffer's "c-transforms" (cultural processes
contributing to the formation of the archeological record) include such specifiable elements of human
behavior as "curation," behavior that at least temporarily keeps some cultural items from becoming part of
the archeological residues of settlements (Schiffer 1976). In Southwest Asia one aspect of "curate behavior"
is the frequently cited removal of roof beams on the occasion of house abandonment. This practice has been
widely (if not systematically) observed to enhance the decay of mud walls. In this instance, a particular
c-transform (curation of beams) is intricately and causally connected with an n-transform (decay of mud
structures, as described by McIntosh) and therefore to mound formation.

3. Obviously, this in itself is an important argument against limiting a sample of a "region" to a single site.

areas — from geography, social anthropology, and archeology — suggests that such variations in functional size of settlements are directly and positively related to variations in settlements' sizes (usually expressed in terms of settlement population, though clearly in some cases also apparent in differences in settlements' areas; Adams 1981). Small settlements, therefore, *tend* to be those exhibiting a smaller range of functions, while those providing more goods and services (functions) *tend* to be larger. Larger settlements are also often "centrally" located with respect to smaller settlements (Johnson 1973, 1975; C. Smith 1976).

It is not implied that all villages are alike. Rather, there is demonstrable variability in the domestic architecture and spatial arrangements of villages in various parts of Southwest Asia today. For example, villages in the Levant and on the Iranian plateau exhibit clear differences from those of the Zagros; even within each of these regions, differences may be observed. Among the axes of formal variability that can be seen from one part of Southwest Asia to another are differences in building materials, presence/absence of internal courtyards, presence/absence of compound walls, type and location of stables, roof type, decorative elements, presence/absence of walls enclosing the village, and degree of nucleation or dispersal of residential structures. Such variations can be seen in the disparity between, for example, those Levantine mountain villages built largely of stone, set on terraced hillsides, with dispersed, free-standing tiled and sometimes gable-roofed houses containing no courtyards, and mountain villages of the Zagros, with their densely packed flat-roofed mud-brick houses, often enclosed by a high compound wall and usually including a large unroofed courtyard, built on an alluvial flat or forming a steplike pattern on a mound or mountain side. Despite these differences, a review of the somewhat limited descriptive literature suggests that there are some widespread uniformities in village architecture and spatial organization, and some of these may reflect underlying and long-established principles of sedentary rural life in this area. Table 1 lists some contemporary villages for which information useful to archeologists is available. This corpus provides much of the background for the following generalizations.[4]

In small rural settlements today, comparatively few activities are unrelated to the maintenance and reproduction of local households, and few structures are devoted exclusively to nonresidential functions. Some villages possess public bath houses (*hammams*), a few scattered shops (in contrast to a market or bazaar, where shops are concentrated and often spatially segregated from residential structures), a religious room or structure, or even two (such as a mosque and a saint's shrine), a "fort" (usually built some time ago and often in a state of disrepair, although sometimes occupied by government personnel or by local residents nonetheless), guest rooms or guest houses, and perhaps a mill, a post office, or a school. Despite this seemingly extensive list, most villages have only one or two such special-function nondomestic structures, and many have none at all. (Most such structures exhibit differences of form — in ground plan and/or building materials — from residential structures, and could, presumably, be distinguished from domiciles in their archeological form.) In addition to a relative paucity of "special" structures, most small rural settlements lack evidence of planning such as may be seen in areally and functionally larger

4. Much of the generalizing that characterizes the following pages is also based on my own experiences in the Iranian Zagros and travels in Turkey and Iran. Off and on since 1976, assistance in measuring village plans, obtaining selected (published) ethnographic data for Southwest Asian villages, and analyzing some of the data from my own ethnoarcheological fieldwork in an Iranian Kurdish village in 1975 has been provided by three students in the graduate program in anthropology of the City University of New York; to Roselle Henn and Richard Smilowitz and especially to Judith Berman, I tender with pleasure my sincerest thanks. Thanks are also due Dr. Sydel Silverman, executive officer of that program, for help in obtaining support for Henn and Smilowitz and to the National Science Foundation and the University Committee on Research, City University of New York, for funding my 1975 fieldwork, the data analysis, and salary for Berman.

Table 1. — Modern Villages in the Zagros-Taurus Mountains and Adjacent Areas[1]

Settlement	Location	Area (ha)[2]	No. of Houses[3]	Data Sources
"Shahabad"[4]	Central west Iran	3.0[a]	67	Kramer 1979, 1980, 1982
"Shahabad" area (n=29)	Central west Iran	X̄=3.5		Ibid.
Hasanabad	Central west Iran	1.4[b]	41	Watson 1966, 1978, 1979
Sar-i Pol-i Zohab area	Central west Iran	2.2		Ed Keall (pers. comm.)
Luristan villages (n=3)	Central west Iran	X̄=2.9	X̄=49	Harvey Weiss (pers. comm.)
Izeh area	Southwest Iran	2.8	100±	Henry T. Wright (pers. comm.)
Tell-i Nun (old)	Southwest Iran	5.7	59	Jacobs 1979
Marv Dasht area (n=110)	Southwest Iran	X̄=2.1		Sumner 1979
Hasanlu	Northwest Iran	6.8[c]	90±	Bob Dyson (pers. comm.)
Rust	Northeast Iraq	6.6	130	Galloway 1958
Walash	Northeast Iraq	.8	12	Leach 1940
Alişar	Central Turkey	4.3[d]	58	Morrison 1939
Sakaltutan	Central Turkey	n.d.	105	Stirling 1965
Hasanoğlan	Western Turkey	n.d.	267	Yasa 1957
Yassihöyük	Western Turkey	1.5	75	M.E.T.U. 1965
Bahtili	Southern Turkey	27.7	122	Kolars 1963
Akdamlar	Southern Turkey	6.0	32	Ibid.
Aşvan	Eastern Turkey	12.6[e]	83±	French et al. 1973
Miyadin	Eastern Turkey	.7[f]	15	Alpöge 1971
Arozik	Eastern Turkey	1.2[g]	20	Ibid.
Aşağı Ağinsi	Eastern Turkey	2.0[h]	30	Peters 1972
Alişam	Eastern Turkey	5.1[i]	125	Ibid.
Raddadeh (old)	Southwest Iran	7.0	30–37	Rouholamini 1973; Geneviève Dollfus (pers. comm.)
Dez Pilot Area (n=54)	Southwest Iran	X̄=1.1	X̄=41	Gremliza 1962

Khanazariya	Southwest Iraq	1.5±	30	Nissen 1968
Sayeh South	Southern Iraq	6.0	16	Wright 1969
B'dair	Southern Iraq	24.0	282	Ibid.
Kufr al Ma	North Jordan	11.0	268	Antoun 1972
Tell Toqaan	North Syria	5.0±	56	Sweet 1974
Lebanese village	South Lebanon	3.0	280±	Peters 1963
al Munsif	North Lebanon	16.0	89	Gulick 1955
Kousar Riz	Southern Iran	28.3	50±	English 1966
Sehkunj	Southern Iran	22.3	80±	Ibid.
Muhiabad	Southern Iran	48.9	125±	Ibid.
Tezerjan	Central Iran	30.0±	100±	Sunderland 1968
Davarabad	North central Iran	10.0	123	Alberts 1963
Baghestan	Northeast Iran	2.0j	33±	Lee Horne (pers. comm.); gov't of Iran 1977
Tauran area (n=13)	Northeast Iran	X̄=1.5		Ibid.

1. Some of these data have been published elsewhere (Kramer 1980, 1982).

2. n.d. (no data) indicates that while settlement plans in the form of published maps or aerial photographs are available, they are without scales; in such cases, it is possible to comment on spatial organization but not on areal values.

3. In some settlements, dwelling units of different households are grouped in one compound, and/or the rooms of one household are dispersed across several componds (e.g., Kufr al Ma, Alişar, Baghestan, and perhaps Sakaltutan). The figures for Tezerjan represent only a sample of that settlement.

4. "Shahabad" was used as a pseudonym for a village in the Kangavar area (Kramer 1979); this name has since been changed.

a. Approximately 40% of this area is nonarchitectural (i.e., alleys, streets, plazas, commons).
b. Approximately 32% of this area is nonarchitectural.
c. Approximately 46% of this area is nonarchitectural.
d. Approximately 54% of this area is nonarchitectural.
e. Approximately 56% of this area is nonarchitectural.
f. Approximately 47% of this area is nonarchitectural.
g. Approximately 39% of this area is nonarchitectural.
h. Approximately 50% of this area is nonarchitectural.
i. Approximately 54% of this area is nonarchitectural.
j. Approximately 34% of this area is nonarchitectural.

settlements in the same area, where some "standardization" in structures may exist and where a grid and/or radial settlement plan may also be evident. While lacking symmetry, many villages are divided into blocks or quarters, and some may, on superficial inspection, look planned, particularly where there are only two blocks, one on either side of a river or road. In some villages, close kin tend to reside near one another. Some of the ethnographic literature suggests that towns' residential wards or quarters are often "tribal," "ethnolinguistic," or "religious" in composition or at least in origin, whereas those in villages may more often tend to be "familial," with more close kin living near one another, and for longer periods, than is the case in larger settlements (Kramer 1982), but more data are required to confirm this apparent dissimilarity.

For present purposes, therefore, a "village" (in contrast to "town" or "city") may be characterized as a small rural settlement with few functions, where most activities pertain to occupants' subsistence and in which the vast majority of architectural structures are secular and residential in nature. Archeologically, such a definition might raise difficulties. For example, Johnson (1975) and Wright, Miller, and Redding (1980) have discussed areally small (and in that respect apparently villagelike) fourth millennium sites that produced artifactual evidence of administrative activities not usually thought to be associated with villages. Archeologists' tendency to conflate areal size and functional size in classifying prehistoric sites therefore presents difficulties, although this problem has not always been acknowledged, or dealt with in practical terms. In the Zagros area today, villages are usually areally small (see table 1 and Kramer 1980). However, some towns (i.e., settlements with more economic and administrative functions than are found in villages in the same regions) also have fairly small populations and/or areas. For an archeologist, therefore, the use of only settlement area data to define settlement type might be problematical, although area is obviously one of the key attributes to be recorded and evaluated. In the modern world, differences in settlements' functional sizes appear to be evident in objects and in settlement layout and architectural structures; one would expect comparable dissimilarities to exist in archeological sites, even if the form they took was not precisely isomorphic with that of the present. It is therefore suggested that in classifying prehistoric sites without benefit of data actually excavated at such sites, archeologists use a combination of data on site area, types of surface artifacts, and the diversity of such artifacts. When archeologists can also excavate at a site or sites, they can confirm or refute classifications based on surface remains.[5] Evaluations of excavated material, as well as strategies used to obtain it, may incorporate assumptions and expectations — "judgments" — based on perceptions of life in modern settlements.

In contemporary Southwest Asian villages large areas of villages are unroofed. A recent review of some published maps suggested that alleys and open areas (commons or plazas) between blocks of houses may constitute as much as half of a village's total area, although in some settlements it is as little as 30 percent if unroofed courtyards are omitted from the measures (see table 1). In Southwest Asia, heat is one reason for high proportions of unroofed area; through much of the year many economic and social activities are carried out in such areas. In addition, villagers "store" livestock in enclosed but unroofed areas for at least part of the year. In courtyards, or "terraces," of those houses built steplike on slopes, household members process food for domestic consumption, and one sees a wide range of activities centering on the collection and processing of wool and hair (shearing, washing, spinning, weaving), construction and modifica-

5. Obviously, decisions about where to excavate are based partly on the distribution and nature of remains on sites' surfaces as these are recorded during an initial stage of surface survey. The relationships between such surface distributions and the subsurface features underlying them have been discussed by Redman and Watson (1970) and Flannery (1976b). One point of the present paper is that while judgments about subsurface features may be based on surface distributions, they can also be based — independently — on assumptions regarding the spatial organization of settlements.

tion of standing structures, and stacking of items to be stored (fuel, structural elements like bricks or wood, dried foods, etc.). Beyond individual house blocks but still within villages' perimeters, other aspects of food and fuel processing are carried out, and there is considerable movement of people, goods, and livestock within the village as well as from the village to fields and roads. Short-term storage of certain forms of fuel (brush, thistles, dung cakes) or of ash (used for fertilizer), the cleaning of household utensils and clothing at the communal village spring or springs, and the discarding of fragments of a wide range of objects and materials take place out of doors but well within village borders.

The surfaces of villages' alleys and "commons" are generally covered with more debris and are more irregular than those of houses' courtyards, despite the fact that both kinds of surfaces are unroofed. Within houses, the walls and floors of different kinds of rooms tend to be accorded different treatment and to accumulate different kinds of residues or discolorations, and are characterized by different kinds of built-in features (bins, ovens, hearths, pits, troughs, niches, etc.). Observations of activities in contemporary villages and of variations in their structural settings therefore suggest that in addition to objects (artifacts) and structures, variations in horizontal surfaces, in walls, and in the spatial distribution of morphologically differing features could be discerned in the archeological record of such villages and could be used to identify houses as well as to differentiate between areas within houses.

It should be noted that modern villages in the Zagros-Taurus area tend to comprise scores of houses, each of which has several rooms, and that houses are generally substantially larger than 20 or 30 m². Activities carried out within modern village houses do not appear to vary widely from one house to another. Where activities within houses appear to be essentially comparable, differing in degree but not necessarily in kind, then variations between domiciles must be due to other causes, such as variations in occupants' "ethnicity," "wealth," household composition, or the relative chronology of houses. While limited, there is some ethnographic and ethnohistoric evidence suggesting that villages become both areally larger and internally more densely settled as they age, and differences in house size (as well as style) might relate partly to such changes in density. A sample of several houses would be required in cases where the identification and explication of households' variability was a component of the research program. This point is discussed below.

Circulation between houses is an important consideration for villagers, and the location of their houses with respect to those of friends and relatives also appears to be a matter of concern. Archeologists might develop hypotheses about the spatial distribution of kin on the basis not only of stylistic analysis of artifacts (see Hill 1970; Longacre 1970) but also on the basis of structural evidence (such as presence or absence of bonding, the nature of plastering on adjoining walls, and the placement of doors within houses as well as into houses). Today, brothers not occupying the same house may reside in adjoining houses which are structural subdivisions of their father's house, or they may face one another across a narrow alley (Kramer 1982). In the latter case, the doors to their houses are more likely to be opposite one another than in the case of neighbors who are not close relatives, since privacy as well as social access through spatial mobility are highly valued. Aspects of circulation within prehistoric villages might best be revealed in the purposive excavation of open areas bordering on structures. Theoretically, one practical difficulty in such an archeological enterprise might be in differentiating between open areas within houses (pens and courtyards) and those between them (alleys and commons), but observations of surfaces in modern villages suggest that such distinctions might be fairly readily drawn. The archeologist might be able to combine soils tests with judgment, based on observations of modern villages, about probable locations and frequencies or proportions of such areas. The high percentage of unroofed space within villages creates potential problems for the archeologist wishing to focus on structures; this point is touched on below.

Finally, archeologically oriented observations in modern villages also suggest that some important activities are consistently carried out at settlement peripheries and beyond. These include the construction of irrigation canals and roads, fuel processing, the threshing of plant foods, some ritual activities, burial of the dead, pitting related to midden accumulation, and earth quarrying for a variety of additional reasons. Trenches restricted to the mounds formed by decayed mud structures are unlikely to locate direct evidence of such activities or of other activities and structures related to food production (e.g., fields, paths to fields, seasonal field huts and silos, stables in pastures, etc.). Artifacts related to subsistence activities, and their indirect traces (such as plough marks in soils and chemical markers both within and outside houses), might also be located beyond the limits of archeological mounds. Archeologists interested in such aspects of prehistoric village life should consider including such areas in their samples.

ARCHEOLOGICAL VILLAGES

There is evidence for substantial time depth for some of the patterns that can be observed in small rural settlements in Southwest Asia today. As it has been reconstructed, the archeological record demonstrates that some of the material features of village life extend back to at least the fourth millennium B.C. and, in some of the areas where earlier data are available, considerably beyond (e.g., in parts of Anatolia). In addition to reliance on the major economic species utilized today, these continuities include the use of comparable building materials and construction techniques, the construction of such built-in features as hearths, ovens, and bins, similarities in house sizes and plans, the spatial organization of settlements, the allocation of areas within settlements to specific activities (such as storing, or livestock stabling), the presence of unroofed courtyards within houses and of plazas between them, the construction of two-storey dwellings, and the absence of demonstrable formal identity or homogeneity of houses within individual settlements. In addition, there are parallels in settlement sizes and in their locations with respect to natural resources (most obviously, rivers) and to one another (e.g., in the existence of settlement pairs or clusters, of distances between nearest neighbors, of linear patterning, and of size hierarchies; F. Hole, forthcoming; Oates 1973, 1977; Watson 1978; Kramer 1982). Site-size hierarchies are reconstructed from differing site areas, from which site populations are generally inferred. (As was noted above, sites' functions may be inferred from sites' areas and/or from type, quantity, and diversity of surface artifacts. Hence the identification of prehistoric "villages" and "centers.") Site hierarchies extend back to about 4000 B.C. in at least the alluvial plains of southern Iraq and Iran, in parts of the adjacent Iranian highlands (Adams 1962, 1965; Adams and Nissen 1972; Dollfus, pers. comm.; Johnson 1973; Kramer 1982; Levine and McDonald 1977; Young 1975), and most probably in a number of other areas as well. They have figured prominently in some discussions of economic and sociopolitical change in the area (e.g., Adams and Nissen 1972; Johnson 1973).

In Southwest Asia, where mud is the basic building material, archeological residues of a single occupation (component) can achieve considerable depth. Multicomponent sites, therefore, are often quite deep and can assume the form of mounds up to 30 or 40 m in height. In the first half of this century, while archeologists were developing the basic descriptive foundation on which subsequent comparative and problem-oriented research was to build, they tended to select multicomponent sites and to sacrifice broad areal coverage in favor of excavating deep stratigraphic columns and establishing long cultural sequences. In contrast to these key sites excavated early in this century, most of the village sites shown in table 2 are small. This list of early villages is not a "random" sample of those excavated, although in providing some indication of the areal scale of some early settlements it is probably not extremely unrepresentative of the sample published to date.

In most cases the figures shown in table 2 are estimates based on site maps drawn at small scales. In fact, of course, the samples removed from these sites were volumes and not planes, but

Table 2. — Sites and Samples: Selected Early Settlements in the Zagros-Taurus Mountains and Adjacent Areas

Site	Approx. Date (years B.C.)[1]	Approx. Area (ha)	Approx. Area Excavated (sq m)	%[2] Excav.	No. of Seasons	References
Karim Shahir	Ca. 8000	.42	500	12	1	Braidwood and Howe 1960
M'lefaat	Ca. 8000	1.10	60	.5	1	Ibid.
Ganj Dareh	8000−6800	.13	310	24	5	P. Smith 1976; Hesse 1978
Ali Kosh	8000−6000	1.43	180	1.3	2	Hole, Flannery, and Neely 1969
Çayönü	7500−6500	2.50	1300±	5	4	Redman 1978
Tepe Guran	6600−5500	.94	120	1.3	1	Meldgaard et al. 1964
Qalat Jarmo	6500−5800	1.30	1370	10	3	Braidwood and Howe 1960
Chagha Sefid	6500−5000	2.00	240	1	1	Hole 1977
Çatal Hüyük	6500−5800	13.00	4050	3	4	Todd 1976; Mellaart 1967
Umm Dabaghiyah	Ca. 5900	.85	3750±	44	4	Kirkbride 1975
Yarim Tepe I	5800−5000	.80	1740	22	7	Munchaev and Merpert 1973
Tell Hassuna	5800−5000	3.00	2550	9	2	Lloyd and Safar 1945
Matarrah	5800−5000	1.00	470	5	1	Braidwood et al. 1952
Tell es-Sawwan	5700−5000	2.50	2750	12	6	Yasin 1970; al-Soof 1971
Tell Shimshara	5600−5000	2.00	400±	2	1	Mortensen 1970
Hacilar	5600−5000	1.50	3540	24	4	Mellaart 1970
Hajji Firuz	5500−5000	2.50	140	.6	2	Voigt 1976
Chogha Mami	5500−5000	5.00	1600±	3	1	Oates 1969
Gawra XX−XI	4500−3400	1.10	4065	36	5	Tobler 1950
Seh Gabi, C	4400−4200	.03	100	38	1	Kramer, forthcoming
Dalma Tepe	4200−4000	.20	100	5	3	Hamlin 1975
Seh Gabi, B	4200−3800	.96	410	4	2	Kramer, forthcoming
Tall-i Bakun A	Ca. 4000	2.00	1825	9	2	Langsdorf and McCown 1942
Seh Gabi, E	3600−3400	.44	145	3	1	Kramer, forthcoming
Seh Gabi, A	3600−3400	.60	150	3	1	Kramer, forthcoming

1. Dates are approximate, based on uncorrected 5730 half-life as reported in a range of publications.
2. Oates (1977) lists areas and sample proportions for some of these sites; in some cases her figures differ from those shown here. It must be remembered that these are measures of area, *not* volume.

it is not possible to consider the volumetric values and stratigraphic complexity of these excavations in the present context.[6] Table 2 suggests that in even fairly small prehistoric settlements, excavated samples (even where more than one field season was involved) are often fairly small. Despite any deficiencies in their excavation and the small size of the samples by which they are represented, the sites in table 2 (and the larger population of early villages that they "represent") serve to reinforce the point — documented in considerable detail by Hole, Oates, and Watson — that many aspects of early villages can be shown to parallel those observable in small-scale rural

6. Given clement weather it is not unreasonable to expect to be able to carry out a two-meter-deep excavation in the course of a single two- or three-month season. Such an excavation might consist of five 10 m × 10 m quadrats, removing about 1,000 m³ of earthen material. A one-hectare site two m in height would have a volume of about 20,000 m³. On the basis of her calculations on house volume and site area, Lee Horne (pers. comm.) has estimated that the current modern (single component) two-hectare village of Baghestan (table 1) would, if flattened to cover its entire area, be a mere 50 cm high; if the earth of which its structures are composed were areally consolidated, just under 10,000 m³ of earth would be involved. The use of "packed house volume" to estimate prehistoric populations has been discussed by Ammerman et al.

settlements today. In other, later, and/or more complex sites, where large block samples were excavated early in this century (e.g., Ur, Nuzi, Sialk, Susa),[7] archeological deposits were frequently removed with insufficient attention to the complexity of stratigraphic relationships. At these and other such sites, although substantial architectural information was obtained and very large samples yielding much useful qualitative data were collected, the excavated material is, for many purposes, useless.

For a variety of reasons, including the history of research in Southwest Asia and the immediate objectives of archeologists at any particular point in time, there are few early village sites for which large excavated samples of any particular component are available, and distributional data for specific village occupations are therefore limited. Certainly in no published case is there a plan of a complete settlement, although a few sites seem to come close (e.g., Tepe Gawra, Umm Dabaghiyah).[8] These do so, of course, partly because they represent the work of several seasons and partly because they are very small sites. Most of the material obtained at these sites comes from quadrats (trenches in the form of squares or rectangles), although some of these excavations involved partial transects in the form of areally short but vertically deep step trenches cut into already eroded and often partly disturbed mound edges. The excavated samples are often substantially less than ten percent of site area. Most of these sites were not excavated according to explicitly formulated probability-sampling designs, and, as a result, it is not possible to argue that each of the areas sampled is representative of that site. Nonetheless, in many if not in most cases, there was an implicit research design, based on "judgment" (although not always necessarily on what we would, today, deem good judgment). In a few instances what might best be termed multistage research designs were employed; sampling procedures and areal focus were modified as new data became available. This was possible in programs of fieldwork which were, from their very inception, defined as long term in nature.

ARCHEOLOGICAL SAMPLING

Archeologists reconstruct the past and explain patterning, variation, and change on the basis of data derived ultimately from excavation and surface survey. Given the nature of archeological

---

(1976, pp. 41ff.), whose computations give a very clear idea of the monumental scale of the sampling problem confronting the archeologist working at a site with scale (and volume) as small as that of Ali Kosh. It can also be noted that, to avoid cave-ins, archeologists often increasingly restrict trench areas as they move downward in deep sites. This practice, coupled with changes as well as continuities in architectural structures (including "spiral stratigraphy"; see Young and Levine 1974, p. 18), suggests that it may be somewhat naive to assume that a probability sample (see below) at even a small village site can be either readily executed or interpreted.

7. These and similar large sites are not tabulated here, because they are (a) generally functionally large "centers" and (b) later in time than the early prehistoric villages that can be used in arguing for the substantial time depth of patterns observable in the present day. The Isin-Larsa component at Ur is at least 60 hectares in extent (R. McC. Adams, pers. comm.), of which just over one hectare was excavated. At the relatively small sites of Tepe Hissar and Nuzi, samples of under 50% were cleared, although at Nuzi (roughly four hectares) the figure was close to this, and at Hissar (whose "nucleus" is approximately six hectares), about 20% of the site area was opened. The period V component at Godin Tepe was probably roughly seven hectares in area. With a large exposure of more than 700 m², the areal sample is only about one percent (though the total volume removed may be on the order of 6,000 to 7,000 m³).

8. The plan of Tell Taya, a site of approximately 80 hectares in the Sinjar region of northern Iraq occupied in the late third and first millennia B.C. and partially excavated by Julian Reade, comes closer than most. This is because the foundations and/or walls of many of the ancient buildings are exposed on the site's surface, so that a town plan could be mapped in detail without its being excavated in its entirety (Reade 1973). Taya, however, is apparently a most unusual site. (This statement is not based on a probability sample!)

data and the resources available for research it can be argued that all archeological work involves sampling (see Redman 1973, p. 62). If it be granted that this is the case, discussions about whether or not sampling is useful are meaningless; what archeologists should do, and what many of them appear to attempt to do, is explicitly identify the population that they wish to sample and specify why they choose to sample it one way rather than another.[9] Several key articles clearly summarize the objectives and the methodology of archeological sampling strategies, and some have evaluated them (Binford 1964; Plog 1976; Ragir 1967; Redman 1974; Vescelius 1960; see Mueller 1975). Partly in response to the influential articles of Vescelius, Binford, and Ragir, many archeologists have for some time incorporated probability sampling in their research designs, although (largely for a set of historical reasons) this has not yet become a widespread practice in parts of the Old World, including Southwest Asia.

In general terms, probability sampling is a means of inferring characteristics of a whole from some of its parts. It is not usually designed to locate rare elements but to "estimate the presence and proportions of common constituents of the population" (Redman 1974, pp. 22f.). It forces the archeologist to minimize bias and, in following certain mathematical principles, permits him or her to subject the data to further statistical manipulations. The work of a number of archeologists, geographers, and ecologists suggests that probability sampling should be incorporated in the research designs that we use in obtaining data to inform us about the past (see Haggett 1965, pp. 191 ff.; Judge, Ebert, and Hitchcock 1975, pp. 90ff.). This work also suggests that different sampling designs are differentially suited to different kinds of research problems, and it shows clearly that there is no single ideal sample size, or fraction.

There are different kinds of probability sampling designs. Simple random sampling treats all sampling units in the same way, such that any of them is equally likely to be selected for detailed investigation. Some archeologists suggest that simple random sampling is the most appropriate approach to a population about which nothing is known (Plog 1976, p. 158; Read 1975, p. 54; Winter 1976). Unlike random samples, systematic samples are laid out in a geometric pattern, and while they are designed to cover the spatial extent of the defined population, they create the risk of masking periodicities inherent in that population. Some have suggested that systematic or stratified sampling provides a more precise estimate of the underlying population than does that obtained in simple random sampling (Plog 1976, p. 143; Read 1975, p. 58), and Redman (1973, p. 63) considers stratified, systematic, unaligned sampling to be the most effective way to obtain an unbiased, geographically dispersed sample in situations where previous knowledge is unavailable. Stratification of sampled populations is designed to explicitly incorporate the investigator's expectations or assumptions about those populations. Populations (such as individual sites) are subdivided into sections (strata), each of which is thought to be internally more homogeneous than the entire population and each of which is therefore sampled separately. Stratification of the population does not require that either objectivity or regularity be built into

9. In the following pages the term *population* follows a distinction made by Read (1975, p. 52). Here, "population" refers to Read's "sampled population (population of cultural material at time of excavation)," in contrast to the "target population (population of cultural material at time of occupation)." The terms *accuracy* and *precision* appear frequently in the literature on archeological sampling and have been defined by Cowgill (1975, pp. 264f.) and Redman (1975, p. 7). *Precision* is a measure of how widely individual sample means are spread out around the mean of their means; *high precision* means that our sample results are highly repeatable, regardless of whether or not they're correct. *Accuracy*, in contrast, is a measure of the extent to which individual sample means are spread out around the true population mean rather than the mean of all sample means. Where sample means are considerably different from true population means, the samples may be considered unrepresentative. One of the main objectives of probabilistic sampling strategies is to obtain representative samples of larger populations. A critical discussion of archeological sampling appears in B. Hole (1980).

the sampling of each stratum. It explicitly utilizes the "knowledge, experience, and intuition of the investigator" (Redman 1975, p. 150), including his or her perceptions of patterning, or "redundancies," in human use of space (see Binford 1975, pp. 255f.).[10] Such judgments may enrich probability sampling, but they do not replace it. Any or all of these approaches to sampling a population may be incorporated into a multistage research design. Here, in sequent stages of research, successively smaller portions of the total population are investigated more intensively. As research progresses, analysis of data obtained with one sampling strategy may be used to redefine one's objectives and, if necessary, to modify one's sampling design.

Since there is no uniformity in archeologists' questions it is impossible to make prescriptive statements about archeological sampling. There is no ideal sampling strategy for locating archeological sites, for collecting surface materials from them, or for excavating samples of them. Nor is there an ideal sample size, or fraction, despite the occasional mention of ten percent as a reasonable sample (see Vescelius 1960, p. 462). The larger the site or region, the more time and money are required to obtain a ten percent sample (Cowgill 1975, p.263; see also Haggett 1965, p. 192; Plog 1976). The size and shape of individual sampling units also vary. Small trenches may be a reasonable way to obtain a sample of deeply stratified material to develop a provisional ceramic sequence or to locate structures that can then be exposed by enlarging the excavation units (Asch 1975; Winter 1976). In general, sampling units should be larger than the phenomena investigated (Cowgill 1975, p. 166), and large blocks (quadrats) — in contrast to small dispersed sample units — are the most appropriate means by which to obtain information about configurational or distributional aspects of phenomena investigated. However, in opening up a few large areas we may obtain a statistically less representative sample of the population (Asch 1975, p. 184ff.; Plog 1976, pp. 151, 157), and linear samples (transects), rather than quadrats, may provide the most accurate estimates of the values in underlying populations that are internally differentiated (Judge, Ebert, and Hitchcock 1975, p. 91). In some circumstances — particularly when dealing with very small populations — archeologists may choose to relinquish any hope of systematically conducting probability sampling, since "one excavation unit located in a favorable area may be worth a hundred other units that sample materials in mediocre contexts" (Asch 1975, p. 186). However, probability sampling permits the archeologist to make an initial identification of the location of mediocre and favorable contexts, and judgment enables him or her to evaluate the promise of these different contexts in terms of specific research objectives. A number of archeologists appear to favor a mixed strategy incorporating both probability sampling and sampling based on assumptions regarding sites' content and organization (Asch 1975; Flannery 1976a).

SOUTHWEST ASIAN VILLAGES AND ARCHEOLOGICAL SAMPLING

Judgment based on observation of populations assumed to be similar to those investigated can be useful in formulating sampling strategies, but its nature and role in decision-making should be explicitly stated. In the case of archeological excavation (as opposed to survey of individual sites or of regions) we might attempt to benefit from our growing understanding of spatial organization within recent settlements by explicitly incorporating such understandings in our sampling strategies. Where formal parallels or similarities between archeological and modern settlements may be presumed to exist, observations on modern settlements may be useful in deciding where to locate trenches, what size and shape to make them, and what sample fraction to collect.

---

10. According to Reid, Schiffer, and Neff (1975, p. 224), the "formation of the archaeological record provides the key to devising sampling strategies"; clearly, archeologists' perceptions of the ways in which the archeological record forms are an important part of what others have called judgment.

Archeologists wishing to minimize bias and to obtain statistically representative samples of larger populations should utilize sampling designs based on probability theory. In view of increasingly fragile geopolitics and the likelihood of continuously shrinking funding levels for archeological field programs, archeologists working in Southwest Asia would do well to "think smaller" than they have in previous years, and for these reasons, if for no other, they should accordingly evaluate more carefully than they have in the past the role of probability sampling in their research.

Tables 1 and 2 show that villages tend to be small in scale. They are often considerably smaller in area than contemporaneous "centers," but, even so, many are two or three hectares in extent, of which 30 to 60 percent may be unroofed,[11] and a single component may have 30, 40, or more houses. Because of their small scale, such villages would need to be excavated almost in their entirety in order to yield a sample sufficiently large that statistically meaningful observations might by made about it. A site of one hectare is, it seems, on the small end of the range. A ten percent sample of a site of this size, or 1,000 m², might be divided among ten trenches, each of them measuring 10 m × 10 m. Clearing a shallow top component in an area of this size might well take a three-month season and a handsome budget, even in areas where labor costs are comparatively low. Obtaining a sample of structures that was statistically representative of such a site could take as much as ten seasons and reveal only one of several components. This hypothetical example ignores two important features of many Southwest Asian sites: their depth and stratigraphic complexity. Initial probability samples may well test only the uppermost component(s), leaving the archeologist with the difficult problem of attempting to compare material from different components and to decide which areas might best be enlarged and to what depth. Even shallow sites of a few meters height may cover a millennium or more of occupation, and probabilistic sampling designs are unlikely to test all components equally. In Southwest Asian mounds, long-term sedentary occupation seems to be the rule rather than the exception. Resultant deep and complex stratigraphy at even the smallest rural sites heightens the difficulty of the archeological decision-making process (see Brown 1975).

If, at such small and shallow sites, we excavate small and dispersed trenches as part of a probabilistic sampling program, it may not be possible to identify different houses (rather than individual rooms) or to clarify stratigraphic relationships among the contents of different trenches. The determination that houses varied, and a specification of the ways in which and the extent to which they did so, would require a sample larger than one house. At most village sites fairly large quadrats would be required to expose even a single house. Contiguous trenches arranged in the form of a transect, particularly in shallow mounds, might be one fruitful approach to the identification not only of differentially distributed features but also of the ways in which these were related to stratigraphy and chronological change. The archeologist interested in stratigraphy, even in short-term chronological change, in distributional information, and in obtaining a statistically reliable sample must find a balance between his or her objectives, the nature of the data base, and the expedient — framed, most likely, in terms of foundation or institutional support, staff availability, and geopolitics. Given the nature of the data and the kinds of questions that archeologists ask, a probability sample at even a small village may yield highly reliable information about remains of poor quality or of low information content. At larger and organizationally more diverse and complex sites, the problem is likely to be greater.

The preliminary identification of frequencies and locations of features, rooms, artifacts and,

---

11. Even in modern North American cities, up to 20% of settlement area may be comprised of streets (Alten 1959). Regardless of important structural and functional differences in the roofed spaces of rural and urban centers, therefore, it appears that large proportions of settlements tend to be unroofed and accordingly *comparatively* low in information content.

perhaps, burials might be based on an initial probability sample. So might the percentage of open space within a village. Given the high proportion of unroofed space within contemporary settlements and the apparently high proportion in ancient settlements as well (see Watson 1978), we are likely to expend considerable time, money, and energy in clearing areas with comparatively low information content even as we expose a high proportion of open space in our unbiased and presumably representative probability samples. This point can be illustrated by summarizing the results of two sampling "experiments" carried out by superimposing graph tracing paper over the detailed plan of a modern village in western Iran (Kramer 1979).

In the first experiment, this three-hectare village was divided into 10 m × 10 m trenches in which (hypothetical) simple random samples, stratified random samples, and systematic samples of one, five, and ten percent were "collected." Briefly, this experiment suggested that although in some cases the amount of unroofed area might be very slightly underrepresented, all sample fractions and all sampling strategies produced comparable and apparently representative proportions of roofed to nonarchitectural area. However, all of these sampling procedures minimize the likelihood of opening up two or more contiguous excavation units. An excavator using any of these sampling designs at such a site would therefore probably get a good idea of the proportion of nonarchitectural to architectural space, and would of course be able to specify some of the locations and more general patterning of features in such spaces, but would not necessarily obtain a particularly useful sense of the range of variation in houses, since all of these sampling strategies entail the use of a fairly standard quadrat size and all exposures are therefore likely to be substantially smaller than many village houses. Such sampling strategies can be used to develop provisional numerical estimates of population values. However, detailed information on metric attributes, ranges of variability, and spatial distributions of houses and house blocks would not be revealed with even a ten percent sample (which at a three-hectare site might require several months of excavation; see table 2). Nonetheless, such sampling would provide crucial data that the archeologist could use in deciding where additional work should be done. In addition, on the basis of the numbers of some artifacts and some room types (e.g., dwelling rooms as opposed to stables and storerooms) it might be possible to attempt household or population estimates, as well as other kinds of reconstruction.

In a second experiment, 10 m × 10 m quadrats were used to excavate ten percent samples of the same hypothetical mound. These "excavations" took the form of a simple random sample, a stratified random sample, a stratified systematic unaligned sample, radial transects, and random transects (see Redman 1974). In all cases, as previously, the site was treated as though it were a plane, and the problems that might be raised by depth, stratigraphic variation, and complexity were completely ignored. All of the samples exposed at least portions of more than one-third of the total number of courtyards actually present in this village. If in carrying out such sampling programs the archeologist could assume that each house had at least one courtyard (which, for this and many Zagros villages, would be a valid assumption), one might use such an ethnographically based judgment to estimate the number of houses present (as well as, of course, to specify their location, one preliminary form of distributional information). In this second experiment, only the random transects revealed a rather low proportion of nonarchitectural space. In all of the other sample designs, comparable and apparently representative samples of nonarchitectural space were exposed in the hypothetical trenches. As in the earlier experiment, of course, even given 10 m × 10 m trenches, very few rooms were exposed in their entirety. No single house was, for in this village, the smallest house (including its enclosed courtyard) is 42 m²; the largest is more than 1300 m² in area, and the median is about 200 m². Although houses in some other villages in the Zagros-Taurus area may tend to be slightly smaller, most of them would not be exposed in their entirety unless large excavation blocks were incorporated into the sampling design. As data reviewed by Watson (1978) show, this has been the pattern in excavations at some well-known early prehistoric villages.

Summary and Conclusions

The existence of architectural variability within even small and socioeconomically fairly uncomplicated villages has been documented elsewhere, (e.g., Kramer 1982; Watson 1979), and the same could no doubt be done for other material aspects of contemporary village life. Until the nature and range of variability within and between villages — and larger settlements — are more clearly specified they cannot be easily explained. To do so, we require a sample greater than one, whether it be pots, burials, rooms, houses, or villages. Theoretically, probability sampling serves to select samples that are representative of underlying populations. However, it can be time-consuming, and it may reveal much information not directly relevant to the investigator's specific research problem. In addition, when such research involves analysis of data whose numerical, spatial, and chronological distributions are discontinuous, probability sampling may well be insufficient (although not unnecessary). Probability sampling is useful in establishing provisional estimates of whole-site populations and in providing information useful in stratifying sites or regions for a second stage of research (Redman 1973; Redman et al. 1978; Redman and Anzalone 1980). It forces the excavator to examine areas that might not otherwise be investigated, thereby minimizing sample bias, and by adhering to mathematical principles it also enables him or her to subject data obtained to further statistical analysis.

Probability sampling pinpoints central tendencies rather than the diversity and spatial organization of cultural materials at a site. In the case of prehistoric villages, probabilistic sampling strategies can provide information on (for example) the proportion of roofed to unroofed space and the number of rooms, features, and artifacts (and the ratios or proportions of such elements, including the differential representation of different types of such elements). An initial probabilistic sample may be followed by additional sampling. It might, for example, be desirable to verify the proportional representation of a particular item identified in a randomizing strategy in a subsequent effort (Collins 1975, p.29). Different strategies, possibly including the excavation of a few but large blocks, could be useful in illuminating configurational aspects of the population rather than simply its "total inventory" (Redman 1975, p. 154). Transects might elucidate the ways in which configurational variability is related to chronological variation.

Archeologists must decide whether they want information about the frequencies with which elements in a population occur, in which case they should use probability samples, or whether they want spatial, configurational information, in which case they require transects and/or large quadrats,[12] thereby running the risk of sacrificing the statistical reliability or representativeness of their sample. If one wishes to achieve both objectives — the assurance that one has obtained a representative sample *and* the detailed information provided by intensive exploration of a subset selected on the basis of judgment — then it *may* be feasible to develop a multistage design, although this can require a substantial commitment of both time and money. In such a case — although enormous difficulties are raised by the sheer size and complexity of the data base, and further magnified by the nature of the questions that we tend to ask — the first stage might incorporate a probability sample in which whole-site estimates could be developed and in which areas for enlarged sample units could be identified. Strata may be defined either before sampling begins or on the basis of the results of such a first stage of work. In either case, judgment can be used in the sampling of subdivisions of a site (or region) subsequent to the initial exploratory and definitional phase of fieldwork. In any case, only the archeologist can decide which sample design, trench shape and size, and sample fraction are most likely to elucidate the population studied.

12. Large blocks of contiguous small quadrats (for example, 2 m × 2 m or 5 m × 5 m trenches) may be useful in cases where the stratigraphy is complex and the excavator wishes to "control" it by monitoring it in numerous vertical profiles.

If one research objective were to determine prehistoric settlements' functions, it would be essential to have as representative a sample as possible of data on activities, areas, and other variables that would help us to classify the population. A probability sample would provide such data. If a sample at one site revealed relatively little artifactual and/or architectural diversity, one might assume that the site in question was functionally small, and if artifacts and structures suggested that activities had related primarily to subsistence and were not necessarily reflective of a wide range of occupational specializations or administrative activities, one might be justified in defining the site as a village. In such a case, if one inferred that activities had been fairly undifferentiated, then it would be reasonable to expect that variation in architecture should be explicable on other grounds, such as chronological variation within the site or the number or socioeconomic rank of occupants in different houses. To establish presence/absence, and the range, of activities, the archeologist may not need too large a sample of households, as expressed in house remains. However, to investigate other questions, a range of extensively cleared houses might be essential. Given the large proportion of unroofed area that is likely to be exposed in a probability sample (even a one percent sample at a small site) detailed architectural and artifactual information might best be obtained in larger block excavations (even if at the expense of statistical reliability). In cases where architectural variation, or differential density of artifacts and structures, may be attributable in part to chronological change, transects rather than large quadrats may be more revealing of the relationships between stratigraphic complexity, chronological change, and distributional variability.

Because some of the isomorphisms in structures and spatial organization of modern and prehistoric villages have been detailed elsewhere, their distribution and content have not been elaborated here. Some specific elements of sedentary rural life — as they are reflected in material remains — extend back for more than six millennia. Although it is not assumed that these similarities in form are due exclusively to similarities in function, it is suggested that such formal similarities can be useful in formulating sampling designs. If judgments based on ethnographic data are to be used in archeological excavations they should, obviously, be clearly stated. A mixed strategy incorporating probabilistic sampling in at least an initial stage and sufficiently flexible to permit sampling that was not necessarily rigorously probabilistic in subsequent stages of excavation would seem, in the 1980s, to be one pragmatic approach to the investigation of prehistoric villages in the hilly flanks of the Fertile Crescent.

BIBLIOGRAPHY

Abu al-Soof, Behnam
  1971   Tell es-Sawwan: fifth season's excavations (winter 1967–1968). *Sumer* 27:3–7.
Adams, Robert McC.
  1962   Agriculture and urban life in early southwestern Iran. *Science* 136:109–22.
  1965   *Land behind Baghdad.* Chicago: University of Chicago Press.
  1981   *Heartland of cities: surveys of ancient settlement and land use on the central floodplain of the Euphrates.* Chicago: University of Chicago Press.
Adams, Robert McC., and Nissen, Hans
  1972   *The Uruk countryside.* Chicago: University of Chicago Press.
Alberts, Robert C.
  1963   Social structure and culture change in an Iranian village. Ph.D. diss., University of Wisconsin.

Alpöge, Ayla
  1971   Anonymous architecture in the Keban region, 1969. In *Keban project 1969 activities*, pp. 135–38. Middle East Technical University Keban Project Publications, series 1, no. 2. Ankara: Middle East Technical University.

Alten, Iven
  1959   Sanandaj: a town plan. United States Operations Missions to Iran. Tehran: Communications Media Division.

Ammerman, A.J.; Cavalli-Sforza, L.L.; and Wagener, D.K.
  1976   Toward the estimation of population growth in old world prehistory. In *Demographic anthropology*, ed. E.B.W. Zubrow, pp. 27–61. Albuquerque: University of New Mexico Press.

Antoun, Richard T.
  1972   *Arab village*. Bloomington: Indiana University Press.

Asch, David L.
  1975   On sample size problems and the uses of nonprobabilistic sampling. In *Sampling in archaeology*, ed. James W. Mueller, pp. 170–91. Tucson: University of Arizona Press.

al-Azzawi, Subhi Hussein
  1969   Oriental houses in Iraq. In *Shelter and society*, ed. Paul Oliver, pp. 91–102. New York: Praeger.

Binford, Lewis R.
  1964   A consideration of archaeological research design. *American Antiquity* 29:425–41.
  1975   Sampling, judgment, and the archaeological record. In *Sampling in archaeology*, ed. James W. Mueller, pp. 251–57. Tucson: University of Arizona Press.

Braidwood, Robert J., and Howe, Bruce
  1960   *Prehistoric investigations in Iraqi Kurdistan*. Studies in Ancient Oriental Civilization, no. 31. Chicago: University of Chicago Press.

Braidwood, Robert J.; Braidwood, Linda; Smith, James G.; and Leslie, Charles
  1952   Matarrah, a southern variant of the Hassunan assemblage, excavated in 1948. *Journal of Near Eastern Studies* 11:1–75.

Braidwood, Robert J., and Reed, Charles A.
  1957   The achievement and early consequences of food production: a consideration of the archeological and natural-historical evidence. In *Population studies: animal ecology and demography*, pp. 19–31. Cold Spring Harbor Symposia on Quantitative Biology, vol. 22. Cold Spring Harbor, Long Island: The Biological Laboratory.

Brown, James A.
  1975   Deep-site excavation strategy as a sampling problem. In *Sampling in archaeology*, ed. James W. Mueller, pp. 155–69. Tucson: University of Arizona Press.

Cockburn, Charles
  1969   Paliwal settlements and the Rajastan canal project. In *Shelter and society*, ed. Paul Oliver, pp. 116–26. New York: Praeger.

Collins, Michael B.
  1975   Sources of bias in processual data: an appraisal. In *Sampling in archaeology*, ed. James W. Mueller, pp. 26–32. Tucson: University of Arizona Press.

Costello, V.F.
  1977   *Urbanization in the Middle East*. Cambridge: Cambridge University Press.

Cowgill, George L.
  1975   A selection of samplers: comments on archaeo-statistics. In *Sampling in archaeology*, ed. James W. Mueller, pp. 258–74. Tucson: University of Arizona Press.

Denyer, Susan
    1978   African traditional architecture. London: Heinemann.

Doumanis, Orestis B., and Oliver, Paul
    1974   (eds.) Shelter in Greece. Athens: Architecture in Greece Press.

English, Paul W.
    1966   City and village in Iran. Madison: University of Wisconsin Press.

Flannery, Kent V.
    1976a   (ed.) The early Mesoamerican village. New York: Academic Press.
    1976b   Sampling by intensive surface collection. In The early Mesoamerican village, ed. Kent V.
                    Flannery, pp. 51–62. New York: Academic Press.

French, David; Aksoy, Behin; Diamant, Steven; Hall, Gerald; Helms, Svend; Hillman, Gordon; McBride,
Sam; Mitchell, Stephen; McNicoll, Anthony; Payne, Sebastian; Riddell, Alwyn; Wagstaff, Malcolm;
Weinstein, Matina; Williams, David.
    1973   Aşvan 1968–1972: an interim report. Anatolian Studies 23:71–307.

Galloway, J.P.N.
    1958   A Kurdish village of north-east Iraq. The Geographical Journal 124:361–66.

Gremliza, F.G.L.
    1962   Ecology of endemic diseases in the Dez irrigation pilot area. Report to Khuzestan, Power
                    Authority and Plan Organization of Iran. New York: Development and Resources Corp.

Gulick, John
    1955   Social structure and culture change in a Lebanese village. Viking Fund Publications in
                    Anthropology, no. 21. New York: Wenner-Gren Foundation for Anthropological Re-
                    search.

Haggett, Peter
    1965   Locational analysis in human geography. London: Edward Arnold.

Hamlin, Carol Kramer
    1975   Dalma Tepe. Iran 13:111–27.

Hesse, Brian
    1978   Evidence for husbandry from the early Neolithic site of Ganj Dareh in western Iran.
                    Ph.D. diss., Columbia University.

Hill, James N.
    1970   Broken K Pueblo. Anthropological Papers, University of Arizona, no. 18. Tucson: Uni-
                    versity of Arizona Press.

Hole, Bonnie Laird
    1980   Sampling in archeology: a critique. Annual Reviews in Anthropology 9:217–34.

Hole, Frank
    1977   Studies in the archeological history of the Deh Luran plain: the excavations at Choga
                    Sefid. Memoirs of the Museum of Anthropology, University of Michigan, no. 9. Ann
                    Arbor: University of Michigan Press.
    1978   Pastoral nomadism in western Iran. In Explorations in ethnoarchaeology, ed. Richard A.
                    Gould, pp. 127–67. Albuquerque: University of New Mexico Press.
    1979   Rediscovering the past in the present: ethnoarchaeology in Luristan, Iran. In Ethno-
                    archaeology: implications of ethnography for archaeology, ed. Carol Kramer, pp.
                    192–218. New York: Columbia University Press.
    forth-   The early village period. In Archaeological perspectives on Iran: from prehistory to the
    coming   Islamic conquest, ed. Frank Hole. Albuquerque: University of New Mexico Press.

Hole, Frank; Flannery, Kent V.; and Neely, James A.
    1969   (eds.) Prehistory and human ecology of the Deh Luran plain. Memoirs of the Museum of
                    Anthropology, University of Michigan, no. 1. Ann Arbor: University of Michigan Press.

Iran, Government of
1977   *Case Study on Desertification, Iran: Turan,* ed. Brian Spooner. International Cooperation to Combat Desertification: United Nations General Assembly Resolution 3337 (XXIX). Tehran: Department of the Environment.

Jacobs, Linda
1979   Tell-i Nun: archaeological implications of a village in transition. In *Ethnoarchaeology: implications of ethnography for archaeology,* ed. Carol Kramer, pp. 175–91. New York: Columbia University Press.

Johnson, Gregory A.
1973   *Local exchange and early state development in southwestern Iran.* Anthropological Papers of the Museum of Anthropology, University of Michigan, no. 51. Ann Arbor: Museum of Anthropology.
1975   Locational analysis and the investigation of Uruk local exchange systems. In *Ancient civilization and trade,* ed. Jeremy A. Sabloff and C.C. Lamberg-Karlovsky, pp. 285–339. Albuquerque: University of New Mexico Press.

Judge, W. James; Ebert, James I.; and Hitchcock, Robert K.
1975   Sampling in regional archaeological survey. In *Sampling in archaeology,* ed. James W. Mueller, pp. 82–123. Tucson: University of Arizona Press.

Kirkbride, Diana
1975   Umm Dabaghiyah 1974: a fourth preliminary report. *Iraq* 37:3–10.

Kolars, John F.
1963   Tradition, season, and change in a Turkish village. University of Chicago Department of Geography Research Paper no. 82.

Kramer, Carol
1979   An archaeological view of a contemporary Kurdish village: domestic architecture, household size, and wealth. In *Ethnoarchaeology: implications of ethnography for archaeology,* ed. Carol Kramer, pp. 139–63. New York: Columbia University Press.
1980   Estimating prehistoric populations: an ethnoarchaeological approach. In *l'Archéologie de l'Iraq: perspectives et limites de l'interprétation anthropologique des documents,* ed. Marie-Thérèse Barrelet, pp. 315–34. Paris: Centre National de la Recherche Scientifique.
1982   *Village ethnoarchaeology: rural Iran in archaeological perspective.* New York: Academic Press.
forth-
coming   Seh Gabi: the chipped stone assemblage.

Langsdorf, Alexander, and McCown, Donald
1942   *Tall-i Bakun A: season of 1932.* Oriental Institute Publications, vol. 54. Chicago: University of Chicago Press.

Lapidus, Ira M.
1969   *(ed.) Middle Eastern cities.* Berkeley: University of California Press.

Leach, Edmund R.
1940   *Social and economic organisation of the Rowanduz Kurds.* Monographs on Social Anthropology, London School of Economics, no. 3. London: Percy Lund, Humphries.

Levine, Louis D., and McDonald, Mary
1977   The Neolithic and Chalcolithic periods in the Mahidasht. *Iran* 15:39–50.

Lloyd, Seton, and Safar, Fuad
1945   Tell Hassuna. *Journal of Near Eastern Studies* 4:255–89.

Longacre, William A.
1970   *Archaeology as anthropology: a case study.* Anthropological Papers, University of Arizona, no. 17. Tucson: University of Arizona Press.

McIntosh, Roderick
    1974   Archaeology and mud wall decay in a west African village. *World Archaeology* 6:154–71.
    1976   Square huts in round concepts: prediction of settlement features in west Africa. *Archaeology* 29:92–101.

Meldgaard, Jørgen; Mortensen, Peder; and Thrane, Henrik
    1964   Excavations at Tepe Guran, Luristan. *Acta Archaeologica* 34:97–133.

Mellaart, James
    1967   *Çatal Hüyük: a Neolithic town in Anatolia.* New York: McGraw-Hill.
    1970   *Excavations at Hacilar.* Occasional Publications, British Institute of Archaeology at Ankara, no. 9. Edinburgh: Edinburgh University Press.

M.E.T.U. (Middle East Technical University)
    1965   *Yassihöyük: a village study.* Ankara.

Morris, Craig
    1975   Sampling in the excavation of urban sites: the case at Huánuco Pampa. In *Sampling in archaeology,* ed. James W. Mueller, pp. 192–208. Tucson: University of Arizona Press.

Morrison, John A.
    1939   Alişar: a unit of land occupancy in the Kanak Su basin of central Anatolia. Ph.D. diss., University of Chicago.

Mortensen, Peder
    1970   *Tell Shimshara: the Hassuna period.* Royal Danish Academy of Arts and Letters, Historisk-Filosofiske Skrifter 5,2. Copenhagen: Munksgaard.

Mueller, James W.
    1975   (ed.) *Sampling in archaeology.* Tucson: University of Arizona Press.

Munchaev, Rauf M., and Merpert, N.I.
    1973   Excavations at Yarim Tepe 1972: fourth preliminary report. *Sumer* 29:3–16.

Nissen, Hans
    1968   Survey of an abandoned modern village in southern Iraq. *Sumer* 24:107–14.

Oates, Joan
    1969   Choga Mami, 1967–68: a preliminary report. *Iraq* 31:115–52.
    1973   The background and development of early farming communities in Mesopotamia and the Zagros. *Proceedings of the Prehistoric Society* 39:147–81.
    1977   Mesopotamian social organisation: archaeological and philological evidence. In *The evolution of social systems,* ed. J. Friedman and M.J. Rowlands, pp. 457–85. London: Duckworth.

Oliver, Paul
    1971   (ed.) *Shelter in Africa.* New York: Praeger.

Peters, Emrys L.
    1963   Aspects of rank and status among Muslims in a Lebanese village. In *Mediterranean countrymen,* ed. Julian Pitt-Rivers, pp. 159–200. Recherches Méditerranéenes, Etudes, vol. 1. Paris: Mouton.

Peters, Eckhart
    1972   Lehmziegelhäuser in der Altinova. In *Keban project 1970 activities,* pp. 173–82. Middle East Technical University Keban Project Publications, series 1, no. 3. Ankara: Middle East Technical University.

Plog, Stephen
    1976   Relative efficiencies of sampling techniques for archeological surveys. In *The early Mesoamerican village,* ed. Kent V. Flannery, p. 136–58. New York: Academic Press.

Prussin, Labelle
    1969   *Architecture in northern Ghana.* Berkeley: University of California Press.

Ragir, Sonia
  1967   A review of techniques for archaeological sampling. In *A guide to field methods in archaeology,* ed. Robert Heizer and John Graham, pp. 181–97. Palo Alto: National Press Books.

Rapoport, Amos
  1969   The Pueblo and the Hogan. In *Shelter and society,* ed. Paul Oliver, pp. 66–79. New York: Praeger.

Read, Dwight W.
  1975   Regional sampling. In *Sampling in archaeology,* ed. James W. Mueller, pp. 45–60. Tucson: University of Arizona Press.

Reade, Julian
  1973   Tell Taya (1972–73): summary report. *Iraq* 35:155–87 (with appendices by J.N. Postgate, George Farrant, and Giles Waines).

Redman, Charles L.
  1973   Multistage fieldwork and analytical techniques. *American Antiquity* 38:61–79.
  1974   *Archaeological sampling strategies.* Addison-Wesley Module in Anthropology, no. 55. Reading: Addison-Wesley.
  1975   Productive sampling strategies for archaeological sites. In *Sampling in archaeology,* ed. James W. Mueller, pp. 147–54. Tucson: University of Arizona Press.
  1978   *The rise of civilization.* San Francisco: W.H. Freeman.

Redman, Charles L., and Anzalone, Ronald D.
  1980   Discovering architectural patterning at a complex site. *American Antiquity* 45:284–90.

Redman, Charles L.; Anzalone, Ronald D.; and Rubertone, Patricia E.
  1978   Qsar es-Seghir. *Storia della Città* 7:11–19.

Redman, Charles L., and Watson, Patty Jo
  1970   Systematic, intensive surface collection. *American Antiquity* 35:279–91.

Reid, Jefferson; Schiffer, Michael B.; and Neff, Jeffrey M.
  1975   Archaeological considerations of intrasite sampling. In *Sampling in archaeology,* ed. James W. Mueller, pp. 209–24. Tucson: University of Arizona Press.

Rouholamini, Mahmoud
  1973   l'Habitation dans la région de Suse Raddadeh (Khuzistan). *Cahiers de la Délégation Archéologique Française en Iran* 3:171–83.

Schiffer, Michael B.
  1976   Behavioral archeology. New York: Academic Press.

Smith, Carol
  1976   *(ed.) Regional analysis.* New York: Academic Press.

Smith, Philip E.L.
  1976   Reflections on four seasons of excavations at Tappeh Ganj Dareh. In *Proceedings of the IVth Annual Symposium on Archaeological Research in Iran* [Tehran, 1975], ed. Firouz Bagherzadeh, pp. 11–19. Tehran: Iranian Centre for Archaeological Research.

Stirling, Paul
  1965   *Turkish village.* New York: John Wiley and Sons.

Sumner, William M.
  1979   Estimating population by analogy. In *Ethnoarchaeology: implications of ethnography for archaeology,* ed. Carol Kramer, pp. 164–174. New York: Columbia University Press.

Sunderland, E.
  1968   Pastoralism, nomadism and the social anthropology of Iran. In *The Cambridge history of Iran,* vol. 1: *the land of Iran,* pp. 611–83. Cambridge: Cambridge University Press.

Sweet, Louise
    1974   *Tell Ṭoqaan: a Syrian village.* Anthropological Papers of the Museum of Anthropology,
                University of Michigan, no. 14. Ann Arbor: Museum of Anthropology.

Tobler, Arthur J.
    1950   *Excavations at Tepe Gawra,* vol. 2: *levels IX–XX.* Monographs of the University
                Museum, University of Pennsylvania, Philadelphia. University of Pennsylvania Press.

Todd, Ian A.
    1976   *Çatal Hüyük in perspective.* Menlo Park: Cummings Publishing Company.

Vescelius, Gary
    1960   Archaeological sampling: a problem of statistical inference. In *Essays in the science of
                culture, in honor of Leslie A. White,* ed. Gertrude E. Dole and Robert L. Carneiro, pp.
                457–70. New York: Thomas Y. Crowell.

Voigt, Mary M.
    1976   Hajji Firuz Tepe: an economic reconstruction of a sixth millennium community in
                western Iran. Ph.D. diss., University of Pennsylvania.

Watson, Patty Jo
    1966   Clues to Iranian prehistory in modern village life. *Expedition* 8:9–19.
    1978   Architectural differentiation in some Near Eastern communities, prehistoric and con-
                temporary. In *Social archeology,* ed. Charles L. Redman, Mary Jane Berman, Edward V.
                Curtin, William T. Langhorne, Jr., Nina M. Versaggi, and Jeffery C. Wanser, pp. 131–57.
                New York: Academic Press.
    1979   *Archaeological ethnography in western Iran.* Viking Fund Publications in Anthropology,
                57. Tucson: University of Arizona Press.

Winter, Marcus S.
    1976   Excavating a shallow community by random sampling quadrats. In *The early Meso-
                american village,* ed. Kent V. Flannery, pp. 62–67. New York: Academic Press.

Wright, Henry T.
    1969   *The administration of rural production in an early Mesopotamian town.* Anthropological
                Papers of the Museum of Anthropology, University of Michigan, no. 38. Ann Arbor:
                Museum of Anthropology. (With contributions by Sandor Bökönyi, Kent V. Flannery,
                and John Mayhall.)

Wright, Henry T.; Miller, Naomi; and Redding, Richard
    1980   Time and process in an Uruk rural center. In *l'Archéologie de l'Iraq: perspectives et
                limites de l'interprétation anthropologique des documents,* ed. Marie-Thérèse Barrelet,
                pp. 265–82. Paris: Centre National de la Recherche Scientifique.

Yasa, I.
    1957   *Hasanoğlan: socio-economic structure of a Turkish village.* Ankara.

Yasin, Walid
    1970   Excavations at Tell es-Sawwan, 1969: report on the sixth season's excavations. *Sumer*
                26:3–12.

Yellen, John E.
    1977   *Archaeological approaches to the present.* New York: Academic Press.

Young, T. Cuyler, Jr.
    1975   An archaeological survey of the Kangāvar valley. In *Proceedings of the IIIrd Annual
                Symposium on Archaeological Research in Iran* [Tehran, 1974] ed. Firouz Bagherzadeh,
                pp. 23–30. Tehran: Iranian Centre for Archaeological Research.

Young, T. Cuyler, Jr., and Levine, Louis D.
    1974   *Excavations of the Godin project: second progress report.* Art and Archaeology Occa-
                sional Paper, no. 26. Toronto: Royal Ontario Museum.

NATURAL AND SOCIAL SCIENCE PARADIGMS IN NEAR EASTERN PREHISTORY

Robert McC. Adams

B Y A DECISION of the editors that is as welcome as it is unusual, the contributed papers in this volume are devoted to the same closely integrated set of themes as the scientific career of the man whom they honor. Having specialized in subsequent chapters of the human record, I would not ordinarily qualify as a contributor to a volume such as this one. Yet it was probably only as an outgrowth of Robert Braidwood's invitation to serve as an archeological field assistant at Jarmo in 1950-51 that I was drawn into the academic pursuit of a related set of interests. The temptation has been irresistible, therefore, to find a basis for inclusion by offering a commentary that is largely about — and certainly is stimulated by — the other studies that this work comprises. I propose to examine, from a perhaps unfamiliar and somewhat partisan but not unsympathetic perspective, two sets of linked assumptions and research strategies that appear to contrast with one another and yet cohabit amicably within a largely shared domain of methods and problems.

The general impression conveyed by these papers is that extraordinary but unevenly distributed progress has been made in the study of the later prehistory of the Near East over the past generation or so. By all odds the most intensive effort has been devoted to what a few (e.g., the Cauvins) still see as a "revolutionary" onset of food production, together with its immediate antecedents and outgrowths. However, the abruptness evoked by the term *revolution* — and perhaps also the implication of an unexpected overturning of the established order through the active, directed efforts of "revolutionaries" — is being increasingly called into question. Thus there has been a continuing, even growing, concentration of attention on an episode (or, as seems to be increasingly felt likely, a series of geographically diffuse and semi-independent episodes) whose boundaries and distinctive character have become progressively more blurred. Meanwhile, only a markedly smaller number of investigators have concerned themselves with the subsequent and final components of the prehistoric record, as Oates accurately observes, even though the people of those times prepared the ground, so to speak, for the subsequent achievement of urban civilization in the fourth millennium. This surprising maldistribution of effort invites attention. My thesis is that it has more to do with the selective adoption of research paradigms, in the sense now made classic by the work of Thomas S. Kuhn (*The Structure of Scientific Revolution*, 2nd ed. [Chicago: University of Chicago Press, 1970]), than with research requirements or findings.

Let us consider first the origins of agriculture and sedentary village life. The foregoing papers reinforce the impression that there is an increasingly detailed and convincing supply of answers to "how," or process, questions. Answers to "why," or explicatory, questions, on the other hand, have been slow to come forth or have proved illusory. There is no reason to deprecate answers to "how" questions; a case can even be made that in most scientific research any other kind is likely to be tendentious or spurious. But straightforward and intelligible regularities of process, co-occurring in different regions and constituting a plausibly comprehensive and interrelated series of directional trends, are distinguished largely by their absence. As Redman writes, "With each new discovery the empirical situation seems to become more complex, rather than clearer."

Perhaps this is only to be expected of any important transformation in the scale, intensity, and complexity of human society, as the onset of sedentary food production certainly was. Debate over attributions of cause in connection with the rise of states and cities or with the industrial revolution is usually fiercer than what is recorded in this volume, and not much less inconclusive. But if the only available explanatory frameworks are necessarily so multifaceted and conditional that even central tendencies remain obscure, then implicit but persistent attempts in some of these papers to treat prehistory as if it were primarily an extension of the natural sciences may be misdirected.

It should be stressed that the progress that has been made is not narrowly circumscribed and unilinear and for this reason incapable of reaching closure on explanations of change. That might have been the case if, for example, major emphasis had been placed on merely filling in the cells in a time-space matrix made up of horizontal rows representing chronological periods and vertical columns representing traditional sequences of localized material culture. Instead, the effort has been powerfully and quite consistently directed at elucidating the processes of domestication and sedentarization, using for this purpose a widening and increasingly sophisticated battery of analytical approaches largely drawn from the natural sciences. Yet the net effect with regard to at least some key questions has been discouraging. The trend of research findings, for example, has been to increase uncertainty about the interregional correspondences of climatic variation that might help to account for other shifts (the Soleckis); to highlight pronounced suboptimal and interrupted occupations that sharply reduce the credibility of most forms of environmental pressure as causative agents (Bar Yosef, the Cauvins, Watson); and to undermine the earlier notion that herding or cultivation would necessarily soon produce discernible morphological changes in previously wild species (Moore, Redman). In spite of the growing accumulations of data, in other words, there appear to be more, not fewer, doubts today than there were two decades or so ago about our ability to ascertain accurately and unambiguously either the degree of attainment of sedentism and agriculture in a given instance or the contribution of environmental forces to it.

A temporal sequence does seem to have been reasonably established in which a substantial degree of sedentism precedes anything more than a marginal reliance on domesticates or protodomesticates. But whether the latter is dependent on the former or both on some other set of factors is left as little more than a matter of assumption (Moore). Initial sedentism in at least the best-documented case of the Natufians turns out, curiously, to involve greater reliance on cave environments (if not necessarily for domiciliary purposes) in that period than in periods prior to the building up of open habitation sites (Bar Yosef). Moreover, only with new forms of analysis (e.g., of microvertebrates) can there be reasonable assurance of sedentism, sharply reducing the usefulness of older research, which does not include comparable data for distributional studies. Perrot's prescription for future advance must also be seen as an expression of grave reservations about the further utility of much of the research that has gone on heretofore: "Les analyses les plus fines ne rendront pas plus solide la documentation dont nous disposons actuellement. Il faut attendre les résultats de nouvelles fouilles, amples et rigoureuses."

Perrot also notes that while the existing data have encouraged a proliferation of theories and models, for the most part it has not been possible to advance beyond the realm of hypothesis. In these papers at least, there is little to show that the useful half-life of theories is any longer than the time it takes to compile the data leading to that theory. Childe's pioneering speculation on the association of domestication with a widespread process of post-Pleistocene dessication, and specifically with enforced propinquity to shrinking oases, was long ago cast into doubt by Braidwood. Reportedly it can be decisively negated today (the Cauvins, Soleckis), although reports of possible very early cultivation in the Nile Valley conceivably could lead to the revival of a modified version of it. According to the Cauvins at least, the proposals of Binford and Flannery that rest on regionally differentiated resource availability and scarcity do not fare much better.

Young and Smith do bring new data to bear in support of their decade-old argument for a dependent relationship between population growth and subsistence intensification. (Among their confrères in this volume, only Moore's paper suggests sympathetic resonances with their position as it was originally formulated). Surely the increased, and increasing, density of occupance that they are now able to document will make their argument more persuasive to a larger group. However, they have yet to begin to demonstrate that prehistoric populations at any point approached the elusive level sometimes termed "carrying capacity." Moreover, their case continues to require a number of plausible but quite speculative assumptions. For example, can the early concentrations they have identified along upper valley margins in the Zagros be adequately accounted for because this ecotone was "somewhat safer and richer multiple-resource" character? If so, how does it become an instance of the operation of population pressure for this niche subsequently to have been partly *abandoned* as population moved to the "slightly more challenging" environs of the open valley floors, where heavy turf presupposed hoe agriculture involving increased labor input? At least *this* nonspecialist finds it hard to escape the impression that throughout the entire Near Eastern prehistoric sequence there was a lot of room to rattle around in. Where, and how densely, people settled, then, is more likely to reflect a culturally constrained choice among subsistence or other locational preferences than a decision imposed by an uncontrollable decline in the net balance of resources over needs.

I certainly do not mean to dismiss population pressure as a factor operating for agricultural intensification in some circumstances. The problem remains, as Young and Smith fully acknowledge, how to define these circumstances and then how to recover archeological evidence that has the potential of demonstrating their existence. Perhaps it is the extreme uncertainty and difficulty of any such undertaking that primarily induces most of their colleagues to turn in other directions, a difficulty that probably extends to any similarly ambitious hypothesis. What is clear in any case, by omission if not by direct statement, is that the position of the substantial majority is one of considerable scepticism about any and all current hypotheses of a formally efficient, causative character. With the Cauvins — and indeed, explicitly following Braidwood — this sort of scepticism can only lead us back to a stress on "l'agent humain et la maturation progressive de son milieu social et culturel." This being so, prehistory must in the long run fall primarily within the domain of the human or social sciences.

At the risk of oversimplification and consequent distortion, it may be worthwhile to sketch out the network of largely implicit assumptions with regard to change and continuity in human society that appears to pervade most of the papers concentrating on the transformation that led to food production. There is a tendency to emphasize individualistic behavioral responses to environmental pressures while giving only slight attention to how they were probably mediated by social and cultural factors. Change is apparently visualized as taking place primarily through a gradually accumulative, directional flow of cost-minimizing, leisure- or resource-maximizing decisions, unimpaired by culturally modulated categories of cognition or perception. Various feedback mechanisms are invoked as a substitute for a socially constituted sense of direction, so that learning primarily takes the form of the unconscious, mechanical imprinting on mental templates of new sets of routines.

As this suggests, consciousness of participation in a process of change, or for that matter in efforts to minimize or avoid change, is apparently felt to have played little or no part. Conscious innovation, propagation, imitation, experimentation fall outside the bounds of those agencies of change to which it is scientifically proper to assign a potential role. Recognition of social as differentiated from individual (preponderantly biological) needs and priorities, or of patterns of social decision-making and action that are more than an aggregate of those of individuals, receive little attention. With the exception of nuclear and perhaps extended families, constituted social groups are seen only as by-products of subsistence requirements. There is little to suggest that instead they might have represented a partly autonomous rationale and tradition that could act to shape the ebb and flow of choice among subsistence alternatives. Correspondingly little weight is given, in accounting for the shift to food production, to the cooperative or competitive interaction of neighboring groups. To the contrary, when an ecological approach is referred to, it is the external, environmental constraints and opportunities that are heavily stressed. Moreover, the environmental factors that receive attention tend to be fairly static or only slowly developing (like population pressure). This is consistent with a narrowly behaviorist framework of explanation in that it provides maximal opportunity for feedback mechanisms to reinforce an unconscious drift into new routines. But it presupposes an unwillingness to consider alternative representations of the adaptive, broadly evolutionary processes of human life. At least during episodes of comparatively rapid change, for example, it is likely that creative modifications of existing patterns were continuously sought out, rationalized in cultural terms, and selectively adopted in order to meet the omnipresent challenges of social as well as environmental risk and uncertainty.

Admittedly, with some justice it may be replied that this alternative construct is largely irrelevant for prehistorians; their theoretical concerns need to maintain a closer congruence with the limitations of their data. The possibility of substantial recovery of realms of consciousness and belief from fragmentary material remains seems hopelessly remote (other than in the programmatic statements of a dwindling handful of "new" archeologists), while on the other hand it can reasonably be expected that a large share of behavior patterns will leave material residues. True enough, but by advancing this alternative perspective we help to call attention to a different paradigm of what archeologists should look for and how they can go about doing so. And barely concealed beneath the surface of this, in other respects, cohesive and harmonious group of papers and contributors are a number of suggestive illustrations, provided primarily by those specializing in prehistoric periods after the transition to food production had been effected.

Most of these papers concern regional or interregional integration, whether under the rubric of trade, exchange, redistribution, religious primacy, or some more overtly political means of articulation. Long-distance trade at least in obsidian is present very early, but its initial manifestations are accorded little significance. Its presence in preagricultural levels as a result of importation is noted but left unassessed by Bar Yosef and the Soleckis, while to Perrot it is merely an indication of "une influence septentrionale en Palestine." Importation continued in appreciably greater quantities after the introduction of agriculture but characteristically now carries a heavier burden of interpretation. Watson is at pains to note the "marked fluctuation" in quantities of obsidian in roughly coeval Halaf sites and to place its circulation within the context of specialized pottery production centers — "a well-organized communications network" — and the emergence of the first integrative and distinctive "horizon style." For Hours and Copeland and for Mortensen, too, obsidian serves as part of a complex of interaction that distinguishes patterns of spatial organization within bioclimatically defined regions or "radiating cultural systems" of permanent and temporary settlements. In the eighth and ninth millennia, it would seem, the trading or other interaction of distant communities with one another falls outside the scope of a discussion of explanatory rather than merely descriptive content, while by the sixth and seventh millennia it has become central. Were the realities of these interrelationships, which in any period surely were initiated and maintained only at considerable cost, so abruptly and profoundly altered? Or does this alteration mark a watershed at which prehistory construed primarily as a natural science becomes prehistory construed primarily as a social science?

Ethnographic and ethnoarcheological analogies play a perceptibly larger part in the papers that gravitate toward social models rather than those of behavioristic or natural science. To be sure, there are always pitfalls in employing such analogies. One may wonder, for example, whether the uniformity of an unplanned, overwhelmingly domiciliary, subsistence aspect that Kramer finds in modern Near Eastern villages permits the same characterization to be inferred for their ancient counterparts. Runaway urban primacy, associated with unprecedented changes in the technology of transport, communications, and coercive political dominance, seriously undermines any comparison. But it is noteworthy that those invoking such analogies do so explicitly and with care. Illustrative suggestions drawn from better-known historical settings or from contemporary life can never be avoided altogether, and it is better that they be put forward openly as refutable hypotheses than introduced in the form of unstated assumptions as to what is logical or universal in human nature. An example of the latter, perchance, is "the acknowledged indolence of man," even though it is given to us by Young and Smith on no less than the authority of Malthus.

In general, the analogies that are invoked help to substantiate the case for the prevalence of social patterning not directly dictated by environmental constraints. Thus Hole persuasively challenges the traditional view of hereditary stratification as based on static patterns of control deriving almost exclusively from economic relationships. Included within the rich variety of organizational modes subsumed under the unrepresentative title of "chiefdom," he argues, are close linkages of status with religious and age hierarchies and, more generally, with fluid, situationally determined assumptions of higher status. Flannery and Oates both note the not uncommon modern juxtaposition of ethnically distinct or complementarily specialized communities, a phenomenon whose ancient analogues might have been slow in coming to light save for the accident of the Jebel Hamrin salvage program. In other words, cultural distributions are more than a dependent variable controlled conjointly by resource availability and by bioclimatic regions. The same concern with aspects of cultural variation is, of course, central to Kramer's paper. She introduces the important distinction between probability-sampling strategies and strategies emphasizing large-scale excavations, noting that the choice between them is inextricably intertwined with an archeologist's choice of overall objective:

> Probability sampling pinpoints central tendencies rather than the diversity and spatial organization of cultural materials at a site.... Archeologists must decide whether they want information about the frequencies with which elements in a population occur, in which case they should use probability samples, or whether they want spatial, configurational information, in which case they require transects or large quadrats, thereby running the risk of sacrificing the statistical reliability of representativeness of their sample.

Kramer adds that multistage strategies can provide a means of having one's cake and eating it, her preference being for probability sampling as the initial step. This may presuppose a degree of continuity with regard to funding, not to speak of political access, which is no longer entirely realistic. More important, the contributors primarily concerned with post-Neolithic phases of prehistory at numerous points seem to favor a different hierarchy of priorities that no longer accords "central tendencies" pride of place. Oates observes that there are "hints in the archeological data of growing economic — possibly even 'political' — authority.... Until a major Ubaid site is extensively excavated, however, we shall remain in ignorance of such more developed facets of Ubaid life." Nissen's emphasis is also on the search for "high-level organizational structures." He sees these not as an irresistibly growing and spreading series of evolutionary emergents but rather as conditionals whose survival and effectiveness depended critically on the scale of administration or interaction. But it is clearly required that, if they are to be identified at all, spatial, configurational, and administrative information be sought in large-scale excavations. Hole, similarly, is preoccupied with ascertaining the nature of Susa's centrality; whether the leadership pyramid is apical or flat topped is not likely to be greatly clarified by probability samples that, properly, are much more adequately representative of the populous base. Lest this all seem excessively elitist, we may call attention to Dollfus's insistence on the need for extensive excavations of complete house plans in a succession of periods in order to clarify changes in family structure. An analogous interest in structural questions requiring a configurational approach is evident in Hours and Copeland's concern to distinguish between simple circulation of utilitarian commodities and the giving or exchange of prestige goods or to delineate the beginnings of the (still much debated) Asiatic Mode of Production. This group of contributors, it seems clear, makes no less use of natural science information where it can be effective than do prehistorians specializing in only slightly earlier periods. In the questions they ask and the strategies they follow, however, they come down more uniformly and firmly on the social science side of the watershed.

"Let a hundred flowers bloom." Sometime, somewhere, limits have to be drawn to preserve the scientific character of a field — to keep it from being dissipated among unprofitable approaches and questions. No one would suggest that this is the case here. Natural and social science paradigms clearly complement one another at this juncture in constructively broadening the range of inquiry, in enlisting the aid of new investigators with different skills and perspectives, and perhaps in approaching a larger group of potential sources for funds. A degree of unstated tension as to basic alliances and objectives may help to keep everybody on their toes. But in the long run, my reading of this collection of evidence as a nonspecialist would lead me to bet on the social science linkage as the more enduring, fundamental one. In its basic orientation, prehistory will be primarily a specialized application of anthropology and history or it will be nothing.